Work Your Way Around the World

Susan Griffith

Work Your Way Around the World
Susan Griffith

This edition first published in Great Britain 2017 by Trotman, an imprint of Crimson Publishing Ltd, 19-21c Charles Street, Bath BA1 1HX

First published 1983
Seventeenth edition 2017

© Crimson Publishing Ltd, 2017

EUROPEAN UNION REFERENDUM:

This edition was revised after the referendum result on 24 June, 2016 regarding the UK's continued membership of the European Union, but before negotiations had progressed with other member states. At the time of going to press, the UK remains a constituent member of the Union, which allows the free movement of people, capital, goods and services across the 28 Member States. Formal proceedings for negotiating the terms of the UK's withdrawal from the Union got underway when the UK government triggered Article 50 of the Lisbon Treaty at the end of March 2017. It is impossible to predict how long it will be after that before the free movement of labour will be curbed. Until that time, the information provided on the European Union remains valid. The publisher acknowledges that the information provided in the book on the European Union will be subject to change following the UK's decision to leave the European Union. At the time of going to press, the UK remains a Member State of the Union and will continue to be subject to its obligations under EU law until it has finalised the terms of its withdrawal with the other 27 Member States.

A catalogue record for this book is available from the British Library.

ISBN 978 1 84455 647 2

Typeset by IDSUK (DataConnection) Ltd
Printed and bound in Malta by Gutenberg Press Ltd

Contents

PART 3: WORK YOUR WAY WORLDWIDE

Preface

The world is always changing, hence the need for a new edition of this book at regular intervals. Some changes are welcome, for example the explosion of bloggers, traders and entrepreneurs successfully funding long stays abroad as 'digital nomads', or the recent price drop for a Working Holiday Visa for Australia, since employers in the countryside are crying out for backpacker labour. The number of young North Americans taking a gap year before university has increased dramatically, and this edition includes a new chapter aimed at all school leavers who are contemplating a year out.

Other developments are not such good news for the adventurous traveller wanting to explore the world. Implementation of the UK decision to leave the European Union may eventually result in the loss of the automatic right to work in Europe. Given that, for many, the idea of escape might be especially appealing now, of heading further afield to work a season at a Canadian ski resort, teach in Turkey or Taiwan, or volunteer at a national park in Costa Rica, out of reach of gloomy headlines and the relentless media coverage of Brexit.

Amid all the changes, I am heartened by how much stays the same, and by the longevity of some shortcuts to seeing the world on a shoestring: the family-run business in Toronto that matches drivers with cars to be delivered to Florida in the autumn, the obscure agency in Essex that recruits seasonal participants for Disney's International Programs in the US, and that hoary old chestnut WWOOF (World Wide Opportunities on Organic Farms) that keeps expanding and welcomes volunteers to work in exchange for food and accommodation.

I often pause to marvel at the wonders of the internet. By typing a few letters into a search bar, anyone can find out about amazing possibilities – tefl.com (for teaching English), wf.is (volunteering in Iceland), swap.ca (work programmes for Canadians) and so on. Yet the internet and social media can be bewildering and discouraging places to pin down paying or volunteer opportunities abroad. This book attempts to introduce you to the panoply of possibilities, and to simplify a preliminary search.

Since the last edition, I have spent a glorious three months in the Bay area of California, and have travelled to Australia, Italy, Poland, Spain, Sweden, Canada, etc., where I have met an impressive range of enterprising travellers. For this 17th edition of *Work Your Way Around the World* my network of informants has encompassed a Belgian man who picked grapes in Beaujolais and worked in a bar on Lake Geneva while living with his Spanish girlfriend in a camper van; a retired American teaching English in Madrid; a 20-something Englishwoman who has set up her own English language school in southern Bolivia; an Australian exchange student living in Berlin; a graduate who joined a post-earthquake reconstruction project in Nepal, and a Cambridge punt guide and model designer who was determined to work on a Mediterranean yacht. Whatever their backgrounds, these folks are happy to expose themselves to the unexpected friendliness and generosity of foreign residents and fellow travellers.

Few of us can simply sail off beyond the blue horizon without giving careful thought to how to finance such a thrilling expedition. Anybody – young or young-at-heart – who occasionally feels the call of the road, the spirit of adventure flicker will, I hope, enjoy reading this book and dreaming. My aim has been to make the information in the following 380 pages as concrete and up-to-the-minute as possible, to cut all the vague generalities and waffle in an attempt to help readers to carve out their own self-funded adventures. Among all the specific contact addresses, websites, hard-headed visa information and realistic practical advice, the stories of working travellers are interwoven to inspire and encourage. This book is written to renew optimism and spark the imagination of all future travellers.

Susan Griffith
Cambridge
May 2017

Acknowledgements

I never get tired of meeting and hearing from those intrepid travellers who are out there, sometimes living the life of Reilly, sometimes living on the edge. Their stories always enliven (and justify) my struggle to keep this book as up to date as possible. This new revised edition of *Work Your Way Around the World* would not have been possible without the help of hundreds of travellers who have generously shared their information over the years. Some have been writing to me over several editions, and their loyalty is greatly appreciated.

I would especially like to thank all those travellers who have crouched over keyboards in remote corners of the world to communicate with me since the last edition. All their pearls of travelling wisdom have been enthusiastically received and have been distilled into the pages that follow. My warmest thanks are owed to the following among many others: Davinna Artibey, Charles Beach, Ben Butler, Alan Chadwick, Miranda Crowhurst, Stephen Dorosewicz, Thibaut Exelmans, Libby Goldsmith, Bradwell Jackson, Imi Letts, Gillian Murphy, Geoff Nunney, Christine Smith, Ben Stefano, Inge Visser and Eve Whitley.

While every effort has been made to ensure that the information contained in this book was accurate at the time of going to press, some details are bound to change within the lifetime of this edition. Wages, exchange rates and government policies in these uncertain times are particularly susceptible to fluctuations, and the ones quoted here are intended merely as a guide.

If in the course of your travels you come across something which might be of interest to readers of the next edition, please write to Susan Griffith at Trotman/Crimson Publishing, or email her at s.griffith@ntlworld.com (she promises to reply). This book depends very much on up-to-date reports from travellers who have worked their way. The best contributions will be rewarded with a free copy of the next edition.

Acknowledgements

Introduction

LIVING THE DREAM

At an airport bus stop in West London one very early November morning, I met James from Wakefield. Within a few minutes of conversation, I realised that he was the archetypal worker-around-the-world. His destination was Aruba, an idyllic Caribbean island just 27km from the coast of Venezuela, where he was hoping to work in the kite-surfing industry or in a dive shop refilling tanks. He had come down overnight to London from Wakefield on a cheap Megabus (£4) and was, like me, catching the easyBus to Gatwick Airport (£2.50); but unlike me he had a one-way ticket on Air Europa to Caracas for which he had paid £404. He was travelling so light it was hard to believe that a sleeping bag and hammock could fit inside his small rucksack. His plan was to try to get from the coast of Venezuela to Aruba by sea but as there is no scheduled boat service he would have to try to wangle his way onto a fishing boat. He was planning to swim every day and wash his clothes in the sea. Fascinated, I asked him about previous travels, of which there have been many. For example, he had worked his way around New Zealand for two years as a barista, parachute packer and fruit-picker on the North Island and in a wacky cookie factory in Christchurch (see New Zealand chapter).

He aims to master a new skill on each of his trips. He is an accomplished unicyclist and would like to ride through Africa on a 36-inch-wheeled unicycle that allows you to reach speeds of 20 miles per hour. In the past he has had a go at mastering juggling, slacklining (like tight-rope walking but looser) and bouldering (climbing without equipment). On this trip to the Caribbean, he was going to take up free diving despite the dangers. He likes the idea of working on a cruise ship but they probably wouldn't hire him because of his appearance (dreadlocks cheerfully adorned with shells, stripy socks, pantaloon-style trousers, trainers). I hope he had a wonderful winter in the sun.

The idea of going off into the unknown to seek adventures holds more than a touch of romance. From the early heroic navigators such as Ferdinand Magellan to the fictional traveller Phileas Fogg, circumnavigators of our planet have always captured the imagination of adventurous souls. More recently Simon Reeve's globetrotting television series and award-winning travel blogs such as www. nomadicmatt.com attract huge audiences, perhaps because so many of us relish a chance to imagine ourselves – impossibly ambitious as it sounds – as round-the-world explorers.

Nothing can compare with the joy of the open road. The sense of possibility and adventure brings feelings of exhilaration, long submerged in the workaday routines of home. Cheap air travel has opened up parts of the globe once reserved for the seriously affluent. When travelling in far-flung corners of the world, you can escape the demands of modern life in the Western world: the chores, the clutter, the technology. Whatever your stage of life, travelling spontaneously means you have the freedom to choose from an infinite spectrum of possibilities. Those who have experienced independent travel normally catch the bug and long to visit more places, see more wonders and spend a longer time abroad. Today, trekking in the hinterland of Rio de Janeiro or diving in the Philippines can be within the grasp of ordinary folk. The longing might stem from a fascination left over from childhood with an exotic destination such as Madagascar or Patagonia. The motivation might come from a friend's reminiscences or a television travelogue or a personal passion for a certain culture or natural habitat. At some point a vague idea begins to crystallise into an actual possibility.

That is the point at which the purple prose of brochure-speak must be interrupted by hard-headed planning. The first question is always: how can I afford such a trip? Magellan had the backing of the King and Queen of Spain, Phileas Fogg was a gentleman of independent means, and Michael Palin could call on the resources of the BBC. How can ordinary people possibly make their dreams a reality? The conventional means to an exciting end is to work and save hard. A grim spell of working overtime and denying yourself a social life is one route to being able to join a safari in Tanzania, a watersport instructor's course on the Mediterranean or a bungee jump in New Zealand. But what if it were possible to skip this stage and head off towards the horizon sooner than that? Instead of trying to finance the expensive trips advertised in glossy travel brochures, what about trying to find alternative ways of experiencing those same places at a fraction of the cost?

The catchy phrase 'work your way around the world' may contain the answer to the thorny question of funding. Picking up bits and pieces of work along the way can go a long way to reducing the cost. Even if it is unrealistic to expect to walk into highly paid jobs in Beijing or Berlin (though they do exist), other informal ways exist of offsetting the cost of travel. Work-for-keep arrangements on a New Zealand farm or Costa Rican eco-lodge will mean that you have to save far less than if you booked a long-haul package holiday to those destinations – in some cases little more than the cost of the flight.

Short of emigrating or marrying a native, working abroad is an excellent way to experience a foreign culture from the inside. The plucky Briton who spends a few months on a Queensland outback station will have a different tale to tell about Australia from the one who serves behind the bar in a Sydney pub. Yet both will experience the exhilaration of doing something completely unfamiliar in an alien setting.

Some spend years toying with the idea, taking a few tentative steps before they finally discover the wherewithal to carry through the idea. Phil Tomkins, a 45-year-old Englishman who spent a year teaching on the tiny Greek island of Kea, describes the thought processes that galvanised him into action:

> *I think it comes down to the fact that we are only on this planet for a finger-snap of time and if you have any kind of urge for a bit of adventure, then my advice would be to go for it! And even if it goes all horribly wrong, you can look people in the eyes and say, 'Well, at least I gave it a try'. You can work 9–5 in an office or factory all day, come home, switch on the Idiot Lantern and sit there watching Michael Palin travelling the world – or you can be bold, seize the day, and do something amazing. One thing I can guarantee: when we are lying on our deathbed many years from now, we will not be saying to ourselves, 'Oh, I wish I'd spent more time at that dead-end job and had a little less adventure in my life!'*

Anyone with a taste for adventure and a modicum of nerve has the potential for exploring far-flung corners of the globe on very little money. In an ideal world, it would be possible to register with an international employment agency and wait to be assigned to a glamorous job as an underwater model in the Caribbean, history coordinator for a European tour company or snowboard instructor in the Rockies. But jobs abroad, like jobs at home, must be ferreted out. The hundreds of pages that follow will help you to do just that.

THE DECISION TO GO

For many, deciding to get up and go is the biggest stumbling block. Often the hardest step is fixing a departure date. Once you have bought a ticket, explained to your friends and family that you are off to see the world (they will either be envious or disapproving) and packed away your possessions, the rest seems to look after itself. Inevitably first-time travellers suffer some separation anxieties and pre-departure blues as they contemplate leaving behind the comfortable routines of home. But these are usually much worse in anticipation than in retrospect. As long as you have enough motivation, together with some money and a copy of this book, you are all set to have a great time abroad.

Either you follow your first impulse and opt for an immediate change of scenery, or you plan a job and a route in advance. On the one hand, people use working as a means to an end: they work in order to fund further travelling. Other people look upon a job abroad as an end in itself, a way to explore other cultures, a means of satisfying their curiosity about whether there is any truth in the clichés about other nationalities. Often it is the best way to shake off the boredom that comes with routine. One contributor to this book felt quite liberated when she decided to drop everything – her *'cushy secretarial job, Debenhams account card, stiletto heels'* – and embark on a working holiday around Europe. Another finally kicked over the traces of what he described as the *'office job from Hell'* when he went off to Thailand to teach English.

When you are wondering whether you are the right sort of person to work abroad, do not imagine you are a special case. It is not only students, school-leavers and people facing unemployment who enjoy the chance to travel and work, but also a large number of people with a profession, craft or trade which they were happy to abandon temporarily. For recent editions I heard from a woman who spent a decade working in the fashion retail industry in her native Holland but was writing from a bush school and wildlife hospital where she was working in South Africa; from a proofreader from Oregon who enjoyed living in Barcelona so much that she is trying to find a way to get back; a middle-aged Australian journalist who created a lovely life in Bergamo, Italy funded by English teaching; a British ski instructor who was so enamoured of the Canadian ski resort Whistler that he stayed on working in a different capacity for the summer; a television writer/producer who quit her job to take a sabbatical which turned into three years of round-the-world travel during which she eked out her funds with a café job in Australia, English tutoring in Istanbul, and PR work for an English Immersion programme in Spain; an administrator and civil servant (married to each other) from Doncaster who taught cricket at a deprived school in Africa; an editor who swapped Edinburgh for Dahab on the Red Sea where she could carry on her freelance work (at least until the events of the Arab Spring cut the internet connection); a 30-something Californian who put his skills as a photographer to good use by getting hired by a British website to record the clubs of Ibiza; and so on. All were motivated not by a desire to earn money but by a craving for new and different experiences, and a conviction that not all events which make up one's life need to be career-furthering or 'success'-oriented.

PREPARATION

It is not the Mr Micawbers of this world who succeed at getting jobs. (Mr Micawber is the character in Charles Dickens's *David Copperfield* who is famous for living in hopeful expectation without taking any practical steps to bring about a successful outcome.) If you sit around as he did 'waiting for something to turn up' you will soon find yourself penniless with no prospects for replenishing your travel funds. If you wait in idleness at home or if you sit in your hostel all day worrying about your dwindling euros or pesos, hesitating and dithering because you are convinced the situation is hopeless or that you lack the necessary documents to work, you will get absolutely nowhere.

Every successful venture combines periodic flights of fancy with methodical planning. The majority of us lack the courage (or the recklessness) just to get up and go. And any homework you do ahead of time will benefit you later, if only because it will give you more confidence. But it is important to strike a good balance between slavishly following a predetermined itinerary that might prevent you from grasping opportunities as they arise and setting off with no idea of what you're looking for. Many travel converts regret their initial decision to buy an air ticket with a fixed return date.

For many people, a shortage of money is the main obstacle. It is the rare individual who trusts to fate and sets off with next to nothing. Other people wait until they have substantial savings before they dare leave home which gives them the enviable freedom to work only when they want to.

SOMETIMES PENURY ACTS AS A SPUR TO ACTION AS IT DID IN THE CASE OF ROGER BLAKE:

I left home with a substantial amount in savings. But they are long gone and for 18 months I have only been living off whatever I make locally. I have been down to just $50 more times than I'd care to remember. But somehow I always seem to come right. When I hear fellow travellers grumbling and sick with worry that they are down to $500, I cannot help but exclaim that they should enjoy it. In other words, when you've got it, flaunt it! Enjoy! There are those (usually with a few hundred dollars in the bank) who are 'looking for work' and those (including myself) who are looking for work. When your funds are REALLY low you WILL find a job, believe me.

Anyone embarking on an extended trip will have to have a certain amount of capital to buy tickets, visas, insurance (see below), etc. But it is amazing how a little can go a long way if you are willing to take a wide variety of casual jobs en route and willing to weather the financial doldrums.

One step you might take when preparing for a job hunt abroad is to tidy up your social media profile and delete any inappropriate rants or evidence of immature behaviour.

Money

It is of course always a good idea to have an emergency fund in reserve if possible, or at least access to money from home should you run into difficulties (see section on 'Transferring Money' in *In Extremis* at the end of this book). How much you decide to set aside before leaving will depend on how tolerant you are of risk. But even risk-takers and gamblers should take only sensible risks. If you don't have much cash, it's probably advisable to keep enough in reserve for a return ticket or even buy a cheap return well in advance as an insurance policy. For example, if you decide to try crewing on a yacht from the Mediterranean, you could buy a one-way easyJet flight London to Nice for £26 and gamble that you'll find something, or buy a cheap return at the same time which you are prepared to waste if you get a place on a boat.

Attitudes to saving vary too. Some people relish the planning stages while saving for a trip. Others find saving over a long period depressing and start to long for nights out and restaurant meals of which they have been deprived. When Xuela Edwards returned after two years of working her way around Europe, she tried to hang on to the travelling mentality which makes it much easier to save money:

> *My advice is to consider your home country in the same way as others. It makes you more resourceful. Try to avoid the car loans and high living that usually make up home life. I'm sure that the reason bulb workers in Holland for example save so much money is because they live in tents (which I admit would be tricky at home).*

Mike Tunnicliffe spent more on his world travels than he intended but didn't regret it:

> *Originally, I intended to finance my year with casual work and return to England having spent only the price of my ticket. In the end, I delved far deeper into my life's savings than I had intended to do, but I was fortunate in having savings on which to draw, and I made the conscious decision to enjoy my year while I had the chance. In other words, fun now, pay later.*

Once you are resolved to travel, set a realistic target amount to save and then go for it wholeheartedly. Don't get just any job, get one which is either highly paid (easier said than done of course) or one which offers as much overtime as you want. Dedicated working travellers consider a 60+-hour week quite tolerable which will have the additional advantage of leaving you too shattered to conduct an expensive social life. If you have collected some assets before setting off, you are luckier than most. Property owners can arrange for the rental money to follow them at regular intervals.

The average budget of a travelling student starts at about $55 a day though many survive in countries such as Laos and Bolivia on half that. Whatever the size of your travelling fund, you should plan to access your money from more than one source: cash, debit card, credit card (kept in a different place), and perhaps one high denomination travellers' cheque for an emergency. The most straightforward way to access money abroad is by using your bank debit card in hole-in-the-wall ATMs. Unfortunately this is an expensive way to access money, since the transaction and loading fees will add a typical cost of £6 or even £8 every time you withdraw. A much better alternative to use in ATMs is a special travel money card pre-loaded with the currency you want (see below). Credit card companies also add punitive charges to purchases abroad, typically a whacking 2.75% of the purchase price. Similarly point-of-sale debit card purchases are routinely marked up by the same amount as a non-sterling transaction fee. If you are going to be abroad for a considerable period drawing on funds in your home account, it would be worth shopping around for the best deal. For example the Post Office credit card and Halifax Clarity credit card add no 'foreign-exchange loading'. Websites like www.moneyfacts. co.uk, www.moneysavingexpert.com and www.moneysupermarket.com provide invaluable comparisons so you can choose the most traveller-friendly cards.

Travel Money Cards sold by a number of companies including the Post Office are prepaid, reloadable cards that can be used like debit cards in ATMs and most shops but are not linked to your bank account. You can purchase a multi-currency card online which allows you to load it with sterling, euros, dollars, etc. Three major players are Moneycorp with its Explorer card (www.moneycorpcard.com), MasterCard with its ICE card (www.iceplc.com) and Travelex (www.cashpassport.com), including their new Travelex Supercard (www.travelex.co.uk/services/supercard). These cards are normally free to purchase, though there may be an initial minimum loading requirement. Be aware that most charge a dormancy fee after 12 months of inactivity.

It is always advisable to keep a small amount of cash handy. Sterling is fine for many countries but US dollars are preferred in much of the world such as Latin America and Israel. The easiest way to look up the exchange rate of any world currency when planning your travels is to check on the internet (eg www.oanda.com or www.xe.com/ucc) though the rate you actually get will always be less favourable than the ones listed. Most banks require a few days' notice to obtain a foreign currency for you. Marks & Spencer's Travel Money offers favourable exchange rates with no commission or handling charges on currency or travellers' cheques. Furthermore these can be ordered online and posted to your home. The Post Office, Thomas Cook and The Money Shop also offer decent rates and people who live in London would do well by visiting one of the 11 branches of Thomas Exchange Global (www.thomas exchangeglobal.co.uk) which offer consistently cheaper rates.

A credit card is useful for many purposes, provided you will not be tempted to abuse it. It can be invaluable in an emergency and handy for showing at borders where the officials frown on penniless tourists; as Roger Blake discovered when he tried to leave Australia on a one-way ticket:

> *On my world travels, I'm usually prepared to be challenged, by having printed bank statements (of borrowed money) at the ready. However, having never been asked before I didn't bother this time and, sod's law, at Melbourne airport they weren't happy about allowing me to leave on a one-way ticket to New Zealand without proof of 'sufficient funds'. I pointed out that it states on my NZ work visa 'outward passage waived' but they were having none of it. I only had about $400 in my pocket. But fortunately I have generous 'credit' available on my credit card. I was able to log onto my account via the internet and that was enough to persuade them to let me through ... eventually ... just one day short of a year to the day after I arrived.*

From London to La Paz there are crooks lurking, ready to pounce upon the unsuspecting traveller. Theft takes many forms, from the highly trained gangs of children who artfully distract people especially in railway stations while their accomplice picks pockets to violent attacks on the streets of US or Brazilian cities. Even more depressing is the theft that takes place by other travellers in youth hostels or on beaches. Risks can be reduced by carrying your wealth in several places including a comfortable money belt worn inside your clothing, steering clear of seedy or crowded areas, avoiding counting your money in public and moderating your intake of alcohol. If you are mugged, and have an insurance policy that covers cash, you must obtain a police report (sometimes for a fee) to stand any chance of recouping part of your loss.

While you are busy saving money to reach your desired target, you should be thinking of other ways in which to prepare yourself – including health, what to take and which contacts and skills you might cultivate.

What to Take

While aiming to travel as light as possible (leave the hair products behind), you should consider the advantage of taking certain extra pieces of equipment. For example many working travellers consider the extra weight of a tent and sleeping bag worthwhile in view of the independence and flexibility it gives them if they are offered work by a farmer who cannot provide accommodation. A comfortable pair of shoes is essential, since a job-hunt abroad often involves a lot of pavement pounding.

Mobile phones are now *de rigueur* for any job-hunt on the road (see section below on 'Staying in Touch' for advice). Other items that can be packed that might be useful for a specific money-making project include a penny whistle or guitar for busking, a jacket and tie for getting work as an English teacher or data inputter, a pair of gloves (fingerless, rubber, as appropriate) for cold-weather fruit picking, and so on. Leave at home anything of value (monetary or sentimental). The general rule is stick to the bare essentials (including a Swiss army knife – but not in your hand luggage if you're flying or it will be confiscated at security). One travelling tip is to carry dental floss, useful not only for your teeth but as strong twine for mending backpacks, hanging up laundry, etc. Some food items are hard to buy abroad (eg British tea bags, peanut butter, etc) so if there's something you can't live without, you'll have to pack it. If you have prearranged a job, you can always post some belongings on ahead.

With Wi-Fi becoming almost universal, most travellers now consider a laptop or smartphone an essential piece of equipment, though carrying an expensive gadget makes you more vulnerable to theft, and recharging can be a hassle. Increasingly travellers consider paper maps and guidebooks passé, choosing instead to rely on their smartphone loaded with a range of travel apps. For questions about travel logistics or recommended places to visit, people turn to TripAdvisor and Twitter as well as to Lonely Planet to find out about destinations and choose where to eat and stay.

And yet I am of the generation that finds that good maps and guides enhance one's enjoyment of a trip. If you are going to be based in a major city, buy a map ahead of time perhaps from the famous map and travel shop Stanfords, which has a branch in Bristol as well as the mother-store in Covent Garden in London; they also have a searchable catalogue online at www.stanfords.co.uk. Also recommended is Daunt Books (83 Marylebone High Street, London W1; www.dauntbooks.co.uk and five other branches in London), which stock fiction and travel writing alongside guidebooks and maps. The Map Shop in Worcestershire (www.themapshop.co.uk) and Maps Worldwide in Wiltshire (www.mapsworldwide.co.uk) both do an extensive mail order business in specialised maps, hiking guides and all kinds of guidebooks.

In North America, Canada's largest travel bookstore is Wanderlust in the hip area of Kitsilano in Vancouver (www.wanderlustore.com), which carries books, maps and travel accessories.

Insurance

Information about health issues for travellers is given at the end of the next chapter, 'Travel'. One of the keys to avoiding medical disaster is to have adequate insurance cover. All travellers must face the possibility of an accident befalling them abroad. In countries such as Thailand and Venezuela the rate of road traffic accidents can be as much as 20 times greater than in the UK. Research carried out by the Foreign and Commonwealth Office revealed that more than a quarter of travellers aged 16–34 do not purchase travel insurance, which means that about three million people are taking a serious risk.

Given the limitations of state-provided reciprocal health cover (ie that it covers only emergencies), you should certainly take out comprehensive private cover which will cover extras, such as loss of baggage and, more importantly, emergency repatriation.

Every enterprise in the travel business is delighted to sell you insurance because of the commission earned. Shopping around online or by phone can save you money. Most companies offer a standard rate that covers medical emergencies as well as a premium rate that also covers personal baggage, cancellation, etc. If you are not planning to visit North America, the premiums will be less expensive. Some companies to consider are listed here, though you can compare these and many others on www.moneysupermarket.com. For a policy lasting a year, expect to pay roughly £25 per month for basic backpacker cover and £30–£40 for more extensive cover. Note that in almost all cases these policies must be purchased before you leave home. If your plans change after departure, one policy that will cover this contingency is World Nomads (wwwworldnomads.co.uk), which is endorsed by *Rough Guides*.

Many policies will be invalidated if you injure yourself at work, eg put out your back while picking plums or cut yourself in a restaurant kitchen, unless you have chosen a policy that specifically covers working abroad. Travel insurers do not always clearly define the type of work that is covered, for example what exactly does 'light' labour mean, or what is 'occasional'? Almost all exclude jobs that involve machinery, and some may impose a height restriction, ie no cover for anyone working more than 2 metres off the ground, ie potentially up a ladder on a volunteer building site or picking fruit in an orchard. Always focus on the fine print.

Coe Connections International: www.coeconnections.co.uk. Offers 12 months of comprehensive worldwide cover for £248 but does not cover manual work.

Columbus Direct: www.columbusdirect.com. One of the giants in the field of travel insurance; £273 for 12 months' worldwide cover with occasional promotional discounts. Globetrotter policy covers non-manual work including bar and restaurant work, being a musician/singer and fruit picking as long as it doesn't require machinery.

Direct Travel Insurance: www.direct-travel.co.uk. Sample cost of 12 months' backpacker cover starts at £226. As usual manual work is excluded, defined as 'work involving the lifting or carrying of heavy items in excess of 25kg, work at a higher level than two storeys or any form or work underground'.

Downunder Worldwide Travel Insurance: ☎ (+44) 800 393908; www.duinsure.com. Six months' Essentials cover costs a bargain £92; the Backpackers rate of £113 adds more cover, as does the Adventurer policy (£147) up to Comprehensive (£159); can be extended while you're on the road.

Endsleigh Insurance: ☎ (+44) 330 3030156; www.endsleigh.co.uk; 12 months' gap year cover from £345. Offers travel insurance specifically designed for travellers planning to live and work abroad for up to 12 months, including adventure sport activities.

Globelink International: www.globelink.co.uk/travel-insurance-for-working-abroad.html. £220 for 12 months, or £265 to include adventure sports.

Hiscox Travel Insurance: www.hiscox.co.uk/travel/gap-travel-insurance. One-year worldwide cover costs £380; extra payment of £20 covers most manual work.

Multitrip.com: ☎ (+44) 333 355 6181; www.multitrip.com. Backpacker policy suitable for trips of long duration; covers non-manual jobs including bar work, restaurant work, volunteering, au pair work and fruit picking. £166 basic for 12 months.

True Traveller: www.truetraveller.com. Policy recommended for the work abroad Canada programme IEC. 12 months' cover for £245, £321 or £394. If you plan to do manual work, you will have to add the Adventure Activity Pack which will increase the cost.

If you do have to make a claim after a theft or medical expenses, keep all receipts and amass as much documentation as possible to support your claim, most importantly a police report.

Recommended US insurers for extended stays abroad are Travel Guard (www.travelguard.com), Travel Insurance Services (www.travelinsure.com) and International SOS Assistance Inc. (www.internationalsos.com), which is used by aid agencies and is designed for people working in remote areas. A firm that specialises in providing insurance for Americans living overseas is Wallach & Company (www.wallach.com).

Security

Travel inevitably involves balancing risks and navigating hazards real or imagined. The Foreign and Commonwealth Office of the UK government (FCO) runs a regular and updated service; the website www.gov.uk/foreign-travel-advice gives frequently updated and detailed risk assessments of any trouble spots, including civil unrest, terrorism and crime.

Some believe that the FCO's travel warnings err on the side of caution to the detriment of national tourist authority efforts to attract visitors and of NGOs struggling to attract volunteers, so try to balance the official warnings with a first-hand account from someone who lives in the place you are considering. The director of the charity Sudan Volunteers Programme describes what he sees as the FCO bias:

> *We continue to be dogged by the negative and, I believe, misleadingly indiscriminate travel advice issued by the FCO which puts off potential volunteers, or more particularly their families. It stems, it seems to me, from the alarming experiences of embassy staff which induces them to put up ever higher fences to guard their premises and of course this siege mentality brings about an ever greater ignorance of the actual conditions.*

The FCO promotes a 'Travel Aware' campaign (www.gov.uk/travelaware) to raise awareness among independent travellers of potential risks and dangers and how to guard against them, principally by taking out a watertight insurance policy.

The site www.travellingalone.co.uk features articles on various topics of interest to the potentially nervous lone traveller. A couple of specialist organisations put on courses to prepare clients for potential dangers and problems on a world trip or gap year (see Gap Years chapter).

Qualifications

These sensible preparations of purchasing maps, buying insurance, finding out about malaria (see section on travellers' health in the next chapter) are relatively straightforward and easy. Other specific ways of preparing yourself, such as studying a language, learning to sail, dive or tend bar, cook or drive, or taking up a fitness programme, are a different kettle of fish. But the traveller who has a definite commitment may well consider embarking on a self-improvement scheme before setting off. Among the most useful qualifications you can acquire are a certificate in Teaching English as a Foreign Language (see Teaching English chapter) and a knowledge of sailing or diving (see Tourism chapter for the address of a course which also offers job placement).

It is a good idea to take documentary evidence of any qualifications you have earned. Also take along a sheaf of references, both character and work-related, if possible, on headed notepaper because scanned copies are not usually acceptable. It is difficult to arrange for these to be sent once you're on the road. If you have prepared a CV, store a copy online with a file hosting service such as Dropbox so that you can access it anywhere and tweak it when necessary.

Language

Having even a limited knowledge of a foreign language is especially valuable for the jobseeker. Consider enrolling in a part-time or short intensive course of conversation classes at a local college of further education or using a self-study programme with books and tapes or an online course. For example the *Oxford Take Off In ...* series from Oxford University Press (global.oup.com) is sold as MP3 downloads, or investigate courses from the BBC (www.bbc.co.uk/languages), Linguaphone (www.linguaphone.co.uk) and Pimsleur, an audio-based learning system whose courses consist of half-hour sessions every day.

More than a million people have turned to technology to teach them a language. Popular language-learning platforms include the popular Duolingo, Babbel and Smigin. Others include www.busuu.com and hellolingo.com which was set up in 2016 to replace the online language learning community livemocha that closed after nearly a decade. Also, check out noticeboards in local cafés, etc or on Facebook for info about language exchanges. A great resource is www.gumtree.com, which has a skills/language swap section and may carry information about informal language learning evenings sometimes called *Intercambios*. If you're lucky, your conversation partner might also be able to help you with advice/contacts for your trip or your job hunt. Numerous organisations offer 'in-country' language courses, though these tend to be expensive. CESA Languages Abroad in Cornwall (☎ (+44) 1209 211800; www.cesalanguages.com), Language Courses Abroad Ltd (www.languagesabroad.co.uk) and Edinburgh-based Caledonia Languages Abroad (www.caledonialanguages.co.uk) offer the chance to learn languages on location. The Worldwide Classroom is an effective US-based search engine for locating courses (www.worldwide.edu).

Another possibility is to forgo structured lessons and simply live with a family, which has the further advantage of allowing you to become known in a community and which might lead to job openings later. Some tourist offices and private agencies arrange paying guest stays, also known as homestays, which are designed for people wishing to learn or improve language skills in the context of family life.

BASED ON HIS YEARS OF LIVING ON THREE CONTINENTS, TILL BRUCKNER THINKS THAT LEARNING THE LANGUAGE IS PIVOTAL:

Learning the local language will not only help you find a job on the spot, it also makes life abroad so much more rewarding. As an extra bonus, you'll find work easier to come by when you return home too. The first thing I do when I arrive somewhere now is to get myself language lessons. The teacher will have met many other foreigners, have local connections and speak some English. In other words, he or she is the natural starting point on your job-hunt. If you make clear that you can only continue paying for your lessons if you find a way of earning some money, you've found a highly motivated ally in your search for work.

Making Contacts

The importance of knowing people, not necessarily in high places but on the spot, is stressed by many of our contributors. Some people are lucky enough to have family and friends scattered around the world in positions to offer advice or even employment. Others must create their own contacts by exploiting less obvious connections.

Dick Bird, who spent over a year travelling around South America, light-heartedly anticipates how this works:

> *In Bolivia we hope to start practising another survival technique known as 'having some addresses'. The procedure is quite simple. Before leaving one's country of origin, inform everyone you know from your immediate family to the most casual acquaintance, that you are about to leave for South America. With only a little cajoling they might volunteer the address of somebody they once met on the platform of Clapham Junction or some other tenuous connection who went out to South America to seek their fortunes. You then present your worthy self on the unsuspecting emigré's doorstep and announce that you have been in close and recent communication with their nearest and dearest. Although you won't necessarily be welcomed with open arms, the chances are they will be eager for your company and conversation. Furthermore these contacts are often useful for finding work: doing odd jobs, farming, tutoring people they know, etc.*

With social networking, international connections are easier to establish than ever. Trip.com (formerly Gogobot) works a bit like a 'travel Facebook' on which people create itineraries and share advice. Maybe you dimly recall that someone you went to primary school with moved to New Zealand or Tenerife with whom you could re-establish contact over Facebook or LinkedIn. By joining online communities and travel forums, you can make virtual friends and find advice from around the world. Some enterprising and imaginative bloggers have benefited from sharing their stories, pictures and videos and attracted offers of hospitality and even sponsorship.

The most high profile online community for hospitality exchange is the Couchsurfing Project (www. couchsurfing.com) where anyone can register free of charge to access members (apparently there are about ten million members). Like so many internet-based projects, the system depends on users' feedback, which means that you can check on a potential host's profile in advance and be fairly sure that dodgy hosts will be outed straightaway. Alternative free sites (with far fewer members) are the Hospitality Club (www.hospitalityclub.org) and Global Freeloaders (www.globalfreeloaders.com). A newer system has originated in France called NightSwapping (www.nightswapping.com), by which you earn the right to stay with a member by hosting a member. If you can't host, you can buy nights that cost from €7 to €49.

Erstwhile carpenter and Royal Marine reserve Christophe Lafosse went on the road for many months, hitch-hiking and benefiting from the kindness of strangers:

> *Some nights I get talking to strangers who offer me a sofa to sleep on, and some nights (mainly in cities) I organise a place via the couchsurfing website. So my only expenses are food and maybe the odd luxury (a €10 massage on a beach in southern Spain). I have learnt a great deal about talking to a person with the intention of getting them to offer me a place to sleep on their sofa. Of all the ways I've travelled before, this type of travelling has offered some very strange, weird, fantastic and random experiences.*

One way of developing contacts is to join a travel club such as the Globetrotters Club (BCM/Roving, London WC1N 3XX; www.globetrotters.co.uk) for £12 a year. Members who live near London, Chester or Toronto can attend local meetings and all can receive the quarterly travel newsletter and a list of members, indicating whether or not they are willing to extend hospitality to other globetrotters.

Servas International is an organisation begun by an American Quaker, which runs a worldwide programme of free hospitality exchanges for travellers, to further world peace and understanding. Normally you don't stay with one host for more than a couple of days. To become a Servas traveller or host in the UK, contact Servas Britain (www.servasbritain.net) who can forward your enquiry to your area coordinator who will arrange the compulsory interview. Before a traveller can be given a list of hosts (updated every autumn), he or she must pay a one-off joining fee of £4 plus £6 annual membership if under 25, £8 otherwise, and then £9/£18 to purchase a Letter of Introduction which allows them to travel and stay with other members. In the US Servas membership costs $98 or $49 if aged 18–30. Hospitality exchange organisations can make travel both interesting and cheap. Bradwell Jackson had been mulling over the possibility of travelling the world for about a decade before he finally gave up his drug abuse counselling job in the USA to take off for an indeterminate period of time. On his earlier travels he had discovered the benefits of joining free accommodation networks and wanted to test the system again. His first destination was Mexico where to his delight he found English teaching work at the first place he happened to enquire in Mexico City:

> *I really must say right away that Servas is not simply for freeloading in people's homes. However, once you take the plunge and commit to wandering the earth, things just start to fall into place. If you belong to clubs such as Global Freeloaders, Hospitality Club, or any of the other homestay organisations, don't be surprised if the family you stay with invites you for an extended stay. The first such family I stayed with in Mexico invited me to stay for six months. All they asked is that I help with the costs of the food they prepared for me and the hot water I used.*

Bradwell has continued his couchsurfing travels in some unlikely locations including Mali where his host in Bamako offered to let him stay for two months in exchange for two hours of English lessons a day. His host was a wealthy man who gave Brad all his meals, internet access, laundry and so on. He commented that *'once one lands into a dream situation like this, you are apt to feel a bit guilty, and such hospitality takes time to get used to. Still, I am certainly not complaining'*. More recently, en route to his teaching job in China, he stayed with a host in Hong Kong, and while completing his CELTA training at International House in London, a Servas host took him to see the Saxon church at Bradwell-on-Sea (no relation to his name).

Other hospitality clubs and exchanges are worth investigating. Women Welcome Women World Wide (www.womenwelcomewomen.org.uk) enables women of different countries to visit one another. There is no set subscription, but the minimum requested donation is £37, which covers the cost of the membership list (with just over 2,000 members) and newsletters in which members may publish announcements. There are currently 2,119 members (aged 16–80+) in 64 countries.

Travelling Alone or in Company

Many travellers emphasise the benefits of travelling alone, especially if job-hunting. Most are surprised that loneliness is hardly an issue, since solo travelling allows you to meet and be befriended by local people. Also, congenial companions are always to be found in travellers' hostels, harbourside pubs, language classes, etc, some of whom even team up with each other if they happen to be heading in the same direction. If you are anxious about the trials and traumas of being on your own, try a short trip and see how you like it.

Women can travel solo just as enjoyably as men, as Woden Teachout discovered when she was 24:

> *I'm female, American and like to travel alone. I have travelled with friends on occasion, which is definitely more 'fun' but it lacks the perilous sense of possibility and adventure that I love most about travelling. Whatever situations you get yourself into when you are on your own, you have to get out of. I have been terribly frightened: I spent the night of my 21st birthday huddled in a cellar hole in downtown Malmo in*

Sweden, wet and shivering, knowing that a local rapist had claimed three victims within the fortnight. But by the same token, the glorious moments, the stick-out-your-thumb-and-be-glad-for-whatever-is-going-to-happen-next moments, the feelings of triumph and absolute freedom, are uniquely yours.

Online communities for women travellers that might be of interest include www.thelmandlouise.com and www.pinkpangea.com.You have to be fairly lucky to have a friend who is both willing and available when you are ready to embark on a working trip. If you don't have a suitable companion and are convinced you need one, you can search through the travel clubs just mentioned, or on appropriate internet forums such as Lonely Planet's Thorn Tree (search for 'travel companions'), www.travbuddy.com, or www.gapyear.com's 'Travel Mates and Meet-ups.'

Staying in Touch

The revolution in communication technology means that anyone with a smartphone can keep in touch with friends via Facebook, check travel information online, book hostels ahead, summon up maps, blog and distribute photos via Instagram. Lots of companies will help you create your own blog free of charge, for example Wordpress (www.wordpress.com) and Tumblr (www.tumblr.com) are free and easy to use. If you do decide to keep a blog, remember that less is more: the folks back home probably don't have the time to read all the ins and outs of your long bus journeys and negotiations with hoteliers. Try to record the most interesting highlights.

Roaming charges for mobiles can cost an arm and a leg. Contact your mobile phone company to check on coverage. Usually if you are going to be in a country for a period of time, it is better to buy a local sim card and insert it into your (unlocked) handset. Alternatively you can reply on WhatsApp or Skype whenever you have access to Wi-Fi. Battery life is limited on smartphones.

A plethora of companies in the UK and USA sell pre-paid calling cards intended to simplify international phoning. You credit your card account with an amount of your choice (normally starting at £10 or £20), or buy a card for $10 or $20. You are given an access code that can be used from any phone. A company called 0044 (www.0044.co.uk) sells foreign sim cards which allow you to take your mobile with you and call at local rates while you're away. Its global sim card costs £15 (with £5 credit, which wouldn't last long) compared with £18 from GO-SIM (www.gosim.com) including $10 of credit, £29 for a data sim card.

Clearly there are advantages to such easy communication, though there are also travellers out there who spend an inordinate amount of time with their nose to a screen, thumbs a-wiggling, instead of looking around the country and meeting locals in the old-fashioned, strike-up-a-conversation way. Some have argued that dependence on instant communication with home hinders rather than encourages self-reliance, and that modern young travellers are more risk-averse than their elders were at their age.

RED TAPE

Passports and Work Permits

A standard 10-year UK passport with 32 pages costs £72.50 by post and £82.25 via the Post Office's Passport Check & Send service. A 48-page passport costs £85.50 or £95.25. The Passport Office warns that it takes at least six weeks to process an application for a first passport so it is important not to apply at the last minute. If you are renewing a passport, they will add the time left on your old passport to the new one. The requirements are clearly set out on the government's website. The fast track (one-week) application procedure for passport renewals costs about £30 extra, whereas the one-day premium service fee is £128 or £137 for 48 pages. Both require you to make an appointment at your nearest passport office either online or by ringing ☎ (+44) 300 222 0000.

Most countries will want to see that your passport has at least 90 days to run beyond your proposed stay. If your passport is lost or stolen while travelling, contact first the police then your nearest consulate.

The free reciprocity of labour within the European Union that Britons have enjoyed for so long means that the red tape has been simplified for travelling workers. As will become clear as you read further in this book, work permits are not readily available to ordinary mortals. With Britain voting to leave the EU, the bureaucratic procedures between the UK and the EU in regard to free movement, capital, goods and services are to be negotiated as part of wider discussions with other Member States, and will only become clear after exit proceedings have been finalised. To be eligible for a work permit, you must invariably have an employer, sponsoring company or approved exchange agency willing to apply to the immigration authorities on your behalf months in advance of the job's starting date, while you are in your home country. This is usually a next-to-impossible feat unless you are a high-ranking nuclear physicist, a foreign correspondent or are participating in an organised exchange programme where the red tape is taken care of by your sponsoring organisation. Wherever possible, we have mentioned such possibilities throughout this book. For general information about ordinary tourist visas, see the next chapter.

Bureaucracy at Large

Having your papers in order is a recurring problem for the working traveller. Andrew Winwood thinks that this book underestimates the difficulties: *'I wish that you would be honest about immigration, obtaining the proper visas, etc. But having said that, I wouldn't have had the nerve to go in the first place if I'd known how hard it would be.'* And for Americans coming to Europe it is even worse: Travis Ball from California was aware that he might encounter bureaucratic difficulties when he showed up in May to look for a job as a bartender in Ibiza, but he had underestimated the problem:

> *I chose Ibiza because I knew that the island would need a ton of workers for the season, and got there early to find the work. Three weeks of searching turned up three job offers; however, all were contingent on my getting the proper paperwork from the government. This was much more difficult than I antici-pated and just wasn't going to happen. All wasn't lost though. I had made a number of contacts during that three weeks searching and turned a bad situation into something that ended up even better. I had studied photography in college and been an 'advanced amateur'. I had my gear and portfolio with me, so I turned around and tried to find work shooting the clubs. After a short trial period, I was working for a British website shooting the clubs five–six nights a week. By the end of the season, I was heading a team of four photographers, requesting press credentials, and basically running a small media depart-ment on the island.*

It is easy to understand why every country in the world has immigration policies that are principally job protection schemes for their own nationals. Nevertheless it can be frustrating to encounter bu-reaucratic hassles if you merely intend to teach English for a month or work on a farm, and there are really no local candidates available. In all the countries with which we deal, we have tried to set out as clearly as possible the official position regarding visas and work and/or residence permits for both EU and non-EU readers. While the UK remains a member of the EU, the information for EU workers remains applicable to UK nationals, and will continue to do so until the UK has finalised the terms of its withdrawal from the EU with the other Member States.

If you are cautious by nature you may be very reluctant to transgress the regulations. People in this category will feel happier if they can arrange things through official channels, such as approved exchange organisations. Other travellers are prepared to throw caution to the winds and echo Helen Welch's view that *'government bureaucracy is the same anywhere, ie notoriously slow; by the time the system discovers that you are an alien you can be long gone'*. This is more serious in some countries and in certain circumstances than in others, and we have tried to give some idea of the enthusiasm with which the immigration laws are enforced from country to country and the probable outcome for employer and employee if the rules are broken. The authorities will usually turn a blind eye in areas where there is a labour shortage and enforce the letter of the law when there is a glut of unemployed local workers. If you do land an unofficial job (helping a Greek islander build a taverna, picking kiwi fruit in New Zealand, doing odd jobs at an orphanage in central Africa) try to be as discreet as possible.

Noisy boasting has been the downfall of many a traveller who has attracted unwelcome attention. It is always important to be as sensitive as possible to local customs and expectations.

Whenever you pass through immigration at airports with only a tourist visa, never let on that you intend anything other than sightseeing. Do not use the word 'work' or even 'volunteer'. If the authorities are suspicious they may search your luggage so do not carry anything as incriminating as was found in the bag of a Mexican man who arrived at Manchester airport, carrying a good luck card for his 'new life in the UK' and was promptly deported the next day.

GETTING A JOB BEFORE YOU GO

The subsequent chapters contain a great deal of advice and a number of useful web addresses and phone numbers for people wishing to fix up a job before they leave home. If you have ever worked for a firm with branches abroad (eg Starbucks, Manpower, EF Language Schools) it may be worth contacting sister branches abroad about prospects. There are lots of 'easy' ways to break into the world of working travellers – for instance working on an American summer camp or joining a two-week volunteer project on the Continent – all of which can be fixed up beforehand through straightforward channels. Inevitably, these will introduce you to an international circle of travellers whose experiences will entertain, instruct and inspire the novice traveller.

Professional or skilled people have a chance of pre-arranging a job. For example nurses, plumbers, coders, motor mechanics, piano tuners, English teachers and dive instructors can sometimes find work abroad within their profession by answering online adverts or scouring specialist journals, by writing directly to hospitals, schools and businesses abroad, and by registering with the appropriate professional association or recruitment agency.

But the majority of people who dream about working their way around the world do not have a professional or trade qualification. Many will be students who are on the way to becoming qualified, but are impatient to broaden their horizons before graduation. The main requirement seems to be perseverance. Dennis Bricault sent off 137 enquiries in order to fix up a summer job as a volunteer at an alpine youth hostel.

Many editions ago, a reader and traveller expressed his longing for a miraculous network of information for working travellers:

> *Wouldn't it be great if someone set up a scheme, whereby people could forward correspondence to an exchange of some kind, for people to swap addresses of places they've worked abroad. For example someone planning to work in Nice could write to some agency to obtain the address of another traveller who could tell him what the manager's like or if the chef is an axe-wielding homicidal maniac or that the accommodation is a hole in the bottom of the local coal mine. This would enable working travellers to avoid the rip-off places; also it might save them turning up in places where the work potential is zero.*

The scheme which was then a pipedream now has a name: the internet. To take just one of a thousand examples, Working Traveller (www.workingtraveller.com) is a free site designed for gap year travellers who want to find work, volunteer or cultural exchanges, with an emphasis on enhancing CVs.

Employment Agencies

Adverts that offer glamorous jobs and high wages abroad should be treated with suspicion. They are often placed by one-man companies who are in fact selling printed bumph about jobs on cruise ships, in the US or whatever, which will not get you much closer to any dream job, whatever their ads promise (eg *'Earn up to £400 a week in Japan'* or *'Would you like to work on a luxury cruise ship?'*). A not-infrequent con is to charge people for regular job listings and contacts in their chosen destination, which may consist of adverts lifted from newspapers or addresses from the *Yellow Pages* long out of date.

By law, UK employment agencies (and those in many other countries) are not permitted to charge jobseekers an upfront fee. They make their money from the company seeking staff. Every so often a bogus agency will place false recruitment advertisements in the tabloid press charging a 'registration fee' or a compulsory charge for extra services. They then disappear without trace. Travellers should be cautious of job offers found online. Never send money upfront to secure or find out more about a job; these are invariably scams. For example not long ago an individual was arrested in England after registering as a 'family' on an au pair matching website and asking applicants to transfer funds in advance of arrival.

There are of course reputable international recruitment agencies in Britain, the USA and elsewhere; many of them operating solely online. Specialist agencies for qualified personnel can be very useful, for example agencies for financial and IT vacancies with branches worldwide. Agencies with a range of specialities from disc jockeys for international hotels to English teachers for language schools abroad are mentioned in the relevant chapters which follow.

International Placement Organisations

Established organisations that assist students and other young people to work abroad are invaluable for guiding people through the red-tape problems and for providing a soft landing for first-time travellers. Specialist gap year agencies are listed in the chapter on Gap Years.

BUNAC: Priory House, 6 Wrights Lane, London W8 6TA; ☎ (+44) 33 3999 7516; www.bunac. org. Previously a non-profit student club and now a travel services company owned by STA Travel. Work and volunteer programmes for students and non-students in the USA, Canada, Australia, New Zealand, South Africa, Nepal, China and a number of others; programme fees usually include an arrival orientation course, UK and in-country support, accommodation and food. BUNAC USA in Texas has outgoing programmes for Americans in Ireland, UK, Spain, Australia, New Zealand, etc.

CCUSA (Camp Counselors USA): www.ccusa.co.uk (HQ in Sausalito, CA). Camp counsellor placement and work experience in the USA. Placements on summer camps in Russia, Croatia and Canada. Volunteering in many developing countries.

Freepackers: www.freepackers.com. Aims to help young travellers find paid work, internships and volunteer placements. Has programmes in France (tutoring English to children while learning French), hospitality internships and volunteer placements in Argentina and many others.

Global Choices: www.globalchoices.co.uk. Working holidays, voluntary work, internships and work experience worldwide from two weeks to 18 months. Placements are arranged for a fee in many fields in a range of countries from Brazil to Cyprus.

InterExchange Inc: New York; ☎ (+1) 212 924 0446; www.interexchange.org. English tutors in Spain, Germany and Italy; au pair placements in France, Norway, Netherlands, Spain, USA, Australia and New Zealand; work and travel in Australia, New Zealand and Ireland; teaching in Thailand and language courses in Peru, Costa Rica and Guatemala. Varying fees.

Intrax Global Internships: www.globalinternships.com. Internships in China, Japan, USA, France, Germany, Spain, Ghana and the UK. A few pay a stipend.

IST Plus Ltd: www.istplus.com. Working programmes for Britons in the USA, Australia, New Zealand, Singapore, Thailand and China.

OVC South Africa: www.ovc.co.za. With more than a dozen offices throughout the country, OVC can organise work and au pair placements for South Africans, arrange hospitality internships in the Middle East and book kibbutz volunteer placements in Israel as well as other programmes in North America, Asia and the Antipodes.

Twin Work & Volunteer: London; ☎ (+44) 800 804 8380; www.workandvolunteer.com. Volunteering on projects in developing countries, internships in professional environments around the world and seasonal paid and unpaid working holidays in developed economies including Norway.

Youth exchange organisations and commercial agencies offer packages that help their nationals to take advantage of the work permit rules. For example Travel CUTS in Canada operates the SWAP programme (www.swap.ca) that sends Canadian students to work in many countries. Approved work-abroad programmes operate for Canadian young people in Australia, New Zealand, Ireland, UK, Austria, Japan plus teaching in Thailand and Vietnam.

Rita Hoek is one person who decided to participate in an organised programme, the Work and Travel Australia programme offered by Travel Active based in Venray, Netherlands:

> *Though I'm not suggesting these programmes are perfect for everybody's specific plans, it's been of great help to me. You can access a discount-group airfare (cheaper and easier), they help with getting a visa and most programmes provide a first week of accommodation, assistance in getting a tax file number and opening a bank account, a service to forward your mail, general information about work and travelling and heaps more. If you don't want to feel completely lost at the airport while travelling for the first time (as I was), I can surely recommend it.*

But clients of packaged working holidays are not always so satisfied, and you should always search for feedback online before committing your money. Negative reviews on the feedback site www. consumeraffairs.com would have most people thinking twice before booking with a work and travel company that originated in Queensland (globalworkandtravel.com) that purports to guarantee jobs for its customers.

Advertisements

If you are thinking of advertising your interest in working abroad, try to be as specific as possible. While surfing the net you will often come across postings along the lines of *'Looking for no-skills job anywhere. Please help me'* which seems worse than hopeless. For a good example of a reader not targeting his self-advertisement carefully enough, see Fergus Cooney's story in the Teaching English chapter. Although the internet makes it possible to access local job adverts, any potential employer is likely to look askance at someone in Dudley or Kirkcaldy who answers an ad for someone to start immediately in a pub on Corfu or a fruit farm in Western Australia.

Web forums can be goldmines. Annelies Van der Plas has used the Dutch travellers' forum www. wereldwijzer.nl to good effect more than once. The advert she placed was very general:

> *Instead of waiting and looking on www.wereldwijzer.nl, we placed an advertisement there ourselves. I was enthusiastic about this forum, because I had got my job on the Greek island of Kos this way. The advertisement was something like this: 'Two hard-working students are looking for a job abroad for July and August'. Our first response was from a man from a campsite where they all walk naked (don't know the English word for it). As you can imagine we waited for other responses. The second response was from a Dutch woman also from a campsite in France. The job was to entertain the children on the campsite and help the owners with cleaning, preparing the barbecue and serving dinner. At first we were a little sceptical, but we looked at their homepage and searched for information and experiences about the campsite. Our contact (Jane) told us that it's not really a party job, but instead you would be part of 'the family'. By this she meant that people at the campsite eat (almost) every night on one long table together. You really get to know the people. This is the thing that persuaded us to take the job. Another plus was that Jane gave us the email address of a girl who worked there before. She told us what we could expect, which was helpful. Within one or two weeks we received our train tickets in the post (worth about €200 each). Also I received a phone call from Jane; we talked about some practical things and fun stuff, like horse riding (she was very glad that for the first time one of her employees liked horses). The best thing to do before you accept a job abroad is to search the internet for experiences, which is what we did.*

Two of the most useful sites are the free community noticeboards Gumtree (www.gumtree.com) and Craigslist (www.craigslist.org); the latter started in San Francisco in 1995 but has spread to hundreds of cities from Auckland to Buenos Aires, Moscow to Cairo. With notification of about half a million new job ads a month, it is probably the biggest job board in the world, as well as carrying accommodation listings and everything else. It also lists many unpaid jobs and internships.

GETTING A JOB ON ARRIVAL

For those who leave home without something fixed up, a lot of initiative will be needed. Many travellers find it easier to locate casual work in country areas rather than cities, and outside the student holiday periods (although just before Christmas is a good time, when staff turnover is high). But it is possible in cities too, on building sites, in restaurants and in factories. If you go for the jobs which are least appealing, eg an orderly in a hospital for the criminally insane, a loo attendant, doing a street promotion dressed as a koala or a hamburger, a pylon painter, assistant in a battery chicken farm, charity collector, dog meat factory worker, or just plain dogsbody, the chances are you will be taken on sooner rather than later.

It always helps to have a neat appearance in order to dissociate yourself from the image of the hobo or hippy. Keenness and persistence are essential. Even if a prospective employer turns you down at first, ask again since it is human nature to want to reward keenness and he or she may decide that an extra staff member could be useful after all. Polite pestering pays off. For example, if your requests for work down on the docks produce nothing one day, you should return the next day. After a week your face will be familiar and your eagerness and availability known to potential employers. If nothing seems to be materialising, volunteer to help mend nets (thereby adding a new skill to the ones you can offer) and if an opening does eventually arise, you will be the obvious choice. If you want a job teaching English in a school but there appear to be no openings, volunteer to assist with a class one day a week for no pay and if you prove yourself competent, you will have an excellent chance of filling any vacancy which does occur. Patience and persistence should become your watchwords, and before long you will belong to the fraternity of experienced, world-wise travellers who can maintain themselves on the road for extended periods.

Despite her tender years when she first started travelling and fending for herself, Carisa Fey had learned the value of quiet observation:

> *My motto was and still is watch the people that do the job you want and then copy them. So my first few days in London I spent walking through the city watching people. After I found out what the businesswomen wore, I went to the shops and bought as cheaply as possible a very neat suit and the right kinds of accessories.*

You may follow the advice in this book to go to Avignon in France in August, for example, to pick plums or to resorts along the Great Barrier Reef to get bar work. When you arrive you may be disappointed to learn that the harvest was unusually early or the resort has already hired enough staff. But your informant may go on to say that if you wait two weeks you can pick grapes or if you travel to the next reef island, there is a shortage of dining room staff. In other words, one thing leads to another once you are on the track.

A certain amount of bravado is a good, even a necessary, thing. If you must exaggerate the amount of experience you have had or the time you intend to stay in order to get a chance to do a job, then so be it. There is little room for shyness and self-effacement in the enterprise of working your way around the world. (On the other hand, bluffing is not recommended if it might result in danger, for example if you pretend to have more sailing experience than you really do for a transatlantic crossing.)

> **AFTER CIRCUMNAVIGATING THE GLOBE AND WORKING IN A NUMBER OF COUNTRIES DAVID COOKSLEY COMMENTS:**
>
> *All the information and contacts in the world are absolutely useless unless you make a personal approach to the particular situation. You must be resourceful and never retiring. If I were the manager of a large company that needed self-motivating sales people, I'd hire all the contributors to Work Your Way Around the world since they have the ability to communicate with anyone anywhere in the language.*

Meeting People

The most worthwhile source of information is without question your fellow travellers, met in hostels, Irish pubs, etc. Other travellers can be surprisingly generous with their information and assistance. Hostel staff may be well versed in the local opportunities for casual jobs. Of course hostels are also the best places for working travellers to stay. Vast numbers of hostels are listed worldwide at specialist sites www.hostelbookers.com, www.hostels.com and www.hostelz.com. You can test bed availability, read reviews and then book if you like the sound of it, paying particular attention to the location; the sites add a small booking fee but it's nothing much.

The original youth hostels federation is called Hostelling International (www.hihostels.com) and consists of 4,000 hostels in 85 countries. Membership costs only £10 per year for those under 26, £20 if you are older, or £5/£15 if put on a direct debit (www.yha.org.uk for YHA England and Wales which is the UK branch of HI). Note that it is no longer necessary to be a member to stay in a YHA/HI hostel but it gives you a good discount. St Christopher's Inns operates a friendly chain of hostels, found across the UK and also in Paris, Berlin, Bruges, Amsterdam, Barcelona, Copenhagen and Prague.

If you have a particular hobby or interest, ask if there is a local club, where you will meet like-minded people; join local cyclists, cavers, environmental activists, train spotters, jazz buffs – the more obscure, the more welcome you are likely to be. Join language courses, find out if the English language bookshop has a useful noticeboard and perhaps even attend the functions of the English language church, where you are likely to meet the expatriate community or be offered free advice by the vicar. Marta Eleniak introduced herself to the local Polish club, since she has a Polish surname and a fondness for the country, to ask if she could put up a notice asking for accommodation. The kindly soul to whom she was speaking told her not to worry about it; she'd find her a place to move into the next day. She has come to the conclusion that learning to be a 'fog-horn' is an invaluable characteristic.

TILL BRUCKNER HAS (RELUCTANTLY) BEEN PERSUADED THAT HOBNOBBING WITH THE RICH AND POWERFUL CAN BE THE KEY TO JOB SUCCESS:

The one lesson I have failed to learn over and over again is the value of socialising. In Bolivia, I shoved a pamphlet advertising myself as a trekking guide under the doors of dozens of agencies without ever getting a reply. It just doesn't work that way. Nobody will ever bother to ring you if they don't know you. A week before I left, I met an old Bolivian friend and when I told him I'd been unable to find work, he said he couldn't believe it because his cousin had an agency and needed a German speaker. In the Sudan, I sent off my CV to all major NGOs offering myself as an unpaid volunteer. All I got was two negative replies. A week before I left (again) I went to a social event at a foreign embassy where I got talking with the head of a big charity. She told me about the problems they had with writing endless reports. I asked her why she hadn't replied to my application and it turned out she'd never seen it. The moral of the story is that in some countries the best place to start looking for a job is down the pub, especially the sort of pub where well-off locals and expats hang out. I absolutely loathe exactly that kind of establishment but you might well hit the jackpot in there. You're unlikely to get hired by someone poor after all.

People who inhabit a world at the opposite end of the earning spectrum can also be invaluable, ie the hippie community. For example, the kinds of people who attend Rainbow Gatherings are the kind who will know about intentional communities and squats where you can stay free of charge, and have advice for musicians, craftspeople, activists and so on. When Anna Ling attended a Rainbow Gathering in New Zealand, she met all sorts of interesting and helpful people, including one who told her of an excellent busking spot in Wellington which she later made use of.

If your contacts can't offer you a real job they might know of a 'pseudo job' or 'non-job' which can keep you afloat: guarding their yacht, doing odd jobs around their property, babysitting, cutting their hair, typing, teaching the children English or just staying for free. These neatly avoid the issue of work permits, too, since they are arranged on an entirely unofficial and personal basis. Human contacts are usually stronger than red tape.

Chance

When you first set off, the possibility of being a sheep-catcher in the Australian outback or an English tutor in Turkey may never have crossed your mind. Chance is a fine thing and is one of the traveller's greatest allies. Brigitte Albrech had saved up leave from her job in the German tourist industry to go on holiday in Mexico. While there, she became friendly with some Québecois who invited her to join them as tree planters in Western Canada, and she never made it back to her job.

There will be times when you will be amazed by the lucky chain of events that led you into a certain situation. 'Being in the right place at the right time' would have made a suitable subtitle to this book, though of course there are steps you can take to put yourself in the right place. Here are some examples of how luck, often in combination with initiative, has resulted in travellers finding paid work:

- Mark Kilburn took up busking in a small Dutch town and was eventually asked to play a few nights a week in a nearby pub for a fee.
- Stuart Britton was befriended by a fisherman in a dusty little town in Mexico and was soon tutoring some of the fisherman's friends and acquaintances (and living in his house).
- While standing in a post office queue in the south of France, Brian Williams overheard the word *boulot* (which he knew to mean odd job) and *cerises*. He tapped the lady on the shoulder and offered his cherry-picking expertise. After an unsuccessful search for the address she had given him, he finally asked directions of someone who offered him a job in their orchard instead.
- On a flight to Reykjavik, Caroline Nicholls happened to sit next to the wife of the managing director of a large fish-packing cooperative in Iceland who told her they were short of staff.
- While strolling round the Sunday market in the Raval of Barcelona, Alan and Sophie were approaching by a woman asking them if they would like to appear in promotional videos.
- After finishing his summer stint as a camp counsellor in the USA, Mark Kinder decided to try one parachute jump. He enjoyed it so much that he learned how to pack parachutes and was able to fund himself at the aerodrome for months afterwards.
- While looking for work on a boat in Antibes, Tom Morton found a job as a goatherd for six weeks in the mountains near Monte Carlo.
- Dominic Fitzgibbon mentioned to his landlady in Rome that he intended to leave soon for Greece since he had been unable to find a job locally in six weeks of looking. She decided he was far too nice to become a washer-up in a taverna and arranged for him to work as a hall porter at a friend's hotel.
- A. Gowing was a little startled to wake up one evening in Frankfurt station to find a middle-aged woman staring down at him. She offered him the chance of working with her travelling fun-fair.
- While getting her jabs for Africa at a clinic in Gibraltar, Mary Hall (a nurse cycling across Europe) noticed a door marked 'District Nurses', barged in and the following week had moved in as a live-in private nurse for a failing old lady.
- While shopping in a supermarket in Cyprus, Rhona Stannage noticed a local man with a trolley full of wine and beer, and assumed it could not be for his own consumption. She approached him, ascertained that he ran a restaurant and a day or two later was employed as a waitress.
- Connie Paraskeva shared a taxi in Bangkok with an American who told her about a vacancy in a refugee camp.

The examples could be multiplied *ad infinitum* of how travellers, by keeping their ears open and by making their willingness to help obvious, have fallen into work. One of the keys to success is total flexibility. Within 10 minutes of a chance conversation with a family sharing her breakfast table in an Amsterdam hotel, Caroline Langdon had paid her bill, packed her bags and was off to Portugal with them as their mother's help.

Of course there is always such a thing as bad luck too. You may have received all sorts of inside information about a job on a Greek island, a vineyard or in a ski resort. But if a terrorist attack has decimated tourism or if there was a late frost that killed off the grapes or if your destination is full of Balkan migrants willing to accept below par wages, there will be far fewer jobs and your information may prove useless. Unpredictability is built into the kinds of jobs that travellers do.

Design

You cannot rely on luck alone; you will have to create your own luck at times. You may have to spend many hours surfing the internet, or apply to 20 hotels before one will accept you or you may have to inform 20 acquaintances of your general plans before one gives you the address of a useful contact.

You must check noticeboards and newspaper advertisements, register with agencies and most important of all use the unselective 'walk-in-and-ask' method, just like jobseekers anywhere. Two important tools for an on-the-spot job-hunt are the *Yellow Pages* and a phone. When Mary Hall was starting her job search in Switzerland, a friend gave her an odd piece of advice which she claims works, to smile while speaking on the phone. Some people say that all initial approaches are best made by telephone since refusals are less demoralising than in person and you need not worry about the scruffiness of your wardrobe.

One old hand, Alan Corrie, describes his approach:

> *The town of Annecy in the French Alps looked great so I found a fairly cheap hostel and got down to getting organised. This meant I was doing the rounds of the agencies, employment office, noticeboards and cafés for a few days. After a matter of minutes in a town, I begin to sprout plastic bags full of maps, plans, lists, addresses and scraps of advice from people I have met on the road.*

Alan sounds unusually cheerful and optimistic about job-hunting and the result is that he worked in Europe for the better part of a decade. Our working wanderers have displayed remarkable initiative and found their jobs in a great variety of ways.

- Waiter in Northern Cyprus: I arranged my job by writing direct to the restaurant after seeing a two-minute clip on a BBC travel programme. Rita wrote back and offered me a job.
- Farmhand on a Danish farm: I placed an advert in a farmers' magazine, and chose one of four replies.
- Au pair to a family in Helsinki: I found work as a nanny in Finland simply by placing advertisement cards in a few playgroups.
- Teacher at a language school in southern Italy: We used the *Yellow Pages* in a Sicilian post office and from our 30 speculative applications received four job offers without so much as an interview.
- Winery guide in Spain: I composed a modest and polite letter and sent it to an address copied from one of my father's wine labels. I was astonished at their favourable reply. Several years later the same contributor wrote to say: I sent a copy of the page in your book where I am mentioned to prospective employers in Australia, and I was offered a job on a vineyard near Melbourne.
- Factory assistant in Ghana: I asked the local Amnesty International representative for any leads.

Implicit in all these stories is that you must take positive action.

REWARDS AND RISKS

The Delights

The rewards of travelling are mostly self-evident: the interesting characters and lifestyles you are sure to meet, the wealth of anecdotes you will collect with which you can regale your grandchildren and photos with which you can bore your friends, a feeling of achievement, an increased self-reliance and maturity, learning to budget, a better perspective on your own country and your own habits, a good sun tan ... the list could continue. Stephen Psallidas summed up his views on travelling:

Meeting people from all over the world gives you a more tolerant attitude to other nationalities, races, etc. More importantly you learn to tolerate yourself, to learn more about your strengths and weaknesses. While we're on the clichés, you definitely 'find yourself, man'.

One traveller came back from a stint of working on the Continent feeling a part of Europe rather than just an Englishman. Sometimes, travels abroad change the direction of your life. After working his way around the world in many low-paid and exploitative jobs, Ken Smith decided to specialise in studying employment law. After deciding to cycle through Africa on an extended holiday, Mary Hall changed her career and ended up working for aid organisations in Africa and the Middle East.

One of the best aspects of the travelling life is that you are a free and unfettered agent. Albert Schweitzer might have been thinking of the working traveller instead of equatorial Africans when he wrote: *'He works well under certain circumstances so long as the circumstances require it. He is not idle, but he is a free man, hence he is always a casual worker.'*

The Dangers

Of course things can go desperately wrong. As the number of young people backpacking to remote corners whether on gap years or otherwise has risen, it is inevitable that accidents will occur and will be widely reported. So if a young man slips down a waterfall in Costa Rica or a British girl is killed by a freak accident with a high voltage cable in Ecuador or a bus carrying overlanding travellers is held up by armed bandits in the Andes, the world hears about it. On the other hand if a student dies of a drug overdose or is killed on his bicycle in his hometown, this is not reported nationally.

A much less remote possibility than murder or kidnapping is that you might be robbed or lose your luggage or become involved in a traffic accident. You may get sick or lonely, or fed up, have a demoralising run of bad luck or fail to find a job, and begin to run out of money (if this is the case, consult the In Extremis chapter).

Many unofficial jobs carry with them an element of insecurity. You may not be protected by employment legislation and may not be in a position to negotiate with the boss. Often the work may be available to travellers like you because the conditions are unacceptable to a stable local population (or because the place is too remote to have a local population). If you have cultivated the right attitude, you will not hesitate to drift on to a new situation if the old one should become undesirable for any reason. Much is now said about 'socially responsible tourism' and perhaps working travellers who put up with dreadful employers are doing both their host community and other travellers a disservice. Stephen Psallidas's advice (based on his own experience of exploitative Greek bosses) is not to put up with it: *'My advice when you are mistreated or your employer acts unprofessionally is to shout back when they shout at you. If things don't improve, threaten to walk out and then do so. You will be doing a favour to future working travellers, and you will almost certainly be able to find something else if you try hard enough.'*

Even when a planned working holiday does not work out successfully, the experience will be far more memorable than just staying at home. This view is held by Stephen Hands who didn't regret his decision to go abroad to look for work (although it didn't work out), but he did regret boasting to all his friends that he was off for an indefinite period to see the world. After writing pages about her dodgy and difficult jobs in Australia, Emma Dunnage concluded with a typical paradox: *'But we did have the best time of our lives.'*

Though travelling itself is seldom boring, a job that you find to help out your finances along the way may well be. True 'working holidays' are rare: one example is to exchange your labour for a free trip with an outback Australian camping tour operator. But in many cases, the expression 'working holiday' is an oxymoron (such as 'cruel kindness'). Jobs are jobs wherever you do them. David Anderson, who found himself working on an isolated Danish farm where he didn't feel at home in any way, recommends taking: (a) your time to decide to accept a job; (b) a copy of *War and Peace*; and (c) enough money to facilitate leaving if necessary. The best policy is to leave home only after you have the reserves to be able to work when you want to.

Work Your Way Around the World

Susan Griffith

trotman | **t**

PART 2: WORK YOUR WAY IN EUROPE

WORK YOUR WAY AROUND THE WORLD

WORK YOUR WAY AROUND THE WORLD

rience of working with young people and preferably of travelling in the developing world. Remuneration depends on experience and starts at £55 a day.

When joining any expedition you are unlikely to escape a financial liability, for most expeditions levy a fee from each participant. Sponsorship, and the amount of it, from companies, trusts and other sources will depend upon the aims of the expedition and the benefits to the donor. And once the money and equipment are forthcoming the expedition then has obligations to its sponsors and forfeits much of its freedom. Raising sponsorship, a job with which all expedition members should help, is probably the biggest headache of all and involves endless letter-writing and the visiting, cap in hand, of dozens of commercial establishments and other possible sources of income.

Enterprise

You don't have to spend eight hours a day serving coffee or stripping a strawberry patch in order to earn money abroad. Many travellers have found or made opportunities to go into business for themselves, exchanging steady wage packets for less predictable sources of income. A huge and growing community of people have mastered the online tools and services that enable them to work from anywhere in our new gig economy. The people who have succeeded in this type of work tend to have a large degree of initiative, determination and often creativity; they have identified some niche in the market and, with a good wifi connection, have gone on to make money from their idea. Some have exploited their own travels by using a blog to attract advertising, though competition is fierce from all the established bloggers out there.

DIGITAL NOMADS

Technology that allows people to work from any location has caused a revolution in working abroad. Graphic designers, English teachers, social media marketers, short-traders, expats of all kinds have succeeded in doing business through their laptops. I have done it myself, writing books and articles during protracted stays in Canberra, California, Canada and Rome, just as I do at home in England. Websites with telling names such as www.NuNomad.com, www.nomadicnotes.com, www.modern daynomads.com and www.locationindependent.com appeal to the market addressed by an article in *Business Week*:

> *Do you ever wish you could win the lottery, chuck the rat race, and take off to explore the world? Heck – who hasn't? These days, however, there's a group of independent-minded, techno-savvy entrepreneurs who are turning that dream into a reality. They call themselves New Nomads, and they've transformed work-at-home into work-anywhere-you-damn-well-please.*

A gigantic infrastructure has grown up to service this sub-culture of aspiring digital nomads. Many individuals (themselves digital nomads) and small start-ups market e-books and workshops to roving entrepreneurs and rent out co-working spaces. You will find invitations to join online communities such as Nomad List (www.nomadlist.com) in order 'to meet 10,000+ remote workers' at a cost of $75 a year. Some pitches over-romanticise the life of a location-independent worker. After all, who realistically can work on a laptop from a deckchair on the beach? It is important not to be taken in by the hype of 'living the dream' and to focus on nitty-gritty realities and the length of time it will take to make a potential profit. Most agree that you need to have savings that will last you at least six months and preferably a year. Travel writer, blogger and publisher, Tim Leffel, has written helpful common sense books such as *A Better Life for Half the Price* (2015, $21.95) in which he profiles 20+ countries with low costs of living and urges readers considering a relocation to spend a trial period in the destination, preferably at a time of year when the weather is at its least comfortable.

A host of other books with a less practical slant may inspire you. For example, Sarah Alderson has written an amusing account of how she and her husband left their high-pressure, long-hours jobs in London to become global nomads with their three year old daughter. *Can We Live Here: Finding a Home in Paradise* describes putting down roots in the Balinese tourist hotspot of Ubud, where Sarah re-invents herself as a blogger and writer of teenage fiction. Meanwhile her husband sets up an attractive bamboo collaborative working space called Hubud.org (Hub Ubud) to cater to 'a diverse community of local and visiting creatives, techies, entrepreneurs and businessfolks, changemakers, downshifters and truth-seekers'. Charges start at $20 for a day pass and go up to $275 a month for unlimited use. It belongs to Copass (www.copass.org), a global federation of more than 600 co-working spaces in 400+ locations in 75 countries. Various levels of membership allow you to access any of these spaces from €49 for three check-ins a month up to €299 unlimited. Most newbies prefer to use the free wifi at Starbucks or similar. A good resource for cafés of interest to digital nomads can be found at www.nomadicnotes.com/cafes.

Plenty of bloggers describe their own journeys, for example a Colombian and Irish couple still running their business remotely blog at www.discoveringice.com. They both work full-time on a digital marketing startup that was initially given a boost by StartUpChile, which prompted them to move to Chile for a time. This is a programme created by the Chilean government to accelerate early-stage startups that want to use Chile as a stepping stone to the rest of Latin America and the world. Other countries have followed suit, so it could be worth applying for a seed grant from one of these once you have a well developed business. Another source of start-up money is crowdfunding through platforms like Kickstarter or Indiegogo.

Digital marketing is a massive business and this book can't hope to cover the topic in detail. Just to give a flavour of location-independent options, an online start-up Tripaneer.com often hires graduates as Online Content Editors to market themed package holidays to a worldwide audience. Jessica Piña from Mexico, who studied in Canada, was paid piece work to write favourable reviews of holiday companies and travel destinations, with very fast work speeds expected. After doing an economics degree at Liverpool University, Hugh Bennett worked in finance for two years, spent a year travelling and then moved to southern Holland where he worked for an online gaming company as a brand manager. While working to increase market share through digital advertising campaigns and social media, he was in constant touch with colleagues he never met because they lived all over the world.

One long-established peripatetic businessman is Charlie Wetherall, originally from Montana, who attributes his current lifestyle to having read *Work Your Way Around the World*, which he describes on his website http://runawaytrader.com:

I was reflecting today about how I got into this runaway mode in the first place and recalled that I can blame Susan Griffith for some of it. Her book offered a glimmer of hope that – someday – I could scrape up enough courage to escape the drudgery of my own existence and see some of the world. I never gave up on the idea of flitting about the globe and inventing a way to pay for that extravagance as I travelled. Now we can do business, that is, make a living, from practically anywhere on the planet. Sure, you may choose an occupation like ditch-digger or a police officer that requires your local presence, but you can also pick an income-producing gig that can be performed from anywhere on the world, without much regard to the local labour force.

Thanks to wireless and other advanced computer technologies, it's now possible to make money buying and selling stocks as I do from almost anywhere in America, and anywhere in the world. As for me, it's strictly pay as you go. If I make money day trading, I go, and keep going. If I don't, I'm marooned. It's as simple as that. I want to know if I can day trade at basecamp on Mount Everest (that's a trip I'm scheduling for spring). I know I can get to all these exotic places. But can I whip out my laptop and make a trade from wherever 'there' is?

Many people earning while travelling have websites that produce a steady income stream. This presupposes that you have valuable material to share with the blogging community. Kirsty Henderson, whose byline on her blog NerdyNomad.com is 'Backpacking around the world on my income from the internet', itemises her earnings from various web ventures, including selling a map she designed of Kigali, the Rwandan capital where she once lived. Link building to get your websites to the top of Google used to be the preferred way to flourish, and patiently building traffic through social networking and blog carnivals. Websites use Google's AdSense to 'monetise' their content, which is measured in clicks.

Hannah Adcock wanted to leave an Edinburgh winter behind in order to work and live in a warm climate. After a month's Arabic course in Cairo, she and her husband Andrew moved to Dahab on the Red Sea as a cheap and sunny place to live while freelance editing, at least until political turmoil resulted in the temporary closing down of internet access. No digital nomad can survive without a good web connection:

After spending an interesting if horribly polluted time in Cairo learning Arabic in December we moved on to Dahab in January. The quality of life really was amazing – we had a third-storey apartment which was a bit like a ship (lots of wood) and had views over the sea and mountains and a terrace. A swimming spot was two minutes away, the weather was hot, and I found a great horse to ride. Plus we had internet so could work – and we did, pretty hard. However, the idyll started to be rocked, as it were, when the Tahrir Square demonstrations started, and the internet blackout really put the boot in. I've followed the protests with great interest, and Dahab has stayed fairly safe, but we decided to move to Tel Aviv (temporarily). This is mainly so we can get some work done without an octogenarian billionaire deciding to switch off the communications network when he feels like it.

Hannah later moved to Berlin, earning from clients who don't mind if she is *'in Edinburgh, Cairo or on the moon, provided I have internet'*. In addition to a laptop, tools of the trade might include a flash gun, hard drive and USB pen drive. When last heard of she was running her business Contented Strategy with tips, advice and case studies for startups, SMEs and social entrepreneurs.

IMPORT/EXPORT

With experience, travellers come to know what items can be bought cheaply in one country and profitably sold in another. Wherever something is exorbitantly priced, it is possible to sell informally to local people or fellow tourists at a profit. But as the world shrinks and trade barriers dissolve, the possibilities are becoming fewer. After his extensive travels in Turkey and Asia, one American concluded:

The enterprise opportunities seem to be vanishing faster than you can say 'free trade'. There weren't many things in high demand that you could buy cheaper in the USA or across a neighbouring border, at least where we were, unless you were dealing in big-ticket electronics. Bringing things back, of course, is a different story.

Perhaps when the UK leaves the EU, which is likely to alter the UK's trading relationship with the EU significantly, there will be new and different opportunities to exploit.

Despite the massive increase of online buying across national borders, niches can always be found. For example, a Derbyshire man realised that Germans in the town twinned with his loved British goods including the obvious things such as tea and marmalade. He went over with a supply of Union Jack beach towels and sold them at the local market in a very short time. Or a Scottish woman had T-shirts printed up with Gaelic motifs and sold them at one of the Canadian Highland Games events every summer. Past readers have recommended carrying around cigarette papers when they were expensive or hard to obtain in certain countries; however with online shopping, this is unlikely to gain much profit. Travellers in Japan and the US with plenty of spare cash to take a punt have been known to buy PlayStation consoles or even iPhones, with a view to selling them discreetly in countries where market conditions, eg in Scandinavia, or exchange rate anomalies, or high import fees as in Brazil make these items much more expensive. Most decide the potential gains are not worth the risk of being unable to find a buyer.

Some travellers think it's worthwhile to load up on bronze trinkets, alpaca sweaters, jade jewellery, rosewood boxes, sisal baskets from Kenya, Tibetan woollens, Turkish carpets or anything else which they know are more expensive or unobtainable elsewhere. Before engaging in this sort of activity first you have to be in a position to assess the quality of what you are buying. I have been approached by minority tribal women in northern Vietnam selling embroidered pencil cases, purses and shoulder bags, silver earrings and bracelets that was clearly imported Chinese tat, whereas the expensive needlework was genuine though the indigo dye would need to be fixed by washing in cold salt water. The next requirement is to be a master haggler, which involves knowledge, patience and good humour. And of course you must know your market and be thoroughly acquainted with customs regulations. Usually it is difficult to make much of a profit on one-off trips abroad. One way of gauging a potential market is to make use of eBay. Depending on the response, you could fill orders as they come in, but make sure the price you charge covers shipping costs as well as makes you a profit.

Do not believe every foreign trader who promises vast profits in your home country, for example selling Tahitian pearls or Sri Lankan sapphires, or who assures you that you will have no difficulty at customs. In fact do not believe any of them. Almost invariably they are inventing a story in order to make a bulk sale. No consumer protection is available to their gulls. Bangkok seems to be the capital of smooth-talking swindlers. A warning notice in a Bangkok hostel, which reads *'These people are vicious and evil and all they say is lies'* was written by a German who parted with $1,100 for '$3,000 plus' of sapphires, only to be told by his 'guaranteed buyer' (an unwitting jeweller in Sydney) that their true value was $250.

Currency Exchange

In countries where there is a soft currency, ie one that cannot officially be used to buy dollars or sterling, or where the government attaches an unjustifiably high value to its currency, a black market often develops. For example the differential in the Uzbek currency, the som, in 2016 was just over 2,800 soms to the US dollar at the bank rate, and nearly 6,000 soms on the black market. Other currencies where the unofficial rate diverges significantly from the official one include the Angolan Kwanza and the Nigerian Naira.

Tempting as the rewards might be, you should be aware of the pitfalls. The black market attracts shady characters who regularly cheat even the canniest travellers, making them regret their greed. Favourite ploys include handing the tourist an envelope full of shredded newspaper or one large denomination bill wrapped cleverly around a wad of lower bills, or pretending to spot a policeman and then vanishing after taking your dollars but before giving you your Egyptian pounds or whatever. To guard against such an outcome, always avoid trading on the street especially after dark.

Familiarise yourself with the appearance of all denominations of currency and take along a friend to assist you. The best place to exchange would be with the proprietor of your hostel or in a shop. These transactions are illegal, so find out in advance what the penalties might be if you are caught.

Second-hand Gear

Outside the consumer societies of the West, there is a fluctuating demand for gadgets and gewgaws, and various items we take for granted can be sold or traded. Even if you don't get cash, you might trade for goods and services or an interesting souvenir. Writing in *Rough News* a few years ago, the newsletter from Rough Guides, one traveller described what he observed on an overland trip through Africa. While shopping in Nakuru, Kenya, he was approached by a vendor looking to sell him one of his handpainted cards. The traveller declined the request; the vendor then asked if he had anything to trade, so he (jokingly) took out his biro. After testing the biro, the vendor accepted, offering a card in return. As he travelled around Kenya, he received many similar requests for clicky pens and items of his clothing; watches in particular proved to be highly coveted trading items, so it might be worth taking an old watch with you if you are travelling around Kenya.

Elfed Guyatt from Wales thinks that Sweden is a particularly promising destination for any would-be entrepreneurs, at least when he was there some while back:

> *In the weekend market stalls people just set up their own table and sell off all sorts of odds and ends. The prices are incredibly high compared to Britain for certain things. You should make 500% profit on selling things like medals, caps, British and American books in subjects that interest the Swedes, in fact anything that looks different and not easily available in their country. They do like showing off possessions here. Souvenirs of London or Shakespeare go well. I saw a very cheap, small brass Big Ben table bell sell for £12.50 and an old battered cricket bat went for £25.*

SPOTTING LOCAL OPPORTUNITIES

The opportunities for finding eager customers on whatever doorstep you find yourself are endless and we can only give some idea of the remarkable range of ways to earn money by using your initiative and your imagination. If you see a gap in the market, try to fill it. For example Stephen Psallidas toyed seriously with the idea of buying a bicycle in the tomato-growing capital of Queensland in order to hire it out to job-seeking tomato pickers since at the time Bowen was, if not a one-horse town, a one-bicycle town. After getting to know the Greek island of Levkas fairly well, Camilla Lambert hired a Jeep at weekends and took three paying passengers out for a day's excursion. One Englishman acquired a chainsaw in Spain and made a killing by hiring himself out to farmers to prune their olive trees. A Canadian who was having trouble being hired by a language school in a provincial city in Taiwan set up his own English immersion social club that easily covered his costs in the two months he ran it. You just need to exploit any manual or artistic or public relations skill you already have or which you have cultivated for the purpose.

Entrepreneurship like this often finds itself on the borderline of the law. If you paint the sun setting over a harbour you are an artist; sell the painting to someone who stops to admire it and you may, in law, become a street trader requiring a permit. If you wash motorists' windscreens at traffic lights, you might be doing them a service, but the police might consider you an obstruction. Usually they do no worse than move you on.

Home-made Handicrafts

A number of people have successfully supported themselves abroad by selling home-made jewellery and other items on the street. Once you master a skill you can move around with it, perhaps following the festival circuit around Europe or wherever mobs of people gather. Careful preparations can pay dividends; for example Jennifer Tong picked up shells from a beach near Eilat and invested £5 in a pair of pliers and some wire, clips and beads when she was in Israel. With these materials she made simple earrings that were bought for a couple of pounds a pair on the Greek Islands. Even more simply, Amy Ignatow collected smooth pebbles in Israel, decorated them with a permanent pen and sold them on the street in Jerusalem for £3 each. Steve Pringle sold earrings in Madrid that he had made from a stock of cheap imitation diamonds he had brought over from London. Braided or knotted friendship bracelets are popular in travellers' resorts and can usually be sold for a few quid and take no more than 15 minutes to make. You have to find something that doesn't require too much time, which Emma Hoare failed to do while on her gap year:

> In the south of France I met up with a girl I had been previously travelling with, and decided to make money by selling bags that we'd sewn. We went on to Spain and quickly discovered that sitting in little pensione rooms stitching minuscule beads onto cheap, flimsy fabric was a recipe for mental deterioration and, at times, uncontrollable hysteria. Then I decided that I had put too much effort into my bags to sell them. They were my little works of art and I was damned if I was going to let some horrible young tourist have it for a fiver and then leave it on the floor in a club somewhere (see what I mean about mental deterioration?).

It is worth looking out for cheap and unusual raw materials such as beads from Morocco, shells from Papua New Guinea or bamboo from Crete. An aspiring sculptress who makes copper wire sculptures found that business was slow at the beginning of the Edinburgh Festival but hotted up, allowing her to fund several months of post-Festival travels. Needless to say, you have to be good at what you do for this to be effective.

If you can draw, knit, sew, sculpt or work with wood or leather then you may be able to produce something that people want to buy. In holiday resorts full of young people, you might be able to exploit the skill of drawing henna tattoos or braiding hair with beads. All you need for the latter is the expertise, some cheap multi-coloured beads and thread with which to tie off the ends. The weather will have an obvious effect on success or failure as Nicole Gluckstern from San Francisco found at the Edinburgh Fringe Festival: *'For cash I did hair wraps. But due to a number of circumstances (closure of the traditional place for setting up called the Mound, inconvenient show time right in the middle of the best selling part of the day and incessant rain), I did not even break even, although I made enough to cover most of my expenses and only spent about $200 of my own money in three weeks, not too bad for a fantastic time.'*

If you are seriously crafty, the online marketplace Etsy.com has become a global phenomenon: 'your place to buy and sell all things hand-made, vintage and supplies'. Café Press (www.cafepress. co.uk) is another online gift shop that helps you to sell your own merchandise such as cards, gifts and T-shirts bearing an image you have designed.

Beaches and Mobs

You should learn to look on any crowd of people as a potential market for what you have to sell. People emerging from a club are often grateful for a hotdog or sandwich or skiers queuing for a lift might appreciate some chocolate. If you loiter in a place where people regularly emerge from a remote place, as at the end of treks in Nepal or New Zealand, you could probably sell some interesting food and drink of which they have been deprived. Stephen Psallidas decided to become a portable off-licence with a view to selling wine to the devotees who flock to see Jim Morrison's grave in Paris. Unfortunately this was not a popular idea with the local cannabis sellers and he ended up drinking the wine himself.

Sunbathers on a wide unspoilt beach may be longing for a cold bottle of beer, suntan lotion or a donut, and won't mind paying over the odds for them. Choose your beach carefully: if a beach is already swarming with cold drinks salesmen (as is the case along much of the French and Spanish Mediterranean), you're unlikely to be welcomed by potential customers. If a beach has none, selling may well be forbidden, as one reader discovered at Sydney's Bondi Beach when the beach inspector chased them off after a few minutes.

International sporting fixtures are a good bet too so creative craftsmen and women might think about heading for the dozen Russian cities that will host World Cup matches in 2018 or the Tokyo Olympics in 2020. A Canadian whom Roger Blake met on his travels in Africa had made $500 painting flags on faces during one World Cup. If a crowd is scheduled to gather for a special occasion, think of the things they may need. Enterprising mechanics might consider taking their tools and some spare parts to a tourist mecca such as Oktoberfest, then set up in the car park to fix and adjust the thousands of travel-weary vans and cars which assemble there. The award for the most original salesman should go to the person who spotted an unruly crowd waiting for the arrival of an unpopular Canadian Prime Minister. He got hold of some eggs and sold them for use as missiles.

Another situation that could be exploited is the refusal to allow scantily clad tourists into certain churches or mosques: renting out a shawl to cover naked shoulders or even pairs of trousers would be a valuable service. If you have the right product, you can sell to a wider market. One traveller earned his way in South America by selling peanut butter he'd made himself from local peanuts to American tourists outside the archaeological sites of Colombia. Ski bums regularly make pocket money by delivering croissants from the local bakery to self-catering holidaymakers. Tessa Shaw picked snails at night by the River Ardèche in southern France and then set up a stall in the market at Carpentras. She found that Fridays were particularly profitable, since restaurateurs and shopkeepers drove down from Paris to buy stock for the weekend.

BASED ON HIS TRAVELS ALAN HADEN EMAILED WITH A SUGGESTION FOR ADDING A STRING TO YOUR MONEY-SPINNING BOW:

Having been inspired by your book to work abroad, I felt that it might be of use for others to learn the skills of palmistry or tarot. These intuitive divination methods will allow a traveller to make plenty of money anywhere in the world. If you're a good palm reader and stuck for cash, just head down to the local tourist area or festival/market place and you'll find it easy to make a bundle of cash for your efforts. After arranging a job abroad, I used my skills to earn extra cash by charging £5–£10 for a quick five-minute reading.

Writing and the Media

A few lucky people manage to subsidise their journeys abroad by selling articles or photographs based on their travels or attracting advertisers or sponsors to their travel blog. The media landscape has changed and print journalism has shrunk to such an extent that few newcomers to the field will be able to sell an article. So many talented bloggers publish their travel pieces free online that space on conventional travel pages – printed, online or both – are far fewer and the ones that survive pay very badly. You can see typical rates of pay at www.thewritelife.com/travel-freelance-writers.

The travel magazine *Wanderlust* receives so many submissions that the editors cannot read them all (see their Writer Guidelines at www.wanderlust.co.uk/aboutus/writers). They pay £220 per thousand words. In-flight magazines of foreign airlines sometimes buy freelance pieces, though these are almost always commissioned to professional travel writers. Illustrated travel articles are best of all.

Enterprising journalists and bloggers have set up sites that make a profit through sponsorship or advertising. This is a long game and generally takes years to make an impact and therefore a profit. Old-style travel journalists have complained that this new kind of travel journalism is anything but impartial, and that 'editorial' turns into 'advertorial'.

One possible outlet for aspiring travel writers is the website www.simonseeks.com which aims to be a high quality travel advice site by publishing travel articles by both paid experts and amateurs who can potentially earn money through advertising revenue (see www.simonseeks.com/get-published). The writing tips on the website are worth checking (www.simonseeks.com/travel-writing-tips#5). Unfortunately the site hasn't become the household name that its founder hoped, based on his very successful earlier venture Travelsupermarket.com, so earnings are likely to be negligible or non-existent.

All media outlets that accept freelance travel writing will be looking for a fresh view and new angle. Feel free to use the first person singular in a travel article. Describe interesting or curious incidents that, while not being of earth-shaking significance, help to brighten up the story. Quote the people you met on the trip: the inn-keeper, the museum guard, as well as giving practical information on how to get there, what to see, where to stay and where to eat. Everything should be delivered in a light, readable manner. In the digital age, attention spans and therefore articles are shorter, so your writing should be arresting from the outset with a punchy style. According to one experienced freelancer, sex really does sell abroad as at home, as do accounts of people coming through tragedies. Editors are usually less interested in arty effects than in photos that tell a story. Be prepared to chase for any payments owed.

If at all possible, persuade an editor to give you a commission before you leave, as Tim Leffel did:

> *I had a few assignments set up before I left New Jersey as a travel writer and have started to sell a few other things from the trip now that I'm back. I've already made over $1,400 from various pieces, though none of the cheques were in hand until after my return. It's not something to do for quick money: 'quick' in an editor's mind means 'less than a year'. I've met lots of would-be writers and photographers who hit me up for advice on financing their travels, having not done the most basic research steps it takes to even get started. In my opinion, you must be someone who has something to say and be good at marketing it to even cover your costs, much less make a profit. I do make a profit, but that's because of a trade publication I've written for for a few years (they pay me good money to review swank hotels).*

You can hone your writing skills and possibly earn a little pocket money by writing reviews of hostels you stay in. Hostelz.com pays $10 for minimum 375-word reviews with photos; details at www.hostelz.com/paid-reviewer.

English language newspapers around the world are struggling to compete with the internet, and long-established titles have been disappearing altogether or going online. There is no harm in approaching any that still exist to ask about a job as a proofreader or assistant.

International firms with branches abroad may need someone to edit their newsletter or brochures. You can offer to correct the English of museum labels, menus or travel brochures. You might get a free meal in exchange for your grammatical expertise (though you may unwittingly be depriving future travellers of a source of amusement). When Carisa Fey translated into her native German the menu of an exclusive restaurant in the Mexican resort of Puerto Vallarta she was paid in margaritas.

One of the most remarkable literary coups was reported in the papers some years ago. A student called Daniel Wilson sent his CV and an example of his verse to the president of the island nation of Kiribati asking if he would like him to become the poet-in-residence. To his astonishment, he had a reply inviting him to occupy a beach hut and become their national poet for a time (although the locals turned out not to welcome the publicity he brought, so his term of office was cut short).

Till Bruckner sent a good tip for would-be journalists: *'In most developing countries there are a few dozen Peace Corps volunteers. If you contact their local rag back in the USA over email, they might be interested in a short feature on what Local John is doing in Uzbekistan. An 800-word piece with photo should net $80–$130. Worked fine for me in Georgia.'*

All you readers who imagine that the ideal job would be to write a travel guide should pay attention to the following description by Woden Teachout who spent one summer researching Ireland for the well-known Let's Go guides (in the days when it was a respected guide book series):

> *I got lucky and was hired by Harvard Student Agency (which hires only students) to update their chapter on Ireland. They gave me my airfare and a daily expense allowance. It was a mixed blessing. I spent most of each day visiting local historical societies and talking to all the Mrs O'Learys who run B&Bs, checking their bathrooms for cleanliness and trying to figure out how to vary descriptions of fluffy white bedrooms. At night I would run around to three or four pubs, trying to encapsulate each atmosphere in a good one-liner and then back to the hostel to write up the day's work. When you're writing a guidebook you can never quite relax, since you are always evaluating in your head. And since you have a fixed itinerary, you are not as free to follow the whims of chance and circumstance. It was definitely nice to get paid to travel, and go to places I otherwise would have missed, but on the whole it felt like indentured servitude.*

Because so many people are now blogging about their travels, some of them extremely entertainingly, it is becoming even harder for publishers to find a market for travel writing in print. Two companies in London offer short courses in travel writing and photography: Travellers' Tales (www.travellers.tales.org) and Travel Writing Workshops (www.travelworkshops.co.uk) are both taught by working journalists and well-known writers. As well as teaching participants ways to focus their observations, these courses also cover the essential topic of how to sell your work. A one-day workshop in London will cost about £100. You will have to be prepared to expose your writing to group criticism. Naturally it is possible to study a travel-writing course online, for example at San Francisco-based https://matadoru.com, costing $475. A cheaper way to acquire some of this practical wisdom would be to look at Lonely Planet's *Guide to Travel Writing* though it is more worthwhile immersing yourself in the writings of travel writers who inspire you.

Those with an ambition to write a novel can learn all about self-publishing from Catherine Howard, quoted in the USA chapter, who published *Mousetrapped* herself, an account of working in Orlando, Florida; see http://catherineryanhoward.com/tag/self-publishing. With the development of affordable print-on-demand (POD) publishing, authors are no longer obliged to buy copies of their book in bulk before selling them on sites such as Amazon.

Photography

A number of online photo libraries in the UK such as iStock (now part of Getty Images) pay a base rate royalty of 15% (paid in US dollars) to the photographer on fees the website earns by selling your photo; see www.istockphoto.com/sell-stock-photos.php. Another major digital library is www.alamy.com, which may have less competition. Others to consider are Snapwire and Shutterstock.

Although digital photography has brought about a revolution, there will always be tourists who will not have the necessary equipment with which to capture a key moment. With the right gadgetry it is possible to set yourself up as a portrait photographer on beaches, near monuments, where people try an adventure activity such as parascending for the first time and so on. If potential customers like the image you show them on your digital camera, you can go ahead and print it out and sell it to them.

Another place to set yourself up as a freelance photographer is at a place that specialises in hosting weddings of holidaying couples. Certain places (and not just Las Vegas) become popular with couples looking for something different from the village church.

A dynamic young company called Urban Adventures (www.urbanadventures.com/become-a-partner) matches up local experts (who could be you if you have been living in a place for long enough) and travellers in its 'Locals on Tap' programme operating in 50 world cities. Local guides work on a self-employed basis. You will have to market and sell your own tours, which could be on a specialist subject such as photographic walking tours of the city, encouraging backpackers and tourists to take their own original photos. Vayable.com is another company that pairs paying tourists with local guides.

Busking

If you can play an instrument, sing, tap dance, juggle, conjure, draw caricatures or act, you may be able to earn money on the streets. Most successful buskers say that musical talent is less important than the spot you choose and the way you collect. You can ask a few backpackers at your hostel to stand and watch and look enthusiastic about your act and in return buy them a beer or two. Passers-by are more likely to stop to watch if there is already a crowd gathered. One of the best ideas we have heard of was reported on the site www.roadjunky.com where an Irishman was spotted in a Berlin park with 'a laptop with a karaoke programme running, a good mike, speakers, an umbrella for the sun and a buggy to carry it all' and also an audience of about 500 people many of whom were stuffing euro notes into the circulating money tin.

To busk, you need the tools of your trade, perhaps an accomplice to collect money and an audience. A favourable climate helps, though some of the most successful buskers we have heard from have played in Northern Europe in mid-winter. One of the keys to success (in addition to talent) is originality. We have had reports from opposite ends of the world (Sweden and Northern Queensland) that kilted bagpipe-playing buskers are always a hit. Most international buskers say that people abroad (especially in Scandinavia, Germany, Switzerland and Spain) are more generous than in Britain, that there is less trouble with being moved on and it is not too difficult to keep yourself by busking around the cafés of Europe.

Anna Ling has busked around the world. She worked up a short fire poi show, ie twirling a rope with two lit ends that makes a pattern in the darkness. In advance of her performances in Seville, Granada, Paris, etc, she checked out which pavement cafés allowed enough space for her routine. When her accomplice circulated with a hat, the vast majority of diners gave a coin. Before starting a world music course at SOAS, Anna travelled with her guitar between festivals in South America. When her bag was nicked from a café in Bolivia, she was glad she still had her guitar because she knew she wouldn't starve (although in the end she was able to contact her parents who transferred a loan to her). The year before she had spent some months in New Zealand where she linked up with some musicians and formed a band. They decided they would move to Wellington to try to get gigs, but this proved more difficult than anticipated (ie impossible). However, she frequented a very good busking spot in a shopping centre out of the city centre, where she often made NZ$20 an hour. She had learned of this spot from her contacts, especially those met at a Rainbow Gathering.

You need a great deal of confidence in your abilities, to go abroad specifically to busk; it may be better to regard performing as a possible way of subsidising a holiday. Festivals and other large gatherings of merry-makers are potentially lucrative; bear in mind that the more potential a position has, the greater the competition is liable to be for it. Guitarist-cum-TEFL teacher Fergus Cooney found that competition can be acute:

> *Please don't ever write a 'Guide to Busking'. We travelling folk would soon be out of business. It's bad enough as it is. For example this year 40 accordion players from Romania swamped Montpellier and killed busking for the rest of us.*

Regulations about street performing vary from country to country, but in general you will be tolerated if you are causing no obstruction or other harm. Often you are supposed to obtain a municipal licence; ask at a youth information bureau or become an expert by attending a busking festival, listed at www.buskercentral.com/calendar.php. Rarely, the question of visas will arise, as it is did for Catriona Rainsford in Mexico who ended up spending a few days in a San Luis Potosí jail. As she was collecting money from the crowd while her then boyfriend, Trico, balanced on a two-metre-high unicycle he had made from junk, a policeman approached and asked to see her work visa which of course she didn't have. She went on to write a gripping book, *The Urban Circus: Travels with Mexico's Malabaristas*, about her two years travelling through Mexico supported by her juggling and fire dancing.

You may find that busking leads to better things. It is said that Eric Clapton, Simon & Garfunkel and Pierce Brosnan all started their careers as buskers. Work-your-wayer Mark Kilburn was offered a job playing guitar in a nightclub in Holland on the basis of his street performances, Armin Birrer was encouraged by a film writer who heard him to try for a job as a film extra in Melbourne, and Kev Vincent was invited to leave the streets of San Tropez behind to entertain on a millionaire's gin palace.

Artists

An artist who paints local scenes or copies local postcards can do well in holiday resorts. If you can draw a reasonable likeness you could set yourself up as a street portraitist. Two friends Belinda and Pandora found it fairly easy to make money in both Britain and the Continent especially among holidaymakers. Belinda used unlined brown paper bought in an industrial roll and oil pastels or children's crayons. You can also use driftwood or smooth pebbles. It is awkward to carry around two chairs with you so she relied on borrowing them from an adjacent café or church hall. Artistically you shouldn't be over-scrupulous; when a disappointed subject asked *'Do I really look that old?'*, Belinda didn't hesitate to erase a few wrinkles.

Apparently boat owners are a particularly vain bunch and will often jump at the chance to have their vessel immortalised on canvas, so loiter around yacht marinas with your sketchbook. Stephen Psallidas noticed a trend in Mykonos for tavernas, banks and other public buildings to display paintings of themselves. Face-painting is a portable skill and there is money to be made from organising children's parties wherever there is an expat community.

Film Extras

If you like the idea of mingling with the stars in Hollywood for a few days and being well paid for it – forget it. In most international film studios even extras belong to trade unions that exclude outsiders. When a film is being shot on location you may have the opportunity of helping to fill out a crowd scene – in fact the accepted term is 'crowd artist' or 'background actor'– but it is a matter of luck coming across these, though your chances are better in some places than others. The picturesque streets of old Budapest together with the relatively lower shooting costs make it a favourite location (in fact the author once spotted an off-duty Ben Kingsley in a restaurant in Budapest).

In the massive Asian film industry, film-makers actively seek out Caucasian faces, especially to be villains, dupes or dissolutes. Agents for film companies usually look for their supernumerary staff among the budget hotels of Mumbai, Bangkok, Hong Kong, Cairo, etc knowing that they will find plenty of travellers only too willing to spend one or two days hanging around a film set in exchange for a few rupees or dollars. In fact by local standards the wage is generous.

Filmmaking

If you are an aspiring filmmaker rather than actor, you will have to be very lucky to make any money from your passion. Zillions of struggling film artists have uploaded their films or film trailers onto YouTube in an attempt to kickstart their careers by attracting an audience and possibly also advertisers.

Casual opportunities in promotional videos are far more numerous than in feature films, as Alan Chadwick and his girlfriend Sophie discovered in Barcelona where they are both living as English teachers. One Sunday in 2016 they were strolling through the trendy flea market in Raval when they were approached by a woman looking for people to be in promotional films. It is likely that the British couple were selected for their attractiveness. They gave their details and not long after were invited to join a shoot. Sophie has been in several online beer ads (for example at www.youtube.com/watch?v=Sb2OT4dZ8ew which stars a famous Spanish actor) for which she got paid €800, and has been doing occasional work ever since, including one advert in which she was filmed running away rather than just sitting around looking decorative. Andrew (Longman) Smith from Cambridge also in Barcelona was in an ad for a US cough syrup and was paid €2,000 (pre-tax) for a fleeting appearance. Many big corporations come to make promotional videos and adverts in Spain because it is cheaper and the weather is so good.

One way to gain experience in the competitive film, video, and multimedia production industry is to undertake unpaid work experience. Holly Tate spent three months working for Pedestrian TV, a media company in Sydney, on a placement that was fixed up (for a sizeable fee) by an internships agency, though you might be able to arrange such a placement independently (www.pedestrian.tv/jobs). She thought it was a great experience:

> *The office is really small, everyone gets on well and it's a pretty fun place to work. I think I've been really lucky. Since I arrived I've learnt a lot of things, like editing, which I'd never done before. They've included me in lots of production meetings and creative brainstorming sessions for new projects, which has been invaluable experience for when I apply for jobs back home.*

ODD JOBS

If you can't or don't want to get a steady job you could consider offering your services as an odd job person. Small towns are probably a better bet than big cities because people are more trusting and word gets around faster. The best areas to look for odd jobs and household maintenance jobs are in expatriate enclaves abroad (especially on the Mediterranean or in Mexico). Fellow backpackers might also need your services if you can cut hair, do tattoos, or fix bicycles. Brian Williams from North Wales, travelling with his partner Adrienne Robinson and their three-year-old son, found his skills as a mechanic in demand wherever he went, including Fiji, New Zealand and Australia. If your sphere of expertise is domestic, you can often find a market for housework and ironing. Hand-deliver a little printed notice in the neighbourhood where you're based and see what happens.

Painters and decorators can often pick up work. Michael Cooley from British Columbia spent some time in northern California where he was offered a job just because he was wearing his painters' whites in town. It is a good policy to suggest a specific job when you are on the doorstep, rather than to ask vaguely if there is anything to be done. Householders are more likely to respond favourably if you tactfully suggest that their garden is not devoid of weeds, or that the hinges on the gate could be brought into the 21st century. You should never underestimate the laziness of other people: in summer lawns need mowing, garages need cleaning, cars need washing, and in winter snow needs clearing. If you propose to specialise in something such as window cleaning you should invest in some basic equipment: people prefer to hire a window cleaner that has his own bucket, chamois and ladder.

Susan and Eric Beney took a break from travelling with their daughters overland to Australia to spend a while on the small Greek island of Halki. They arrived in April, before the tourist rush, and there was no evidence of any work around. But they successfully created a job from scratch:

> *The beach was a terrible mess with rubbish washed up in the winter storms, so we set ourselves the task of cleaning it up and asked the mayor for rubbish bags. After we had been here for five weeks and our funds were sadly depleted, Eric was asked if he would like the job of 'port cleaner'. This job entailed sweeping the harbour and cleaning the streets three days a week and cleaning the loos daily. The job hadn't been done for a month so was quite a task in the beginning but I helped Eric get the loos to a reasonable standard and after that the job was quite a nice little number with plenty of time off. The pay was more than £100 a month and of course it has endeared Eric to the locals, none of whom would do such a job. Apparently a council allowance is made for this job so it could be worthwhile searching out the local mayor and offering your services. Even the police are happy about it or turn a blind eye.*

Because we have now been here a while Eric has also done lots of other odd jobs for people as there is very little spare labour on the island (or the locals are too lazy!).

BUSINESS AND INDUSTRY

This book does not set out to advise jobseekers who are looking for professional posts. A raft of recruitment sites and careers databases such as www.eurograduate.com address the needs of those who are looking for skilled jobs. Information about cross-border applications is widely available in the corporate sector and there are firms that advise on just that such as Rotterdam-based ELM (Expertise in Labour Mobility, www.labourmobility.com). Until Britain exits the EU, the European job mobility portal, EURES, will be of interest to international job-seekers.

Although work in offices, mines, shops and factories is not generally seasonal in the way that work in orchards and hotels is, casual and temporary opportunities often arise. You might be needed in a shop during the pre-Christmas rush, or in a swimming pool firm before the summer, or on an Easter egg production line in February/March. Just as Russia and the former Eastern bloc countries allowed energetic individuals in the 1990s to flourish if they could spot an emerging business opportunity, that mantle has passed to China, which has been rushing pell mell towards commercial expansion. Some predict that China will be the world's biggest economy inside 15 years. Westerners with specific skills to offer such as in financial services, consultancy, editing, IT and telecommunications may still be able to find opportunities in trade and joint ventures. According to a recent estimate, some 850,000 foreigners are living and working in the country.

Shops

Even monolingual people may find shop work outside the English-speaking world by approaching shopkeepers who sell primarily to tourists. For instance you could present yourself to a carpet merchant in a coastal Turkish town or to an electronics shop in a Japanese shopping precinct favoured by American tourists and offer to sell (initially) on commission. Not only will your fluency in English be an asset but your enthusiasm about the product for sale may also inspire confidence in your compatriots. Make sure the percentage you are given is worthwhile; the range will be 2%–20% depending on the value of the goods (lower for electronic goods and higher for cheap souvenirs).

Mystery shopping is something that might allow you to earn some extra cash, but not a living. Mystery shopping agencies send individuals who fit the appropriate demographic to visit shops, restaurants, car dealers, banks, etc as anonymous shoppers, in order to report back objectively on customer service. Further information about this and completing surveys for pay can be found at www.borntoloaf.co.uk. To become a 'mystery evaluator' for the company Bare International (www.bareinternational.com) for example, no specific experience is required. The company is headquartered in the US but has offices worldwide and pays between $5 and $35 per assignment.

Commercial and Secretarial

Students and recent graduates in business, management science, marketing, etc. may be interested in an organisation run by a global student network that extends to 126 countries. AIESEC – the French acronym is now redundant since its remit is far wider than for Students of Economics and Management – can organise paid internships in its member countries, aimed at giving participants an insight into living and working in another culture. Positions advertised on its Opportunities Portal cover everything from software development in the Czech Republic to trouble-shooting for a tour company in Tokyo. The registration fee is £450.

A number of commercial companies charge candidates a hefty fee for arranging a work experience placement in a foreign business, usually with the primary aim of allowing the foreigner to improve his or her knowledge of the local language in a working environment. For example Twin Work & Volunteer in London (www.workandvolunteer.com) offers professional internships of varying durations in France, Valencia (Spain), Berlin, London and Buenos Aires for a fee starting at £750.

Trained secretaries who are fluent in a European language may be able to arrange work in Europe. Most major European cities have a British Chamber of Commerce where it may be possible to deposit your CV for inspection by local businesses, or the Chamber of Commerce may run a website on which your request for work can be posted. It will normally be necessary to join the Chamber before you will be offered this service.

Specialist cross-border employment agencies can help the highly qualified. Multilingual Europe Ltd is an online job board that specialises in the recruitment of contract multilingual customer service, sales and marketing, IT and finance in Europe (www.multilingualvacancies.com).

GAMBLING

Well used by a practised operator, a pack of cards, a backgammon board or set of poker dice are a possible source of extra income. Chess, poker, bridge and backgammon are widely played for money throughout the world; if you become proficient there is every reason to use your skills for profit. The great thing about poker and backgammon is that they are comparatively simple games in which at every stage there is a mathematically correct play. The vast majority of players in amateur schools never take the trouble to learn the percentages. If you do, and so long as you keep out of the professional games, you will win.

The 'three card trick' or 'spot the lady' requires a definite element of dexterity but with regular practice you will become competent in a few weeks and can confidently invite customers to place their money on the Lady, which hopefully is never the card they choose.

Rolling two dice for someone and getting them to bet on what number will come up is another possible ruse. The possible numbers are 2 to 12 so the odds about any one number appear to be 10/1. In fact they range from 35/1 for a 2 or 12 to 5/1 for a 7. Actually it is better to get the pigeon to roll the dice and let you bet on 6s 7s and 8s (6/1, 5/1, 6/1) and keep him paying out at 10/1 until he can stand it no longer.

PART 1

WORK YOUR WAY

**TOURISM
THE COUNTRYSIDE
TEACHING ENGLISH
CHILDCARE
VOLUNTEERING**

Tourism

Despite the potentially destablising changes of 2016, the international tourism industry continues to grow at about 4% each year and is predicted to carry on like that for the next ten years. The sector represents nearly a tenth of world GDP, and now supports 284 million people in employment, about 1 in 11 jobs on the planet, which is a staggering statistic. The tourist industry is a mainstay of the mobile worker. The seasonal nature of hotel and restaurant work discourages a stable working population, and so hotel proprietors often rely on foreign labour during the busy season. Also, many tourist destinations are in remote places where there is no local pool of labour. For this reason travellers have ended up working in hotels in some of the most beautiful corners of the world from the South Island of New Zealand to Lapland.

AGENCIES AND WEBSITES

People with a background in hotels and catering may be able to fix up overseas contracts while still in the UK. EURES, the European job mobility portal, registers foreign vacancies in the tourist industry (particularly in France and Italy) via the UK's Jobcentre Plus, at least while the UK still belongs to the EU. Specialist agencies will be of interest to qualified hotel staff including chefs, hotel receptionists and restaurant staff.

While opening up an enormous range of possibilities, the internet can be a bewildering place to job-hunt. One of the best specialist recruitment websites is www.seasonworkers.com, which is designed to help people find a summer job, outdoor sports job or ski resort job. Another website that can prove invaluable for job-seeking travellers is the non-commercial, free Jobs Abroad Bulletin, www.jobsabroadbulletin.co.uk, which will send on request a free monthly jobs listing by email. Early spring is peak time for looking: in a single issue, JAB included job details for bartending at a beach resort in the British Virgin Islands, work experience at a holiday equestrian centre in the west of Ireland, hotel entertainer in Mallorca, chambermaid on the Greek island of Skopelos and karaoke hosts in Spain. Otherwise try www.anyworkanywhere.com, www.jobmonkey.com (especially for North America), www.coolworks.com (ditto) and so on. Jobs.natives.co.uk started out as a winter resort recruitment site, but now deals with summer season jobs too. Everywhere you look on the internet potentially useful links can be found. A surprising number of tour operator home pages feature an icon you can click to find out about jobs/recruitment/careers.

HOTELS AND RESTAURANTS

If you secure a hotel job without speaking the language of the country and lacking relevant experience, you will probably be placed at the bottom of the pecking order, eg in the laundry or washing dishes. Some hotels might confuse you by using fancy terms for menial jobs, for example 'valet runner' for collector-of-dirty-laundry or 'kitchen porter' for pot-washer. Reception and bar jobs are usually the most sought after and highly paid. However, the lowly jobs have their saving graces. The usual hours of chamber staff (7am–2pm) allow plenty of free time.

Even the job of dish-washer, stereotyped as the most lowly of all jobs with visions of the down-and-out George Orwell as a *plongeur* washing dishes in a Paris café, should not be dismissed too easily. Nick Langley enjoyed life far more as a dish-washer in Munich than as a civil servant in Britain.

Many people thrive on the animated atmosphere and on kitchen conviviality. Nick Langley maintains that once you're established you'll gain more respect by shouting back if unreasonable demands are made, but adds the proviso, *'but not at the powerful head cook, please!'* Heated tempers usually cool down after a couple of beers at the end of a shift.

The earlier you decide to apply for seasonal hotel work the better are your chances. Hotels in a country such as Switzerland recruit months before the summer season, and it is advisable to apply to as many hotel addresses as possible by March, preferably in their own language. Even though English holds sway in many resorts, a knowledge of more than one language is an immense asset for work in Europe. If you have an interest in working in a particular country, get a list of hotels and contact the largest ones (eg the ones with over 100 rooms) and then apply in the language of the country. Mass emailing of your CV will be much less effective than applying in writing or in person. You could also sign up for free vacancy bulletins from www.hotel-jobs.co.uk.

On the other hand you might not be able to plan so far ahead, or you may have no luck with written applications, so it will be necessary to look for a hotel job once you've arrived in a foreign country. All but the most desperate hoteliers are far more willing to consider a candidate who is standing there in the flesh than one who emails from afar. One jobseeker recommends showing up bright and early (about 8am) to impress prospective employers. Perseverance is necessary when you're asking door to door at hotels. One of our contributors was repeatedly rejected by hotels in Amsterdam on the grounds that she was too late in the summer (ie August). Her last hope was the Hilton Hotel and she thought she might as well give it a try since it might be her only chance to see the inside of a Hilton. She was amazed when she was hired instantly as a chambermaid. It also might be necessary to return to the same hotel several times if you think there's a glimmer of hope.

KATHRYN HALLIWELL DESCRIBED HER JOB HUNT IN LES GETS IN THE HAUTE-SAVOIE OF FRANCE:

I had to ask from hotel to hotel for three days before finding the job, and experienced what I have come to know through experience and others' reports is the normal way to hire a casual worker. The boss told me blankly that he had no work. As I was leaving he said, what sort of work? I told him anything. He said I could come back the next day in case something came up. I did and was told he was out, come again tomorrow. I eventually did get the job and realised he had just been testing my attitude as he had every other employee when they first applied.

When going door-to-door, try to get past the receptionist to ask the manager personally. If you are offered a position (either in person or in writing) try to get a signed contract setting out clearly the hours, salary and conditions of work. If this is not possible, you should at least discuss these issues with the boss.

Colm Murphy took a two-year leave of absence from his job in the airline industry of Ireland to work his way around Australia and New Zealand. He describes how it doesn't pay to be a wallflower in this business:

You have got to sell yourself. Nobody else is going to get you your first job, only your skills, experience and references and most importantly the first impression you make. The manager or human resources person who interviews you has to have a gut instinct that you will be honest and hardworking. When you get a trial or a job, it is very important to have a good attitude and create that vital first impression with work colleagues, management and, most importantly, the customers.

Only in a handful of cases can agencies and leisure groups place people without any expertise in foreign hotels; however, wages in these cases are normally negligible.

Catering Jobs

Hotels represent just one aspect of the tourist trade, and there are many more interesting venues for cooking and serving, including luxury yachts, holiday ranches, safari camps and ski chalets. (For information about working on cruise liners, see Working a Passage chapter.) People with some training in catering will find it much easier to work their way around the world than the rest of us. The serious traveller might even consider enrolling in a catering course before embarking on his or her journey.

Of course, there are opportunities for the unskilled. You might find a job cooking hamburgers in a fast food chain, bearing in mind that the *Oxford English Dictionary* includes the coinage 'McJob' to refer to any form of dead-end, low-paid employment. Pay is low, hours unreliable or inconvenient and the attitude to discipline more worthy of school children. When you are applying for jobs like this, which are not seasonal, you should stress that you intend to work for an indefinite period, make a career of fast food catering, etc. In fact staff turnover is usually very high. This will also aid your case when you are obliged to badger them to give you extra hours.

A good way of gaining initial experience is to get a kitchen job with a large organisation in Britain such as Butlins (owned by Bourne Leisure; www.bournejobs.co.uk) or PGL Adventure in Ross-on-Wye (www.pgl.co.uk). Those taken on without much experience join the apprenticeship programme which lasts for 34 weeks and pays £138.60 a week less a deduction of £42 a week for accommodation. After that the staff package increases to £191–£260 a week depending on age, minus the deductions for board and lodging and an optional deduction of meals for £40 a week. PGL also have seven holiday centres in France and one in Spain.

OTHER OPPORTUNITIES WITHIN TOURISM

Your average big-spending pampered tourist, so often ridiculed by budget travellers, indirectly provides great scope for employment. He wants to eat ice cream on the beach or croissants in his ski chalet, so you might be the one providing this service. He would be most distressed if he got dripped on in his hotel bed, so you may get hired to tar the roof before the season begins. He doesn't want to be pestered by his children, so you spend the day teaching them how to swim or draw at a holiday camp. She is not happy unless she goes home with a genuine sachet of Ardèche lavender or a Texan 10-gallon hat sold by a charming souvenir shop assistant, who will be you. He needs to be entertained so you get a job in an amusement arcade, the local pub or windsurfing school. And so it could continue. The point is that casual jobs proliferate in tourist centres.

Of course there are also many opportunities at the budget end of tourism, in travellers' hostels and so on. Check out www.hosteljobs.net for worldwide vacancies as managers, volunteers and so on.

DUSTIE HICKEY DESCRIBES THE WAY SHE WENT ABOUT GETTING A JOB IN THE AVIGNON YOUTH HOSTEL, WHICH IS TYPICAL:

I checked out all the hostels in Avignon and had help to write a letter in French. Then I telephoned because I did not get a reply. The hostels could not promise me any work till they met me. Before I left the farm in Brittany where I was working, I telephoned again to remind them I was on my way. When I arrived the hostel I'd chosen was very busy. For free B&B, I just had to keep the dormitory clean, but I pitched in and helped with cleaning, laundry, breakfast, etc. The manager was pleased and gave me a little money. At the end of July the paid assistant left so I was given her job, and eventually I had a room to myself.

Several companies based on the Continent recruit numbers of so-called 'animators', ie people to organise and lead the entertainment and sports programmes for adults or children in holiday resorts. For example the company TMC Tourist Services (www.tmc247.com) with offices in Cyprus and Denmark places international staff in resort hotels in Greece or Cyprus. The number of vacancies warrants a massive campaign of conducting Skype interviews around January. Experience and knowledge of languages is helpful but the right personality is crucial. Another company is the Greek-based Agency Remarc (www.sunseafun. com), which sends animators and entertainers also to resorts in Greece and Cyprus. Note that wages are paid into a local bank account, not a British one. More companies are listed in the chapter on Italy.

Not many working travellers will be able to face selling timeshare properties but any who are interested should look at www.timesharestaff.com which is now more active in Asia (Thailand, Vietnam, Bali) with only one European location, Madeira.

Pubs and Clubs

Bars and clubs should not be omitted from your list of likely employers. Caroline Scott looked at the club magazine *Mixmag* in the winter and contacted a number of Ibiza clubs, one of which hired her for the summer season. If you want to job-hunt after arrival, you might consider carrying a set of 'black and whites' (black trousers/skirt and white shirt) in case you pick up a job as a bartender or waiter. If you have no experience, it can be worthwhile volunteering to work at your local pub before you leave home for a week or two and then ask for a reference.

Once you are abroad, ask at English-style pubs that are found from the Costa del Sol to the Zamalek district of Cairo, from Santa Monica, California to Austrian ski resorts and try to exploit the British connection. Irish people are at an even greater advantage since there are Irish bars and pubs around the world from Molly Malone's in Paris to Irish Village in Dubai. In ordinary bars on the Continent you may be expected to be proficient in the prevailing language, although exceptions are made, particularly in the case of glamorous-looking applicants and in Scandinavia where so many locals speak English. Women (especially blonde ones) can find jobs from Amsterdam to Hong Kong, but should be sure that they can distinguish between bars and brothels.

Places such as the Canaries, Ibiza, Corfu, Rhodes and the Caribbean islands are bursting at the seams with clubs of one kind or another. As long as you investigate the establishments in the place you want to work before accepting a job, you should not encounter too many unpleasant surprises. Handing out promotional leaflets for bars and clubs (known as 'PR-ing') is a job that travellers frequently do, especially in Spain.

Special Events

Great bursts of tourist activity take place around major events like the Olympics. Normally volunteers have to be over 18, have access to accommodation in the host city and preferably have experience in sport or volunteering. Applications will be accepted online a long way in advance, for example volunteer requirements for the 2020 Olympics in Tokyo were released in summer 2016. The organisers are looking for people with communication skills in more than one language, to go through three stages of training and an interview, to pay for their own transport and accommodation and to work for eight hours over ten days. No wage is paid and perks are few in many of these world events since the organisers know that there will be no shortage of eager participants.

On a smaller scale, annual arts festivals and sporting events, trade fairs and World Fairs are all useful providers of casual employment possibilities, both during and before or after when facilities are set up and then dismantled. It is not possible for an event such as Oktoberfest in Munich (held every year in late September) to host nearly seven million visitors without a great deal of extra labour being enlisted to prepare all those barbecued chickens and sausages and to dispense the 2,000,000 gallons of beer consumed. The main problem is finding affordable accommodation during these peak-time events.

Sometimes recruitment for major events is contracted out to employment agencies such as Adecco, which is the chosen partner of the Cirque du Soleil. Richard Ferguson worked for the Cirque when it came to Auckland, and he would have followed it to Australia except he had to complete a course:

> *I was an usher, and they also employ people for selling tickets, merchandise, food and beverage and for the VIP tent. The work is not hard and you can have a great time and get to know a lot of the 'stars' as it were (as long as you don't become a 'groupie' and get star struck).*

TOUR OPERATORS

Acting as a tour guide, representative or courier for a tour operator is one way of combining work with travel. In most cases employers want staff that will stay at least for the whole summer season, April to October inclusive. The peak recruitment time is the preceding autumn, though strong candidates can be interviewed over the winter. Knowledge of a European language is always requested, though it is unusual for reps in Greece or Portugal to speak those languages. Debbie Harrison was taken aback at the ease with which she got a season's work as a rep in Greece without relevant experience or qualifications. Personality and maturity seem to be what count most and a commitment to the company, and possibly also to tourism as a career. By all accounts interviews can be fairly gruelling as they try to weed out the candidates who will crack under the pressure of holidaymakers' complaints and problems.

Considering the rigours and pressures of the job of package tour company representative, wages are low, though of course accommodation is provided. Often wages are paid into a bank account at home. Employers usually expect their reps to supplement meagre wages by accepting commissions from restaurants, shops, car hire firms, etc, not to mention tips from clients.

A qualification in childcare is highly marketable in this sphere since more and more tour operators are attempting to woo families. In the first instance, search the internet and see which tour operator's style suits you. Most big companies devote some of their web pages to recruitment, some with online application facilities. The giant companies TUI and Thomas Cook have swallowed up a number of others and have centralised recruitment systems, mainly done online.

Thomas Cook: www.thomascook.com/recruitment. The Thomas Cook Group employs 21,800 people.

TUI UK & Ireland: www.tuijobsuk.co.uk. Includes First Choice, Crystal Holidays, Thomson, Sunsail and many other brands, employing 54,000 people worldwide.

Other sizeable tour operators include the following:

Club Med: www.clubmedjobs.co.uk. Range of staff (who must be able to speak French) to work as GOs (*Gentils Organisateurs*) for their 65 holiday villages in countries worldwide with plans to open up to 25 new resorts by 2020. As well as behind-the-scenes hotel and catering staff (for whom French is an advantage but not a requirement), they require sports instructors, children's reps, hostesses, shop staff and tour guides.

Mark Warner Ltd: Resorts Recruitment Department, 20 Kensington Church Street, London W8 4EP; www.markwarner.co.uk/recruitment. Runs Beach Resorts in Corsica, Sardinia and Greece for which it employs hotel managers, customer service officers, childcare staff, chefs, bar and waiting staff, watersports, tennis and aerobics instructors, pool attendants, health and beauty staff, maintenance/drivers and night watchmen. Wages are low but benefits include use of watersports facilities, accommodation, meals, travel, medical insurance and the potential for winter work at their ski chalet hotels in Europe in France, Austria and Italy.

Monarch/Cosmos: Wren Court, 17 London Road, Bromley, Kent BR1 1DE; www.monarch.co.uk/jobs. Monarch now concentrates more on its Luton-based aviation business but still employs reps, children's reps, etc for the Mediterranean and beyond.

Neilson Overseas: Brighton; ☎ (+44) 1273 666130; www.neilson.co.uk/recruitment. Recruit for beachclub activity holidays and ski resorts worldwide.

Working in Africa, Asia and Latin America as an adventure tour leader is discussed in the chapter Working a Passage: Overland Tours. Special interest and activity tour operators to whom people with specialist skills like diving and cycling can apply can be searched at www.aito.com, site of the Association of Independent Tour Operators. In the USA, consult the *Specialty Travel Index* (www.specialtytravel.com).

A number of companies specialise in tours for school children, both British and American. For example the London office of the American Council for International Studies (www.acis.com/about/join) annually hires 100 clever linguists to become tour managers to lead groups of American high school students around Europe. Abbey Road Programs (www.goabbeyroad.com/summer-teaching-jobs-abroad) looks for summer teachers and resident advisors for summer language immersion and pre-college programmes in Spain, France, Italy, Greece and the US for high school students. A student group tour operator that takes on linguists as group leaders and ski reps in France, Germany and Italy for short periods in the university vacations is Halsbury Travel Ltd in Nottingham (www.halsbury.com/about/jobs). The weekly allowance for group leaders starts at £100 plus half-board while ski reps receive £200 and ski pass.

Contiki (www.contiki.com/jobs) specialises in coach tours for clients aged 18–35 and hires EU citizens and those with UK work visas as tour managers and coach drivers, and also to work on-site at Contiki villages. Another youth-oriented European tour operator is Busabout which posts full recruitment information for prospective drivers and guides at www.busa-bout.com/recruitment. Both Contiki and Busabout belong to the Travel Corporation along with 28 other travel brands that maintain several recruitment websites for Australia, Canada, the USA, Europe and the UK (www.ttc.com/careers).

With scores of city walking tours running in 18 cities from Amsterdam to Jerusalem, Lisbon to Liverpool, Sandeman's New Europe, headquartered in Berlin, facilitates work for more than 400 freelance guides. Tours are marketed as 'free' however punters have to be pressurised into tipping because otherwise the guide would earn nothing. The phrasing on Sandeman's recruitment page is: '... guides employ us to bring travellers to their tours'. Obviously it is an asset to know the city very well and to speak the language, but the company is mainly looking for confidence, charisma and good presentation skills. Details may be found at www.neweuropetours. eu/main/en/work-with-us. The tours-for-tips idea is so popular that other companies have sprung up; for leads see www.freetour.com.

Campsite Couriers

British camping holiday firms (addresses below) hire large numbers of couriers to remain on one campsite on the Continent for several months. The courier's job is to clean the tents and mobile homes between visitors, greet customers and deal with difficulties (particularly illness or car breakdowns) and introduce holidaymakers to the attractions of the area or even arrange and host social functions and amuse the children. Some couriers are employed exclusively to work in the children's programme. All of this will be rewarded with a wage starting at £160 a week in addition to free tent accommodation. Many companies offer half-season contracts March/April to mid-July and June/July to the end of September.

Setting up and dismantling the campsites in March/April and September (known as *montage* and *démontage*) is often done by a separate team. The work is hard but the language requirements are nil. The company Brad Europe Ltd (www.bradeurope.com) provides a linen hire service to over 300 campsites in France, Italy, Spain and the UK, so hires drivers and laundry operatives to work for three to six months.

Some camping holiday and tour operators based in Britain are as follows (with the European countries in which they are active).

Alfresco Holidays: Bury, Lancashire; ☎ (+44) 161 250 7990; overseas@alfresco-holidays. com; www.alfresco-holidays.com/work-with-us. Reps hired to work on mobile home parks in multiple locations in France plus Spain, Italy and Croatia, May to mid-September.

Canvas Holidays: Dunfermline, Scotland; ☎ (+44) 1383 629012; www.canvasholidays recruitment.com. Mainly France but also Italy and Spain.

Eurocamp: Overseas Recruitment & Training Department; Northwich, Cheshire; ☎ (+44) 1606 787522; www.eurocampjobs.com. Hires staff for 180 campsites in ten countries; applications accepted from October; interviews held in Cheshire over the winter.

Vacansoleil: Eindhoven, Netherlands; ☎ (+31) 40 844 7748; camping-jobs@vacansoleil.com; www.campingjobs.co.uk. 1,200 seasonal staff for almost 500 campsites in 16 European countries, mainly France, Spain, Italy and Germany.

Be warned that an offer of a job may be more tentative than it seems, as Karen Martin describes:

Before we left in May, we had both been interviewed for the job of campsite courier. We got the jobs and signed the contracts, and our rough start date was the 7 July. They did not make the position clear that an offer 'subject to terms and conditions' means that it is possible that a week before the start date you can be told that there is no longer a job due to lack of customers, which is what happened to us. We really felt let down.

Successful couriers make the job look easy, but it does demand a lot of hard work and patience. Occasionally it is very hard to keep up the happy, smiling, never-ruffled courier look, but most seem to end up enjoying the job. Alison Cooper described her job with Eurocamp on a site in Corsica as immensely enjoyable, though it was not as easy as the clients thought:

Living on a campsite in high season had one or two drawbacks: the toilets and showers were dirty, with constant queues, the water was freezing cold, the campsite was very very noisy and if you're unfortunate enough to have your tent in sunlight, it turns into a tropical greenhouse. Of course we did get difficult customers who complained for a variety of reasons: they wanted to be nearer to the beach, off the main road, in a cooler tent with more grass around it, etc, etc. But mostly our customers were friendly and we soon discovered that the friendlier we were to them, the cleaner they left their tents.

I found it difficult at first to get used to living, eating, working and socialising with the other two couriers 24 hours a day. But we all got on quite well and had a good time, unlike at a neighbouring campsite where the couriers hated each other. Our campsite had a swimming pool and direct beach access, though nightlife was limited. The one disco did get very repetitive.

Caroline Nicholls' problems at a campsite in Brittany included frequent power failures, blocked loos and leaking tents: *'Every time there was a steady downpour, one of the tents developed an indoor lake, due to the unfortunate angle at which we had pitched it. I would appear, mop in hand, with cries of "I don't understand. This has never happened before." Working as a courier would be a good grounding for an acting career.'*

The big companies interview hundreds of candidates and have filled many posts by January. But there is a high dropout rate (over 50%) and vacancies are filled from a reserve list, so it is worth applying as late as April. Anyone who has studied a European language and has an outgoing personality stands a good chance if he or she applies early and widely enough.

Activity Holidays

Many specialist tour companies employ leaders for their clients (children and/or adults) who want a walking, cycling, watersports holiday, etc. Companies that operate in only one country are included in the country chapters.

Acorn Adventure Ltd: Stourbridge, West Midlands; www.acornadventure.co.uk/jobs. Seasonal activity instructors and centre managers to work in centres in the UK, France, Spain and Italy. UK staff are paid the minimum wage for 42 hours, less living expenses; overseas staff receive a weekly cash allowance of €75 in addition to food and accommodation.

Camp Europe e.V.: Hamburg, Germany and Ottawa, Canada; www.campeurope.ca. Camp counsellors and English language coaches for children's summer camps in Germany, Spain and Ireland; this company is unusual in encouraging applications from young people outside the EU to come as volunteers and trainees.

Headwater Holidays: Northwich, Cheshire; ☎ (+44) 1606 720006; mike.wheeler@headwater.com; www.headwater.com. Hires staff to look after clients on independent or guided walking and cycling holidays, mainly in France and Italy but throughout Europe; wages from £120–£140 including accommodation.

In2action Ltd: Cowes, Isle of Wight; Recruitment Department: ☎ (+44) 1983 297607; recruitment@in2action.co.uk; www.in2action.co.uk. Recruits staff for resorts on behalf of First Choice Holidays and children's programmes for Canvas Holidays. Action Team members lead children in a range of sports and activities, in resorts from Turkey to the Costa del Sol.

King's Camps: Sheffield, South Yorkshire; ☎ (+44) 114 263 2155; www.kingsrecruit.com. King's Recruit is part of The King's Foundation, a registered charity that uses sport and activity to help children and young people; it's a specialist recruitment service provider for the sports and childcare sector on cruise ships and holiday destinations abroad.

PGL Travel: Ross-on-Wye, Herefordshire; recruitment@pgl.co.uk; www.pgl.co.uk. Recruit for about 1,000 seasonal vacancies for activity instructors, group leaders, catering and support staff at their holiday centres in Britain, France and Spain plus for ski resorts.

Ramblers' Holidays Ltd: Welwyn Garden City, Hertfordshire; ☎ (+44) 1707 331133; mandyd@ ramblersholidays.co.uk. Tour leaders (preferably mature people) needed for programme of walking holidays worldwide. Must speak a foreign language, be resident in the country or have a mountain leadership qualification. Work placements and internships available for students.

Sunsail International: ☎ (+44) 2392 222322; marine.recruitment@specialistholidays.com; www.sunsail.eu. Part of TUI, the company recruits for the activity sector employing staff for flotilla and bareboat sailing holidays in the Mediterranean, especially Greece and Turkey, and also the Caribbean. March to October positions are available as flotilla skippers, engineers and hosts.

Village Camps: Recruitment Office, Nyon, Switzerland; ☎ (+41) 24 493 3064; personnel@ villagecamps.com; www.villagecamps.com. Camp counsellor and outdoor education positions in Switzerland, Austria, Spain, France and England; vacancies for activity specialists, language teachers and nurses. Room and board, accident/liability insurance and an expense allowance are provided; staff must be at least 21.

Any competent sailor, canoeist, diver, climber, rider, etc should be able to market their skills abroad. If you would like to do a watersports course with a view to working abroad, you might be interested in the instructors' courses offered by Flying Fish (www.flyingfishonline.com) or UKSA (www.uksa.org) both on the Isle of Wight. They offer training as instructors in windsurfing, diving, dinghy sailing and yachting. A typical six-week sailing instructor course in Greece will cost about £3,300 including shared self-catering accommodation but excluding flights. The website allows access to water sport job vacancies around the world.

Diving resorts around the world from the Red Sea to the Great Barrier Reef are staffed by people who started out as recreational divers with the basic PADI (Professional Association of Diving Instructors) Open Water Diver qualification. PADI members can access an Employment Bulletin Board. Dive centres in exotic locations around the world accept trainee divers willing to work in exchange for living expenses and dive training. To take two examples, Hurricane Divers in Playa Santa Cruz (Oaxaca, Mexico; www.hurricanedivers.com) operate a three-month Divemaster Internship programme for anyone over 18 who is willing to spend long hours taking bookings, filling tanks and cleaning toilets. In Thailand, Mermaid's Dive Centre in Pattaya is allied to an internship programme called Learn in Asia Dive Internships Co. Ltd (www.learn-in-asia.com).

WINTER RESORTS

Ski resort work is by no means confined to the Alps. Skiing centres can be found in Finnish Lapland and Argentine Patagonia, from the dormant volcanoes of North America to the active ones of New Zealand. And there are dozens of ski resorts in North America, in addition to the most famous ones such as Whistler and Banff in the Canadian Rockies, or Aspen and Vail in Colorado.

Winter tourism offers some variations on the usual theme of hotels and catering. Staff are needed to operate the ski tows and lifts, to be in charge of chalets, to patrol the slopes, to file, wax and mend hired skis, to groom and shovel snow, and of course to instruct would-be skiers and snowboarders. The season in the European Alps lasts from about Christmas until late April/early May. Between Christmas and the New Year is a terrifically busy time as is the middle two weeks of February during half-term holidays.

If you are lucky you might get a kitchen or dining room job in an establishment that does not serve lunch (since all the guests are out on the slopes). This means that you might have up to six hours free in the middle of the day for skiing, though three to four hours is more usual. However, the hours in some large ski resort hotels are the same as in any hotel, ie eight to 10 hours split up inconveniently throughout the day, and you should be prepared to have only one day off per week for skiing. Because jobs in ski resorts are so popular among the travelling community, wages can be low, though you should get the statutory minimum in Switzerland. Many employees are (or become) avid skiers/boarders and in their view it is recompense enough to have easy access to the slopes during their time off.

Either you can try to fix up a job with a British-based ski tour company before you leave (which has more security but lower wages and tends to isolate you in an English-speaking ghetto), or you can look for work on the spot.

Ski Holiday Companies

In the spring preceding the winter season in which you want to work, contact ski tour companies to find out their application procedures and interview timetable. Most of the recruitment takes place online and the websites of most major ski tour operators feature a 'Recruitment' icon. Most companies are looking for resort representatives (for which language skills are needed), chalet staff (described below), cleaners, qualified cooks, odd jobbers and ski guides/instructors. An increasing number of companies are offering nanny and crèche facilities, so this is a further possibility for women and men with a childcare qualification and a DBS check (Disclosure and Barring Service, formerly the Criminal Records Bureau). A certain number of staff have been hired by mid-June, though there are always vacancies until the beginning of the season and during it as well.

Specialist ski recruitment websites can be helpful. The superb www.jobs.natives.co.uk posts current vacancies on behalf of a selection of the major operators and also includes detailed resort descriptions (natives.co.uk). Registered users can upload their CVs. Try also Season Workers (www.seasonworkers.com), which aims to keep up to date with the latest jobs, courses and gap year placements worldwide including recruitment of winter staff for Europe and North America. The smaller Ski-Jobs.co.uk mainly lists vacancies in France.

Here are some of the major UK ski tour operators. Some have a limited number of vacancies that they can fill from a list of people who have worked for them during the summer season or have been personally recommended by former employees, so you should not be too disappointed if you are initially unsuccessful.

Alpine Elements: www.jobsite.alpineelements.co.uk/winter-ski-jobs. Recruits for ski resorts in France. Sample pay is €280 per month for 54 hours a week over 6 days as a hotel assistant. Free lift pass, free food and free accommodation.

Crystal Ski Holidays: http://tuijobsuk.co.uk/work-at-tui-travel/abroad/crystal-ski-jobs. Part of mass tour operator TUI; hundreds of resort reps and chalet/hotel staff for scores of ski resorts in Europe (especially France, Austria and Italy) and North America (visa required).

Equity Travel: Part of same travel group as SkiPlan and Pavilion Tours; www.equitytraveljobs.co.uk.

Hotelplan Group (combining Inghams, Esprit Ski and Ski Total): Surrey; ☎ (+44) 1483 791010; www.workaseason.com. Hundreds of reps and in some countries chalet staff for alpine resorts mainly in France and Austria, but also some in Switzerland, Slovenia, Andorra and Finland. Also extensive ski programmes in Canada and USA. Perks include free ski pass, ski and boot hire, meals, accommodation and return travel from the UK.

Powder Byrne: London SW15; ☎ (+44) 20 8246 5342; www.powderbyrne.com/work-for-pb. Upmarket company with strong family programme in Flims, Laax, Grindelwald, Zermatt, Davos, Arosa, and Lenzerheide in Switzerland, Zurs, St Christoph, and Lech in Austria and San Cassiano and La Villa in Italy. Also recruits resort teams for summer programme in Spain, Portugal, Greece and Italy.

Scott Dunn: London SW15; www.jobs.scottdunn.com. Established in 1986, offers both summer and winter season recruitment.

Skibound: Brighton. Recruits French-speaking hotel and bar staff for France, among others, through partner recruitment brand www.getupandgojobs.com.

Skiworld: London W6; ☎ (+44) 870 420 5914/3; www.skiworld.co.uk/recruitment. Catered chalet and hotel holidays in France, Austria, Switzerland, Italy, Canada, USA and Japan.

Supertravel Ski: London SE1; ☎ (+44) 20 7962 1369; www.supertravel.co.uk/ski/seasonal jobs.aspx. Takes on winter staff mainly for Courchevel (France) and St Anton (Austria); all applicants must hold a passport from an EU member state and have a National Insurance number.

VIP Ski: ☎ (+44) 208 870 6310; www.vip-chalets.com/work-for-us. Employs scores of staff, especially chalet hosts and childcare staff. Usual minimum age 21.

You can find other ski company addresses by consulting ski websites, magazines and travel agents. Another good idea is to attend the Telegraph Ski & Snowboard Show held in late October in London where some ski companies hand out job descriptions and application forms. An added bonus is that you can attend the Natives Jobs Fair free at the same time.

The wages paid by most tour operators are fairly dire, though they are on top of bed, board and a ski pass. One of the excuses given for the low pay is that staff can supplement their wages with tips, something that made Susan Beney and her husband uncomfortable when they worked for Le Ski in France:

> *We did make good tips which became our spending money, so no tips, no treats. Being Aussies (with joint UK nationality), it goes against the grain to expect tips. And then you find yourself judging guests by how much they tip you – horrible way to be. We worked long hours six days a week, and were probably a bit too conscientious due to our age (we have just become grandparents). It's still a good way to experience a season in the Alps, but just be prepared to be overworked and underpaid. Listen to the young folk who have got the work down to a fine art and really know how to cut corners since they are there to ski and socialise.*

Applying on the Spot

The best time to look is at the end of the preceding winter season though this has the disadvantage of committing you a long way in advance. The next best time is the first fortnight in September when the summer season is finishing and there are still plenty of foreign workers around who will have helpful advice. The final possibility is to turn up in the month before the season begins when you will be faced with many refusals. In November you will be told you're too early because everything's closed, in December you're too late because all the jobs are spoken for. If you miss out on landing a job before the season, it could be worth trying again in early January, since workers tend to disappear after the holidays.

EVERY NEGATIVE EXPERIENCE IS COUNTERBALANCED BY OTHERS LIKE MARY JELLIFFE'S ACCOUNT OF OPPORTUNITIES IN THE FRENCH RESORT OF MERIBEL:

At the beginning of the season there were many 'ski bums' looking for work in Meribel. Many found something. People earned money by clearing snow, cleaning, babysitting, etc. You do need some money to support yourself while looking for work but if you are determined enough, I'm sure you'll get something eventually. One group of ski bums organised a weekly slalom race from which they were able to make a living. Another set up a video service; another made and sold boxer shorts for £10 a pair.

Chalet Staff

The number of chalets in the Alps has hugely increased over the past decade with the biggest concentrations in Méribel, Courchevel and Val d'Isère in France, Verbier in Switzerland and St Anton in Austria. Chalet clients are looked after by a chalet girl, chalet boy or chalet couple. The chalet hosts do everything from cooking first-class meals for the 10 or so guests to clearing the snow from the footpath (or delegating that job). They are responsible for keeping the chalet clean, preparing breakfast, packed lunches, tea and dinner, providing ice and advice, and generally keeping everybody happy. Fifteen-hour days are standard.

Although this sounds an impossible regimen, many chalet hosts manage to fit in several hours of skiing in the middle of each day. The standards of cookery skills required vary from company to company depending on the degree of luxury (ie the price) of the holidays. Whereas some advertise good home cooking, others offer cordon bleu cookery every night of the week (except the one night which the chalet host has off). In most cases, you will have to cook a trial meal for the tour company before being accepted for the job or at least submit detailed menu plans. Many aspiring applicants do a cookery course tailored to chalet work such as the Ultimate Chalet Cookery course in La Rosière (www.chaletcookerycourse.co.uk) or the all round one-week chalet hosting course in Morzine (www.chalethostcourse.co.uk) which has good links with hiring ski companies. Courses take place in September and October, cost from £549 and include instruction on cleaning, Jacuzzi-mending, etc, as well as menu-planning and shopping. Chalet cookery courses offered in London, for example by the Wyld Seasonaire Cookery Course and the Avenue Cookery School, are far more expensive, eg more than £1,300+ for a two-week course.

Eighteen-year-old Dan Hanfling baked a creditable cake for his interview and was pleased to be offered a chalet job. But on arriving in the Alps, he learned that chalet staff in their first season are not always assigned their own chalet, but are expected to service a number of them by carrying supplies, cleaning toilets, etc. This job was a lot less glamorous than he had imagined, and he returned to England after just a few weeks (to the consternation of his parents who had booked a Christmas holiday in the same resort).

Ski Instructors

To become a fully-fledged ski instructor, qualified to work in foreign ski schools, costs a great deal of time and money. Freelance or 'black' instructors – those who tout in bars offering a few hours of instruction in return for pocket money – are persecuted by the authorities in most alpine resorts. The main legitimate opportunities for British skiers without paper qualifications are as instructors for school parties or as ski guides/ski rangers. The situation is especially difficult in France which bans ski leaders or ski hosts. These are volunteers who ski and socialise alongside holidaymakers, logging experience, through a scheme operated successfully by the venerable Ski Club of Great Britain in European and North American resorts.

If you are already a good skier or snowboarder and interested in qualifying as an instructor, contact BASI, the British Association of Snowsport Instructors (www.basi.org.uk), or one of the gap year instructor courses offered from Courchevel to Ruapehu in New Zealand by companies such as Basecamp (www.basecampgroup.com), Peakleaders (www.peakleaders. com) and New Generation (www.instructorcourses.skinewgen.com). Be warned that these are very expensive, typically £8,000+ for an 11-week course. The recent explosion in snowboarding has resulted in many young people qualifying as instructors, though with not much demand, since snowboarders tend to be self-taught. Most instructors teach from two to six hours a day depending on demand, and are expected to participate in the evening entertainment programme.

SKI RESORTS AROUND THE WORLD

FRANCE	SWITZERLAND	AUSTRIA	ITALY
Chamonix	Davos	Kitzbühel	Cortina d'Ampezzo
Les Contamines	St Moritz	Söll	Courmayeur
Val d'Isère	Zermatt	Lech	Sestriere
Courchevel	Gstaad	Badgastein	Bormio
Méribel	Klosters	St Anton	Campitello
St Christoph	Villars	Mayrhofen	Canazei
Flaine	Wengen & Mürren	Kaprun	Livigno
Avoriaz	Crans-Montana	Alpbach	Abetone
Les Arcs	Kandersteg	Brand	Corvara
La Plagne	Adelboden	Kirchberg	Selva
Tignes	Verbier	St Johann	Sauze d'Oulx
Montgenèvre	Grindelwald	Solden	Asiago
La Clusaz	Arosa	Obergurgl	S Stefano di Cadore
Alpe d'Huez	Saas Fee	Zell am See	Alleghi

SPAIN	GERMANY	NORWAY	SCOTLAND
Sol y Nieve	Garmisch–Partenkirchen	Voss	Cairngorm (Aviemore)
Formigal	Oberstdorf	Geilo	Glenshee
Cerler	Berchtesgaden	Telemark	Lecht
		Lillehammer	Glencoe
		Gausdal	Nevis Range
		Synnfjell	

ANDORRA	FINNISH LAPLAND	BULGARIA	ROMANIA
Arinsal	Levi	Borovets	Poiana Brasov
Soldeu	Ylläs		
Pas de la Casa			

NEW ZEALAND	AUSTRALIA	CANADA	USA
Queenstown	Falls Creek (VIC)	Whistler/Blackcomb	Aspen/Snowmass (CO)
Coronet Peak	Mount Hotham	Banff	Copper Mountain (CO)
Mount Hutt	Mount Buffalo	Lake Louise	Steamboat (CO)
Mount Ruapehu	Mount Buller	Sunshine Village	Vail (CO)
	Thredbo (NSW)	Fernie	Breckenridge (CO)
	Perisher	Hidden Valley	Alpine Meadows (CA)
	Mount Field (Tas)	Blue Mountain	Heavenly Lake Tahoe (CA)
	Ben Lomond	Mont Tremblant	Mt Bachelor (OR)
		Mont Sainte-Anne	Timberline (OR)
			Alyeska (AK)
			Park City (UT)
			Sun Valley (ID)
			Jackson Hole (WY)
			WhitefishMountain Resort (MT)
			Waterville Valley (NH)
			Stowe (VT)

The Countryside

HARVESTING

Itinerant workers have traditionally travelled hundreds of miles to gather in the fruits of the land, from the tiny blueberry to the mighty watermelon. It might even be possible to pick your way around the world, by following the seasons and the ripening crops. In Europe, large numbers of East European migrant pickers looking to earn Western wages are joined every year by young travellers.

Living and working in rural areas is a more authentic way of experiencing an alien culture compared to working in tourism. It is easy to see why farms, vineyards and orchards play a large part in the consciousness of those who want to work their way around the world, especially in Australia and New Zealand.

Although the problem of work permits does dog the footsteps of fruit pickers abroad, there is always a good chance that the urgency of the farmers' needs will overrule the impulse to follow the regulations. The availability of harvesting work for travellers in Europe has been reduced by the large numbers of Romanians, Albanians, Moroccans, etc roaming every corner of Europe. When Aaron Woods arranged through a friend to work in the maize fields of a farm in Baden-Württemberg in southern Germany, he was paid €4 an hour on top of room and board. However, his 10 Polish colleagues told him that this was four times the equivalent rate of pay in their home village.

Where to look for work

The vast majority of this kind of work is found only after meeting the farmers face-to-face either well in advance of the busy season or once it's underway and the growers are desperate if they don't have enough labour. However, in a few isolated cases, specialist agencies try to match up farmers and travelling harvesters. One is the excellent Dutch company Appellation Contrôlée (www.apcon.nl) set up by two ex-travellers who wanted to help people find work on farms offering good pay and conditions in France (see France chapter).

As usual the internet can play a key role. Check www.pickingjobs.com for some useful links to farms that are perennially short of workers such as in the cherry harvest on the South Island of New Zealand and the massive berry harvests in Denmark. There are some country-specific sites as well such as www.seasonalwork.co.nz.

State-run employment offices are worth a try, especially in France, Canada and Australia. After visiting the French equivalent of a jobcentre and also a private agency in Epernay one September, Anna Ling and her boyfriend were given a list of phone numbers of potential farm employers. Preparing for a marathon of phoning, they bought a local phone card but struck lucky on their very first call. They visited the vineyard in Champagne, were interviewed in the home of the wine-grower and told to come back when the harvest started, which was 20 September. They were not so lucky with following up this harvest. In their search for apple-picking work south of Epernay and near Bordeaux, they followed up every imaginable lead only to hit a series of brick walls. You win a few, lose a few.

Asking around in backpacker hostels, campsites and local pubs is often successful, though not always; Jon Loop says this is great for people who are good at meeting prospective employers in pubs, unlike him who just gets drunk and falls over. If you are in a densely farmed area, it might even be worth trying to visit farmers personally. Farm hands and people already picking in the fields will be able to offer advice as well. You may want to consider hiring or borrowing a bicycle, moped or car for a day of concentrated job-hunting.

One of the jobseeker's best allies is Google maps. It is easier to find a rural location after you have had the route pointed out on a map than it is just following verbal instructions (possibly in a language you barely know).

An excellent reference book for prospective grape-pickers is Hugh Johnson's and Jancis Robinson's *World Atlas of Wine* (published by Mitchell Beazley, 2013 edition) which includes splendidly detailed maps of wine-producing regions from Corsica to California. Unfortunately it is far too expensive and bulky to carry with you. Alternatively, get a second hand copy of the concise edition (though the cartography is far less detailed) or a list of vineyards from the regional tourist offices or wine producers' association so that you can contact or visit the proprietors, asking for work.

Technique

Picking fruit may not be as easy as it sounds. If you are part of a large team you may be expected to work at the same speed as the most experienced picker, which can be both exhausting and discouraging. Be assured that your speed will quickly improve with experience, a fact you will need to hang on to for the first few days if you are being paid according to the quantity you pick, known as piecework, which is how the vast majority of picking jobs are paid. When Andrew Walford was tempted to feel envious of the people who could fill seven or eight bins of apples a day in Shepparton, Australia, he consoled himself that, even if his record was only five, at least he wasn't as eccentric as they were. Rather than succumb to feelings of inferiority, watch their technique closely.

There are often external limitations to the amount you can earn. Sometimes picking is called off in bad weather. Sometimes you are forced to take some days off while the next crop ripens fully or because the price on the market has dropped. Be prepared to amuse (and finance) yourself on idle days.

Informal competitions can enliven the tedium. Alan Corrie describes his fellow tomato-picker on a farm near Auch in the Gascony region of southern France, with undisguised admiration:

> *In August I was taken on by a farmer to join his contracted Moroccan worker picking tomatoes. This is paid by the crate, and iron discipline and single-minded determination are needed to breach the 50 crates barrier per 10-hour day, and get in amongst the good earnings. When my first half-century had been verified, I was punching the air in triumphant salute. The next day, toying with extremis, 53 was achieved, and I had the distinct feeling while unloading at the depot that the workers there were nudging one another and confiding 'c'est lui, mon dieu, comme une tempête dans les tomates!' Ahmed, meanwhile, was touching 70 crates a day. Any day now, I reasoned, we'd be on a par, sending the boss off to buy a calculator and to order extra crates. This was not to be, however. I had peaked. Desperation set in; the crates were becoming bigger, tomatoes always lying awkwardly, the heat blistering; I began to flounder, drained and dejected in the low 40s. My colleague when I last asked him was turning in a cool 80 a day, which if you knew anything about tomato picking I would not ask you to believe. You would have to see it for yourself. I'm thinking of giving guided tours of the scene of his campaign for knowing seasonal workers and aficionados: 'Yup,' I'll nod my head – greyhaired as it now is after the experience – in the direction of a little altar-like structure, 'I was there, seen it wi' m'own eyes. I swear it, them little rascals wuz up'n jumpin' in that thaar bucket of his.' Anyway, good luck to him. It was with some relief that I was transferred to the shady plum groves across the road.*

During August in the South of France the only equipment you'll need is a sun hat. But if you are planning to pick apples in British Columbia or olives in the Greek winter, you will need warm clothing, waterproofs and possibly also rubber boots for muddy fields and gloves for wet fruit. Gloves can also be useful if you are picking fruit which has been sprayed with an insecticide that irritates cuts or stains your hands an unsightly colour. If it is too awkward to pick wearing gloves, you can tape up your hands with surgical tape to prevent blistering.

FARMING

Not all casual work in rural areas revolves around fruit and vegetable harvests. There are a lot of miscellaneous seasonal jobs created by the agricultural industry, from 'castrating' maize (which means plucking the flowers) to crutching sheep (removing dirty wool from around the tail), from scaring birds away from cherry orchards to herding goats (something which seems to reduce most novices to tears), from weeding olive groves to spraying banana plantations. There is always the chance of work if you knock on farmers' doors.

Many farms, especially in Europe, are relatively small family-run businesses, and the farmer may not need to look any further than his or her own family for labour. But often farmers are looking for one able-bodied assistant over the summer months, and if you are fortunate to be that one, you will probably be treated as a member of the family, sharing their meals and their outings. It is more important to be able to communicate with the farmer than if you are hired as a fruit picker, since the instructions given to farm hands are more complicated. It also helps to have some tractor-driving or other farm experience or at least an aptitude for machinery.

Even if the work you are given is tedious, this might be exactly what you want, as was the case with Joseph Tame who spent a few weeks working on an organic farm in Switzerland one spring: *'The type of work can at times be tremendously repetitive (such as the four hours a day every day spent scraping cow shit from the yard!). Yet in this repetitiveness you have a freedom, a freedom of the mind that enables you to mull over any thoughts or feelings that in England would be swept aside by the stress of everyday life. Here I have all the time in the world; and in this world, time is not money.'*

AS SO MUCH DEPENDS ON THE GENEROSITY OF THE HOSTS, KAREN MARTIN AND PAUL ANSELL WERE LUCKY AT THEIR MAIZE AND APPLE FARM IN FRANCE:

It is, I imagine, like many farms out in the sticks, but the wife is happy to drive us to the supermarket or train station if you fancy going to big places like Angers or Saumur. They have given us loads of fresh fruit, washed our clothes, given us lots of their very good (very strong) drink, let us use their internet and even lent us money when we first arrived.

Advertising Online

Placing an advert in the national farmers' journal is especially worthwhile for people who have had some relevant experience. Gary Tennant placed the following advert in a Danish farmers' publication and elicited four offers: *'23 year old Englishman now in Denmark would like farm work. Have been working on a kibbutz in Israel (4 months) in the fields and tractor work. Just finished gardening work in England and want to try different farming. Telephone 06191679, ask for Gary.'*

Targeting small rural newspapers can also pay dividends partly because it will almost certainly be a novelty. Ken Smith noticed a small ad in the *Oamaru Mail* in New Zealand published every Friday: *'Young German man seeks farm work. Has tractor experience and good work habits.'*

Range of Opportunities

Many long-term itinerant workers meet up with people who are interested in alternative lifestyles that may include organic farming or goat-cheese production as a way of earning a living, or advocates of the Slow Food movement. In rural areas, a polite request for room and board in exchange for half a day's work often succeeds. Rob Abblett has worked on farms all over the world from Mexico to Malawi, Sweden to Salt Spring Island, Canada. He simply gathers lists of contacts from organisations like the ones listed in this section and gets in touch with the ones that sound appealing:

I've visited, worked and had many varied experiences on over 30 communes around the world. I like them because they are so varied and full of interesting people, usually with alternative ideas, beliefs, but also because I almost always find someone that I can really connect with, for sometimes I need to be with like-minded folk.

Tree nurseries are often a good source of casual work and in some countries (especially Canada) tree planting is a job often done by nomadic types. Without any formal training in agriculture, it is possible to get some preliminary experience. A few European countries have programmes whereby young people spend a month or two assisting on a farm, eg Norway and Switzerland (see chapters). A farming background is not necessary for participating in these schemes, though of course it always helps.

It is not impossible to find work on farms and ranches that have diversified to accept paying visitors. For example in Italy the *agriturismo* movement is particularly thriving, and it could be worth making contact with member proprietors. This is also popular in the USA (where guest ranches are called 'dude ranches') and Australia. These establishments need both domestic and outdoor assistants to lead guests on trail rides, show them places or events of local interest, etc.

Volunteering your labour on a farm in exchange for bed and board is an excellent way to gain agricultural experience at the same time as a cultural exchange. A free internet-based exchange of work-for-keep volunteers can be found at www.helpx.net where more than 7,500 Australian and 4,500 New Zealand hosts are listed, with a growing number in Europe and worldwide as well. Membership of this excellent online community costs €20 for two years.

Another superb resource is www.workaway.info for rural jobs, among other paid and volunteer opportunities worldwide including many in the developing world. Potential work-for-keep volunteers can access the listings by paying a fee of US$29 for a year.

WWOOF

With growing fears of unsustainable farming methods and genetically modified foods, the organic farming movement is attracting an ever growing following around the world, from Toulouse to Turkey. Organic farms everywhere take on volunteers to help them minimise or abolish the use of chemicals and heavy machinery. There are various co-ordinating bodies, many of which go under the name of WWOOF.

WWOOF stands for World Wide Opportunities on Organic Farms, changed some while ago from Willing Workers on Organic Farms, with an eye to the sensitivities of immigration officers around the world who always bridle at the word 'work'. (If the topic arises at immigration, avoid the word 'working'; it is preferable to present yourself as a student of organic farming who is planning an educational farm visit or a cultural exchange.)

The International WWOOF Association (IWA) has a global website www.wwoofinternational.org with links to both the national organisations in the countries that have a WWOOF co-ordinator and to those which do not, known as WWOOF Independents. Each national group is autonomous with its own aims, system, fees and rules. Most prefer applicants to have gained some experience on an organic farm in their own country first, though this is not essential. WWOOF is an exchange: in return for your help on organic farms, gardens and homesteads, you receive meals, a place to sleep and a practical insight into organic growing. The work-for-keep exchange is a simple one that can be immensely satisfying. Visitors are expected to work for about six hours per day in return for free accommodation and can stay from a few days to many months depending on whether or not they click with the owners and, of course, how much work needs to be done. Idealists might like to choose their destination carefully. Anna and Rachel Frayling-Cork, two sisters from Cambridge, organised a WWOOF stay with a family living on a remote property in the Pyrenees before Rachel's A level year so that she could improve her French. The family was friendly, the food delicious but the work they were asked to do was not much different from free labour to help them build an extension to their house. When it rained, the WWOOF volunteers had to work indoors. One day Rachel spent the day sitting on planks to steady them while the father of the family sawed them into lengths. It was hard to see how this helped to further the aims of the organic movement. And the heavy regional accent also made it difficult to further her aim of learning French.

CANADIAN LEONA BALDWIN AND PARTNER DECIDED TO GO DOWN THIS ROUTE TO FIX UP A WORK-FOR-KEEP PLACEMENT AT A TREKKING CENTRE IN NEW ZEALAND:

From the Bay of Islands to Invercargill, WWOOFing opportunities were advertised everywhere, at Yoga retreats, ski resorts, cattle farms and horse trekking centres. Our preference was for the latter. Ever since my 'My Little Pony' days of youth, dazzled by storybook images of unicorns and Black Beauty, I had loved horses. As it transpired, it was destined to be a love affair from afar. My first riding experience at the age of 10 had found me clinging helplessly to the saddle and then face down in the snow. The best thing you can do in those circumstances is get right back on. But I hadn't, and now 15 years later, I decided to make amends.

Luckily, our first choice in horse-trekking farms had a vacancy for two WWOOFers, and we were invited to come and stay in the scenic Ruapehu district. Soon after arrival I found myself in the paddock ready to confront the four-legged demons of my past. And there they stood, 14 pairs of ears pricked up, eyes wild, muscles taut and ready for action. My knees went weak. As I reached up over my head to attach the rope to its neck, heart in my throat, I took a step and to my great surprise, it moved obediently behind me. I was in control!

If you want to WWOOF in countries that have their own WWOOF organisation like Italy or Korea, it is necessary to join the national WWOOF organisation before you can obtain addresses of their member properties. This usually costs €15–€40 per year. At present there are 58 countries with their own WWOOF co-ordinators from Canada to Kazakhstan, Austria to Australia, many of which are mentioned in the following chapters of this book with the price of joining. New countries are joining the federation all the time, most recently Norway and Togo. You can almost always see a preview of the properties online but must pay to join in order to get contact details.

Organic farms in all the countries without their own national organisation are known as WWOOF Independents (www.wwoofindependents.org), whose list contains multiple addresses in Finland, Croatia, Morocco, etc, but only one or two in countries such as Belarus and Mauritius. To obtain the addresses of properties in all the left-over countries, go to www.wwoofindependents.org; joining WWOOF Independents costs £15. In many cases, if you join a national WWOOF organisation, you will automatically be entitled to access WWOOF Independents as well.

Mike Tunnicliffe joined the long-established WWOOF New Zealand to avoid work permit hassles and his experience is typical of WWOOFers' in other countries: *'My second choice of farm was a marvellous experience. For 15 days I earned no money but neither did I spend any, and I enjoyed life on the farm as part of the family. There is a wide variety of WWOOF farms and I thoroughly recommend the scheme to anyone who isn't desperate to earn money.'*

Before arranging a longish stay on an organic farm, consider whether or not you will find such an environment congenial. Many organic farmers are non-smoking vegetarians and living conditions may be primitive by some people's standards. Although positive experiences are typical, Craig Ashworth expressed reservations about WWOOF, based on his experiences in New Zealand, and claims that a proportion of WWOOF hosts are 'quite wacky'. (See Denmark chapter for a first-hand account of total incompatibility in this context.) Bear in mind that the work you are given to do may not always be very salubrious: for example Armin Birrer, who has spent time on organic farms in many countries, claims that the weirdest job he ever did was to spend a day in New Zealand picking worms out of a pile of rabbit dung to be used to soften the soil around some melon plants. With such a loose network of individuals around the world, the system is bound to be hit and miss. Danny Jacobson was willing to take that gamble and on the whole was happy with his WWOOF experiences in South Australia.

One was an organic fig/garlic farm and the other a vineyard. Both were great though the farmers can be really bizarre and sometimes anal about how things are done. On the fig farm, the lady even gave us grades according to how we'd done that day and it was pretty annoying. Still it was really beautiful and the work was good. On the vineyard, the guy was very nice and extremely enthusiastic about making the best wine in the world.

Communities

Many communities (formerly called communes) welcome foreign visitors and willingly exchange hospitality for work. Although not all the work is agricultural, much of it is. Some are radical or esoteric in their practices so find out as much as you can before planning to visit. The majority are vegetarian. The details and possible fees must be established on a case-by-case basis. The following resources are relevant:

Diggers and Dreamers: The Guide to Communal Living: Published by Edge of Time (www. edgeoftime.co.uk); £14.50. The 2015 edition marks the book's 25th anniversary; contains a listing of communities in the UK.

Eurotopia: Directory of Communities and Ecovillages in Europe: www.eurotopia.de. Lists 336 international communities in 23 countries (mainly Europe and the UK).

Fellowship for Intentional Community: Main Office (at Sandhill Farm in Missouri), RR 1 Box 156-W, Rutledge, MO 63563–9720, USA; ☎ (+1) 660 883 5545; www.ic.org/directory. Publishes *Communities Directory: A Comprehensive Guide to Intentional Communities and Co-operative Living* (2016 edition costs $35/£27). It lists about 1,200 communities world-wide including *'eco-villages, rural land trusts, co-housing groups, kibbutzim, student co-ops, organic farms, monasteries, urban artist collectives, rural communes and Catholic Worker houses'*; much of the information is available on their website. The majority of communities listed are in the US.

Global Ecovillage Network (GEN): GEN-Europe Office, Ökodorf Sieben Linden, Sieben Linden 1, 38489 Beetzendorf, Germany; www.gen-europe.org. GEN functions as the umbrella organisation for a wide range of intentional communities and eco-villages all over the world, many of which welcome guests and volunteers.

Agricultural Exchanges and Apprenticeships

An organisation that started out in the early 1970s as a small group of dairy farmers in Minnesota has grown into CAEP (Communicating for Agriculture Educational Programs; www.caep.co.uk) still based in rural Minnesota, but with representatives in many countries. It offers paid apprenticeships in the US (assigning candidates a J-1 visa) and in Canada, Australia and New Zealand, mainly for US partici-pants. Candidates must be aged 18–28 (or 21–35 for the oenology placements) with an interest or background in agriculture, horticulture, equine or wine-making. Placement dates, durations and fees differ; for example a field crop apprenticeship in the US lasts from March to December.

Equipeople is an Irish company that supplies staff not just to the horse sector but to the agricul-tural industry more broadly in Ireland and abroad (www.equipeopleabroad.com). It runs work exchange programmes in Canada, the US, New Zealand, Australia and the Netherlands for people aged 18–28/30 who have at least one year's relevant experience. Their agency fee is €300–€400 plus the partner organisations impose their own fees, eg €475 in the case of the Dutch exchange foundation SUSP, or NZ$1,195 in the case of Rural Exchange New Zealand. For a list of agricultural exchange organisations around the world, check the list of members of the Grow Abroad International Alliance (www.grow-abroad.com). The British representative is an agency in Rutland called IEP-UK (vanessa. peach@iepuk.co.uk).

A specialist online recruiter based in Florida, Equistaff (www.equistaff. com) has an international clientele for its farm, ranch and equine jobs worldwide. Experienced grooms, riding instructors and stable staff may consider registering with a specialist online matching service such as Career Grooms (☎ (+44) 20 7289 6385; www.careergrooms.co.uk) with vacancies mainly in the UK and Germany.

Other agencies advertise in the specialist press, for example *Horse & Hound*. Stable staff and light-weight riders are needed for work on studs and in racing establishments around the world. For those who like horses but lack experience, becoming a volunteer at a riding stable might be the answer, which can be arranged in some countries through the WWOOF exchange.

Teaching English

This chapter used to begin with a quotation from a traveller-turned-professional-EFL-teacher, Dick Bird:

> *It is extremely difficult for anyone whose mother tongue is English to starve in an inhabited place, since there are always people who will pay good money to watch you display a talent as basic as talking. Throughout the world, native speakers of English are at a premium.*

But this rosy view of the traveller's prospects must now be moderated somewhat. Although the English language is still the language that millions of people around the world want to learn, finding work as an English teacher is not as easy as many people assume. Furthermore, there is a worrying trend even for people with a qualification to have difficulty getting an entry level job with decent pay and conditions. The number of both public and private institutes turning out certified TEFL teachers has greatly increased in the past 15 years, creating a glut of teachers all chasing jobs, especially in the major cities of Europe.

Having sounded that warning note, it must be said that there are still areas of the world where the boom in English language learning seems to know no bounds, principally China, Korea and Taiwan, though demand is strong in many other countries from Ecuador to Vietnam. In cowboy schools and back-street agencies, being a native speaker and dressing neatly are sometimes sufficient qualifications to get a job. But for more stable teaching jobs in recognised language schools, you will have to sign a contract (minimum three months, usually nine) and have some kind of qualification which ranges from a university degree to a certificate in education with a specialisation in English Language Teaching (ELT is the term now preferred to Teaching English as a Foreign Language or TEFL).

One of the best sources of information about the whole topic of English teaching (if I may be permitted to say so) is the 2017 edition of *Teaching English Abroad* (Trotman). This chapter can only provide the most general introduction to such topics as TEFL training and recruitment; for specific information about individual countries, see the country chapters.

ELT TRAINING

The only way to outrival the competition and make the job-hunt (not to mention the job itself) easier is to do a training course. The British Council's www.teachingenglish.org.uk is a good starting place for information. There are two standard recognised qualifications that will improve your range of job options by an order of magnitude. The best known is the Certificate in English Language Teaching to Adults (CELTA) administered and awarded by the University of Cambridge ESOL Examinations (www.cambridgeeng-lish.org). The other is the Certificate in TESOL (Teaching English to Speakers of Other Languages) offered by Trinity College London (www.trinity-college.co.uk). Both are intensive and expensive, with the cost ranging from £1,000 to £1,400 for a full-time course. These courses involve 100–130 hours of rigorous training with a practical emphasis (full-time for four weeks or part-time over several months). Although there are no fixed prerequisites apart from a suitable level of language awareness, not everyone who applies is accepted. And almost no one finds these intensive courses a breeze. Fergus Cooney says that on his CELTA course, they barely had time for a coffee during the day and that several trainees broke down in tears during breaks, himself (almost) included.

The hundreds of centres in the UK and abroad offering the Cambridge CELTA are linked from the Cambridge English website (www.cambridgeenglish.org/find-a-centre/find-a-teaching-centre). CELTA courses are offered at more than 300 centres in 48 countries from the Middle East to Queensland, including 24 in the USA and 29 in Australia and New Zealand.

A number of centres offer short introductory courses in TEFL, which vary enormously in quality and price. Among the main providers are i-to-i.com, StarTEFL.com and UK-TEFL.com, all of which sell online training courses as well. These may be less challenging and the qualification not widely recognised, but this did not deter the self-confessedly unacademic Roger Blake who felt that he benefited greatly from a short TEFL course:

> *Of the many things that I have achieved over the past few years, one of the most significant must be my certificate in TEFL. Partly inspired during a backpacker-style holiday to New York where I saw a subway advertisement asking for English teachers, I followed it up and did a crash weekend course with i-to-i. To my surprise I enjoyed it so much that I then did their language awareness module by home study to improve my understanding and ability to teach. (It is worth noting that i-to-i's courses are aimed at casual would-be teachers not career professionals.) Not being the academic sort, I amazed myself in completing 40 hours but it was worth it. Since then I have been particularly keen to get off on my travels.*

Other training centres for American readers to consider apart from CELTA ones are Transworld Schools in San Francisco (☎ (+1) 415 928 2835; www.transworldschools.com) and the School of Teaching English as a Second Language in Seattle (☎ (+1) 206 781 8607; www.schooloftesl.com) which offer their own four-week certificate courses 10 times a year for about $3,000. The TEFL Academy (www.internationalteflacademy.com) offers four-week training courses in Boston, New York, Chicago, Seattle and Honolulu, costing $2,395–$2,980. The same course is offered in many other countries from Nicaragua to Vietnam.

What English Teaching Involves

It is difficult to generalise about what work you will actually be required to do. At one extreme your job will be to listen to Korean businessmen reading English novels aloud to correct their pronunciation. At the other extreme you may have a gruelling schedule of lesson preparation and teaching recalcitrant adolescents. Whatever the teaching you find, things probably won't go as smoothly as you would wish.

BARRY O'LEARY HAS TAUGHT ENGLISH IN THAILAND, AUSTRALIA, ECUADOR, BRAZIL AND NOW SPAIN. HE DESCRIBES HIS JOB IN QUITO:

The teaching varied. In one school I was responsible for conversation classes. I had no guidance with the type of lessons they wanted so had to use resources from my course, the internet and my imagination. In every lesson a local teacher was there to help with any language barriers. The working conditions were very relaxed, no lesson plans or meetings, I was just given a timetable and left to get on with it. As long as the students were smiling, I was seen to be a good teacher.

I was lucky enough to find an apartment with an Ecuadorian family through an advertisement in an internet café. I made enough money to pay for my rent, food and some social activities and even managed to travel a bit with my last pay packet – and the dollars went much further in Peru.

The students were all great, the teenagers tending to be cheeky, a few times they changed the theme of the lessons to 'make the teacher dance like a fool' before they did any work, but this was all part of the fun. It was a very relaxed atmosphere most of the time. I really enjoyed working with local teachers and they were all very open and friendly and interested in my life in England since many of them had never left Ecuador.

Native speaker teachers are nearly always employed to stimulate conversation rather than to teach grammar. Yet a basic knowledge of English grammar is a great asset when pupils come to ask awkward questions. The book *English Grammar in Use* by Raymond Murphy is recommended for its clear explanations and accompanying student exercises.

The teaching of young children is a booming area of TEFL from Portugal to Taiwan, and usually involves repetitive drills, sing-songs, puzzles and games. Intermediate learners can be difficult, since they will have reached a plateau and may be discouraged. Adults are usually well motivated though may be inhibited about speaking. Teaching professionals and business people is almost always well paid. Only 18 himself, Sam James had to teach a variety of age groups in Barcelona during his gap year and, despite the problems, ended up enjoying it:

> The children I taught were fairly unruly and noisy. The teenagers were, as ever, pretty uninterested in learning, though if one struck on something they enjoyed they would work much better. Activities based on the lyrics of songs seemed to be good. They had a tendency to select answers at random in multiple-choice exercises. On the other hand they were only ever loud rather than very rude or disobedient. The young children (8–12) were harder work. They tended to understand selectively, acting confused if they didn't like an instruction. Part of the problem was that the class was far too long (three hours) for children of that age and their concentration and behaviour tended to tail off as the time passed.

Most schools practise the direct method (total immersion in English), so not knowing the language shouldn't prevent you from getting a job. Some employers may provide nothing more than a scratched blackboard and will expect you to dive in using the 'chalk and talk' method. Brochures picked up from tourist offices or airlines can be a useful peg on which to hang a lesson.

FINDING A JOB

Teaching jobs are either fixed up from home or sought out on location. Obviously it is less nerve-racking to have everything sorted out before you leave home, but this option is usually available only to the qualified. It also has the disadvantage that you don't know what you're letting yourself in for.

In Advance

Everywhere you look on the internet potentially useful links can be found for job-seeking English teachers. Hundreds of websites are devoted to EFL/ESL jobs, many in Asia. Tefl.com is a crucial resource, having gained in authority and popularity over recent years. When subscribing (for free), you can specify whether you want to be notified of vacancies by email on a daily or weekly basis. The site claims to have more than 23,500 registered employers. At the time of writing, the countries with the most vacancies listed were Spain (89), China (91) and Italy (64). Another long established linchpin site is Dave Sperling's ESL Café (www.eslcafe.com). 'Dave' provides a mind-boggling but well-organised amount of material for the future or current teacher including accounts of people's experiences of teaching abroad (but bear in mind that these are the opinions of individuals). It is possible to post your CV which will often attract job offers, though it is important to be fairly specific as Fergus Cooney discovered:

> I posted a message simply stating 'Qualified teacher seeking job'. Within two days I was inundated with many dozens of replies requesting my CV and, more surprisingly with job offers everywhere, although the majority were from Korea, Taiwan and China. 'Jackpot' I thought (I have since realised that many schools/agents must have an automatic reply system which emails those who advertise in the way I did). I quickly began sifting through them, but not as quickly as they kept arriving in my inbox. Before a few more days had passed, I had become utterly confused and had forgotten which school was which, so I deleted them all, got a new email address and posted a second, more specific message on Dave's.

Here is a list of some of the other key recruitment sites:

www.eslbase.com: Reasonably reliable links to language schools, country by country plus current vacancies; useful TEFL forum.

www.eslteachersboard.com: Vast site and free community for EL teachers with current job postings (dated and with email addresses revealed) and teachers' CVs.

www.englishjobsabroad.com: Dated and archived job postings with addresses revealed.

http://teflen.com/tefl-tesol-jobs-board-employment-job-portal.html: Mainly recruitment agencies with live vacancies.

www.tefljobs.net: Dated vacancies with possibility of clicking through to contact details; free to register but must upload a CV in order to apply.

www.TEFLworld.com: Calls itself a vertical search portal with a search engine that crawls major job boards across the Internet and finds posted positions matching the criteria of the job seeker. Strongest in vacancies in Asia.

TEFLnow.com: Online TEFL training provider. Worldwide vacancies posted on Facebook (www.facebook.com/TEFLnow) as they arise.

www.esl101.com: Database of recent job postings with web addresses but no contact details.

Other websites that are country-specific, eg www.ohayosensei.com (jobs in Japan) and www.ajarn.com (teaching in Thailand) are listed in the relevant country chapters. The major language school chains hire substantial numbers of teachers, many of whom will have graduated from in-house training courses. Among the major employers of EFL teachers are Berlitz (www.berlitz.com) who have been expanding their summer programmes for young learners in Germany, Spain, etc, EF English First (www.englishfirst.com/ESL-Jobs) which recruits teachers on an ongoing basis for 200 EF schools in Russia, China and Indonesia, International House with 160 affiliated schools in 52 countries (www.job.ihworld.com), Language Link in London (www.languagelink.co.uk), Marcus Evans Linguarama (www.linguarama.com) which caters to the business English market, and Wall Street English (teach@wallstreetenglish.com; www.wallstreetenglish.com).

Scope for untrained but eager volunteers exists for those willing to pay an agency to place them in a language teaching situation abroad, for example by many of the placement agencies listed in the Gap Years chapter. For example Global Nomadic in London (www.globalnomadic.com) tries to minimise costs in its placements worldwide, offering paid teaching in Thailand, China, Costa Rica, Czech Republic and Spain, sometimes in conjunction with an in-country training course.

The British Council (10 Spring Gardens, London SW1A 2BN; language.assistants@britishcouncil.org) administers language assistant placements to help local teachers of English in secondary schools from France to Colombia. Applicants for assistant posts must normally be aged 20–30, native English speakers, with at least two years of university-level education in the language of the destination country.

North American Organisations

A selection of key programmes and organisations in the USA includes:

Global Crossroad: Irving, Texas; ☎ (+1) 866 205 6515; www.globalcrossroad.com. Volunteer teaching and internships in 18 countries from Uganda to Peru. For volunteer programmes in many countries, application fee is $299 plus varying weekly fee.

Greenheart Travel: Chicago; www.greenhearttravel.org. Cultural exchange organisation that arranges teaching jobs in South Korea, China, Myanmar, Thailand, Vietnam, Colombia and Italy. (Greenheart won top prize at the Global Youth Travel Awards 2016 as Outstanding Volunteer Project.)

LanguageCorps: Sudbury, Massachusetts; ☎ (+1) 978 562 2100; toll-free (North America): ☎ (+1) 877 216 3267; www.languagecorps.com. Company offers four-week TESOL training course in many places worldwide, and then job placement in South-East Asia, Latin America, etc.

WorldTeach: Cambridge, MA (☎ (+1) 857 259 6646; www.worldteach.org). Non-profit organisation that provides college graduates with one-year contracts (EFL or ESL) in American Samoa, Colombia, Ecuador, Guyana, Namibia, the Marshall Islands, China, Bangladesh, Chile, Pohnpei (Micronesia) and Thailand. Summer programmes are available in Ecuador, Poland, Namibia, Morocco, Nepal, Micronesia and South Africa. Participants pay a volunteer contribution ranging from zero to $3,990; several programmes are fully funded by the host country including Samoa, the Marshall Islands and Micronesia.

On the Spot

Jobs in any field are difficult to get without an interview and English teaching is no different. In almost all cases (especially in Europe) it is more effective to go to your preferred destination, CV in hand, and call on language schools and companies. The director of the Mainz branch of a chain of language schools is just one language school director who has emphasised the importance of applying locally:

Schools like ours cannot under normal operating circumstances hire someone unseen merely on the basis of his/her resumé and photo. Moreover, when the need for a teacher arises, usually that vacancy must be filled within a matter of days that, for people applying from abroad, is a physical impossibility. I would suggest that an applicant should arrange for a face-to-face interview and make him/herself available at a moment's notice. Of course, I do appreciate the compromising situation to which anyone in need of employment would thus be exposed. Regrettably, I know of no other method.

When looking for work at private language schools, it is helpful if you can claim some qualifications, and be prepared to provide proof of the same. If you have a degree (in any subject), take along the certificate. In countries from Mexico to Japan, travelling teachers have stressed the importance of dressing smartly, having a respectable briefcase and a typed CV with no spelling mistakes.

Check job ads on Craigslist, Gumtree, Kijiji or equivalent. Trawl the internet and the *Yellow Pages* (print or online) in order to draw up a list of addresses where you can ask for work.

An alternative to working for a language school is to set yourself up as a freelance private tutor. While undercutting the fees charged by the big schools, you can still earn more than as a contract teacher. Normally you will have to be fairly well established in a place before you can attempt to support yourself by private teaching, preferably with some decent premises in which to give lessons (either individual or group). Bear in mind the disadvantages of working for yourself such as frequent last-minute cancellations by clients, unpaid travelling time (if you teach in clients' homes or offices), no social security and an absence of professional support and teaching materials.

Private students can be found online, which is much easier than the old way of having to put up eye-catching posters and promote yourself unashamedly. Specialist language tutor search sites may be of help such as Angoltanarok.com in Budapest or GetStudents.net in Japan. Creating a profile on these sites is usually not expensive. A site that operates internationally is Findmyfavouriteteacher.com where you can post your bio and the prices you charge for a discounted trial lesson and for normal lessons.

Telephone teaching or teaching by Skype is a growing market, so if you have a laptop and a good internet connection, you could investigate this avenue. Specialist online platforms are now a common way to supplement a teaching income or even to become a full-time job. A growing number of companies such as Learnlight, SpeakPlus, FluentU and Learnship (for business English) have created marketplaces that connect language learners with tutors or coaches. Even a chatting-app like NiceTalk Tutor popular among Chinese language learners may earn you a bit of money.

Childcare

The terms au pair, mother's help and nanny are often applied rather loosely, since all are primarily live-in jobs concerned with looking after children. Nannies normally have some formal training and take full charge of the children. Mother's helps work full-time and undertake general housework and/or cooking as well as childcare. Au pairs are supposed to work for no more than 30 hours a week and are expected to learn a foreign language while living with a family.

One of the great advantages of these live-in positions generally is that demand is so great that they are relatively easy to get (at least for women). Occasionally, young men can find live-in jobs, and slowly the number of families and therefore agencies willing to entertain the possibility of having a male child-carer (sometimes referred to as a manny) is increasing. Au pairs can often benefit from legislation that exempts them from work permit requirements.

The standard length of stay is for one academic year, typically September to June. Summer stays can also be arranged to coincide with the school holidays. The advantage of a summer placement is that the au pair will accompany the family to their holiday destination at the seaside or in the mountains; the disadvantage is that the children will be your responsibility for more hours than they would be if they were at school, and also most language classes will close for the summer. Make enquiries as early as possible, since there is a shortage of summer-only positions.

A new development is for countries outside the usual European–New World axis to introduce live-in helper schemes. Young men and women have started to be placed in families in China to do 25 hours of childcare and to set the children on the path to learning English (see China chapter and Almondbury agency below).

One high profile agency, Smart Au Pairs, ventured the following opinion post-Brexit: *'We do not believe the vote to leave will affect au pairs for the foreseeable future and feel very positive that European au pairs will be welcomed in the UK for many years to come.'*

PROS AND CONS

The term au pair means 'on equal terms' and often the terminology 'hostess' and 'hospitality' is used rather than employer/employee. Therefore the success of the arrangement depends more than usual on whether individuals hit it off, so there is always an element of risk when living in a family of strangers. The Council of Europe guidelines stipulate that au pairs should be aged 18–27 (though these limits are flexible), should be expected to work about five hours a day, five days per week plus a couple of evenings of babysitting, must be given a private room and full board, health insurance, pocket money and opportunities to learn the language.

Once you have arrived in the family, it is important to clarify immediately what your hours and duties will be, which day you will be paid, whether you can expect a rise and how much notice either party must give if they wish to terminate the arrangement. This gets everyone off to a business-like start. But no matter how well defined your duties are, there are bound to be occasions when your extra services will be taken for granted. It may seem that your time is not your own. Kathryn Halliwell worked for a family in Vancouver, Canada for a year and describes this problem: *'A live-in job is a very committed one. It is extremely difficult to say no when the employers ring at 6pm to say they can't be home for another two hours. Children don't consider a nanny as an employee and tension develops if a child can't understand why you won't take him swimming on your day off.'*

At one extreme you have the family (with one well-behaved child) who invites you along on skiing trips with them and asks you to do a mere 24 hours of child-minding and light housework a week. On the other hand you might be treated like a kitchen skivvy by the mother, and like a concubine by the father, while at the same time trying to look after their four spoiled brats. So it is advisable to find out as much as possible about the family before accepting the job. If you do not like the sound of the situation at the beginning you should insist that the agency offer any available alternatives.

Different national temperaments and mores can cause problems. In conservative families in countries such as Turkey, southern Italy or even the USA, it is unacceptable for young women to go out alone at night, so your social life may be very restricted.

ON THE OTHER HAND, GILLIAN FORSYTH'S EXPERIENCE WHEN SHE AU PAIRED IN BAVARIA WAS A GREAT SUCCESS:

I had no official day off or free time but was treated as a member of the family. Wherever they went I went too. I found this much more interesting than being treated as an employee as I really got to know the country and the people. In the evenings I did not have to sit in my room, but chatted with the family. Three years later we still keep in close contact and I have been skiing with them twice since, on an au pair/friend basis.

If you do not have a friendly arrangement with the family, it is easy to feel lonely and cut off in a foreign country. Many au pairs make friends at their language classes. Some agencies issue lists of other au pairs in the vicinity. Despite all the possible problems, au pairing does provide an easy and often enjoyable introduction to living and travelling abroad. A family placement is a safe and stable environment for young, under-confident and impecunious people who want to work abroad.

Pay and Duties

The standard pocket money paid to au pairs in Europe nowadays starts at €250 a month in Italy and rises to €450–€500 in Belgium and Luxembourg. With a strong euro this represents a reasonable income in addition to room and board. In Switzerland, au pairs earn (by law) the equivalent of £400–£600 a month, and statutory minimums are also high in Austria (€425.70 per month (gross) for 20 hours a week).

Nannying can be an excellent passport to spending a season in a summer or winter resort for those with a qualification or experience. Most large tour and campsite holiday operators such as Mark Warner, Thomas Cook and TUI Holidays (addresses in Tourism chapter) employ nannies with qualifications or experience in childcare to look after the children of holidaymakers. Companies that specialise in arranging summer and winter holidays for families, such as Esprit Holidays, employ a considerable number of childcare staff as well as other employees for their summer programme in the Alps (www.workaseason.com).

Most au pairs' duties revolve around the children. For some, taking sole responsibility for a child can be fairly alarming. You should be prepared to handle a few emergencies (for example sick or lost children) as well as the usual excursions to the park or collecting them from school. The agency questionnaire will ask you in detail what experience you have had with children and whether you are willing to look after newborn infants, etc.

APPLYING

Many au pair agencies now operate only as online matching services, and the era of the old-fashioned one-woman agency is all but over. Au pairs and nannies seeking positions generally pay nothing but families must pay a registration fee. Because of the low profit margins, many agencies that used to send British girls abroad are now concentrating almost exclusively on placing foreign girls with paying client families in the UK.

If you are already abroad, check in the local English language newspaper or visit an au pair agency office in the country where you are (addresses provided in country chapters). Many European agencies charge a substantial fee of €200+, which they claim is necessary to guarantee a minimum quality of service.

Other ways of hearing about openings are to consult Craigslist or equivalent and also to check the noticeboards at the local English-speaking churches or ask the head teacher of a junior school if she/he knows of any families wanting an au pair. Online communities among expats can be invaluable. One tip for finding babysitting jobs in resorts is to introduce yourself to the *portiere* or receptionist on the desk of good hotels, show them some references and ask them to refer guests looking for a babysitter to you, possibly offering them a small commission. With more suspicion around these days, informal arrangements like this are less likely to succeed; some potential clients might be reassured if you have good references and, assuming you have worked in the past through an agency that has applied on your behalf, a DBS enhanced check (current cost is £44).

The Internet

Cyberspace buzzes with an exchange of information about live-in childcare. Au pair placement was something that was always done by telephone and correspondence rather than requiring a face-to-face interview, so it is an activity that is well suited to an online database. Among the most popular sites are www.aupair-agency.com (run by Almondbury Care International), www.greataupair.com, www.findaupair.com and www.aupair-world.net (based in Germany but operating internationally in English). Agencies online enable families and applicants to engage in DIY arrangements. They invite prospective au pairs to register their details, including age, nationality, relevant experience and in many cases a photo, to be uploaded onto a website which then becomes accessible to registered families. The families then make contact with suitable au pairs after paying an introduction fee to the web-based agency. Registration is invariably free for the jobseeker.

One problem identified by the traditional agencies is that this method makes it very difficult to carry out any effective screening of either party. On the other hand, the same could be said for sits vac advertising in the conventional way (see below). If relying on the internet it is essential to ascertain exactly the nature of the situation and the expectations of your new employer. Work out in your mind what you will do in the event the arrangement does not work out; if the agency is simply a database-provider, they will be able to offer no back up. Jean-Marc Cressini, owner of the French agency Oliver Twist, thinks that this book *'should really warn applicants about free websites, as we have just been informed by Interpol that some girls have paid large amounts of money to families who do not exist. A person pretending to be a family has been arrested in England for asking applicants for large bank transfers.'* You should be suspicious of any individual or company that asks for money upfront.

Agencies in the UK

Arguably there is too little regulation in the world of au pair agencies, and things can go wrong in even the most tightly controlled programmes. Many leading au pair agencies and youth exchange organisations in Europe belong to IAPA, the International Au Pair Association, an international body trying to regulate the industry. The IAPA website www.iapa.org has clear links to its member agencies around the world.

Most reputable agencies will ask prospective au pairs to submit written references (not from family or friends), a letter of introduction about their family background and experience, an up-to-date medical certificate, a police check, a first-aid certificate (if possible) and a driving licence (preferred).

Agencies that specialise in one country are mentioned in the country chapters. The following UK au pair and/or nanny agencies all deal with a number of European countries.

Almondbury Au Pair & Nanny Agency: London W14; ☎ (+44) 20 7097 5135; admin@aupair-agency.com; www.aupair-agency.com. It is not merely an internet matching site but can be consulted by phone. In addition to all the usual countries, it runs an Au Pair China programme.

Childcare International Ltd: Borehamwood, Herts; ☎ (+44) 800 652 0020 or (+44) 20 8731 4551; www.childint.co.uk. Separate divisions for incoming and outgoing childcarers to Europe, Canada, Australia, New Zealand and China.

Edgware & Solihull Au Pair & Nanny Agency: Radlett, Hertfordshire; ☎ (+44) 1923 289737; www.the-aupair-shop.com. UK, Europe and the USA.

Janet White Agency: Leeds, West Yorkshire; ☎ (+44) 113 266 6507; www.janetwhite.com. Europe and the USA.

My Travelling Nanny: Letchworth, Hertfordshire; ☎ (+44) 20 8133 3126; www.mytravelling nanny.co.uk. An agency that specialises in placing nannies for short periods of 1–3 weeks, typically to accompany a family or pair of families on holiday, eg skiing or diving, or to a music festival. Only nannies with at least a year's childcare experience and checkable references will be added to the database.

Nora Roche Au Pairs: Abingdon, Oxfordshire; ☎ (+44) 1235 525115; au.pairing@gmail.com; http://noraroche.wixsite.com/au-pairing. Au pair placements arranged in Spain, Germany, Italy and sometimes other countries.

Total Nannies: London, W1; ☎ (+44) 20 7060 1213; www.totalnannies.com. So-called cultural exchange programme by which female candidates are placed with professional families mainly in Italy.

Twinkle Au Pairs: Oxfordshire; www.twinkleaupairs.com. Placements in France, Spain and US.

Agencies Worldwide

Many North Americans are eager to learn the language and absorb the culture of European countries, and indeed some do become au pairs, though the term is not universally recognised in the USA and Canada. The red tape is more difficult for them because they can stay for no more than three months according to the rules of the Schengen zone. Some youth exchange organisations recruit all nationalities to live in, such as the Au Pair Berlin Agency (www.aupair-to-germany.com). Agencies that can help include the following.

InterExchange/Working Abroad: New York, USA; ☎ (+1) 212 924 0446; www.interexchange. org. Au pair placements in France, Netherlands, Spain, Norway, Australia, New Zealand and USA; admin fee is $795 for most programmes except Au Pair in Netherlands where the fee is $40. Most placements last 6–12 months except in Spain where it is two-three months.

Scotia Personnel Ltd: Halifax, NS, Canada; ☎ (+1) 902 422 1455; www.scotia-personnel-ltd. com. Au pair placements in England, France, Spain, Germany, Netherlands, Iceland, Italy, Japan, China, Korea, Australia and New Zealand.

Au pairing is very popular among South Africans especially in the Netherlands for obvious linguistic reasons (since Afrikaans is based on the Dutch that the Boers took to southern Africa). A youth exchange agency OVC makes placements in the Netherlands (www.ovc.co.za/pages/aupairholland. asp) or try Youth Discovery Programs (www.ydp.co.za/au-pair-around-the-world).

Agencies in New Zealand include Nannies Abroad Ltd/International Working Holidays in Auckland (☎ (+64) 9 632 1138; www.nanniesabroad.co.nz or www.iwh.co.nz) which places New Zealanders and sometimes other nationalities in au pair and live-in language-assistance positions in France, Germany, Netherlands, Italy, Spain, the UK, Canada, USA, Australia and China.

Volunteering

Volunteering can open doors in exotic places that would otherwise be out of reach. Everyone should be aware that volunteering almost always costs the volunteer money, sometimes substantial sums. Yet the cost will be less, sometimes far less, than a mere tourist would pay and can be an economical way to visit an expensive or exclusive destination. You won't get the first-class amenities but you will get to see the same things the tourists are paying a much higher price to see. For example joining a voluntary scheme on a lion reserve in Zimbabwe will allow you to have more exposure to the animals than the tourists who have paid five times as much.

Many volunteer schemes are open to all nationalities and often avoid work permit hassles. By participating in an organised project such as building a community centre in a Turkish village, looking after refugee children or just helping out at a youth hostel, you have the unique opportunity to live and work in a remote community, and the chance to meet up with like-minded people from many countries who can point you towards new job prospects. You will gain practical experience, for instance in the fields of construction, archaeology or social welfare which will stand you in good stead when applying for paid jobs elsewhere.

Volunteers with no medical, technical or other relevant background and with no knowledge of the local language inevitably find it difficult to make a concrete difference to the lives of others. They learn the hard though valuable lesson that the giving of aid is a messy and complicated business, and that quite often they benefit from the experience far more than those they aim to help. It is a fact of life that many young people from moneyed backgrounds join volunteer schemes abroad primarily to enhance their CVs. Most fixing organisations charge volunteers to cover the cost of recruiting, screening, interviewing, pre-departure orientation, insurance, etc on top of travel, food and lodging. Many of these are profit-making companies though some do give a proportion of the fees paid by volunteers to support the projects with which they're linked. If you are thinking of signing up with a company or organisation with which you are not familiar, it is a wise precaution to carry out some investigations and if possible check with former volunteers. Be sure that you are aware whether the agency is a charity/non-profit or a commercial enterprise and ask for a breakdown of the costs.

In any case it is worth giving careful thought to whether or not you need to go through a mediating organisation. After chunks of time spent working and travelling in Latin America and having fixed up a teaching placement in Africa that turned out not to be as it was described by the placement agency, Till Bruckner knows his mind on this question:

> It strikes me as weird to collect volunteers from Britain who have to pay a fee plus their airfares to teach the children of the better-off in universities. In a country with poverty on that scale, there's more useful things you can do with £500 to help people in need. If you want fun, go elsewhere. If you want to help, put the £500 in an Oxfam charity box. I can see that some people might appreciate organisational support if they want to volunteer, but except in very restrictive countries, it's not really necessary. I met two girls in Bolivia who had just walked into a home for street kids and volunteered there and then. They got free board and lodging and all they did was talk to the kids and play with them since nobody ever did that. Those girls really did something valuable there. But if they had found themselves not able to contribute anything they would have had the freedom to walk out on the spot.

After participating in several prearranged voluntary projects in the United States, Catherine Brewin did not resent the fee she had paid to Involvement Volunteers:

> The whole business of paying to do voluntary work is a bit hard to swallow. But having looked into the matter quite a bit, it does seem to be the norm. While it may be a bit unfair (who knows how much profit or loss these voluntary organisations make or how worthy their projects are?), most people I've met did seem to feel good about the experience. The group I was with did raise the odd comment about it all, but did not seem unduly concerned. However, I should mention that most were around 18 years old and their parents were paying some if not all the costs.

A succession of natural disasters, including cataclysmic earthquakes in Nepal in April 2015 have focused minds on helping in an emergency in an unprecedented way. The outpourings of financial help from around the world after a natural disaster like the 2004 tsunami or the typhoons in the Philippines are always accompanied by an upsurge in the number of people wanting to donate their time to help. As with all emergency relief work, skilled and experienced professionals mobilised by agencies like United Nations Volunteers (www.unv.org). are in demand while well-meaning amateurs potentially get in the way. All Hands Volunteers mobilises volunteers to help at scenes of devastation, mainly to rebuild houses (www.hands.org/volunteer); at the time of writing they were still recruiting volunteers to work in a rebuilding programme in Nepal.

In the autumn of 2016, Eve Whitley decided to go travelling on her own and wanted to incorporate some worthwhile volunteering. From the excellent Workaway.info, she heard about the charity All Hands which makes no charge to volunteers. She signed up to join their post-earthquake reconstruction project in the village of Prithvi a few hours east of Kathmandu and bought a London–Kathmandu return flight for £400. The volunteer accommodation consisted of one big on-site tent, cheerfully slung with hammocks, though it took a little while to get used to sharing one dunny with 30–40 volunteers and having cold bucket showers after sweaty days of clearing a hillside and doing manual labour. She tried a variety of tasks but avoided one which she couldn't get the hang of, tying rebar, a reinforcement technique when building with concrete. She felt the organisation was less than perfect on the occasions when the volunteers spent the day doing a task, only to be told it had been done wrong and their day's labours had been wasted. However overall she enjoyed many aspects of the experience: the tasty dal bhat cooked by local women, the camaraderie with the other volunteers from all over the world, the local masons and villagers and the insights into Nepali culture. She left to hike the Annapurna Circuit when yet another festival came along to disrupt the work and scatter the volunteers.

The International Citizen Service (ICS) programme is a UK government-funded global volunteering experience that gives young participants aged 18–25 a chance to live and work with other youth volunteers in a developing country for up to three months (www.volunteerics.org). Placements are made through partner organisations including VSO (www.vsointernational.org/volunteering/ICS-youth-volunteering) and other approved agencies such as Restless Development and Skillshare. Participants are expected to fundraise £800 for their project and the government pays for the rest. For information about other programmes of primary interest to gap year students, but also to other prospective volunteers, see the chapter on Gap Years earlier in this book.

SOURCES OF INFORMATION

The long-established company WorkingAbroad.com maintains a searchable database of volunteer organisations. It also recruits for a selection of projects. The World Service Enquiry (www.wse.org.uk) provides information and advice to people who are thinking of working overseas, whether short or long term, voluntary or paid. They offer a one-to-one consultancy service via Skype or WhatsApp ranging in price from £80 to £240 depending on level of contact. The best of the volunteering websites have a multitude of links to organisations big and small that can make use of volunteers. For example www.idealist.org is a US-based, easily searchable site that will take you to the great monolithic charities such as the Peace Corps as well as to small grassroots organisations. It lists 111,000 non-profit and community organisations in more than 100 countries. When American Katie White was planning a year out, she spent hours browsing the amazing opportunities on www.idealist.org and www.goabroad.com and felt 'like a kid in a candy shop'.

Non-profit Ecoteer (www.ecoteer.com) has a database of around 150 projects worldwide that need volunteers and are willing to provide food and accommodation at no, or at little, cost. Ecoteer provides contact information to members who pay a membership fee of £25 or £100 for lifetime membership and a personal consultation. Other databases and matching services to try are www.givingway.com (US$25 membership), the comparison site www.volunteerworld.com, www.omprakash.org, www.work away.info (US$29 to join, $39 for a pair), www.freevolunteering.net (UK-based), www.truetravellers.org and www.the7interchange.com. Yet another is One World 365 (www.oneworld365.org), a travel company in London that maintains a directory of meaningful travel opportunities including volunteer programmes, gap year and career break ideas, TEFL jobs, etc. When trying to decide among competing options, check feedback sites online for candid reviews, as on the site www.abroadreviews.com which offers 'unbiased reviews of international programmes'. The site www.gooverseas.com links to a searchable online directory of opportunities to teach, study, volunteer and intern abroad and includes in some cases first-hand reviews of employers and programmes.

PROS AND CONS

Bear in mind that volunteer work, especially in the developing world, can be not only tough and character building but also disillusioning (see Mary Hall's description of her year at a Uganda clinic in the Africa chapter). And just as the working traveller must be alert to exploitation in paid jobs, so he or she should be careful in voluntary situations as well. Occasionally eager young volunteers are forced to conclude that the people in charge of an organisation have not been upfront about where the fees go. Fortunately the experiences of one volunteer in Africa are rare: he claims to have discovered that the community development projects described in the literature from an organisation in Sierra Leone did not exist and furthermore the director had previously jumped bail from Freetown CID. Always check online reviews and if you are not satisfied, ask for the names of one or two past volunteers whom you can contact for an informal reference. Any worthy organisation should be happy to oblige.

Not all placement organisations are the same. A couple of years ago a scandal was uncovered in Nepal (though the problem is not confined to Nepal) of bogus children's homes whose owners routinely duped village parents into sending their children away, primarily to extract money from foreign volunteers. In response Tourism Concern (www.tourismconcern.org.uk) launched a campaign 'Stop Orphanage Tourism'.

Disillusionment can be a problem for even the most privileged volunteers working for the most respectable charities. When Danny Jacobson visited Bulgaria, he found the country stuffed full of Peace Corps volunteers:

I had always envisioned Peace Corps volunteers to be off in Third World countries living in huts, repairing trees and teaching English to tribal children. In fact, in Bulgaria they all had sly apartments, decent salaries and an average of about 20 hours a week to commit to the cause. Everything from toothpaste to toilet paper was provided and twice a year they were all carted out to some fancy hotel to practise the language and bond. Pretty much everyone we met had a similar story: they joined to try to make a difference and were now left disenchanted and feeling useless. Since the Peace Corps is pretty relaxed about assigning duties – basically you are dropped off in a town and left to your own resources with no supervision – Chris had to start teaching English and later worked with a couple of guys to help build mountain huts and maintain hiking trails. Everyone was pessimistic because it seemed to take forever to get anything done.

This is just a snapshot impression. Morale might well be higher now and in other locations.

WORKCAMPS AND OTHER PLACEMENT ORGANISATIONS

Voluntary work in developed countries often takes the form of workcamps, now generally referred to as short international projects, that accept unskilled labour. As part of an established international network of voluntary organisations they are not subject to the irregularities of some privately run projects. As well as providing volunteers with the means to live cheaply for two or three weeks in a foreign country, workcamps enable volunteers to become involved in what is usually useful work for the community, to meet people from many different backgrounds and to 'increase their awareness of other lifestyles, social problems and their responsibility to society' as one volunteer has described it. In 2020, the movement will celebrate its centenary as an international network working towards conflict resolution and community development, providing an inexpensive and personal way to travel, live and work in an international setting.

Worldwide there is a massive effort to coordinate workcamp programmes. This normally means that the prospective volunteer should apply in the first instance to the appropriate organisation in his or her own country, rather than to a centralised international headquarters. The majority of camps take place in the summer months, and camp details are normally published online in March/April with a flurry of placements made in the month or two following. It is necessary to pay a registration fee which has become standard across the different agencies recruiting volunteers, normally £200 for a project in Europe, more for one in a developing country to help finance future projects or to pay for specialised training. The fee covers board and lodging but not, of course, travel. Each national body can respond quickly to the needs of their country, for example the Japanese workcamp organisation NICE set up projects that foreign volunteers could join to supervise sports, activities and crafts for children displaced by the earthquake and tsunami.

The largest workcamp organisation is Service Civil International with branches in 44 countries (www.workcamps.info/icamps). The UK branch is International Voluntary Service (IVS-GB) in Edinburgh; ☎ (+44) 131 243 2745; info@ ivsgb.org; ivsgb.org. The cost of registration on IVS workcamps outside the UK is £160–£200, in addition to a £50 membership in IVS; prices are discounted for unwaged volunteers.

The other organisations in the UK workcamp network are as follows:

Concordia International Volunteers: Brighton, East Sussex; ☎ (+44) 1273 422218; www.concordiavolunteers.org.uk. Programme of workcamps in 20 countries; registration fee £225–£250; for projects in Latin America, Asia, Middle East and Africa volunteers pay an extra fee of £80–£250 to cover food and accommodation, interpreters, etc.

UNA Exchange: Cardiff; ☎ (+44) 29 2022 3088; www.unaexchange.org. Fee £225 for overseas projects, £250–£350 for longer term ones.

Voluntary Action for Peace/VAP: London, SE22; ☎ (+44) 844 209 0927; www.vap.org.uk. Workcamps held in many countries in Western and Eastern Europe, plus Mexico, the Middle East and Bangladesh; administrative fee £210–£230.

Xchange Scotland: Glasgow; ☎ (+44) 141 237 2430; www.xchangescotland.org. £250 fee.

European Voluntary Service (EVS) is a fully funded initiative of the European Commission to encourage young Europeans (aged 17–30) to join projects lasting from two weeks to 12 months, in social care, youth work, outdoor recreation and rural development elsewhere in Eastern and Western Europe. This programme is remarkable because volunteers do not have to pay to participate; EVS provides volunteers with free travel, food, accommodation and an allowance. Applicants need to apply through an approved sending organisation (http://europa.eu/youth/volunteering/project_en).

North American workcamp volunteers should apply to one of the following:

Cadip (Canadian Alliance for Development Issues and Projects): Vancouver, British Columbia; ☎ (+1) 604 628 7400; www.cadip.org. Also hosts volunteers at Canadian workcamps.

SCI-IVS (Service Civil International-International Voluntary Service): Great Barrington, Massachusetts; www.volunteersciusa.org. International workcamps.

Volunteers for Peace: www.vfp.org. VFP publishes an online 'International Project List' with more than 2,500 programme listings in 100 countries, available from early April; registration for most programmes costs $500.

The majority of international projects are environmental or social. They may involve the conversion/reconstruction of historic buildings and building community facilities. Some of the more interesting past projects include building adventure playgrounds for children, renovating an open-air museum, organising youth concerts in Armenia, helping with the orange harvest in a Japanese village grappling with depopulation, looking after a farm-school in Slovakia during the holidays, working at a summer day camp for children with autism on Vancouver Island, plus a whole range of schemes with the disabled and elderly, conservation work and the study of social and political issues.

ARCHAEOLOGY

Taking part in archaeological excavations is another popular form of voluntary work, but volunteers are usually expected to make a contribution towards their board and lodging. Also, you may be asked to bring your own trowel, work clothes, tent, etc. Unfortunately Archaeology Abroad based at University College London, which used to publish details of excavations needing volunteers has ceased to do so. Some relevant information on digs that accept paying volunteers is published by the Biblical Archaeology Society (http://digs.bib-arch.org)

One of the largest resources is the listing from the Archaeological Institute of America (www.archaeological.org/fieldwork), which invites you to search the globe for a dig. An online source of archaeology field schools is the memorably named Shovelbums (www.shovelbums.org) run on a shoestring by an archaeologist in Ohio. For those who are not students of archaeology, the chances of finding a place on an overseas dig will be greatly enhanced by having some digging experience nearer to home. For information about excavations in Britain, see chapter on the UK. Anthony Blake joined a dig sponsored by the University of Reims and warns that *'archaeology is hard work, and applicants must be aware of what working for eight hours in the baking heat means!'* Nevertheless, Anthony found the company excellent and the opportunity to improve his French welcome. See the chapter on France for information about joining one of the hundreds of summer digs.

Israel is another country particularly rich in archaeological opportunities, many of them organised through the universities. Digs provide an excellent means of seeing remote parts of the country though Israeli digs tend to be more expensive than most, typically from $50 a day plus registration.

CONSERVATION

People interested in protecting the environment can often slot into conservation organisations abroad. One enterprising traveller in South Africa looked up the 'green directory' in a local library, contacted a few of the projects listed in the local area and was invited to work at a cheetah reserve near Johannesburg in exchange for accommodation and food.

Green Volunteers maintains a database of volunteering opportunities that can be accessed after joining for £4. The general volunteer databases listed earlier in this chapter can be searched according to type of opportunity sought. A number of companies and charities offer 'conservation holidays' which cost almost as much as a regular holiday, for example Earthwatch. A California-based organisation Conservation Volunteers International Program (www.conservationvip.org) charges hefty prices for its trips.

The Australia-based Involvement Volunteers International (☎ (+61) 7 5535 7982; www.volunteering.org.au) arranges individual placements worldwide open to all. A few projects are concerned with conservation but many more cover other fields like animal welfare, social and community service and education. Projects last one to 12 weeks and can be arranged back-to-back in different countries. The one-off application fee is A$275 and a sample programme fee is A$2,965 for two months of marine conservation in Cambodia and about half that for a clean-up project in Bali.

The volunteer agency Go Eco (www.goeco.org) registers conservation and humanitarian volunteer openings in Israel and worldwide. GoEco has contact phone numbers in the UK, USA and Australia.

DEVELOPING COUNTRIES

Commitment, no matter how fervent, is not enough to work in an aid project in the developing world. You must normally be able to offer some kind of useful training or skill unless you are prepared to fund yourself and don't mind that your effort to help will be more a token than of lasting benefit. Many organisations offer ordinary people the chance to experience life in the developing world by working alongside local people for a brief period and these are mentioned throughout the chapters on Africa, Asia and Latin America later in this book.

> **GEOFFROY GROLEAU FROM QUÉBEC SPENT SOME MONTHS VOLUNTEERING FOR AN NGO IN INDIA:**
> *Volunteers should expect to learn more from the people than they will ever be able to teach. Remember that the villagers know much more about their needs than we do, and they have learned long ago to use effectively the resources around them. On the other hand, the contact with the outside world that the volunteers provide is a valuable way for the villagers to begin to understand the world that surrounds them. In my experience, the hardest things were to adapt to the rather slow rhythm of life and to the fact that as a volunteer you will not manage to change significantly the life of the villagers other than by putting your brick in a collective work that has been going on for many years.*

The pre-eminent professional voluntary and aid organisation in the UK is VSO (www.vsointernational. org) which mainly recruits professional volunteers for two-year assignments in the fields of education, health, natural resources, technical trades and engineering, business and social work, among many others in 24 developing countries. VSO pays a modest local wage, various grants, national insurance, provides accommodation, health insurance and return flights. Volunteers are mainly aged 20–75 – the average is now 43 – and qualified and experienced.

Another long-established and respectable global agency is Inter-Cultural Youth Exchange (ICYE) (☎ (+44) 20 7681 0983; www.icye.co.uk) which arranges for students and others aged 18–30 to spend six or 12 months abroad with a host family and volunteering, for example in drug rehabilitation, protection of street children and ecological projects in one of 30 countries in Latin America, Africa and Asia. No specific skills are needed as this is a skills development programme. The fees are from £1,600 for a four-week short-term programme, £3,995 for six-month placements, and £4,795 for a full year with some bursaries available.

To find the smaller more obscure organisations, you will have to spend time searching. For example Just Volunteers (www.just-volunteers.org) is a one-woman organisation that works with a small group of charities in Hong Kong, China, Myanmar, Mongolia and Malaysia.

NORTH AMERICAN OPPORTUNITIES

Here is a selection of major organisations, some of which offer short volunteer vacations, popular in the USA, lasting no more than the length of an ordinary holiday:

Abroader View Volunteers: Elkins Park, Pennsylvania; www.abroaderview.org. Scores of volunteer projects lasting one to 12 weeks in 21 countries including Rwanda and Cameroon as well as the usual suspects. From $820 for a week in Africa to $2,240 for 12 weeks in Central America.

Cross-Cultural Solutions: New Rochelle, New York; ☎ (+1) 800 380 4777; www.crossculturalsolutions.org. Volunteers join projects worldwide for one to 12 weeks. Costs from $2,250 for one week to $8,968 for 12 weeks.

Global Crossroad: Irving, Texas; www.globalcrossroad.com. Volunteer teaching and internships in 18 countries, from Uganda to Peru. For volunteer programmes in many countries, application fee of $299 plus varying weekly fee.

Global Routes: Northampton, Massachusetts; www.globalroutes.org. Offers 12-week voluntary internships to students over 17 who teach English and other subjects in village schools in Tanzania/Zanzibar, Costa Rica/Panama, Ecuador/Galapagos and Nepal; participation fee $9,000–$10,000 for 12 weeks.

Global Service Corps: San Francisco, California; www.globalservice-corps.org. Cooperates with grass-roots organisations in Cambodia and Tanzania and sends volunteers and interns for a semester, summer or short stay.

Global Volunteers: St Paul, Minnesota; ☎ (+1) 800 487 1074; www.globalvolunteers.org. 'Granddaddy of the volunteer vacation movement' with some unusual destinations such as St Lucia and the Cook Islands; fortnight-long trips cost $2,500–$3,600 plus airfares.

World Endeavors: Minneapolis, Minnesota: ☎ (+1) 866 802 9678; www.worldendeavors.com. Volunteer, internship and study programmes lasting two weeks to three months in many countries.

GOING IT ALONE

In the course of your travels, you may come across wildlife projects, children's homes, special schools, etc in which it will be possible to work voluntarily for a short or longer time. You may simply want to join your new Tongan, Turkish or Tanzanian friends in the fields or wherever they are working. You may get the chance to trade your assistance for a straw mat and simple meals but more likely the only rewards will be the experience and the camaraderie.

PART 2

WORK YOUR WAY IN EUROPE

United Kingdom

Many readers of this book will begin to plan their world travels in Britain, and it is in Britain that they will want to save up an initial travelling fund. Savings targets will vary depending on the ambitiousness of the travel plans and on the individual's willingness to wing it and rough it once he or she sets out. Some people are lucky enough to have a reasonably well-paid and stable job in a shop or as a maths tutor or software developer before they set out on their adventures and will be in a position to save. Others will have to gather together as many funds as possible from doing casual work at home before pursuing the same activities abroad.

Readers in other countries will also be interested in the information contained in this chapter if they are planning a working holiday in the UK. Armies of young people from continental Europe, the Antipodes and so on arrive year round and quickly plug into the network of like-minded travellers looking for work in London and beyond. Everyone knows that London is an expensive city and not a pleasant place for people with few funds. But thousands of young people from overseas overlook its defects for the excitement of spending time in one of the world's great cities.

The rate of unemployment achieved an 11-year low of less than 5% in 2017 with the highest proportion of part-time workers since records began. The biggest increase has been in the expansion of the so-called 'gig economy' or on-demand economy in which huge numbers of people work freelance or on short-term contracts without employment rights such as access to the minimum wage, redundancy pay, paid holidays or sick pay.

RED TAPE

At the time of writing, Prime Minister Theresa May was poised to announce the end of free movement of labour for EU citizens. The assumption is that the rights of EU nationals already living in the UK at the time that Article 50 triggering Brexit was invoked will be protected, however this is still under debate. Arrivals from the European Union after that date will no longer have the automatic right to live permanently. However EU nationals play a crucial role in the labour force and will be needed to fill jobs for many years to come. One possible compromise would be for EU migrants to be entitled to five-year working visas but barred from claiming in-work benefits while they are in Britain.

For non-EU citizens, most of whom enter on six-month tourist visas (which can normally be renewed on re-entering the country after an absence), it is increasingly difficult to find legal work. In general the Home Office does not issue work permits to unskilled and semi-skilled workers. Employers are now required to see documentary proof of status and, as they have always done, record your National Insurance number. The UK is gradually becoming a more bureaucratic country than it used to be, and the penalties for flouting the law are becoming more punitive.

The UK has a five-tiered immigration system based on points. As is true throughout the world, skilled workers must have a job offer in hand before their prospective employer can apply for a work permit on their behalf. Many immigration websites explain all the permutations, such as www.workpermit.com. The official government site is www.gov.uk/browse/visas-immigration/work-visas. Several categories under Tier 5 of the immigration rules (Temporary Worker) allow foreign nationals to enter the country for up to one year, including charity workers who intend to do unpaid work for a sponsoring agency. Note that visitors may undertake incidental volunteering (ie to supplement a holiday rather than as the main purpose of their visit), for up to 30 days in total provided it is for a charity registered in the UK.

Commonwealth citizens who can produce documentary evidence that a parent or grandparent was born in the UK can gain permission to stay and work under the ancestry or patriality rules. After completing five continuous years of work they can apply for indefinite leave to remain (current fee £1,875).

Youth Mobility Visas

The long established working holiday scheme was radically overhauled at the end of 2008. Only eight nationalities are eligible for the new Youth Mobility Scheme (in contrast to the 50 Commonwealth countries previously eligible): Australia, New Zealand, Canada, Japan, Taiwan, Hong Kong, South Korea and Monaco. These are based on reciprocal visa provisions offered by those countries to British nationals with quotas, ie 35,500 for Australians, 13,000 for New Zealanders, 5,500 for Canadians and 1,000 for the others.

To be eligible you must be between the ages of 18 and 30 inclusive with no dependants. The YMS working holiday permit entitles the holder to work in Britain at any job or jobs for up to a maximum of two years. It is essential to apply from outside the UK and you must prove that you have £1,890 available in cash funds. Application forms and details are available at www.gov.uk/tier-5-youth-mobility; the cost of applying for the visa is £230 (2017).

Commonwealth nationals can apply for a Youth Mobility Scheme permit independently or, if they want the security of a package arrangement, they can make use of the services of expert agencies. Canadians for example can participate in the Student Work Abroad Programme (SWAP) for a fee of C$395 excluding the visa fee.

Backpacker agencies in Australia and New Zealand have links with London agencies and sell packages that make arrival and the initial job-hunt easier. For example Student Flights (www.studentflights.com.au/gap-year), part of Flight Centre Ltd with offices throughout Australia, sells starter packs to working holidaymakers bound for the UK. A scheme that includes a pre-departure job offer in Central London, accommodation in a shared house and other arrival services costs A$895, whereas a basic orientation costs A$80 ('UK Arrival Pack Lite'). Working Adventures Worldwide in New Zealand (www.iep.co.nz) offers a similar selection of assistance packages.

The UK Pub Co (www.ukpubco.com) with its main office in Melbourne and branches in the UK, Canada and New Zealand can sort out live-in jobs for individuals and couples before arrival for a fee starting at A$895/NZ$950/C$895. As usual experienced cooks and chefs are always in demand, while people with no relevant experience can be placed as kitchen porters.

Britbound (www.britbound.co.uk) is a London-based service that provides a sociable arrival experience for anyone with a Youth Mobility visa heading to the UK. Their 'Hit the Ground Running' packages cost from £85 to £525 and include various kinds of assistance, for example with visas, bank accounts, accommodation, sim cards, National Insurance numbers, etc. They also run a social events club.

Other Visas

Non-EU students at bona fide higher education institutions in the UK are allowed to work up to 20 hours a week during term-time and full-time in the vacations without applying for a work permit. Those attending courses below degree level are permitted to work up to ten hours.

Anyone entering the country as a visitor or tourist who intends to stay longer than a few weeks should be able to prove that they have no intention of staying, so should be able to show a print-out of a return or ongoing ticket out of the UK, specific reasons why you want to stay for a long period, details of where you will be staying in the first few days, proof of how you can afford your proposed stay, eg a bank statement or credit card, proof that you will need to return to your home country eg a job you will return to, registration for college, ownership or lease on a house, etc, proof of private travel insurance and preferably a tidy appearance, since as at all international borders, scruffy candidates often attract unwanted attention. If you are questioned, the immigration officer will probably stamp your passport with a 'Code 3' stamp that will mean you will be questioned more closely on future arrivals. See www.gov.uk/uk-border-control/overview for official information about what to expect at border control.

Some years ago, American Woden Teachout arrived without having prepared a watertight story:

Coming into the UK I had a horribly distressing immigration experience. On the advice of my travel agent, I had bought a six-month return ticket rather than an open return and expected no problems. Everything went awry. I think it was when I wavered over how long I meant to be in the country that the immigration official became suspicious. The lady-turned-ogre forced me to produce my passport, ticket, money, address book and wrote down my entire life's history in cramped cursive on the back of my entrance card. I portrayed myself as a spoilt and privileged child, funded by mummy and daddy in her aimless intercontinental wanderings. When she at last grudgingly stamped me into the country, she called after me in a voice thick with derision, 'Do you think you'll ever work for a living?'

A few weeks later Woden had five different jobs.

SPECIAL SCHEMES AND EXCHANGE ORGANISATIONS

A number of English language schools, companies and non-profits in the UK offer work experience placements for EU and non-EU citizens, usually unpaid and often in conjunction with an English language course. For example Twin Work & Volunteer (London; ☎ (+44) 20 8297 3278; www. workandvolunteer.com/uk-professional-internships) has links with hundreds of companies and hotels throughout the country; internship programme costs start at £500. Many commercial agencies on the Continent sell packaged working holidays to young people. Caution should be exercised when paying over large sums to a mediating agency since some offer a very poor service, as Emiliano Giovannoni from Italy explains:

Every year there are hundreds of Italian, French, German and Spanish guys and girls who get to London 'thanks' to the service of some unscrupulous agencies which operate in these countries and have the monopoly on 'advising' youngsters. These agencies charge enormous fees, promising jobs, accommodation and English lessons which they don't always deliver. I have met very many people in London who, after having paid a lot of money, had to live with rats and, after weeks, still haven't been given the chance of attending one interview for a job that they usually ended up finding themselves or thanks to the local Jobcentre. All this just because they did not have access to some genuine information.

For Americans

With the demise of the long-lived Work in Britain Program, the main opportunity for US nationals now is as an intern for up to six months via BUNAC (www.bunac.org/usa/intern-abroad/professional/britain), which is more restrictive than the old working holiday. To be eligible you must be a full-time degree level student or within a year of having finished your studies, and already have an offer of an internship; the programme fee is $755.

US citizens who wish to spend seven weeks from mid-June volunteering in a social service programme in London (eg working with inner city youth, the elderly, homeless and people with mental health problems) and then travel independently for two weeks should request an application from the Winant & Clayton Volunteers (☎ (+1) 212 737 2720; www.winantclayton.org.uk). Free room and board plus travel expenses are provided, but the volunteers must fundraise a minimum of $2,850/£1,750 to participate.

The UK's largest volunteering organisation, Volunteering Matters (formerly Community Service Volunteers) (☎ (+44) 20 3780 5870; www.volunteeringmatters.org.uk) runs a full-time residential volunteering programme in which people aged 18–35 are placed in projects with people who need help, such as children with special needs, adults with learning difficulties, teenagers at risk of offending and homeless people. Volunteers do not need any previous experience, special skills or minimum qualifications to join. During the projects, which last six to 12 months, food (equivalent to £40 a week), accommodation and £34 weekly allowance are paid. Volunteering Matters accepts some international volunteers via partner agencies, some of which charge placement fees.

Tax

One clear advantage of obtaining legal working holiday status is that you are entitled to apply for a National Insurance number from the local Jobcentre Plus (☎ (+44) 845 600 0643; www.gov.uk/apply-national-insurance-number), which you should do promptly. A face-to-face interview is required, which has to be scheduled two to three weeks in advance. Single people are entitled to a personal tax allowance, currently £11,000, after which they start paying 20% in income tax. If your employer is deducting tax at source under the PAYE (Pay As You Earn) system, you will have to reclaim at the end of the tax year if you have earned less than your personal allowance in the tax year starting on 6 April. The relevant form for applying for a rebate is R38.

Foreign nationals can claim the personal allowance if they have been in the UK for at least 183 days in any tax year. If the total is less than 183 days, they may be able to claim as a foreign national and/or resident of a country with which the UK has a double taxation agreement. HM Revenue & Customs maintains a clear and informative website (www.hmrc.gov.uk). If you might need to claim, keep all tax documents such as the P60 (end-of-year tax certificate). When you finish work, send both parts of the P45 that your employer has to give you to your employer's tax office. When you are ready to leave Britain and want to claim a tax rebate, complete and submit form P85, a leaving certificate that asks your intentions with respect to returning to the UK to work. Always take the precaution of making photocopies of any forms you send to the tax office for the purposes of chasing later, and be prepared to wait at least six weeks. You can make things easier for yourself by using an accountancy firm that specialises in tax rebates. They normally keep a percentage (about 18%) of whatever they get back for you but don't charge if you don't get a refund. Try, for example, one of the London firms that advertise in the expat press such as 1st Contact (www.1stcontact-taxrefunds.com) or Taxback (www.taxback.co.uk).

In addition to income tax, you must also pay National Insurance Contributions of 12% on taxable earnings above £155 a week.

EMPLOYMENT PROSPECTS

At the time of writing, the British economy was showing encouraging recovery, with the rate of unemployment continuing to fall. Seasonal and temporary vacancies in agriculture, tourism, childcare and so on are less affected than the public sector and manufacturing.

The National Minimum Wage from April 2017 is £7.50 per hour for workers over 25, £7.05 for workers aged 21–24, and £5.60 for workers aged 18–20. For details contact the Pay and Work Rights helpline ☎ (+44) 300 123 1100 or check the government website www.gov.uk/national-minimum-wage-rates. Unless you are lucky in finding cheap accommodation, it will be very difficult to save on the minimum wage especially in south-east England where the cost of living is higher than elsewhere. Some employers pay the Living Wage which is higher than the Minimum Wage, currently £9.75 an hour in London and £8.45 elsewhere.

Temp Agencies

Thousands of employment agencies do business in the UK, though times are tough with so much job recruitment happening online. Major companies like Reed and Capita Resourcing, with dozens of branches in London alone and many more nationwide, fill more permanent vacancies than temporary ones.

Catering agencies abound and anyone with a background as a chef will probably be in demand. (See section below on Tourism and Catering.) Temping allows a great deal of flexibility, though most agencies you approach will want to be reassured that you are not about to flit off somewhere. Most will ask foreign temps for evidence of permission to work.

COLIN ROTHWELL FROM SOUTH AFRICA FOUND INDUSTRIAL AGENCY WORK A VERY SATISFACTORY WAY TO SAVE FOR HIS FUTURE TRAVELS, THOUGH HE COULDN'T STOMACH ALL HIS ASSIGNMENTS:

In England I found the easiest way to find work was through temping agencies. However, it was also the most inconvenient way as they liked you to have an address and a phone number. They were also the biggest sharks around and you got paid half the going wage as they took a very healthy cut from your hard-earned blood, sweat and tears. It did have its advantages though; you worked when and where it suited you, and some agencies sent you all over the place to do all kinds of weird jobs. For example, the worst job I did on my whole trip was at a dog meat factory. You arrived at the crack of dawn and were sent into a massive fridge where you were met with tons of semi-defrosting offal, with blood everywhere, and a stench like you wouldn't believe. So, as desperate for money as I was, I only lasted two days.

One recommended website for people with Youth Mobility visas or EU citizens is Workabout (☎ (+44) 1202 848455; www.workabout.uk.com) which specialises in the leisure and hospitality industry. The Australian-linked temp agency Bligh Appointments (70 North End Road, London W14 9EP; (☎ (+44) 20 7603 6123; www.bligh.co.uk) always has vacancies for childcare/nursery assistants and catering staff, and welcomes travellers with the legal right to work in the UK.

Adverts

As each year goes by, fewer job ads appear in print and more on recruitment websites such as www.indeed.co.uk and free classified ads sites like www.gumtree.co.uk with local sites from Cornwall to Edinburgh. In London http://london.craigslist.co.uk carries hundreds of job ads, many of them unsavoury ('looking for cleaner naked'). Sites that specialise in employment for students may be help-ful such as www.student-jobs.co.uk, www.studentjob.co.uk, www.e4s.co.uk, www.studentgems.com, www.fish4.co.uk and the government's job-finding service at www.gov.uk/jobsearch.

Several free newspapers and magazines in London aimed at the expat communities, mainly of Australians, New Zealanders and Canadians, can prove to be sources of agency information and casual jobs. Look for *TNT*'s distribution boxes around the capital or check adverts online (www.tnt-magazine.com). Recruitment agencies advertise for nurses and professionals in accountancy, banking, IT, law, etc and for unskilled and semi-skilled jobs as mother's helps, in call centres, bars and farms.

One job that is advertised aggressively (possibly because there is such a high turnover) is as a 'charity fundraiser'. Commercial companies are regularly hired by mainstream charities such as the Red Cross to raise money on the streets of British cities. Companies such as Flow Caritas (www. flowcaritas.co.uk) and Inspired People (www.inspiredpeople.org) use worthy sounding lines such as 'championing the search for a better world' in their bid to hire an army of young people to accost passers-by and try to persuade them to sign direct debit donation forms. This activity has been dubbed 'charity mugging' and hence the employees are sometimes referred to as 'chuggers'. A high percent-age of those hired are foreign young people on working holidays, including 18-year-old David Cox from Ontario who was hired soon after arriving in London. He was invited to attend a day's training in Oxford before being dispatched to his first location, and looked forward to a chance to see different places:

The last three weeks have been very interesting, and I'm starting to get into the swing of things. So far I've been posted in Brighton, Portsmouth and Newcastle areas and am leaving for Manchester tonight. I love the job but it's literally seven days a week and can be very stressful so I'm looking forward to time off, I'm going to Norway in two weeks.

Not everybody ends up loving the job by any means. Anna Ling was attracted partly by idealism to do this job in Bristol but came to consider it iniquitous since so much of the money raised goes to the 'middle-men'. In addition to a basic wage, street fundraisers earn a commission per donor.

HARVESTS

Currently there is a shortage of workers in the British countryside, and businesses welcome people from outside the area and from overseas who are legally allowed to work in the UK. The principal fruit growing areas of Britain are: the Vale of Evesham over to the Wye and Usk Valleys; most of Kent; Lincolnshire and East Anglia, especially the Fens around Wisbech; and north of the Tay Estuary in Scotland (Blairgowrie, Forfar). But there is intensive agricultural activity in most parts of Britain so always check with the Jobcentre or Farmers' Union in the area(s) where you are interested in finding farm work. Harvest dates are not standard throughout the country, since the raspberries of Inverness-shire ripen at least two or three weeks later than the raspberries on the Isle of Wight; nor are the starting dates the same from one year to the next.

Some of the biggest agricultural employers in the country belonged to the Seasonal Agricultural Workers Scheme (SAWS) that for many years granted permission to foreign nationals to enter the country to work on farms for three to six months, with the peak season falling in May. After 2014 when Romanian and Bulgarian nationals were allowed to work in the UK the scheme was cancelled, though post-Brexit, a successor is very likely to be reinstated. The prospect of losing access to EU workers has farmers in agricultural regions such as Kent, East Anglia and Herefordshire very worried that they will find it impossible to recruit enough seasonal workers to harvest their crops. In 2017, British Members of Parliament were in discussion with representatives from agricultural businesses and recruitment companies that rely on hiring staff in the EU to work seasonally on farms, picking apples, salad, flowers and vegetables. While government policies are intended to encourage British nationals into employment, farmers contend that Britons are not willing to undertake farm labour.

Agricultural Agencies

Agencies that recruit on behalf of farms throughout the UK are:

Concordia (YSV) Ltd: 19 North Street, Portslade, East Sussex, BN41 1DH; ☎ (+44) 1273 422293; www.concordia.org.uk/farms. Non-profit organisation.

Fruitful Jobs Ltd: Windy Hollow, Upton Bishop, Ross-on-Wye, Herefordshire HR9 7TT; ☎ (+44) 1989 500130; info@fruitfuljobs.com; www.fruitfuljobs.com. For example they recruit asparagus pickers for Shropshire in the spring.

HOPS Labour Solutions: c/o National Federation of Young Farmers' Clubs, YFC Centre, Stoneleigh Park, Kenilworth, Warwickshire CV8 2LG; ☎ (+44) 2476 69 8000; www.hopslaboursolutions.com.

Sastak Ltd: 1&7, BDC, Long Lane, Craven Arms, Shropshire, SY7 8DZ; ☎ (+44) 1588 673636; www.sastak.com. Recruits on behalf of farms in the Midlands and Cotswolds.

CARISA FEY, AN 18-YEAR-OLD GERMAN TRAVELLER, JOINED THE RANKS OF THE AGRICULTURAL WORKERS IN THE EAST OF ENGLAND AFTER ANSWERING AN ADVERT IN *TNT* MAGAZINE:

Together with a South African girl I'd met in Scotland, I went to Wisbech, the most boring place on earth. So we didn't mind working 12 hours every day with an hour and a half travel to and from work. We managed to save around £100 each a week. And working in the factories wasn't that bad; one just has to entertain oneself. It is very easy to get a job in the factories through the agencies that advertise. The good thing is that they handle everything like accommodation, job, bank account, but you have to be lucky to find a fair one. If you have enough money for your own job search, go to the Jobcentre in Peterborough or Wisbech or ask at the factories directly.

The press frequently reports cases of exploitation, particularly of foreign workers with little knowledge of English. A large proportion of employment in UK agriculture is in the hands of the unattractively named 'gangmasters'. If you are concerned that you may be getting involved with something dodgy, make sure that your employer is licensed under the Gangmasters (Licensing) Act 2004 whose site has a searchable database of licensed agencies (www.gla.gov.uk).

In 2017 a basic hourly wage for harvesting was £6.21 with an hourly rate of £9.32 for overtime (above 39 hours a week). Higher grade workers with qualifications earn correspondingly more. Working conditions are regulated; for example the maximum deduction for caravan accommodation provided is about £34 per week.

The organisation WWOOF UK (World Wide Opportunities on Organic Farms) maintains a list of 669 farm hosts throughout the UK who offer free room and board in exchange for help. Membership costs £20 (£30 for a couple) and entitles you to a copy of their list (printed or online); details from WWOOF UK, PO Box 2207, Buckingham MK18 9BW (www.wwoof.org.uk).

TOURISM AND CATERING

There is nothing much that the UK tourist industry can do about the weather, but it has been making huge strides in improving standards of hospitality, particularly in pub catering. With the recent strength of the euro against sterling, more Britons have been choosing to take their holidays at home in the UK. In any case Britain attracts millions of tourists from abroad: 37.3 million last year to be exact. It has been estimated that one in 10 of the employed labour force of Britain is involved in the tourist industry.

Hotel staff with silver service or other specialist experience can expect to earn a decent wage though the majority of people working in pubs and restaurants earn the minimum wage or close to it. People who are available for the whole season, say April to October, will find it easier to land a job than those available only for the peak months of July and August. Most hotels prefer to receive a formal written application with CV in the early part of the year, complete with photos and references; however, it can never hurt to telephone (especially later in the spring) to find out what the situation is. Anyone who has acquired the Basic Food Hygiene Certificate online or in person will have an advantage when looking for catering work. As usual, many companies use online recruitment sites such as www.careersincatering.co.uk.

A few training and exchange organisations place foreign students in service jobs; try for example the European Work Experience Programme Ltd (www.ewep.com) that currently assists young EEA nationals to find jobs in hotels, airport outlets, fast food restaurants, etc. Their job-finding service is free to all comers though those who pay the administrative and accommodation fee of £272 receive extra benefits.

Working holidaymakers should be able to fix up work in bars, cafés, hotels, etc without going through a mediating agency. Twenty-two-year-old Sarah Zimmerman from the USA decided to support herself in the UK by picking up jobs, but encountered a few problems she hadn't anticipated when her first job was in a fancy hotel:

> *You'd think it would be easier for me since I understand English, but no, the entire menu and bistro – everything was in French, I couldn't even figure out what the word for green bean was! And, I know they said that the head chef was speaking English, but I begged to differ because I have yet to understand a word he shouted at me. The others whom I worked with from Austria, Poland, Sweden and Venezuela were very nice and seemed to grasp it all better.*

Sarah set off to find a job in a non-French-speaking environment but wasn't convinced it was preferable: 'The English are self-proclaimed laid-back people, so maybe that is why it takes so long to secure something. I had a trial day at a funky/expensive bakery/restaurant that really was fun, minus the two-hour lunch rush where I was serving hot food and felt so much like a cafeteria lady from elementary school that I almost asked where my hair net was!'

Americans often have trouble with the different accents they will encounter, as Woden Teachout found: *'I had a hard time deciphering the orders over the music; "Bakes" does not sound remotely like "Becks" to the American ear.'*

Pubs

Live-in pubs abound throughout England, especially in London and the south east with a sprinkling further afield. Staff work 39–45 hours a week with a couple of days off, and usually earn the minimum wage. Many people work some evenings in a pub in addition to their day job to boost their finances for future travelling.

Waiting for an ad to appear is usually less productive than going pub to pub. A traveller found himself nearly penniless in the popular tourist town of Pitlochry in Perthshire and made the rounds of the pubs asking for work. In each case the management were either fully staffed or were too concerned about his lack of a work permit. He claims that in the 34th and final pub, they asked him if he was free to start work that minute, and he gleefully stepped behind the bar and began work, without knowing shandy from Guinness. Foreign holidaymakers may need to be reminded that you do not get tips in a British pub.

Scotland

Although unemployment is traditionally higher in Scotland than England, plenty of tourist-related jobs are available.

CARISA FEY FROM GERMANY IS JUST ONE TRAVELLER FROM THE CONTINENT WHO WAS INSTANTLY SMITTEN WITH SCOTLAND:

Before all my money was gone I took the bus up to Scotland because I heard that it would be very easy to get a job in the Highlands in a hotel. As the bus came through Aviemore on my way to Inverness it was love at first sight. One visit to the Jobcentre in Inverness and two days later I was back in Aviemore to work at the Freedom Inn plus extra nights at the Cairngorm Lodge (better paid but less fun). My planned stay of three months worked out to be 10 and by the time I left I was speaking with a Scottish accent, could clean a room in record speed, carry four plates and still talk normally after consuming an amount of alcohol that would kill an average middle European man. I had a wonderful time.

Agents sometimes advertise in London for live-in hotel and pub work in Scotland. Keith Flynn answered such an ad (www.livein-jobs.co.uk), and ended up working in an isolated place 10 miles from the nearest town and with no public transport, which made it an ideal place to save money: *'I saw Dee Cooper's advert and decided to ring up. Basically you just call and say what job you do, eg kitchen porter, bar, waiter/waitress and she gives you a list of vacancies around Scotland at no cost to you.'*

Dee Cooper continues to place single candidates and couples/ friends in jobs in isolated places as well as pubs and hotels within an hour of the big cities. All bar/ waiting/housekeeping/kitchen positions are live-in and last 3–6 months (dee@livein-jobs.demon.co.uk).

Paul Binfield from Kent travelled further north in Scotland and was rewarded with a healthy choice of casual work in Orkney:

Unemployment was low at that time, and from March to September there is an absolute abundance of summer jobs. We worked in one of the several youth hostels on the islands, have done voluntary work for the Orkney Seal Rescue and I am currently earning a very nice wage working at the historical site Skara Brae on a three-month contract. There is loads of seasonal work available in hotels and bars, cutting grass for the council and other garden contracts, etc.

Holiday Camps and Activity Centres

Anyone with a qualification in canoeing, yachting, climbing, etc should be able to find summer work as an instructor. The 20+ centres that belong to the British Activity Providers Association (www.thebapa.org.uk) are a good starting point and the BAPA website allows you to forward a job enquiry form to member organisations.

Plenty of jobs as general assistants exist for sports-minded young people, especially at children's multi-activity centres. Suzanne Phillips, who worked at an adventure centre in North Devon, claims that 'a person's character and personality are far more important than their qualifications'. The pay is not high but may be supplemented by an end-of-season bonus at some centres. Applicants intending to work with children must undergo a DBS check and foreign candidates will have to show police clearance forms. Normally it is the responsibility of the employer rather than the individual to apply to the DBS.

One of the largest employers is PGL Travel, with a staggering number of vacancies for activity instructors, group leaders, etc for its 14 UK holiday centres (as well as in France and Spain). The season lasts from February to October though most vacancies are for the summer season. PGL's Recruitment Team can be contacted by phone on ☎ (+44) 333 321 2123 or recruitment@pgl.co.uk (www.pgl.co.uk/recruitment).

Many activity holiday centres also double as English language camps for children from abroad. These also need a range of support and leadership staff in addition to EFL teachers (see list in section on Teaching below).

Here are some holiday activity centres that may require domestic as well as leadership staff:

Barracudas Summer Activity Camps: St Ives, Cambridgeshire; ☎ (+44) 1480 497533; jobs@barracudas.co.uk; http://recruitment.barracudas.co.uk. 150 activity instructors, 50 arts and crafts instructors, 150 group coordinators, 50 lifeguards, etc for residential and day camps at about 40 centres throughout southern England; 5–6 weeks of school holidays only.

Kingswood Group: ☎ (+44) 1273 648298; www.kingswoodjobs.co.uk. Large number of apprentice instructors and group leader positions at educational activity centres on the Isle of Wight, north Norfolk coast, etc; also hires large numbers of seasonal staff for residential camps run by Camp Beaumont.

Super Camps Ltd: Abingdon, Oxfordshire; ☎ (+44) 1235 467300; www.supercamps.co.uk/work-for-us. 1,000 openings for seasonal instructors at all levels at nearly 80 centres, all over England but mainly in the Midlands and southern England.

For catering, domestic and other work at family holiday centres try Butlins with centres in Bognor Regis, Minehead and Skegness, Pontins which hire for five coastal family holiday centres (www.pontins.com/pontinsrecruitment), and HF Holidays offering activity and special interest holidays at country house hotels (www.hfholidays.co.uk). Butlins along with Warner Leisure Hotels and Haven Holidays all belong to the Bourne Leisure Group, which is responsible for hiring up to 12,000 staff (www.bournejobs.co.uk).

Theme parks such as Alton Towers and Legoland have large seasonal staff requirements, though do not offer accommodation. As well as filling the usual skivvying jobs, they require ride operators, entertainers for both children and adults, lifeguards, DJs, shop assistants, etc.

Hostels

Hundreds of general assistants are taken on in a voluntary capacity by the Youth Hostels Association (England and Wales) from March to October each year (https://jobs.yha.org.uk) to help in the running of YHA's 140 or so youth hostels. Scotland has its own network of 60 hostels. The job can involve cooking for large numbers, general cleaning, cash handling and some clerical work. Accommodation and food are provided with the possibility of some pocket money.

There are also a number of independent hostels and budget accommodation around the country. Several hundred are listed in the pocket-sized *Independent Hostel Guide* from the Backpackers Press in Derbyshire (www.independenthostels.co.uk), whose hostel listings are searchable online. Independent hostels are a good source of temporary work, often providing a few hours a day of work in return for bed and board.

Special Events

Events such as the Henley Regatta in June, Test matches at Headingley in Leeds, the Edinburgh Festival in August/September and a host of golf tournaments and county shows need temporary staff to work as car park attendants, ticket sellers and in catering. Sporting events such as the British Open and Wimbledon employ a myriad of casual workers. Ask the local tourist information office for a list of upcoming events and contact the organisers.

Outside catering and other companies that hold the contracts for staffing special events:

Berkeley-Scott Hotels, Hospitality & Catering Recruitment: www.berkeley-scott.co.uk. With offices in Birmingham, Bristol, Guildford, Leeds, London and Manchester.

Citrus Events Staff Ltd: Newcastle upon Tyne; www.citruseventstaffing.co.uk. Stewards, promotions, bar staff, security, etc for sporting events and festivals.

FMC (Facilities Management Catering Ltd): London SW19; ☎ (+44) 20 8971 2465; www. fmccatering.co.uk. One of the largest outdoor caterers in Europe that has the contracts for Wimbledon where 1,800 people are hired for the fortnight.

Jam Staffing: London W4; ☎ (+44) 20 7237 2228; www.jamstaffing.com. Bar and waiting staff recruited for special events held across London.

NDSS Ltd: Cardiff Bay, South Glamorgan; www.ndssltd.co.uk. Events stewards and security personnel for major events.

Peppermint Bars & Events: London SW19; ☎ (+44) 20 8687 2774; www.peppermintbars. co.uk. Crew including bar staff to work at festivals such as Bestival.

If mass catering and cleaning seem a little tame, more interesting possibilities for entrepreneurs crop up at major events, especially at such a buzzy event as the Edinburgh Fringe Festival.

NICOLE GLUCKSTERN FROM THE USA DISCOVERED POSSIBILITIES AT THE EDINBURGH FESTIVAL:

Work available breaks down into two basic categories: street vending and theatre work. Street vendors of jewellery, hairwraps, caricatures, etc should bring their own supplies and a raincoat. In theory, you need a permit which has to be applied for one year in advance.

Theatre work itself is for technicians and flunkies who sell tix, make popcorn, mop floors (how much theatre experience do you need?). If you just breeze into town the week before the festival you can probably find work pasting up posters all over town; otherwise you probably have to do some advance planning. Unless you live in Bohunk Montana, you might try to find a group in your hometown who's going and offer to work as an unpaid assistant. Every group is required to bring a stage manager but a lot of them find it hard to find one at the last minute. Unlike rock festivals or Christmas markets, working the Fringe is not going to make you any fortunes but the sheer value of the experience is well worth going out of your way for.

Keith Larner recommends a variation on the classic summer job of erecting marquees for weddings and parties: *'Now I can tell you about another good avenue for casual work. I've just completed a job erecting temporary grandstands for sporting events such as golf, racing and tennis. It is very physical work, extremely heavy-going, but financially rewarding because you work seven days per week (but only between April and October).'*

Less financially rewarding but probably a lot more fun would be to attend one of the big summer music festivals such as Glastonbury, WOMAD or Latitude as a steward. Oxfam recruits up to 5,000 volunteer stewards for festivals (www.oxfam.org.uk/stewarding). Other festivals are manned by volunteers that sign up through www.festivalvolunteer.co.uk. Volunteer litter picker-uppers, stewards, wrist-banders, etc are taken on for summer festivals such as the Isle of Wight and Glastonbury; see www.festaff.co.uk.

CHILDCARE AND DOMESTIC

At one time, au pairing was the easiest way for young foreigners to spend time in the UK improving their English. But changes in immigration regulations have curtailed possibilities, even before Brexit comes into effect. To quote the UK Border Agency website: *'Au Pairs: This immigration category closed on 26 November 2008. Please refer to the Youth Mobility Scheme under tier 5 of the points-based system.'* Whereas large numbers of au pairs used to arrive (legally) from non-EU countries such as Turkey and Bosnia-Herzegovina, those nationalities are now banned. Few candidates from the Youth Mobility countries such as Canada, Australia, New Zealand and Japan are interested in au pairing. For now, of course, European Union nationals are free to work as au pairs or anything else. The great majority of au pairs come from the EU accession countries of Slovakia, the Baltics, Bulgaria and Romania. Despite the abolition of the au pair immigration category, au pairs are not entitled to the minimum wage or paid holidays (www.gov.uk/au-pairs-employment-law).

The old Home Office guidelines, deeply ingrained in the system, stipulate that au pairs should work caring for children and doing light housework for no more than 25 hours and five days a week, plus a couple of evenings of babysitting. The recommended minimum pocket money range for au pairs is currently £70–£85 a week.

Young women (and a few men) from the EU or with a Youth Mobility visa, wishing to work longer hours than an au pair, can become au pairs plus, mother's helps or nannies. An untrained, unqualified childcarer with good references can expect to be paid from £130 a week in addition to room and board. Mother's helps with some experience often earn twice this amount and nannies even more.

Nannying in the UK is the option that many young women from Australia and New Zealand choose, partly because it takes care of accommodation and pays a reasonable wage. Those with the Youth Mobility visa can make use of agencies or answer private ads.

If you decide to register with one of the approved agencies, your references will be verified and a police check will be carried out on you. The British Au Pair Agencies Association is a good place to start (www.bapaa.org.uk); all but one of their 30 member agencies make inbound placements in the UK from Kent to Scotland. At least one London agency now specialises in supplying male childcarers or 'mannies'. My Big Buddy (www.mybigbuddy.com) recruits casual and part-time nannies as well as live-in full-timers (though there are fewer of these positions than the live-out ones).

If you want a live-in position but not looking after children, many agencies specialise in providing carers for the elderly and disabled, for example Cura Domi-Care at Home in Surrey (☎ (+44) 1483 420055; www.curadomi.co.uk) pays from £450 a week to residential care workers. Oxford Aunts is another venerable agency in this field (☎ (+44) 1865 791017; www.oxfordaunts.co.uk).

Obviously most job-finding has moved online, and there are dozens of relevant sites to match families seeking childcare with candidates looking for live-in or live-out positions (see the introductory chapter on Childcare for more information). One of the largest is www.childcare.co.uk; childcare providers and tutors can add their profile to this site free of charge and wait to be contacted by parents interested in engaging them

TEACHING

Although there is a veritable epidemic of English language schools along the south coast and in places such as Oxford and Cambridge, you may find it more difficult to get a job as a language tutor in

Torquay than in Taipei, harder in Brighton than in Bogota. It takes more than a tidy appearance to get one of the well-paid summer jobs at one of up to 800 summer language schools operating in Britain. In recent years, there has been a huge increase in the number of students coming from Russia and the Far East.

The majority of language schools in Britain insist that their teachers have a formal qualification in TEFL (Teaching English as a Foreign Language) or at the very least a university degree, teacher's certificate or fluency in a foreign language. If you satisfy any or all of these requirements you should apply to a number of language schools several months prior to the summer holiday period. The average salary for certificate-qualified EFL teachers with experience is £300–£400 per week. Many employers provide staff accommodation for which there will be a deduction from wages.

If you lack the necessary qualifications to teach, you might still consider blitzing the language schools, since many of them also run a programme of outings and entertainments for their foreign students and they may need non-teaching supervisors and sports instructors.

The British Council has an accreditation scheme and a searchable database at www.educationuk. org/english, which allows you to search by region and type, eg junior vacation courses in Southern England. Schools are located throughout the UK including Wales and Scotland, but are concentrated in London and the South East, Oxford, Cambridge and coastal resorts such as Bournemouth and Hastings.

Some of the major language course organisations that offer a large number of summer vacancies are as follows:

Anglo Continental Educational Group: 29–35 Wimborne Road, Bournemouth BH2 6NA; ☎ (+44) 1202 557414; jhaine@anglo-continental.com; www.anglo-continental.com.

Anglophile Academics: 140–144 Freston Road, London W10 6TR ;☎ (+44) 20 7603 1466; tutors@anglophiles.com; www.anglophiles.com. Teachers needed for summer camps and schools in England plus Ireland and the continent.

Ardmore Language Schools: Hall Place, Berkshire College, Burchetts Green, Maidenhead, Berkshire SL6 6QR; ☎ (+44) 1628 826699; jobs@theardmoregroup.com; www.theardmoregroup.com or www.ardmore-language-schools.com/working_for_ardmore.aspx. Successful applicants will be DBS-checked to work in one of about a dozen residential summer centres.

Bell Summer Schools: Red Cross Lane, Cambridge CB2 0QU; ☎ (+44) 1223 275594; jobs. uk@bellenglish.com; www.bellenglish.com/jobs. Schools in Cambridge and St Albans, plus Oxfordshire and Berkshire. Pay rate for CELTA-holder from £375 per week plus statutory holiday pay.

Concorde International Summer Schools: Arnett House, Hawks Lane, Canterbury, Kent CT1 2NU; ☎ (+44) 1227 453315; recruitment@concorde-int.com; www.concorde-int.com/recruitment.

Discovery Summer: 33 Kensington High St, London W8 5EA ☎ (+44 20 7937 1199; www. discovery summer.co.uk/employment.php). EFL teachers for various locations in England such as Radley (Oxfordshire) and Shrewsbury (Shropshire).

EC English Language Centres: (www.ecenglish.com/en/work-for-ec). International company with UK summer schools in Brighton, London, Oxford, Cambridge, Bristol and Manchester. Teaching rate of about £16 per hour (including holiday pay).

EF Language Travel: 22 Chelsea Manor Street, London SW3 5RL; ☎ (+44) 20 7341 8612; www.ef.co.uk/summer-jobs. Centres in Oxford, Torbay, Brighton, Hastings, London, etc.

EJO: Eagle House, Lynchborough Road, Passfield, Hampshire GU30 7SB; ☎ (+44) 1428 751549; www.ejo.co.uk/work-with-us.

Embassy English: http://jobs.embassysummer.com. Teachers and other staff needed for 2–8 weeks at many summer schools. Also summer teaching jobs at three Embassy Academies.

Harrow House: Harrow Drive, Swanage, Dorset BH19 1PE; ☎ (+44) 1929 424421; www. harrowhouse.com).

Kent School of English: 10 and 12 Granville Road, Broadstairs, Kent CT10 1QD; ☎ (+44) 1843 874870; enquiries@kentschool.co.uk; www.kentschoolofenglish.com).

LAL UK Summer Schools: Conway Road, Paignton, Devon TQ4 5LH; ☎ (+44) 1803 558555; jobs.england@lalgroup.com; careers.lalschools.com. Summer schools held in Tavistock, Taunton, Winchester, Brighton, Berkhamsted and Twickenham. Up to £350 per week.

OISE Youth Language Schools: OISE House, Binsey Lane, Oxford OX2 0EY; ☎ (+44) 1865 258346; ylsrecruit@oise.com; www.oiserecruitment.com. 120 summer teaching jobs at 11 summer schools.

Oxford International: 259 Greenwich High Road, London SE10 8NB; www.oxfordinternational.com/recruitment. 800 teachers, activity leaders, etc.

Pilgrims Young Learners: 38 Binsey Lane, Oxford, OX2 0EY ☎ (+44) 1865 258336; recruitment@pilgrims.co.uk; www.pilgrims.co.uk).

Plus International: 8–10 Grosvenor Gardens, London SW1W 0DH; ☎ (+44) 20 7730 2223; www.plus-ed.com. 120 summer teaching positions in the UK plus Dublin. Non-residential pay of £13–£18 per hour.

Project International: 19 Catherine Place, London SWIE 6DX; ☎ (+44) 20 7916 2522; recruitment@projectinternational.uk.com; www.projectinternational.uk.com/employment). Jobs at 10 centres from Dover to Brecon.

Stafford House Study Holidays: 19 New Dover Road, Canterbury, Kent CT1 3AS; ☎ (+44) 1227 811506; recruitment@staffordhouse.com; www.staffordhouse.com. Part of Cambridge Education Group, with 14 centres. Recruitment season opens in January.

SUL Language Schools: 31 Southpark Road, Tywardreath, Par, Cornwall PL24 2PU; ☎ (+44) 1726 814227; claires@sul-schools.com; www.sul-schools.com/teachers. Base pay for starting teachers £258 per week, £278 with CELTA/TESOL.

Thames Valley Summer Schools: 13 Park Street, Windsor, Berkshire SL4 1LU; ☎ (+44) 1753 852001; recruit@thamesvalleysummer.co.uk; www.thamesvalleysummer.co.uk/working-for-us.aspx. Salary from £365 per week for CELTA/TESOL certified teachers.

XUK: 48 Fitzalan Road. Finchley, London N3 3PE; ☎ (+44) 20 8371 9686; www.xukcamps.com/jobs. 2 residential summer camps in East Anglia (Ipswich and Attleborough, Norfolk). £325–£375.

Outside the summer period, private tutoring might be a possibility. MyTutor.co.uk provides one-to-one online exam support for children studying for A levels or GCSEs. They take on as tutors university students who are enrolled at one of the 24 Russell Group universities and who obtained A or A* grades at A-level. The promised wage range is £10–£24 an hour.

The shortage of certified teachers for primary and secondary schools in deprived areas is still acute, both in London and elsewhere. Many local Education Authorities, mainly in inner and outer London, are constantly in need of supply or temporary short-term teachers who are paid a daily rate ranging from £150 to £195. Agencies such as EduStaff (www.eductaff.co.uk) can advise.

APPLYING LOCALLY

British readers may decide that it is easiest to save money by working close to home. If you have had no luck through Jobcentre Plus, by answering ads on Gumtree or elsewhere or by registering with private employment agencies, you may want to spread your net even wider. Personal visits are also a good idea, for example to the personnel managers of large department stores, supermarkets, national retailing chains, fast food restaurants or canneries in your area, especially well before summer arrives.

A huge increase in the number of easy-come easy-go jobs as deliverers, drivers, cleaners and handymen/women has been made possible by the popularity of apps like Uber and Deliveroo. Participating in the gig economy, as it is known, can be a good way of supplementing an income though it is usually not brilliant as a sole means of support. These companies have come into conflict with the law in not paying the minimum wage. Deliveroo pays £7 an hour plus £1 per delivery, so the maximum you can make for a three-hour shift is about £30. Cleaners working through www.handy.com earn £8.50 an hour though travel time and down time between jobs are not compensated.

One enterprising young American woman pieced together several jobs in Cambridge within a couple of weeks: *'In my terror at my shrinking funds, I accumulated five jobs: two cleaning, one nannying, one behind the bar at a red plush Turkish nightclub and one (which has stood me well) as a personal assistant to a professor.'* The latter job, which was advertised on a noticeboard at the Graduate Student Centre, was by far the most interesting and also lucrative. Similar notices for research assistants are posted in universities around the world, mostly in department offices and teaching buildings rather than in student unions.

One way of earning a bit extra is to register on the panels of market research companies such as YouGov. Earnings for joining focus groups and completing surveys can range from zilch up to £150; try for example www.focus4people.com, www.sarosresearch.com and www.surveyspot.com.

MEDICAL EXPERIMENTS

As many as one hundred clinical research units in the UK conduct ongoing pharmaceutical testing, many of which rely on healthy human volunteers for Phase 1 trials. The demand for willing volunteers is so great that some of the larger pharmaceutical companies such as GlaxoSmithKline (GSK) advertise in the mainstream media. The case in 2006 of six healthy volunteers suffering catastrophic organ failure after acting as guinea pigs for a leukaemia drug damaged the reputation of clinical drug testing, and fewer volunteers have been willing to come forward ever since. Drug testing is of course very carefully monitored and overseen by ethical committees, but the case at London's Northwick Park Hospital proved that safety cannot be guaranteed. Less dramatically, many people fear that the long-term consequences of taking unlicensed drugs cannot be safely predicted.

Nevertheless, many people rely on drug testing as a regular source of income, earning as much as £200 a day, or £3,500 for a complete trial. Most company literature states that expenses will be reimbursed, but payment is normally more generous than this. The UK Clinical Trials Gateway (www.ukctg.nihr.ac.uk) provides background information on the process and links to trials around the UK. To obtain details about GSK's programme of experiments in Cambridge and London, see www.volunteers.gsk.co.uk. Other clinics to try include:

Covance Clinical Research Ltd: Leeds, West Yorkshire; ☎ (+44) 113 394 5200 or 800 591570; www.covanceclinicaltrials.com.

Hammersmith Medicines Research: London NW10; ☎ (+44) 800 783 8792; recruit@ hmr-london.com; www.londontrials.com.

Parexel Early Phase Clinical Unit: Northwick Park Hospital, Harrow, Middlesex; ☎ (+44) 800 389 8930; drugtrial@parexel.com; www.drugtrial.co.uk.

Richmond Pharmacology Volunteer Recruitment: Croydon; ☎ (+44) 800 085 6464; www.trials4us.co.uk. Recruiting volunteers at time of writing for a trial that was paying £1,445.

Simbec Research Ltd: Merthyr Tydfil, South Wales; www.simbec.co.uk/volunteers.

In some cases, volunteer subjects must produce a medical certificate from their own doctor attesting to their good health, and in most cases foreign volunteers must prove that they are in the country legally. Reluctantly Rob Abblett signed up for a study of hayfever tablets in his home town (Leicester) to revive his flagging fortunes between world trips: *'Lots of blood samples and lots of TV. Thankfully, my veins are too fine so I won't be making a career out of this. I'll get about £950 if I last the distance from 16 June to 11 July. This includes two nights residential and two return visits each week.'*

The majority of opportunities are in London. If you qualify as a participant for a current trial, you will be asked to attend for screening by the volunteer recruitment officer. After passing the screening (you must have taken no medications or drugs in the previous fortnight), you must undertake to abstain faithfully from nicotine, alcohol, tea, coffee, cola and chocolate for 48 hours on either side of the test. Between swallowing the experimental medications and having tests (eg blood tests, blood pressure, etc), you will be given meals and entertained with television and DVDs, *Coma* or *Love at First Bite*). If the thought of subjecting your body to unknown drugs upsets you, then psychological experiments provide an easier (if less lucrative) alternative. Psychology researchers constantly need volunteers and often receive grants specifically to pay subjects. It is worth enquiring at any university's psychology department about this opportunity.

Men who once would have unthinkingly donated sperm in exchange for a small fee must now register their details so that the children born subsequently can trace their genetic fathers. More than two-thirds of prospective donors are rejected. For the nearest clinic, contact the National Gamete Donation Trust (www.ngdt.co.uk). Accepted donors may be able to claim up to £35 per clinic visit to cover expenses, and it is not unusual to donate two to three times a week for up to four months. The London Women's Clinic, Harley Street (www.londonwomensclinic.com) is the UK's largest sperm bank.

BUILDING AND OTHER SEASONAL WORK

The building trade has been picking up after years of stagnation. Skilled and unskilled jobs are widely advertised on sites like www.jobsite.co.uk/jobs/construction. Labourers should obtain a CSCS (Construction Skills Certification Scheme) card after doing a one-day health and safety course. You may have better luck finding work building temporary rather than permanent structures. The work of erecting marquees is strenuous and pays fairly well, especially since time spent travelling to the destination is also paid, and there is usually plenty of overtime. Try, for example, Field and Lawn (Marquees) Ltd who operate throughout the UK with offices in Manchester, Edinburgh, London and Bristol (www.fieldandlawn.com/about-us/careers/crew-support). The company Danco based in Bristol has a history of hiring backpackers for marquee erecting (www.danco.co.uk). Check the online *Yellow Pages* for other firms to contact.

Certain agricultural jobs are very seasonal in nature, such as turkey plucking in December.

ERIC MACKNESS BRAVED THE GRUELLING JOB OF WORKING ON A CHRISTMAS TREE PLANTATION IN OXFORDSHIRE FOR ONE MONTH FROM 10 NOVEMBER:

I was recruited at the end of the summer tourist season on Sark by an Irish company that has outlets in Ireland, Scotland and Kent, as well as Abingdon near Oxford where I worked. The job consists of sorting, pricing and loading Christmas trees. It's not that well paid an hour but because of the potential for working a hideous number of hours (80–90 a week with no days off) it is possible to earn a tidy sum. Accommodation is provided and the food is excellent. The work was the hardest I have ever done (and I have done some hard jobs). Working on top of a trailer loaded with frozen trees in a snowstorm is not for the faint-hearted.

Apparently many of the workers return from one year to the next, but new vacancies do crop up with the Emerald Group; applications to the Irish office in Wexford (☎ (+353) 53 912 2033; www.emeraldgroup.ie).

LONDON

Most new arrivals in the capital report that there is no shortage of work. The problem is finding affordable accommodation that allows you to save from what is seldom a startlingly good wage. Ian Mitselburg from Sydney went through the usual processes: *'The first job I got was through a hostel noticeboard: labouring for a shifty hotel owner, who was restoring his hotel in the Paddington/Bayswater area (where else?) for a few weeks, paid cash in hand. After that I worked through an agency in Earl's Court run by a couple of Kiwis who favoured Australasians.'*

The advertising pages of free magazines aimed at the expat community, notably *TNT*, carry scores of ads for employment agencies specialising in everything from banquet catering to landscape gardening. You can expect to earn minimum wage as a kitchen porter (the most lowly job) and up to twice that as an assistant chef. Ask your agency about obtaining hygiene certificate training which isn't compulsory but assists in the job hunt. Also check out cleaning and security work, for which there seems to be an insatiable demand in London. An active agency in the field of horticulture and land-scape labouring, as well as the usual retail and catering, is the Target Group in Canada Water, East London (☎ (+44) 20 7232 1010; www.target-jobs.com).

Pubs

Anyone who has been on a pub-crawl in London will know that a huge percentage of the people working behind the bar are not English, but rather Polish, Australian or one of a hundred nationalities. Although there are employment agencies specialising in bar work, they aren't usually very helpful to people looking for casual bar work. Gumtree is a better bet.

Some pub jobs come with accommodation, in which case you would expect to have the permitted sum of £42 a week deducted from your wages of £324 for a 45-hour week before tax (for those over 25). Many pubs operate primarily as restaurants now so you can expect to earn tips in some positions.

Couriers

Driving is a standard stop-gap job, for example of vans or as a courier. Uber will be of interest only to those with their own four-door sedan vehicle. Motorcycle owners might be tempted by the money that can be earned by despatch riders. For those who don't own their own bikes, they can be leased from the firm. Despatch riders can earn £700+ a week. But the high earnings only come when jobs come thick and fast, and if you have a good knowledge of London streets. There is also a high risk of serious injury; hence insurance premiums will be very high if you declare your occupation for insurance and tax purposes.

The firm City Sprint is always looking for people willing to become self-employed drivers and couriers out of their 31 offices around the UK, and seems sympathetic to the erratic habits of people working for relatively short periods to fund their travels (www.citysprint.co.uk/workwithus/courier work). They were also taken to court in 2017 by one of their couriers in a test case to demand employment rights such as holiday pay and the minimum wage; the judge found in favour of the courier.

Bicycle couriers are also needed, for example by visa agencies. Top couriers cover 50+ miles a day doing up to 40 deliveries. The job carries on in all weathers (except snow which is considered too dangerous).

Accommodation

Most new arrivals in London go to one of the scores of (relatively) cheap hostels where overseas travellers congregate. Expect to pay from £15 for a dorm bed, though the cheapest listed at www.londontoolkit.com/accommodation/hostels.htm start at £10. Hostels can serve as a launch pad for money-saving careers and shared houses. If you are lucky enough to have friends with whom you can doss, offer to contribute at least £5 a night towards bills. When sharing private accommodation, budget for £150 a week for a room in a not very central part of London (which can be halved if you are sharing with a partner); twice that for a studio flat or self-contained bedsit. Websites can be very useful for London accommodation such as www.spareroom.co.uk. www.accommodationlondon.net and www.roombuddies.co.uk.

An interesting alternative is to investigate anti-squatting agencies that rent out empty premises for short periods at very low rents, referred to as 'license fees'. Flats and houses whose owners may be waiting for planning permission to renovate or buildings in line for demolition may be on the agency books. Office spaces, studios, warehouses and pubs may also need caretakers. You must be prepared to move out at short notice, but with luck you can stay for a decent period of time. Agencies to check out are Guardians of London (www.guardiansoflondon.com), Ad Hoc (www.adhoc.eu), Camelot

Property (www.camelotproperty.com) and Property Guardians (www.propertyguardians.org). Obviously these companies will check references and legal status if you're not a Briton, and expect you to be in employment or a mature student. You may be charged a registration fee of about £75 and have to pay a returnable bond of £500.

Carisa Fey arrived in London from Stuttgart at the tender age of 18 determined to make a go of long-term working and travelling, and soon moved out of a hostel and into rented accommodation:

> *Once in London I went – where else? – to Earls Court, and met my first fellow travellers in a hostel. I planned to be the very first one on Monday morning to grab the hostel copy of TNT and to start my hunt for a job. Well, unfortunately, we were in one of those, ahem, social hostels and until 3pm on Monday I couldn't even walk. I thought my chance was gone and that no-one was going to give a job to me considering the state I was in. But just to practise I put on my suit and decided to look for a place to stay. The third letting agency I went into (I was still a spoiled brat then and believed in things like letting agencies) seemed nice, professional and not too expensive. While filling in the form, I left the space 'occupation' empty and said that I was looking for a job. The agency's boss sat on the next desk, looked up and asked 'Do you want to work here?' So I found in one afternoon a job and a place to stay.*

Free food and accommodation in exchange for some duties is a great bonus in London. A number of charities recruit full-time volunteers to assist people with severe physical disabilities to live independently in the community. For example Independent Living Alternatives (www.ILAnet.co.uk) recruits volunteers, who are required to stay for a minimum of four months, and in turn receive a shared place to live and an allowance of £63.50 a week. A shift system is worked by volunteers allowing plenty of free time to explore London. ILA's office is in North London (☎ (+44) 20 8369 6032).

DEBBIE HARRISON ARRIVED IN LONDON AFTER A FRENETIC SEASON AS A HOLIDAY REP IN GREECE, EAGER TO SAVE SOME MONEY:

After the constant dining out, excessive drinking and sunbathing, my current job as a live-in carer for an old lady in a quiet part of Surrey is quite a contrast. I went to the agency interview with no experience or qualifications but was introduced by a friend already employed by them and I was offered a job straightaway. The pay is good and the long hours mean temporary death to the social life so it's a great way to save.

The kind of clientele served by certain agencies means that they will be selective, so you will need to look respectable and have a background to match, with contactable references. A driving licence is often essential.

VOLUNTEERING

Volunteering Matters (formerly Community Service Volunteers) mentioned at the beginning of this chapter offers volunteer placements to anyone aged 18–35 who commits him/herself to live away from home for six to 12 months supporting people who need help, such as children with special needs and homeless people. Volunteers do not need any special skills, qualifications or experience. Volunteers receive a modest weekly allowance in addition to accommodation and meals; consult www.volunteeringmatters.org.uk/volunteering-information/full-time-volunteering or ring ☎ (+44) 20 3780 5870. Another organisation that provides board, lodging and pocket money to volunteers willing to work at centres for the homeless is the Simon Community in North London (☎ (+44) 20 7485 6639; www.simoncommunity.org.uk) whose preferred minimum stay is six months after a trial month. Volunteers over 19 receive an allowance for travel, etc in addition to room and board.

Many shorter-term opportunities for volunteers can be found, especially during the summer months when disability charities recruit volunteers to assist at holiday centres to give disabled people and their carers a break. Revitalise runs holiday centres in Southampton, Southport and Epping Forest that depend on willing volunteers (British or otherwise). The charity pays all board, lodging and travel to the centres from within the UK; an application form can be downloaded from the site www.revitalise. org.uk.

If you are more interested in conservation work, several national bodies arrange one to three week working holidays where volunteers repair dry stone walls, clear overgrown ponds, undertake botanical surveys, archaeological digs or maintain traditional woodland. You will be housed in comfortable volunteer basecamps with about a dozen other volunteers. For a listing of the hundreds of working holidays organised by the National Trust, go to www.nationaltrust.org.uk/working-holidays. TCV (The Conservation Volunteers) has cut way back on its residential volunteering programme but runs projects in the South Downs National Park (www.tcv.org.uk).

Bird-lovers can become volunteer wardens for up to four weeks with the Royal Society for the Protection of Birds (RSPB) and undertake many other volunteer roles (☎ (+44) 1767 680551; www. rspb.org.uk/volunteering). Accommodation is provided free but the volunteers must provide their own food. The Waterway Recovery Group (☎ (+44) 1494 783453; www.waterways.org.uk) runs week-long voluntary Canal Camps costing only £70 a week for accommodation and meals.

Anyone who wants to participate on an archaeological dig should consult information from the Council for British Archaeology in York; some of its fieldwork listings are freely available on their site (http://new.archaeologyuk.org/fieldwork). Participation costs vary from free to £200–£250 per week.

In Wales, the Centre for Alternative Technology, Machynlleth, Powys SY20 9AZ (www.cat.org.uk/volunteers) takes on short-term volunteers (who pay £10 a day for room and board) and those able to stay up to six months. Accommodation is available on a first-come first-served basis or can be found locally. CAT can pay travel expenses up to £16.50 a week for volunteers who live off-site.

Buddhist communities throughout Britain offer working visits whereby volunteers stay free of charge. For example the Manjushri Mahayana Buddhist Centre in Cumbria (www.manjushri.org/volunteering-visits) gives one week's free dormitory accommodation and three vegetarian meals a day in exchange for 35 hours of work. Alcohol, tobacco and loud music are not permitted. The Madhyamaka Centre in Yorkshire has the same arrangement in place for those willing to work 25 hours a week, and also takes on longer-term volunteers (www.madhyamaka.org/volunteering-visits). Shona Williamson once enjoyed a working holiday here so much she decided to make it her home for an extended period. In exchange for gardening, decorating and other duties she got free dormitory accommodation, vegetarian meals and the chance to attend evening meditations and teachings.

Laura Hitchcock from New York State managed to fix up two interesting three-month internships in the field of her career interest by agreeing to pay her own expenses if they would take her on and help her find accommodation in local homes. Her jobs were in the publicity departments of the Ironbridge Gorge Museum Trust near Telford in Shropshire, and then in a theatre-arts centre in East Anglia. This was some time ago, and it is likely that unemployed British graduates will already have tracked down potential unpaid work experience placements like this.

Ireland

Ireland's economy has been on a rollercoaster in recent years. The heady 'Celtic tiger' days came to an ignominious end during the 2008 collapse when the country's debt ballooned, property markets crashed and unemployment climbed to 15%. Somehow the economy is now surging ahead again, with unemployment halved since the peak. Yet it is not quite an economic miracle since unemployment among the young is still high, and about a quarter of the jobs in the country pay the minimum wage of €9.25. But that shouldn't bother those who arrive for a working holiday.

WORKING HOLIDAY SCHEMES

Full-time American students in tertiary education or within 12 months of graduating are eligible to apply for a Working Holiday Authorisation valid for four months over the summer or 12 months year round. Applications can be made directly to the nearest Irish consulate in the US, located in New York, Boston, Chicago, San Francisco and Washington, for a fee of $339. Canada and Ireland have a reciprocal working holiday arrangement by which Canadians aged 18–35 (not necessarily students) can apply for visas valid for up to two years. These are available from the Irish embassy or can be obtained through the student travel organisation SWAP (www.swap.ca) for a fee of C$560. The partner organisation in Ireland is the student travel and exchange agency USIT (19–21 Aston Quay, Dublin 2; ☎ (+353) 1 602 1906; www.usit.ie). If you visit the USIT office on the south side of the River Liffey, you can inspect a large noticeboard with Jobs Available notices and get a lot of solid support while you're job-hunting, plus access to photocopying for your CV and a quiet space for Skype interviews.

Once in Ireland, non-EU citizens intending to stay and work for longer than 90 days must register with the Garda National Immigration Bureau (GNIB) and pay a fee of €300, in Dublin at 3/14 Burgh Quay or at your local Garda (police) station outside Dublin. USIT can advise on this as well as advising on job opportunities.

All applicants for a working holiday visa will have to prove that they have access to the equivalent of €1,850 as support funds.

US nationals who can prove Irish ancestry may be eligible for unrestricted entry to Ireland and even Irish nationality (which would confer all EU rights). There may be processing delays, since the Irish consular service has been inundated with applications for nationality after the Brexit vote in 2016.

Obviously there will be many who are not eligible for these visas. Again informal arrangements with private hostels can make it possible to extend your stay in Ireland. One enterprising Californian contacted hostels via www.hostels.com and, after a brief exchange of emails and references and a phone conversation, was hired by a start-up hostel which gave her accommodation plus $150 a week.

THE JOB-HUNT

Intreo centres around Ireland combine the functions of an employment service and welfare support for unemployed Irish people. Job vacancies throughout the country are listed at www.jobsireland.ie. Commercial recruitment sites such as www.jobs.ie and www.irishjobs.ie are two of the country's biggest online recruitment sites, which register employers' vacancies in hotels, restaurants, bars and leisure centres, sales, childcare, etc throughout Ireland. Chefs and experienced hotel receptionists are particularly in demand.

Note that some agencies arrange unpaid work experience placements for young people from the Continent, such as Vocation Relocation Career Training Internships in Cork (www.vocationrelocation. ie). The same can be arranged for Americans, for example by World Endeavors (www.worldendeavors. com) which charges substantial programme fees, eg $3,190 for a one-month career-specific internship and private accommodation mainly in Dublin.

Tourism

The tourist industry is the main source of seasonal work in Ireland. Outside Dublin, the largest demand is in the south-western counties of Cork and Kerry, especially the towns of Killarney (with well over 100 pubs) and Tralee. Contact the addresses from any hotels listing for Ireland.

When applying, you should mention any musical talent you have, since pubs and hotels may be glad to have a barman who can occasionally entertain at the piano. Directly approaching cafés, campsites and amusement arcades is usually more effective than writing. One hundred thousand people a year visit the Aillwee Cave in County Clare; the company which manages the attraction recruits cave tour guides, plus catering and sales staff for all of July and August (Aillwee Cave Co. Ltd, Ballyvaughan,

Co. Clare; ☎ (+353) 65 707 7036; www.aillweecave.ie/employment-opportunities-at-aillwee-cave). Recruitment starts in mid-March and hostel accommodation is provided at a cost.

Experienced assistants and instructors may be needed by riding stables and watersports centres throughout Ireland. Instructors and pony trek leaders are needed mainly for children at Errislannan Manor Connemara Pony Stud (Clifden, West Galway; ☎ (+353) 952 1134; errislannanmanor@eircom. net); the minimum stay is two months and applications must be made before March.

Innumerable musical and cultural festivals take place throughout Ireland, mostly during the summer. Big-name bands often perform at concerts near Dublin. A small fortune can be made by amateur entrepreneurs (with or without a permit) who find a niche in the market. Heather McCulloch had two friends who sold filled rolls and sandwiches at a major concert and made a clear profit of over £1,000 in a short time.

'The Rose of Tralee', a large regional festival held in Tralee, Co. Kerry in the third week of August, provides various kinds of employment for enterprising workers, as Tracie Sheehan reports: *'As 50,000 people attend this festival each year, guest houses, hotels, restaurants and cafés all take on extra staff. Buskers make great money, as do mime artists, jugglers and artists. Pubs do a roaring business, so singing or performing in a pub can be very profitable.'*

Dublin

According to Mig Urquhart *'crappy jobs are very easy to get in Dublin, whereas real jobs are scarce'*. Mig has worked in a Dublin hostel, a bed and breakfast, the Irish-owned fast food company Supermac's (recruitment@supermacs.ie), the canteen of a government department and for the boat taxi on the River Liffey (which closed when the Samuel Beckett Bridge opened). Check the noticeboards in the main travellers' hostels such as the Dublin International Youth Hostel at 61 Mountjoy Street. The hostel is always looking for volunteers and interns for marketing, maintenance and mountain guiding; you can join their volunteer database online at www.anoige.ie/inspire-me/job-positions-volunteers-and-interns.

Try the trendy spots in Temple Bar and around Grafton Street in the city centre for restaurant and pub work.

Buskers and street entertainers can do well in and around Dublin's Grafton Street since the Irish are a generous nation and appreciate musical talent.

Au Pairing

European Union citizens who want to learn English and some Commonwealth passport holders may wish to consider au pairing in Ireland via one of a number of agencies; for example the Shamrock Aupair Agency in County Carlow (www.aupairireland.com) makes the usual family placements in Dublin and the rest of the country.

Another member of the International Au Pair Association is SK Dublin Au Pairs in Co. Wicklow (www. skdublin.ie/au-pairs) while Cara International in Co. Mayo (www.carainternational.net) has been around for a long time. The recommended pocket money for au pairs is €110 a week for 25 hours of duties plus two evenings of babysitting, €120 for 30 daytime hours and one evening, and €140 for 35 hours and an evening. The agencies that are offshoots of language schools usually make it a requirement that au pairs sign up for English courses with them. Experienced nannies may wish to contact the childcare and elder care specialist Hynes Agency in central Dublin (www.hynesagency.ie).

Agriculture and Fishing

The horse industry continues to flourish in Ireland; anyone with experience of horses might have success by contacting stables, riding holiday centres or equestrian recruitment agencies. Equipeople in County Laois is a specialist agency providing work experience on Irish farms especially for European students (www.equipeopleworkexperience.com) and also supplies horsey staff to the equine sector in Ireland and abroad (☎ (+353) 57 864 3195). Another site to check is www.yardandgroom.com.

Robert Abblett gave a lift to an Irish fisherman who passed on some tips on finding work in the fishing industry:

> He mentioned three places to try. I visited a fish factory in Rossaveal west of Galway and could have got a job easily extracting the roe from herrings. The work was paid piecework for a maximum of five days a week (weather permitting). Most people only last a few days as the work is dirty, smelly and boring. The season here lasts from mid-October till February only. I then visited Dingle and enquired at the fish factory. I didn't bother checking Castletownbere on the Beara peninsula which is a large whitefish port. Work on the fishing boats and factories is apparently available most of the year.

The Netherlands

British and Irish young people no longer pour off cheap flights and ferries, check into hostels and begin looking for jobs. After years of having the lowest unemployment in the EU, the rate is currently almost 7%. However the market for unskilled non-Dutch-speaking workers is not entirely saturated so prospects for picking up work are fair. The standard of English spoken throughout the Netherlands is astoundingly high.

REGULATIONS

The Dutch have tightened up regulations to control squatters, drug abusers and others perceived to be undesirable, although a policy of benign tolerance of drugs is still in place unless it is perceived to be causing social harm.

All job-seeking EU citizens must follow the bureaucratic procedures that the majority of agencies and employers follow. EU citizens who intend to stay for more than three months are obliged to register with the authorities and obtain a Citizen Service Number (*Burger Servicenummer* or BSN) which serves as ID for employment, tax and health care purposes. You will need this before you can for example register with employment bureaux or take up a job. You can carry out this procedure at any town hall; in Amsterdam it is located at Amstel 1 and it is possible to make an appointment, which would save some hassle. An alternative, billed as being more 'streamlined', is to pay a fee (eg €210) and get the Expatcenter in the World Trade Center in Amsterdam Zuid to deal with the red tape, though their clientele is mainly expat employees of big companies. In either case you will need a passport from an EU country and registered address.

Job agencies may not be willing to sign you up unless you have a Dutch bank account and some banks are reluctant to open accounts. Look for the major branches of ABN-AMRO or ING.

Non-EU Citizens

The situation for non-EU citizens is predictably more difficult. North Americans, Antipodeans and others who require no visa to travel to the Netherlands are allowed to work for less than three months, provided they register for a BSN as above, which is no longer permitted at the Amsterdam City Hall so will have to be done through the Expatcenter within three days of arrival.

Non-EU citizens wishing to stay for longer than three months must obtain a sponsor, such as an employer willing to obtain a *tewerkstellingsvergunning* (also called a TWV) from the UWV Werkbedrijf (employment service). Since procedures were streamlined with the adoption of the Modern Migration Policy, the employer can also apply for a residence permit (*verblijfsvergunning*) at the same time, but before the prospective employee arrives in the country. In practice, a TWV will not be issued for casual work.

For detailed information, search the website of the Dutch Immigration Service, called Immigratie en Naturalisatie Dienst or IND (www.ind.nl which is fully accessible in English) or ring ☎ (+31) 88 0430 430. Canadians, Australians and New Zealanders up to the age of 30 can obtain a working holiday visa valid for up to a year.

Red Tape

The Dutch have some of the most progressive laws in the world to minimise exploitation of workers. Compulsory holiday pay of at least 8% of gross salary should also be paid on all but the most temporary casual jobs. Do not count on receiving the holiday pay immediately after finishing a job because it may have to be sent to your home bank account months later. Similarly tax rebates may be owing at the end of the tax year, and so employees should save all pay slips showing income and deductions. Health insurance contributions (*Ziekenfonds*) are compulsory: a full time worker should expect to pay €90–€100 a month for cover.

If you feel that you are not being treated fairly by an employer or landlord, you can get free legal advice from any Jongeren Informatie Punt or JIP (Youth Information Points; www.jip.org) or you can make enquiries at any employment office. Current minimum monthly wages stand at €1,551.60 for those 23 or older, but less than half that for 18 year olds.

PRIVATE EMPLOYMENT AGENCIES

The majority of employers turn to private employment agencies (*uitzendbureaux* – pronounced and meaning 'out-send') for temporary workers, partly to avoid the complicated paperwork of hiring a foreigner directly. Therefore, they can be a very useful source of temporary work in Holland. They proliferate in large towns, for example there are more than 200 in Amsterdam alone.

Look up *Uitzendbureau* in the telephone directory or the *Gouden Gids* (*Yellow Pages*; www.detele foongids.nl) and register with as many as you can in your area. Not all will accept non-Dutch-speaking applicants. You should visit or at least phone the office daily at opening time and perhaps twice a day since often the allocation of jobs is not systematic and once the phone is put down the agency forgets about you. Ian Kent thinks that Amsterdam is far more promising than the provinces for non-Dutch speakers:

> In Amsterdam it is easy to get work in cafés, hostels and coffee shops. However, outside Amsterdam it is somewhat tricky. It took me three months of asking round farms, greenhouses and being told by all of the uitzendbureaux that there is no work unless you speak Dutch. By chance I found work packing fruit and veg through an uitzendbureau in Rotterdam who at the time were giving work to anybody with an EU passport. The work was boring and the shifts long, 10–12 hours. I would advise anybody who does not speak good Dutch to go to Amsterdam to look for work.

Uitzendbureaux deal only with jobs lasting less than six months. Most of the work on their books will be unskilled work. The area in the industrial west of the Netherlands encompassing Amsterdam, Rotterdam, the Hague and Utrecht, called the Randstad, has the most work. Many international companies are based in the Netherlands, so there are vacancies for experienced native English secretaries and data-inputters, usually through the *uitzendbureaux*. Kerian Parry spent several years when she was in her early 20s working in Sassenheim and Noordwijk-aan-Zee near Leiden.

> Leiden has a lot of uitzendbureaux, and in my experience about half of them will take on English speakers who don't speak Dutch. Adecco, Olympia, Manpower, First Start and one branch of Luba definitely signed up foreign workers when I was there and all except one or two offered me jobs during my stay. They are nearly always looking for people who have office experience and/or typing skills, but I didn't feel my typing was good enough. I supported myself with the following jobs: worker in flower-factories, order-picker in a clothing warehouse, cleaner of fire-damaged objects and kitchen assistant/cleaner in a hospital canteen. I hated starting at 7am, although most low-paid jobs in Holland seem to start

between 7am and 8.30am. Like all employment agencies uitzendbureaux gain their income by charging the employer a percentage of the wage, which in some cases is 100% or more.

Among the largest *uitzendbureaux* are Randstad (incorporating Tempo Team and Dactylo) with up to 700 branches, Manpower, and Adecco, all of whose websites are only in Dutch.

For seasonal work in agriculture and horticulture, look at www.seasonalwork.nl which at the time of writing in the winter had fruit tree pruning, campsite cleaning and nursery work in three different provinces of southern Holland.

THE BULB INDUSTRY

Traditionally, the horticultural sector has had difficulty in finding enough seasonal labour for the processing of flower bulbs for export and related activities. Young travellers, especially from the accession countries of Eastern Europe, descend on the area between Leiden and Haarlem in the summer. Unskilled workers are employed in fields and factories to dig, peel, sort, count and pack bulbs, especially in the early spring and through the autumn. Important export companies (*Bloembollen Groothandel*) can be found in the north around Andijk and Breezand. The Dutch *Yellow Pages* online can be a useful ally in the search for work. For example dozens of addresses of bulb companies are listed showing their locations on linked maps.

Finding the Work

Some farmers use agents or middlemen to recruit casual labour. Some years ago Rob Abblett travelled to Holland after the *vendange* in Switzerland, just because he'd never been before. He headed for Andijk near Enkhuizen north of Amsterdam: *'By great luck and effort I managed to find a job on foot, but later discovered that I had to go through a job agency anyway, unless I had worked there the year before. The job agencies helped me and, now that I have their telephone numbers, I can even phone them from England, say, to check on work availability.'*

Work in the Andijk factories is available mid-July to September and mid-October till February. He returned to Hillegom in September armed with an address given to him by a fellow traveller, and this connection made it much easier to land a job. Eighty caravans were parked behind the factory, full of Polish workers with German passports. His job was to sprinkle glitter on waxed pinecones for the Christmas market. After a month, he couldn't face it any more and returned home.

The busy times differ among bulb employers according to their markets. For example mail-order companies need employees to pick and pack customers' orders from February until the end of April and again from September to December. The busy time for bulb peeling is the second half of June. Look for signs (*Bollenpellers Gevraagd*) in Hillegom, Lisse, Noordwijk, Sassenheim and Bennebroek. New arrivals should have no trouble locating the properties of the bulb barons once they arrive. In Hillegom head for Pastoorslaan or Leidsestraat where many of the factories are concentrated and in Lisse, look along Heereweg. Note that the greenhouses and flower auction houses in and around Aalsmeer also provide employment, but not so seasonal.

The majority of bulb exporters consider only candidates who are around when there are vacancies and with changes in immigration patterns more of them are able to find enough workers and students already resident in the Netherlands. It is always worth trying the famous bulb exporter Bakker.com, which employs 500 seasonal staff at busy times (February–May and September–December) working 7.30am to 4.30pm Monday to Friday in Lisse and nearby DeZilk. Seasonal production workers all come through one of two agencies: Otto Workforce (bakker.com@ottoworkforce.eu) and Unique (inhouse.bakkercom@unique.nl).

The long established firm Frijlink & Zonen in Noordwijkerhout (☎ (+31) 252 343143; www.frylink. com) receives plenty of applications via word of mouth. You can also try enquiring about *vakantiewerk* (vacation work) at Van Zanten b.v. in and around Hillegom (www.royalvanzanten.com) and René Vink in 't Zand (☎ (+31) 224 591984; info@renevink.nl).

In Robert Abblett's experience, the bad reputation that seasonal workers have among local land-lords, etc. is not undeserved: *'Lots of the workers smoke dope from waking up, at work (if they can) and the rest of the day. But I can't blame them, for the work requires a positive mental attitude to withstand the boredom and if you haven't got it, then you must choose insanity, oblivion or just leave.'* Obviously if the competition is like this, it is not too surprising that his boss at De Jongs Lily Factory in Andijk made him supervisor of the night shift line (☎ (+31) 228 591400; www.dejonglelies.nl).

Competition for jobs remains stiff, though less so at the more far-flung factories. Mark Wilson recommends having some transport: *'Along with a tent, a necessity when looking for bulb work is a bicycle. While out exploring on my bike I came across an area full of factories just outside Noordwi-jkerhout, a village west of Lisse.'* Second-hand bicycles can be picked up fairly easily and affordably.

Pay and Conditions

Overtime paid at a premium rate is what makes it possible to save though there seems to be less on offer than there used to be. Like most agricultural work, earnings fluctuate according to the weather; on a rainy day when the flowers don't open people are lucky to get four hours' work.

In a post on the web forum www.ukhippy.com one young woman described her experience of this seasonal work, advising that future travellers should aim to make their way to Noordwijkerhout in Holland in late April. Those who arrive early enough may be able to find work in the bulb factories as a packer, collecting stock from shelves, packing boxes and completing online orders. Several former workers have commented that you can earn enough from working in the factories to see you through the rest of the year from three to four months' work.

Bulb-peeling is a much more unpleasant job than bulb packing as Martin and Shirine recall: *'The work was hard on our hands and we soon resorted to wearing rubber gloves or plasters. The hours of work were 8am–5pm with an hour's lunch break and the choice to work until 10pm. That was a long time to spend crouched over a table, sitting on an old wobbly stool that was the wrong height for you.'*

Mark Wilson had an even more miserable experience as a bulb peeler: *'The first job I had was peeling the skin off the bulbs which was the most mind-numbingly boring job I have ever done. Later I was condemned to two weeks in the hyacinth shed which is kept away from the main factory. While working on a sorting machine in a loose T-shirt I found to my horror and my Dutch workmates' amuse-ment that bulb dust is a very powerful irritant, so after a couple of hours of itching like a madman, I resigned on the spot, ran back to the campsite and dived into the shower to relieve my tormented skin.'*

AGRICULTURE

From mid-April to October jobs might be available picking asparagus, strawberries, gherkins, apples and pears. During the same period jobs exist in greenhouses and mushroom fields, though these jobs are popular with locals and usually can be filled with local students and other jobseekers.

Many harvests take place in fertile pockets of southern Holland, for example in the Baarland in the extreme south-west and in Limburg to the east along the Belgian border. Garrett Mohan travelled to the tiny village of Kwadendamme near Goes in the Baarland (Zeeland) in early September (after local school children had returned to school) to join the apple and pear harvest that ends in early November. An agency that may be able to assist is Unique Uitzendbureau in Goes (☎ (+3) 1 113 211223; goes.office@unique.nl).

Limburg and Brabant

The area around Roermond in the 'deep south' of Holland (about 50km south-east of Eindhoven and north of Maastricht in the province of Limburg) is populated by asparagus growers and other farmers who need people to harvest their crops of strawberries (June to mid-July), potatoes and other vegeta-bles, especially in the spring. The agencies around here are less accustomed to dealing with non-Dutch applicants but that doesn't mean that they won't try to be helpful.

Asparagus picking starts just after the middle of April and lasts through to mid-June. A tent is a great advantage here to be able to stay at campsites such as the one Murray Turner stayed at in Helden north of Roermond. Despite initial hopes that earnings would be high in the peak season, he ended up earning a modest wage based on piecework rates. He moved on to the strawberry harvest where earnings from piecework were unreliable because of the weather. The asparagus harvest is similarly affected by weather; if it's hot you can work as long as you are able.

Westland

The area between Rotterdam, the Hook of Holland and Den Haag is known as the Westland. The principal villages in the area are Naaldwijk, Westerlee, De Lier and Maasdijk, but the whole region is a honeycomb of greenhouses. The tomato harvest begins in early to mid-April and this is the best time to arrive, although work is generally available all year round if you are prepared to work for at least one month. Although the work is boring and dirty with long hours – it is not unusual for workers to start work at 5am and finish at 7pm or 8pm – conditions can be reasonable with barn accommodation provided.

Try *uitzendbureaux* in Naaldwijk, 's-Gravenzande and Poeldijk for work picking cucumbers, peppers, flowers, etc. Also try the flower and vegetable auctions (*bloemenveiling/groenteveiling*) in Westerlee/ De Lier and Honselersdijk which need people to load the stock for auction buyers, etc. Ian Govan's overtime pay (in cash) increased his basic earnings for a 38-hour week by about two-thirds.

TOURISM

Dutch hotels and other tourist establishments employ some foreigners, especially those with knowledge of more than one European language. A few tour operators such as Eurocamp (see Tourism chapter) with three sites in Holland employ some British young people as staff for the summer season, although competition is keen from young Dutch people who are generally such good linguists. The luxury camping holiday operator Vacansoleil whose head office is in Eindhoven hires entertainers, food and beverage staff and receptionists for Europe including Holland (www.campingjobs.co.uk).

In Adam Skuse's year off before university, he almost succeeded in finding hotel work but not quite:

> *I got a list of hotels online and then systematically emailed them all asking for a job. Most had no vacancies, a couple told me to call them when I was in Amsterdam, and one actually arranged an interview with me. But even the knockbacks were pleasant. Quite a few offered to buy me a drink anyway. Alas, I never managed to find the hotel in time, ran out of funds and am now back in Blighty.*

Although you may be lucky enough to obtain a hotel job through an *uitzendbureau*, your chances will normally be better if you visit hotels and ask if any work is available, or keep your ears open in pubs and hostels.

While visiting a friend in the seaside resort of Zaandvoort south of Haarlem, Martin and Shirine tried to find work washing dishes for one of the many bars which line the beach. They knew that without speaking Dutch this was the only job they could reasonably expect to get.

A range of boating holidays for leisure, business and school parties is managed by Naupar, which employs 300 crew and a catering team of 100 for its fleet of 140 traditional sailing boats such as Platbodems. Applicants must have knowledge of German as well as English.

OTHER WORK

Labouring work may be available in some of the massive docks of Rotterdam and Ijmuiden north of Haarlem. According to Shelly Harris's partner Terry, who got work straightaway unloading fishing boats, it's just a case of turning up at the offices on the docks early (about 5.30am) and asking for work. The money is good but the work is hard, cold and irregular. It used to take Terry two hours to thaw out in front of a fire after knocking off work about 3.30pm.

Teaching

Urban Dutch people have such a high degree of competence in English after they finish their schooling that there is not much of a market for basic EFL teaching. An increasing need for advanced levels of English within both companies and universities means that institutes are always on the lookout for qualified native speaker teachers. Language schools tend to look for people who have extensive commercial or government experience as well as a teaching qualification. For example UvA Talen in Amsterdam (trainers@uvatalen.nl) with links to the University of Amsterdam offers part-time assignments to registered and well-qualified freelancers, and Language Partners with offices in Amsterdam, The Hague, Rotterdam, Amersfoort, Zwolle, Breda and Nijmegen (www.languagepartners.nl) looks for experience in business-to-business training. Rates of pay start at around €27 per hour.

Amsterdam

As throughout the world, hostels employ people to clean, cook, do maintenance and night porter duties. Carolyn Edwards was not dissatisfied with the wage which was paid in addition to room and board since it was equivalent to what she had been earning as a temp in London (minus the food and accommodation). More usually, people work a few hours a day for free bed and breakfast but no wage.

Saffery Ruddock enjoyed this arrangement as a *Whapper* (willing helper at the Pig) at the Flying Pig hostel near the Vondelpark, though there are two other locations, one at the beach near Leiden (www.flyingpig.nl/aboutus/pigjobs.php). She exchanged 29 hours of work over five days cleaning, serving breakfast and doing odd jobs for a dorm bed, food and a *'brilliant atmosphere, busy, friendly and relaxed'*. Workers must be of European descent or hold a passport from an EU member country or a working holiday visa. The London parent company Beds and Bars recruits for these hostels as well as other brands including St Christopher's and Winston's Hostels in Amsterdam (www.bedsandbars.com/careers).

Justine Bakker recommended her workplace in Amsterdam as a *'great place for travellers because it hires a lot of international people, especially for promotion'*. Boom Chicago (www.boomchicago.nl) at Rozengracht describes itself as an 'English language comedy institution' and employs scores of people as cooks, waiters, bar staff, performers and for distributing promotional leaflets around Amsterdam.

One way to get very cheap accommodation if you are going to be staying some time in Amsterdam, Utrecht and other cities is to investigate anti-squatting agencies. Their remit is to protect vacant buildings and discourage squatters from moving in (which they are legally entitled to do after a building has been unoccupied for a year). One anti-kraak agency to try for cheap digs is www.bewaaktenbewoond.nl based in Amsterdam, which manages properties nationwide and does not require an introduction by someone already on their books. You will have to undertake to move out with little warning if required.

Busking is an ever-popular way to earn some money and the tolerance for which the Dutch are famous extends to street entertainers. The best venues are in the Vondelpark (where many Amsterdammers stroll on a Sunday) and in the city squares such as Stadsplein and Leidseplein. Some pitches (such as the one outside the 'smoking' coffee shop the Bulldog Palace) are in such demand that you may have to wait your turn. Regular buskers have their favourite pitches, so be cautious about muscling in.

'Proper' jobs may not be outside the reach of non-Dutch speakers with relevant experience, as Paul Jones from Australia discovered:

> *Having been working for a number of years at home in Australia and having transferable skills in IT, it made sense to find work in Europe in my field to finance my trip. Prior to leaving, I found a job by using the internet and having interviews over the phone. I still like the fact that I got my first job by having an interview on my mobile phone that was the clearest while standing on a city street that provided a nice drowning out kind of noise. Not the best conditions for an interview but it worked. The job happened to be in the Netherlands where I had never wanted to go but that was the job that I was accepted for first, so I took it as a stepping stone.*

Au Pairs

Since Dutch is not a language that attracts large numbers of students, au pairing in the Netherlands is not well known. Private agencies can place au pairs with Dutch or international families. Working conditions are favourable, with pocket money of €300–€340 per month, two days off a week and insurance and language class costs met by the host family. The minimum stay is one year unless you are from the EU or North America in which case you can stay for six months. The main agencies are reputed to offer solid back up, guidance on contacting fellow au pairs and advice on local courses and excursions.

The agency with the largest incoming au pair programme is Au Pair Nederland (part of Travel Active in Venray; (☎ (+31) 478 551910; www.aupair-nederland.nl) which places au pairs aged 18–30 with Dutch families as well as sending Dutch young people abroad on various work exchanges. The programme is free to incoming au pairs, although some cooperating agents abroad may charge a fee.

Jill Weseman from the States was very pleased with her au pair placement in a village of just 500 people 30km from Groningen:

> *After graduation I accepted an au pairing position in Holland, mainly because there is no prior language requirement here. I really lucked out and ended up with a family who has been great to me. Though the situation sounds difficult at best – four children aged one and a half, three, five and seven, one day off a week and a rather remote location in the very north of Holland – I have benefited a great deal. The social life is surprisingly good for such a rural area.*

Other agencies include Au Pair Interactive in Doorn (www.aupairinteractive.com), Au Pair Agency Mondial (www.aupairfamily.nl) whose au pairs mainly come from Russia, Ukraine, Argentina, Colombia and South Africa, and the House-o-Orange Au Pairs (☎ (+31) 70 324 5903; www.house-o-orange.nl) which has families in Belgium as well. These agencies all belong to the Dutch Au Pair Association, BONAPA (Branche Organisatie Nederlandse Au Pair Agentschappen; www.bonapa.nl).

Belgium

Belgium is a country that is often ignored. Sandwiched between France and the Netherlands, its population of 11.2 million can be broadly divided between the French-speaking people of Wallonia in the south (about 40% of the total population) and those who speak Flemish (which is almost identical to Dutch) in the north.

Belgium has no large agricultural industry comparable to those of its neighbours: it needs neither the extra fruit pickers that France does, nor the unskilled horticultural processors that Holland does. The unemployment rate has been gradually rising and now stands at 8.3%, unchanged for the past few years.

As in neighbouring Holland, employment legislation is strictly enforced in Belgium with favourable minimum wages, compulsory bonuses, sickness and holiday pay for all legal workers. The demand for temporary workers is especially strong in Belgium because of the generous redundancy regulations that discourage employers from hiring permanent staff. Of course the many multinational companies, attracted by the headquarters of the European Union in Brussels, have a constant and fluctuating demand for bilingual office and other workers.

REGULATIONS

As throughout the EU, Belgium requires foreign residents with European Union nationality to register with the local authorities. Within four months of your arrival you should take to your local Town Hall

(*Hôtel de Ville*, *Maison Communale* or *Gemeentehuis*) a valid passport from an EU member country and proof that you can fund your stay (by working, being self-employed, studying, supported by a spouse, etc). Some local authorities will also request photos, a housing contract, birth certificate and/ or European Health Insurance Card (EHIC).

Non-EU citizens will have to find an employer willing to apply for a work permit (*carte profession-nelle*) on their behalf from the Office National de l'Emploi. Assuming they want to stay longer than three months in paid employment, they must also be in possession before arrival in Belgium of a temporary residence permit (*Autorisation de Séjour Provisoire* or *Voorlopige Verblijfsvergunning*).

SEASONAL WORK

Although Belgium's seaside resorts such as Knokke-Heist, Blankenberge and De Panne, and other holiday centres such as Bouillon in the Ardennes are hardly household names, there is a sizeable tourist industry in Belgium where seasonal work is available. The more mainstream tourist centre of Bruges is very busy in the summer. Travellers have a chance of being given free accommodation in exchange for some duties at one of the city's private hostels such as St Christopher's Inn (info@bauhaus.be). Ski Ten International takes on French-speaking sports instructors (especially tennis) and English monitors to work at summer camps (☎ (+32) 81 213051; www.skiten.com).

The best way of finding short-term general work, apart from contacting possible employers directly, is to visit a branch of the Belgian employment service *Agences Locales pour l'Emploi* or ALEs. The T-Group (www.t-groep.be) registers temporary and other vacancies on behalf of several major recruit-ment agencies including T-Interim and Luba. Most jobs will require a good knowledge of at least one foreign language. For Brussels, a useful employment site in English can be found at www.be.brussels/working-and-doing-business.

AU PAIRS

As the capital of the European Union, Belgium has a high demand for au pairs. The government stipulates that au pairs be paid a generous €450 a month for 20 hours of work a week and €500 for au pairs plus (an au pair with experience or relevant qualifications). Non-EU au pairs are required to enrol in a language course; most study four to six hours a week. Most family positions are arranged over the internet via www.greataupair.com etc, though the House-o-Orange mentioned in the Netherlands chapter fills vacancies in Belgium too.

TEACHING

The casual EFL teacher will probably have trouble finding work in Belgium where there is a great deal of competition from highly qualified expatriates. Yet, despite the large number of well-qualified expat spouses and others who take up teaching, some schools are always recruiting, among them Call International in Brussels (www.callinter.com) which uses up to 150 freelance teachers. Almost all foreign teachers who begin to work for an institute do so on a freelance basis and will have to deal with their own tax and social security. The starting pay at most schools falls between €15 and €30 an hour.

Berlitz have several language centres in Belgium which employ a number of native English speakers with a university degree after they have done the compulsory Berlitz training and a trial teaching period of three months; contact Berlitz at Avenue Louise 306–310, 1050 Brussels; (joke.vandaele@berlitz.be). They pay €15 per lesson to freelancers.

Other organisations in Brussels to try if you have a TEFL background include Kiddy & Junior Classes asbl (☎ (+32) 2 218 3920; www.kiddyclasses.net), LC Language Centre in Brussels (www.lclanguage centre.com), and CLL (Centre de Langues) based in Louvain-la-Neuve which employs about 100 teachers to work on a freelance basis. Prolinguis runs language courses for children, teenagers and adults in remote countryside near Arlon in the province of Belgium called Luxembourg (6717 Thiaumont;

www.prolinguis.be). EFL-trained teachers are hired by Prolinguis on 12-month or two-month summer contracts and are paid €12.50–€14 an hour plus board and lodging on campus.

CONTACTS

The Federation Infor Jeunes Wallonie-Bruxelles is a non-profit making organisation which coordinates youth information offices in French-speaking Belgium (www.infor-jeunes.be). These can give advice on work as well as leisure, youth rights, accommodation, etc. The website of the Brussels branch has links to useful job info at www.inforjeunesbruxelles.be/emploi-chomage. Advising French speakers on temporary and holiday jobs is among Infor Jeunes' services.

Newcomer is a bi-annual publication which remains in print, though its sister English language monthly magazine *The Bulletin* ceased publication a few years ago in order to go entirely digital (www.xpats.com). *Newcomer* contains information and contact addresses of interest to the newly arrived teacher, including a listing of major language schools (look for it in newsagents).

VOLUNTARY OPPORTUNITIES

Young people interested in participating in residential archaeological digs in Namur lasting one to three weeks in the summer should contact Archeolo-j (www.archeolo-j.be). Residential archaeological digs accept paying volunteers, some for teenagers, some for adults. The fee is €665 for 15 days (2017).

Luxembourg

If Belgium is sometimes neglected, Luxembourg is completely by-passed. Yet it is an independent country with the highest per capita GDP in the world and an unemployment rate of 6.3%, no longer among the lowest in the EU. It is estimated that more than 40% of inhabitants are immigrants. One summer Felix Turner met a Spanish painter in his hostel who had come in search of work, who claimed that he could earn at least five times as much as he could at home.

The national employment service (Administration de l'Emploi or ADEM) at 10 rue Bender, L-1229 Luxembourg (www.adem.public.lu) operates a *Service Emploi des Jeunes* for students and young people looking for summer jobs in warehouses, restaurants, etc. To find out about possibilities, you must visit the office in the capital or in Esch Belval in person. Or it might be more fruitful, keeping your eyes and ears open in hostels.

With a total population of just over half a million and an area of 999 square miles, job opportunities are understandably limited. However, they do exist especially in the tourist industry for anyone who has mastered a European language in addition to English. While cycling through the countryside, Mary Hall was struck by the number of travellers working on campsites and in restaurants in Luxembourg City. Check an online directory of hotels such as www.hotels.lu for leads or the specialist job site www.hotelcareer.com/jobs/luxembourg.html where the five-star Hôtel le Royal in Luxembourg City may be advertising positions (recruitment@leroyalluxembourg.com).

The main language is Luxembourgish (variously called Luxembourgeois and Letzeburgesch) but both German and French are spoken and understood by virtually everyone. Casual workers will normally need a reasonable knowledge of at least one of these. Temporary office work abounds for linguists since many multinational companies are based in Luxembourg. Addresses of potential employers and recruitment firms can be obtained from the membership list of the British Chamber of Commerce in Luxembourg (www.bcc.lu). Temp agencies belonging to the association FES can be seen listed at www.fes.lu/fes/membres.

HELPFUL ORGANISATIONS

The Centre Information Jeunes (CIJ), 87, route de Thionville, L-2611 Luxembourg (☎ (+352) 26 293200; www.cij.lu) runs a holiday job service between January and August for students from the EU. Wages in Luxembourg are very high; the minimum for those over 23 is a massive €1,923 per month.

Officially Luxembourg does not recognise the special status of au pairs so they are treated like nannies, ie like all foreign workers, which means they must have a written contract of employment and pay social security contributions. Demand from families exists, so the best way is to browse through online childcare matching services such as www.aufini.com and www.findaupair.com.

France

Although you may occasionally encounter the legendary hostility of the French towards the English, more often you will be treated with warmth and helpfulness especially in the countryside. So many English-speaking people reside in France that expatriate grapevines and online communities are invaluable sources of job information. Yet economic woes and generous compulsory benefits are making it difficult for businesses to flourish in France. Unemployment is among the highest of the old EU countries, just a shade above the EU average of 9.8% (2016), and the rate among young people is more than two and a half times as high. It would be a mistake to expect to walk into a job just because you have a GCSE in French and enjoy eating *pains au chocolat*.

Although the French tourist industry offers many seasonal jobs, there are even more in agriculture: approximately 100,000 foreign workers are employed on the grape harvest alone. Workers come from all over, but mainly from eastern Europe and the Balkans, north Africa and southern Europe. You may find yourself working in the fields next to a student from Québec, an Albanian migrant worker or a young Dane or Scot who is touring Europe as a nomadic worker. It is possible to support yourself throughout the year in France by combining work in the various fruit harvests with either conventional jobs such as tutoring in English, or more unusual occupations from busking to gathering snails.

One important feature of working in France is that you should be paid at least the SMIC (*salaire minimum interprofessionel de croissance*) or national minimum wage. There are slightly different rates for seasonal agricultural work and full-time employees: at present the basic SMIC is €9.76 per hour or €1,480 per month (gross) based on a working week of 35 hours, the normally observed maximum in France. These are adjusted annually to take account of inflation.

REGULATIONS

Tax inspectors and immigration officers carry out spot checks in tourist resorts, and employers in even the most out of the way places have refused to hire anyone who lacks the right documents. Wine-makers in Bordeaux have been told that if they are caught employing non-EU citizens without papers, they will not be allowed to bring in their harvest the following year.

EU Citizens

As throughout the EU, citizens of EU member states do not need to obtain a residence permit, but only to register their address if they intend to stay for more than three months. Once you take up paid employment in France, your employer must complete all the necessary formalities for registering you with social security (*La Sécu*) at the local URSSAF office where you will be issued with a registration card and start to have contributions deducted from your wages. You will be asked to provide a certified and translated copy of your birth certificate, which it is wise to sort out before you leave home.

Currently, UK-registered companies employing European nationals on British contracts are expected to pay salaries into British bank accounts, and submit two months' worth of pay slips that show National Insurance and PAYE contributions in the UK. This enables the employer to apply for the A1 form from URSSAF confirming that their staff remain subject to UK social security legislation. EU legislation does not exempt the employer from paying posted workers the minimum wage of the country in which the employee is working.

Non-EU Formalities

Australians, New Zealanders, Canadians and some other nationalities under 30/35 are eligible for one-year working holiday visas for France. Non-EU citizens must obtain work documents before they leave their home country in order to work legally and this can be fiendishly difficult since it depends on finding an employer who can argue that no French or EU citizen could do the job. Non-Europeans must also register with the OFII (Office Français de l'Immigration et de l'Intégration) and pay the required fee.

A more manageable approach is to turn yourself into a student. French language students with a long-stay visa who are enrolled in an institution that registers its students with the national health insurance system have the right to work during their studies. The maximum number of hours worked in a year is 964, which equates to approximately 15–20 hours a week in term time and full-time in the vacations. In order to obtain a student visa, you will have to have good French language skills, two years of higher education (which may be waived if attending art college) and proof of financial support in the form of a notarised statement from a bank or benefactor that you can access enough per month to live on. Students based in Paris should apply at the Préfecture de Police at 92 Boulevard Ney in the 18th arrondissement.

Special Schemes for North Americans

Several youth exchange organisations administer a Work in France programme for higher education students over 18 or occasionally new graduates from outside Europe. Centre d'Echanges Internationaux (CEI) in Paris charges a fee for assisting with job and internship placements for candidates who are conversant in French. Details are available from CEI Paris (☎ (+33) 1 44 166250; workinfrance@cei4vents.com; www.cei-europe-tours.com). Another company, Aquarius (www.jobsandinternshipsabroad.com/jobs-france), also in Paris, charges €996 for an internship placement service in the tourist industry.

The long-established English Teaching Assistants programme places hundreds of undergraduates and graduates under 30 with a good working knowledge of French in schools around France; British applicants currently apply through the British Council (www.britishcouncil.org/language-assistants/become/france), North Americans should consult www.tapif.org and other nationalities should go to www.ciep.fr/assistants-etrangers-france. The programme runs from 1 October for seven to nine months, and the gross monthly stipend is €965 (around €794 net).

Americans who are interested in arranging an internship in France may contact the French–American Chamber of Commerce in New York, which oversees an International Career Development Program (☎ (+1) 212 867 0123; icdp@faccnyc.org). The programme is for students or graduates aged 18–35 with relevant experience. The Chamber can assist suitable candidates with arranging a visa lasting 3–18 months.

The French American Center in Montpellier (☎ (+33) 4 67 923066; www.frenchamericancenter.com) arranges au pair placements for Americans aged 18–25 with families in the Languedoc region plus internships in local businesses lasting up to three months. It also runs a local English language teaching programme for adults and young people.

Special exchange visas are available for students who are residents of Québec through the Association Québec-France (prog@quebecfrance.qc.ca). They can issue special work permits to cover the grape harvest or a summer job in youth hostels, holiday camps, etc for a paltry fee of C$750 including airfares.

THE JOB-HUNT

Potentially useful websites include www.angloinfo.com/france which has reams of practical information and classified adverts specific to 20 regions, while the monster recruitment search engine www. indeed.fr may help. As usual the *Yellow Pages* are available online (www.pagesjaunes.fr) which can prove a great help when drawing up a list of relevant places to ask for work.

Once you get into the countryside, the French can be remarkably generous not only in offering lifts but in helping their passengers to find work. If you are offered seasonal work ahead of the start date and plan to leave the area in the meantime, stay in constant touch with the employer; not only can start dates vary but farmers and hotel managers don't always keep their promises.

Pôle Emploi (Jobcentre)

Jobcentres in France are known as Pôle emploi (www.pole-emploi.fr). The national employment service of France has dozens of offices in Paris and hundreds throughout the country. The website lists all the branches by region or postcode and for those who can navigate in French carries lots of valuable info about jobs favoured by working holidaymakers, eg try searching for *vendangeur* if you want tips on how to get a grape-picking job. For example the Pôle in Narbonne will have seasonal hotel vacancies from May to September, and others can provide details of when agricultural work is available. Although EU citizens should have equal access to the employment facilities in other member states, this is not always the case in France unless the jobseeker speaks good French and has a stable local address. If possible foreign jobseekers should work with a EURES Adviser.

Seasonal employment offices are set up in key regions to deal with seasonal demands such as the *vendanges* for the grape harvest and in ski resorts.

CRIJ

There are 27 regional Centres Régionals d'Information Jeunesse (CRIJ) and hundreds of smaller youth information points in France that may be of use to the working traveller. Helping people to find jobs is only one of their activities: they can also advise on cheap accommodation, the legal rights of temporary workers, etc. They publish a 24-page booklet *Jobs d'été et petits boulots* which is free online (www. informationjeunesse-centre.fr/portail/uploads/Guides/Guide_Jobs.pdf). The national centre in Paris is CIDJ (Centre d'Information et de Documentation Jeunesse), whose foyer noticeboard is a useful starting place for the jobseeker in Paris. CIDJ may be visited at 101 Quai Branly, 75740 Paris Cedex 15 (☎ (+33) 1 44 491200; www.cidj.com); it opens 1–6pm Tuesdays to Saturdays. Employers sometimes notify centres of their temporary vacancies; some offices just display the details on noticeboards, while others operate a more formal system in cooperation with the local employment office (eg, CIDJ in Paris registers hundreds of summer jobs).

Private Employment Agencies

Agences de travail temporaire (temporary work bureaux) or *agences d'intérim* may be of some use. Among the largest are Manpower (www.manpower.fr) and Adecco (www.adecco.fr); others can be found in the *Yellow Pages* under the heading *Travail Intérimaire* or from the Franco-British Chamber of Commerce in Paris (☎ (+33) 1 53 308130; www.francobritishchamber.com). Almost all will require good French, and many specialise in a field such as industrial, medical or office work. Although vacancies for unskilled jobs are few and far between, some travellers have made good use of agencies.

TOURISM

The best areas to look for work in the tourist industry of France are the Alps for the winter season, December–April, and the Côte d'Azur for the summer season, June–September, though jobs exist throughout the country. The least stressful course is to fix up work ahead of time with a UK campsite or barge holiday company in summer or ski company in winter. For example the giant TUI Travel plc (www.tuijobsuk.co.uk) hires people, not necessarily with qualifications, to work in many regions of France. Esprit Holidays is one among many that recruits for both the summer and winter seasons (www.workaseason.com).

Eurolingua offers a Hotel Internship programme in the south of France lasting three to six months to students who are already connected to the hospitality sector (non-EU as well as EU). The work is paid and comes with free staff accommodation and meals in the hotel. The programme is preceded by an appropriate French for Tourism course in Montpellier; details at www.eurolingua.com/hotel-internships/France. The combined programme fee is €1,550.

If you set off without anything pre-arranged, one of the easiest places to find work is at fast food establishments such as Pizza Hut France (http://restaurant.pizzahut.fr/recrutements) or Quick fast food hamburger restaurants (number two in France); the latter employs 10,000 people in France and is chronically short of workers. Americana continues to be trendy in France and English-speaking staff fit well with the image. The hardest place to find work is with reputable French-owned hotels and restaurants, where high standards are maintained. Your best chances will be in small family-run hotels where the hours and conditions vary according to the temperament of the *patron*.

Hotels and Restaurants

The vast majority of restaurants are staffed by waiters rather than waitresses. Newspapers in holiday towns may carry adverts, eg *Nice Matin* (http://emploi.nicematin.com). But most people succeed by turning up at a resort and asking door-to-door and, in the opinion of veteran British traveller Jason Davies, 'door-to-door' should be just that:

> Before I was down to my last few coins I had been choosy about which establishments to ask at. 'That doesn't look very nice' or 'that's too posh' or 'that's probably closed' were all thoughts that ensured that I walked past at least three in five. But in Nice I discovered that the only way to do it is to pick a main street (like the pedestrianised area in Nice with its high density of restaurants) and ask at EVERY SINGLE place. I visited 30–40 one morning and I would say that at least 20 of those needed more employees. But only one was satisfied with my standard of French, and I got the job of commis waiter.

Speaking French to a reasonable standard greatly improves chances of finding a job, though fluency is by no means a requirement. Kimberly Ladone from the American east coast spent a summer working as a receptionist/chambermaid, also in Nice:

> I found the job in April, at the first hotel I approached, and promised to return at the start of the season in June. While there, I met many English-speaking working travellers employed in various hotels. No-one seemed bothered by work permit regulations as most jobs paid cash in hand. My advice to anyone seeking a job on the French Riviera would be to go as early in the season as possible and ask at hotels featured in English guidebooks such as Let's Go: France, since these tend to need English-speaking staff. My boss hired me primarily because I could handle the summer influx of clueless tourists who need help with everything from making a phone call to reading a train schedule.

It must be said that not everyone finds work easily, as Alison Cooper found: *'Last summer I tried to find work along the French Riviera, but was unsuccessful. I met many people at campsites who were in the same position as myself. From my experience most employers wanted people who could speak fluent French, and German as well. Otherwise you have to be very very lucky.'*

The best time to look for work on the Côte d'Azur is the end of February when campsites well known to working travellers, such as Les Prairies de la Mer and Camping de la Plage at Port Grimaud near St Tropez host representatives from camping holiday companies trying to get organised in time for Easter. If you are on the spot you can often wangle free accommodation in exchange for three or four hours of work a day. If you can't be there then, try the middle of May at the beginning of the peak season. When Ben Butler and Emma Johns couldn't find work on boats in Antibes in September 2016 as they had hoped, because many of the boats had already left, they were befriended by a French neighbour in Cagnes who wanted to help them find work cleaning or in a bar or restaurant which would have been possible, but they decided to cut their losses and return to England.

Campsites

An estimated 7,000 campsites in France employ an army of seasonal staff even though some of them are small family-run operations that need one or two assistants. You can make direct contact with individual campsites listed online at www.campingfrance.com/UK or in a printed guide to French campsites such as Michelin's annual *Camping France*. As is typical for France, recruitment information is usually only in French, as with the company Yelloh (www.yellohvillagejobs.com) which has a network of upmarket campsites throughout the country. The alternative is to show up and look for a job on the spot. Jobs are not glamorous, such as cleaning the loos, manning the bar or snack bar, doing some maintenance, etc. Even if there are no actual jobs, you may be given the use of a tent in exchange for minimal duties, outside the peak season.

A number of British-based travel companies offer holidaymakers a complete package providing pre-assembled tents and a campsite courier to look after any problems that arise. Since this kind of holiday appeals to families, people with a childcare background or who can organise children's activities are especially in demand. In addition to the Europe-wide companies such as Eurocamp and Vacansoleil (addresses in Tourism chapter), the following all take on campsite reps/couriers and other seasonal staff:

Carisma Holidays: ☎ (+44) 1923 284235; www.carismaholidayjobs.co.uk.
Matthews Holidays: East Horsley, Surrey; ☎ (+44) 1483 284044; www.matthewsfrance.co.uk/jobswithus.html. £200 per week less £50 for mobile home accommodation provided; positions in Brittany and the Vendée.
Venue Holidays: Ashford, Kent; ☎ (+44) 1233 629950; jobs@venueholidays.co.uk; www.venueholidays.com/UK/work_for_us. 10 campsites around the edges of France.

The best time to start looking for summer season jobs from England is between November and February. In most cases candidates are expected to have at least A level standard French, though some companies claim that knowledge of French is merely 'preferred'. It is amazing how far a good dictionary and a knack for making polite noises in French can get you. Many impose a minimum age of 21.

The massive camping holiday industry generates winter work as well. Brad Europe Ltd has depots in Nantes, Beaucaire and Albertville that clean and repair tents and bedding on behalf of many of the major companies. Staff (who need not speak French though it is an advantage) are needed for the laundry and distribution for three to six months in winter and summer. Gite accommodation is provided free of charge in addition to the UK minimum wage. A driving licence is essential for the delivery drivers but not for the laundry operatives. Brad Europe's UK office is in Wigan (☎ (+44) 1942 829747; info@bradeurope.com; www.bradeurope.com).

Short bursts of work are available in the spring (about three weeks in May) and autumn (three weeks in September) to teams of people who put up and take down the tents at campsites, known as *montage* and *démontage*. For example the Dutch company Vacansoleil takes on English-speaking people to work in small international teams between March and May and again in September/October to set up and then break down and store tents for the following season (www.campingjobs.co.uk).

Holiday Centres

Siblu Villages (www.siblu.com/jobs) need reps and children's staff to work at mobile home and tent parks, and at adventure centres from early May to the end of September. Siblu has 17 villages across France: in Brittany and Normandy, the Loire Valley, Charente, Maritime and Vendée, Aquitaine, Languedoc, and Côte d'Azur. The company recruits separately for its entertainment programmes at www.siblu-entertainment.com.

Outdoor activity centres are another major employer of summer staff, both general domestic staff and sports instructors. Try the companies mentioned in the chapter on Tourism such as PGL and Acorn Adventure (www.acornadventure.co.uk/jobs). Manor Adventure based in Shropshire (☎ (+44) 1584 862126; www.manoradventurejobs.com) hires holiday coordinators and sports instructors for its adventure centre Le Chateau du Broutel along the coast from Boulogne and for another in Somme. Travelbound is one of hundreds of TUI's brands, and hires staff for a holiday centre in Normandy, Chateau du Molay; hiring is done through partner recruiter www.getupandgojobs.com. After one season with a TUI brand, it is easy to move to other jobs within the company.

Camps for French school children whose parents want them to be exposed to English in a fun environment are run by several companies. The American model of the summer camp thrives in France and dozens of camps have a strong ESL component. Anglophone counsellors and tutors are employed, many of them from the US staying for less than 90 days on a Schengen visa. One of the biggest companies is American Village (www.job-americanvillage.fr) which hires 200 language counsellors for English-immersion residential camps in six locations in France, attended by children aged 6–17. The monthly salary in 2016 was €770 (less 11% for deductions) in addition to board and lodging. Site transfers to different camps provide a change of scene. Christine Smith from the US reports that her days at camp started around 8.30am and finished any time up to midnight:

It is a long day and you need energy, but a lot of the work is fun, if you enjoy playing games and doing crafts and being silly. etc. We did lots of games and songs and not a lot of worksheets. One nice thing about this job is that if you are new to teaching, you get to have a new group of kids every week or two weeks. If you really don't like one group of kids, or if you really mess up and don't bond with the kids, you get to change kids! The attitudes of the pupils range from extremely enthusiastic to 'I'm only here because my parents made me come and I hate them for it.' It is a crash course in teaching.

Christine goes on to describe the rewards of spending the summer in France (or six summers in her case): *'Camp is a place that you can form very deep bonds with other people. There are times sitting at a fire cooking marshmallows when you can be completely free and open about life. Also, you share with the other counsellors many first time experiences – first time eating some strange food, first time hitchhiking, etc.'*

Keen cyclists could seek work with a cycling holiday company active in France such as BSpoke Tours (www.bspoketours.com/work-for-bspoke) and its affiliate company Cycling for Softies (www.cycling-for-softies.co.uk) whose staff must speak French and have clean driving licences. Headwater Holidays in Cheshire (www.headwater.com/all/work) looks to hire French-speaking reps who spend about 40% of their time driving a minibus and are prepared to be trained in bicycle maintenance. The basic rep wage starts at £120–£140 a week. One other to try is Belle France in Kent (www.bellefrance.co.uk).

For work in a more unusual activity holiday, contact the hot air balloon company Montgolfière-Evasion based in a village near Troyes (contact@montgolfiere-evasion.com). Ground crew who can speak French are hired for the summer season May to October and must have physical fitness and strength, a cheerful personality and a trailer driving licence.

Ski Resorts

France is the best of all countries in Europe for British and Irish people to find jobs in ski resorts, mainly because it is the number one country for British skiers, 200,000 of whom go there every year. Most of the resorts are high enough to create reliable snow conditions throughout the season. The main problem is the shortage of worker accommodation; unless you find a live-in job you will have to pay nearly holiday prices or find a friend willing to rent out his or her sofa. Since many top French resorts are purpose-built, a high proportion of the holiday accommodation is in self-catering flats or designed for chalet parties. This means that not only is there a shortage of rental accommodation, but there are fewer jobs as waiters, bar and chamber staff for those who arrive in the resorts to look for work. There are an increasing number of English and Irish style pubs which are good places to find out about work.

If you are employed by a British tour operator, be aware that you will not be paid according to French employment law and your employer will be exempt from paying the very high social charges. The French authorities have estimated that 10,000 staff are employed to work for ski chalet companies and all of them are being paid less than the SMIC, even factoring in accommodation and lift passes, although technically the SMIC should pertain. Note that every winter, stories emerge of British workers, especially ski instructors, guides and hosts, being persecuted by the French police.

Excellent ski recruitment websites include www.jobs.natives.co.uk and www.seasonworkers.com, which post current vacancies and profile the main alpine operators. Up to 30 British tour companies are present in Méribel alone, so this is one of the best resorts in which to conduct a job-hunt. It may even be worth calling into the tourist office to ask about seasonal employment, though it is more promising to ask for work in person at hotels, bars, etc. Looking for work out of season in October and November has the added advantage that well-placed youth hostels such as the one in Séez les Arcs are empty and relatively cheap.

Resorts such as Méribel are flooded with British workers just before the season and eventually by British guests, many of them school groups. The functioning language of many establishments is English. British chalet operators have also established a strong presence in Courchevel; at least one UK tour operator has its French office in the picturesque village of Le Praz, one of the five villages that comprise the resort of Courchevel. If you are not already familiar with the resorts, try to do some research beforehand, something Susan Beney regretted not doing: *'We took pot luck with the resort and on reflection should have done a bit more homework on resorts we might have preferred. La Tania was very limited; La Plagne would have been 100% better.'*

Most jobs with British companies pay low wages but allow workers to ski or snowboard between 10am and 4pm. UK operators that recruit staff for Méribel and France generally include the following:

Alp Leisure Ltd: Courchevel, France; ☎ (+33) 4 79005942; recruit@alpleisure.com; www.alpleisure.com/recruitment.htm. Hosts for luxury chalets in Courchevel and Méribel, and other roles.

Esprit Holidays/Ski Total: Godalming, Surrey; ☎ (+44) 1483 791010; recruitment@workaseason.com; www.workaseason.com.

Family Ski Company: Malvern, Worcestershire; ☎ (+44) 1684 540333; www.familyski.co.uk/recruitment. Offer many jobs in the French Alps.

Inghams: also recruit via www.workaseason.com.

Le Ski: Huddersfield, West Yorkshire; ☎ (+44) 1484 548996; recruitment@leski.com; www.leski.com/ski-jobs. Jobs in Courchevel, La Tania and Val d'Isère.

Meriski: Cirencester, Gloucestershire; ☎ (+44) 1285 648518; www.meriski.co.uk/jobs. Chalet cooks and nannies in greatest demand.

Scott Dunn: London SW6; http//jobs.scottdunn.com. Summer season jobs also.

Ski Beat: Brighton; jobs@skibeat.co.uk; www.skibeat.co.uk/cms/ski-jobs. Jobs in La Plagne, Les Arcs, Tignes, Val d'Isère, La Tania and several others.

Ski Olympic: Doncaster, South Yorkshire; ☎ (+44) 1302 328820; www.skiolympicjobs.com. Full range of chalet jobs in Courchevel, Méribel, Les Arcs, La Plagne and La Rosière.

Supertravel Ski: London SE1; www.supertravel.co.uk/ski/seasonaljobs.aspx. Takes on winter staff for Courchevel, Val d'Isère, Méribel and Val Thorens, primarily chalet chefs, chalet hosts with excellent cooking skills, chalet assistants with customer service skills, chalet managers fluent in French, and handymen/drivers; all applicants must hold a passport from an EU member country and have a National Insurance number.

Qualified/experienced nannies are often sought after in ski resorts. Specialist nanny agencies supply nannies to skiing families, for example Merinannies (www.merinannies.com) offer professional private nannies in Méribel, Courchevel, Chamonix, Megève and La Clusaz, and Cheeky Monkeys (www.cheekymonkeysmorzine.com) cover the Portes du Soleil area. Nannies must have a childcare qualification and be DBS-checked. Matt Tomlinson, who spent a year near Paris as an au pair, spent the winter season in Courchevel:

> I'm not sure if I just lucked out getting work or whether it is a question of having done most jobs, being presentable and enthusiastic. There certainly doesn't seem to be any shortage of employment opportunities in Courchevel and Le Praz during the busy periods. My first job was as a private nanny: easy work, good pay plus extra for babysitting. I moved on to doing Children's Club with one operator and then Snow Club with Ski Esprit. Not everyone was NNEB qualified though all had substantial childcare experience and most were hired in England. I would recommend anyone thinking of doing a nanny job in the Alps to think seriously before taking it on. The days were very long and tiring, especially when you have to keep track of 18 sets of ski gear.

Success is far from guaranteed in any on-the-ground ski resort job-hunt and competition for work is increasing. Val d'Isère attracts scores of ski bums every November/December, many of whom hang around bars or the employment office for days in the hope that work will come their way.

Yachts

Kevin Gorringe headed for the south of France in June with the intention of finding work on a private yacht. His destination was the British favourite of Antibes, where he began frequenting likely meeting places such as La Gaffe English pub and the Irish bar as well as the agencies such as Blue Water. Links to crewing agencies can be found in the directory at www.angloinfo.com/riviera, including the long-established Peter Insull's agency in La Galerie du Port, 8 Blvd d'Aguillon, 06600 Antibes.

Kevin recommends staying at one of the cheap campsites at Biot on the other side of Antibes, which is easily reached by public transport. Alternatively there are several crew houses such as the Crew Grapevine (www.crewgrapevine.com) located a minute away from Port Vauban Marina, though this is expensive at €37.50 a night. Others in Antibes include Debbie's Crewhouse (www.debbies crewhouse.co) and The Glamorgan Crewhouse (www.theglamorgan.com). These places are goldmines of information.

Ben Butler and his girlfriend went round the quays of Antibes and all marinas within a generous radius asking for work in August and September 2016. See the chapter *Working a Passage* to see how they fared. To find work in Antibes you have to be persistent, focused, personable and lucky.

Look tidy and neat, be polite and when you get a day's work, work hard, for example if hired to help refit a yacht in preparation for the charter season. The first job is the hardest to get, but once you get in with this integrated community, captains will help you find other jobs after the refitting is finished. Of course many continue through the summer as deckhands on charter yachts and are paid a wage plus a share of the tips (which often exceed the wage). The charter season lasts until late September by which time yachts have organised their crew for the trip to Fort Lauderdale and thence to the Caribbean.

A British tour company that hires instructors, reps, chefs and entertainers for its three sailing holiday centres in South-west France is Rockley Watersports based in Poole (☎ (+44) 1202 677272; www.rockley.org/about/join-the-team). Try also Club Correze near Meymac in the Massif Central region of Southern France (www.clubcorreze.com/site/recruitment) whose owners recruit watersports and multi-activity instructors as well as domestic staff for the season.

Barges

The holiday barges that ply the rivers and canals of France hire cooks, hostesses, deckhands and captains. The best time to apply to the companies is in the New Year. All prefer to employ only people who feel comfortable functioning in French even if the majority of their clientele is American or British.

European Waterways with an office in Berkshire (☎ (+44) 1753 598555; www.gobarging.com/vacancies) employs seasonal staff for its hotel barges in Europe. The season lasts from April to October and vacancies exist for barge pilots, chefs, deckhand mechanics, tour guides and hosts/hostesses for the luxury barge fleet. All applicants must have a passport from an EU member country (or the right to work in the UK), a current driving licence, and some knowledge of French culture and language. Positions include on-board accommodation, meals and uniform as well as a salary from £180 a week.

GRAPE PICKING

Every year the lure of the *vendange* attracts many hopefuls, whether for financial gain or the romance of participating in an ancient ritual. Past participants agree about the negative aspects of the job: the eight to 10 hours a day of back-breaking work, often for seven days a week, and the weather, which is too cold and damp in the early autumn mornings and too hot at midday. Waterproofs are essential because you will be expected to continue picking in the pouring rain and mud. The accommodation may consist of a space in a barn for a sleeping bag, and the sanitation arrangements of a cold-water tap. But despite all this, every year the grape-growing regions of France are flooded with jobseekers.

Part of the attraction is the wage. Although it is just the minimum of €9.76 (*le SMIC*) for pickers (though porters sometimes earn a little more, especially when the vineyards are located on steep hills), there is little opportunity to spend your earnings on an isolated farm and most people save several hundred pounds during a typical fortnight-long harvest. Anna Ling joined the *vendange* in Epernay a couple of years ago, and after working 10 straight days for eight hours a day, earned a lump sum in cash of €800. However many people manage to clear less than that, on average €55–€60 a day.

If you work for the same *patron* for seven consecutive days, you should be paid an overtime rate. Be prepared for at least 15% to be deducted for social security.

A major continuing threat to jobs comes from mechanisation. In some regions such as Cognac and south of Bordeaux, great noisy juggernauts harvest day and night, and have almost completely replaced human beings. However, in other cases as in Champagne, Beaujolais and Alsace, grapes must be picked by hand to qualify for the Appellation d'Origine Contrôlée (AOC) seal of approval, which guarantees that hand-pickers will be needed in large numbers for the forseeable future. An estimated 100,000 grape pickers are still taken on each year, making the *vendange* by far the largest employer of casual labour in France.

Work and Conditions

Working and living conditions can vary greatly from farm to farm. Obviously it is easier for the owner of a small vineyard with a handful of workers to provide decent accommodation than for the owner of a château who may have over 100 workers to consider. Farmers almost always provide some sort of accommodation, but this can vary from a rough and ready dormitory to a comfortable room in his own house. Food is normally provided, but again this can vary from the barely adequate to the sublime: one picker can write that *'the food was better than that in a five-star hotel, so we bought flowers for the cook at the end of the harvest'*, while another may complain of instant mashed potatoes or of having to depend on whatever he or she can manage to buy and prepare. When both food and accommodation are provided there is normally a deduction of one or two hours' pay from each day's wage.

Free wine is a frequent feature of the job, for example Dustie Hickey was allowed a seemingly endless supply of wine, which *'lifted up the workers' spirits but often left me falling into the bushes'*. (When she was offered the same perk during the olive harvest later in the autumn, she wisely sold her daily two litres of wine.) Eddy Van de Werken's motivation for joining the *vendange* (as he arranged to do several times) was not merely financial:

> *I'm a wine lover and I read a lot about the winemaking process. I wanted to experience more of the things that are done before the wine is bought in my local store. Winemaking is complex and requires a*

lot of equipment, knowledge and time. So grape picking was the easiest way to get near to the process and also give me the opportunity to participate in the production process.

My French is not good enough to arrange all the issues by myself so I signed up with the agency www. apcon.nl [see below] who arranged a job in Fleurie near Macon for eight straight days. All the workers were gathered in a barn at 6.45am and then loaded into a trailer to be transported to the vineyard. For the cutting the grapes you could choose a special knife or scissors. We worked from 7am till 12 and from 1.30 till 6pm, 10 hours a day. Working this way was physically heavy. The first days most of the people needed pain killers against the muscle pain. But working with other people in a field, with beautiful sights, nice conversations and the sun shining on your body compensates a lot.

The farmer had two barns (one for men, one women) where basic beds were placed. Simple showers and toilets were provided. Not luxury, but enough to sleep and wash. It is a nice experience. You learn local traditions and work attitudes, eat local food and drinks, and meet a lot of international people aged 20–55. It is quite relaxing for your mind. After the vendange this year, I will travel further south and use the money to buy wine for a couple of years for my own usage (and as presents for friends).

Hours can vary. Whereas one traveller found the structuring of the working day ridiculous, with an hour and a half lunch break and no other breaks between 7am and 6pm, others have found themselves finishing the day's picking at lunchtime, especially in the far south near the Spanish border, where the sun is unbearably hot in the afternoon.

The work itself will consist of either picking or portering. Picking involves bending to cut the grapes with secateurs or a mini scythe-like tool from a vine that may be only three and a half feet tall, and filling a pannier that you drag along behind you. Gloves are useful if you don't want your hands stained by grape juice (white grapes are the worst) and rubber boots are the footwear of choice. The panniers full of grapes are emptied into a *hotte*, a large basket weighing up to 100lb which the porters carry to a trailer. The first few days as a *cueilleur/cueilleuse* or *coupeur* (picker) are the worst, as you adjust to the stooping posture and begin to use muscles you never knew you had. The job of porter is sought after, since it does not require the constant bending and is less boring because you move around the vineyard. The further south you go the more likely you are to find yourself competing with migrant workers from Spain, Portugal and North Africa. Large and famous châteaux (such as Lafite) often use a contracted team of pickers who return every season and who can stand the fast and furious pace. These immigrant workers tend to return to the same large vineyards year after year, where they work in highly efficient teams, which are normally preferred to individual travellers.

How to Find Work

Provided you are prepared to disregard their advice if it is discouraging, the local Pôle in a wine-growing region is worth visiting in case they are able and willing to tell you which farmers need workers. As mentioned they are not usually helpful unless you speak good French. But if you can navigate a computer in French, you can conduct a DIY job-hunt and print out relevant numbers to phone. One traveller who was informed *'C'est complet'* by the Pôle (then called the ANPE) in Saumur, the tourist office, a *maison de vin* and a private employment agency, decided to persevere and, after a 10-mile walk east along the Loire, found a job.

When Michael Jordan was looking for grape-picking work in Alsace, he noticed that every *mairie* (town hall) had a poster up advising jobseekers to present themselves to the employment office in Colmar. According to the local winegrowers' syndicate, L'Association des Viticulteurs d'Alsace, the harvest generates thousands of jobs in Alsace lasting two to three weeks. Alsace Vendanges is a seasonal service in Colmar, Guebwiller, Molsheim and Sélestat which you can contact by phone on ☎ (+33) 3 89 208070 from when they launch their campaign to match workers with growers, usually at the end of August. The jobs that tend to go unfilled are for people with their own accommodation (tent, caravan) and their own transport. Because of its more northerly location and because some late-picked varieties are grown, the latter part of the Alsace harvest can be cold, which puts some potential competition off.

Below are listed some major wine-producing regions, with rough guidelines as to the starting dates of the harvest. It should be stressed that these dates can vary by days or even weeks from year to year. After a very hot summer, the harvest can start a full month early. Even vineyards a few miles apart may start picking up to a week apart.

Alsace: 15 September, harvest of late varietals finishes at end of October; *Pôle emploi* offices in Colmar, Strasbourg and many others.

Beaujolais: 10 September; *Pôle emploi* in Villefranche-sur-Saone.

Bordeaux: 25 September; *Pôle emploi* in Bordeaux and Pauillac.

Burgundy: 6 October; *Pôle emploi* in Mâcon and Dijon.

Champagne: 1 October; *Pôle emploi* in Reims and Epernay.

Languedoc-Roussillon: 15 September; *Pôle emploi* in Perpignan, Carcassonne, Nimes, Bagnols sur Cèze, Beziers, etc.

Loire: 6 October; *Pôle emploi* in Tours and Angers.

For those who do not want to go it alone, there is an easier way. A Dutch agency called Appellation Contrôllée (☎ (+31) 50 549 2435; info@apcon.nl; www.apcon.nl) mediates between grape-growers (in Beaujolais north of Lyon, Burgundy, Chablis and Champagne) and up to 500 Europeans looking for jobs in the *vendange*. Work lasts between one and three weeks in September/October. In exchange for working at least eight hours a day, seven days a week you will earn a net wage of €57 a day in addition to full board and lodging. The ApCon agency fee is €99 and they have a good website and message board. Participants must be flexible enough not to know until early September when the start date will be.

After signing up with ApCon, Thibaut Exelmans from Belgium was set up with a grape-picking job in Beaujolais. He had no trouble identifying the good and bad aspects of his experience:

> *My first experience with travelling abroad was as a vendangeur in the Beaujolais region in France. As recommended in your book I contacted the Dutch organisaton Apcon to arrange a job as grape picker. It has been a fantastic experience in terms of meeting people, social contact while working and integrating in the very local community. On the other hand it was fiscally very hard and the weather conditions were often unfavourable; rain or no rain, the job needed to be done.*
>
> *Financially I didn't come home with much profit after deduction of the Apcon fee and the costs charged by the farmer for food and stay. Furthermore the farmer insisted on paying us with paper cheques which, as we found out later, could only be cashed in our own banks. And to make it even worse a fee had to be paid for cashing the cheques. All in all it was a great experience but if I would ever do it again I would try to get work directly through a farmer to avoid fees, and I'd ask about the way of payment before starting.*

Danielle Thomas who also picked grapes through Apcon listed a few practical tips for the benefit of future grape pickers: bring waterproof clothing and Wellingtons, as the weather may change at any moment. Also, bring rubber washing-up gloves (not cloth gloves), since in the mornings the grapes are wet and your hands get very wet. Hand cream is also a good idea. And most importantly do not expect the French to be able to speak English, so bring a phrase book.

Tom Alber was too late in contacting ApCon for the harvest but decided to go to France in any case at the beginning of September. He went to Nice and ended up helping out at a hostel whose owner did his best to find Tom a spot on a picking team but without success.

The demand for pickers in all regions is highly unpredictable. Whereas there is usually a glut of pickers looking for work at the beginning of the harvest (early to mid-September), there is sometimes a shortage later on. Harvests differ dramatically from year to year; a late spring frost can wreak havoc. The element of uncertainty makes it very difficult to fix a starting date from afar.

Experienced grape pickers recommend visiting or phoning farms well before the harvest starts and asking the farmer to keep a job open. According to Jon Loop the key to success is serial phoning: *'The best time to phone is July. Then phone in August to ask when to phone for starting dates. Then phone in September to say you are coming, to ask when it starts. You may also have to phone a week before the start to confirm.'*

OTHER HARVESTS

Although the *vendange* may produce the highest concentration of seasonal work, numerous opportunities for participating in other harvests can be tracked down and with potentially less competition for the available work. While increasing mechanisation threatens the future of grape picking by hand, there are not yet any machines that can cope with apples, plums and peaches.

When researching options, it will be very advantageous to speak and read French. For example the Association Nationale Emploi Formation en Agriculture (www.anefa.org/emplois-saisonniers) produces superb information for seasonal workers, searchable by harvest with the relevant telephone numbers and email addresses of employment offices with vacancies and addresses of *maisons de l'agriculture*.

France is an overwhelmingly rural country. The *départements* of Hérault, Drôme and Gers are among the most prolific fruit and vegetable producers, especially of plums, cherries, strawberries and apples. Crops ripen first in the south of the country, and first at lower altitudes, so it is difficult to generalise about starting dates. For example the strawberry harvest on the coastal plain around Beziers normally takes place between mid-May and late June, whereas 60km inland in the Haut Languedoc near Sauclieres, it starts in mid-July. Cherries and strawberries are the first harvests, normally taking place between May and July. Blueberries are picked throughout July and August. Peaches are picked from June after the trees have been pruned, while pears are picked throughout the summer but especially (like apples) from mid-September to mid-October. Apples are grown throughout France including in Normandy. Maize is a crop that needs 'castrating' in the summer which means picking off the flowers of the male maize plants, called *l'écimage*. A recent internet search revealed that the Centre Sem in Reignac-sur-Indre was inviting applications in the spring for a few weeks work from mid July.

THE BELGIAN TRAVELLER VINCENT CROMBEZ WROTE FROM THE VILLAGE OF MONTIERAL-LEMONT (BETWEEN GAP AND SISTERON) TO RECOMMEND THIS AREA OF THE HAUTES-ALPES SOUTH OF GRENOBLE:

Apple picking starts about the 1 September and lasts until the end of October. I was paid the SMIC and worked nine or 10 hours every day except Sunday. It's no problem to save £400+ a month if you don't go to the only pub in this wonderful village every day. Now I'm back here for the apple-thinning. I'm working nine hours a day, but it's easy, always sunny and I will save £800 for the two months.

After landing a job in the *vendange* with her first phone call to a proprietor in Champagne, Anna Ling's luck ran out when trying to follow up with an apple-picking job. She and her boyfriend followed up every imaginable lead but were led on a wild and unproductive goose chase. Apple growers all seemed to want relevant experience, certainly for the months of pruning following the harvest.

Harvest work is paid either hourly (normally *le SMIC*) or by piece rates. If you are floundering with piecework, you may be transferred to a different job where you can earn an hourly wage. It is normally up to workers to provide their own food and accommodation, and so a tent and camping equipment are essential. If a farmer does provide board and lodging he will normally deduct the equivalent of two hours' wages from your daily pay packet. If you are planning to leave as soon as the harvest is over, bear in mind that agricultural wages are often not paid until seven to 10 days after the harvest finishes (to ensure workers do not leave prematurely). Furthermore the wages may have to be cashed at a local bank, so be prepared to hang around.

The Loire Valley

Strawberries, apples, pears and many other crops can be found along the River Loire: the towns of Segré, Angers and Saumur are especially recommended. For example the strawberry harvest around Varennes-sur-Loire lasts six to eight weeks from early/mid April.

Two unusual crops are grown round Saumur, both of which are picked from the beginning of June, mushrooms and blueberries or bilberries. While working on a farm in Kent, Andrew Pattinson-Hughes found out that the farm secretary owned a blueberry farm a few kilometres north-east of Saumur:

> *After hounding her to write us a letter of recommendation, she gave in. I borrowed money from my dad for the coach fare to Tours, then caught a train to Saumur and an over-priced taxi to the farm, Anjou Myrtilles (myrtille is French for blueberry). The farmer spoke fluent English and agreed to hire us. We stayed on a campsite in Brain-sur Allonnes about a 40 minute walk away, as the farm is in the middle of the sticks.*

It is possible to print out an application form from the site www.anjoumyrtilles.fr and submit it to Service Emploi Saisonnier, Sarl Anjou Myrtilles, 2 rue du Vau de Chevré, 49390 La Breille les Pins (☎ (+33) 2 41 528381). It may be possible to continue picking until the end of August and then move on to the apple harvest in the nearby village of Parcay les Pins where it will be easy to save most of your earnings.

Apple picking takes place around Tours throughout September and October; try the villages of Brèches and further west, Les Rosiers sur Loire.

Organic Farms

The organic movement is powerful in France, and now WWOOF France (86 bis, rue Principale, 33460 Lamarque; www.wwoof.fr, also in English) maintains an up-to-date list of 1,400 hosts looking for volunteers. The membership fee is €25 for one, €30 for two for an electronic list, €17 extra for printed booklets and postage. In his gap year, Jack Standbridge was looking for 'an experience', which he found first on the grape harvest and later by WWOOFing in France:

> *I went to a WWOOF place where there was no electricity, no running water, no heating or a house or anything, because I thought it would be interesting. The work has been difficult in places, like when I had to build a dry-stone wall for pretty much a month solid with stones that weighed quite a good deal more than myself.*

TEACHING

So many expatriates live in Paris and throughout France that being a native speaker of English does not cut much ice with prospective employers of English teachers. Without a TEFL qualification, BA or commercial flair (preferably all three) it is very difficult to get a teaching contract. Of course if you can make yourself look ultra-presentable and have an impressive CV, you should ring to make appointments and then tramp round all the possible institutes and training centres to leave your CV. (As is usual in Europe, there is virtually no hope of success in July and August.)

Googling for *Écoles de Langues* and your destination city is usually the best way to come up with contact details for language schools. The *Pages Jaunes* (Yellow Pages; www.pagesjaunes.fr) are a useful search engine; search under the heading *Cours Langues Étrangeres* or *Formation Langues*. A great many of these cater for the business market, so anything relevant in your background should be emphasised. Most schools pay between €15 and €25 (gross) per lesson. As is increasingly common, schools are reluctant to take on contract teachers for whom they would be obliged to pay taxes, social security and holiday pay of 12%, and so there is a bustling market in freelance teachers who work for themselves and are prepared to teach just a few hours a week for one employer.

Language exchanges for room and board are commonplace and are usually arranged through advertisements (in the places described below in the section on Paris) or by word of mouth. This is one way for Americans and other non-Europeans to circumvent red tape difficulties, as Beth Mayer from New York found in Paris:

> *I tried to get a job at a school teaching, but they asked for working papers which I didn't have. I checked with several schools that told me that working papers and a university degree were more important than TEFL qualifications. So I placed an ad to teach English and offer editing services (I was an editor in New York City before moving here) and received many responses. I charged a decent fee but after I had spent time going and coming, I earned only half that. It would be better to have the lessons at your apartment if centrally located. I not only 'taught' English but offered English conversation to French people who wanted practice. I met a lot of nice people this way and earned money to boot.*

The usual methods of scouring online message boards, advertising in local newspapers, and sticking up photocopied ads in libraries could work.

University language students who would like to spend a year as an English language *assistant* in a French school should contact the Language Assistants Team of the British Council (www.britishcouncil.org/language-assistants). They send hundreds of undergraduates studying French at British universities and recent graduates aged 20–35 to spend an academic year in primary or secondary schools throughout France. This arrangement is coordinated through the Erasmus+ scheme; following the referendum on the UK's membership of the EU, the UK government issued a statement confirming that the result would not impact on those considering applying in 2017. Beyond this point, the UK's future participation in the Erasmus+ programme is to be determined as part of formal discussions with the EU, which got underway after UK triggered Article 50 of the Lisbon Treaty. While the UK remains a member of the EU, and until it has finalised the terms of its exit with the other Member States, UK nationals will continue to have access to the Erasmus+ scheme under the current terms of the programme. *Assistants* give conversation classes for 12 hours a week and are paid €965 (gross) a month (€794 net) for seven months from 1 October. As mentioned earlier, Americans can also become *assistants* in France through the French Embassy in Washington (http://highereducation.frenchculture.org/teach-in-france).

Emily Sloane from the USA was posted as an *assistant* to a small town in Lorraine (where the quiche comes from), unknown to any English-language guidebook that she could find:

> *I taught English to about 170 students in three different primary schools, two 45-minute sessions per class per week, for a total of 12 hours of work each week. In general, the teaching and lesson planning were thoroughly enjoyable, although I wasn't given much guidance and received no feedback throughout the year, so I'm sure the fact that I was already comfortable and experienced with teaching and working with children made a big difference in my enjoyment. The kids, although adoring and very enthusiastic, were a lot rowdier than I had expected, and I was obliged to spend a lot more time on behaviour management than I'd anticipated. The kids were never mean, just excitable and chatty, especially so because my class offered a break from their usual blackboard-and-worksheet style routine. The fact that I was the only assistant in my town meant that my French improved noticeably, especially my slang and listening comprehension, although it made for some lonely weekends, because I was forced to get by in French all the time.*

Outside the bigger cities, your chance of picking up freelance teaching work is quite strong, something Emily Sloane discovered. Through word of mouth and no active self-promotion, numerous townspeople contacted her about private English tutoring and by the middle of the school year she had five private students, whom she taught once a week each for €10, with sometimes a free meal thrown in. This is at the very lowest end of the tutoring range; in Paris most charge double that amount.

In Paris it is often a case of offsetting the high cost of living by doing some tutoring which sometimes shades into au pairing. Part-time work tutoring children in a family context should be easy enough to fix up through a company like Speaking Agency (www.speaking-agency.com) which recruits up to 1,000 native speakers over 18 to work for a few hours a week either babysitting children aged 3–12 focusing on teaching English through play, or teaching older children. These are all live-out positions so the company is interested in hearing from people already living in France. As well as in Paris, it places tutors in Lyon, Lille, Bordeaux, Nantes and Toulouse. The hourly rate is €10–€13 for the childcare positions, €13–€20 for the tutoring, depending on number of children and travel distance. Details of the online application procedure are at www.facebook.com/jobinfrance. Other companies with similar programmes are Babylangues (http://job-in-france.babylangues.com) which arranges for native English speakers in Paris, Lyon, Marseille, Lille, etc to fill part-time babysitting and teaching positions, as does Eveil Bilingue in the greater Paris area (www.eveilbilingue.com/we-are-recruiting).

Not only is it hard to find work in Paris, but of course rents are also very high in the capital. Sara Breese described her job-hunt in Paris and the style of life teaching can pay for:

> *Finding work in France is a rather arduous process; however, with determination and zeal one can easily find work. I moved to Paris in September as a jeune fille au pair and doing side-work teaching children English. The next year I decided to get my ESL teaching certificate at TEFL Paris, which was one of the best decisions I ever made. Not only did I love the process of getting my certificate, but I also discovered a love for teaching. ESL is probably the number one industry for Anglophones and is your best investment in terms of success in the job search. In order to find a teaching job I looked in the FUSAC [mentioned below] and applied to every English teaching organisation in the magazine. After about two weeks, I received some calls asking for interviews. I interviewed with three different places, accepting a job where I still work. I am paid €20 per hour gross, €16 euros after taxes. I immediately signed a CDII, which is the ideal type of contract for a business English teacher in Paris. It translates to basically a long-term intermittent contract meaning that you will receive work when it is available but you will not stop being considered an employee.*
>
> *I have not been able to save money because Paris is very expensive. I can make anywhere between €1,000 and €1,600 a month. Rent in Paris is very high and I have never heard of a teaching organisation providing housing for their teachers. When I first moved to Paris I lived in what they call a chambre de bonne (maid's quarters). These are rented for about €450 per month, so as a teacher you can expect at least half your pay cheque to go to rent.*

CHILDCARE

Au pairing has always been a favoured way for young women to learn French and for young men too. The pocket money for au pairs in France is normally €80–€100 per 30-hour week plus a city transport pass if you are in Paris. Au pairs plus and nannies should earn more. Most agencies make enrolling in a French course a necessary condition.

Quite a few foreigners are too hasty in arranging what seems at the outset a cushy number and only gradually realise how little they enjoy the company of children and how isolated they are if their family lives in the suburbs (as most do). Unless you actively like small children, it might be better to look for a free room in exchange for minimal babysitting (eg 12 hours a week). Matt Tomlinson went into his au pair job with his eyes open:

> *I'd heard too many horror stories from overworked and underpaid au pair friends to be careless, so chose quite carefully from the people who replied to my notice on the upstairs noticeboard of the British Church (just off the rue de Faubourg St Honoré). My employers were really laid back, in their mid-20s so more like living with an older brother and sister. The little boy was just over two whilst the little girl was three months old, and they were both completely adorable. On the whole it was great fun. Baking chocolate brownies, playing football and finger-painting may not be everybody's idea of a good time but there are certainly worse ways to earn a living (and learn French at the same time).*

Applying directly through a French agency is commonplace. The most established agencies are members of UFAAP, the Union Française des Agences Au Pair, an umbrella group set up in 1999. The

12 member agencies have links from their website www.ufaap.org. Registration fees vary, but can be steep, eg €160+. UFAAP agencies warn applicants against free online matching services, which have the potential for leading to problems and swindles.

Here are some agencies to contact:

Accueil International Services: Saint Germain en Laye; ☎ (+33) 1 39 730498; au-pair@accueil-international.com. Au pair positions in Paris region (Île de France) plus Picardie, Haute Normandie, Champagne-Ardennes, Centre and Bourgogne.

Apitu: Dol de Bretagne; ☎ (+33) 2 99 732236; www.apitu.com. Family placements in Brittany, Normandy and the Loire; EU citizens pay service charge of €40 on arrival, Australians, New Zealanders, Canadians and Americans pay €80.

Association Familles & Jeunesse: Nice; ☎ (+33) 4 93 822822; info@afj-aupair.org; www.afj-aupair.org. Places more than 400 au pair girls and boys, mainly in the South of France plus the French Riviera and Corsica.

Europair Services: Paris; ☎ (+33) 1 43 298001; europairservices@wanadoo.fr; www.europairservices.com. Member of IAPA.

Oliver Twist Work & Study: Pessac and Ingrandes; ☎ (+33) 5 57 269326; www.oliver-twist.fr.

By law, families are supposed to make social security payments to the local URSSAF office on the au pair's behalf, though not all do and you might want to enquire about this when applying. Au pairs in or near Paris should obtain the *Navigo* card, ideally given by their host family, that costs €22.15 for a week and €73 for a month of unlimited travel in the whole Paris region.

BUSINESS AND INDUSTRY

You will normally need impeccable French in order to work in a French office, which eliminates the sort of temping jobs you may have had back home. Fee-paying training programmes can provide an opening to employment and boost the quality of a participant's CV. Expensive internship programmes cater to Americans, for example Global Experiences (www.globalexperiences.com) organise eight-week internships in Paris for $8,500.

A cheaper way to find a base in France from which to improve your knowledge of the language is to track down your own internship, by using a website like iAgora.com. Alternatively you can try to participate in a work exchange, for example the one offered by the Centre International d'Antibes, a French language school on the Côte d'Azur, which sometimes advertises *stages*, ie temporary placements (www.cia-france.com/career).

A number of British-run building firms (not all of them licensed) are active in areas like the Dordogne where many English people renovate homes. You are more likely to come across building work informally as the American Peter Goldman did:

> *I was hitching south from Paris when a kind woman stopped near Tours. She was heading to her farmhouse near Bordeaux where a Dutchman was putting a new roof on the house. I explained that I had some experience in construction and I was hired on the spot. I worked for 10 days, received good wages plus tons of food, beer and wine and a bed. The Dutchman was happy with my work and took me to Biddary near Bayonne to help him renovate another house. There I earned a small wage on top of all living expenses, learned a lot about European building methods, rural France and met some great people.*

VOLUNTEERING

France has as wide a range of opportunities for voluntary work as any European country, and anyone who is prepared to exchange work for subsidised board and lodging should consider joining a voluntary project. Projects normally last two or three weeks during the summer and cost between €10 and

€20 a day. The word for a workcamp or working holiday in this context is *chantier*. Many foreign young people join one of these to learn basic French and make French contacts as well as to have fun.

Archaeology

A great many archaeological digs and building restoration projects are carried out each year. Every year the Ministry of Culture (Direction de l'Architecture et du Patrimoine, Sous-Direction de l'Archéologie) publishes a national list of summer excavations throughout France requiring up to 5,000 volunteers which can be consulted on its website (www.culture.gouv.fr/fouilles) from March/April. Most *départements* have *Services Archéologiques* which organise digs. Without relevant experience you will probably be given only menial jobs but many like to share in the satisfaction of seeing progress made.

Anthony Blake describes the dig he joined which the History Department of the University of Le Mans runs: *'Archaeology is hard work. Applicants must be aware of what working 8.30am–noon and 2pm–6.30pm in baking heat means! That said, I thoroughly enjoyed the working holiday: excellent company (75% French so fine opportunity to practise French), weekends free after noon on Saturday, good lunches in SNCF canteen, evening meals more haphazard as prepared by fellow diggers. Accommodation simple but adequate.'*

Conservation

France takes the preservation of its heritage (*patrimoine*) very seriously and numerous groups both local and national are engaged in restoring churches, windmills, forts and other historic monuments. Many are set up to accept foreign volunteers, though they tend to charge more than archaeological digs:

Chantiers, Histoire et Architecture Médiévales (CHAM): Paris; ☎ (+33) 1 43 351551; www. cham.asso.fr. Volunteer projects to protect historic buildings, not just in mainland France but in farflung places including Réunion Island (a *département* of France in the Indian Ocean near Mauritius); see the CHAM website (which is in English) for details; camps cost €12 a day plus €30 registration fee.

Etudes et Chantiers: Clermont-Ferrand and Île de France; ☎ (+33) 4 73 319804; www.etudes etchantiers.org. Hundreds of international volunteers for short-term conservation projects and longer-term professional training, accepted via partner agencies.

La Sabranenque: Saint Victor la Coste; www.sabranenque.com. Paying volunteers are needed between May and October to restore a mediaeval village and pave its walkways, located not far from Avignon. €300 for 6 days.

REMPART: Paris; ☎ (+33) 1 42 719655; www.rempart.com. Similar to the National Trust in Britain, in charge of endangered monuments throughout France. Volunteers are needed in July and August. Prices differ and are posted on the website from March.

Solidarités Jeunesses: Paris; ☎ (+33) 1 55 26; www.solidaritesjeunesses.org. Fee for one of several environmental and renovation projects is €120 for one week.

Try to be patient if the project you choose turns out to have its drawbacks, since these organisations depend on voluntary leaders as well as participants. Judy Greene volunteered to work with a conservation organisation and felt herself to be *'personally victimised by the lack of organisation and leadership'* or more specifically by one unpleasantly racist individual on her project. Tolerance may be called for, especially if your fellow volunteers lack it.

PARIS

Like all major cities in the developed world, Paris presents thousands of ways to earn your keep, while being difficult to afford from day to day. Unless you are very lucky, you will have to arrive with some money with which to support yourself while you look around. When house-hunting, check noticeboards (see below) and local papers or (if you can afford it) use an agency which will cost you at least a month's rent but will help to ensure that you get your deposit of two months' rent back.

The fashion for English and Irish pubs is still in evidence. The chain of British-style Frog Pubs hires lots of English speakers for its 11 branches in Paris and in fact has its recruitment pages in English (www.frogpubs.com/jobs.php). The company targets gap year students as well as more career-minded people.

The Grapevine

Expatriate grapevines flourish all over Paris and are very helpful for finding work and accommodation. Many people find accommodation as well as jobs through one of the city's many noticeboards (*panneaux*). The one in the foyer of the CIDJ at 101 Quai Branly (*métro* Bir-Hakeim) is good for occasional studenty-type jobs such as extras in movies, but sometimes there are adverts for full-time jobs or *soutien scolaire en anglais* (English tutor).

The other mecca for job and flat-hunters is the American Church at 65 Quai d'Orsay (☎ (+33) 1 40 620500; www.acparis.org; *métro* Invalides). Official notices are posted on various noticeboards inside and out; the corkboard in the basement is a free board where anybody can stick up a notice, which is open for viewing 9am–10pm on Monday to Saturday and 1pm–6pm on Sunday.

The American Cathedral in Paris at 23 avenue George V (www.amcathparis.com; *métro* Alma Marceau or George V) has a noticeboard featuring employment opportunities and housing listings. The Cathedral also offers volunteering opportunities, for example at its Friday mission lunches.

Arguably the most eccentric bookshop in Europe is Shakespeare and Company at 37 rue de la Bûcherie in the fifth *arrondissement* (on the south side of the Seine). It has a noticeboard and is also useful as a place to chat to other expats about work and accommodation. The shop operates as an informal writers' guesthouse. The late American owner George Whitman has passed on the shop to his young daughter Sylvia who carries on the tradition of allowing what he calls his 'tumbleweeds' to stay free, as long as they work two hours a day (and as long as there is space).

HANNAH ADCOCK DESCRIBES HERSELF AS A 'RATHER SOLEMN' 18-YEAR-OLD WHEN SHE READ AN EARLIER EDITION OF THIS BOOK AND SET OFF FOR PARIS:

Soon after, I found myself living at this hippy Parisian bookstore with a view of Notre Dame, a treat of inedible pancakes to look forward to and orders to clean the floor using newspaper and cold water. Kids staying at Shakespeare's do most of the jobs for free. You'll only get a paid job if: (a) the owner really likes you, (b) you went to a university like Cambridge or Harvard and (c) you're really cute. The room overlooking Notre Dame is lovely but when I was there it smelt foul and a highly evolved species of bed bug lurked, as big as rats (ok – exaggeration). Shakespeare's is brilliant, but working there has its 'interesting' aspects!

The bilingual English magazine *France-USA Contacts* or *FUSAC* (www.fusac.fr) is now published exclusively online. *FUSAC* carries mainly classified adverts including some for English teachers. The cost of an ad for example under the heading 'Work Wanted in France' starts at €36 for 20 words. Another possible source of job and accommodation leads is the free ads site www.paris-annonces.com.

Disneyland Paris

The enormous complex of Disneyland Paris, 30km east of Paris at Marne-la-Vallée, employs about 8,000 new recruits every year, both on long-term and seasonal contracts, though the number of seasonal staff has been reduced in recent years. Seasonal positions from March or May to September are open to EU citizens or others with permission to work in the EU. The minimum period covers the high season from the end of June to the end of August.

'Cast members' (Disneyspeak for employees) must all have a conversational level of French and preferably a third European language. It has been often noted that when there is a shortage of bilingual candidates, they may be prepared to accept people with borderline French. You might get away with having very little French if you work in the parades, where the emphasis is on dancing ability, or in the more menial positions as sweepers, etc. Working conditions are not as good as they were, with many employees working a six-day week. But travel costs are reimbursed (currently €76 from the UK for open-ended contract, €152 for return journey for fixed-term contracts) and accommodation is provided in shared flats a bus-ride away from the park with the cost (subsidised but still expensive) deducted from wages.

The majority of jobs are in food and beverage, housekeeping, merchandising and custodial departments, though one of the best jobs is as a character such as Mickey Mouse. The French standard working week is 35 hours long for which staff are paid a salary which is slightly above the SMIC less monthly social security deductions of at least €170. Further details are available at http://careers.disneylandparis.com/en. Casting tours are conducted around Europe in the winter, especially for entertainment roles, with pop-up recruitment desks in colleges and universities where queues of applicants can be long for an initial screening of your French and your motivation. For all jobs the well-scrubbed look is required (though the no-facial-hair rule has been dropped), and of course they are looking for the usual friendly, cheerful and outgoing personalities. Whether you will be impressed by the fringe benefits is a matter of individual taste; they consist of discounts on merchandise and in the hotels and some free entrances to the theme park itself.

KEITH LEISHMAN FROM DUNDEE WAS A CAST MEMBER A FEW SUMMERS AGO BEFORE TAKING A LAW DEGREE (WITH FRENCH):

Getting the job was initially quite frustrating. I first sent a letter to the company around November. After another couple of letters and emails without reply I was just about giving up hope. Finally around March I received notification of an interview in Edinburgh and was offered the job. After that you are pretty much left to your own devices and simply expected to turn up at Disney the day before your contract begins. (This was rather a shock to me after working for Eurocamp the year before who provided transport to France and some preparatory material beforehand.)

I was employed on the ticketing side of operations. I had to wear a Prince Charming costume and supervise the entrance of guests to the Park, stamping their hand for re-admission. This meant standing for the whole shift in what were often scorching conditions. This was very beneficial for my French as people would ask a whole range of weird and wonderful questions.

The staff apartments were comfortable enough and equipped with kitchens, though I did not cook much due to the cheapness and accessibility of Disney canteens; I could eat well for a few euros a day. Another of the main advantages of working at Disneyland is the mixture of nationalities. The sheer number of young people from all over the world means there are always lots of parties and barbecues in the residences. On days off I usually went into Paris, which is only 40 minutes away on the train. I stayed for two months of the peak summer season and found it quite hard to keep up the Disney smile when I was hot and tired. The job is demanding because you are creating an illusion. All the same I would urge anybody with an interest in people and a desire to improve their French to try the experience. I intend to return at Christmas and Easter.

Survival

Talented musicians should consider joining the army of buskers on the Left Bank on a Friday or Saturday night and graduating to the highly competitive *métro*. Transit authorities issue licences (free of charge) that allow you to perform in prescribed locations. Playing on the trains themselves is not allowed, though many ignore the regulations. Anna Ling from Cambridge developed a short and dazzling fire poi show (spinning two flaming balls on a flexible chain), which she performed outside restaurants one August, wherever she could find enough space, while her accomplice circulated with a hat.

Robert Abblett enjoyed his stay on a community a few years ago:

> *From the WWOOF list, I found the address of Domaine de Courmettes. This was my favourite WWOOF for it was situated on an 800-metre plateau above the Côte d'Azur. I spent a wonderful three and a half weeks here one August in a most peaceful place camping and swinging in my hammock, contemplating life and exploring the top of the mountain nearby. On my days off I would go swimming in some of the most beautiful rivers and swimming holes with the other volunteers. I would work four days washing up followed by three days off. My French really helped me enjoy the experience.*

For an expenses-free week or four in the countryside of Creuse in central France, you can offer your services at a holiday centre for disabled people through the Association Le Puy Batard (www. puy-batard.org/eng/volunteers.html). Volunteers simply befriend the clients, accompany them on outings, help care for them and share domestic duties.

If you are more into private enterprise, you may wish to follow Tessa Shaw's example (from many moons ago). She learned that there were many edible snails to be found along the canals and river-banks in the *département* of Vaucluse which she could sell in the market. The snails move about only on still, dank nights: so Tessa would be found between the hours of 2am and 7am scouring the waterside with the help of a torch. She would then keep them in a sack or bin for four or five days until they exuded all the poison in their systems, rinse them well and then sell them in the market of Carpentras. There is a closed season for snail collecting between 1 April and 30 June. Note that the increased use of pesticides in recent years has reduced the harvest dramatically so most edible snails are now imported from Poland and Romania.

While you're waiting for something to turn up, it is possible to sleep in parks, railway stations or on beaches, though this is unlikely to be trouble-free. If you are sleeping overnight in a station, you may be asked to show a valid ticket; otherwise the patrolling police will not be over-gentle when evicting you.

A few years ago, Bradwell Jackson tried and failed to get an English teaching job in Marseille, because he is American. After travelling and teaching on several continents since then, as a personal challenge, he decided to return to the 'town of his former ignominy' to see if he could survive:

> *What I found is that it's not so difficult to make it in Marseille without having enough money. The homeless shelters are remarkably easy to get into and they aren't so bad. You get two meals a day and the people aren't even dangerous. They were actually kind of interesting to get to know.*

Germany

With its seemingly impregnable reputation for being the economic powerhouse of Europe, foreign workers continue to flock to Germany. More than eight million people live in Germany without a German passport. Whereas in the years following reunification, thousands of unskilled workers poured in from the former Yugoslavia, the Balkans and eastern Europe, now it tends to be skilled professionals such as engineers and IT specialists from Mediterranean countries suffering from the Eurozone debt crisis. And more recently Angela Merkel's policy of admitting Syrian refugees into Germany on humanitarian grounds has swelled the numbers. This influx from all over Europe and the Middle East has left fewer vacancies for British and other students and travellers. The rate of unemployment remains stable at a creditable 5.8%. Work experience placements for students of German are still numerous, albeit unpaid in many cases. Perseverance by anyone who has a reasonable command of German has every chance of being rewarded with a decently paid job.

REGULATIONS

EU citizens are free to travel to Germany to look for and take up work, but like all German nationals must register their address with the relevant district authority (*Einwohnermeldeamt*). For this you will need proof that you are living locally, eg a copy of your contract with your landlord, and ID to prove your date of birth.

A high number of self-employed artisans and sellers continue to work black (*Schwarzarbeit*), though huge fines on employers caught employing unregistered workers under the table has reduced the number in the construction and cleaning industries. For jobs that involve serving food, you need to obtain a *Belehrungsbescheinigung* from the local *Gesundheitsamt* (health department) where you must watch a video, listen to a talk, confirm you have no contagious diseases and pay the fee of €25.

Australians, New Zealanders and a few other nationalities under 30 are eligible for one-year working holiday visas for Germany. Canadians aged 18–35 can obtain a Youth Mobility Visa also valid for a year. There are two categories: Work and Travel, and Young Professional, and it is possible to apply for a second year in a different category. The first is open to people who want to supplement 'tourism and cultural discovery' by earning along the way, and the second to those who are looking for a professional traineeship. The site www.experience-germany.ca has links to mediating programmes. Other citizens of privileged countries (Australia, New Zealand, Canada, the USA, Israel, Japan and South Korea) are permitted to apply for a residence/work permit after arrival in Germany provided they have found an employer willing to support their application and assuming they can tolerate the oft-reported hostility of the bureaucrats encountered at the *Ausländeramt* or *Ausländerbehörde* (Foreigners' Registration). You will have to present a raft of documents including the *Anmeldebestätigung* (registration of residence), evidence that you have health insurance and proof of job or funds (minimum €700 a month) plus a fee of €50.

Other nationalities must apply through the German consulate in their home country. The German government bans the recruitment of foreign labour for unskilled or low-skilled jobs, so it will be very difficult for non-Europeans to obtain permission to stay in Germany for an extended period. The discussion forum at www.info4alien.de may be useful for German speakers.

If you have a student visa for Germany, you are allowed to work up to 120 days or 240 half-days per year without a work permit.

Those who earn more than €450 per month or work more than 19 hours a week are obliged to pay tax and contributions so must obtain a tax card (*Lohnsteuerkarte*). Above that level, you will start to pay contributions on a graduated scale. Everyone in employment must pay social security contributions for health insurance, pension and unemployment, which can amount to about a fifth of your income.

SPECIAL SCHEMES

Internships for American students and graduates up to the age of 30 who can function in German are available in business, finance, engineering or technical fields through Cultural Vistas, an organisation that formed from the merger of two long-established exchange programmes, CDS International and AIPT (www.culturalvistas.org). Funded one-year fellowships combining study and interning are available to 75 Americans aged 18–24. The competitive Congress-Bundestag Youth Exchange for Young Professionals (CBYX) programme starts with a two-month language course in Cologne, Radolfzell or Saarbrücken followed by three months' university study in the assigned German city, followed by an internship (normally paid) in a relevant field. The only outlay for participants is the cost of travel to the orientation in Washington DC and spending money.

InterExchange in New York (www.workingabroad.org) runs a conversation coaching programme in Germany whereby young Americans aged 18–30 live with a family and spend 15 hours a week tutoring the children in English for between one and three months. The programme fee is US$895.

The IJAB (International Youth Exchange) in Bonn has a EuroDesk that administers European student exchanges and maintains a website www.rausvonzuhaus.de with a section in English 'Come to

Germany' with links to internships, courses, etc. Praktikum.de provides a free internship database for companies, students and anyone else who is offering or searching for internships in Germany and elsewhere. (The word for internship in German is *praktikum*.)

ACCOMMODATION

Considering that a one-bedroom flat in one of the big cities can easily cost €475–€675 per month, excluding bills, salaries need to be high. Most newcomers search online communities for rooms in shared houses or flats to rent. Ben Stefano who lived in Berlin for part of 2016 describes the best sources of accommodation in Germany:

> *As far as accommodation in any German city goes, www.wg-gesucht.de is definitely the first website that most people recommend. You can rent a whole apartment or a single room in a shared flat ('Wohnge-meinschaft', abbreviated to WG), which is what I did. I was paying €300 a month for my room in a 3-bedroom WG in the well-connected suburb of Wedding, although in Berlin it's common to pay €350 or even up to €480 for a room in a hip area like Kreuzberg, Friedrichshain or gentrified Prenzlauer Berg. Another similar website Immobilienscout24.de is also popular. These sites are free to use, but searching them can be difficult and time-consuming. Also you have to be wary of scammers, especially for apart-ments that are too good to be true in the big cities. Lots of young people also use Facebook groups where you can advertise your free room or write a post telling people you're on the hunt for a room. People often write profiles for themselves so others can get an idea of what kind of person they are.*

Cities may have their own portals of use to German speakers, such as http://schwarzesbrett. bremen.de for Bremen (*Schwarzesbrett* means Bulletin Board). An alternative to classified ads web-sites is the local *mitwohnzentralen*, which charges commission (usually one month's rent) for finding flats or less for a sub-let. It is customary to pay your rent directly out of a bank account, so open a basic current account (*girokonto*) as early as you can. Often you pay the rent to the person whose name is on the lease (*Hauptmieter* or main renter).

WORK EXPERIENCE

Internships are commonplace in German companies. Work placements can be organised in a wide range of sectors including tourism, trade, telecommunications, marketing and banking depending on timing and availability. Most internships are organised in conjunction with an intensive language course. Normally an upper intermediate level of language ability is required for work experience to be successful. Most are unpaid or are rewarded only with a subsistence wage. Board and lodging will generally be provided only in the tourism sector.

The federal employment service (see next section) can assist with arranging internships for post-graduate students and recent graduates who wish to gain international work experience in a German company. The preferred faculties are engineering, economics, business administration and tourism management. The duration of the internships should be at least three months and not longer than one year. The students should have a good knowledge of the German language. Applications should be sent to the international department ZAV's Project-Team Incoming (☎ (+49) 228 713 1313; www. arbeitsagentur.de).

DID-Deutsch Institute in Frankfurt (☎ (+49) 69 2400 4560; www.did.de) is a major language course provider which can arrange two to six month internships following their language courses in Berlin, Frankfurt and Munich; the processing fee for a work placement is €480 in addition to the preceding language course lasting a minimum of six weeks (eg €1,100). Similarly GLS (www.gls-berlin.de) combines a minimum four-week language course with an unpaid internship in a Berlin-based company of six, eight or 12+ weeks; the internship placement fee is €600. Host companies want their trainees to speak German to at least an intermediate (B-1) level.

GERMAN NATIONAL EMPLOYMENT SERVICE

The whole of Germany is covered by the network of employment offices run by the state Bundesagentur für Arbeit (www.arbeitsagentur.de). All branch offices are connected by a number of coordinating offices that handle both applications and vacancies that cannot be filled locally. If you speak German and aren't in a hurry, it's probably worth registering.

The Zentrale Auslands-und Fachvermittlung (International Placement Services), ZAV, part of the German Federal Employment Agency, has an international department (Auslandsvermittlung) for dealing with applications from German-speaking students abroad. Details and application forms are available from ZAV (Info Centre, Villemombler Strasse 76, 53123 Bonn; ☎ (+49) 228 713 2000; zav-Bonn@ arbeitsagentur.de). All applications from abroad are handled by this office. Although people of any nationality can apply through the ZAV, only citizens of EU countries (who have German language skills) are entitled to expect the same treatment as a German.

This special department of the ZAV called Ferienbeschäftigung finds summer jobs for students of any nationality, because this is felt to be mutually beneficial to employers and employees alike. The deadline for students who wish to participate in this scheme is 31 January, since summer vacancies start to be notified to the department from October. Students must be at least 18 years old, have a good command of German and be available to work for at least two months but no more than three, which is the maximum allowed. ZAV places students in all kinds of jobs, but mainly in hotels and restaurants, in industry, cleaning and agriculture. The ZAV assigns jobs centrally, according to employers' demands and the level of the candidate's spoken German. For example those with fluent German may be found service jobs while those without will be given jobs such as chambermaiding and dishwashing. If you decline the first job offered by the ZAV, there is no guarantee of being offered another.

OTHER SOURCES OF WORK

Anyone with office experience and knowledge of German should look for branches of private employment agencies such as Adecco and Manpower in the big cities; these will be listed in the *Gelbe Seiten* (*Yellow Pages*) under *Personalberatung* or *Stellenvermittlungsburo*.

BZ in Berlin (www.bz-jobs.de) has a selection of vacancies for unskilled people or check www. toytowngermany.com/jobs for English language jobs in Germany. Berlinstartupjobs.com might be of interest to techies.

TOURISM AND CATERING

The German tourist industry depends heavily on migrants and students during the busy summer months. Despite the high percentage of immigrants from Eastern Europe and the Balkans who are often willing to work for exploitative wages, other nationalities do find jobs in hotels and restaurants.

If you are conducting a door-to-door search of hotels and restaurants in the cities, you will be at an enormous advantage if you speak decent German. For example every time Danny Jacobson turned around in Freiburg (after a fruitless search for harvesting work in the countryside), he met young people from around the world working at campsites and in bars. You may be lucky and find a manager who speaks English and who needs someone behind the scenes to wash dishes, etc. Robin Gray lived to regret accepting a job in a kitchen without really understanding what he was meant to do:

> *The manageress told me she was looking for a salad chef and I said I was a chef. The waitresses were coming in with the orders, but I didn't know there were about seven different salads. I was just putting a couple of slices of lettuce, tomatoes, bit of cucumber, etc on all the plates and they were going off their heads because there wasn't enough watercress or no tomatoes with that certain salad. I started at 10am and got the sack at 2pm, but I got paid for it so I wasn't too bothered.*

Tom Alber fared much better more recently. Without knowing a word of German and after being in Berlin for only three days, he found a job in a restaurant making the traditional German pizza *Flamm-kuchen* and got on famously with the head chef.

You can try to fix up a summer job ahead of time by sending off speculative applications. Sometimes the more remote places have the most trouble filling vacancies. One reader of this book once worked as a dishwasher in Berchtesgaden on the Austrian border: *'I spent two and a half months working in a very orderly and efficient kitchen on the top of a mountain in the Kehlsteinhaus (Eagle's Nest) with the most amazing view I've ever seen.'* By contrast, magnets such as Berlin where so many thousands of young foreigners gather have a far more competitive scene as Richard Ferguson discovered:

> *I can tell you one thing about getting work in Berlin – it's not easy. It seems all the bar jobs go to friends and girlfriends, etc, who seem to have never worked behind a bar before. Frustrating when you have three years' experience like me.*

Munich is estimated to have more than 2,000 pubs and restaurants and Berlin is similarly well endowed with eateries (try the American style places on Kurfürstendamm). The Munich beer gardens, especially the massive open-air Chinese Tower Beer Garden, pay glass collectors and washer-uppers (most of whom have lined up their jobs at the beginning of the season) the minimum wage of €8.84 an hour (2017) and at the height of the season, some people work 14-hour days. Look for adverts in *Abendzeitung* in Munich (job ads at http://mjobs.sueddeutsche.de), Craigslist in Berlin, www.jobcafe. de or www.quoka.de with job classifieds. Key words to look for on notices and in adverts are *Notkoch und Küchelhilfe gesucht* (relief and kitchen assistant required), *Spüler* (dishwasher), *Kellner, Bedienigung* (waiters/waitresses), *Schenkekellner* (pub type barman); *büffetier* (barman in a restaurant), *Büffetkräfte* (fast food server), or simply *Services*.

Be prepared for hard work. In hotels, it is not unusual to work 10 or 12 hours a day and to have only a day or two off a month. Those whose only experience of hotels and catering has been in Britain are usually taken aback by German discipline. Waitresses are normally expected to keep all customers' payments until the end of a shift, when the total is calculated and handed over as a lump sum. Those who lose track while being shouted at in German will not last long.

The punitive hygiene laws do not help matters. Once you realise that restaurants and hotels are frequently visited by the health department you will appreciate why it is that the head cook orders you to scrub the floors and clean the fat filters regularly. Paul Winter worked several seasons on the lakes near Munich:

> *I found that it is best to apply around April/May in person if possible. What they usually do is to tell you to come back at the beginning of June and work for a couple of days to see how you get on. As long as you are not a complete idiot they should keep you on until September. Even as late as July I knew of places looking for extra staff but as a rule most places are full by the end of May. I worked for the summer as a barman/waiter earning a good net wage. With the tips I got I generally managed to double this.*

Both Ammersee and Starnbergersee can be reached by S-Bahn from Munich. These two lakes are ringed by towns and villages which all have hotels and restaurants, popular mainly with German tourists. Be warned that competition for work from German students and migrant workers will make it difficult.

Other recommended areas to try for a summer job are the Bavarian Alps (along the border with Austria), the shores of Lake Constance (especially in and around Friedrichshafen), the Bohmer Wald (along the Czech border), the Black Forest (in south-west Germany), and the seaside resorts along the Baltic and North Seas. One employer on the Baltic coast hires a number of general assistants, food and beverage staff, child carers and sports instructors at a coastal campsite/golf and holiday park. The hours are long and you must be able to speak German but the wages are good. Students only should apply in the spring to Wulfener Hals Camping, 23769 Wulfen/ Fehmarn (www. wulfenerhals.de/stellenangebote.html). Movie World employs between 400 and 500 staff for food concessions (restaurants, bakeries, ice cream stalls, fast food, etc). Applicants should be able to converse in German as well as English, and preferably Dutch too since the park is not far south of the Dutch border. Accommodation is not provided (www.movieparkgermany.de/jobs).

Winter Resorts

Germany is a good place to pick up jobs in ski resorts although few British tour companies operate there compared to France and Austria. The two main skiing areas are Garmisch-Partenkirchen (which also has hotels and services for the American Army) on the Austrian border 50 miles south-east of Munich, and the spa resort of Oberstdorf in the mountains south of Kempten. Seasonal vacancies are mostly in the kitchen or housekeeping departments.

As always, timing is crucial. One highly qualified jobseeker with experience in hotels and restaurants, a knowledge of German, French and English, and a good skier went on the old 'hotel-trot' in Garmisch-Partenkirchen and was repeatedly told that they wouldn't be hiring until the beginning of the season (circa 15 December). Up-to-date job listings, including entry-level jobs, can be found on http://jobs.meinestadt.de/garmisch-partenkirchen.

Work on Military Bases

Cutbacks in military spending have necessitated the withdrawal of resources and personnel from British and American military bases in Germany. In fact the British government will close its remaining bases by 2019. Yet there are still some jobs around for Americans and on the relevant bases. Wiesbaden has become the HQ for the US Army in Europe, home to thousands of serving soldiers and their families, which creates many ancillary jobs. For the estimated 3,100 servicemen and women at Wiesbaden, there is a total population of nearly 20,000 including family members and 4,000 civilian workers.

Military bases throughout Germany have Civilian Human Resources Agencies Personnel Advisory Centers (CHRAs) that are responsible for recruiting auxiliary staff to work in bars, shops, etc, on base and as ski instructors. The best bet for US citizens to obtain entry level jobs in the hotel and recruitment department for a period of 15 months is at Edelweiss Lodge and Resort in Garmisch-Partenkirchen, an American Forces Recreation Centre. Details are available from the Human Resources Department Unit 24501, APO AE 09006; (☎ (+49) 8821 9440; www.edelweiss-lodgeandresort.com/employment). They interview exclusively in the United States several times a year, and candidates must go through rigorous interviews and background checks before being selected. Edelweiss never hires Americans who are already in Europe. Americans do not require work permits to work on US bases.

Special Events

Oktoberfest starts each year on the second last Saturday of September and lasts a fortnight. They begin to erect the 14 giant tents for the festival about three months ahead so you can begin your enquiries any time in the summer. Some of the hiring is done directly by the breweries, so it is worth contacting the Hofbräuhaus and Löwenbräu for work, as well as pubs, restaurants and hotels. Nicole Gluckstern from California wrote to confirm that Oktoberfest is always looking for people to sell pretzels, wash glasses, take photos, etc but she advises jobseekers to set their dignity temporarily aside since the atmosphere will be zoo-like. There is also work after the festival finishes as Brad Allemand from Australia discovered: *'On the Monday after Oktoberfest finished I went around to all of the Beer Halls which were being taken down asking for some work. The first one I went to was Spatenbräu and the boss obliged. Even though my German was almost non-existent, I managed to understand what was needed of me. Many other foreigners were also on the site – English, Australian, Yugoslav, etc.'* Brad enjoyed the work, which lasted about six weeks. He worked 7am–5pm five days a week.

Many other international trade fairs and special events may need large numbers of people to set up stands and deal with maintenance, catering, etc. Some of the major ones include the Frankfurt Trade Fair in March and the Hannover Trade Fair in April. Hamburg hosts a big festival ('DOM') three times a year, for a month before Christmas, over Easter and in August. Casual labour is needed to dismantle the place at the end of the events, so look for 'Help Wanted' signs on the stalls. Many high-profile trade fairs are held at the huge Frankfurt Exhibition Hall (*Messe*), such as the Frankfurt Book Fair in mid-October. Applications for work at one of the numerous fairs held in Frankfurt can be addressed to Messe Frankfurt GmbH, Ludwig-Erhard-Anlage 1, 60327 Frankfurt (www.messefrankfurt.com). Only people with a stable base in Frankfurt and a good command of languages (for example for running messages) can be considered.

TEACHING

If you enquire at an *Arbeitsamt* about teaching, translation or secretarial work in the major cities, you will probably be told (truthfully) that there is a surplus of people offering those services. However, you may find that they are more helpful outside the honeypot cities of Berlin, Heidelberg and so on.

Graduates with a background in economics or business who can speak German have a better chance of finding tutoring work in a German city than arts graduates, since most of the demand comes from companies. Private language schools have multiplied in the eastern *Länder*, many with an American bias. Try for example ICC Sprachschule in Leipzig and Chemnitz (www.icc-sprachinstitut.de) which employs about 50 teachers; and Lingua Franca in Berlin (www.lingua-franca.de) which makes use of a similar number of freelancers at any one time. A wage of €15–€20 per 45-minute lesson is typical.

Berlin is the city which is both exquisitely trendy and reassuringly relaxed, and it is the city that appeals most to people in search of European culture at its finest. After graduating from the University of Bath with a degree in Italian and German a couple of years ago, Nino Hunter decided to make his way in Berlin, but he found it a struggle:

> *I did find it extremely difficult to find teaching posts in Berlin. I think the main reason would be the sheer number of English speakers in Berlin, many of whom wish to stay in this amazing city. Given the lack of industry, they have little alternative but to fall back on teaching English, with or without a CELTA/TEFL certificate. The English community is huge in Berlin (check the online Toytown Berlin at www.toytowngermany.com/berlin which has tons of new postings every day). There are of course a huge number of language schools in Berlin but given the number of teachers and the decreasing demand over the last two years due to the global economic crisis many of them have become exceptionally picky about who they choose to take on, often asking for at least two years' experience, etc. There was a particular demand for English teachers able to teach advanced students (Cambridge levels 1 & 2) and a few schools simply wouldn't take people on who didn't have experience teaching higher level students. All of which means that the market in Berlin is extremely saturated and sending a CV off to each and every school usually doesn't help. The best way of finding teaching positions in the city is putting on a suit and going to the schools with a CV, introducing yourself and trying your hardest not to get fobbed off by a secretary, but rather to get an actual interview where they offer you a course. This obviously requires a little courage and a fair amount of energy but is the only way of being sure your CV isn't deleted immediately and is in fact the only way I or any of my colleagues got jobs at private language schools. The teachers at the Berlin School of English where I did my CELTA course assured me that no-one would pay less than €15 for 45 minutes to a teacher with a CELTA. My first school paid me just €12 and it took me 10 weeks to get up to €14, which was not at all uncommon.*
>
> *Two pieces of advice I could give would be firstly to try to get on the lists for the Volkshochschulen (I think there are about seven in Berlin), as these pay more (if you have a university degree even more) and the classes are large and quite fun. I would also recommend joining ELTABB (English Language Teacher's Association – www.eltabb.com), which costs €40 a year but is undoubtedly the best place to network and sometimes perfect positions come up. Basically one needs to be as proactive as possible and not be too fussy. If Berlitz offers you a course, take it.*

If you do intend to look for a teaching job, take some good references (*zeugnisse*), which are essential in Germany. You can always try to arrange private English lessons to augment your income, though you are unlikely to be able to make a living this way.

Language teaching organisations whose addresses are included in the introductory chapter Teaching English have a sizeable presence in Germany: Berlitz Deutschland (www.berlitz.de) with 68 institutes, Bénédict with 25 branches, inlingua (www.inlingua.de) with 76 branches and Marcus Evans-Linguarama which specialises in language training for business. The latter (www.linguarama. com) employs between 25 and 70 teachers at its eight centres in Germany. At the time of writing (winter 2017), 48 branches of Berlitz were advertising vacant posts as English teachers. To the surprise of many, Wall Street English has closed its 23 schools in Germany after more than two decades of operating there. According to the telling statement on their website: 'With a higher level of English being spoken by a larger amount of people in Germany, we feel it will, in the future, be increasingly difficult to deliver the full, high quality, WSE student experience.' In other words, they couldn't sustain their business with the number of clients they were attracting.

Many commercial institutes employ teachers on a freelance basis, often resident expatriates willing to work just a few hours a week. The best source of language school addresses is once again the *Yellow Pages*, which can be consulted online (www.gelbeseiten.de). Another way of accessing potential employers is via the local English Language Teachers Association, a branch of which can be found in some major cities in addition to Berlin as mentioned above. The Munich Association (MELTA) is especially vigorous and devotes one page of its website to potential jobseekers (www.melta.de/jobs.htm).

A more realistic option might be summer language camps which take on lots of native speakers to help kids improve their English through interactive play, sports, music, etc during the school holidays. Try for example:

Berlitz Kids: www.berlitz.de. Largest summer programme in Germany, employing 250 native English speakers who work freelance at holiday camps; €450 per week but no accommodation provided.

Camp Adventure: www.campadventure.de. English camps in various locations from the Baltic to Bavaria; affiliated to Camp Europe (headquarters in Hamburg) which aims to create an international network of summer camps throughout Europe to enable Canadian and American university students to gain international work experience; instructors must be over 19 and have training.

KCA (Kids Camp America): www.kidscampamerica.com/en/jobs. English immersion camps in Frankfurt, Wiesbaden, etc. €600 per week.

LEOlingo Sprachcamps: www.leo-lingo.de. Camps in north-eastern Germany (Hamburg, Baltic Sea, Mecklenburg-Vorpommern) last 6–7 weeks from mid-June, and in Bavaria from mid-July to the beginning of September; day counsellors are paid €200 a week, night counsellors €100 a week, plus room and board, with host families, at youth hostels, etc; staff are hired from North America, Australia, etc.

Oskar Lernt English: www.oskar-lernt-englisch.de/jobs.php. Native speaker teachers and counsellors should have a working knowledge of German.

Penguin Camp: www.penguincamp.de/jobs. Language counsellors wanted.

Sphairos: ☎ (+49) 89 18 70 31 56; www.sphairos.de.

Sarah Paschke has worked several summers for LEOlingo in Bavaria. She first applied after finishing her degree in the US when she knew she wanted to live in Europe and had to find something to justify this decision to her father. So she googled 'Summer Camps' knowing that she wanted to work for a small personal outfit rather than one of the giant language camp companies. To further overcome her parents' possible objections, she wanted to find a summer job that paid a wage and would assist with the visa issue:

> *LEOlingo was delightful and timely in the application process. A couple of the 'megas' sent automated rejection replies to my email account or I never received any word back at all. After sending my resumé and questionnaire, a Skype interview was scheduled within a matter of two weeks. I had a background of teaching and tutoring youths; however, nothing with the intensive responsibilities of directing children 24/7. When I was applying around Europe, I was disappointed that so few employers offered a wage in addition to accommodation and food. LEOlingo pays well and gives you accommodation and food, which allowed me to save money to travel after camp.*

The LEOlingo programme is a balance of language games, sports and crafts to keep the campers engaged, excited and interested in the topics. From writing and acting mini-dramas, to playing a camp-wide game of Capture the Flag, there is little time for campers to be bored! I knew it was going to be demanding, a high-energy and 'on-top-of-your-game' sort of job, and I was up for that challenge. LEOlingo really pushed me to interact with the German culture since from the start we were staying with German host families in town. I don't speak German so I was lucky to have a family that knew English and was equally interested in me as I was in them. I still keep in contact with my host family and go to visit them a couple times a year when I can. Encounters with my pupils were always unpredictable, and they never failed to amaze me. Germans in general have a higher knowledge and capacity to learn English. Schools teach it well and the students at the summer camps are highly motivated and intrigued by the LEOlingo staff. Last summer my fellow teachers and counsellors represented all but two English-speaking countries. The highlight of camp is the correspondence between cultures, whether it is between counsellor and camper, or counsellor and counsellor. I learned so much about my own culture.

Many secondary schools in Germany (including the former East) employ native English-speaking *assistenten*. Applications are encouraged from candidates under 30 who have studied at least two years of German, preferably at university level. UK applicants should contact the Language Assistants Team at the British Council (language.assistants@britishcouncil.org; www.britishcouncil. org/language-assistants/become/germany), which has over 250 places available in schools across Germany. The salary is €800 a month (net) for 12 hours of work a week, unchanged for many years. Beyond 2017, the UK's future participation in Erasmus+ programmes, including the Language Assistants Scheme, is to be determined as part of formal negotiations with the EU.

CHILDCARE

Au pairs must have some knowledge of German and experience of childcare and those from outside the European Union must be aged 18–26. Among the longest established agencies is the non-profit Roman Catholic agency IN VIA with headquarters in Freiburg (☎ (+49) 761 200206) and 14 branches throughout Germany (www.aupair-invia. de). Its Protestant counterpart is affiliated to the YWCA: Verein für Internationale Jugendarbeit headquartered in Frankfurt (☎ (+49) 69 4693 9700; www.au-pair-vij. org). VIJ has ten offices in Germany (as well as Paris, Ukraine and Russia) and places both male and female au pairs for a preferred minimum stay of one year, though six-month stays are also common.

Scores of private agents operate all over Germany, many of them members of the Aupair-Society e.V. (www.au-pair-society.org) which has links to its 34 members (many of which specialise in sending German au pairs abroad). Commercial au pair agencies do not charge a placement fee to incoming au pairs.

Abroad Connection: Bremen and Munich (plus Desenzano del Garda in Italy); www.abroad connection.de.
Au Pair Berlin: www.aupair-to-germany.com.
Au-Pair Vermittlung AMS: c/o Anna-Maria Schlegel, Freiburg; www.aupair-ams.de.
MultiKultur AuPair Service: Köln; www.multikultur.info. Places hundreds of international au pairs throughout Germany.

The minimum monthly pocket money for an au pair in Germany is fixed by the government at €260. Most families contribute a further €50 a month towards a language course and travel expenses. In a few cases families contribute to your fare home but this is discretionary. In return they will expect hard work that may involve more housework than au pairs normally do, as Maree Lakey found during her year as an au pair in Frankfurt.

I found that Germans do indeed seem to be obsessed with cleanliness, something which made my duties as an au pair often very hard. I also found that from first impressions Germans seem to be unfriendly and arrogant; however, once you get to know them and are a guest in their home, they can be the most wonderful and generous people. The Germans I met were sincerely impressed by my willingness to learn their language and at the same time genuinely curious about life in Australia, my home country.

If you are based in a German city and want some part-time work looking after children or helping in private households, check out the online listings at www.haushaltsjob-boerse.de. This is linked from the government agency Minijobs (www.minijob-zentrale.de) which has a Jobs Offered and Jobs Wanted area searchable by location. Mini-jobs refer to part-time work that is below the tax threshold, ie up to €450 a month.

FARM WORK

Farms in Germany tend to be small and highly mechanised: most farm work is done by the owner and his family, with perhaps the help of some locals or regular helpers from Poland, etc at busy times. Only on rare occasions are harvesting vacancies registered with the local *Arbeitsamt*.

Aaron Woods from Ireland was determined to secure some farm work on the Continent. He was lucky enough to have a friend whose cousin owned a maize farm in the village of Breisach am Rhein, 65km north of Basle near the French border. The farmer needed a team of people to help with the flower-plucking stage in July:

> My friend secured the job for three others and myself, all from the same college. It was my friend's cousin's farm that we worked on. We were given free bunk accommodation on the farm in an annex connected to the main house that had a nice kitchen and comfortable bedrooms. We were given a food allowance every week and we got paid at the end of the picking session. Our job was as corn pickers, or rather cornflower pickers. We were to extract the flower of every plant across 75 acres of farmland. The hours were pretty extravagant – six day weeks and working between 8am and 6pm, sometime until 7pm. It was often tough being in the sun for such prolonged periods, and your hands got quite painful, so too did your back and legs. All in all it was pretty tiring work with early starts and very long days.
>
> There was lunch cooked for us every day – the food was delicious, always home cooked by the grand-mother of the family. The surrounding countryside was also filled with vineyards and the family made their own wine (and we were given a few free bottles). The pay was €4 per hour, which is half that of what it is in Ireland. However, our Polish colleagues said it was equivalent to four times their basic rate of pay. The Polish workers seemed to come from the same place (about 10 of them). I think they were the usual workers that worked that farm every year.
>
> In our spare time, we swam in the local lake, went cycling in the countryside or just relaxed out the back with a few beers. Sometimes we'd go to the local city but more so toward the end of the season because we rarely had time off. We also played a lot of basketball and table tennis, facilities that they had in the house. The Polish guys were extremely good at table tennis.

Grape production is the only branch of agriculture that employs casual workers in any number. The harvest, which takes place mostly in the west of the country, is usually later than the one in France, taking place throughout the month of October. While hitching through the Rhine Valley, Danny Jacobson asked repeatedly about grape picking and every response included a reference to Polish migrant workers who appear to have a monopoly on the harvest work.

As usual your chances are better if you can visit the vineyards a month or two before the harvest to fix up work. Ask any German tourist office for a free leaflet about wine festivals which is bound to include sketch maps of all the grape-growing regions of Germany. The main concentration of vineyards is along the Rivers Saar, Ruwer, Mosel and Nahe, centred on places familiar from wine labels such as Bernkastel, Bingen, Piesport and Kasel. There are 10 other areas, principally the Rheingau (around Rüdesheim and Eltville), Rheinpfalz (around Deidesheim, Wachenheim and Bad Dürkheim) and Rhein-hessen (around Oppenheim and Nierstein).

Apart from grapes, the most important area for fruit picking is the Altes Land, which lies between Stade and Hamburg to the south of the River Elbe and includes the towns of Steinkirchen, Jork and Horneburg. The main crops are cherries, which are picked in July and August, and apples in September and October. Apples and other fruit are grown in an area between Heidelberg and Darmstadt called the Bergstrasse, and also in the very south of the country, around Friederichshafen and Ravensburg near Lake Constance. The Bodensee area has been recommended for apple picking: small villages such as Oberdorf, Eriskirch and Leimau sometimes employ migrant workers.

An account of the strawberry harvest near Wilhelmshaven in northern Germany from a Polish contributor Kristof Szymczak goes some way to explaining why so few travellers work on German fruit harvests: *'I was strawberry picking in June/July, and I don't recommend this kind of work to anybody who isn't desperately short of money. Strawberry picking for me is really hard work, almost all day under the sun or rain. Of course it's piecework. The pickers are only from Vietnam and Turkey (already resident in Germany) and of course Poles like me. After travel and living costs, there wasn't much left.'*

Germany has long been at the forefront of the Green movement and organic farming has a high profile. Those who wish to volunteer to work on organic farms should contact the German branch of WWOOF or World Wide Opportunities on Organic Farms (www.wwoof.de). Membership costs €18 for online access, €25 for a printed list of more than 500 addresses in Germany.

VOLUNTEERING

Most of the international organisations mentioned in the introductory Volunteering chapter operate schemes of one sort or another in Germany. Justin Robinson joined a workcamp to restore an old fortress, formerly a concentration camp. Many organisations concentrate their efforts on arranging projects to protect the environment or preserve old buildings. For example Internationale Jugendgemeinschaftsdienste (IJGD) organise summer 'eco-camps' and assist with city fringe recreational activities. This organisation was highly praised by a former volunteer who wrote: *'The camp was excellent value both in the nature of the work and in that the group became part of the local community. These camps are an excellent introduction to travelling for 16 to 26 year olds.'*

As usual workcamps organisations in Germany normally recruit through national partners:

IJGD: workcamps-incoming@ijgd.de; www.ijgd.de. Scores of camps in Germany; British applications accepted by Concordia, VAP, UNA Exchange and Xchange Scotland; basic cost €120.

Internationale Begegnung in Gemeinschaftsdiensten (IBG): www.ibg-workcamps.org. Many projects in both eastern and western Germany; applications in UK as above plus via VFP (www.vfp.org) in the USA.

Mountain Forest Project (Bergwald Projekt e.V.): Würzburg; www.bergwaldprojekt.de. 85 week-long education and conservation projects in the alpine forests of southern Germany; basic knowledge of German is useful since the foresters conduct the camps in German; hut accommodation, food and insurance are provided free though participants must pay an annual membership fee of SFr60/€50.

NIG: Rostock; www.campline.de. Registration for camps at which the language is English, mostly in northern Germany; camps cost €110.

Vereinigung Junger Freiwilliger (VJF): Berlin; www.vjf.de; registration fee €60.

Longer-term possibilities can also be found. The European Voluntary Service (EVS) programme is well established in Germany, which is a fully funded initiative of the European Commission to encourage young Europeans (aged 17–30) to join projects in social care, youth work, outdoor recreation and so on. Internationaler Bund (http://ib-freiwilligendienste.de) takes on young people through this scheme for a period of six or 12 months in various social institutions such as hospitals, kindergartens, and homes for the elderly or disabled people. In some German states, young people aged 16–27, including foreign nationals, may work on ecological projects for a year starting at the end of the summer (www.foej.de). Pocket money, insurance contributions and sometimes even board and lodging are provided by the scheme.

Local opportunities to volunteer can be sought out by anyone staying in a city. For example, Sitske de Groote wanted to spend time with her boyfriend in Berlin. With a background in biological sciences and a liking for working outdoors, she approached the Botanical Gardens to ask about volunteer work. At first they said no because they were worried that her German was not good enough to understand instructions and that she did not have a German tax card. But when she pursued it with the director, he said that she did not need a tax card because the work would be unpaid and that they would take her on, and she ended up really enjoying the experience.

Greece

While many backpackers have been moving further afield to Turkey, Thailand and Tahiti, thousands gather on the islands and mainland of good old Greece every summer. They laze on the beaches, indulge in calamari and Kalamata olives, and try to work out how to afford to stay longer. Jobs in cafés, bars and hostels pop up throughout the busy season and are usually (and regrettably) given to attractive young women.

In the past agricultural jobs in the orange and olive fields that were readily available to travellers now go almost exclusively to jobseeking Albanians, Serbs, Romanians, Bulgarians, Georgians, etc. Outside Athens the hiring of itinerant workers to pick fruit, build houses, unload lorries, etc, often on a day-to-day basis, tends to take place in the main café or square of the town or village, where all the locals congregate to find out what's going on and possibly offer a day's work to willing new arrivals. The work that remains for Western Europeans in addition to resort work is in English language schools, as holiday reps and looking after the children of foreign tourists or in private households where English is prized.

The financial crisis that has battered Greece over the past five years means that Greece is considered an economic basket case, especially by Germans who have contributed billions of euros to prop up the Greek economy. It is estimated that wages have fallen by up to a quarter since 2010 and almost one in four workers is unemployed. Every business is suffering at the time of writing, including private language schools because, when money is tight, language learning is what some companies and families decide to axe. Of course their suffering is as nothing compared to that of the Syrian refugees who have poured into Greece. Altogether Greece is not in a happy place and working travellers should not pin too many hopes on easily stepping into paid employment in Greece at the moment.

Many people from around the world have been so moved by media reports of the suffering of Syrian refugees arriving in Greece with nothing but scarred memories that they have decided to try to help. Some have worked on Lesbos, others in Skaramangas, the huge government-run camp outside Athens. Many volunteers have ended up feeling helpless and traumatised by the stories they have heard and by the inadequacy of the provision for these suffering people. Willing hands have been plentiful but professional preparation and guidance have been minimal, leading in many cases to secondary trauma stress and compassion fatigue, exhaustion and guilt in the face of this overwhelming humanitarian crisis.

REGULATIONS

A European Union directive states that EU citizens who intend to stay for more than three months should apply for a registration certificate (*veveosi eggrafis*) at the local aliens bureau, which is valid indefinitely. This is free of charge and should be issued on the spot after the applicant produces the necessary documents, ie a passport from an EU member country and proof of employment, self-employment or (if not working) proof of funds and medical insurance. EU citizens who do not register will be subject to a fine.

It is mandatory for Greek employers to register full-time employees with the Greek national health insurance scheme, EOPYY, which covers less than the scheme that preceded it (IKA).

The situation for non-Europeans is complex and confused. The reality is that the people working with non-European passports, mainly in resorts, are doing so informally and without permits. The immigration police conduct occasional raids on bars or clubs hiring people under the table, but usually the rumour of a raid provides some advance warning. The sad truth is that they are more concerned about undocumented migrants and refugees. For more high profile and longer-term jobs such as English teaching, most employers will hire outside the EU only if they are desperate.

According to Schengen rules, non-EU citizens can enter Greece (or any member state) for up to 90 days. Be careful not to stay longer than the three months or you risk a hefty fine when leaving.

Remember that you can't return before you have been out of the country for a further 90 days (see section on Border Formalities in introductory chapter on Travel).

TOURISM

Recession, serial street protests, strikes and uncertainty leading to a bad press have prompted a drastic fall in the number of tourists visiting Greece, especially from France and the US (in 2016) but also Britain and Germany. The decline has been less marked in island resorts than in Athens so many young Europeans will still be needed to work in bars, clubs and restaurants. Women have the advantage, although young men are hired as well including as touts to persuade groups of young women into clubs. A good time to look is just before the Orthodox Easter (usually in April) when the locals are beginning to gear up for the season. In a few cases there is work outside the May to September period especially if you are willing to work on a commission-only basis.

You are more likely to find work in places that are isolated from the local culture, in American/ European style bars and clubs in the cities and resorts. Well-known party resorts such as Faliraki in Rhodes, Gouvia in Corfu and Malia and Hersonissos on the north coast of Crete tend to employ young European and English-speaking staff. As long-time expat writer and entrepreneur Louis Tracy concludes, *'The work scene for students is the same as always – people need to prepare well, speak some Greek, arrive early and have lots of chutzpah and determination.'* Party animals might want to consider signing up with a company like Air-Pro Working Holidays in Liverpool (www.air-pro.co.uk) whose base is in Zante. They have taken over a hotel in the resort to house all their clients. Punters pay £68 to register and from £300 to cover four weeks' accommodation plus a €50 in-resort fee for training and assistance with the job hunt (but no guarantees). Similarly the agency PlayaWay (www.playawaya-broad.com) arranges Greek working holidays in the clubbers' resorts of Malia (Crete) and Zante. For a fee from £261 to £379, the company provides a month's accommodation, advice from a PlayaWay rep and introductions to local bar and club owners who may hire you. The range of jobs available may not hold a great deal of appeal, including shot girls, glass collecting, laughing gas selling and so on.

Greeka.com provides links to many local travel and tourism companies throughout Greece that may be hiring. You can check out their job vacancy page at www.greeka.com/greece-jobs.htm which for 2017 included jobs in a surf shop on Rhodes and boat crew for a yacht charter in Halkidiki in the north. Patient internet surfing will lead to the websites of individual bars and restaurants that have a 'Jobs' icon, for example the Tex-Mex restaurant Escoba with branches in Kifissia, a suburb of Athens, and on Naxos (www.escoba.gr) or the Hotel Galini on the large island of Euboea north of Athens (www.pefki-galinihotel. gr); in both cases they are looking for female staff only. The monthly electronic jobs listing Jobs Abroad Bulletin (www.jobsabroadbulletin.co.uk) carries a sprinkling of vacancies in Greece in the spring. While surfing online for a suitable summer vacancy, Annelies van der Plas made use of www.wereldwijzer.nl, the largest online travel community in her native Holland. After spending days of online searching and placing adverts, she finally received a reply from a Dutch man who asked her if she would like to work behind the bar at the Camel Bar on Kos (www.camel.gr). She was asked to send a picture to the Greek boss (which, alas, is typical) and was soon offered a job but no contract (again typical):

> *It was a kind of gamble to go alone as a blonde girl of 19, and my parents were a little bit worried, but they did not object to it, especially because many Dutch people worked on Kos. The boss had an apartment ready for me, for €200 per month or €100 if I shared. The apartment itself was nothing special but the beautiful view of the harbour from the balcony made it worth the money.*

> *When I was working at the Camel bar I saw that it was not hard to find another job on the island. Mostly jobs behind the bar were already taken so the jobs consisted of getting people in. I noticed that the salary was most of the time the same, about €30 a night. I luckily received my money every week, although I did not get my salary for my last week, which means I worked a whole week for nothing. There was nothing I could do; the police were very corrupt.*
>
> *A good feature of the job was the free drinking and the contact with the people. I met a lot of people and every evening seemed like a night out. The tips were much better on the terrace and I could talk more to the people.*
>
> *In two months I have seen that most Greek people see the tourists as idiots. Most bosses think only of money, and they don't care if the customer is not happy with their drink because they will never see them again. My last piece of advice: if you are a (blonde) girl, be careful of the Greek men.*

Undoubtedly the motives of some employers in hiring women are less than honourable. If you get bad vibes, move on. On her gap year, Emma Hoare lasted precisely 20 days in a job as receptionist in a hotel on Mykonos before realising that: (a) she was being totally ripped off and (b) her boss was a *'big fat disgusting immoral bully'*, whom another disgruntled ex-employee described as *'feral'*.

According to the expat website www.livingincrete.net/employment.html, adverts for seasonal work in hotels, cafés, tavernas and shops can be found in the Greek language newspapers *Haniotika Nea* and *Patris* in February/March. The site also has an employment forum with a few job vacancies. LivinginCrete.net also recommends the noticeboard at the secondhand shop, To Pazari, on Daskalogianni St in Chania, which sometimes has ads in English for job vacancies, or you can advertise your services here. Another source of possible job info is www.jobincrete.com with a handful of up-do-date vacancies. Corfu, Zakynthos, Ios, Kos, Rhodes and Naxos seem to offer the most job openings in tourism, though Paros, Santorini and Mykonos have all been recommended. One web poster makes the situation sound hopeful:

> *Last summer me and my friend from New Zealand went over to Santorini and worked in a bar. We got over at the start of June which was the start of the season but if you're looking at going to Ios (where all the Australians and Kiwis go) you would have to go in May to get the good jobs and good accommodation. We worked every second night over June as it wasn't too busy. Come mid-July till the end of September, you work every day of the week, often till closing time at 4am. We were only doing bar work but saved about €6,000 between us so that was good! We had the best time ever in Santo and are going back to do it again!*

It should be noted that it is more usual even for careful savers to end up with a lot closer to zero than to €6,000 after a long busy season. Flamboyant personalities might want to investigate Agency Remarc near Athens which supplies entertainers, animators and sports services to hotels and resorts in the region (www.sunseafun.com); the promised wage starts at €500 per month plus room and board after an unpaid one-week training course in April. Another company that hires people to work in the entertainment programmes of hotels in Greece as well as Cyprus and Spain is TMC Tourist Services (www.tmc247.com) which is part of TUI Travel and has offices in Denmark and Cyprus.

Working in very heavily touristed areas can leave you feeling jaded. Although Richard Ferguson had a great season in Faliraki, he was relieved when he finally had a ticket out of 'ChavLand'. He had had enough of his PR job outside Q Nightclub with the nightly patter, *'Hullo luff, yoo awright? Where yoo goin' tanite? Come ta Q Club. I'll give ya sum free shots I will 'n awl.'* Q Club Nightclub on Club Street is the one favoured by other foreign workers in Faliraki who go along at the end of their shifts. Blogger Turner Barr includes among the jobs you might get 'door whore' (male enticing people in) and 'floor whore' (female who dances and drinks with customers to give them a good time).

To find out about occasional openings for people to deliver cars for car rental firms or to act as transfer couriers, ask around at those local travel agencies which act as the headquarters for overseas reps. Some enterprising long-stay foreigners have moonlighted as freelance guides. For example you could hire a Jeep and offer to take small groups on an off-the-beaten-track tour of a region you know well, taking in the cheapest tavernas and most remote beaches.

Seasonal jobs can be arranged from the UK, preferably by contacting relevant tour operators in February or March. Mark Warner (www.markwarner.co.uk/recruitment) runs watersports holidays at resorts in Kos, Rhodes and Lemnos. As usual, jobs are easiest to find if you are a nanny or a watersports instructor. Similarly Neilson (www.neilson.co.uk/recruitment) takes on a range of summer staff for its seven Greek beachclubs from Sivota in northwest Greece to Lesbos.

Other possibilities exist with Olympic Holidays, which is based in London and has opportunities in the UK and overseas (overseas-jobs@olympicholidays.com; www.olympicholidays.com), and who are always on the lookout for outgoing applicants with relevant experience to work a season as resort reps (minimum requirement: decent GCSE grades in Maths and English). Tax-free wages are £450–£550 per month including commission for selling car hire, excursions, etc plus flights and accommodation.

TOUR OPERATORS SEEM TO BE MORE INTERESTED IN FINDING THE RIGHT ATTITUDE RATHER THAN EXPERIENCE WHEN RECRUITING REPS, AS DEBBIE HARRISON DISCOVERED;

Despite the fact that I had no qualifications or relevant experience, had never been to Greece and had never even been on a package holiday, I was offered a job on the island of Kos immediately at the end of my interview. Perhaps this had something to do with the fact that it was mid-March, less than a month before training began and they obviously still had positions to fill. However, tour operators do hire reps as late as May or June to help out with the extra workload of high season. Six or seven months is a long time to stay in one place.

In-Globe Agency is a recruitment agency based in Thessaloniki and registered with the Ministry of Labour. It aims to find staff from all over Europe to fill positions in holiday resorts in Greece and Cyprus and recruits up to 2,000 Europeans aged 18–55 for summer jobs in tourist hotels on the islands and also in its internship programme for trainees. Summer jobs and internships open to students (primarily students of hospitality and tourism) last four months (June to September) whereas professional work experience placements can be for up to 18 months. Basic monthly salaries start at €350–€450 net in addition to free accommodation, meals, social insurance and the possibility of paid flights. CVs an be uploaded onto the website www.inglobe.com.gr or ring ☎ (+30) 2310 588200.

Some hotel chains such as Grecotel (www.grecotel.com) implement their own training and work experience hospitality programmes, though they obtain their entertainment staff from Agency Remarc.

Selling and Enterprise

Creative entrepreneurs often find a ready market in the tourist ghettoes of the Greek islands. In the past people have sold sunglasses at a big mark-up, made jewellery and cut hair to supplement their travel fund.

Anyone who can paint or draw quick portraits may be in for a bonanza in the main resorts. There may be work painting signs and noticeboards (primarily at the beginning of the season) or decorating the walls, doors and menu boards of tourist places themselves. This can be quite well paid if you are good at it and get a good reputation. One reader reported that after noticing so many misspelled signs on Zakynthos (her favourite advertised 'daft Cider'), she was sure that someone with both artistic and orthographic talents could persuade Greek bar owners to pay for a sign.

The island of Santorini boasts a cutting-edge English language bookshop called Atlantis (www. atlantisbooks.org), which struggles to stay afloat, so they are unlikely to have job vacancies.

Boating

Yachting holiday companies are a possible source of jobs, which can be fixed up either ahead of time or on the spot. Major UK-based tour operators hire the full range of summer staff, for example

Sailing Holidays based in North London runs holiday programmes in the Ionian and Saronic Islands and the Sporades, for which it needs skippers, engineers, flotilla 'hosties' and shore-based crew (hr@sailingholidays.com). Similarly Island Sailing (www.island-sailing.com/sailing-jobs) is a major employer. A youth oriented sailing tour operator operated by New Zealand yachties hires seasonal staff; contact MedSailors (careers@navigatetravel.com). Seafarer invite applications in January (including at the London Boat Show) for their flotilla sailing holidays and beach clubs on Kos and Lefkas. The company has been expanding so needs more crew and staff than ever (http://seafarersailing. co.uk/crew-wanted-now). Plenty of charter boats and sailing holidays set off from the Halkidiki Peninsula east of Thessaloniki. For example BabaSails Yachting (www.babasails.eu) needs boat crew from early June to the end of September. You have to be friendly and smiling and also (preferably) speak Russian.

RYA cruising instructors and skippers are taken on by Sail Ionian (www.sailionian.com/job-opportunities) in Levkas. Keen sailors might choose to qualify as instructors at courses offered in Greece which would make it easy to step into a job. The Yacht Academy trains unqualified people to work though the cost of their Zero to Hero course costs an eye-watering £8,750.

For casual work it is worth doggedly enquiring around yacht marinas on any island from Corfu (Gouvia) to Crete (Agios Nikolaos).

Scuba diving centres may also offer free accommodation and training in exchange for hard work for a season. Two to try on Crete are European Diving Institute in Lygaria, 20km west of Heraklion (admin@eurodiving.net) and the Stay Wet Diving Centre in Heraklion where you can turn yourself into a divemaster if you stay from March to October (www.staywet.gr/certifications_en.html).

AGRICULTURE

Working in the English-speaking environment of tourism is not for everyone and certainly does not conform to Ben Nakoneczny's philosophy of travel:

> *If you are to work abroad it is preferable to be employed in a capacity which allows an insight into the people of the country you are visiting. To serve English tourists bottled beer in a Western-style bar is merely to experience the company of those travellers who cling to what they know, unprepared to risk the unfamiliarity of an alien culture. I believe that the best way of breaking cultural boundaries is to work outside the tourist areas, probably in agriculture.*

Unfortunately these days you might end up deserting an English-speaking environment only to find yourself in an Albanian, Bulgarian or Romanian one. Recent feedback about harvesting in Greece has been all but non-existent of late or if it does exist reads more like an epitaph than a how-to guide.

For example Siôn from Wales revisited the Peloponnese on a sentimental journey, recalling his experiences as a fruit picker and casual worker when he was a contributor to this book in its infancy: *'The citrus pickers I watched in the Sparta region seemed to be Romanians and Greeks. I didn't notice any of the sort of seasonal workers in Kalamata, Mystras and Sparta that I knew in the early 80s in Greece. I remembered my time on the mainland when I and others had been offered seasonal work by drivers merely by walking along roads.'*

Inevitably, travellers will continue to meet farmers in cafés and be asked to lend a hand here and there in the harvesting of oranges, olives, grapes and other crops. But the employment of young international travellers does not take place on the massive scale it once did. The orange harvest between Corinth and Argos runs from late November or early December to late February, with the crop at its peak between mid-December and mid-January.

Crete, the largest of the Greek islands, was once able to provide a huge amount of work to travellers, from the bananas in Arvi on the south coast (the most northerly commercial banana plantations in the world) to the potato harvest around Ayios Georgios in the Lassithi Plain in August, but mainly involving the grape and olive crops and the massive greenhouses around Ierapetra. The olive harvest begins in late November though mechanisation has replaced much of the hand picking.

Although much of northern Greece is rugged and forbidding, parts of Central Macedonia are very fertile. The area west of Thessaloniki, encompassing the market towns of Veria in the prefecture of Imathia, and Yiannitsa in Pella province, comprises a rich agricultural plain, producing asparagus, peaches, pears and tobacco. The asparagus harvest takes place in the spring while the peach harvest gets started in mid-July and peaks after 1 August. As elsewhere, this area once attracted armies of migrant workers, both Greek and Western European. Now the work has been taken over by Albanians and Bulgarians (whose borders are not far away).

WWOOF Greece (www.wwoofgreece.org) has expanded since it launched in 2011 and now has 65 hosts. When you preview the host list, you may be tempted to join so that you can, for example, help cultivate vegetables, olive trees and vineyards, help make soap, cheese, bread, olive oil and *tsipouro* (a kind of grappa), and look after a rare breed of pony. Membership costs €15.

OTHER WORK

It is sometimes worth checking the classified ads on Craigslist.gr, though quite a few of the listings seem to be looking for models and companions. A few are for au pair, nanny or English-tutoring jobs in private households. The Athens Chamber of Commerce and Industry (7 Academias Str, 106 71 Athens; www.acci.gr) may be able to advise skilled candidates on jobs with Greek companies though in the current economic climate, proper jobs are as scarce as hens' teeth.

Childcare

Living with a Greek family is one of the best ways of organising an extended stay. Yet au pairing hours tend to be longer in Greece than elsewhere, partly because there is no expectation that an au pair will need time off to study the language. The Nine Muses Agency (www.ninemuses.gr) is now primarily a Greek language teaching organisation and no longer accepts applications from young European and American women for au pair positions. Riitta Koivula from Finland moved from an unsatisfactory situation on Kos to a much better one in Athens:

> I started my work as an au pair on Kos when I was 19. At first I was so excited about my new family and the new place since I had never been to Greece before and I loved the sun and the beach. I lived in a small village called Pili where almost no-one spoke English. But soon I got tired of the village because winter came, tourists left and it wasn't so warm to spend time on the beach any more. I also got tired of the family. The three little girls didn't speak English and they were very lively. The working hours were also terrible: 8 to 12 in the morning and then 4 to 10 in the evening every day except Sundays. I was very homesick on Kos and decided I wanted things to change. So I went to Athens in November and changed to a new family. I fell in love with Athens and its people right away. My new family was the best and we are still very close.

An agency in Greece that potentially places au pairs year round is In-Globe in Thessaloniki (inglobe. com.gr) mentioned above.

The advantage of waiting until you get to Greece to look for a live-in job is that you can meet your prospective family first. It is far better for both parties if you can chat over a cup of coffee and bargain in a leisurely fashion for wages, time off, duties, etc. Most families looking for nannies live in the well-off suburbs of Athens such as Kifissia, Politia, Pangrati and Kolonaki as well as in Thessaloniki, Patras and the islands.

Experienced nannies should be able to find summer work with holidaymaking families. For example Kids in Greece (www.kidsingreece.com) wants to hear from candidates with at least two childcare references, a DBS check and first aid certificate, for possible placement in Athens, Thessaloniki, the Ionian and Aegean islands plus Crete, Rhodes, Kos and Halkidiki.

Teaching English

Thousands of private language schools called *frontisteria* are scattered throughout Greece, creating a demand for native English speaker teachers. This is one job for which there will be no competition from Albanians, though it should be noted that EU citizens are strongly preferred over non-EU. Australians, South Africans and North Americans of Greek ancestry are often given teaching jobs in preference to people with non-Greek surnames.

Standards at *frontisteria* vary from indifferent to excellent, but the run-of-the-mill variety is usually a reasonable place to work for nine months. By no means all of the foreign teachers hired by *frontisteria* hold a TEFL qualification, though all but the most dodgy or desperate schools will expect to see a university degree (which is a government requirement for a teacher's licence) and EU citizenship.

The majority of jobs are in towns and cities in mainland Greece. Athens has such a large expatriate community that most of the large central schools are able to hire well-qualified staff locally. But this may not be the case in Edessa, Larisa, Preveza or any of numerous smaller towns of which the tourist to Greece is unlikely to have heard.

The minimum hourly wage has dropped to €8.13 gross which becomes a niggardly €6.84 net, though this is not too bad if accommodation is provided free. The average number of hours assigned to teachers has been shrinking to 18 per week, which further reduces earnings. Teachers with superior training or experience may be able to ask for a higher rate, and all teachers will hope to receive holiday pay plus Christmas and Easter bonuses, which seem to have survived in the private sector at least, despite the imposition of so many austerity measures.

A couple of teacher recruitment agencies actively seek teachers to work for one academic year, though numbers have fallen in the past few years. Interviews are carried out in Greece or the UK during the summer for contracts starting in September. These agencies are looking for people with at least a BA and normally a TEFL certificate (depending on the client *frontisterion*'s requirements). The following undertake to match EU teachers with *frontisteria* and do not charge teachers a fee:

Anglo-Hellenic Teacher Recruitment: 13 Vasilou St, Vrahati, PO Box 263, 20006 Corinth, Greece; ☎ (+30) 2741 053511; applications@anglo-hellenic.com; www.anglo-hellenic.com. Posts in choice of locations for university graduates from the UK, preferably with a recognised 120-hour TEFL Certificate; Anglo-Hellenic offers a one-month training course from TEFL Corinth (www.teflcorinth.com) for €1,295 plus €250 for shared accommodation; note that some graduates of the course have found it more difficult to find jobs than expected, because they do not speak Greek.

Cambridge Teachers Recruitment: 8 Daskalou-Kitsou, Maroussi, 15124 Athens; ☎ (+30) 21 0258 5155 or (+30) 694 655 8217; also in UK in August: ☎ (+44) 20 8686 3733; macleod_smith_andrew@hotmail.com. Teacher applicants must have a degree and a TEFL Certificate, a friendly personality and conscientious attitude.

Peter Beech, Director of Anglo-Hellenic in Corinth has noticed an increasing interest from people who have already had a career in the UK, in teaching or in any field, who want to move abroad. One of his trainees, Jerry Melinn, enjoyed teaching English at an institute in Athens so much that he has renewed his contract several times since:

> *I suppose you could say I don't fit the profile of a TEFL teacher. Usually they are unattached, young and out to see the world after finishing their university studies. I worked in the telecommunications industry in Ireland for almost 40 years and took advantage of an early retirement scheme when I was 56 years old. I didn't want to stop working and, as my four children were grown up, I decided with the agreement of my wife, to try my hand at teaching English in Greece. I was interested in Greece because we have friends here and had been coming to Greece on holidays for many years.*
>
> *I have read some horror stories on the internet about teaching in Greece but my experience has been great. The TEFL training course in Corinth (www.teflcorinth.com) prepared me well for teaching at the Katsianos*

School of Foreign Languages in Athens. I have learned so much, made many new friends and grown very attached to the school and especially the students. I have nothing but admiration for them as they come to lessons twice a week after Greek school and the vast majority are well behaved and good humoured. The pay and conditions are the same as most schools in Greece, beginning at €700 a month with accommodation provided and all bills paid as well as health insurance, which I thought was very good.

Private lessons, at least in the provinces, are possible to find, especially if you are already familiar with the most popular exams, eg First Certificate (Lower) and Certificate of Proficiency mainly administered by Cambridge and Michigan. The going rate can be €25–€30 an hour for tutoring candidates to pass the B2 (Independent User) and C2 (Proficient User), the EU-wide standards.

Volunteering

Elix-Conservation Volunteers Greece in Athens (☎ (+30) 21 0382 5506; www.elix.org.gr) is a non-profit organisation promoting intercultural exchanges and nature and heritage conservation. Projects include education programmes for refugee and migrant children, work in protected landscapes, conservation of traditional buildings and assistance with social care. Applications can be sent directly or through a partner organisation such as UNA Exchange and Concordia in the UK.

Earth, Sea and Sky (www.earth-sea-sky-global.org), a private NGO which grew out of a travel agency, recruits volunteers to carry out island-based wildlife research, conservation and tourist awareness work on the Ionian island of Zakynthos. The SOS Sea Turtle Rescue Centre near Gerakas Beach is still being developed. Volunteers with a range of skills are needed for short or long-term placements between April and October. On the same island, a project to protect sea turtles actively uses volunteer helpers. Volunteer fees are from £390 for a fortnight to £1,610 for 12 weeks plus €5–€15 a day for food.

Archelon is the Sea Turtle Protection Society of Greece (☎ (+30) 21 0523 1342; www.archelon. gr) that carries out research and conservation on the loggerhead turtle on Zakynthos, Crete and the Peloponnese. A free campsite is provided for those who stay at least a month; volunteers will need at least €15 a day for food plus pay a registration fee of €300. One traveller worked for Archelon in Zakynthos; her duties included giving explanations to tourists on the turtles, presentations and talks to raise public awareness, manning the information booth. She also spent a short time on the island of Marathonissi conducting surveys in the morning and evenings and recording data found from turtle tracks on the beach.

Another turtle conservation organisation is the Katelios Group working on the island of Kefalonia during the nesting season (June/July) and the hatching season (August/September). Volunteers stay for a minimum of one month in rented rooms near the turtles' habitat and spend days and sometimes nights patrolling the beaches, occasionally travelling between them by kayak. The cost is reasonable (www.kateliosgroup.org/volunteer); subscription costs €50 plus estimated living costs are about €400 a month in shared accommodation which must be arranged privately.

Medasset (Mediterranean Association to Save the Sea Turtles; ☎ (+30) 21 0361 3572 or in the UK: ☎ (+44) 20 3286 6189; www.medasset.org) offers volunteers free accommodation at the Head Office in Athens in exchange for working for a minimum of three weeks. Volunteer work is office-based only and includes assisting staff with projects, letter writing, computer orientated and archiving tasks, database updating, internet research, etc. No prior knowledge in sea turtle conservation is required, just a passion and interest in the environment.

Bears are even more threatened than marine turtles. Arcturos accepts short-term volunteers at its environmental centre in the Prefecture of Florina in northern Greece, which serves as a bear protection centre (☎ (+30) 23860 1150; www.arcturos.gr). Yet another project for animal lovers is the Donkey Rescue Centre in Corfu (www.corfu-donkeys.com), which takes on about six students to be interns or volunteers for at least a fortnight.

Another interesting possibility for people willing to work for at least three months from April or July is at the holistic holiday centre on the island of Skyros (www.skyros.com) in the northern Aegean. A number of 'work scholars' help with cleaning, bar work and domestic and maintenance duties in exchange for weekly pocket money of £50 plus the opportunity to join one of the 250 courses on offer, from yoga to windsurfing. Childcare staff are also sometimes needed for short summer stays. Details are available from Skyros's UK office on the Isle of Wight (☎ (+44) 1983 865566; jobs@skyros.com).

Cyprus

The Cypriot economy has made an impressive recovery in the four years since the banking system suffered a meltdown in 2013. However the rate of unemployment of nearly 15% is troubling. Like its Greek counterpart, it has relied heavily on agriculture and tourism. The sharp decline in tourist numbers arriving in Cyprus after the global financial crash and economic downturn, has been reversed and is now steadily climbing. An estimated 10% of the population is employed in the tourist sector of the Republic of Cyprus. (The Turkish Republic of Northern Cyprus is dealt with separately at the end of this chapter.)

A visitor to Greek Cyprus will be struck by the similarities with Greece (language, cuisine, architecture, landscapes and culture) but then surprised by the relative prominence of English and the widespread British influence left over from when Cyprus was a British colony until 1960. They are also sometimes shocked by the extent of the concrete jungles along the coast catering to mass tourism.

REGULATIONS

Cyprus is a full member of the EU so nationals of all the other EU countries have the automatic right of residence in Cyprus. Those who intend to work and stay in the country are obliged to apply for a registration certificate within four months of arrival. In Nicosia this can be done at the Migration department; elsewhere applicants must visit the Immigration Police.

Australians are lucky that there is a reciprocal working holiday scheme whereby people aged 18–30 can apply in Australia for a one-year working holiday visa for Cyprus.

Anyone with qualifications and experience, particularly in IT, should look at the job vacancies listed by the recruitment agency Global Recruitment Solutions with offices in Limassol and Nicosia (www.grs recruitment.com) or consult recruitment sites such as www.jobscyprus.com and www.jobsincyprus. com. Although these sites are in English, most vacancies are for people with knowledge of Greek.

TOURISM

Most big tour operators consider placement in Cyprus as a perk to be offered to staff who have worked well for the company elsewhere, especially if they have worked in Greece and picked up some of the language. Cyprus has the advantage of offering work during the winter as well as the summer, though it has special short seasonal attractions when it is especially busy, such as for the spring flowers.

To track down companies to which you can apply check any Winter Sun travel brochure or check recruitment websites. Hotel chains such as Louis Hotels (human.resources@louishotels.com) and Amathus Hotels (www.amathus-hotels.com) are worth investigating. An extensive list of hotels can be found on the site of the Cyprus Hotel Association (www.cyprushotelassociation.org). As in Greece, women are at an advantage when looking for work in cafés, bars and restaurants, but they should exercise caution according to Karen Holman:

> *In my two years there I heard stories about Cypriot employers expecting more of their barmaids than just bar work. I worked in two pubs and I would say that both bosses employed me with an ulterior motive. I was lucky – both of them were shy. By the time they realised I wasn't going to be their girl-*

friend, they had found me to be a good worker and were used to me being around. Many employers will sack the girls, or threaten to report them for stealing.

Tom Parker had little success with a job search along the seafront in Limassol in April:

We headed for the tourist area and were soon told that we would stand a better chance if we bought a drink for the manager before asking about jobs. The only concrete result was that we got very drunk. No job opportunities (they told us we were too early). The next day we concentrated on the small cafés in the back streets of the old town. Here my two companions (both girls) were offered jobs in separate cafés.

TURKISH REPUBLIC OF NORTHERN CYPRUS

As is well known, Cyprus is a divided island. The southern part is the Republic of Cyprus, a member of the British Commonwealth and European Union. The north, occupied by Turkey since the intervention of 1974, is called the Turkish Republic of Northern Cyprus (Kibris) and tens of thousands of Turkish troops are stationed there. It is not recognised by any country except Turkey. In early 2017, promising talks were held which represented the best chance there has been to reunite the island. Ironically some commentators fear that reunification might spell the end of the North's special undeveloped, under-visited character.

However, there is a sizeable expat community that has acquired many properties along the north coast of the island. One factor that has suppressed growth in the tourist industry is the lack of direct flights. At one time, you had to fly via mainland Turkey, however the restrictions have been relaxed and several land border crossings exist. Because Northern Cyprus is off the beaten track, the pool of potential seasonal or casual labour is smaller than it is elsewhere on the Mediterranean.

Turkish Cyprus is a very small place (population just over 300,000) and job vacancies become known as soon as they exist. For every one advertised in the English language weekly *Cyprus Today*, there are dozens heard of on the grapevine. The noticeboard outside the Post Office in the main town of Kyrenia (Girne) is a possible source of information on jobs, accommodation, etc. The active British Residents' Society can be found in 'the hut' behind the post office on Saturday mornings and also maintains a website (www.brstrnc.com) with good, up-to-date information. You can meet expats (most of whom own property in the TRNC) at their favourite haunts such as the Cafe George in Girne.

Opportunities may exist in restaurants and holiday apartments, especially those owned or managed by expats. The wages are low by British standards, but food and accommodation may be provided. The highest concentration of restaurants and bars is along the picturesque harbour of Girne, with a further concentration in Lapta, Karaman and Alsancak to the west.

Tour Companies

Northern Cyprus is not a cheap package holiday destination and tends to attract a more discerning clientele, who are interested in visiting the sites as well as enjoying the marvellous scenery and climate. It is a popular destination for Germans, so some knowledge of German would be an advantage.

Some time ago, Pat Kennard landed a job with a ground-handling agent for a number of UK tour operators. She enjoyed a fantastic season as a holiday rep even though, as she admits, it is a very demanding job having to do early morning and late night airport runs, sort out clients' problems with their accommodation and conduct tours of the island. Nowadays, they prefer people who can speak Turkish as well as English.

Red Tape

The red tape for foreign workers is more difficult than it used to be. The prospective employer must prove that no local citizen can do the job, and arrange a work permit while the employee is out of the country. If you stay on a 90-day tourist visa, it will be necessary (as in Turkey) to leave Cyprus every three months to renew your tourist visa; this entails a two-hour passenger-only catamaran trip from Kyrenia to Tasucu on mainland Turkey at a cost of about €78 return. Reports have been becoming more frequent of the authorities being reluctant to give an automatic further 90 days. Do not overstay your three-month stay because you will be fined for every extra day.

In order to work legally in Northern Cyprus, you must obtain either a work permit (if working for a TRNC company) or a business permit. The cost of a work permit is 160TL (about £35) for six months; the business permit costs six times as much for the same period. Individuals caught working without a permit will face deportation and a huge fine, as will the company that employed them.

Italy

Italy is a remarkably welcoming country. Once Italians accept you, they will go out of their way to find you a place in their communities, without any emphasis on the barriers of nationality. Once you get a toehold, you will find that a friendly network of contacts and possible employers will quickly develop. Without contacts, if only a sympathetic landlady at your *pensione*, it is difficult to find work.

In Italy you find the best-dressed and most sophisticated people in the world. Image counts for a great deal in Italy, and it has to be said that good-looking, smartly dressed people have far more chance of success than their dowdy careless counterparts. With a high rate of unemployment that has been stuck stubbornly at around the 12% mark for a few years and is predicted to drop only slightly before 2020, it is going to take more than a pair of stylish shoes to find a job. The situation for casual jobseekers has been made more difficult by the arrival of more than a million Romanians since 2007 when Romania joined the EU.

REGULATIONS

EU citizens intending to stay in Italy longer than 90 days are required to register at the *Anagrafe* office of the local town hall with documentary evidence that they are working or studying in Italy.

If non-EU citizens want to stay longer than the 90 days permitted on a Schengen visa, they must apply for a *permesso di soggiorno* (temporary permit to stay). They will have to show proof of a short-term job or a course. It is possible to apply at a post office as well as at the *Questura* (police department). Detailed information can be found at www.portaleimmigrazione.it (for which you will need Google translate) including templates of the forms needed to apply for the *permessi*.

Australian, New Zealand and Canadian citizens aged 18–30 are eligible for a 12-month working holiday visa in Italy. The best chances for other non-EU citizens (*extracomunitari*) of getting their papers in order are to be a dual national, to obtain a student visa which permits 20 hours of work a week (living in or out) or to arrange a firm offer of a job while they are still in their home country. Note that American citizens may be able to avoid work permit hassles by working for the US military. The American Garrison base in Vicenza sometimes hires catering and other staff, although most jobs go to dependants of stationed personnel; contact the Vicenza Civilian Personnel Advisory Center. If you want to open a bank account, you need to take proof that you are resident and proof of income (tax return or contract). Tax is a further headache for long-stay workers. As soon as you sort out the work documents, you should obtain a tax number (*codice fiscale*) from the Agenzia delle Entrate. The rate of income tax (*ritenuta d'acconto*) is usually about 20% in addition to social security deductions of up to 10%.

Remember that medical expenses can be very high if you're not covered by the Italian Medical Health Scheme (ASL or *Azienda Sanitaria Locale*). Once you locate the local office, you must apply for an EU Health Insurance Card for Italy (*Tessera Sanitaria*).

FINDING WORK

If you can't speak a word of Italian, you will be at a distinct disadvantage. Provided you can afford it and are sufficiently interested, you should consider studying a little Italian before you set off on your travels or enrolling in one of the many short Italian language courses offered in most Italian cities. Italian is one of the easiest languages to pronounce and learn, especially if you already have some knowledge of a Latin-based language.

Although you should not neglect scouring the newspapers and online recruitment sites for job adverts, you may be disappointed. Sometimes requests by *stranieri* (foreigners) for work outnumber the situations vacant, eg in the free ads paper *Secondamano* (www.secondamano.it/lavoro). English-language publications both online and print can be useful, such as the fortnightly *Easy Milano* (www.easymilano.it) and *Wanted in Rome* (www.wantedinrome.com), which has a good selection of job vacancies for teachers, au pairs, etc, as do the free ads sites www.kijiji.it and www.bakeca.it ('Career Builder').

Contacts

Contacts are even more important in Italy than in other countries. Many of the people we have heard from who have worked in Italy (apart from TEFL teachers, au pairs, etc) have got their work through friends. They may not necessarily have had the friends or contacts when they arrived, but they formed friendships while they were there as visitors.

Language school noticeboards are always worth checking; at the Centro di Lingua & Cultura Italiana per Stranieri where Dustie Hickie took cheap Italian lessons in Milan, there was a good noticeboard with adverts for au pairs, dog-walkers, etc. Dustie got a cleaning job this way.

Even with contacts you are not guaranteed to find work, as Edward Peters found one summer: *'After travelling through Eastern Europe and Austria, we had hoped to find something in Italy; but three sets of contacts were unable to find us anything – perhaps because it was August (national holidays) or perhaps because we were too busy enjoying ourselves in Milan, Rome and Ischia.'*

TOURISM

Italy's tourist industry employs a high proportion of the Italian workforce and has limited openings for unskilled non-Italians. Anyone who has had the pleasure of dining out in Italy or even buying 200 grams of cheese or salami at a delicatessen will know that Italian standards of service are very professional and indeed people (usually men) consider waiting on tables as a career. Any openings for casual bar staff that come along are likely to be in (for example) Irish-themed pubs or American-style bistros.

Although less well known than the seaside resorts of other Mediterranean countries, there may be seaside possibilities for foreign jobseekers, especially in the resorts near Venice. Lake Garda resorts such as Desenzano, Malcesine, Sirmione and Riva del Garda are recommended as are the seaside resorts near Venice such as Lido di Jesolo, Bibione, Lignano, Caorle and Chioggia, all of which are more popular with German and Austrian tourists than Britons, so a knowledge of German would be a good selling point. Apart from the job of *cameriera ai piani* (chambermaid), knowledge of Italian will be necessary.

The Blu Hotels chain manages 25 hotels and holiday villages in Lake Garda, Sardinia, Umbria, Abruzzo, Tuscany, Rome, Palinuro and Calabria (as well as Austria); its website www.bluhotels.it has a jobs icon (*Lavora con noi*). Michael Cullen worked in three hotels around Como and Bellagio and found '*a nice friendly and warm atmosphere, despite the heat and long hours*'. Even in flourishing resorts such as Rimini, there seem to be enough locals and Italian students to fill the jobs in hotels, bars and on the beach, although one company has been advertising heavily in the English-speaking media. The Life Club in Rimini (www.liferimini.com/job.html) hires young people to work as promoters, bartenders, photographers and DJs in the club scene over the summer; they want to see a photo of prospective staff.

If you don't get a job in a hotel, you might get work servicing holiday flats or gardening. If you plan far enough in advance (and speak some Italian) you might get a job as a campsite courier with one of the major British camping holiday organisers such as Canvas Holidays or with a tour operator such as Headwater Holidays (see introductory chapter on Tourism). The smaller Venue Holidays (☎ (+44) 1233 629950; jobs@venueholidays.co.uk; www.venueholidays.com/UK/work_for_us) employs summer season reps at campsites on the Adriatic coast, Lake Garda and in Tuscany. Similarly Bolero Holidays (www.boleroholidays.co.uk) look to hire campsite couriers and children's couriers at their mobile home holiday park at Union Lido near Venice; and European Camping Services Ltd (formerly Happy Camp Family Holidays) conduct interviews in the UK between November and February for customer service reps (www.eucsltd.co.uk). A company tent and the use of a bicycle is provided.

Catherine Dawes enjoyed her campsite job near Albenga on the Italian Riviera – '*a fairly uninspiring part of Italy*' – even more than she did her previous summer's work on a French campsite. She reports that the Italians seemed to be more relaxed than the French, especially under high season pressure, and would always go out of their way to help her when she was trying to translate tourists' problems to the mechanic or the doctor.

The British company Brad Europe Ltd (www.bradeurope.com) provides a linen hire service to over 300 campsites in Europe, and operates a laundering facility near Vicenza. Staff are paid the UK minimum wage and provided with free accommodation.

Many mountain resorts with busy ski seasons (see section below) also need workers from outside the area for the summer. One UK tour operator that takes on domestic staff and summer reps with language skills to work in the Dolomites is Collett's Mountain Holidays (☎ (+44) 1799 513331; www.colletts.co.uk/work).

You can also try Italian-run campsites that often have a large staff to man the onsite restaurants, bars and shops. The two main campsites in Rome including the Flaminio Village may take on English help before the season begins (ie March). Boat mechanics and other staff can approach holiday barge companies; for example the cruise company LeBoat (www.leboat.co.uk/careers) which is part of TUI Travel, has bases in Casale near Treviso, Precenicco on the Adriatic and Porto Levante south of Venice in the Po delta.

Holiday Animators and Entertainers

A surprising number of the European agencies that recruit animators, musicians, singers, DJs and entertainers for holiday villages and summer resorts are based in Italy. All of these want their summer entertainment teams to speak two European languages. The companies seem to favour English names like 'Sounds Good Animation'. Here are a few companies that hire substantial numbers of young people normally aged 18–30:

Associazione Nazionale Animatori: Rome; ☎ (+39) 06 678 1647; www.associazione nazionaleanimatori.it. Trade association for the industry.

DarwinStaff Srl: Florence; ☎ (+39) 055 292114; www.darwinstaff.com. Company casts large numbers of mini club animators to arrange children's holiday programme plus hostesses, DJs, musicians, etc.

Like It Srl: Grosseto, Tuscany; ☎ (+39) 0564 49 7273; risorse.umane@likeit.red. Entertainment specialists (see their Facebook page). Hire teams to organise daily activity programmes for holidaymakers eg in sport/fitness/kids' clubs.

Planet Villager Animazione Turistica: Rimini; www.planetvillager.com. This company recruits hundreds of staff not only in Italy but also throughout Europe.

RDS World: Foggia; lavoro@rdsworld.it; www.rdsworld.it; recruits reps in Rome, Bari and Naples for about 15 resorts in Italy; four-day training course held in May.

Sounds Good Animation: Verona; www.soundsgoodanimation.com/en. Hire holiday club entertainment and animation staff, event or show organisers, costume party organisers for children, etc.

Hostels

As throughout the world, backpackers' haunts often employ travellers for short periods. Check out www.hosteljobs.net that at the time of writing was advertising seasonal vacancies in the WikiHostel in Zagarolo located in the hills half an hour east of Rome. A hostel in Rome that has been recommended is Fawlty Towers at Via Magenta 39 (www.fawltytowers.org) near the Termini Station in Rome, where many native English speakers find work in reception, maintenance and cleaning.

Raised in New York and largely cut off from her family's Italian roots, one traveller decided at age 30 to spend some time in Italy.

BY MAKING USE OF WWW.HOSTELS.COM STEPHANIE FUCCIO HAD LITTLE DIFFICULTY PRE-ARRANGING A HOSTEL JOB:

Never in a million years did I think that watching MTV would be part of my daily life in Rome, Italy. But it was. I was working at a really cute, small hostel in Rome, seven days a week. The shifts would alternate from evening to morning every day: one day doing the morning shift when the hostel was cleaned and the next day the evening shift. As well as getting to stay there for free, they paid me and my co-worker 20 euros per day in cash, which was really nice. Rome was so cheap (from a San Francisco point of view) and with great weather, it was easy to save. I came to Italy with $700 cash and a plane ticket; I left with about $600 and a plane ticket to England and Ireland. I was there about five weeks total.

Winter Resorts

On-the-spot opportunities are possible if not plentiful in the winter resorts of the Alps, Dolomites and Apennines. Many of the jobs are part-time and not very well paid, but provide time for skiing and in many cases a free pass to the ski lifts for the season. Sauze d'Oulx and Courmayeur are the best resorts for job-hunting.

Cathy Salt describes her success in Sauze d'Oulx:

Upon arrival at Sauze d'Oulx on 14 November, we found we were much too early for on-the-spot jobs. The place was practically dead. Only a few bars were open. Fortunately an English guy working in a bar informed us that the carpenter was looking for help. My partner Jon was able to get four weeks' work with him, sanding down and varnishing, also enabling him to be on the spot for other work that would come up. The same day I found a babysitting job for a shop owner's son, but I wouldn't start until 5 December. We were both fortunate in finding this since we came up on a Thursday and have since found out that the weekend is a much better time to look because the ski shops and restaurants are open.

Such stories are counterbalanced by the inevitable failures: Susanna Macmillan gave up her job-hunt in the Italian Alps after two weeks when she had to admit that her non-existent Italian and just passable French were not getting her anywhere. Perhaps she was looking in the wrong resorts such as Cortina d'Ampezzo, which is sophisticated and expensive and has a high percentage of year-round workers.

After passing his Level 3 BASI (British Association of Snowsports Instructors) exams, Laurence Young went to work at Pila in the Valle d'Aosta of Italy, an instructor's job that was arranged by his course provider in Courchevel. Crystal Holidays, part of the TUI Travel Group hire resort reps and chalet staff for work in the Italian Alps as well as staff for summer holidays. Interski based in Nottinghamshire specialise in ski holidays in the Aosta Valley and recruit lots of winter staff over 21 (☎ (+44) 1623 466333; www.interski.oo.uk/employment). Mark Warner (www.markwarner.co.uk/recruitment) also hires winter staff for Courmayeur.

Not nearly as many chalet jobs can be found in Italy as in France, due to the strict regulations that govern chalets in Italy. You are more likely to find a job in a small family-run bar or hotel than in one of the big concerns. The large hotels tend to recruit their staff in southern Italy and then move them en masse from the sea to the mountains in the autumn.

AU PAIRS

Many European au pair and nanny agencies deal with Italy, so you should have no trouble arranging a family placement. The London-based agency www.totalnannies.com (☎ (+44) 20 7060 1213) specialises in Italy and has short and long-term vacancies year round.

> **ANGIE COPLEY WAS DELIGHTED WITH THE SITUATION TO WHICH HER BRITISH AGENCY SENT HER:**
>
> *After finding the address of agencies in your book, I wrote to one and before I knew it they had found me a family in Sardinia. I couldn't believe it was so easy. All I had to do was pay for a flight out there and that was that. When I arrived, the family met me and took me to their house. Some house. It wasn't just a house but a castle where the Italian royal family used to spend their holidays. What was even better was that the family had turned it into a hotel, the best possible place for meeting people. I ended up having the best summer of my life in Sardinia. Once I picked up the language I went out, met lots of people, had beach parties. My work involved not much more than playing with their two-year-old boy all day and speaking English to him. Basically it was one big holiday.*

Summer-only positions are readily available. Most Italian families in the class that can afford live-in childcare go to holiday homes by the sea or in the mountains during the summer and at other holiday times which did not prove as idyllic as it sounds for Jacqueline Edwards:

> *My first job as an au pair in Italy was with a family who were staying in the middle of nowhere with their extended family. It was a total nightmare for me. I could just about say hello in Italian and couldn't understand a word of what was going on. After three weeks I was fed up, homesick and ready to jump on the next plane to England. But a few days later we moved back to town (Modena) and from then on things improved dramatically.*

The average wage for au pairs is in the range €65–€90 per week, mother's helps €800 monthly and trained nannies upwards of €1,200. Wages are slightly higher in the north of Italy than central and southern parts of the country because the cost of living is higher. The demand for nannies and mother's helps able to work 40+ hours is especially strong since a high percentage of families in Italy have two working parents. Some cushy jobs are sometimes advertised, for example a family in Cagliari, Sardinia were advertising on Totalnannies.com for an 'au pair' to live in and spend four hours each afternoon speaking English to their 18 year old son, for a generous €145 per week (net).

Most of the Italian agencies speak English and welcome applications from British au pairs, and many will assist Canadians, Americans, Australians and New Zealanders. Agencies do not charge a registration fee to au pairs though a few may charge for ancillary services, so always enquire. Try any of the following:

Bambini Divini Agenzia di Intermediazione per Au-Pair: Via Aurelio Saffi 15, Milan ☎ (+39) 342 828 0023; bambinidivini@hotmail.com.

Celtic Childcare: Via Sant Antonio Da Padova 14, 10121 Turin; ☎ (+39) 011 533606; www.celticchildcare.com. IAPA member.

Euroma: Rome; ☎ (+39) 06 8069 2130; www.euroma.info. Member of IAPA; placements not just in Rome.

Europlacements Italy SRL Recruitment Agency: Piazzale Biancamano 8, 20121 Milan; ☎ (+39) 02 76018357; www.europlacements.it. Also places qualified English language teachers.

Living Au Pair: Lucca; www.livingaupair.it.

Roma Au Pair: Via Pietro Mascagni 138, 00199 Rome; www.romaaupair.com. No placement fee for au pairs.

TEACHING

Hundreds of language schools around Italy employ native English speakers. Unfortunately for the ordinary traveller, the vast majority of the jobs require a degree, TEFL qualifications and some knowledge of Italian. Just being able to speak English is not enough.

Doing a TEFL course will improve your chances, as always. After '*stressing and sweating*' his way through a CELTA course in Edinburgh one summer, Fergus Cooney posted a message on Dave's ESL Café (see introductory chapter Teaching English): 'Teacher with degree + CELTA seeks job in Italy/Spain' and soon his inbox began to fill (and not only with job offers from Korea). He chose a school in Calabria (but it is unlikely that the Calabrian Tourist Promotion Board will be giving him a job in the near future):

> *To cut it short (forgive the pun), I was sacked after two months for what might well be the most unreasonable reason ever in the field of TEFL, for falling ill with appendicitis. My appendix burst and I nearly died. The small private school in the village far from anywhere wanted me back at work two days after the operation. I could barely walk and couldn't talk for a week. I certainly couldn't shout loudly which was necessary in the south of Italy in a class full of screaming 12-year-olds. After a week, the bosses told me that I was no longer needed and that I had to be out of their flat by Monday. I found a job in a nice school run by two English guys in the city 50km away although I had problems there too trying to obtain a contract. I now know that getting a contract is of the utmost importance and next time I will not plunge into a job before researching the school, town, amenities, etc. To inexperienced teachers: don't go to Reggio Calabria. It has to be Europe's most boring and ugly city. There is nowhere to eat during the day except Mc-bloody-Donald's; there is nowhere in the city centre to sit down, no cinema, no pubs, no live music and a general lack of culture. OK the local food and, especially the oranges in winter, are fantastic. But I would definitely NOT go back to Calabria.*

GLOBETROTTING AUSTRALIAN JOURNALIST ALEXANDRA NEUMAN DESCRIBES HOW SHE SET ABOUT FINDING TEACHING WORK IN THE TOWN OF BERGAMO WHERE SHE AND HER PARTNER HAD DECIDED TO SPEND A YEAR OR TWO:

The first step these days is to go online. I quickly found three or four English schools in Bergamo: Shenker, Wall Street, inlingua and two small local firms run by individuals. I decided I should also look in Milan since it is only 45 minutes by train from Bergamo.

This is where you quickly realise this is not like job-hunting in your own country and in your own language. Few Italians answer emails from strangers. You have to pick up the phone – a challenge when your language is rusty but as these were English schools most had an English-speaking receptionist. Then I discovered the vagaries of the private teaching system which basically is out to make as much money as possible while paying as little as possible to teachers and expecting infinite flexibility on the teacher's part and no flexibility on the school's part!

You will need patience and a sense of humour at this stage. I quickly got an interview with Wall Street Institute and Shenker and was accepted at Shenker. Being accepted is not a problem it's actually getting onto the payroll and teaching that takes time. It was three months before I got on a two-week training course where we were promised €150 a week. In fact I received this money in December – two months after I'd done the course and five months after the initial interview. So it is best to have plenty of spare cash to see you through the first six months of finding work.

Shenker was good for me because I had no formal teaching qualification. It is based around a system, so all your lesson plans are provided and you simply turn up and teach the system. For this you will be paid about €13.50 an hour before tax. I get about 15 hours work a week, although they promised 20. But as I started working for them during the financial crisis their student numbers were considerably down.

They do offer 30 hour-a-week contracts but at a much reduced rate of pay. This will suit some people as it means you can stay in the country if you have a work contract. However, the pay is truly abysmal and you have to do 30 hours a week, which can often involve split shifts including working till 8.30pm every evening and Saturday mornings. Plus these contracts only run from September to July so you don't get paid in August.

The upside to teaching is that the actual Italians working in the schools are great on the whole. Everyone knows that the system is bad and tries to help each other through it. The students are also great and if you have a class you get to know, teaching can be really fun. It's a good way to get to know people and the Italians are by and large extremely friendly and always willing to help you out if they can. It also gives you a sense of belonging and really getting involved.

Fortunately, the online version of the Italian *Yellow Pages* is reasonably user-friendly. Go to www. paginegialle.it and search under *Scuole di Lingue* in the cities and towns in which you're hoping to work or choose the handy English version of the site. Typing in 'English language school' will produce more than 2,000 entries. The search engine allows you to search by city or more generally by region. International language school groups such as Benedict Schools, Linguarama, Berlitz and inlingua are major providers of English language teaching in Italy. Wall Street English now has 70 centres in Italy and actively recruit native speakers (www.wallstreet.it has a link to *lavora-con-noi*).

Several Italian-based chains of language schools account for a large number of teaching jobs, though most operate as independent franchises so must be applied to individually. Chains include the British Schools Group (www.britishschool.com/teaching-opportunities.html) with 70 member schools; the branches in Taranto, Brindisi, Ravenna, Casale Monferrato, etc were all advertising for teachers at the time of updating. You can get contact details for all 150 British Institutes on the website www.britishinstitutes. it (click on 'Sedi'). Smaller chains to investigate include My English Schools (www.myenglishschool.it) which hire teachers for Bari, Bologna, Monza, Palermo, etc; Morgan Schools (www.morganschool.it) with a network of 25 schools around Italy; and Shenker Schools with 16 (www.shenker.com/work-with-us).

A useful starting place for resources and information on training and teaching English in Italy is www.teachingenglishinitaly.com, a site maintained by Sheila Corwin, an American resident in Florence who has been working and living as an English language teacher and teacher trainer in Italy (on and off) since 2002. The company offers affordable online options in basic TEFL certification (from €200), a 20-hour weekend TEFL course in Florence (€195) about ten times a year and other teacher refresher courses; details from sheila@teachingenglishinitaly.com.

Another possibility is to set up as a freelance tutor, though knowledge of Italian is even more of an asset here than it is for jobs in schools. You can post notices in supermarkets, tobacconists, primary and secondary schools and advertise in a free paper. As long as you have access to some premises, you can try to arrange both individual and group lessons, and undercut the language institutes significantly. One enterprising traveller presented himself to a classroom teacher who asked her class of 12 and 13-years-olds if they would like to learn English from a native. They all said yes and paid a small sum to attend his after-school class.

Summer Language Camps

As in other European countries, summer camps for unaccompanied young people usually offer English as well as a range of sports. ACLE (Associazione Culturale Linguistica Educational) Summer & City Camps in San Remo, Liguria (☎ (+39) 0184 506070; www.acle.org) advertises heavily for up to 400 native English-speaking tutors aged 19–30 to teach English and organise activities including drama at summer camps all over Italy from Sicily to the Dolomites. The promised wage starts at €520 for the minimum three-week commitment plus board and lodging with local families, insurance and transport between camps. Summer staff must enrol in a compulsory five-day introductory TEFL course for which a deduction of €150 will be made from earned wages. The deadline for applications is the middle of March.

A less well-known organisation also based in San Remo is Lingue Senza Frontiere (☎ (+39) 0184 533661; raffaella.lsf.application@gmail.com; www.linguesenzafrontiere.org). They promise to pay their tutors €450 net plus board and lodging every two weeks in their English immersion summer camps. They also take on English-speaking actors for the academic year. An expanding outfit to try is The English Camp Company (www.theenglishcampcompany.com) based in Assisi with summer camps all over Italy. Teachers attend a week-long orientation course in Assisi in early June and then are contracted to work for two months. The pay is €175 a week.

Philip Lee from New Zealand wanted to spend his summers working in Europe and had gained some camp experience in Switzerland before turning his attention to Italy. Although he didn't have direct experience of teaching English as a foreign language, he had worked with children and given tuition and revision classes. He describes the highs and lows of the job:

I searched online for work over the summer in Italy. There were a lot of random jobs that didn't really lead to anything and a lot of misleading job adverts. However, I found some English teaching websites that were credible and I applied. After completing a written application on my background and experience in teaching, working with children and art/drama/games/sport and providing references, I was hired by Lingue Senza Frontiere. I taught English through playing games and sports or completing an activity conducted in English, so there was very limited traditional 'classroom' teaching. Because a lot of the children were not very familiar/comfortable with English I had to be very energetic, positive and supportive throughout the day to keep them encouraged.

I stayed with the most hospitable and generous families, most of whom lived by the seaside. The families were very accommodating and understood that non-Italians did do some things differently, such as eating more than one biscuit for breakfast. They also understood that I wanted to experience as much of Italy as possible and took me out to vineyards, restaurants, farms, relatives' houses, shops, the beach, holiday homes, bars, pools, concerts and neighbouring towns and cities. They were also quite happy when I went out to socialise at night.

The wages are not high; however, I considered the English camp as a working holiday and was not aiming to leave with many savings. The training sessions that the camp organisation provides are really vital and it would have been a great benefit if I had written down all the ideas for games and activities for future reference. Altogether it was a great opportunity to meet people from all over the world as well as Italians, to spend time in Italy not as a tourist, and incredible fun working with children, as all day is spent playing games or doing activities.

Companies that hire native speakers for English language summer camps include the following:

Bell – Beyond English Language Learning: Liguria; recruitment@bellbeyond.com; www.bellbeyond.com/en/tutorsleaders. Minimum stay two weeks; €470 (gross) per fortnight.

Berlitz Italy: summercamps@berlitz.it; www.berlitz.it. Candidates must be native English speakers and experienced with children to work at two camps in Tuscany. Two-week minimum stay in June/July.

The English Experience: www.englishexp.co.uk. Advertises two-week summer contracts, including flights from UK, full board and accommodation, and a wage. Applications and interviews handled in Norwich office.

English is Fun: Bologna; direzionedidattica@englishisfun.it; www.englishisfun.it. Proprietary teaching method for young children taught on compulsory three-day training course costing €610.

M B Scambi: Padua; www.mbscambi.com. Summer camp for month of July held on the beach at Lignano Sabbiadoro in the Venice area. Experienced teachers are paid €380 (gross) per week plus free room and board in shared en suite rooms.

Nowbootlo Viaggi Ctudio: Jesi; www.newbeelleviaggistudio.it. Language camp at Montecopiolo in the Marches.

Smile Modena: www.smilemodena.com. Employs summer tutors to mount English language theatre productions with groups of children. Summer staff are chosen after auditioning, including in London in October.

AGRICULTURE

In most Italian harvests, there is no tradition of hiring large numbers of foreign young people. With the arrival of so many migrant workers from Romania, the Balkans and elsewhere joining the traditional Moroccan workers, the situation has become even less promising. Seasonal jobs in the grape and olive harvests are reserved and carefully regulated among locals and other Italian unemployed. However, if you have local friends and contacts or if you speak some Italian it is worth trying to participate in one of the autumn harvests which by most accounts can be thoroughly enjoyable.

There may be seasonal agricultural work in the strawberry harvests of Emilia Romagna. Cherries are grown around Vignola (just west of Bologna) and are also picked in June. The Valtellina area, near the Swiss border, is another area with a multitude of orchards. Olives are almost never picked by foreigners. Andrea Militello investigated possibilities for olive pickers in Tuscany (around San Miniato) but the wages were so low he didn't pursue the idea.

The poor working conditions that migrant agricultural workers endure is highlighted in the press from time to time. For €200–€300 per month, mainly Africans harvest oranges, tomatoes and many other vegetables in areas such as Saluzzo in the north to Rosarno in Calabria.

The contact for World Wide Opportunities on Organic Farms (WWOOF) in Italy is Bridget Matthews in Castagneto Carducci in Livorno (www.wwoof.it). After joining WWOOF Italia for €35, which includes accident and liability insurance, you will be sent the impressively long list of rural properties throughout Italy looking for volunteers.

Val di Non Apple Harvest

The main exception to the shortage of harvest jobs for foreign travellers is the apple harvest in the Val Venosta and Val di Non around the town of Cles in the valley of the River Adige north of Trento.

ANDREA MILITELLO (FROM ANOTHER PART OF ITALY) HAS PARTICIPATED IN HARVESTS FROM SPAIN TO TASMANIA, BUT HIS FAVOURITE IS THE APPLE HARVEST IN REVO NEAR CLES WHERE HE HAS PICKED FRUIT FOR MANY YEARS:

This year I had a great time with the other pickers. The harvest starts about the 20–25 September and lasts until 25 October, but it's better to arrive at least 10 days early. In the beginning it's best to go to Cles. This harvest unites people from everywhere, South America, Spanish, black people ... so there's a meeting of many cultures.

Women normally sort the apples that the men have picked (for a slightly higher wage). To get the crop picked as quickly as possible, the farmers expect workers to pick 10 hours a day with no days off. The standard arrangement is for a proportion of the hourly wage to be deducted for lunch and accommodation.

Of course not everyone is successful at finding a job. Kristof Szymczak from Poland described the area as a tower of babel and couldn't find an orchard owner willing to hire him. But if you do manage to break in, it sounds one of the most enjoyable harvests in this book, at least as described some years ago by the American Natalia de Cuba:

Apple picking is great on the ground. The ladders require much more concentration (beware of drinking too much wine!) and are considered a man's job. Lunch with the family was included – pasta, salad, wine and a shot of grappa. It was delicious and friendly, as all the pickers – many of them family members – ate together and gossiped and joked. There is always plenty of opportunity to chat while working, especially if you are assigned the job of sorting the fruit. The Italian pickers really do sing opera in the orchards.

Grape Picking

Several people have reported success in finding a place on the grape harvest (*vendemmia*). Italy was called Oenotria by the ancient Greeks meaning 'the land of wine' and it remains the biggest producer of wine in the world. Today there are no regions of Italy that are without vineyards. Once you are in a fruit-growing area, a good place to look for work is the warehouse run by the local cooperative where all the local farmers sell their produce to the public. There may even be a list of farmers who are looking for pickers. Try visiting the Societá Agricultura Vallagarina in Rovereto in the region of Trentino, a major agricultural area. In the German-speaking South Tirol, strawberries are picked in June in the Val Martello and Val Isarco.

The style of grape picking is reputed to be easier than in France since the plants are trained upwards onto wire frames, rather than allowed to droop to the ground, so that pickers reach up with a clipper and catch the bunch of grapes in a funnel-type object, which is less strenuous than having to bend double for hours at a stretch. Accommodation can be a problem since farmers do not normally provide it.

VOLUNTARY OPPORTUNITIES

Many Italian organisations arrange summer work projects that are as disparate as selling recyclable materials to finance development projects in the developing world to restoring old convents or preventing forest fires. Here is a selection of voluntary organisations that run working holidays. In some cases, it will be necessary to apply through a partner organisation in your home country.

Abruzzo, Lazio and Molise National Park: Villetta Barrea; centroservizi.villetta@parco abruzzo.it; www.parcoabruzzo.it. Volunteers for Nature programme accepts volunteers for seven or nine days to carry out research and protection of flora and fauna in remote locations, eg in Pescasseroli and Villetta Barrea, between April and early October; website links to an application form in English for international volunteers, who pay a reasonable registration fee.

AGAPE: Prali; ☎ (+39) 0121 807514; campolavoro@agapecentroecumenico.org; www.agape-centroecumenico.org. Volunteers help run this ecumenical conference centre in the Alps, about 80 miles from Turin; stays usually last three–five weeks in summer but can be shorter at other times of the year.

Emmaus Italia: Boves; campi@emmaus.it; www.emmauscuneo.it. Workcamps throughout Italy to collect, sort and sell second hand equipment to raise funds for social and community projects worldwide.

Inachis: Florence; www.inachis.org/wordpress/?page_id=1685. Conservation holidays of varying durations in Italy's national parks (including Parco Abruzzo above). Low participation fees of €70 for 9 nights, €140 for 19 nights.

International Building Companions (Soci Costruttori): Ferrara; www.iboitalia.org. Renovation projects in deprived communities; €150 fee for Italy workcamps.

LIPU (Lega Italiana Protezione Uccelli): Parma; www.lipu.it. Long-established environmental and bird conservation association (equivalent to the RSPB) which organises summer projects at its bird reserves (*oasi*) throughout Italy; membership of LIPU costs €25.

Lunaria: Rome; www.lunaria.org. Workcamps, from agricultural work in Sicily to helping at a comedy festival in Rome.

Volunteers can also join archaeological camps. The national organisation Gruppi Archeologici d'Italia in Rome (www.gruppiarcheologici.org) is the umbrella group for regional archaeological units that coordinate two-week digs (*campi di scavo*). It has website links to local branches around Italy that arrange archaeological digs, some of which accept paying volunteers. For example participation at a dig in Arlena di Castri in Viterbo province costs €350 for the second two weeks of August (www.gruppoarcheologico.it/chi-siamo/sezioni).

Malta

Malta joined the European Union in 2004, after which EU citizens have been entitled to work in Malta. Despite its small size and population (less than half a million) and resulting fear of having its labour market swamped, Malta welcomes all EU citizens to enter freely and look for work. Australians and New Zealanders under 30 may apply for a working holiday visa to Malta valid for one year.

Although small in area (30km by 15km), Malta has much of interest for the traveller. Its economy is doing well and recently its declining rate of unemployment was at a record low of less than 5%. The procedure for non-EU nationals wishing to obtain an employment licence is to obtain a signed form (Employment Engagement Form) from their prospective employer and submit it to the Department for Citizenship and Expatriate Affairs (Identity Malta) at Evans Building, St Elmo Place, Valletta. In order to succeed, the proposed appointment must pass the labour market test as carried out by the national employment body Jobsplus. An up-to-date online database can be found on the Jobsplus site www.jobsplus.gov.mt with vacancies ranging from skilled tradesmen to part-time waitresses. Many of these job openings overlap with the ones registered by EURES. Tourism plays such a large part in the island's economy that it may be possible to get a job on the spot. Try cafés, bars, hotels and shops in Sliema, Bugibba and beach resorts in the north. Wages are far from high. Spring and summer see far more listings than winter.

Birdlife Malta (www.birdlifemalta.org) needs volunteers to attend raptor camps in the autumn to guard against hunting and trapping. They recruit people through the RSPB in Britain (www.rspb.org.uk/volunteering).

TEACHING

Malta has undergone an English language teaching boom over the past decade and a number of private language schools cater to groups of language learners from around the Mediterranean, especially for holiday summer courses where English-speaking monitors and tour leaders are needed. The Malta Tourism Authority promotes language courses; you can check the list of language schools on www.visitmalta.com/en/language-learning. The EFL Monitoring Board of the Ministry for Education and Employment publishes online a list of 42 licensed language schools.

The interests of mainstream English language institutes are represented by FELTOM, the Federation of English Language Teaching Organisations Malta in Sliema (☎ (+356) 2131 0927) whose website www.feltom.com has good links to its 19 member schools such as the Maltalingua School in St Julian's (www.maltalingua.com/jobs) and, in that same resort, EC English Language Centre (http://jobs.ecenglish.com) which offers summer jobs to entry-level teachers provided they are able to do an intensive induction course for the first half of June.

The student and youth travel organisation NSTS whose English Language Institute is in Gzira (☎ (+356) 2558 8000; www.nsts.org/vacancies) markets English courses in conjunction with sports holidays for young tourists to Malta. NSTS runs weekly vacation courses from June to August, and hires animators to organise the social programmes; applications to apipe@nsts.org are due by early February. NSTS was keen to hire Robert Mizzi from Canada, especially when they learned he was half-Maltese:

> *I was offered a job quite casually when NSTS found out I was volunteering conversational English in the main youth hostel in Valletta. Perhaps one reason they wanted to hire me was they knew the visa would not be a problem. However, I was surprised by how relaxed the offer was. It was just mentioned in passing rather than at an actual interview. I guess it is the Maltese way; once you are one of them, then everything is gravy.*

Scandinavia

The Scandinavian countries of Denmark, Sweden, Finland, Norway and Iceland exercise their own fascination, though working travellers must be prepared for the notoriously high cost of living and of travel in this region, especially Norway. Iceland has come out the other side of its economic collapse and prices have climbed back up again.

Denmark, Sweden and Finland are full members of the European Union, whereas Norway and Iceland have decided to stay outside of it. However, they are part of the European Economic Area (EEA) which permits the free movement of goods, services and people from the EU. European citizens are entitled to enter any Scandinavian country for up to three months to look for work. When they find a job and get a 'Confirmation of Employment' from their employer, they can then apply to the police for a residence permit that, in the case of open-ended (ie permanent) jobs, will be for five years; otherwise it will be for the duration of the job. At least in principle, the only prohibition in the two non-EU countries is that foreign workers are not entitled to claim social security.

The accession of new member countries into the European Union has had a major impact on the job markets of Scandinavia over the past decade. A large number of students and migrant workers from Poland and other countries have been attracted to the high wages and low unemployment that contrast so strongly with their home countries. For example the hourly rate in Norway for an unskilled job such as cleaning, house renovations or in farm work can easily reach 200 Norwegian kroner (US$25), many times what would be paid in Poland, though of course the relative costs of living must be taken into account.

Australian and New Zealand citizens aged 18–30 may obtain a one-year working holiday visa for Denmark, Sweden, Norway and Finland and Canadians too in Denmark, Norway and Sweden. In the case of Iceland only Australians are eligible for a working holiday programme. No such reciprocal schemes exist for Americans. In all the programmes, participants must undertake not to work for the whole 12-month validity of the visa and be able to show sufficient back-up funds, eg DKK18,000 (A$3,400) for Australians going to Denmark.

In order to work legally, people not eligible for working holiday visas have to obtain work permits before leaving home, which is well nigh impossible. The American-Scandinavian Foundation in New York (☎ (+1) 212 779 3587; www.amscan.org) places a small number of American university students and graduates (within two years of graduation) aged 21–30 each summer in internships in the fields of engineering, chemistry, computer science and business in Scandinavia, primarily Finland and Sweden. The ASF can also help 'self-placed trainees', ie those who have fixed up their own job or traineeship in a Scandinavian country, to obtain a work permit.

Knowledge of a Scandinavian language is not essential in landing a job since English is so widely used throughout Scandinavia. One contributor humorously points to the few areas where English will not cut any ice (literally): *'among migratory Lapp shepherds, among polar Eskimo hunters in North Greenland and among Russian coal miners in Spitzbergen'*.

One of the features that unifies these countries is that the cost of living and travel is very high. One possibility for keeping costs down is to join WWOOF and work four to six hours a day in return for bed and board at organic farms (national contact details below). Susan and Eric Beney, a couple from Australia with two grown-up daughters, did this when they found themselves 'pretty broke' driving their camper van from Norway to France where they had been hired as chalet hosts for the winter season. Busking, begging and street selling are illegal in many places; however, prosecutions are rare. As long as you are not causing a nuisance or blocking traffic you should be left alone by the authorities but will attract the attention of many passers-by for whom busking is a novelty. Scandinavians have the reputation of being both rich and generous.

AU PAIRING

The demand for English-speaking au pairs is very small, possibly because childcare and nursery provision is so good in Scandinavia. Au pair agencies in the Nordic countries seem to offer almost exclusively outgoing programmes. In addition to the online matching services like GreatAuPair.com (see introductory Childcare chapter), one specialist online agency is the Scandinavian Au-Pair Center (scandinavian@aupair.se; www.aupair.se) in Helsingborg, Sweden whose website lists quite a few family vacancies in Sweden and the odd one in the rest of Scandinavia. It lists far more profiles of experienced au pairs looking to work for a family in Sweden. Many Scandinavian families employ au pairs from developing countries such as the Philippines and Thailand. Extensive information about the rules governing non-European au pairs may be found on the relevant immigration sites, for example www.nyidanmark.dk. Wages vary but expect the monthly minimum in Denmark to be DKK4,000 (£460) and in Iceland 12,500 Icelandic kroner per week (£88).

DENMARK

Denmark has the highest average wage of any EU country and the second highest spending power. Most wages are at least DKK110–120 per hour. The rate of unemployment has been gently declining and stands at about 6.5%. Denmark is an undeniably rich country and there are still many opportunities for casual work. Employers are obliged to pay legal workers an extra 12.5% holiday pay *feriepenge*).

Work exists on farms and in factories, offices and hotels: the main problem is persuading an employer to take you on in preference to a Danish speaker. May Grant from Glasgow corroborated that the attitude in the jobcentres seemed to be 'Denmark for the Danes' and to find work it was necessary to explore other avenues.

Although initial impressions are that non-Danish speakers have little chance of finding work, some find that the reality is not so bad, provided you speak English. Partly because benefits are so generous in Denmark, many unemployed people are reluctant to move to find work, to take on unpleasant jobs or work at unsocial hours, which leaves some opportunities for the energetic foreigner.

Regulations

The rules on how to obtain a work or residence permit, all set out in beautiful English, can be found on the Immigration Service's website at www.nyidanmark.dk and in the Ministry of Employment manual on residence and work at www.uk.bm.dk. EU citizens who intend to stay longer than three months should apply for a registration certificate or residence card from the regional state administration where they are based, which serves as proof of the rights already conferred on an EU citizen. Take the approved form, two photos, passport and, if possible, a contract of employment or, alternatively, proof of means of support. The contract should show that you are employed for a minimum of 10 hours a week and that your monthly wages before tax reach a required minimum (more for people over 25). If your application is straightforward, you should be sent the permit within a week.

Non-EU citizens will find it much more difficult, though certain categories may be eligible (such as au pairs). As usual, work and residence permits must be applied for at a Danish consular representative in the applicant's home country. Four International Citizen Service offices were opened in Copenhagen, Aarhus, Odense and Aalborg to act as one-stop centres for newly arrived foreign workers; addresses can be found at http://icitizen.dk. The office and service centre of the Immigration Service is at Ryesgade 53, 2100 Copenhagen Ø.

The minute you find employment, even if it is going to be very temporary, apply for a tax card in the municipality where you are working (or where your employer has its head office). You can find contact addresses at www.skat.dk (☎ (+45) 7222 1818) or you can get it from the International Citizen

Service. You will need a CPR (Civil Registration for social security) number from the Folkeregisteret in order to apply. Give your tax card to your employer the day you get it. Without one, you will be taxed at a punitive 52% on all earnings. The tax card entitles you to a personal allowance of DKK43,400 per year (and then a tax rate of 30%–35%). Farmers who regularly hire foreigners may be able to help you get an exemption card, though there is no way of avoiding the universal 8% deduction for the *arbejds-markedsbidrag* (labour market tax).

Copenhagen

Copenhagen, the commercial and industrial centre of the country, is by far the best place to look for work. It is also the centre of the tourist industry, so in summer it is worth looking for jobs door-to-door in hotels, restaurants and the Tivoli Amusement Park. The highest concentration of restaurants is located from Vesterbros Torv to Amalienborg Slot and from Torvet to Christiansborg Slot. Many of the large hotels have personnel offices at the rear of the hotel that should be visited frequently until a vacancy comes up. Also try the trendy burger restaurants like Cock's & Cows on Gammel Strand in Copenhagen and British style pubs including the Old English Pub, the Scottish Pub and Rosie McGee's bar/nightclub (job@rosiemcgee.dk) at Vesterbrogade 2A which despite its name serves TexMex food.

Some jobseekers may have no trouble finding hotel work, as in the case of the Dutch traveller Mirjam Koppelaars:

> *My Norwegian friend Elise and I rather liked Copenhagen but realised that money was going quick again and decided to try to find some work. After filling in an application form and having a very brief interview at the Sheraton, we both got offered jobs as chambermaids starting the next day.*

Jobcentres (*Arbejsformidling*) in Copenhagen should be able to assist EU citizens with a sought-after skill and a knowledge of Danish. They can do nothing for people who send their CVs. Private employment agencies (*Vikarbureauer*) will also expect clients to speak Danish. It may still be worth registering with a few of those listed in the *Yellow Pages* (www.degulesider.dk) such as the multinational Adecco, which is the largest in Denmark.

Among the largest employers of casual staff in Denmark are newspaper distribution companies. More than 100,000 Danes subscribe to a daily or weekly newspaper and an army of 3,000 workers is needed to deliver them. The main distribution company is Bladkompagniet A/S (www.bladkompagniet. dk.) which has an online application form. So great is the demand for deliverers that a dedicated English language website gives further information at www.papercarrier.dk/eng_thejob.html. This job is not done by school children as in Britain and North America because most of the deliveries are done late into the night. Typically, papers must be collected from a local depot at 8pm (or an hour or two earlier at weekends) and delivered by 2am. If delivering in the city you need your own bicycle or moped, if in rural areas, you need a car.

Bear in mind that the reason for the chronic shortage of workers is that the work is no doddle. Mr Stonemann describes what is involved:

> *Few buildings in Denmark have private mail boxes at the entrance, so deliverers must go up to the fourth or fifth floor to put the paper through the right slots. Hence this is physically demanding work, especially in winter. Payment is according to quantity of work done. New workers take only one or two routes, whereas some veteran workers can do six or seven by themselves. After the first week of practice, a new worker can usually earn in less than two nights enough to finance a bicycle, especially if he chooses to work on Sundays and holidays. In winter the payment is 10% more. Payment is made every 14 days by bank transfer, so the worker needs to open a bank account before beginning a contract.*

Another big hiring company is DAO Distribution (hr@daoas.dk) that distributes the morning paper *Morgenavisen Jyllands-Posten* in South and Central Jutland.

Agriculture

Farming plays an important part in the Danish economy and farm work is arguably the easiest door by which to enter the working life of Denmark. The main crops are strawberries (picked in June and July), cherries (picked in July and August), apples (picked in September and October), maize (August) and Christmas trees (October–December). The Danish fruit industry is flourishing and worker shortages can be a problem, although a number of farms now concentrate on the pick-your-own (*selv pluk*) side of their businesses. EURES estimates that 2,000 foreigners are offered jobs in seasonal harvests so it would be worthwhile calling in to a local employment office in the spring. Note that recruitment is normally completed by May when the strawberry season begins.

The hours of strawberry picking are normally early in the morning, typically 5am until between 11am and 1pm leaving the afternoons free for cycling, swimming and socialising. Most employers expect you to bring your own tent and cooking equipment, and in most cases will make a daily charge from kr25 to cover the cost of electricity, water and rubbish collection. The island of Fyn has often been recommended for fruit-picking work, especially the area around Faaborg. But Samsø is where most pickers head in June. Over the years farmers always stress that they can accept only people with a passport from an EU member country and an EHIC (European Health Insurance Card). One of the major employers is Kræmmergård (Kræmmergård-vej 50, 7660 Bækmarksbro; ☎ (+45) 9788 1034; http://sommerfrisk.dk/job/english.aspx) where about 35 seasonal staff pick strawberries for five–eight weeks from early June, plus also peas and blackcurrants. Also try Duborg Jordbær (Duborgvej 30, 6360 Tinglev; (☎ (+45) 7476 2434; info@duborgjordbaer.dk). Grete and Peter Schmidt carry out their hiring between January and March in advance of the season that runs from 1 June to mid-July.

Starting dates and picking hours are unpredictable so do not count on making a quick fortune. Whereas you will get 40 or 50 hours of work one week (and can expect to pick between 10kg and 20kg of strawberries an hour), you might only get 10 hours the next. A standard return is €1 per kilo plus a bonus of 6.75% and 12.5% holiday pay. Some farms will not allow you to stay on unless you achieve a certain minimum number of kilos per hour, eg 14. Be sure to take wet weather gear since picking carries on through the rain. And even in July the 5am starts can be chilly. Other crops such as apples, pears and cherries are paid either by the hour (which because of the high minimum wage is usually very worthwhile) or by piecework.

The long-established WWOOF Denmark distributes a list of their 68 member hosts, most of whom speak English. In return for four to six hours of work per day, you get free food and lodging. Always phone, email or write before arriving. The list can be obtained only after joining WWOOF in Denmark for €25 (www.wwoof.dk). May Grant and her boyfriend Ian visited two organic hosts, one very relaxed where they only had to weed the garden, the other more strenuous. Rob Abblett had a very positive experience working briefly for a friendly farmer who took him to Copenhagen to visit the Botanical Gardens and other sites.

If communal living appeals, you may want to visit the Svanholm Community, which consists of about 120 people including lots of children. Numbers are swelled in the summer when a few extra volunteers arrive to help with the harvest of the organic produce. This possibility is open to all nationalities. Guests can stay for a month and work 30 hours a week for food and lodging but no pocket money. If interested, write to the Visitors Group, Svanholm Gods 4A, 4050 Skibby (gaestegruppen@svanholm.dk; www. svanholm.dk).As usual it is best to find out as much as you can about what you're letting yourself in for.

DAVID ANDERSON MADE PRIVATE ARRANGEMENTS TO WORK ON AN ORGANIC FARM ON MORS IN THE NORTH OF JUTLAND. HE REGRETTED HIS HASTE IN DECIDING TO TAKE THE JOB:

I arrived at the doorstep with the equivalent of £10. The owner was a strict vegetarian (all home-grown) and expected me to be the same. And there was no hot water. I was the only staff to pick the fruit and vegetables plus I had to help him build a greenhouse in the shape of a pyramid since he was convinced pyramids have some special power. When I received my pay for the first three weeks, I left and headed straight for the McDonald's in Esbjerg.

Volunteering

The main volunteer agency in Denmark, Mellemfolkeligt Samvirke (www.ms.dk), is mainly active in the developing world. In some years MS coordinates month-long summer workcamps in Greenland (minimum age 20) to undertake tasks such as renovating a Viking village. The fee for Greenland is at least €2,000 including airfares (enquiries in the UK to Concordia; www.concordiavolunteers.org.uk).

Survival

Contributors have suggested various ways to survive, including bottle collecting from bins early in the morning or from annual festivals such as the Roskilde Festival. The pickings are rich along certain Copenhagen streets especially on Sunday morning when only a few supermarkets are open to accept returns; try for example the Aldi on Rantzausgade. The giant Roskilde Festival uses volunteers year round but up to 25,000 volunteers are needed during the eight days of warm-up and festival starting at the end of June each year; no wage is paid but you gain free camping and free admission to hear the 160 bands. Applications should be made during a specified fortnight in April (see Volunteer information in English at www.roskilde-festival.dk).

Denmark is one of the most prolific sources of sperm for infertile couples in the world. Cryos is a franchised network of sperm banks with four centres in Aarhus, Copenhagen, Aalborg and Odense, as well as New York and India (http://dk.cryosinternational.com). The company recruits both anonymous and non-anonymous donors from all races and ethnicities. No minimum commitment period is necessary but they ask donors to deliver at least 10 ejaculates. Be warned that nine out of 10 men's sperm is rejected. Payment is at least DKK250 and DKK430 according to quality and volume and can top DKK600, all paid tax-free to preserve the donors' anonymity. A laborious registration process means that future recipients of the sperm can hear a recording of the voice, see a handwriting sample and of course check medical and educational records. You may even be asked to submit childhood photos.

Buskers head for the pedestrian streets of Central Copenhagen such as Købmagergade and Strøget where, on a busy summer's day, it is not unusual for a talented musician, juggler or acrobat to earn DKK200 in an hour. Buskers do not require a permit but they must not use amplifiers and must not perform in groups of more than three. Hours are restricted in some places, though Rådhuspladsen and Kongens Nytorv are open to buskers between 7am and 10pm, with more limited hours elsewhere in the city finishing at 8pm on weekdays and 5pm on weekends. Whereas most musicians need not apply for a licence, street performers such as magicians and jugglers do.

FINLAND

British students and graduates who want an on-the-job training placement lasting between one and 18 months in the field of agriculture or in technical subjects should apply to IAESTE for technical placements, which cooperates with IAESTE Finland (www.iaeste.fi).

In 2017 CIMO, the Centre for International Mobility, was absorbed into the new Finnish National Agency for Education (PO Box 380, 00531 Helsinki; ☎ (+358) 295 331 000; www.oph.fi) which was set to take over the trainee placement programme for students in higher education administered by CIMO. Details are yet to be clarified of the short-term summer training programme that used to operate. The affiliated Study in Finland service advises on work but mainly for foreign students both EU and non-EU studying in Finland (www.studyinfinland.fi/living_in_finland/working).

Applicants in the USA should contact the American-Scandinavian Foundation mentioned above. If an individual does succeed in fixing up a traineeship, work and residence permits are granted for the specific training period offered by a named Finnish employer. Immigration queries can probably be answered by looking at the English language website of the Finnish Immigration Service whose customer service desk is at Lautatarhankatu 10 in Helsinki (☎ (+358) 295 419 600; www.migri.fi).

Teaching

Anyone with experience of the business world might persuade Richard Lewis Communications with offices in Helsinki, Turku, Tampere, Jyväskylä, Kuopio and Oulu (info.finland@rlcglobal.com; www.riversdown.com/careers) to hire them to teach communication skills to corporate clients on a freelance basis. RLC has its headquarters near Southampton in the UK (☎ (+44) 1962 771111).

For a quite different clientele wanting to learn English, a Russian language school (☎ (+7) 812 303 8696; www.nordicschool.ru) hires native speakers of any nationality to teach conversational English to Russian teenagers at fortnight-long summer language camps in northern Finland. In addition to board and lodging, a payment of €400–€500 is paid per fortnight plus transport to other locations for those working at consecutive camps.

Freelance writer, blogger and graduate, Emma Lander, became a fan of Nordic School after spending a summer in Finland:

> *My school sat next to one of Finland's many lakes so in our free time we were able to swim, row boats and explore the forest area around the camp on bikes. As there was nothing around the area (and the bikes and boats were free for teachers) there was nothing really to spend money on, which made it a great place to save the €500 we were paid at the end of each two-week camp.*
>
> *The atmosphere at the school was great; everyone was always excited, active and happy to be there and the students were fun to teach. Because it was a summer school we were free to teach what and how we wanted and we often joined classes together to create big treasure hunts and other fun games.*

Casual Work

EU nationals are entitled to use the employment service which is called TE Services (www.te-palvelut.fi/te/en) although, without knowledge of the (difficult) Finnish language, you are unlikely to receive much help.

Finland's rate of unemployment is about 8%, which is considerably higher than that of its neighbouring Nordic countries, so job opportunities are not going to be abundant. However, certain areas of employment do experience occasional labour shortages, such as the flower nurseries around Helsinki, private language tutoring and in hotels, especially in resorts such as Hämeenlinna and Lahti. Check the centralised recruitment site www.duunitori.fi (vacancies in Finnish only).

Jobs with UK tour operators are rare but possible: Esprit Santa's Lapland have positions for hosts, assistants and elves for their Finnish Lapland programme in Saariselka and Rovaniemi which operates for the month of December (Esprit Holidays; ☎ (+44) 1483 791010; www.workaseason.com/work-for-us/winter-jobs/santas-lapland). Hotels in the Lapland ski resort of Sirkka-Levi even further north sometimes look for hospitality trainees for the winter season. The Lapland Hotel Group (www.laplandhotels.com) has nine hotel-restaurants and the recruitment icon on their website says that they take on 800 seasonal workers for their hotels, restaurants and ski schools. The hourly wage for shift work is about €10 with deductions of between €150 and €500 per month for rent and €4.13 per day for meals. Much of their recruitment is carried out by the recruitment agency StaffPoint Oyin Helsinki (Ruoholahdenkatu 14; ☎ (+358) 20 720 6200; www.staffpoint.fi) who also recruit for smaller places including Akaslompolo, a ski resort in Lapland.

The area around Suonenjoki 350km north of Helsinki produces about 15% of the country's strawberries and needs between 3,000 and 4,000 extra workers to tend the plants and harvest the berries between the end of June and early August. Pickers will already need to have a tax card for Finland and be prepared to be out in the fields bent double from 5am to noon. Some farmers provide accommodation for a small deduction of €3–€5 a day. Other berries are also grown in the region such as *vadelma* (raspberries) and *herukkoita* (redcurrants). Two fruit growers' associations that have been seen advertising are: Suonenjoen Seudun Marjanviljelijäin Yhdistys RY (marja.suonenjoki@gmail.com; www.marjanviljelijat.fi) and Jokiniemen Berry Farm, Veijo Karkkonen, Jokiniemenranta 35, 77600 Suonenjoki (www.jokiniemenmarjatila.fi/tyopaikat.php; with a job application form in English).

Babysitting and live-in tutoring jobs can be found. Try for example advertising on www.finlandforum. org. Some time ago, Natasha Fox fixed up her own work with private families:

I found work as a nanny in Finland simply by placing advertisement cards in a few playgroups. The best area to place them if you are in Helsinki, is Westend Espoo, the most affluent area of the capital. If you have Finnish friends, ask them to translate newspaper advertisements for you. Helsingin Sanomat, Finland's daily newspaper, has several vacancies for domestic positions each day. It's certainly worth ringing up and asking if they would like an English speaker for the children's benefit. (Since so many Finnish parents want their children to learn English, this often works.) If you advertise yourself, try to write in Finnish; it shows you aren't an arrogant foreigner. You probably won't have to speak a word of it in the job.

Here is the advert I put up:

Haluaisitko vaihtaa vapaale', lasten hoidon lomassa? Iloinen, vastuullinen Englandtilais-tytto antaa sinulle mahdollisuuden! Olen vapaa useimpina päivinä/iltoina.

This translates as: 'How would you like a break from the kids? Responsible cheerful English girl will give you the chance! I am free most days and evenings.'

On a more frivolous note, busking might be one way of stretching your travel fund, especially outside Helsinki. According to a correspondent in Finland, buskers (especially Russian accordionists) are a familiar sight; average hourly earnings are €8–€15. As in Denmark, collecting empty bottles, both alcoholic and non-alcoholic, can be profitable.

Volunteering

The coordinating workcamp organisation in Helsinki is called KVT, the Finnish branch of Service Civil International (www.kvtfinland.org). They organise 10–15 summer camps each year undertaking lots of interesting projects, for example helping to organise a peace festival or doing maintenance work in a national park. The short-term workcamp joining fee is €100 in addition to the €20 KVT membership fee.

An affordable place to head is the Keuruu Ecovillage near a small town 280km north of the capital. You can stay here for a week or two between spring and autumn, paying €9 a day for food and accommodation, and in exchange help out in the gardens or at one of the volunteer 'bee' weeks at the end of May and August (www.keuruunekokyla.fi).

The Finnish Youth Cooperation organisation, Allianssi (www.alli.fi), cooperates with the members of the Alliance of European Voluntary Service Organisations placing volunteers sent by their counterparts in other countries in workcamps in Finland.

ICELAND

At less than 3% Iceland's rate of unemployment is even lower than that of Switzerland, which means that the majority of the working population out of the total of 330,000 are gainfully employed.

Demand for labour is traditionally within the farming, tourism and service industries and often during the summer season only. Fishing, along with other production industries, has declined in recent years, mainly because the seas are yielding much less fish. A few foreigners find unskilled jobs in agriculture and hotels.

There are eight regional Employment Offices in Iceland in addition to the one in the capital where the EURES Advisers can be consulted: Vinnumalastofnun (Employment) service centre at Kringlan 1, 103 Reykjavik (www.vinnumalastofnun.is/en). Efforts are concentrated on recruiting workers from other Scandinavian countries primarily through the Nordjobb scheme that arranges summer jobs for Nordic citizens aged 18–28 in other Nordic countries for at least four weeks (www.nordjobb.org).

The private employment agency Ninukot (Síðumúli 13, 108-Reykjavik, (☎ (+354) 561 2700; ninukot@ninukot.is; www.ninukot.is) originally specialised in agricultural and horticultural jobs throughout Iceland but has now branched out to offer jobs in tourism and is especially strong on au pair placements. Their welcoming website is in English and holds out the prospect of an easy-to-arrange working holiday in Iceland for EEA citizens. Live-in childcarers are paid about ISK12,500 a week pocket money plus room and board. After completing six months, the family pays for a one-way airfare to Iceland and return fare after 12 months. Any hours in excess of 30 are paid at a rate of ISK650 from 2017. Au pairs from outside the EU must be aged 18–25 and should apply from outside Iceland.

Qualifying Europeans may stay up to six months before they need a residence permit. Processing of permit applications takes an average of 90 days and proof of payment of the ISK12,000 fee must accompany the application. Information in English is available from the Icelandic Directorate of Immigration (Skógarhlíð 6, 105 Reykjavik; www.utl.is). If you are planning to take advantage of the freedom of all EEA citizens to go to Iceland to look for work, take plenty of money to cover the notoriously high cost of living. If touring, accommodation costs can be very high unless you are hardy enough to camp (and it is often cold). An alternative is *svefnpokaplass* which means 'sleeping bag accommodation', whereby you pay from £25 for hostel-style accommodation, possibly with a farming family. Another way of solving the problem is to arrange to live with a family in exchange for minimal duties (housekeeping, English conversation, etc).

The Fishing Industry

The fishing industry is fairly labour intensive, directly employing less than 5% of the working population (a fraction of what it was 20 years ago). Yet fish products account for a large proportion of the country's exports. It is a seasonal industry and the busiest season coincides with the long dark winter. The demarcation of jobs seems to be strictly adhered to according to sex: men go to sea or do the heavy lifting and loading in the factories and women do the processing.

Fish processing in Iceland was once upon a time one of those classic travellers' jobs where you could earn a lot in a relatively short time in an unexpected part of the world. But the work is much more scarce now, though still well paid. Provided you are prepared to stay for at least five months from January in an Icelandic town or village, you might be able to find a job in a fish factory by visiting the relevant villages well in advance. Average earnings were significantly bumped up in 2015 so that the basic monthly pay is now ISK325,000 (gross) which is more than £2,250. The employer may assist with or provide reasonably priced accommodation. The peak seasons are late January/February, April/May and again in September/October. The large seafood company H B Grandi (www.hbgrandi.com) has an online application form on its website, all in English, for work at its fish processing plants in Reykjavik, Akranes just north of the capital and Vopnafjörður in the far east of the country.

The factories are always located by the seaport. Work is pressurised because the fish must be processed quickly to maintain freshness. Shifts of 12 or 14 hours with few breaks are the rule. Tasks to be done in a fish-processing plant include sorting, cleaning, filleting, weighing, de-worming, de-boning and packaging. The worst job is in the *Klevi* or freezer where the temperature is around −43°C (−45°F). The work of packing and shifting boxes of fish would not be too bad were it not for the intense cold. Without proper gear including fur-lined boots and gloves, a balaclava and layers of sheepskin, this work is unendurable. In the rest of the factory the temperature is 10°C–16°C (50°F–62°F).

It takes weeks of practice before you can fillet and pack fish expertly. Standards are usually very high and if the supervisor finds more than two bones or worms, the whole case will be returned to you to be checked again. Since pay is normally according to performance, your earnings will increase as your technique improves, but the wages will not be wonderful in view of the high cost of living. Some years ago, Debbie Mathieson described her work at a small factory in Hnfisdal as '*not really difficult, but mind-blowingly boring*'.

Conventional social life is almost non-existent in the fishing villages of northern Iceland, though many are so prosperous that they offer facilities that would be unheard of in a village of similar size elsewhere. The five dark months of winter, when villages are cut off from their neighbours, can be depressing. Vicki Matchett signed a six-month contract with a factory in the village of Vopnafjörd in north-east Iceland and describes the life: *'Fishing villages usually have about 800 inhabitants with almost no social life, no pubs, not even any wildlife, and the weather between December and May made sightseeing risky. For the sake of saving £1,000 I'm not sure it's worth vegetating for six months. I must admit I spent most of my spare time reading travel journals to remind myself that civilisation still existed.'*

Other

Agriculture is a major enterprise in Iceland. Haymaking is an important summer job; much of the grass is cut by scythe as tractors cannot work the steep slopes, particularly in the narrow valleys where many of the farms are located. However, this work is mainly done by school children.

Ninukot specialises in finding agricultural and horticultural jobs throughout Iceland. Many jobs are in picking and packing plants or greenhouses in the south and west of the country, but can also be with riding stables, on holiday farms between May and September or planting trees. The pay starts at ISK243,000 a month plus 10% holiday pay less ISK68,000 for room and board, and terms for flight reimbursement are the same as for au pairs mentioned earlier.

It is also possible to fix up this kind of summer job independently or through EURES, especially if you know more than one European language. Janet Bridgeport was staying as a tourist at a guesthouse in Hvolsvöllur which happened to be next door to a horse trekking centre: *'Because I'd worked with horses and wasn't in any rush to get home, I knocked on the door of the trekking centre and asked if they needed any casual help for the summer. I was really amazed when they said they'd take me on (for board and lodging only). A lot of the riding guests spoke English so I suppose that weighed in my favour.'*

Volunteering

The Icelandic Environment Agency runs a popular summer programme of projects (not for the faint-hearted) at several locations throughout Iceland. Transport from Reykjavik is usually provided, as is the food but participants have to bring their own tents. The destination is Skaftafell in Vatnajökull National Park. Recent projects have been mainly involved with building and maintaining paths and steps. The cost for a fortnight is £395, and for four weeks £550 excluding flights. Places can be booked through the British volunteering organisation WorkingAbroad (www.workingabroad.com/projects/iceland-volunteer) though they get filled quickly. You could try to make direct contact with Iceland Conservation Volunteers (volunteer@ust.is).

Volunteering is well developed in Iceland and the international SCI network sends volunteers to more than 150 projects around the country, through partner organisations in Iceland. For example Worldwide Friends (Veraldarvinir in Icelandic) offers an interesting range of two-week projects (work-camps) that international volunteers can join. Many are concerned with the environment, sometimes in exotic locations such as the remote fjords of the east coast. WF can be contacted at Hverfisgata 88, 101 Reykjavík (www.wf.is). Another agency SEEDS (www.seeds.is) also arranges many interesting-sounding projects, both short and long term, involving photography, excavating a monastery, etc. Both add fees to the normal workcamp registration fees.

NORWAY

Norway has been more resistant than most countries to embracing Europe and sometimes this attitude is apparent when foreigners look for jobs in Norway. Robert Abblett is not convinced that equality of opportunities is being taken seriously enough in employment offices in Norway:

Before I flew out to Norway, I thought I would test the water a bit by phoning the Oslo Jobcentre and a private employment agency. I think I was a bit naïve, really. When I phoned Oslo I was passed on to three different people each of whom flatly refused to give me any information because I could not speak Nor-

wegian. The same happened when I phoned Manpower in Bergen. In perfect English we argued over the point that this was a racist barrier against foreign workers from Europe from claiming their legal right to work in Norway.

The EURES department of the Norwegian Labour & Welfare Administration (☎ (+47) 75 42 64 04; eures@nav.no; www.nav.no/english) may be more willing to assist jobseekers in person.

No matter how long the duration of your employment, you will need to apply for a tax card (*skatte-kort*) from the local tax office (*Likningskontor*) before starting work; otherwise half of your wages will be withheld for tax. EU citizens intending to stay longer than three months must apply for a residence permit. SUA (Service Centre for Foreign Workers) is a one-stop shop for information on immigration, tax and employment for all foreigners arriving in Norway for work. The website http://www.sua.no/en/sua/ links to the addresses in Oslo, Stavanger, Bergen, Trondheim and Kirkenes.

To make contact with private temp agencies, look up *Vikartjenester* in the *Yellow Pages* (www.gulesider.no) or look for the usual suspects such as Manpower, Adecco and Kelly Services. Not surprisingly most advertisements specify that a good knowledge of Norwegian both written and oral is required. Also check ads in the main daily paper *Aftenposten* or try placing one yourself. As in Denmark, the delivery departments of the main newspapers employ lots of people especially during the six weeks of the school holidays from 1 July; check the website for *Aftenposten*'s delivery or '*Avisbud*' department, http://avisbud.aftenposten.no. Early morning deliverers who work between 3.30am and 6am six days a week earn a tidy NOK7,000–10,000 a month, with a bad weather supplement paid in winter. Those with their own vehicles are especially in demand.

Even by Scandinavian standards, wages in Norway are high and many Swedes come to work in Norway, though the high cost of living means that a sizeable proportion of wages must be spent on living costs. Travellers have commented on how friendly and generous Norwegian people are. Buskers can do well. Mary Hall plucked up the courage to do some busking in Bergen on her newly acquired penny whistle. Although she knew only two songs, she made £15 in 15 minutes, mostly due to the fact that her audience was drunk. In Oslo, a recommended spot to try late on Fridays and Saturdays is next to the Stortinget T-Bane exit on Karl Johan Gate where there is a steady procession of appreciative listeners.

Oslo has a young person's travel information service called Use It (*Ungdomsinformasjonen*) which might be able to advise on longer term accommodation and job options. Use It is located at Møllergata 3, 0179 Oslo; (www.use-it.no) and is open year round from 11am to 5pm with longer opening hours during the summer. Their free online and print guide to Oslo called 'Streetwise' appears in English with lots of concrete tips for making the most of your stay in Oslo (but doesn't deal with employment issues at all).

A cleaning agency called City Maid with ever expanding demand for its services, and offices in Oslo, Stavanger, Bergen, Trondheim, Drammen and Østfold, recruits cleaners year round (☎ (+47) 4000 6330; www.citymaid.no).

Tourism

English-speaking staff might find openings in the summer tourist industry as well as in winter resorts such as Geilo, Hemsedal, Lillehammer, Nordseter, Susjoen, Gausdal and Voss. For either season, you can try to get something fixed up ahead of time by emailing or writing to hotels listed on websites such as www.visitnorway.com. There is a greater density of hotels in the south of Norway including beach resorts along the south coast around Kristiansand, and inland from the fjords north of Bergen (Geilo, Gol, Vaga, Lillehammer, and in the Hardanger region generally). Remember that even in the height of summer, the mountainous areas can be very chilly.

A destination that might not come immediately to mind is the group of Lofoten Islands off northern Norway inside the Arctic Circle. As a tourist destination on the route of the Hurtigruten coastal cruise, a service industry has grown up often staffed over the summer by Scandinavian university students who come to work in hotels and bakeries, cafés and shops. It might be possible for foreign workers to find employment cleaning hotel rooms, as American David Michael did. His job at the Best Western hotel paid a remarkable NOK150 per hour basic with increments for working after 9pm and on Sundays when the wage climbed to nearly $30 an hour. Staff were expected to be able to clean up to three rooms in an hour.

Wages and deductions for board and lodging for the hotel industry are revised annually. Expect to lose up to 40% of your gross wage for these as well as for tax.

The ski holiday market is much smaller in Norway than in the Alps and not many British tour operators hire staff for holidays in Norway. Lillehammer is probably the best bet. Travellers have shown resourcefulness in extending their time in ski resorts (primarily to ski), by doing odd jobs such as snow clearing and car cleaning, waitressing, DJing (since the British are thought to know their way around the music scene), au pairing and English teaching.

Norwegian Working Guest Programme

Atlantis Youth Exchange in Oslo (www.atlantis.no) runs the 'Working Guest Programme' which allows mainly Europeans aged between 18 and 30 to spend two to six months in rural Norway, sometimes helping on farm or in family-run tourist accommodation. The only requirement is that they speak English.

Farm guests receive full board and lodging plus pocket money of at least NOK1,100 a week (just over £100) for a maximum of 35 hours of work. The idea is that you participate in the daily life, both work and leisure, of the family: haymaking, weeding, milking, animal-tending, berry picking, painting, house-cleaning, babysitting, etc. A wardrobe of old rugged clothes and wellington boots is recommended.

Application should be made through partner organisations where available; all are listed on the Atlantis website. British participants can apply through Twin Work & Volunteer in London (JongFox@ twinuk.com; www.workandvolunteer.com) after paying a fee of £750. Atlantis distributes submitted applications with photos, references, medical certificate, etc to Norwegian farm families participating in the scheme, and then host families that want to offer a placement contact applicants directly to conduct a telephone interview.

ROBERT OLSEN ENJOYED HIS STAY SO MUCH THAT HE WENT BACK TO THE SAME FAMILY AN-OTHER SUMMER:

The work consisted of picking fruit and weeds (the fruit tasted better). The working day started at 8am and continued till 4pm, when we stopped for the main meal of the day. After that we were free to swim in the sea, borrow a bike to go into town or whatever. I was made to feel very much at home in somebody else's home. The farmer and his daughter were members of a folk dance music band, which was great to listen to. Now and then they entrusted me to look after the house while they went off to play at festivals. Such holidays as these are perhaps the most economical and most memorable possible.

Outdoor Work

One of the best areas to head for is the strawberry growing area around Lier, accessible by bus from Drammen. Wages are notoriously bad in this area and, as a result, the majority of harvesters are foreign. Kristen Moon and her Italian friend Maurizio were given jobs at the first farm they phoned, but earned a pittance. The strawberry season here reaches its peak in early July.

The steep hillsides on either side of the many fjords support abundant wild blueberries. It is possible to freelance as a berry picker and then sell the fruit to the local produce and jam cooperatives. In Lapland it is not permitted to pick certain berries in certain seasons, since only native Lapps have the right, so make local enquiries first. Autumn brings wild mushrooms – Norway has about 2,500 varieties. Since 2015, funding has been stopped for the mushroom control that were once manned by experts advising on poisonous varieties.

The major industry in the far north of Norway is fishing. Not enough locals are prepared to work in the fish processing plants, as Rob Abblett had confirmed when he rang a fish factory in Vardø:

> *I spoke to a manager who had picked up an American accent somewhere and he told me almost everyone at the factory was Finnish because the local people don't want to do the work. Speaking Norwegian was not a pre-requisite here (hurray) but he did say that he would only consider long-term applicants, minimum one year, as it takes up to six months to train someone in the finer arts of fish processing, which sounded a little incredible to me.*

The repository of volunteering opportunities Workaway.info includes openings in Norway including several in the remote Lofoten Islands. An opportunity open to anybody is to volunteer at a lighthouse on one of the smallest Lofoten islands, which sounds idyllic in the account of one summer volunteer:

> *The work we did whilst I was there was extremely varied, from working on the land draining and digging the potato patch, planting seeds and caring for them in the top of the lighthouse until they were ready to be planted out in the prepared soil at the front of the island, to sanding, scraping and painting in the lighthouse, and tons of other little projects. The work was often hard, but always rewarding and never unenjoyable! Cooking and eating together was fun and delicious, from the fresh baked bread in the morning to the tea and cakes sitting out in the snow with woollen blankets looking over the sea and Lofoten Islands. There was plenty of time for exploring the island, talking, reading and watching films by the fire in the cosy little library, jumping over rocks and on a special Easter occasion dipping into the icy waters. I still think about my stay on this wonderful little island and the amazing people I met there all the time. It is hard to describe such an unusual and magical place.*

Au Pairs

The situation is promising for au pairs of many nationalities (provided they speak some English), though the red tape is still considerable for non-Europeans and the majority of au pairs are from the EU.

Atlantis runs a programme for 200 incoming au pairs who must be aged 18–26 and willing to stay at least six months but preferably nine–12 months. The programme has become so popular that applications are accepted only through partner agencies, and there isn't one in the UK or USA. Interested Britons should seek advice from Atlantis since it may be possible to apply through an agency in another country.

Information about the programme is readily available on their website www.atlantis.no. Au pairs from an EEA country can obtain the residence permit after arrival; others must go through a complicated procedure in their home country that can take months. The pocket money in Norway is NOK5,600 per month though at least 15% will be deducted for taxes.

SWEDEN

EU/EEA citizens may enter Sweden to look for work as in any other member state. All information on the regulations and fees are set out in the admirably clear English-language website of the Swedish Migration Board: Migrationsverket (www.migrationsverket.se). Immigration queries should be addressed to one of the immigration offices in Swedish cities or by phone to ☎ (+46) 771 235235.

The addresses of employment offices around Sweden can be found on the website of the Swedish Employment Service (www.arbetsformedlingen.se). Once you find work, you must register at the local taxation office (addresses linked from www.skatteverket.se) and get a *personnummer* (ID card) for a fee of 400 krona.

Casual Work

State handouts are so generous in Sweden that many natives are unwilling to undertake jobs such as dishwashing and fruit picking. Even without the benefit of having the right stamp in your passport, there are possibilities, as the American Woden Teachout discovered:

> *In southern Sweden I did the cleaning lady's tour of Swedish mansions. I found the first job through a couple that picked me up hitch-hiking and who contacted a friend of theirs. There are a great number of large country houses in Skane, and all the families I worked for were the acme of respectability, so a neat appearance is probably very important. I had several weeks of sweeping out from behind stoves, washing windows, and generally helping with the spring clean. Housework has never been my great speciality, but the living was easy since the relics of Swedish gentry are both rich and hospitable. I had my own room, four-course meals under the evening sun and they took me merrily along to celebrate midsummer, or on outings to the beach or theatre.*

A rather more elevated casual job has been found by well-educated foreigners as proofreaders and polishers. So many documents in Sweden are translated into English that it is worthwhile phoning publishing companies for freelance work.

New Zealander, Richard Ferguson, arrived in Stockholm one winter with a one-year working holiday visa (Australians and Canadians are also eligible for this visa). His plan was to find work in a bar, café or restaurant as he had in Portugal and Greece the year before. Not surprisingly, he found January was not the ideal month to job-hunt. Despite his nationality, he trawled all the Irish pubs to submit his CV, and soon was given a job at Galways in the city centre at Kungsgatan 24 (www.galways irishpub.se):

> *Anyone who speaks English has about a 95% chance of getting a job there. The reason I am stoked with the job is that Turkish families run it. Most importantly you do get paid, no question. I get 96 kroner an hour and maybe 10–15 kroner an hour tip-wise. Also I get paid extra after 8pm and more still after midnight. In the winter it's hard to work 40 hours there but it's enough to pay rent and basic costs. From what I hear it's easier to get a job in the summer. Apparently in Gamla Stan (the old town and main tourist area), the bars and restaurants are more relaxed about visas and language, often employing anyone to serve drinks and clear tables. I imagine they don't get paid much but again, if you need to start somewhere ... It's very difficult (some say impossible) to find accommodation, but somehow I found an apartment in three days; www.thelocal.se is a good site to search for apartments. Just email every single ad and you will get something.*

A friend of Richard's, also a New Zealander, who has been living on and off in Stockholm for several years, works in construction which can be tough in the cold dark months of winter and requires some experience. The government has a scheme by which employers are subsidised a considerable percentage of a worker's salary, provided the employee enrols in a free Swedish language course. However, these are so intensive that it would be impossible to combine a course with a full-time job.

It may be worth trying to find work in hotels, usually in the kitchen. Your best bets are hotels in remote areas where if you are touring before the season begins you may find jobs going. Alternatively try popular tourist areas in summer such as the Sunshine Coast of western Sweden including the seaside resorts between Malmö and Göteborg, especially Helsingborg, Varberg and Falkenberg. Other popular holiday centres with a large number of hotels include Orebro, Västeras, Are, Ostersund, Jönköping and Linköping. The chances of fixing up a hotel job in advance are remote. After writing to dozens of Scandinavian hotels, Dennis Bricault's conclusion was 'Forget Sweden!'

For outdoor work, try the southern counties, especially Skåne, where a wide variety of crops is grown, especially strawberries. Peas, cucumbers, spinach and many other vegetables are grown under contract to canneries and if you can't find work in the fields, you might find it in the processing plants. In the eastern part of Skåne there is specialised fruit growing: apples, pears, plums, cherries, strawberries and raspberries. The short wild berry season depends on lots of foreign workers who traditionally are paid very badly. The Migration Board addressed this problem and will no longer give work permits unless the applicant can prove that he or she will earn at least SEK13,000 a month.

Au Pairs

Au pairs are subject to the same regulations as other foreign employees so non-EU citizens must obtain a work permit before leaving their home country. It is possible to apply for a permit online or by post, provided you have the necessary documents including a job offer from a family (showing hours and pay) and a certificate of intended studies in Swedish. The Swedish Migration Board stipulates that au pairs must work no more than 25 hours a week, must be serious about studying Swedish and must earn at least SEK3,500 a month before tax.

An agency that sends many Swedish au pairs abroad will try to place British and other girls as au pairs in Sweden: Au-Pair World Agency Sweden in Uddevalla (☎ (+46) 522 140 00; www.aupair sweden.com).

Teaching

Casual work teaching English is rarely available in Sweden. For many years the EFL market has been in a slow but inexorable decline, as standards of English among school leavers have improved. The Folkuniversity of Sweden has a long-established scheme (since 1955) by which British and other native English speakers may be placed for one academic year in a network of nearly 50 adult education centres throughout the country, but they no longer have a policy of actively recruiting applicants from abroad. They take on new staff who are already resident in Sweden and even then, the work is part-time, at least initially (www.folkuniversitetet.se).

Voluntary Opportunities

WWOOF is represented in Sweden (www.wwoof.se). In order to obtain the list of 200+ WWOOF hosts you must pay the membership fee of €25 online. Susan and Eric Beney enjoyed rural Sweden a few summers ago: *'When we were looking for work in Sweden the number we rang no longer took WWOOFers but they put us on to someone who did. Lotte and Matthias had a smallholding with a lovely old farmhouse not far from Orebro. Their greenhouse had collapsed after a huge snowfall so our job was to dismantle it so they could erect a new one. They were very friendly, fed us very well and sent us on our way with fresh meat and vegetables. During our time off we would explore the local area – beautiful forest walks were close by.'*

Stiftelsen Stjärnsund (Bruksallén 16, 77071 Stjärnsund; www.frid.nu) is located among the forests, lakes and hills of central Sweden. Founded in 1984, the community aims to encourage personal, social and spiritual development in an ecologically sustainable environment. It operates an international 'Participating Guest' programme lasting one week to three months though at the moment openings are restricted and best negotiated on the spot after you have spent some time as an ordinary paying guest.

Another possibility for lovers of the outdoors is the Falsterbo Bird Observatory (www.falsterbo fagelstation.se) on the south-western tip of Sweden, where they need people who are familiar with bird ringing to work during the autumn migration (late July–November). The observatory's funding has been cut so it is less common for long-term volunteers to be given an allowance.

Survival

Collecting discarded bottles and cans can be a fairly profitable way to earn some money anywhere in the country. The carnivals and music festivals that take place in July and August are recommended as prime targets for bottle collecting. British and American souvenirs are trendy, so you can make up to 500% profit by selling such things at local weekend markets. Medals, caps, books, etc are worth stocking up on at home for possible sale in Sweden.

Spain

Spain's economy is in really dire straits, with the building industry among many sectors showing only faltering signs of recovery. Since the peak of unemployment when it hit 26% in 2014 with a staggering rate of more than double that for young people under 25, the situation has been slowly but steadily improving with the figure dropping below 19% in 2017. Yet, the demand for foreign labour, particularly in English language teaching and tourism, has not evaporated, and Spain's tourist industry continues to absorb foreign young people in temporary and part-time jobs.

REGULATIONS

All EU nationals working in Spain should possess a resident permit (*Certificado de registro de ciudadano de la Unión*) and a foreigner ID number (NIE), which can be obtained from the Foreigners' Office (Oficina de Extranjeros) in the province of residence or at a designated police station (http://extranjeros.cmpleo.gob.es/es). An NIE (*Número de Identidad de Extranjero*) is essential for all bureaucratic purposes from opening a bank account to obtaining a job contract. The application charge is €15. You must demonstrate that you have medical insurance while in Spain and that you have an income of at least €400 a month, either from your employer, as a registered self-employed worker or from independent means (a credit card might be sufficient accompanied by a letter from your bank that you are well under the credit limit). If you are working legally, you will automatically be registered with the Social Security system for medical treatment; otherwise you will have to show a private policy that satisfies the requirements.

To supplement the basic guidance offered by the British Embassy in Spain (www.gov.uk/guidance/residency-requirements-in-spain), check expat forums such as Spain Expat (www.spainexpat.com), Spain Made Simple (www.spainmadesimple.com) and Eye on Spain (www.eyeonspain.com).

Non-EU Citizens

The immigration situation for people from outside Europe is very difficult. Most employers refuse to tackle the lengthy procedures involved in obtaining work permits which involve submitting an official job offer form, original official company fiscal identity document, certification that the job on offer has already been advertised in the official Provincial Unemployment Office, and so on. Once your home country's Spanish Consulate has processed your work visa, you have to fetch it in person.

All people with an address in Spain including foreigners are obliged to register on the *padrón* (municipal register) at their local town hall (*ayuntamiento*), which is free of charge. Any non-Europeans who work on a tourist visa will have to renew it every three months by leaving the Schengen zone for 90 days. An independent company called COMO Consulting run by two young American expats can advise on moving to Spain to live and work (www.comoconsultingspain.com) for varying consultation fees.

Strict rules make it almost impossible for people from outside Western Europe to pick up casual work legally. Americans, Canadians, Australians, etc sometimes find paid work as monitors in children's camps, tutors at language schools and in private households, touts for bars and discos, etc. When their 90-day Schengen visa is about to expire, they are obliged to leave the Schengen area (most of Europe) for 90 days before returning. Youth mobility visas that entitle the holder to work for up to a year can now be obtained by Australians, New Zealanders and Canadians. Quotas pertain based on reciprocal agreements, eg 500 for Australians and 1,000 for Canadians.

One possibility for Americans and other non-Europeans of independent means, perhaps those with established location-independent businesses, is to apply at a Spanish consulate for a Non-Lucrative Residence Visa. This allows you to reside in Spain without engaging in earning anything in Spain. Among the documents you will have to provide are a notarised and officially translated explanation of why you want the visa, the purpose, the place and length of your stay in Spain and proof of a minimum income of €25,560 per year.

Since 2014, the government has offered a special visa for entrepreneurs to encourage start-ups, of which there are a great many in Barcelona and the other main cities. According to the *Ley de Emprendedor* (law of entrepreneurship), you must be legally resident for at least a year in Spain before you can apply, and your business plan must be approved by a local trade union.

Cultural exchange organisations in North America such as InterExchange in New York (www.inter exchange.org) and Scotia Personnel in Canada arrange Teach English in Spain programmes whereby fee-paying young North Americans live with a family for one to three months in exchange for speaking English and providing 15–20 hours of tutoring a week; the programmes are similar though the fees differ ($895 for InterExchange). The Californian company Adelante (www.adelantespain.com) places interns (for a sizeable fee) in Barcelona, Madrid and Seville. The programme is meant to be about half work experience in a company, and the other half cultural immersion and Spanish language learning.

See the section on Teaching below for other leads and for details of an exchange programme open to North American candidates who work in Spanish schools for an academic year on a student visa.

Americans can gain access to the EU if they are fortunate enough to be able to prove European ancestry and acquire dual nationality. After coming to the end of a career in his native United States, Stephen Dorosewicz and his wife decided to embark on a teaching adventure in Spain, partly because their son is living and working in Madrid. First Stephen obtained a Polish passport through ancestry which gave him access to Europe.

TEEMING TOURISM

Year on year, Spain's tourist industry has been expanding so that in 2016 the country hosted a staggering 75.3 million visitors, including nearly 13 million Britons. The proverbial British tourist to the Spanish Costas is not looking for undiscovered villages but wants to have the familiar comforts of home along with the Mediterranean sunshine.

You almost always have to be on hand to secure a job, so people should take a cheap flight to the area that interests them in April and ask door to door. The going rate for a bar job is around €6–€7 and not more than €10 per hour without accommodation and not counting tips. Community job sites carry a few adverts for cleaners, live-in babysitters, chefs, bar staff, etc. Spainexpat.com mentioned above carries an annotated list of job sites at www.spainexpat.com/spain/information/jobs_in_spain. Among these are www.loquo.com, which describes itself as the premier classifieds site in Spain, and uses a format similar to that of Craigslist. Also try www.recruitspain.com for mainly sales jobs. If you can arrange to visit the Spanish coast in March before most of the budget travellers arrive, you should have a good chance of fixing up a job for the season. The resorts then go dead until late May when the season gets properly underway and there may be jobs available. If you are heading for the Canary Islands, the high season for British package tourists is November to March.

All these pale-skinned northerners are often in need of sun protection. The company Suncare (www.suncarecentral.com/Career.asp) markets natural skin and suncare products and hires English-speaking teams as 'Suncare Advisers' to sell these on beaches in the Balearics and Costa Blanca. (The Balearic Islands comprise Mallorca, Minorca, Ibiza and Formentera.)

Competition for jobs is predictably keen in the popular cities and so without EU citizenship chances are very poor, as New Zealander Richard Ferguson found:

I went to Barcelona to work but it is very very hard to get work without the right papers. Saying that you can get jobs in hostels or handing out flyers, doing walking tours of the city, but these didn't go my way so I went to Palma de Mallorca to try there. Palma is THE place to try to get a job on a superyacht but everyone knows this so nowadays there are heaps and heaps of Kiwis, Aussies, Saffas and Brits trying their luck. All have their STCW [see the chapter Working a Passage]. But few have any experience, which is really what the yachts are after. It seems the most demand was for stewardesses (boys need not apply), engineers and chefs. If you do land a job you can get well paid.

Anyway I was never going for one of these jobs but found a job in a pub. Palma is also very hard to get jobs without papers, but luckily I was taken on. But it was not great, the boss was a dragon and apparently thinks New Zealand is in Europe as she thought I was legal. She began to cut my hours down drastically, and earning €6 an hour in Palma on only 20 hours you can't survive. So after a month I decided to leave, without my tips – she promised to send them to me which I figured should be €200–€300, but she is only sending €115.

Clubs

Year-round resorts such as Tenerife, Gran Canaria, Lanzarote, Magaluf and Ibiza afford a range of casual work as bar staff, DJs, beach-party ticket sellers, timeshare salesmen, etc. For Tenerife, check out www.jobsintenerife.com. If you are in Ibiza, a good meeting place is the Queen Victoria Pub in Santa Eulalia, which sometimes posts jobs and accommodation on its noticeboard. Anyone can drop by and consult these though it is polite to buy a drink as well. If you are on the other side of the island around San Antonio ask around at the British-style Ship Inn in West End; according to its Facebook page it has been 'a mecca for workers and tourists alike since it opened in 1972'. In Gran Canaria, ask around at the English and Irish bars in and around Playa del Inglés.

CAROLINE SCOTT, WHO HAS WRITTEN A DISSERTATION ON YOUTH CULTURE IN IBIZA, DESCRIBES THE EMPLOYMENT SCENE SHE FOUND A FEW SUMMERS AGO:

Bar work was the highest paid, then waitressing, postering and, worst, touting which is what I did, where wages were enough to get by. Accommodation becomes harder to find in July, so it's recommended to go in May/June when the better jobs are also available. This year I went back for a second season working for a different club, which I obtained by sending my CV to British clubs in January. (I got the addresses from Mixmag, a club magazine.)

Wherever there is a demand for jobs, there will be agencies charging clients to make the necessary arrangements. Sunkiss in Dublin (www.sunkisstravel.net) and Playaway (www.playawayabroad.com) arrange for sun-worshipping party types to find work in Tenerife, Ibiza, Marbella, Magaluf and Santa Ponsa also on Mallorca. Working abroad packages that cost from £273 to £429 include a month's accommodation, advice of reps and a guaranteed job, for example as a 'shot girl', who circulates around a bar or club, flirting with the men and persuading them to buy jelly shots (shots in a test tube or syringe) for which they get €1 commission each.

The big clubs such as Privilege and Amnesia are on the road between San Antonio and Ibiza. A good site for up-to-date information on clubs is www.ibiza-spotlight.com. Thousands of Britons try to find work on Ibiza each year so it is important to offer a relevant skill. If you haven't got one it is probably best to get your face known round the neighbouring pre-club bars before approaching the clubs for a job.

While preparing for some open-ended world travel, Californian Travis Ball made sure he got some bartending experience, because he wanted to pick up work in Ibiza:

In Ibiza, the red tape actually prevented me from my planned work as a bartender. I managed to get around that by working for a British company that needed photographers covering the clubs. I am even appreciative of the fact that I had difficulty as I never would have had the amazing time I had working four months doing something I love. I would typically go out to start shooting around midnight, and expected my peak shooting time to be between 2am and 4am. I would leave a club sometime between 4am and 6am depending on the energy of the club and how I felt about what I captured that night. When I got home I'd have to spend about one or two hours processing the images and then another hour uploading them. That time would also be spent emailing team members and press contacts, dealing with scheduling issues, and miscellaneous tasks that needed attention. I would usually get to sleep between 9am and 11am. Perks included free entry to the clubs and free drinks while there.

Tour Operators

Jobs with British tour companies such as Canvas and Eurocamp (see Tourism chapter) can be fixed up months in advance from home. Outdoor activity centres are a major employer of summer staff, both general domestic staff and sports instructors. Try the companies mentioned in the chapter on Tourism which have watersports centres on the Costa Brava, such as PGL at La Fosca, and Acorn Adventure (www.acornadventure.co.uk/jobs) at La Cala Canyelles, and In2Action (www.in2action.co.uk). Voyager School Travel (www.voyagerschooltravel.com/staff-recruitment) hires assistant watersports instructors and resort staff for three to six months at Tossa de Mar on the Costa Brava.

Agencies in the major Spanish cities may be able to assist, for example the Easy Way Association (www.easywayspain.com/ingles/employment.htm) in Madrid charges a fee starting at €370 for placing Spanish-speaking or hospitality-trained people in restaurant jobs for a minimum of two or four months. Their other programmes are much more expensive since they include a formal Spanish course. Agencies of a different kind supply teams of entertainers and animators to Spanish resorts. AnimaJobs (www.animajobs.com) is a recruitment portal linked to the Acttiv entertainment agency that posts current vacancies. Casting (ie hiring) events are held between January and March in Spanish resorts and elsewhere in Europe. They also fill different positions in resorts. For example at the time of writing, Acttiv's Facebook page was trying to entice applicants: 'Are you dynamic, funny and a good dancer? Do you speak several languages and have experience, studies or training as a kids' educator or fitness-wellness instructor? Come to meet us and find out which job possibilities you have!'

Odd Jobs and Touting

There is a job which is peculiar to the Spanish resorts and which allows a great many working travellers to earn their keep for the season. The job is known variously as 'PRing', 'propping', 'blagging' or touting, that is to entice/bully tourists to patronise a certain bar or club.

MANY READERS HAVE FOUND 'PROPPING' A GOOD WAY TO SPEND THE SEASON, AMONG THEM IAN GOVAN FROM GLASGOW IN LLORET DE MAR ON THE COSTA BRAVA:

There are literally hundreds of British props and a fair number of other nationalities too. I worked as a prop for over a dozen bars in three months and by the end I was earning several hundred pounds a month with free beer to boot. Be warned that saving is virtually impossible, but you will have one hell of a social life, and will soon enjoy the job and the challenges that arise as you try to match the experienced props and develop your own routine. The highest compliment is when the old hands start using your lines. It's pure unadulterated showbiz.

The job can involve dressing up to promote a themed event, putting up posters or sticking leaflets under windscreen wipers, as well as simply leafleting and chatting up passers-by. Some pay a nightly wage, while others pay a commission, eg €2 for every 'capture' plus a bonus after every 20. Sometimes new people are taken on on a drinks-only basis for one or two sessions and, after they have proved their effectiveness in drawing in customers, begin to earn a wage. When you first arrive, try to get a toehold by working at one of the less sought-after places. The authorities normally turn a blind eye to this activity provided props carry out their work discreetly. The hours of work are usually midnight onwards, as late as 7am.

Timeshare touting is far less common than it once was, and most of the shared ownership developments are stably owned now. One company that does occasionally hire holiday sales consultants out of its office in Malaga is CLC World Resorts (www.clcworld.com/corporate/careers) for its four resort complexes on the Costa del Sol and three in Tenerife.

The English and Irish pubs that advertise in the English language press are usually good places in which to make contact with like-minded jobseekers, for example McCarthy's Bar and Flaherty's in Barcelona; and O'Connor's and the Irish Rover in Madrid. Good sales people and sometimes photographers are taken on by companies such as Barcelona Vibes and BCN Events & Crawls (mail@ bcneventsandcrawls.com) to trawl the beach and promote pub crawls and other backpacker events around Barcelona.

TEACHING ENGLISH

Language schools continue to attend to the brisk demand from students and young adults just out of university keen to improve their CVs, and from parents who continue to send their young children and teenagers to English classes, so they can pass school exams and have a chance of competing in a shrinking job market by being able to function in English. Young Spaniards have been leaving Spain to look for work in the UK where the employment situation is considered more favourable, and for this move they need a working knowledge of English. Thousands of foreigners find work as English teachers in language institutes from the Basque north (where there is a surprisingly high concentration) to the Canary Islands. The entries for language schools run to more than 800 in the online *Yellow Pages* for Madrid.

Job-Hunting on the Spot

Most teaching jobs in Spain are found on the spot and, with increasing competition, it is necessary to exert yourself to land a decent job. Many jobseekers use the usual method of pounding the pavements of likely neighbourhoods. The best time to look is at the end of August or very beginning of September, after the summer holidays are ended and before most terms begin on 1 October. Spanish students tend to sign up for English classes during September and into early October. Consequently, the academies do not know how many classes they will offer nor how many teachers they will need until quite late. It can become a war of nerves; anyone who is willing and can afford to stay on has an increasingly good chance of becoming established. Barry O'Leary wrote from Seville, having been a teacher there for a number of years. In his first year he worked for a disorganised and crafty academy where there was no mention of a contract, classes started at 8am and were staggered throughout the day until 10pm, and it was difficult to predict how much you would earn from month to month because of all the unpaid festivals in Spain

Luckily in his second year, after mingling with the other expat teachers, he was able to land himself a job with a more professional establishment. He now works fixed hours from 4pm until 10pm, Monday to Thursday leaving the mornings free, and there are excellent ongoing training sessions on Friday mornings:

The students, who are often passionate and keen to learn English, range in age from six to 60 so there is never a dull moment. Classes have a maximum of 12, all material is provided and there is scope to move away from the syllabus now and then. A lot of extra work is necessary in February and June when the exams take place but it's worth the agony. Life in Seville is fun and varied, with an abundance of festivals including the religious Semana Santa and the livelier Feria. The city is a great place to live and a base for exploring Andalucía. Evenings can be spent in the many bars enjoying tapas, watching flamenco or Sevillanas (a local dance) or just mingling with the locals. Seville is generally safe and with the year-round blue skies it's a great place to brush up on your Spanish and experience a different way of life.

With a CELTA qualification and experience of teaching English in Argentina and Chile, Alan Chadwick chose Barcelona as his next destination. He is convinced that it is better to look for a job after arrival than apply in advance. He has just completed two years of employment at BCN Languages in Barcelona (www.bcnlanguages.com) and is on the whole satisfied with the experience. Working conditions are reasonably good with small classes, plenty of freedom in lesson planning and few admin or training requirements, so he finds that he has an easy and comfortable life. He and his girlfriend Sophie supplement their earnings from teaching by doing promotional film work. (See chapter on Enterprise: Film Making for details.)

The great cities of Madrid and Barcelona act as magnets to thousands of hopeful teachers, some of whom struggle to get as many hours as they want and any job security because the supply of willing teachers is so endless. For this reason, other towns may answer your requirements better. There are language academies in cities all over Spain, especially in the north, and a door-to-door job-hunt in September might pay off. This is the time when tourists are departing so accommodation may be available at a reasonable rent on a nine-month lease.

Berlitz is a long established player in Spain though it is notorious for paying low wages starting at €13 an hour. Contact details for the several branches in Madrid, two in Barcelona and others in Seville, La Coruña, Santander, Huesca, etc can be found at www.berlitz.es. Applicants must have a degree but not necessarily teaching experience or qualifications.

Other sources of job vacancy information include www.loquo.com (mentioned above), www.lingobongo.com, Vibbo.com (formerly *Segundamano*, the free ads paper) and for Spanish speakers the Madrid daily newspaper *El Pais* (http://empleo.elpais.com) which usually carries a few relevant classifieds. In Barcelona the classified section of the magazine *Barcelona Metropolitan* (www.barcelona-metropolitan.com) carries teaching vacancy notices. One way to make contact with the local community is to attend (or organise) an *intercambio* in which Spanish speakers and English speakers exchange conversation in both languages, often held in pubs.

In Advance

Anyone with an ELT component on his or her CV might try to fix up work ahead of time. Addresses of language centres that have been known to hire native speaker teachers can be found in the 2017 edition of my book *Teaching English Abroad* (Trotman). One option which makes the job-hunt easier is to do a TEFL training course in Spain, of which there is a considerable choice. Specialist websites can be invaluable sources of information and potential employers, such as www.madridteacher.com.

Without a TEFL qualification, the best chance of a teaching job in Spain would be on a summer language camp which are very popular for children aged 5–18. Some pay a reasonable wage; others provide little more than free board and accommodation. Try for example TECS Summer Camps in El Puerto de Santa María, Cádiz (☎ (+34) 956 853000; www.tecsemployment.com), which recruit up to 200 camp support staff and monitors for at least a month for eight residential locations in Cádiz, Salamanca, Andalucía and Madrid region. Other companies to try include ModLang in Zaragoza (www.modlang.es), English YA in Basque country (www.englishya.es), Eurobridge International in Cazorla and Alicante (www.eurobridge.net), McGrogans Summer School (www.mcgroganschool.com) and the Farm Summer Camp in the Basque country (www.campamentosthefarm.com).

It must be reiterated that language academies consistently say that they cannot employ non-EU citizens unless they already have official permission to work and reside in Spain (through marriage to a Spaniard, etc). An excellent way for North Americans to get round the draconian immigration laws is to join a teaching assistant programme that can bestow a student visa and pays a modest salary. The NALCA programme (North American Language and Culture Assistants in Spain) is administered by the Spanish Ministry of Education to further its bilingual schools campaign. Native English speakers from North America work as assistants in state and private schools, at both the primary and secondary levels (details at www.mecd.gob.es/eeuu/convocatorias-programas/convocatorias-eeuu/auxiliares-conversacion-eeuu.html). About 2,500 Americans and Canadians are placed in schools for the academic year October to May to work at both the primary and secondary levels in state and private schools. Applicants must have a degree and at least an intermediate knowledge of Spanish for some programmes, though school leavers are accepted on the Conversation Assistant Programme for Schools (CAPS, www.capsassistants.com) in Catalonia and Valencia, and are paid a study grant of €315 per month in addition to home stay accommodation.

Applications for these various programmes open in early January and are due by early April. Assistants receive a monthly allowance (*ayuda mensual*) of €700 (more in Madrid where the academic year finishes at the end of June); see http://comunidadbilingue.educa2.madrid.org/aux.conversacion for details of the Madrid language assistants programme. Note that mediating agencies in the US such as CIEE (www.ciee.org/teach/spain) ease the application process for a fee of $1,100–$2,000. Various companies and organisations are involved with recruitment of native-speaker assistants, such as Multilingual Education Development & Support (Meddeas) in Navarra (www.meddeas.com/recruiting-language-assistants-spain), UP International Education (www.upteachinspain.com), which places graduates as assistants in private schools throughout Spain and rewards them with grants of up to €845 per month, and the Instituto Franklin (www.institutofranklin.net) affiliated to Universidad de Alcalá in Madrid, which offers enrolment in an MA programme alongside teaching in its Teach and Learn in Spain programme (www.institutofranklin.net/en).

Note that Britons can also currently participate through the British Council administered Language Assistants scheme, though this situation may change after the UK has exited the EU.

The company Spain Internship (www.spain-internship.com) in Valencia has a teaching programme, among others in design, IT, hospitality, etc, whereby participants from Europe and outside earn €500 a month.

Live-in Positions

As mentioned above in the section 'Regulations', positions as live-in volunteer teachers are widely available. Relaciones Culturales, the youth exchange organisation at Calle Ferraz 82, 28008 Madrid (☎ (+34) 91 541 7103; www.worktravelstudyinspain.com) places native speakers with Spanish families who want to practise their English in exchange for providing room and board; the programme fee is €300. No TEFL experience is required.

The company Culture Go Go (www.culturegogo.com) provides an online platform for native speakers from UK, Ireland, USA and Canada to arrange live-in stays; access to the host list costs $20 for a month, $48 for a year. Some arrangements may shade into au pairing where you are looking after children while helping them improve their English (see section on Au Pairing below).

It is also possible to arrange an informal exchange of English conversation for a free week in Spain. At least two companies, Vaughan Town (http://volunteers.grupovaughan.com) and Diverbo (www.diverbo.com/en/volunteer-abroad/adults), offer programmes whereby holiday centres in Spain are 'stocked' with native English speakers and Spanish clients who want to improve their English. In exchange for making English conversation all day and all evening, participants receive free room and board, and transport from Madrid. Diverbo's 'Pueblo Ingles' programme lasts eight days and the average age of participants from all over the world is 40.

Back in June I took part in an English Language immersion programme in Spain. They want native English speakers (any flavour, although in practice North Americans predominate) to go and talk a lot of English to Spaniards. The Spaniards are generally professional manager-types paid to be there by their companies to improve their English. All people have to do is get themselves to Madrid in time for the pick-up. At the end of the week, you will be delivered back to Madrid, unless you have extraordinary stamina and can manage two (or more) continuous weeks in the programme. It isn't a way to make money, but of course people can and do make friends and contacts both with the other 'Anglos' and with the Spaniards. It's also a week off worrying about food, drink and where to sleep.

Conditions of Work

Salaries for English teachers at *academias* are not high in Spain. The standard net salary starts at €1,000 per month for a full-time load of about 25 hours a week. Wages in Madrid are a little higher (say €1,100–€1,300) but then the cost of living is higher. As a rough guide to living expenses, most people spend about half of a full-time wage, ie about €600 per month on rent, bills, food, phone and city transport. Alan Chadwick reported recently that the standard price for a room in a shared house in Barcelona is €300 a month which is often inclusive of all bills and internet. Compulsory social security (*seguridad social*) payments are between 6% and 9%.

One of the worst problems in the classroom is the difficulty in motivating students. Many are children or teenagers whose parents enrol them in classes in order to improve their performance in school exams. David Bourne echoes this complaint after completing a nine-month contract in Gijón: *'I have found it very hard work trying to inject life into a class of bored 10-year-olds, particularly when the course books provided are equally uninteresting. The children themselves would much rather be outside playing football. So you spend most of the lesson trying (unsuccessfully in my case) to keep them quiet.'*

Private Tutoring

As usual, private tutoring pays much better than contract teaching because there is no middleman. Rates start at €20 an hour in the main cities and go up to €50 per lesson. If you teach several people at once, obviously you charge less. Most freelancers have put in time as employees of a school so know the local ropes. It is difficult to start up without contacts and a good knowledge of Spanish; and when you do get started it is difficult to earn a stable income due to the frequency with which pupils cancel. Getting private lessons is a marketing exercise and you will have to explore all the avenues that seem appropriate to your circumstances. Obviously you can advertise on relevant websites as well as on noticeboards at universities, corner shops and wherever else you think there is a market. The main difficulty is choosing the premises. It doesn't seem professional to teach out of your flat or at a café, and it will cost at least €150 a month (in Barcelona) to rent an office space with a whiteboard.

Freelance teachers must register as an *Autonomo* for tax purposes, ie an independent professional. *Autonomos* must pay a flat rate of €265 per month to cover compulsory social security contributions, no matter how little they earn.

AU PAIRS

Au pair links between Spanish agencies and those in the rest of Europe are strong because Spanish continues as one of the most popular modern foreign languages. The pocket money for au pairs in the big cities at present ranges from €70 to €80 a week plus a possible contribution to a monthly transport pass. Increasingly agencies offer positions as 'au pair teachers', ie a combination of childcare and English language tutoring duties. If you deal with a Spanish agency, you may have to pay a sizeable placement fee. Here are a few Spain-based agencies, some of which are branches of language schools:

B.E.S.T.: www.bestprograms.org. Au pair placements for Americans and Europeans in Barcelona; fee €1,100 for three months as an 'au pair English teacher'. Males as well as females aged 18–26 welcome.

Globus Idiomas: Murcia; www.globusidiomas.com. Member of IAPA; registration fee €100.

Instituto Hemingway de Español: Bilbao; www.institutohemingway.com. Accepts most nationalities for a €300 fee; also places interns in local companies, hotels, etc (for a fee of €800).

Language Job Spain: A Coruña; www.languagejobspain.com. Au pair placements in Galicia, with a teaching component in the 25–30 hour working week.

Planet Au Pair: Madrid; www.planetaupair.com/aupairspain.htm. €303 fee for au pairs; €363 for au pair teachers.

Relaciones Culturales: Madrid; ☎ (+34) 91 541 7103; www.worktravelstudyinspain.com. €395 fee for 12-month placement, €195 for 1–3 months.

Spanish Teachers: Madrid; www.spanishteachers.es. Au pairs learn Spanish and/or teach English in a family setting according to programme chosen; IAPA member.

AGRICULTURE

Reports of people finding harvesting work in Spain are far less common than in France, but they do filter through every so often. Traditionally there is an excess of migrant labour from Africa and landless Spanish workers especially from Andalucia to pick the massive amounts of oranges, olives, grapes, and latterly avocadoes and winter strawberries. Lepe, Moguer (from which half of Columbus's sailors came) and Cartaya in the Andalucian province of Huelva not far east of the Portuguese border are among the main centres of the strawberry harvest that begins in late February. More and more locals are competing with migrants now that unemployment in Spain has soared, so the struggle becomes ever harder to find work, possibly by going to a hiring café at 6am in the hope of being picked up by a farmer, and to earn decent money. Other major harvests that attract roving pickers are the apple harvests of Catalonia and the olives around Jaen in Andalucia.

Tomatoes and many other crops are grown on Tenerife. The Canaries are normally valued by working travellers only for their potential in the tourist industry, but there is a thriving agricultural life outside the resorts. Just a bus ride away from Los Cristianos, the farms around Granadilla, Buzanada, San Isidro and San Lorenzo may take on extra help between September and June.

A couple of years ago Anna Ling looked into almond picking but concluded it was almost impossible to find an opening or to make it worthwhile since the pay was terrible.

Spain now has a WWOOF organisation (http://ruralvolunteers.org) with more than 300 member properties. As always, access to these is available to members, and membership costs €20. In the days before WWOOF got organised in Spain, Brendan Barker hitched to an organic farm near Granada (whose address he had noticed on a card displayed in a health food shop in Brixton!) and worked happily there on a work-for-keep arrangement for six months, while picking olives at a neighbouring farm in his free time.

Jon Loop is one contributor who succeeded in linking up with an organic farmer in southern Spain whore he soon got down to some serious work weeding, building a pig enclosure, searching for water when the mountain stream dried up, etc with no days off. But the surroundings were stunning, and the desolate beauty and harshness of the semi-desert made his stay very enjoyable. He even managed to enjoy goat-herding, that most challenging of rural activities:

This could be quite difficult since their range was 10km by 5km, and they could get through dense undergrowth while I had to follow dried-up rivers and footpaths. Also they had a habit of disappearing, even though they wore bells. The family were quite friendly, the food was exquisite, the accommodation adequate but the temperatures were unbearable. Walking out of the house at 5pm for the evening stint was like walking into a Swedish sauna without the steam. After three weeks I decided to call it a day, and headed up north in search of rain.

Sunseed (www.sunseed.org.uk) is an off-grid ecovillage in the arid south-east of Spain (near the village of Sorbas in Almería) where new ways are explored of reclaiming deserts. The centre is run by short-term (one to three weeks), medium term (four to six weeks) and long-term volunteers (minimum seven weeks). Weekly charges vary from £100 to £150 depending on length of stay and hours of work (25 or 35 a week). Typical work for volunteers might involve germination procedures, forestry trials, organic gardening, designing and building solar ovens and stills, mapping footpaths and building and maintenance. Living conditions are basic and the cooking is vegetarian. In special circumstances, volunteers don't have to pay, for example in the winter of 2017, a storm damaged a watercourse and people to repair it were urgently needed.

VOLUNTEERING

The Atlantic Whale Foundation (www.whalenation.org) is working to protect whales and dolphins in the Canary Islands. Volunteers pay a reasonable £100 a week to cover accommodation and half-board and the chance to go out on the whale-watching boats. Jacqueline Edwards wanted a live-in position but her status as the single mother of a two-year-old boy made her quest more complicated. She used her initiative and contacted vegetarian/vegan societies around Europe, asking them to put her details in their newsletter. Several of the replies she received were from Spain including from a natural therapies retreat centre in Zamora.

Squats and Communities

Not long after arriving in Granada, 19-year-old Anna Ling bumped into an English girl who was involved in squatting. She and a number of other people of various nationalities were setting up a new one, and Anna was invited to join. The building had been abandoned for at least 10 years and was absolutely vile, with no water supply. With very little money, Anna took up 'skipping', ie rescuing edible food from skips near supermarkets. Anna earned her keep by helping prepare meals, paint her room, etc. Almost all squatters are musicians and try to earn some money by busking. She stayed for about a month and in that time developed a quickfire 10-minute fire poi show that she performed outside restaurants. One of her record bad days earned her €5 an hour but mostly it was quite a bit more. Seville proved a more lucrative destination than Granada. It has more of a shopping culture and here she earned €10–€11 per hour.

Anna also spent time at the famous community, Beneficio, in the foothills of the Sierra Nevada, two hours from Granada. Beneficio is a 30-year-old commune in a beautiful location, where the resident hippies and musicians welcome visitors willing to work for their keep, for instance by collecting wood, preparing meals, etc. Rugged, ragged-looking members can be seen on market day in nearby Orgiva.

Gibraltar

Gibraltar is an anomaly, an accident of history. It is a tiny British dependent territory on the Spanish coast, 2.6 square miles and with a population of about 32,000. It has the same currency, the same institutions, the same language (though with a unique accent) as the UK. Gibraltar is still separated from Spain by a wire fence and border guards, although about half of the workforce lives in and commutes from Spain. More than 95 per cent of Gibraltarians voted for Britain to remain in the European Union in the 2016 Referendum, the highest proportion of any British region, because the enclave has a great deal to fear if free movement of goods and labour ends. Under the 1713 Treaty of Utrecht, Gibraltar must revert to Spain if Britain ever gives up sovereignty, and the government in Madrid sees a chance to regain sovereignty over the Rock once the UK has departed from the EU. So these are very worrying times for Gibraltarians who have built up their economy based on the benefits of the single market.

Unlike in Spain where the building industry is in crisis, it continues to flourish in Gibraltar, where the rate of unemployment remains low at just 1%. The majority of the population is employed in the main industries of financial services, e-commerce and online gaming. However casual jobs continue to crop up in the many bars and clubs in the busy summer tourist season.

EU citizens are free to take up any offer of employment made to them in Gibraltar. Non-EU citizens must obtain a work permit from the Ministry of Employment, Unit 76–77, New Harbours (employment. service@gibraltar.gov.gi) after the employer has applied for one. To have an application for a work permit approved, the prospective employer must prove that no Gibraltarian or EU citizen is available to fill the vacancy, undertake to repatriate the worker if necessary and show that suitable accommodation has been found.

Tourism continues to flourish, partly because Gibraltar's VAT-free status makes it a popular shopping destination. Candidates with experience in a field such as admin, marketing, IT, engineering, online gaming and so on should look at online recruitment websites for Gibraltar (and Spain) such as www.recruitgibraltar.com and www.castlehillrecruitment.com, a specialist in the gaming industry which employs 3,500 people in Gibraltar.

But work-your-wayers are more likely to be interested in jobs on yachts moored in the marinas or picking up bar work. Without contacts, it will be difficult to pick up work and expensive to stay while you're looking.

Adam Cook complained of the shortage of work in 'that litter-strewn blob of all that's undesirably British', yet managed to find a little yacht-varnishing work, and then was taken on to help redecorate a restaurant, before his big break came and he was taken on as paid crew on a private yacht bound for England.

ACCOMMODATION

There are no campsites and only one overpriced hostel (Emile's) on the Rock and free camping is completely prohibited on the beaches. A property boom in the wake of the expanding gambling businesses means that rental property is almost non-existent. Most non-resident workers choose to commute from La Linea, the port town in Spain just across the border, where accommodation is cheaper.

Sheppards Marina is where most of the yacht work is carried out; whereas Marina Bay with more than 200 berths and the brand new Mid-Harbour Marina with 700 berths is where the long cruising yachts are moored. A good source of information on jobs and lodgings in the marinas is the newsagents next door to Bianca's Bistro in Marina Bay and to a lesser extent the Star Bar on Parliament Lane or Aragon Bar on Bell Lane in central Gibraltar. A noticeboard worth using is located in Sheppard's Marina chandlery shop in Marina Court.

Opportunities for fixing up a crewing position on a yacht exist, though normally on a shared-expenses basis; see the chapter Working a Passage.

Portugal

Portugal's economy weathered the global crisis a little better than Spain, and its unemployment rate is currently just over 10% and heading slowly in the right direction.

One sign of recovery is that the national minimum wage was raised in 2016 to €618 per month (up from €565). Average net wages are the lowest among the original EU member states, just over half of what they are in Spain: €984 as opposed to €1,718. Chances of finding work are best with tour operators or in hotels, restaurants and holiday clubs along the Algarve coast.

There is a long and vigorous tradition of British people settling in Portugal, and the links between the two countries are strong. Large numbers of expatriates live around Lisbon and on the Algarve, many of whom are retired. English-speaking travellers might expect to find odd jobs in this community by asking expatriates for help and advice. Although the Portugal job vacancy listings on Angloinfo.com aren't usually promising, there is no harm in looking. The Portuguese language site www.trabalhar.pt has more choice including hospitality jobs (*cozinheiro* means cook).

REGULATIONS

Portugal has always had comparatively liberal immigration policies, possibly because it has never been rich enough to attract a lot of foreign jobseekers. EU citizens are supposed to apply for a registration certificate (by the end of the fourth month after arrival) if they intend to stay longer than that. The usual documents will be needed: proof of accommodation and means of support (job, pension, etc). Wage earners must prove that they are being paid at least the Portuguese minimum monthly wage. The registration certificate should be obtained from the nearest immigration office SEF (*Serviço de Estrangeiros e Fronteiras*) or the local town council (*Câmara Municipal*). Forms can be downloaded from the SEF site. More information about working can be found at www.angloinfo.com/how-to/portugal/working/work-permits.

Non-EU citizens must provide the usual battery of documents before they can be granted an *Autorização de Trabalho*, including an entry visa obtained from the Portuguese Consulate in their home country, a document showing that the Ministry of Labour (*Ministerio do Trabalho*) has approved the job and a medical certificate in Portuguese. The final stage is to take a letter of good conduct provided by the applicant's own embassy to the police for the work and residence permit. All of this takes an age, as the blogger Andrea Smith from Washington DC describes in painful detail at http://americanin-portugal.blogspot.it/2012/02/so-you-want-to-move-to-portugal-heres.html. She could only achieve legal status with the ongoing help of her Portuguese boyfriend. She refers to using *recibos verdes* or 'green receipts' for non-contract work in order to work legally. Since then, the system has changed and these invoice receipts used by freelancers called *faturas-recibo* are now all logged online.

TOURISM

UK-based tour operators needing seasonal staff include Powder Byrne (www.powderbyrne.com) which operates hotel holidays in Sintra near Lisbon. Thousands of Britons and other Europeans take their holidays on the Algarve creating many job opportunities in bars and restaurants in resorts such as Lagos and Albufeira.

Unfortunately, incidents of gang violence against tourists in busy resorts such as Vilamoura and Albufeira are not unknown. The notorious Montechoro Strip is lined with bars, clubs and restaurants. Finding somewhere to stay can be more difficult than finding employment. Not surprisingly, accommodation is quite expensive during the high season. Ask around so you can avoid the dodgy landlords. It would be cheaper to camp especially if you can negotiate a discount for a long stay.

ACCORDING TO MANY TRAVELLERS SUCH AS EMMA-LOUISE PARKES, THE ALBUFEIRA AREA IS THE PLACE TO HEAD:

I arrived at Faro Airport in June, and went straight to Albufeira. A job-hunter here will be like a kid in a sweet shop. By 12.15pm I was in the resort, by 12.30pm I had found somewhere to stay and had been offered at least four jobs by the evening, one of which I started at 6pm. All the English workers were really friendly individuals and were a goldmine of information. Jobs-wise, I was offered bar work, touting, waitressing, cleaning, packing ice cubes into bags, karaoke singing, nannying for an English bar owner, timeshare tout, nightclub dancer … I'm sure there were more. Touts can earn £16 a night with all the drink they can stomach while waitresses can expect a little less for working 10am–1pm and 6pm–10pm. Attractive females (like myself!) will be head-hunted by lively bars, whereas British men are seen by the locals as trouble and are usually kept behind bars (serving bars that is) and in cellars.

Lisbon will be a harder nut to crack, although Richard Ferguson managed it, helped by his knowledge of the language. He suggests trying the bars and restaurants at the docks (*docas*), especially the Irish bars, all of which are full of tourists in the summer. The other key area of the city is the Bairro Alto, jammed with revellers and clubbers till the wee small hours.

I've been working in Lisbon for two months now. Through a friend in New Zealand, I met a local who got me my first job in a pizzeria. We simply asked the owner when we were eating there and I was told to start the next day. I was working six days from 11.30am to 4pm then an evening shift 7pm till late for €750 a month plus tips of about €80. All the workers were immigrants and these wages were below par as the minimum should be about €1,000 per month. After five weeks I was offered a job by a rival pizzeria where I'm now working evenings only for €650 a month plus about €40 a week in tips. Finally I have some decent free time. It's an awesome environment – like a family – living with colleagues in an apartment owned by the owner for next to nothing. I'm loving it.

Any budding surfies might look into the possibility of working, paid or unpaid, at a surf camp. For example the Portugal Surf Camp at Ericeira (on the coast north of Lisbon) accepts trainees for up to a month to act as 'more or less a maid-of-all-work' between April and November. Applicants must be over 21 and 'stress-resistant' (jobs@portugalsurfcamp.com). Surprisingly there isn't just one all-female surf and yoga holiday centre, but two. Female surfers should investigate openings at Wave Sisters located on the Costa da Caparica (www.wavesisters.com/en/jobs_en) and Chicks On Waves (www.chicksonwaves.com) whose base is at Salema between Lagos and Sagres.

TEACHING

The market for English tuition is fairly buoyant, especially in the teaching of young children and especially in northern Portugal. As of 2016 a government initiative assists preschools and primary schools to join the new Bilingual Schools Programme in cooperation with the British Council. As a result parents are eager to start their children very young in private English classes. Apart from in the main cities of Lisbon and Oporto, jobs crop up in historic provincial centres such as Coimbra and Braga and in small seaside towns such as Aveiro and Póvoa do Varzim. The Cambridge Certificate (CELTA) is widely requested by schools, but a number (especially those advertising vacancies in June, July and August) seem willing to consider candidates with a BA plus a promising CV and photo.

One of the most well-established groups of schools is the Cambridge School group (www.cambridge.pt) which every year imports up to 110 British teachers for its five centres in Lisbon and one each in Porto, Coimbra, Almada and Funchal (Madeira). Other chains of language schools to try are the Bristol Schools Group (www.bristolschool.pt) with four schools in the Oporto area, two in the Azores and three inland; and the Oxford School in Lisbon and Cacém, which hires 40 teachers (www.oxford-school.pt).

The consensus seems to be that wages are low, but have been improving at a favourable rate in view of the cost of living. On the positive side, working conditions are generally relaxed. Some schools offer a low salary but will subsidise or pay for flights and accommodation. Teachers being paid on an hourly basis should expect to earn between €12 and €17 an hour.

A company that specialises in teaching children aged 3–13 is Fun Languages/Kids Club (www. kidsclub.pt), with dozens of clubs throughout the country. It is possible to submit an online application form, which is circulated round all the clubs and any with vacancies will make contact.

BUSINESS

If you know some Portuguese, you might find an opening in an office; without knowing the language, chances are remote. For agencies specialising in temporary work, google *Trabalho Temporário*. A couple of temp agencies are Randstad (www.randstad.pt) and Adecco (www.adecco.pt).

The British-Portuguese Chamber of Commerce (*Camara de Comércio Luso-Britanica*) is in Lisbon (www.bpcc.pt). CVs of members may be sent by email to info@bpcc.pt, though the Chamber cannot respond unless they have already been notified of a relevant opportunity, which is rarer in the tough economic climate than it used to be. They attempt to match qualified jobseekers with their members who might be looking for staff.

AGRICULTURE

Although it is the fifth largest wine producer in the world, we have never heard of any traveller picking grapes. The farms are generally so small that hiring help from beyond the local community is simply not done. On the other hand, a large strawberry producer and packer in Brejão (info@sudoberry.com) near the Atlantic coast south of Lisbon hires pickers for the harvest season which is between January and June, with the peak season for the spring crop lasting from March until the end of May. It also posts occasional vacancies for tractor drivers, people with computer skills, etc on its Facebook page.

Portugal has a national WWOOF association (www.wwoof.pt); membership costs €15 and allows you to access the list of about 145 member organic farms, including romantic sounding olive groves and cork tree woodlands. Descriptions such as the following looking for volunteers sound alluring if you are into alternative lifestyles:

> *O Monte is situated 7km from the small town of Aljezur and 10km from the natural and wild beaches of the west coast. We are a Portuguese/English couple. The farm belonged to Rui's grandparents in the past. We have been working, cleaning and maintaining the land for six years. The vegetable gardens are extensive enough for us to be more or less self-sufficient through the year and provide produce to sell at the local farmers' market. Everyday tasks can include … harvesting wild produce, eg mushrooms and medronho, preserving of produce … Accommodation is a 4m yurt and we have a solar and wind powered shower and wash area.*

Switzerland

Switzerland is not a member of the European Union; however, it is in the Schengen area and for all intents and purposes operates an immigration system that is harmonised with the rest of Europe. In a referendum in 2014, the Swiss people voted to introduce quotas on EU migrants from 2017; however this was overturned in the Swiss parliament so as to avoid being expelled from the European Single Market, because the imposition of quotas would violate the terms of Switzerland's free movement treaty with the EU. The proposed compromise is to introduce measures that would give residents priority for jobs over foreigners. In any event, EU jobseekers can continue to enter Switzerland for up to three months (extendable) to look for work. If they succeed they must show a contract of employment to the authorities and are then eligible for a short-term residence permit (valid for up to one year and renewable) or a long-term permit (up to five years) depending on the contract.

With a stable low rate of unemployment (3.3%) it is difficult to understand why the Swiss are so keen to curb immigration. It has been the case for a long time that a high proportion of the working population – about a quarter – is non-Swiss. The high cost of living while job-hunting and the (deserved) Swiss reputation for hard work discourage many travellers from going to Switzerland to look for work. But many people who have spent time working in Switzerland and have come to know the Swiss have nothing but compliments. According to Tony Mason who picked grapes four seasons running and worked as a builder: *'The Swiss are a genuinely friendly and hospitable people and we are often invited to local homes for meals and on outings to the mountains. I can't say enough good things about the Swiss.'*

REGULATIONS

No permit is needed for EU citizens who stay for less than three months. If they want to stay beyond that, eg to continue job-hunting or to do a seasonal job, they must apply for an L permit (short-term residence permit). The L-EC/EFTA permit (*Kurzaufenhalter/Autorisation de Courte Durée*) is issued for periods of work lasting less than 12 months and can be renewed once for a further year. EU citizens simply need to take their passport and contract of employment to the local cantonal office. Permits are no longer tied to a particular job or canton.

If the contract of employment is going to extend beyond 12 months, it is possible to apply for a B-permit, valid for between one and five years. This is also the permit available to self-employed people after they prove that they can support themselves. Detailed information about the regulations is published by the State Secretariat for Migration (www.sem.admin.ch). Detailed information in English is sometimes available from the cantonal authorities, for example downloadable brochures about living and working in Zurich are available at www.awa.zh.ch. The canton of Zurich also allows foreigners to apply for a work permit online (German language only), which shortens the application time. The searchable forum www.englishforum.ch can also be helpful on technical matters.

Non-EU citizens will find it just as hard to gain access to Switzerland's labour market as throughout the European Union, unless they apply in special categories such as spouse or au pair or trainee. If a non-EU national does find an employer willing to sponsor their application, the applicant will have to collect the documents from the Swiss Embassy in his or her home country.

All legal workers are eligible for the high wages but also the very high taxes and contributions. Accident insurance is compulsory for all foreign workers and often the employer pays this. However, health insurance, also compulsory, is the responsibility of the individual. Anyone near a border can save a lot of money by doing their grocery and other shopping in a neighbouring country.

Trainee exchanges between Switzerland and a number of non-EU countries including the USA, Canada, Australia and New Zealand are available to young professionals aged 18–35 who have completed their vocational training (or a degree in the case of Americans) and are working in that field. Permits for temporary trainee placements (*stagiaires*) lasting up to 18 months can be obtained from the Swiss Federal Office for Migration in Bern (young.professionals@sem.admin.ch). Normally the Swiss embassy administers the programme abroad, but in some cases a cooperating partner organisation such as Cultural Vistas in the USA handles the formalities for a fee of $450. Guidance may be given to applicants on how to find an employer, though the programme is for individuals who can find a suitable position in their field independently.

CASUAL WORK

Particularly in the building trade and for agricultural work, the local supply of labour is so clearly inadequate that people without a residence permit do find jobs.

DANNY JACOBSON FROM WISCONSIN SPENT SEVERAL SUCCESSFUL SEASONS PIECING TOGETHER ODD JOBS IN THE TOWN OF BULLE:

I still feel Switzerland is a working traveller's best friend in Europe. If you're willing to get dirty, there's tons of work around. If you can speak French or German, head into the more rural parts or the less touristy towns. I've based myself in Bulle, an over-sized village in the Préalpes. The word on the street is that in the off-the-beaten-track parts of Switzerland, the authorities look the other way because the hotels and restaurants are usually desperate for workers. The hotel owner has offered me a full-time position cleaning the staircases and washing dishes five days a week for a generous wage paid cash in hand plus food. If I choose to stay here for a bit, I shouldn't need to work again for a long time when I hit the road again.

He clearly preferred this boss to a previous one, a *'drunken madman with 800 ways to mop a floor, of which a new one would be demonstrated each day because I was too inept to realise I was using yesterday's'*.

In winter you may be able to find occasional work chopping firewood or mending roofs and be paid a handsome SFr120+ per day. A special opportunity for odd jobbers – assuming global warming doesn't kill it off – is afforded by the Swiss law that prohibits snow on roofs from reaching more than two metres depth.

Although Switzerland doesn't go so far as to demand that buskers get a work permit, Leda Meredith was surprised to find that the city of Bern (a 'goldmine for buskers') publishes a leaflet about when and where busking is permitted. In fact it hosts an annual buskers' festival in August, which feeds and houses eligible musicians and entertainers for three days (www.buskersbern.ch). Assaf de Hazan from Israel found Switzerland a Shangri-La for buskers: *'If you have a guitar (and can play it) here in Geneva, you are a king. If you have a bit of impudence and are willing to go around cafés and bars (not too fancy) and ask to play three songs, you are more than a king. I was getting more than £50 for a day's playing around the train station part of the lake. You just go and ask and they always say yes. After playing just three songs, you go around with an ashtray and get money, and lots of it.'*

TOURISM

It has been said that the Swiss invented tourism. Certainly their hotels and tourism courses are still the training ground and model for hoteliers worldwide. For the hotels and catering industry, a rapid short-term injection of labour is an economic necessity for both the summer and winter season – June/July to September and December to April.

Swiss hotels are very efficient and tend to be impersonal, since you will be one in an endless stream of seasonal workers from many countries. The very intense attitude to work among the Swiss means that hours are long (often longer than stipulated in the contract): a typical working week would consist of at least five nine-hour days working split shifts.

On the other hand, the majority are *korrekt*, ie scrupulous about keeping track of your overtime and pay you handsomely at the end of your contract. Alison May summarised her summer at the Novotel-Zürich-Airporthotel: *'On balance, the wages were good but we really had to earn them.'* Remember that from the gross (*brutto*) monthly wage of SFr2,500–4,000, up to half will be lost in deductions for board and lodging, tax and insurance (with slight cantonal variations). For example a Swiss tour operator was offering a gross monthly salary of SFr2,850 to domestic and maintenance staff, and SFr4,000 to chefs; the net equivalents worked out at SFr405 and SFr620 a week.

The Job-Hunt

Provided you have a reasonable CV and knowledge of languages (preferably German), a speculative job-hunt in advance is worthwhile. One hotel group worth trying (provided you are a European national) is Mövenpick at www.moevenpick.com, while the Park Hotel Waldhaus, 7018 Flims-Waldhaus (www.waldhaus-flims.ch) always seems to be recruiting staff with EU citizenship to become *Zimmer-frauen* and *Serviceaushilfen* (temporary service staff) among others. Try also the Ski Lodge Engelberg (www.skilodgeengelberg.com/en/work-here) right in the middle of the country.

The Swiss Hotel Association's online recruitment site www.hoteljob.ch typically will list more than 1,000 vacancies, most for German speakers with professional experience. Another source of similar jobs is www.hotelcareer.com/jobs/switzerland.

Quite a few British travel companies and camping holiday operators are active in Switzerland such as Eurocamp with campsites in Interlaken, Susten and Lauterbrunnen. Venture Abroad in Derby (www.ventureabroad.co.uk) hire a few '*practical, resourceful and calm*' people to work as resort reps at their centres in Adelboden and Kandersteg for scouts and guides. The work consists of meeting and guiding youth groups in the Bernese Oberland.

Most ski tour operators mount big operations in Switzerland, such as Crystal Holidays and a trio of companies including Ski Total (www.workaseason.com). The main disadvantage of being hired by a UK company is that the wages will be on a British scale rather than on the much more lucrative Swiss one. Working conditions might be better at smaller companies such as CK Verbier (www.ckverbier.com/careers) who hire non-cooking chalet hosts among other roles. A Swiss company that advertises for resort staff and ski instructors is Viamonde in Anzère (www.viamonde.com/personnel).

The Swiss organisation Village Camps advertises widely its desire to recruit staff over 21 in their multi-activity language summer camp for children in Leysin. Jobs are available for EFL teachers, sports and activity instructors, nurses and general domestic staff. For jobs with Village Camps, room and board are provided as well as accident and liability insurance and weekly pocket money. The recruitment office in Nyon gears up just after the new year (personnel@villagecamps.com; www.villagecamps.com).

New Zealander Philip Lee spent his summers during university working at English language summer camps in Europe including one summer with Village Camps. The application for the position of counsellor involved a formal application and phone interview, plus he had to complete a basic first aid/ CPR course at his own expense. This opportunity is open to Antipodeans and Americans as well as European nationals as Philip reported:

> There wasn't much of a visa problem as most tutors from outside the EU (USA/Canada/Australia/NZ) had a three-month tourist visa I believe. I never encountered any problems in relation to my visa and working and even when I was working in Switzerland, where I expected more regulation and controls, there wasn't a problem at all. I worked in Switzerland for a two-week camp. But there were people who stayed there for up to 12 weeks working without problems. I was paid cash-in-hand for the Swiss camps. I think payment was always a bit of a concern for people working in this line of work for the first time, in the sense that there were no 'employment rights', but at the organisations I worked with, payment was always managed very professionally.

Another camp operator looking for seasonal summer or winter staff is Les Elfes in Verbier (www. leselfes.com/about-us/jobs). Most of its staff are over 20, though younger candidates are eligible to do work experience. The Haut-Lac International Centre (1669 Les Sciernes; www.haut-lac-camp.ch) is a language and sport camp for adolescents that employs teacher-monitors and domestic staff for seasonal language camps held year round. The American School in Switzerland (TASIS) also employs TEFL tutors and children's counsellors for their Summer Language Programs, 6926 Montagnola-Lugano (http://summer.tasis.com/page.cfm?p=303). Hiring takes place between January and March. Net salaries for the complete session, June 20–August 13, are SFr2,600 for counsellors and SFr4,000 for teachers; American staff may be eligible for a SFr1,300 contribution to their transatlantic airfares and Europeans up to SFr500.

International Camp Suisse is a British-based language camp with an office in West Yorkshire and the camp held in Torgon. Activity leaders and language teachers are needed to fill many summer positions (www.campsuisse.com/job-description/language-teachers).

On the Spot

Although many people fix up jobs ahead with a tour operator or via an online seasonal recruitment site, others go out armed with a couple of references and try to fix up a winter job in the lesser known resorts such as Les Portes de Soleil at Champery or Les Crosets as well as the major resorts of Leysin, Verbier, Thyon and Crans Montana. This valley is a major road and rail route and is ideal for concentrated job-hunting. Another area that has been recommended is the Jura between La Chaux-de-Fonds and Delémont. Timing is tricky. September is the favoured time, though some employers will already have promised winter season jobs to people they know from previous seasons or ones who approached them earlier. In fact many companies do their recruitment for the winter season the previous May/June. November is a bad time to arrive since most of the hotels are closed and the owners away on holiday.

Surprisingly, tourist offices may be of use both winter and summer. Naturally their lists of local accommodation and restaurants are a useful starting point for a door-to-door job search, but tourist information staff may also offer advice on employment. In May 2016, a Belgian reader of this book, Thibaut Exelmans, wrote from Switzerland where he was getting by, living with his Spanish girlfriend Marta in a campervan which they parked up around Lake Geneva. He was impressed that lakeside car parks were provided with good facilities including hot showers. Their job hunt proved tougher than anticipated:

> *Attracted by the enormous wages and the flourishing economy of the country we decided to come here at the end of April. Although the unemployment rate is very low there isn't much demand for people willing to do odd jobs, possibly because of the big load of 'frontaliers' (French people working in Switzerland). We applied in almost all the buvettes (little lakeside bars) from Geneva to Lausanne, only to hear that we were quite late with our job hunt for the season. The recommended period to apply seems to be mid-March. After this we tried some chalets and buvettes higher in the mountains, mainly in the Swiss Jura, but here also it seemed to be a bit late to apply.*
>
> *In the end we got a job in a buvette at the lake through a friend who had worked there before. From the other 20–30 applications we received only one actual job offer. As with most jobs, experience in the desired job is a big plus. The Swiss are very disciplined when it comes to serving clients! In my experience chances for a job are better in the smaller towns and villages than in big cities like Geneva. In small places there is less competition from other job hunters and the demand for experience is often lower. Tourist offices can be a big help as they often provide lists of employment agencies, as well as hotels and bars.*

Joseph Tame's surprising tip is to go up as high as possible in the mountains. After being told by virtually every hotel in Grindelwald in mid-September that they had already hired their winter season staff, he despaired and decided to waste his last SFr40 on a trip up the rack railway. At the top he approached the only hotel and couldn't believe it when they asked him when he could start. Although he had never worked in a hotel before, they were willing to take him on as a trainee waiter, give him full bed and board plus the standard Swiss wage. At first he found the job a little boring since there were few guests apart from Japanese groups on whirlwind European tours. But things changed at Christmas:

Christmas and New Year was an absolute nightmare. Three shifts a day for everyone with very little sleep and no time off. When a promised pay rise didn't materialise, I decided I had had enough and handed in my notice. But by 5 January, business had slumped and we had at least two hours off daily to ski. When my overdue pay rise came through I withdrew my notice. If you can stick the Christmas rush, things do get better. Switzerland was definitely the best thing that ever happened to me.

Joseph enjoyed his first season so much that he returned for three subsequent seasons and says that he is very glad that he stumbled across this 177-year-old hotel in a blizzard. The proprietors sometimes have trouble filling vacancies and so he recommends sending a CV with photo to Hotel Bellevue des Alpes, Scheidegg Hotels AG, 3801 Kleine Scheidegg (welcome@scheidegg-hotels.ch).

An Amazon reviewer of this book recalls a similar happy outcome in Switzerland when she was 22:

I had always wanted to live in Switzerland, since seeing the childrens' drama Heidi on TV! I thought why don't I just go for it?! Things can't get worse, I've got nothing to lose! ... So I quit my work and booked a flight to Zurich. Work Your Way Around the World was actually slightly negative about the possibility of finding official work in Switzerland. It was one country in Europe that was very strict with visas, etc. But after a great week of staying in hostels, meeting new people and walking miles through the snow in gorgeous Switzerland and knocking on hotel doors, I eventually was offered a job as a chambermaid in Grindelwald, and had a brilliant three months, earnt very good money, lived in a chalet with the other staff (mostly from Spain) ... one of the best times of my life. After that experience, I knew I didn't want to go back to office work so, upon returning to the UK, I got a job as an air hostess.

A recommended meeting place is Balmer's Herberge and Campsite in Interlaken (www.balmers.com). They take on English-speaking seasonal staff as all-rounders who can work in 'housekeeping, food preparation, grill and bar service, shuttle driving, ticket desk, reception and maintenance'. The staff here may also know of other job openings in the area as the hostel is sometimes contacted by local hotels asking for workers.

Casual work opportunities crop up in some alternative establishments in Bern and the other big cities. One reader found weekend bar work at the Reitschule in Bern, a socialist collective arts centre housed in the former city stables, where he had some fairly wild and woolly times. For serving drinks over the pounding electro-beats and cleaning up as dawn broke, he was paid SFr15 an hour cash in hand.

AGRICULTURE

Official Schemes

Young Europeans who are interested in experiencing rural Switzerland may wish to do a stint on a Swiss farm. Through the Horizon Ferme scheme, Agriviva based in Winterthur (☎ (+41) 52 264 0030; www.agriviva.ch) places young people aged 16–25 on 800 'peasant' farms (their translation of *paysan*) throughout Switzerland for short stays. Young volunteers must be nationals of the old EU countries and know some German or French to become a *stagiaire* with a rural family helping in the stables, fields at harvest time and in the household generally.

Despite Switzerland's reputation as an advanced nation, thousands of small family farms practise traditional farming methods, especially in the German-speaking cantons. Part of the reason for this is that not many mechanical threshers or harvesters can function on near vertical slopes (neither can every human harvester for that matter). In addition to the good farm food and comfortable bed, farm volunteers will be paid SF20 per day worked. On these small Swiss farms, English is rarely spoken and many farmers speak a dialect which some find incomprehensible. The hours are long (typically

48 per week), the work is hard and much depends on the volunteer's relationship with the family. Most people who have worked on a Swiss farm report that they are treated like one of the family, which means both that they are up by 6am or 7am and working till 9pm alongside the farmer and that they are invited to accompany the family on any excursions, such as the weekly visit to the market to sell the farm-produced cheeses.

Ruth McCarthy gives an idea of the range of tasks to do on the farm, and a taste of village life, which sounds like something out of *Heidi*:

> *The work on my farm in the Jura included cleaning out cow stalls, haymaking, grass cutting, poultry feeding, manure spreading, vegetable and fruit picking, wood cutting, earth moving, corn threshing and also housework, cooking and looking after the children. The food was very wholesome and all produced on the farm: cheeses, fresh milk, homemade jam, fresh fruit, etc. The church bells struck throughout the day and pealed at 6am and 9pm to open and close each day. As well as church bells the sound of cowbells was also present so that it was quite noisy at times. There was little nightlife unless you went to a gasthof bar in the village. Anyway it's probably better to get a good night's sleep.*

WWOOF Switzerland (wwoof@gmx.ch; http://zapfig.com/wwoof) keeps an updated list of more than 100 farmers around the country. To obtain the list you must join WWOOF at a cost of SFr30/€30/$35 via PayPal. Volunteers must apply with a photocopy of their passport and an accompanying letter of introduction stating why they want to become WWOOF volunteers.

You can also try to arrange a paid harvesting job directly with mainstream farmers. One farm located about nine miles east of Zurich that accepts seasonal workers from the end of May is owned by Jürg and Priska Morf (Ruetihof 5, 8602 Wangen; ☎ (+41) 44 833 21 28; www.erdbeer-feld.ch). The season gets underway with their main crop which is strawberries and with vegetables like mange tout and beans, though exact start dates are, as always, unpredictable and you are asked to keep in daily touch before and during the harvest. Piecework rates per kilogram are paid.

> **JOSEPH TAME MADE USE OF THE WWOOF WEBSITE TO FIX UP A PLACE ON A FARM IN THE SPRING:**
>
> *I can honestly say that it has been an absolutely fantastic experience. The hours could be thought fairly long by some (perhaps 35 per week) considering there is no money involved, but I absolutely love the chance to work outside in this land that reminds me so much of the final setting in The Hobbit. From our farm your eyes take you down the hillside, over the meadows covered in flowers, down to the vast Lake Luzern below and over to the huge snow-capped mountain Pilatus. It really is paradise here. The family have been so kind, and as I put my heart into learning all that I can about the farm they are only too happy to treat me with generosity. I really feel a part of the family.*

Grape Picking

Like every country in Europe south of Scotland, Switzerland produces wine. The main area is in the Vaud north of Lake Geneva, but also in Valais around Sion and Sierre, where the harvest begins in late September though sometimes a few days in October. Every year scores of hopeful *vendangeurs* begin pouring into the region. Robert Abblett calculated that if he had arrived in time to catch the beginning of the harvest, he could have saved £350 from 11 days of work.

Almost everyone who over the years has written about the Swiss harvest writes in glowing terms. A Canadian Kyle MacDonald travelling with his girlfriend at the beginning of September was delighted to see a small notice pinned up in the hostel in Lyon just a few hours after arriving in Europe. They made haste to the destination, St Saphorin, on the shore of Lake Geneva and were soon put to work at a chateau in Chexbres. Kyle recorded his experiences:

The next day we were aboard the appropriately named 'Le Train des Vignes' zipping along high above the shores of Lake Geneva. The thousands of acres of vineyards we passed through were going to fill thousands of bottles with Swiss wine. A cheerful Madame greeted our arrival at the train station in St Saphorin and drove us up the road, stopping at a massive four-storey Chateau overlooking sparkling Lake Geneva and the vineyards below. In the distance were the glacier-covered peaks of the Alps. If a handful of experts had ever sat down to agree where the best place on earth to harvest grapes was located, this had to be it.

Dominique's job was to cut bunches of grapes from each vine. Using a small set of garden clippers, she filled plastic containers left along each row and were picked up by 'un porteur' like me. My job was to carry 'small' containers of grapes to a 'large' container waiting on the closest roadway. Each 'small' container weighed about 35 pounds and we carried three containers at a time on our backs using a metal rack. The incredibly steep terrain made work difficult. Hauling grapes down steep staircases was tricky, but the real test came when grapes had to be hauled up staircases. We were called 'les porteurs' but I think of myself as a wine and chocolate-fuelled Swiss grape sherpa.

In addition to free room and generous board, *vendangeurs* usually earn SFr75 (£60) per day, and in some cases even more.

Vineyards are found along the north shores of Lake Geneva on either side of Lausanne. One district is known as La Côte, between Coppet and Morges west of Lausanne, and the other is the Lavaux, a remarkably beautiful region of vineyards, rising up the hillside along the 25km between Pully on the outskirts of Lausanne and the tourist city of Montreux. The vineyards, enclosed within low stone walls, slope so steeply that all the work must be done by hand, and the job of portering is recommended only for the very fit.

The winemakers' association of Lake Biel (Bielersee) lists the 80 growers in their region at www.bielerseewein.ch/winzer.asp August and early September can be a good time to approach the vineyard owners since you might be taken on early to help with netting the grapes, to minimise bird damage. Try also the northern shores of the two adjoining lakes Murtensee and Lac de Neuchâtel.

TUTORS AND AU PAIRS

Private tutoring is a possibility for those who lack a permit, as an American world traveller discovered when he was living with his Swiss girlfriend (now wife) in Bern:

A Swiss friend advised me to apply at one of the English schools but I didn't think it would work without a permit. So I just made my own flyer and put it up around town and the next thing I knew I had a bunch of people calling me up to help with proofreading seminar papers/assignments and to give private lessons. I figured I'd go for quantity and low-ball the market, charging only SFr20 per hour. But I found a few adverts for people looking for teachers and with those, I went with their offered price, which was sometimes twice as much.

Note that a qualified EFL teacher can charge SFr80 an hour in the cities, so a rate of SFr40 might strike some as a bargain.

For those interested in a domestic position with a Swiss family there are rules laid down by each Swiss canton that principally apply to non-EU citizens since Europeans can work in Switzerland in any capacity. Au pairs and nannies from any country of the world are able to work in Switzerland, provided they come through one of the handful of authorised agencies (contact details below). Non-EU candidates must be under 26, can stay as an au pair for one year only and are required to spend at least three hours a week studying German or French (depending on which part of Switzerland they are in). Families usually pay the language school fees or at least make a substantial contribution. The agencies are at pains to remind potential au pairs that Swiss German is very different from the German learned in school, which often causes disappointment and difficulties.

Au pairs in Switzerland work for a maximum of 30 hours per week, plus babysitting once or twice a week. The monthly salary varies among cantons but the normal minimum is SFr700–800. Rates may be slightly higher for older girls and are generally higher in Geneva than Zurich. In addition, the au pair gets a four or five week paid holiday plus SFr18–20 for days off (to cover food). Au pairs are liable to pay tax and contributions that can mean a deduction of up to a fifth of their wages unless the family is willing to pay or subsidise these costs.

Pro Filia in Zurich (☎ (+41) 44 361 5331; www.profilia.ch) is a long-established Catholic au pair agency with four branches in German-speaking Switzerland for incoming au pairs and one in French-speaking Vaud. The agency registration fee is SFr45 plus a fee of SFr360 is to be paid on taking up the placement.

Independent au pair placement agencies include Perfect Way in Brugg (☎ (+41) 56 281 3912; www.perfectway.ch) which vets all families and distributes a list of other au pairs and their contact details. The agency Au Pair Link (part of Wind Connections) in Erlenbach near Zurich (☎ (+41) 44 915 4104; www.aupairlink.ch) accepts au pairs from Australia, Canada and the USA, where it has in-country interviewers, as well as other countries. It even has a few client families in Liechtenstein as well as Switzerland.

VOLUNTEERING

Several of the international workcamp organisations operate in Switzerland mainly to carry out conservation work. Workcamp Switzerland based in Zurich is expanding its programme and now carries details in English of its 21 workcamps and longer projects at www.workcamp.ch, from teaching English on teen summer camps to alpine gardening. The workcamp joining fee is SFr150.

The Mountain Forest Project (www.bergwaldprojekt.ch) runs one-week forest conservation projects in the alpine regions of Switzerland and southern Germany. MFP welcomes foreign volunteers who know some German (or French in the case of the camps at Champéry, Trient and Blonay). It provides hut accommodation, food and accident insurance during one-week education and conservation projects free of charge, but if you register and cancel you have to pay SFr60. For details see the website (in English) or contact MFP in Trin (☎ (+41) 81 650 4040).

Austria

With thriving winter and summer tourist industries, Austria offers much seasonal employment. Its rate of unemployment has been climbing and now stands at 8.3%, the highest it has been since the 1950s, but still below the European average of nearly 10%. However in some industries there are net labour shortages, for example 29% of people employed in tourism are not Austrian citizens. A good knowledge of German will be necessary for most jobs, apart from those with UK tour operators. The government website www.help.gv.at gives information in English about immigration and social security procedures for those working in Austria.

Once you are in Austria, you should visit the state-run employment office AMS (*Arbeitsmarktservice*) though it would be virtually essential to speak German before they could assist. The AMS runs offices at the national, provincial and regional levels. The AMS web pages (www.ams.at) including its e-JobRoom might be of assistance to German speakers. The site also provides links to EURES Advisers in each of the regions, for example to the Vienna office specialising in youth employment at Gumpendorfer Gürtel 2b (eures.wien@ams.at).

For seasonal workers in tourism, the AMS organises special job fairs. Most *Saisonstellen im Hotel und Gastgewerbe* (seasonal hotel jobs) for the winter season are notified in November for the start of the season at the end of November. Jobcentres that specialise in seasonal work are called

BerufsInfoZentren or BIZ. The BIZ office in Innsbruck can be especially helpful, as it registers many hotel and catering vacancies in the South Tyrol (Schöpfstrasse 5, 6010 Innsbruck; ☎ (+43) 512 5903). Anyone under 25 might find it worthwhile asking for advice about the Tirol at InfoEck, the Youth Information Centres in Innsbruck, Imst and Wörgl (☎ (+43) 512 57 1799; www.mei-infoeck.at) where you can consult a Summer Job and Internship database. Their online job platform which includes babysitting is called Jobscope (www.jobscope.at).

Nationals of non-European countries must find an employer willing to apply for a work permit on their behalf. The Austrian government has special quotas for seasonal workers from outside the EU in the tourism and agricultural sectors. Employers may apply to employ a non-EU citizen for varying maximum periods. Up-to-date information is available from www.migration.gv.at/en (search for 'Seasonal Workers').

The Austrian Consulate in the US has good information about the procedures for applying for an entry visa (valid for stays of three–six months) and a residence permit (more than six months) linked from www.austria.at/do-you-need-a-visa. Canadians under 30 may get a six-month youth workers exchange visa through SWAP (www.swap.ca/austria) for a programme fee of C\$420.

THE JOB-HUNT

Tourism

There is no shortage of hotels to which you can apply either for the summer or the winter season, especially in the west of Austria. Get a list from the local tourist office or online. The largest concentration is in the Tyrol, though there are also many in the Vorarlberg region. Wages in hotels and restaurants are lower than they are in Switzerland, but reasonable.

Adventure activity organisers in Kirchberg and elsewhere may require guides for white-water rafting, mountain biking or hiking. For example Fankhauser Rafting needs guides for these activites as well as support staff (www.tirolrafting.at).

Austrian ski resorts have traditionally been popular with British skiers, which creates a demand for English-speaking staff. The main winter resorts to try are St Anton, Kitzbühel, Mayrhofen, Saalbach, St Johann in Tyrol, Obergurgl, Ischgl, Lech and Söll. The ski season in the Innsbruck region is fairly reliable since the Stubai Glacier normally ensures snow from early December until the end of April. The Kaprun Glacier allows skiing between the end of October and December, and some ski instructor courses take advantage of this, such as the Deutsch Institut Tirol (www.deutschinstitut.com) which markets an intensive four-week German language course in October followed by a ski instructor course both costing from €6,700 which precedes a ski season job. The Ski Instructor Academy in Taxenbach (www.siaaustria.com) in the Kaprun Zell-am-See area guarantees winter employment in the Austrian Alps to anyone who completes one of its instructor courses.

As usual, it will be necessary to enquire everywhere for jobs in hotels, shops, as an au pair, in specialist areas such as the *skiverleih* (ski hire), as a technician or just working on the drag-lifts. It is probably best to target one or two villages where there are a lot of guesthouses and hotels. The Tourist Information office and the bus drivers who convey skiers from hotels to slopes are both good sources of information. You could try to fix up a job with a British tour operator beforehand, ideally in September, for example with Esprit/Inghams/Total Ski (www.workaseason.com) or Crystal (http://tuijobsuk.co.uk/work-at-tui-travel/abroad/crystal-ski-jobs). Vacancies are posted on the specialist recruitment sites SeasonWorkers.com and www.jobs.natives.co.uk. Supertravel (www.supertravel.co.uk/ski/seasonal jobs.aspx) takes on winter staff for St Anton, primarily chalet chefs, chalet hosts with bubbly personalities, chalet managers fluent in German, and handymen/drivers over 23. All applicants must hold a passport from an EU country and have a British National Insurance number.

English Teaching

As in Germany, the market for EFL in Austrian cities is primarily for business English, particularly in-company. Most private language institutes such as SPIDI in Vienna (www.spidi.at) depend on freelance part-time teachers drawn from the sizeable resident international community. The hourly rate at reputable institutes starts at €26, which is none too generous when the high cost of living in Vienna is taken into account.

Berlitz is well represented with 10 centres in Austria including several in Vienna (www.berlitz.at). In fact all centres recruit new English trainers of British, Irish, American or Australian nationality. Candidates must have permission to work in the EU, while a business and university background would be advantageous.

Summer language and sport camps provide more scope for EFL teachers and others. Village Camps based in Switzerland (www.villagecamps.com) run a summer activity camp at Piesendorf near Zell-am-See from late June to July. Some experience of teaching children and a knowledge of a second European language are the basic requirements.

Two Vienna-based organisations active in this field are the similarly named English for Children (www.englishforchildren.com) and English for Kids (www.e4kids.co.at) both of which are looking for young monitors and English teachers with experience of working with children and preferably some TEFL background. English for Kids promises a salary up to €1,650 per month gross, plus full board and accommodation and travel costs within Austria. Try also LETA e.U. (Learn English Through Action) based in Vienna but with camps elsewhere (www.leta.co.at/en/careers) and The English Camp Company (www.theenglishcampcompany.com) for summer jobs teaching English and supervising activities. The latter hires lots of American counsellors.

Au Pairs

Austria, together with Switzerland, was one of the first countries to host au pairs, though the practice is not as popular as it once was, and the number of agencies active in the field has declined.

Au pairs from EU countries will have no trouble sorting out the paperwork in Austria whereas non-EU candidates must obtain an entry visa (National Austrian Visa D) in advance for stays of less than six months, and a full-blown residence permit (*Aufenthaltstitel*) for longer stays which are issued by the Austrian authorities while you are out of the country. The D entry permit costs $107 in the US and has to be applied for in person.

According to the regulations revised in 2017, all au pairs must receive €523 per month for working 18 hours per week. Placement agencies include: Au Pair Austria, Vermittlungs-agentur in Linz and Vienna (www.aupairaustria.at/english.aspx) and Friends Au Pair Vermittlung (www.aupairvermittlung. at) which charges a placement fee of €50 for au pairs from the EU and considerably more for others, €100–€250.

It should be possible to find babysitting work if you are based in a resort. Ask for permission in the big hotels to put up a notice. The going rate according to InfoEck which matches babysitters with families is €12.75 an hour.

Outdoor Work

WWOOF Austria is in Puch/Weiz (☎ (+43) 676 505 1639, with limited hours; www.wwoof.at). Membership costs €25 per year which entitles you to online access to contact details for around 260 Austrian organic farmers looking for work-for-keep volunteer helpers.

The fact that the Austrian government grants thousands of short-term labour permits specifically for harvest helpers indicates that demand for seasonal workers is strong. The farmers prefer workers who know some German since few of them speak any English. Normally you will be expected to stay for the whole season though people who are free to work for the first four weeks before the school holidays begin are in demand. Try the large cooperatively run farms rather than the small ones that usually rely on family members.

Central Europe and Russia

As the European Union expanded to embrace Bulgaria and Romania as well as Hungary, Poland, the Czech Republic, Slovakia, Slovenia, Lithuania, Latvia and Estonia, the divide between Eastern and Western Europe has been almost completely eroded. The English language has been now long established as the preferred second language. The demand for native speakers to teach English continues to be strong in the cities and far-flung corners of this vast region, though it is nothing like it was in the first 15 years after the collapse of Communism.

Thousands of foreigners continue to fall under the spell of Prague, Budapest and Kraków. Even those who find themselves in the less prepossessing industrial cities normally come away beguiled by Central European charm. The English language teaching industry in those cities has grown up, and is now much more likely to hire teachers with proven experience or an appropriate qualification.

TEACHING ENGLISH

In the early days, foreigners were welcomed into the state education system but nowadays most foreigners teach in the private sector that offers less job security but better pay. Fewer vacancies in Central and Eastern Europe are being advertised in the educational press and on the internet, even in Poland, but it is still worth checking the main EFL job sites such as www.tefl.com which at the time of writing carried job ads for about 30 different employers, with more than half being in the Russian Federation.

The major chains have multiple franchise schools in the region, chief among them International House, EF English First and Language Link (see Teaching English chapter). Certification is almost always required and one attractive option is to train on the spot. Training centres such as LIVE TEFL in Prague (www.liveteflprague.com) and International House in Budapest (www.teacher-training.hu) can offer graduates of their monthly four-week courses job-finding assistance. Language Link (www.jobs. languagelink.ru) is active in Russia and Kazakhstan. Contracts for new teachers pay from roughly $1,100 per month in Moscow with various perks, less in smaller cities.

Once you have a work base, the supply of private teaching is usually plentiful. The pay for private lessons can be excellent compared to wages offered by schools. A small notice placed on a prominent university noticeboard or online announcements site would have a good chance of producing results.

Teaching in the Czech Republic

There seems to be an equally strong demand for English in the Czech and Slovak Republics, though the majority of TEFL teachers gravitate to the former. In Prague, the glut of well-qualified teachers is so bad that salaries are actually lower than in smaller cities such as Brno, even though the cost of living is higher.

Most people wait until they arrive in Prague before trying to find teaching work, which is what Linda Harrison did: *'If you persevere there are jobs around. A lot of teaching work here seems to be in companies. Schools employ you to go into offices, etc to teach English (though not usually business English).'* Most private language schools in the major cities can count on receiving plenty of CVs on spec from which to fill any vacancies that arise. Anyone who is well qualified or experienced should eventually find employment. The *Yellow Pages* or *Zlaté Stranky* (www.zlatestranky.cz – search for Jazyková Anglictina) is an excellent source of school addresses. Advertisements for teaching jobs frequently appear on www.expats.cz, especially for vacancies in nurseries and pre-schools. Otherwise you can post your bio and prices on www.findmyfavouriteteacher.com. The pattern is to offer a discounted trial lesson and then charge the going rate of 300–400 crowns.

The market in Brno is booming, with dozens of language schools operating in the country's second largest city (many will be one-person outfits), catering to a population of just 385,000.

Among the schools with the largest demand for teachers are:

Akcent International House: Prague; www.akcent.cz. Degree plus CELTA or equivalent is minimum requirement. Prefer teachers who have obtained a freelancers' licence (*živnostenský list*).

Brno English Centre: Brno; www.brnoenglishcentre.cz.

Caledonian School: Prague; jobs@caledonianschool.com. Employ 100 teachers for schools in Prague, and throughout the Czech and Slovak Republics; teachers must have a Trinity or Cambridge Certificate or equivalent; approximate net salary of 18,000–20,000 crowns per month.

Spevacek Group: Prague; www.spevacek.info. Recruitment info on website. Affiliated to Live TEFL training mentioned above.

Tutor School: Prague; www.tutor.cz. Most vacancies in Prague and Brno.

Self-employed freelancers can invoice companies for 20,000–30,000 crowns a month. Private sector wages can be as high as 24,000 crowns per month before an average of 15% is deducted for tax. When a much lower wage is offered it usually includes a range of benefits such as holiday pay and health insurance. Hourly fees start at 200 crowns net. For summer jobs try Wattsenglish which runs city summer day camps in Prague, Liberec, Karlovy Vary and České Budějovice, and a residential camp in the Giant Mountains (www.wattsenglish.cz/for-teachers/employment-opportunities). Teachers are paid 6,000 crowns per week gross (4,000–5,000 net).

EU citizens do not have to apply for a visa or work permit. For non-EU citizens the sought-after document is the blue card that entitles foreign nationals with good qualifications (minimum university degree) to both live and work in the country. Information can be found on the Immigration section at www.mvcr.cz. This requires gathering a raft of documents including employment contract, proof of accommodation, proof of health insurance, etc and presenting it at the Czech embassy in your home country. Foreigners do sometimes pick up work on their Schengen tourist visa but before it expires after 90 days, the holder must exit the country and is not allowed to return until a further 90 days has elapsed.

The Czech Republic has Youth Mobility agreements with New Zealand and Canada which allow young people aged 18–35 who meet the acceptance criteria to reside and work in the Czech Republic for up to 12 months; the administration fee is currently 2,500 crowns.

Teaching in Slovakia

As the poor cousin in the former Czechoslovakia, the republic of the Slovaks has been somewhat neglected not only by tourists but by teachers as well. As one language school director put it: '*Many teachers are heading for Prague, which is why Slovakia stands aside of the main flow of the teachers. That's a pity as Prague is crowded with British and Americans while there's a lack of the teachers here in Slovakia.*'

The density of private language schools in the capital Bratislava and in the other main cities such as Banska Bystrika makes an on-the-ground job-hunt promising. The largest semi-private language school in Slovakia is the Akadémia Vzdelávania (www.aveducation.sk) with academies around the country hiring native speaker teachers from time to time.

Geoff Nunney has enjoyed teaching in Slovakia on and off for a number of years and returned in 2016. He was pleased when one of the 30 schools in Nitra to which he had applied offered him an interview and then a job starting in March though he didn't stay the course since the boss was a control freak and he was barely earning enough to cover his costs. He has now returned part-time to a previous employer in Nitra, the Lingua School, where he hopes to fill up his timetable eventually. Geoff summarises his impressions of teaching in Slovakia:

The best thing you need in Slovakia is a sense of humour. I have been in school plays, and they are a very friendly nation of people. Their standard of English is very good, and they are great fun to teach. For example last Friday, a student stopped me and said, 'Geoff, the walls have ears' to demonstrate his mastery of an English idiom. Although wages aren't great here, the locals and the scenery and the supportive staff make up for it. I love it out here, and it has stunning mountains and walking country.

Teaching in Hungary

English is compulsory for all Hungarian students who wish to apply for college or university entrance, and university students in both the arts and sciences must take courses in English, creating a huge market for English teachers. But because of the high calibre of Hungary's homegrown teachers, native speakers do not always have the cachet they have elsewhere.

Yet native speakers continue to find teaching opportunities in Hungary, especially in the business market. The invasion of foreigners in Budapest was never as overwhelming as it was (and is) in Prague. Gillian Murphy from Ireland concluded that there was a shortage of native English teachers in Budapest when she was teaching business people in private institutes until summer 2016. She attributes this to the low pay and complicated tax system. She reported that her pay ranged from 2,700 forints (£7.50) for 45 minutes to 4,000 forints (£11) for one hour, depending on the arrangement between the school and the student. There is enough demand for private tuition to support several websites that allow language learners to find English teachers including www.LearnEnglish Budapest.com, www.angoltanarok.com and www.AnyanyelviAngolTanarok.hu.The US-based Central European Teaching Program (CETP, 3800 NE, 72nd Avenue, Portland, OR 97213; ☎ (+1) 503 287 4977; www.cetp.info) places up to 100 native speakers of English mainly in state schools around Hungary. The programme offers cultural immersion through teaching and is open to native English speakers with a university degree, preferably some experience of TEFL and overseas teaching/study experience and a willingness to pay the programme fee of US$1,900–$2,500. A co-teaching model is used whereby classes are taught by a native Hungarian and a native English speaker.

Before the 93rd day of an EEA citizen's stay, he or she should report their presence to their nearest regional Office of Immigration and Nationality. The office will issue a registration certificate, which permits indefinite stays. EU citizens working full-time in Hungary are subject to the same social security and pension obligations as Hungarians. Employees must make payments into the National Health Insurance Fund and into a pension fund.

A non-EU employee cannot be legally paid until she or he has a work permit, which must be supported by a Hungarian employer who is entitled to apply for a work permit from the relevant Regional Employment Office. General information about residence permits is available from the Office of Immigration & Nationality (www.bmbah.hu).

Teaching in Poland

Prospects for English teachers in Poland, western Poland in particular, remain reasonable, even if the demand for English teachers is more moderate than it was in the early days after democracy was restored. Poles are still keen to learn English but, with the improvement in education and the explosion of cheap flights to and from Poland, millions of Poles simply get on a plane and come to Britain or Ireland, mainly to work and improve their English in situ.

Even the major cities of Warsaw, Wroclaw, Kraków, Poznan and Gdansk are worthwhile destinations, though the job-hunt is usually easier in the many lesser known towns and cities of Poland. After obtaining some addresses, would-be teachers should dutifully 'do the rounds' of the *Dyrektors*. Some of the bigger schools include:

Angloschool: 4 schools in Warsaw area; www.angloschool.com.pl.
BELT (Business English & Language Training) Schools: www.belt.edu.pl. Centres in Gdansk and Gdynia, plus Szczecin (www.belt.szczecin.pl) and Program Bell in Poznan (www. program-bell.edu.pl/english/work_for_us.htm). Formerly Bell Schools.

Lektor Szkola Jezykow Obcych: Wroclaw; www.lektor.com.pl. 70 British, American, Canadian or Australian teachers with certificate in TEFL.

York School of Language: Kraków; www.york.edu.pl; 30 qualified teachers.

The current average gross salary in the private sector starts at about 45–60 zloties an hour (£8.75–£11.50). Generally speaking, private language schools in Poland offer reasonable working conditions, with few reports of profit-mongers and sharks.

Some private language teaching organisations run short-term holiday courses in summer and sometimes winter which require native speakers. To take one example, the Perfect English private language school (www.perfectenglish.pl) in the foothills of the Beskidy mountains in Southern Poland fills vacancies for its summer courses as well as for the academic year. American young people might be interested in volunteering to work at one of the many English language immersion camps run by the Kosciuszko Foundation's Teaching English in Poland (TEIP) Program (www.thekf.org/kf/programs/teaching_english_in_poland). The four-week programme takes place in July and early August; the deadline for applications falls early in the calendar year. International House (www.ih.com.pl) maintains several language schools in Poland employing certificate-qualified EFL teachers, in Wroclaw, Bydgoszcz and Bielsko-Biala.

Short holidays in which paying language learners mingle and interact with native speakers who are given free room and board and transport from the nearest city are organised by Angloville (www.angloville.com). Enthusiastic conversationalists willing to engage in English lessons and informal conversation with Polish adults or teenagers for up to 12 hours a day over six days receive transport from Warsaw and free accommodation (some more luxurious than others) and meals.

Poland's requirements for EU teachers are broadly in line with the rest of Europe. They no longer need to apply for a work permit; however, teachers wishing to stay for more than three months should obtain a residence card from the regional governor of their chosen city/town. Applicants will need to justify their stay in Poland and confirm that they have sources of income (eg a statement from a bank account). Employers should assist with the documentation and the necessary translation of official documents into Polish. Most employers who take on non-EU teachers will be aware of the procedures which, according to one, could fill a book. The Polish Embassy in Washington can provide information for US citizens (www.washington.mfa.gov.pl).

RUSSIAN FEDERATION

The Russian economy is in dire straits. The rouble has been tumbling, mainly because of the fall in the world price of oil and EU sanctions after Russia annexed Crimea. However at the time of writing the Russian currency had made a gain and was trading at just less than 60 roubles to the US dollar, which may be an indicator that recession can be stayed. Yet national morale is low, not helped by the disgrace of the doping scandal that resulted in the ban of so many of its athletes from the Rio Olympics. The geopolitical situation is no rosier, with mounting hostility over Russia's assistance to President al-Assad of Syria. Yet the English language market continues to be strong, especially in the corporate sector, and old and new language training businesses are eagerly recruiting teachers via advertisements abroad. Hosting the 2018 FIFA World Cup may act as a spur just as the Winter Olympics of 2014 did.

Many qualified teachers work for the major foreign-owned language chains such as Benedict, Language Link and EF English First (see below). The situation in the Central Asian Republics is somewhat different because demand for English there is largely funded by international oil investment or in the case of Georgia by the government (see below).

Barry Robinson spent a number of years in Moscow working the EFL circuit:

When living in Moscow patience is priceless. Expect to queue, wait longer, and endure a certain amount of discomfort when travelling around the city from lesson to lesson. Yet Moscow is an expansive, vibrant, culturally rewarding city in which to live. The people at first appear a tad abrupt, but this is usually just to cope with the breakneck pace of life in Russia's capital. When you make friends – and you will as Russians are quite sociable and always interested in native English speakers – you'll find them warm and generous people, who will let you into their hearts and homes if they genuinely like you.

Be warned: Moscow is a very expensive city. Increasing prosperity and the influx of foreigners have driven up rents so, if you don't want to rent a roach-infested shed, you'll have to spend hundreds of dollars on some living space. Often teaching contracts will include a flat, but these tend to be rather manky and often shared with another teacher. Freelance opportunities are abundant, and extremely lucrative. However, you'll have to wade through the quagmire that is Russia's ever-muddled, ever-changing visa and entry requirements.

Finding a Job

Anyone with a qualification and contacts in the region or who is prepared to go in order to make contacts should be able to find a teaching niche on an individual basis. Many educational institutes outside Moscow and the other major urban centres can't afford to attract Western teachers through the usual recruitment channels. Experienced TEFLer Bradwell Jackson found that in negotiations with a school in the obscure city of Shakhty in southern Russia, he had the upper hand:

> The fact that Russia was the first to offer a favourable contract may say something about their need for native speakers. I only agreed to start the visa procedure after I saw that the contract specifically stated that I couldn't work over 22 hours a week. I believe that this particular town of Shakhty was willing to agree since they are such a small town it's not easy for them to inveigle a foreigner to come to live. This makes this a perfect symbiotic relationship, as I am happy to live in such a village-like atmosphere where I don't need to have a car and can walk to work. The teachers are quite friendly to me, and the manager almost never does anything to ruffle my feathers, since she probably doesn't want to see me take off (as some previous foreign teachers have done apparently). Upon arriving in-country, I didn't notice as much of the supposed 'Russian cold exterior' as I have been apprised of. It is true that I couldn't just smile at people on the street. My colleague told me that people will think that I'm crazy if I do that. I asked him 'even if I smile at the girls?', and he said yes. I found out that he was right.

The monthly salary of 35,000 roubles (less than $600) is at the low end, though more than three times what the local Russian teachers are paid. In Brad's case, the easy workload and comfortable free apartment are sufficient compensations. Small town pastimes seems to suit Brad too: *'For the most part, Russians seem just as sociable as any other people I've known. When I go out for dancing or karaoke, I'm often inundated by the local tipsy Russians who demand that I come over to their table for a drink which they say is a Russian tradition.'*

It is generally accepted among Moscow employers that most if not all teachers supplement their income by freelancing, which causes no problems unless a teacher is trying to poach students.

Check the online message board community for English speakers living in Moscow www.expat.ru which always carries a selection of clearly set out adverts for native English-speaker teachers, preferably already resident in Moscow. An advert seen in 2016 invited native speakers, qualified teachers and tutors of English (and other languages) with a linguistic background or TEFL Certificate to join the teachers team of the Native Speakers Club which arranges private lessons at the teacher's or student's place (www.nsc24.org).

Among the major language teaching organisations, the following employ substantial numbers of native speaking teachers with a TEFL qualification:

BKC – International House: Moscow; recruit@bkc.ru; www.bkcih-moscow.com/jobs. Around 200 contract and hourly-paid teachers in Moscow, plus 50 more in the Moscow region.

EF English First: www.englishfirst.com/ESL-jobs/teaching-jobs-in-russia. Teachers for 35 schools in Moscow, St Petersburg, Vladivostok, etc.

Language Link Russia: www.jobs.languagelink.ru. 200 teachers throughout Russia (Moscow, St Petersburg, Volgograd, Siberia, Urals, etc); freshly certified EFL teachers can be placed in Russian schools; unqualified people can join Teacher Internship Training Programme.

ROBERT JENSKY, DIRECTOR OF LANGUAGE LINK RUSSIA, IS CONVINCED THAT HIGH STANDARDS ARE ESSENTIAL:

I have personally seen many unqualified teachers fail because they did not fully realise the difference between speaking English and teaching English. Although Russians can vary in temperament and personality, they share a respect for education. Their only concern is that they get their full money's worth from each and every lesson. Russian students are demanding and place high expectations on their teachers, and so do the companies that employ them (including those that hire EFL teachers illegally). Given these circumstances, it is strongly recommended that any teacher coming to Russia have with him or her a good grammar book, a dictionary and a concise guide to TEFL methodology.

Russians have taken to the internet with unbounded enthusiasm and opportunities may be discovered by doing some concerted surfing. A few schemes offer volunteers the chance to teach English at any level from university to businesses to summer camps. For example the youth exchange company CCUSA with offices in the UK and California (www.ccusa.com) runs a Summer Camp Russia Programme whereby teacher/counsellors are placed in youth camps in Russia lasting four or eight weeks between mid-June and mid-August. Camps are widely scattered from Lake Baikal in Siberia to the shores of the Black Sea. The programme fee of £999/$2,900 includes round-trip travel from London/ USA to Moscow, visa, travel, insurance, orientation on arrival and room and board. Australian Paul Jones gradually came to enjoy the programme:

I worked as a counsellor in a summer camp near the city of Perm. When I first arrived, my heart sank because it looked like a gulag (for which the area around Perm is famous). But you soon forget the physical conditions, mostly anyway. If I didn't like the food at the start, I definitely learnt to like it by the end and now reminisce about the worst of it. My job, as with American summer camps for kids, was to help lead a group of up to 30 children for their three-week stay at the camp. Because I did not speak the language, I was placed with two other leaders so my services weren't really necessary. However, this region of Russia doesn't exactly get many international visitors so the role I played at camp sometimes felt more like being rockstar! The types of activities the kids did ranged from football, basketball and swimming (the colour of the pool was scary) to singing, dancing and crafts. But while I tried as best I could to lead my group of kids in their daily activities, every single kid in the camp wants a piece of you because you're the foreigner! So a lot of the job is to just be there and share a different culture with the kids (and their parents sometimes), other Russian counsellors and the Camp Director. In return, they also shared their culture. I've actually stayed in contact with a number of the local counsellors. The ones that don't speak English very well make up for it with sign language and friendliness. I found that a few words in Russian go a long way to bridging the culture gap. And if possible take some souvenirs for the kids. Even a pack of cards with the British flag on them provides 52 little gifts.

The expansion of the oligarch classes has been accompanied by a rise in the number of jobs for English speakers to tutor and look after young children in kindergartens or as nannies. Agencies as well as individual families post adverts in newspapers and on websites such as www.expat.ru. Specialist agencies such as Gouverneur International (www.guvernior.ru) and Bonne International (www.bonne-int.com) take on native English speakers for a number of vacancies, mainly in and around Moscow. ESL-qualified native candidates are needed to tutor children aged four to 10. MsPoppins (www.mspoppins.com) also advertises for native English tutors for children aged from four to 12.

Volunteering

A Russian youth organisation called SFERA based in Nizhniy Novgorod organises short voluntary projects in the Russian Federation (http://dobrovolets.ru/eng) and can assist with getting a visa.

The list of projects is published every March. Since 1992 the Serendipity Russian–English Program (www.serendipity-russia.com) has been sending American graduates to work at the American Home in Vladimir, a city 200km east of Moscow. Not only do they teach English but also deliver lectures on American culture. Contracts last 10 months (renewable) starting in mid-August. The annual deadline for applications is 1 March. Participants are billeted with a Russian family, receive three hours a week of Russian lessons and are paid a stipend.

Regulations

A double-entry tourist visa for Russia costs £65 and you will have to provide proof of accommodation and other tricky documentation. For people participating in established international exchanges, the red tape is usually manageable. The Russian tourist office can assist for a fee (www.visitrussia.org.uk) as can specialist visa agencies such as Real Russia (www.realrussia. co.uk) and VFS Global (http://ru.vfsglobal.co.uk) both in London.

Russia is a place where the regulations change as often as the government ministries responsible. In the commercial sector, work permits are problematic, because few Russian companies are willing to embark on the time-consuming and expensive process. A sponsored visa is necessary to live and work legally in Russia.

The difficulty lies in finding a company or organisation that is registered with the authorities and has permission to invite foreigners to Russia for the express purpose of working for them. Many language schools would prefer to avoid this route as it means they have to pay both income and social welfare taxes on their foreign employees. Obviously, the easiest way for language schools to avoid these costly taxes is not to employ teachers legally. In order to crack down on this abuse, the authorities now stipulate that foreigners who enter the country on multiple entry business visas can remain in Russia for only three months during any six-month period. This has cut down on the number of foreigners working without proper authorisation, apart from those working for very short periods. Agencies such as Legal Stay (www.legalstay.ru) advertise in Russia their ability to provide working visas for teachers for a colossal fee (eg €1,450 a year). In order to qualify for a long-stay permit, teachers must provide apostilled (legally certified) copies of their passport, TESOL certificate and university degree certificate, and must undergo an HIV test.

BALTIC STATES

As traditionally the most Westernised part of the old Russian Empire, the Baltic countries of Lithuania, Latvia and Estonia were all admitted to the European Union in 2004. Despite new business and tourism links with cheap fares offered by budget airlines, the market for English language teachers is not large and few vacancies are advertised abroad.

Even voluntary opportunities are few and far between. Karen Rich decided in her 30s to get some TEFL training and do something completely different from her career as airline cabin crew. The country that took her fancy was Latvia, so she made contact with the agency Changing Worlds (which has since dropped Latvia from its list of destinations), and ended up enjoying herself enough to extend her three-month stay to a full year:

> *It's truly been a life changing year for me. I changed careers, I moved to the small town of Tukums where I'm the only English person and I've travelled to many new and exciting countries including Russia, Lithuania and Estonia. I hadn't expected to have so many students and classes. I had to call a halt at around 50 students and working weeks of 40 hours. I felt so proud that students who had been shy and reserved at the beginning of the year were relaxed and able to chat to me quite openly at the end. However, loneliness was a problem. All my colleagues in the school were Latvian and had their own families, so it was difficult to mix with the local people as the culture was different and it's not acceptable for a single woman to sit in a café and drink coffee. I noticed that the people didn't laugh much.*

UKRAINE

The vast republic of the Ukraine's EFL market is still undeveloped, although demand seems to be increasing since the EU and Ukraine signed a Deep & Comprehensive Free Trade Agreement (DCFTA) in 2016 which is opening markets in goods and services and should lead to modernisation and reform. English teachers are in higher demand than they have ever been, including in a reviving corporate sector. After having withdrawn all its volunteers in the wake of Russia's annexation of Crimea and the ensuing violence, the Peace Corps is in the process of implementing a TEFL Project in Ukraine, whereby volunteers will work in secondary schools and universities to enhance the English communication skills of students and teachers. A handful of language schools advertise vacancies on the main job sites like www.tefl.com.

GEORGIA

Six years ago the Georgian Ministry of Education took the dramatic decision to fund a native English-speaker teaching programme called Teach and Learn with Georgia (TLG). Semester start dates fall in August/September and January/February. The programme offers foreigners the chance to teach in state schools throughout the country, as part of a cultural exchange programme. Airfares, homestay accommodation, medical insurance and a round-trip ticket for one vacation are all covered by the programme plus a modest stipend of 750 lari per month. After taxes are withdrawn and the host families are reimbursed for food and utilities, only 400 lari (US$140) are left for spending. Full details can be found on the TLG website www.tlg.gov.ge. Reviews of the programme on sites like www.gooverseas.com are generally favourable.

CENTRAL EUROPE

Romania

English was barely taught before the downfall of Ceaucescu in 1989 and the collapse of communism. Demand for English has been intense ever since though there are still relatively few private language institutes, even now that Romania is in the European Union. The association of quality language services (QUEST Romania; www.quest.ro) based at the Prosper-ASE Language Centre in Bucharest does not seem at all active and is of little use to foreign teachers.

Wages are low, so that a salary of 3,500 lei (US$800) a month is considered a good salary by Romanian standards. Teachers would be advised to take as many teaching materials as possible, eg magazine articles, postcards, language games, photos and pictures. Information about the teacher's hometown always goes down well.

Many years ago, Minna Graber arrived in Romania to celebrate the New Year and became besotted with the country:

> We went straight into a Carpathian village at the top of a mountain complete with gypsy fiddlers and not an internal combustion engine for miles around. I fell for the place hook, line and sinker and haven't been able to kick the habit. I wanted to teach in the north-east of the country and so contacted the British Council in Iasi who in turn referred me to SOL [no longer recruiting volunteer teachers]. I met the director Grenville Yeo at a café and we talked for a long time about the challenges, rewards and requirements. In the end the job offer was with one of the best schools in Bucharest where the students all go on to university (and a significant minority are these days applying for British university places). The wages sound terrible: 1,100 lei a month after deductions for tax and National Insurance. The other teachers have to pay for accommodation out of this so in comparison I have a big advantage (the school's parents association provides and pays for my very simple small studio flat and for the running costs). I am very good at living frugally but find that I still have to take on a couple of private students to make ends meet. The rest of the staff work long hours giving these private lessons.

According to Minna, native speakers of English can command a high fee for giving private tuition. She charged the equivalent of $18 an hour in Bucharest. If you work in a private kindergarten, as she did at one point, you can charge even more. Despite her modest earnings, she is far from discontent with her lifestyle that includes concerts, martial arts classes, mountaineering and lots of travel in many tourist-free areas.

Apart from teaching, few opportunities present themselves to foreigners who don't speak Romanian. Even people who are married to Romanian nationals struggle to find employment. IT skills are in demand and IT companies in the capital are doing quite well. Otherwise jobs in call centres can be found with a low starting salary of 2,000 lei.

Bulgaria

Since Bulgaria joined the EU in 2007 it has attracted EU tourists in large numbers, whilst property speculators and foreign businesses have not been far behind. There is a substantial demand for English teachers, although opportunities in the private sector are still scarce. Almost all schools ask for at least a degree and teaching certificate.

A Bulgarian agency of long standing appoints 60–80 native speakers to teach in specialist English language secondary schools for one academic year for which the deadline is the end of May. Details are available from Teachers for Central and Eastern Europe (21 V 5 Rakovski Boulevard, Dimitrovgrad 6400; (☎ (+359) 391 24787; tfcee@usa.net; www.tfcee.8m.com). Students, preferably with a TEFL background, are accepted from the USA, UK, Canada and Australia to spend an academic year teaching. The weekly teaching load is 19 40-minute classes per four-day week. The monthly salary in Bulgarian levs is equivalent to $100. Benefits include furnished accommodation, 60 days of paid holiday, paid sick leave and work permit. A summer programme is also available at Black Sea resorts for which the application deadline is 20 June and the monthly wage equivalent to US$200. TfCEE charges an application fee of US$60.

Slovenia

As in Croatia, there are a good many private schools and many opportunities can be created by energetic native speakers both as freelance teachers for institutes or as private tutors. The hourly wage should start at €11. Berlitz has a sizeable operation in Slovenia with schools in Maribor, Novo Mesto, Kranj and Celje as well as Ljubljana (workinslovenia@berlitz.si). Another private language school that hires native speaker teachers is Nista Language School in Koper on the Adriatic (www.nista.si).

Albania

A decade ago Albania was a rather desperate and lawless place, but its economy has been growing and the country is more stable. Private schools have opened, though are staffed mainly by Albanian teachers. Wages are low while the cost of living is rising. The organisation LSIA (Language Schools in Albania) was founded to improve the knowledge of foreign languages, but it seems to be dormant, and it is not clear whether it can be of any assistance to aspiring teacher-volunteers despite its having a 'Careers' tab on its website (www.lsiaal.org).

VOLUNTARY OPPORTUNITIES

Service Projects

The main workcamp organisations in Britain (IVS, Concordia, UNA Exchange and VAP) and in the USA (SCI-USA and VFP) can provide up-to-date details of projects and camps in all the countries of the region. The site of Service Civil International (www.sci.ngo) links to the national partner organisations in 21 countries of Eastern Europe and the Balkans, such as www.cvs-bg.org for Bulgaria and www.alternative-v.com.ua/en in Ukraine.

The registration fee will be £160 minimum, but usually closer to £250 which of course does not cover travel to the destination. The national workcamp partners handle the travel and insurance arrangements once you arrive in their country and provide food and accommodation usually for an extra though reasonable fee. The language in which camps are conducted is usually English. Projects vary from an archaeological dig in Belarus to organising an activity programme for elderly clients in Slovakia. Applications for workcamps should be sent through the partner organisation in the applicant's own country (see introductory chapter on Volunteering). If you are particularly interested in one country it is worth checking the websites of the main voluntary organisations at regular intervals.

Environmental Volunteering

A number of non-profit organisations are involved in protecting the ecology of Lake Baikal in Siberia. One of the best known is the Great Baikal Trail (GBT), whose main aim is to protect the unique environment of Lake Baikal by creating a network of environmentally friendly trails and by developing eco-tourism. The GBT conducts summer camp projects in national parks and reserves where volunteers have a chance to spend two weeks on the shores of the lake in pristine Siberian taiga (www.greatbaikaltrail.org). Volunteers pay a contribution of 25,000–28,500 roubles (approximately $450 or £375).

Organisations in the countries of the region organise workcamps independently, such as HUJ in Armenia with an office in the capital Yerevan (www.huj.am). It accepts 150 foreign volunteers to do ecological and renovation work, take care of sick and disabled children, and so on.

WWOOF now operates in the majority of Eastern European countries, sometimes with just a handful of host farms, including the Czech Republic, Hungary, Bulgaria, Romania, Poland, Lithuania, Estonia, Moldova, Macedonia and Serbia. A sprinkling of organic properties in other countries such as Slovenia, Croatia, Latvia and even Kyrgyzstan and Georgia may be found among the WWOOF Independents (www.wwoofindependents.org), ie without a national association of their own. Lindsay Whitlock and her family paused in their round-the-world adventure to spend some time on a WWOOF farm in Hungary, which turned out to be one of the highlights of their year-long travels. The family arranged to stay on a goat farm in a remote area about 25km from Kaposvár where they picked fruit and helped in the kitchen and where 10-year-old Tom helped look after the herd of goats, meanwhile all staying in an idyllic old farmhouse.

Volunteers who are willing to pay €880–€940 for 12 days spent assisting researchers to monitor dolphin behaviour and habitats along the coast of Croatia should contact the Blue World Institute which operates the Adriatic Dolphin Project (www.blue-world.org). Students with a background in biology or geography may be accepted as interns.

CCUSA (mentioned earlier in this chapter) runs a summer camp in Croatia (www.campcalifornia.com), where English-speaking counsellors are needed from early June till the end of August; details and an application form can be found at www.ccusa.co.uk or www.ccusa.com. The programme fee is £245.

The Laboratory of Geoarchaeology, a department of the Kazakh National University, recruits international volunteers and students for archaeological fieldwork. The work consists of documenting petroglyph sites and ancient habitats by river valleys, with training in mapping, geomorphology, palaeoenvironmental study, etc. Details are available from the Department of Geoarchaeology in Almaty, Kazakhstan (ispkz@yahoo.com; www.lgakz.org/VolunteerCamps/Volunteer.html). The three camps last 15 days between June and October and cost $300 per week.

Social Projects

Ecologia Youth Trust (☎ (+44) 1309 690995; www.ecologia.org.uk) is a small, Scottish charity with close links to a community of foster families in Russia that is dedicated to giving orphans and abandoned children a new start in life. For over 20 years, Ecologia has been recruiting volunteers, particularly Russian language students, to spend two or, preferably, three months working and living in the community, which is based in the countryside south of Moscow. Extensive preparatory information is provided, along with 24-hour support from a resident volunteer coordinator. The joining fee is £1,055 for one month to £1,470 for three months, and includes food, accommodation, visa support and an airport transfer, but not airfares to Moscow. Knowledge of Russian or TEFL is preferred.

OTHER OPPORTUNITIES

Many people based in the cities of Eastern Europe over the past two decades have taken advantage of the rampant entrepreneurial spirit by engaging in conventional employment. Companies and agencies occasionally advertise on expat sites and other places for computer programmers, administrators, etc. The major capitals have recruitment agencies that specialise in placing foreigners with specific skills (eg Dorset Recruitment in Prague). However there are now so many well qualified locals who speak excellent English as well as their native tongue, it is not easy for a monolingual foreigner to find a job.

The Westernising democracies of Eastern Europe are all targeting tourism as a means of aiding their economies and are encouraging foreign tour operators to develop resorts, etc with large staff requirements. Ski tour operators such as Balkan Holidays (London W1; jobs@balkanholidays.co.uk) recruit children's reps and entertainers outside the countries, but mostly try to hire locals.

Young people in east European capitals are so eager to embrace Western culture that American-style restaurants and Irish pubs are plentiful, and some hire English speakers as chefs, waiting staff, etc. Such jobs will be heard about by word of mouth or possibly advertised in the English-language press such as expats.cz or www.job-poland.com. If you are looking for casual work, ask discreetly in hostels, around the universities or among expatriates teaching English. Your services as anything from a DJ to a freelance marketing consultant may be in demand.

PART 3

WORK YOUR WAY WORLDWIDE

Australia

In some ways this chapter is superfluous. Australia has developed a magnificent industry to cater specifically for backpackers and working holidaymakers. Most hostels both in the cities and the countryside are well informed about local jobs available to travellers; some act as informal employment agencies. Bus companies have routes that shuttle between fruit-picking regions for the benefit of working travellers. Outback properties offer training in the skills necessary to work on a station and then double as a placement agency. Recruitment agencies and employers with seasonal requirements target the backpacking community by advertising in the places they frequent. Free newspapers, magazines and websites specifically address an audience of backpackers, carrying employment advertisements. Employers even cooperate with regional tourist offices to find seasonal staff, as in the south-eastern fruit-growing region of the Riverina. So there is no shortage of information and assistance available for the newly arrived working holidaymaker.

After years of expansion, the working holiday programme has been shrinking over the past couple of years. In 2016, a total of about 214,500 working holiday visas were granted, compared to 265,000 three years before. The demand for working holidaymakers among employers is as great as ever. In fact the Australian government is considering ways to attract more applicants. It reduced the visa fee in 2017, and is considering raising the maximum age from 30 to 35. It was announced in late 2016 that the government would spend $10 million on a campaign to market jobs to backpackers.

As of January 2017 the unemployment rate stands at a healthy 5.7%, which has been unchanged over the past three or four years, with continuing economic growth forecast. However, optimism needs to be tempered with realism. The Australian dollar has lost value, especially against the US dollar. Picking up casual work to cover all your travelling expenses is not as straightforward in the Australia of today as it was a dozen years ago. In the areas that backpackers have colonised, such as certain suburbs of Sydney and some Queensland Island and beach resorts, travellers on working holiday visas are unpopular since they have a reputation for 'Ibiza'-type behaviour.

The working holiday visa is for people intending to use any money they earn in Australia to supplement their holiday funds. The rules encourage working holidaymakers to move away from the cities and to country areas to work. If you can prove that you have done paid work for at least 88 days working in regional Australia, for example fruit picking, pearling or sheep-shearing (but not nannying or waitressing at a roadhouse), you can apply to extend your one-year working holiday visa for a further 12 months or apply outside the country for a future second year of combining holiday and work.

The working holiday scheme works because the majority of unemployed Australians do not want to pick fruit, collect for charity, do telesales, work on a sheep station or do any of the other kinds of work visitors to Australia do. This is the conclusion to which Armin Birrer, contributor to *Work Your Way Around the World*, came when he worked as recruiting officer at a vineyard in northern Victoria:

> *Local unemployment was high at that time, and yet I had severe problems getting pickers. Most of the unemployed didn't want to pick grapes because it is too hard for them. Plus lots of them don't think it's worthwhile to go off the dole for three to four weeks and then wait to go back on again. I came to the conclusion in Mildura that I can always find some work even if unemployment rises to 20%, if I go to where the work is. People who can work hard and don't make trouble are always in demand.*

Provided you arrive with the right visa, positive references (most Australian employers are sticklers for references and will check them) and some decent clothes, you should find a way to earn a crust. Or even more than a crust. The national minimum wage is more than £10 per hour (A$17.70) and casual workers get paid a premium in many kinds of employment. (Note that dollar rates quoted throughout this chapter are in Australian dollars.)

Roger Blake who spent two separate spells as a working holidaymaker in Australia is someone who is willing to turn his hand to anything and has successfully 'blagged' (talked) his way into all manner of jobs around the world. Yet he found Australia an uphill struggle, certainly compared to New Zealand.

Although he managed to survive on his occasional earnings (having arrived with next to nothing), he warns to expect a 'rough ride': *I have met SO many travellers who are leaving Australia after just three months or less of their WHV, thoroughly disgusted with the attitude of employers towards backpackers and the associated struggles of finding an (often lousy) job in the first place … But it is not all doom and gloom and I've had fun between troublesome times.'*

On a more positive note, there are still plenty of easy-come, easy-go jobs. For example of the three newly graduated friends Seb, Alan and Ali, who arrived in Melbourne with their shiny new working holiday visas, one quickly found work in a smart city restaurant, another in a call centre (a job redeemed by the good wages and camaraderie among the staff, many of them Britons on the same visa), and the third found part-time work at a garden centre helped by his diploma in horticulture. These jobs funded a brilliant lifestyle in Melbourne but none found it very easy to save for travelling further or even for surf weekends at the nearby resorts along the Great Ocean Road.

The kinds of job you are likely to get in the rural areas are of a very different nature from city jobs. To discover Australia's more exotic features, you will have to penetrate into the countryside. While some experienced travellers declare that the big cities are the only places you can work on a steady basis at reasonably good wages, others advise heading out of Sydney as soon as you've seen the harbour. Chris Miksovsky from Connecticut found office work in both Sydney and Melbourne with ease. However, after a few months he realised that the reason he had left home was to get away from spending his days in an office, so he headed north to look for station work. Work in the country or the outback often comes with accommodation whereas city rents can eat into your wages, as can the social life.

WORKING HOLIDAY VISAS

Australia has reciprocal working holiday arrangements with a large number of countries divided into two groups. The one-year Working Holiday Visa (sub-class 417) can be obtained by nationals aged 18–30 without children from the UK, Ireland, Canada, Netherlands, Germany, France, Japan, Korea, SAR of Hong Kong, Taiwan, Sweden, Denmark, Finland, Norway, Cyprus, Malta, Belgium, Italy and Estonia. A similar but slightly more restricted Work and Holiday Visa (sub-class 462) is available to nationals of a second group of 16 countries that includes the USA, China, Turkey and Chile. Working full-time for more than six months for the same employer is not permitted, though you are allowed to engage in up to four months of studies/training. During the 12-month period of validity of the Working Holiday visa, you can leave and re-enter Australia but this does not alter the maximum duration of the visa. Most people apply for a Working Holiday Maker (WHM) visa online, though you can also submit a paper application to any Australian representative outside Australia (for an extra $80). When you apply online for an e-WHM visa there is no need to provide proof of funds nor do you send in your passport. Applying online via the Australian Department of Immigration website www.border.gov.au is normally straightforward and hassle-free and should result in an emailed confirmation inside the promised 48 hours, which is sufficient to get you into the country. Your passport isn't physically inspected but your eligibility to work is registered online, which prospective employers can check. The fee for the WH visa was reduced to $390 from $440 in 2017.

If for some reason you want to apply through a specialist visa service (for which you will have to pay a premium of course), try Visa First (www.visafirst.com) or the Visa Bureau in London and Edinburgh (www.visabureau.com). Even if you do not use these services, their websites may answer some of your questions.

A top tip when filling out the application form is to answer the question: 'What type of employment do you intend to seek in Australia?' with the reply 'fruit harvest/seasonal work'. This is primarily what the government wants WHMs to do while in Australia and therefore they are more likely to approve a visa application on this basis. Once you have the visa you are free to seek any job and do any kind of work (within the terms of the visa).

The second step is to save as much money as you can. On arrival you may be asked to submit a bank statement proving that you have sufficient back-up funds of $5,000. Anyone intending to work in health care or a childcare centre must undergo medical tests by an approved doctor.

If you overstay your visa and they notice on the way out, you will be automatically barred from returning to Australia for a minimum of three years. People found working without the necessary visa will be placed on the Movement Alert List (whose acronym means 'bad' in French) which may count against them in future visa applications.

The rules for applying for a second WHV are clearly set out on the immigration website (google 'form 1263'). The postcodes are all listed that qualify as 'rural Australia' as well as the kinds of eligible work, ie plant and animal cultivation, forestry, construction and a few others. If you work as a nanny for a farmer, for instance, this does not qualify. Rumours circulate that you can find a tame farmer to sign the Employment Verification Form for a negotiated fee, without doing the requisite 88 days of qualifying work. However, it has become routine for the authorities to verify the information; fraudulent claimants will be summarily deported and can face huge fines and even prison. Note that exchanging your labour for board and lodging does not qualify for a second WHV; you must be able to show pay slips.

Alternative Visas

Those not eligible for a working holiday visa may want to investigate the range of alternative options. People with a skill in short supply, anything from carpentry to dental hygiene, architecture to IT, may be eligible for the Temporary Business Visa (457) which requires sponsorship from an Australian employer. Special allowance is made for those willing to work in regional Australia. It is even possible to be sponsored by an employment agency such as Geoffrey Nathan (www.geoffreynathan.com). In that case you must already be in Australia on a valid visa, be looking for work in an area of skills shortage, have a degree and/or five years' relevant experience in your profession, and be available to work for at least three months and up to four years. A separate range of Business Visas is available to senior managers and investors with significant assets. All of these visa programmes are described on the Department of Immigration site (www.border.gov.au) and further helpful information can be found on the websites of specialist immigration law firms such as Parish Patience in Sydney (www.parish patience.com.au) that specialise in assisting clients with visa applications.

Obtaining a resident's visa (for permanent migration) is, predictably, much more difficult, though not impossible if you have a skill in short supply (such as nursing or teaching and are prepared to work in a rural area) and/or a close relative in Australia.

Pre-departure Schemes

A number of competing travel and youth exchange agencies can assist those who want some back-up on a working holiday. They offer various packages that may be of special interest to first-time travellers. Some are all-inclusive especially the gap year placement organisations; others simply give back-up on arrival. Given how relatively straightforward it is to orient yourself and find work, you should weigh up the pros and cons carefully and check online and Facebook reviews before paying a substantial fee. Typically, the fee will include airport pick-up, hostel accommodation for the first few nights and a post-arrival orientation which advises on how to obtain a tax-file card, suggestions of employers and so on. Some even claim to guarantee a job, though it is unlikely to be the kind of job you will want. Various perks may be thrown in like a telephone calling card and free maps.

BUNAC: London W8; ☎ (+44) 033 3999 7516 www.bunac.org/uk/workaustralia. Offers several Work Australia packages costing £155, £359 and up to £899, the latter for a five-day skills course on a ranch.

Get Australia: London SW7; www.getaustralia.com. Arrivals packages arranged by same organisation as runs Camp America. £410–£1,179.

OzIntro: Plymouth, Devon; ☎ (+44) 203 397 9790; www.ozintro.com. With office at 22 Market St, Sydney 2000; sells a package for £499 which includes your first week in Sydney.

VisitOz: Goomeri, Queensland; ☎ (+61) 7 4168 6106; www.australianworkingadventures.com. Year-round programme to introduce WHV holders to farm working techniques over a 5-day course, preceding the guarantee of a job; package fee is $2,399.

Companies also exist to place graduates and others in unpaid internships in professional fields such as marketing, design and hospitality. For example Australian Internships (www.internships.com.au) with offices in Brisbane and Sydney places candidates in suitable work places for up to a year.

Backpacker Agencies

Any travel agency that specialises in the backpacker market will almost certainly promote their ability to assist clients on working holidays, since such a high proportion of that market wants to work. There is a maze of alliances between travel and recruitment agencies, hostel groups and working holiday providers though most of them seem to be offering similar services. Try to shop around if you have the stamina.

Australian Backpackers, Woolloomooloo, Sydney; www.australianbackpackers.net. Kick-start services for working holidays from $69.

Go Work About: Perth; www.goworkabout. com. Assistance to working holidaymakers in Western Australia. Sample package costs $770.

Job Search Australia & New Zealand, offices in Sydney, Brisbane, Melbourne, Cairns and Darwin; www.workingholiday.co. Packages focus solely on job alerts and services relevant to working. $50 for one month, $175 for 12 months.

The Job Shop: Northbridge, Perth; www.thejobshop.com.au. Offices also in Kununurra and Katherine, NT. Licensed employment agency in Perth's backpacker district of Northbridge that tries to find jobs for backpackers free of charge.

The Work & Travel Company: Goulburn St, Sydney; also Bourke Street, Melbourne; www. worktravelcompany.com. In-house recruiters match backpackers with jobs in hospitality, retail, call centres, etc. Package costs $569.

Ultimate Oz: 2 Lee Street, Sydney, NSW 2000; www.ultimate.travel/ultimateoz-sydney package for $849 that includes seven days of accommodation and activities in Sydney, plus airport transfer, access to Job Search service, bar skills course, etc.

Workstay Australia: Perth; www.workstay.com.au. Online source of info on getting jobs in country pubs, offices, mines (for professionals and trade), fruit picking and packing, etc.

Backpacker agencies tend to outsource their recruitment service to specialist agencies such as Travellers at Work in Sydney (☎ (+61) 2 9281 2700; www.taw.com.au).

Unofficial Work

Concern about illegal immigration means that measures to root out visa-less workers have become more punitive. Tax file numbers and bank accounts are compulsory (see below) and immigration raids are not uncommon especially in the horticulture industry. Employers who at one time did not check working holiday visas are more likely to do so these days to avoid paying huge fines of more than $20,000 if caught.

Jane Harris thinks it should be stressed that anyone working without a visa alongside others in a similar position should be very careful, and suspicious of anyone nosing around. She describes what happened at the campsite she was staying on in Stanthorpe, Queensland:

> *I got back to our campsite to discover that immigration had raided farms throughout the area. Apparently, a local man had been running an illegal bus service to all the local farms from the three campsites in town. Someone from immigration started checking the visas of everyone on the bus, and found seven people with tourist visas. They were told to leave the country within two weeks. That evening, four car-loads of immigration officials turned up at the campsite. They had lists of local farm employees and were matching these with people's passports. They do not have to see you physically working but can act on circumstantial evidence.*

According to recent press reports, the authorities are more likely to raid farms and properties that employ illegal workers from Asia recruited by exploitative labour contractors.

Tax

All people in employment in Australia must either provide their employer with a nine-digit tax file number (TFN) or be taxed at a punitive emergency rate. Therefore it is greatly to your advantage to obtain one. We have heard in the past of people being deported for inventing tax file numbers (but giving their real names).

Foreigners must apply at a tax office, for example in downtown Sydney, where queues are long (national telephone number ☎ (+61) 132861; www.ato.gov.au). Processing normally takes between four and six weeks. You must submit a passport with appropriate visa plus one of a number of documents such as an original or certified copy of your birth certificate, Australian driving licence, bank statement at an Australian address, etc.

The ultimate tax liability for non-residents of Australia is 32.5% of all earnings whereas residents are taxed at 19% above the tax-free threshold of $18,200. In 2016 the government was proposing to tax working backpackers at the non-resident rate with no personal allowance. However employers, especially in the farming sector, and other interested parties mounted a vigorous campaign to prevent this and were successful. Working holidaymakers are now liable for the resident rate of 19% tax on all earnings. If you are lucky enough to have obtained a Resident's Visa on the basis of your education and skills, you can legitimately claim the tax status of a resident and pay no tax until you have earned more than $18,200. In this case, you should obtain a Group Certificate (statement of earnings and tax deducted, equivalent to a P45) after you leave each job, arranging to have it posted on to you if necessary. The tax year runs from 1 July and all earners are supposed to submit a tax return by 31 October.

Note that many employers will pay wages only into a bank account. Anyone who can show that they will be resident in a certain place for more than three months is eligible for a Medicare card which allows you refunds on doctors' fees and prescriptions.

THE JOB-HUNT

Although everybody finds some kind of job in the end, it isn't always easy. You are likely to encounter a surprising degree of competition from others on working holidays, many of whom are chasing the same kinds of job. For example, a company that operates tours of Sydney Harbour received 50 replies to an advertisement for waiting staff and a receptionist, 42 of which were from Poms. The glut of travelling workers is especially bad in Sydney, Perth and in Queensland resorts before and after Christmas. In addition to asking potential employers directly (which is the method used by at least a third of successful jobseekers in Australia), the main ways of finding work are online recruitment sites such as www.backpackerjobboard.com.au, www.jobs4travellers.com.au, www.jobaroo.com and www. bestjobsau.com, plus online job adverts on sites such as Gumtree and Craigslist, and noticeboards especially at backpackers (ie hostels).

Anyone intending to work in Australia should have an up-to-date and properly thought-out CV. With few exceptions (such as fruit picking) prospective employers will ask to see your CV before they'll so much as entertain your application and often they'll ask for references from an Australian too. A further frustration is the rampant bureaucracy and government insistence on paper qualifications which means that employees must have specific certificates to work in certain industries, for example the RSA (Responsible Service of Alcohol) and RCG/RSG (Responsible Conduct/Service of Gambling) for jobs in hospitality and the Occupational Health and Safety (OHS) green or white (formerly blue) card for the building and construction industry. Most hospitality training courses last a half or a full day and cost $100–$150 from course providers such as TCP Training in Sydney (www.tcptraining.com). Check that a certificate issued in one state will be recognised in another.

The door-to-door job-hunt will require reserves of stamina and patience, as Roger Blake discovered:

Another frustrating aspect of the job-hunt downunder is the oh-so-frequent scenario where I have walked into a bar, restaurant or wherever (CV in hand) to express an interest in the job seen advertised in their window. The response has varied from: 'Sorry, the job has been taken, we just haven't taken the sign down' (yet two weeks later the sign is still up in their window), to 'Sorry, we're looking for a female', to 'We want a local, sorry, mate'. Obviously they're not allowed to put that on their advertisements.

Private Employment Agencies

As in Britain, private employment agencies are very widespread and are a good potential source of jobs for travellers with hospitality experience or office skills, computer, data processing or financial experience. In addition to the specialist backpacker agencies mentioned earlier, a surprising number of mainstream temp agencies positively encourage English speakers on working holidays. Competition will be most acute at those agencies that court the backpacking market so some people purposely avoid those.

Big international agencies such as Drake and Adecco have branches in every state, though sometimes it is better to target your search on smaller agencies that have a range of temp jobs. You should make an appointment to register and allow up to an hour for each one to have your skills assessed and your references checked. George Street in Sydney has dozens of agencies including the long established Bligh Appointments (Level 7, Dymocks Building, 428 George St, Sydney NSW 2000; ☎ (+61) 2 9235 3699; www.blighappointments.com) who welcome working holidaymakers.

In Melbourne head for Collins Street downtown where there is a concentration of agencies including specialist and general ones that deal with the usual range of urban jobs for travellers: data entry clerks for people who can type, call centre workers, furniture removers, market research interviewers, general labourers, and so on. Periodic shortages of temporary office support staff crop up, so if you've got decent skills, you've got a good chance of being hired promptly. Some agencies specialise in certain kinds of work for example work on stations and farms, in tourist resorts or as nannies and au pairs (see relevant sections). Troys Hospitality Staff (☎ (+61) 2 9290 2955; www.troys. com.au) have been recommended for placing casual catering staff in Sydney including for functions and events paying $20–$30 an hour, while Pinnacle Hospitality & Travel People recruitment agency have offices in Melbourne and all the state capitals (www.pinnaclepeople.com.au).

Hostels and Noticeboards

Youth hostels and backpackers' lodges everywhere are a goldmine of information for people working their way around the world. And nowhere are they better than in Australia. The average cost of a dorm bed in a backpackers is $23–$30, with beds costing more than $40 in central Sydney. Often a double room costs only a little more per head, but these are often booked up ahead. A growing number of hostel managers, especially in the major fruit and vegetable growing areas of Queensland, run their own informal job-finding service and try to put backpackers in touch with local employers.

You may find employment in the hostels themselves of course. Stephen Psallidas describes the proliferation of work, especially on the 'route' between Sydney and Cairns:

> *I've met loads of people working in backpackers' hostels. Typically you work two hours a day in exchange for your bed and a meal. Work may be cleaning, driving the minibus, reception, etc and is always on an informal basis so there are no worries about visas, etc. I will be jumping on the bandwagon myself soon. I'll be completely shattered from picking tomatoes so I'm going to 'work' in a hostel in Mission Beach, where the owners invited me to work when I stayed there earlier. I'm to rest up in a beautiful place before continuing my travels, and not spend any of my hard-earned dollars.*

In addition to the network of YHA hostels (www.yha.com.au), several successful groups of private backpackers' hostels operate including VIP Backpackers Resorts of Australia, which is especially strong in New South Wales and Queensland (www.vipbackpackers.com). A booklet listing its Australian hostels is distributed far and wide or can be obtained from overseas by purchasing the VIP card for

$47, which gives discounts and benefits and includes postage. Many VIP hostels have noticeboards advertising jobs, flats, car shares, etc.

The Nomads Backpacker chain has 18 hostels in Australia, many of them renovated pubs. Nomads (www.nomadsworld.com) sell a discount card called MAD membership for $19.

The disadvantage of using hostels as your main source of jobs is that they are full of your main competition for available work. Andrew Owen was discouraged to find that every backpackers' hostel seemed to be populated almost entirely with Brits on working holidays. Also be a little suspicious of claims such as 'Plenty of farm work available for guests' since this may just be a marketing ploy on the part of the hostel (see section on Queensland).

Most Sydney hostels are well clued up on the local job scene, especially in the main backpackers' areas such as King's Cross, Glebe and Coogee (pronounced Cood-jee).

ROGER BLAKE COULD NOT AFFORD TO BE TEMPTED BY THE SOCIAL LIFE OF SYDNEY AND GOT STRAIGHT DOWN TO FINDING A JOB:

Having enjoyed the East Coast to the full, I arrived in Sydney at make or break point with $70 to my name, leaving me with no choice but to sort myself out and quickly. I found a reasonable and certainly afford-able place to stay in King's Cross on day one. I found a job on day two, once again through scouring the backpacker noticeboards and making a hundred and one phone calls. A desperate backpacker is willing to turn his or her hand to anything for a dollar (no choice but). I spent six hours a day, seven days a week pounding the city streets in a sandwich board handing out flyers promoting of all things, tapestry, knitting and needlecraft. This went on for about three weeks and I was one of the few who stuck it out from start to finish. I only made it through this mind-numbing, leg-cramping job because of the comedy moments and observations of life on Sydney's streets. A couple of times I saw buskers being casually thrown a $50 note and on several occasions beggars being given $10–$20 as if they were 20 cent coins. The owners took us out for a nice meal and all the drinks paid for at the end of the sale. I did quite well out of it actually and didn't mind being paid to parade the city streets looking like a fool ... all too easy and good fun. I did two brilliant tours of the outback paid for by my antics in Sydney.

The Cronulla Beach YHA (www.cronullabeachyha.com/backpacker-jobs.html) actively assists back-packers to find local jobs as waiting staff, labourers, nannies, etc. By asking around you will quickly learn which hostels are regularly contacted for casual workers and day labour, usually bright and early in the morning. Apparently it helps if you are built like a barn, especially if they are looking for someone to move grand pianos. It is also worth sticking close to reception in the evenings when employers ring with their requirements for the next day. When working like this, insist on being paid daily.

When I was researching a former edition of *Work Your Way*, I visited Glebe Village Backpackers in Sydney in the winter. While chatting to the Canadian backpacker manning the desk about job oppor-tunities in Sydney, the hostel phone rang. As if on cue, the phone call was from an employer in North Sydney looking for a casual employee to start work the following day and my obliging informant invited me to watch her informal job agency in action. I followed her into the courtyard of the backpackers' hostel where the first person we bumped into eagerly jotted down the phone number of the employer and within five minutes had fixed up a job doing manual work for a decent hourly wage of $23.

In fruit-picking areas, certain hostels and campsites are populated almost exclusively by workers; see the relevant sections below.

Online Resources

Many of the sites listed above in the section on Backpacker Agencies will provide an excellent starting point. Searching the web for employment leads is especially productive in Australia. Dozens of routes exist for finding out about job vacancies. The government's http://jobsearch.gov.au is a superb resource listing up-to-date vacancies throughout the country in an easily searchable format with contact details, normally to a local employment agency.

Jobaroo.com mentioned above is a well-maintained work site for backpackers with pages on outback and harvest jobs. Plenty of other search engines cater for more corporate jobseekers, such as www.seek.com.au, www.adzuna.com.au and www.careerjet.com.au.

RURAL AUSTRALIA AND THE OUTBACK

Most of Australia's area is sparsely populated, scorched land that is known loosely as the outback. Beyond the rich farming and grazing land surrounding the largest cities, there are immense properties supporting thousands of animals and acres of crops. Many of these stations (farms) are so remote that flying is the only practical means of access. Sandra Gray describes the drawbacks of spending time on a station:

> *Be warned! Station life can be severely boring after a while. I managed to land myself on one in the Northern Territory with very little else to do but watch the grass grow. If you have to save a lot of money quickly station work is the way to do it since there's nothing to spend it on. But make sure the place is within reasonable distance of a town or at least a roadhouse, so you have somewhere to go to let off steam occasionally.*

Your chances of getting a job as a station assistant (a jackaroo or jillaroo) will be improved if you have had experience with sheep, riding or any farming or mechanical experience. Several farmers are in the business of giving you that experience before helping you to find outback work, such as the one mentioned above in the VisitOz Scheme. Shaun Armstrong thoroughly enjoyed a similar four-day jackaroo/jillaroo course in Queensland:

> *I braved the jackaroo course with three other travellers (all Dutch). Horse riding, cattle mustering, ute driving, trail biking (the 'ings' were numerous) and other tasks occupied our days: wonderful hospitality ended each evening. Memorable days. Station placement was arranged afterward as was transport if needed. I was sorry to leave really. I'd say the course did prepare me for most experiences encountered in the job. For example I was able to muster cattle on horseback with four experienced riders having spent only 15 hours in the saddle. It wasn't easy, but I did it.*

Such an outback training course is available from the Leconfield Jackaroo and Jillaroo School (Kootingal, NSW 2352; ☎ (+61) 2 6769 4230; www.leconfieldjackaroo.com) which runs an 11-day outback training course costing $900. On completion successful participants will be guided in the direction of paying jobs.

Another cowgirl/cowboy course is offered by Jackaroo Jillaroo Downunder (www.jackaroojillaroo downunder.com) in Bingara in northern New South Wales. The five-day course costs $670, though stays of two and four weeks are also on offer. One recent participant was 30-something Jenny from Hertfordshire, who wanted a change from the stress of working as an intensive care nurse in a London hospital. She could never have foreseen that she would choose to extend her stay by working on the Garrawilla property, fall for a sheep shearer and start a family while living among camels and carriage horses.

Shearing is out of the question for the uninitiated. Although the post of 'roustabout' (the job of fetching, carrying, sweeping and trimming stained bits from the fleeces) is open to the inexperienced, jobs are generally scarcer on sheep stations than they once were because of the decline in the wool industry. Try the backpacker job agencies in Perth or check adverts in agricultural journals such as *Queensland Country Life* (www.queenslandcountrylife.com.au/classifieds).

Chris Miksovsky was not impressed with the assistance he received from two outback placement services in Alice Springs so resorted to cold-calling stations after looking them up in the phone book for northern Western Australia, the magical land where Baz Luhrmann's film *Australia* is set. After making more than 40 calls (and spending as many dollars on phone cards) he found a cattle station willing (or desperate enough) to take him on. He advises against exaggerating your experience: if you say you can ride a horse, the station manager will probably put you on 'Satan the Psycho-mare' your first day.

CHRIS MIKSOVSKY DESCRIBES STATION LIFE AS HE EXPERIENCED IT:

The days were long (breakfast sometimes at 3am), never-ending (I worked 32 days straight once), often painful and sometimes gruesome. But then again, where else can you gallop across the outback chasing for (or being chased by) a Brahman bull and sleep out under the stars listening to other jackaroos spinning yarns around a campfire, all while getting paid? Three months on the station earned me about $3,000 net. It was the best thing I've done since I started travelling.

Have a look at the 'Work and Travel' pages at www.outback-australia-travel-secrets.com, a site maintained by an ex-backpacker turned web entrepreneur based in the Kimberley region of Western Australia. Follow the links to agencies for finding work on cattle stations, fruit picking, etc.

Some city-based employment agencies deal with jobs in country and outback areas, primarily farming, station, hotel/motel and roadhouse work. In Western Australia try the Rural Enterprises Employment Agency in a suburb of Perth (☎ (+61) 8 9477 6600; www.ruralenterprises.com.au). Experienced farmworkers and tractor drivers are paid at least $25 an hour for 10–12 hour days, seven days a week at seeding time (April to June) and harvest time (October to December). Housekeeping, nannying and cooking positions are available for two or three months at a time throughout the year. While travelling back from Ayers Rock, chef Sara Runnalls popped into an employment office in the Northern Territory town of Katherine to ask about local jobs. That day she was driven 80km to a property at Scott Creek:

Here I found 15 hungry workers and a disgustingly dirty, dusty, insect haven for a kitchen. I had few fresh ingredients, ample beef, plenty of salt and tomato ketchup. My mission was to feed them five times a day with a variety of beef dishes and homemade cakes. I came up with some typically English cuisine and no complaints. I saw plenty of wildlife and enjoyed my two weeks on the cattle station. They asked me to stay the whole season but I'm here to travel.

Anyone with experience of the horse industry might be interested in a scheme administered by International Rural Exchange (IRE) in rural Western Australia (☎ (+61) 8 9064 7411; www.ire.org.au). They place trainees from many countries on Temporary Activity Visas (408). An Adelaide-based firm, Bibber International, oversees exchanges primarily for the wine industry (☎ (+61) 8 8374 0077; www.bibber.com.au) though they have extended the range of placements – who could resist the invitation to 'Work in a Piggery'? They encourage applicants abroad to make a one- to three-minute YouTube video of themselves to be submitted to potential employers. The agency charges start at $2,670. Anyone with a background in horse racing can investigate the activities of the specialist international agency Ryen Racing Solutions (www.ryenracingsolutions.com) or check the job ads on www.racingjobs.com.au.

Although you may not be forced to eat witchetty grubs for tea, there are some obvious disadvantages to life in the outback: the isolation, the heat and to some extent the dangers. A blogger reported that she and her boyfriend did a runner in the night to get away from the Northern Territory cattle station where they were working, in order to get away from the 'knives being pointed at people, skinning a cow and casual racism'.

Even if you have had experience of living in the rural areas of Europe, it may be hard to adjust to life in the outback. Lots of towns have nothing more than a post office and small shop combined, a hotel (pub) and petrol pump. The sun's heat must not be underestimated. It is important to cover your head with a cowboy hat or a towel and to carry a large water bottle with you. Droughts are common and, in drought-afflicted regions, be prepared to cope with severe water restrictions.

Finally there is the ever-present hazard of spiders and snakes, which Tricia Clancy describes: *'The hay barn attracted mice and the mice attracted snakes, so whenever we entered the barn we had to make a loud rumpus to frighten them away. Huntsmen spiders proliferated. These great tarantula-like creatures were not poisonous; however, it was still frightening when they emerged from behind the picture frames in the evenings.'* Once you get into the habit of checking inside your boots and behind logs for snakes, and under the loo seat for redback spiders, the dangers are minimised. The outback is often a rough male-dominated world, and not suited to fragile characters.

Conservation Volunteers

Several organisations give visitors a chance to experience the Australian countryside or bush. The main not-for-profit conservation organisation in Australia is called, predictably enough, Conservation Volunteers Australia (www.conservationvolunteers.com.au). They cooperate with agents in many countries to place volunteers from overseas in their projects. Partner agencies in the UK include Gap360, BUNAC and WorkingAbroad.com which offer varying packages. It is also possible to book a conservation project directly with one of the CVA offices linked from the main website, especially if you are already in Australia. Sample projects include weed removal, tree planting, seed collection from indigenous plants, building and maintaining bush walking tracks. Volunteering for just a day is free of charge, since no food or accommodation is provided. Eco-volunteering holiday escapes are listed at www.naturewise.com.au.

DANIELE ARENA FROM ITALY STUMBLED ACROSS AN INDEPENDENT PROJECT ON THE COAST OF QUEENSLAND THAT APPEALED TO HIM:

One of the most amazing experiences I had in Oz was the time I was volunteering at the Turtle Rookery in Mon Repos Beach. We could pitch our tent for free, and gave a small daily contribution for food. The work was to patrol the beach waiting for nesting turtles and, when they come in, to tag and measure them and the nest. This goes on between November and March. I was fortunate enough to get this by chance but normally there are quite a few people who want to do it, so you should probably contact the Queensland Parks and Wildlife Service for info.

The Willing Workers on Organic Farms (WWOOF) organisation is very active in Australia and has a huge supply of unpaid work opportunities on organic farms, etc. WWOOF Australia headquarters are near Buchan in Victoria (☎ (+61) 03 5155 0218; www.wwoof.com.au) though their publicity is widely distributed through backpacker haunts. The Australian WWOOF Book contains more than 2,000 addresses throughout Australia of organic farmers and hosts looking for short or long-term voluntary help or to promote cultural exchange. The list with membership is sold with accident insurance at a cost of $70 within Australia ($5 extra to cover postage within Australia).

An internet-based exchange of work-for-keep volunteers can be found at www.helpx.net where more than 7,500 Australian hosts are listed. To register for the premier service of this excellent online community that allows you to contact hosts, it is necessary to pay €20 for two years' membership. Before becoming a volunteer with Conservation Volunteers, Susan Gray joined WWOOF Australia and worked on several farms on a work-for-keep basis. *'They are all growing food organically and usually in beautiful countryside. Most are very keen to show you around and show off their home region to you. The work was as hard as you wanted it to be, but about four hours of work were expected. I usually did more as I enjoyed it, and I learned a lot from those experiences.'*

Interesting research projects take place throughout Australia and some may be willing to include unpaid staff looking for work experience. For example a rainforest field research station in far northern Queensland operated by the Australian Tropical Research Foundation (PMB 5, Cape Tribulation, Qld 4873; ☎ (+61) 7 4098 0063; www.austrop.org.au or www.facebook.com/austrop) welcomes paying volunteers who usually stay two or three weeks, though extensions are possible. Volunteers assist in research and station activities such as radio-tracking bats, assessing fig phenology, stomping grass for forest regeneration, tree-planting, invasive weed control, constructing buildings and running the Bat House visitor centre. Volunteers are asked to pay US$35 a day to cover food and accommodation, unchanged for a number of years. AUSTROP also caters for interns (who do a small formal research project), undergraduates and postgraduate students.

Speaking of bats, a dedicated bat hospital on the Atherton Tableland of northern Queensland takes on self-funding volunteers who contribute $30–$70 a day for food and accommodation, depending on the length of their stay, and must arrive with proof that they have been vaccinated against rabies. The busy season is November to January, which is in the middle of the tick paralysis season when many young flying foxes are orphaned and need to be cared for. See details at www.tolgabathospital.org/volunteers_home.htm.

The Australian Institute of Marine Science (AIMS) at Cape Ferguson near Townsville (☎ (+61) 7 4753 4260; www.aims.gov.au) maintains a register of applicants interested in temporary or casual work at this marine research centre, and also has some places for graduates and undergraduates looking for work experience in marine research; it would be most unusual for a school leaver to be accepted, although anyone with a scuba diving certificate and a keen interest should make contact with relevant members of permanent staff who might be willing to support an application.

Wildcare is a Tasmanian NGO (www.wildcaretas.org.au) that anyone can join for just $25 and then request a volunteer placement, from monitoring orange-bellied parrots to becoming a temporary caretaker on a remote southern island.

Fruit Picking

In the rich agricultural land between the coastal ribbon of urban development and the outback, a multitude of crops is grown: grapes around Adelaide and in the Hunter Valley of New South Wales, tropical fruit on the Queensland coast and north of Perth, apples in the south-west part of Western Australia and in Tasmania, etc. Although fruit farms may be more fertile than the outback, the same considerations as to isolation, heat and dangers from the fauna hold true. The standard hours for a fruit picker working in the heat are approximately 6am–6pm with two or three hours off in the middle of the day.

Each year backpackers make up one quarter of the workforce on farms. During certain harvests, the farmers are desperate for labour and put out appeals over the radio, on the noticeboards of back-packers' hostels and via harvest employment agencies. On one Queensland farm where Mary Anne Mackle from Northern Ireland worked, the farmer had to bring in a team of prisoners to finish off the cucumber harvest since there was such a shortage of pickers. If you find yourself falling behind your fellow-workers during the first few days of the harvest, you should console yourself that some may be professionals who have been following harvests round the country for years.

Since it became possible to apply for a second year's working holiday if you have spent at least three months in a rural area, eg harvesting or packing produce, the numbers of working holiday makers seeking rural work has escalated. Competition is keener than it was but if you are prepared to stay for a spell on a farm, opportunities abound. A short surf of the internet will soon take you to a huge amount of harvesting information. The National Harvest Labour Information Service based in Mildura, Victoria (☎ (+61) 1800 062 332; www.harvesttrail.gov.au) is funded by the federal government and therefore free to users. The fruitpicking hub www.fruitpickingjobs.com.au lists new vacancies as they occur. Feedback on its forums can be useful as well as its Facebook page. Access to job listings is free though enhanced access is available for $5 a month.

Harvest seasons are often diverse: crops ripen first in Queensland and finish in Tasmania as you move further away from the equator. Even the two major grape harvests take place consecutively rather than simultaneously. For easy reference, we have included tables showing crops, regions and times of harvest (omitting grapes, which appear on a separate chart) for the most important fruit-growing states of New South Wales, Victoria, South Australia, Western Australia and Queensland.

Quite often farmers will offer a shack or caravan for little or no money. Not all fruit farmers can supply accommodation, so serious jobseekers carry a tent. On the other hand backpackers' hostels are never far away and in the main picking districts organise minibus transport between hostels and farms. Camper vans are of course very versatile and comfortable but expensive to run and expensive to buy.

MARY ANNE MACKLE PARTICIPATED IN A NUMBER OF HARVESTS DURING HER WORKING HOLIDAY AND OFFERS THESE TIPS TO UNSUSPECTING FRUIT PICKERS:

1. *Although a car is not essential, it is often necessary in looking for work, and then getting to town to shop.*
2. *Be prepared for extremes of temperature. Although it may be in the 80s during the day, the nights are often very cold.*
3. *Don't expect any nightlife. A typical evening for us involved showering, washing dishes, making dinner, reading, writing and chatting with fellow fruit pickers.*
4. *Forget about vanity. You will stink at all times even after a shower. Your socks will never be the same again and your skin won't like the sunblock and build-up of dirt either.*
5. *Forget about modesty. Don't expect to have the use of toilet facilities out in the fields.*
6. *On an optimistic note, you will be a fitter person and, if things go well, a wealthier one too. You can then go off and take a dive course on the Great Barrier Reef, snorkel in Coral Bay, canoe down Katherine Gorge, get drunk in Darwin, hike in national parks, swim in waterfalls, until your money runs out and you start all over again.*

Mary Anne's conclusion is that harvesting is certainly preferable to packing boxes in a warehouse in Sydney or selling hotdogs. Hang on to the fact that you will definitely improve with practice, so don't give up after the first couple of days of earning a pittance from piecework.

The Grape Harvest

Australian wines have made a startling impact on the rest of the world as the volume, quality and consumption increase each year. Regardless of their quality, the important fact for itinerant workers is that there is a large quantity of grapes to be picked. The main centres for grape picking are the Mildura region of Victoria, the Riverland of South Australia (between Renmark and Waikerie) and the Hunter Valley of New South Wales (around Pokolbin and Muswellbrook), though grapes are grown in every state including Tasmania. Detailed tables are set out below. The harvests usually get under way some time in February and last through March or into April. If you work solidly for six weeks, it is possible to earn more than $2,000.

Picking for a winery is easiest; it doesn't matter too much if the grapes are squashed or there are a few leaves left in (a blockie would have a fit if he read that). Picking for drying means the grapes shouldn't be squashed and picking for market (ie table grapes) demands extreme care and is usually paid as wages or at a higher rate per box.

The fairest way to pick is by weight. The only time you are likely to get a break in the afternoon is when it is too hot to leave the grapes out in the sun, though adverts have been seen in the past promising 'smoko' time, ie breaks.

Certainly the demand for pickers is intense in many regions. After deciding that the Sydney employment scene was unremittingly grim, Henry Pearce phoned some employment agencies in mid-February and decided that Griffith in New South Wales was the best bet. When he arrived, he was delighted to see that the job board was full of grape-picking jobs. He was hustled into the harvest office, allocated to a farmer and driven to a farm in the region, where he began work the next morning. The Explorers Hostel at 72 Benerembah Street in Griffith (☎ (+61) 2 6964 4638; www.explorers hostel.com.au) helps with finding work and transport to the farms.

Across the River Murray the situation is the same around Mildura in Victoria, the grape capital of the area. Armin Birrer reported from the town of Cardross that 300 picking jobs were advertised in the local papers and on roadside signs. This is the area to which agencies in Melbourne are most likely to send you if you arrive in January/February. The Western Australian wine industry is flourishing. Some vacancies for pruning work between June and September and harvesting February to April in Margaret River and Busselton are filled through the Margaret River agency Down to Earth Labour (☎ (+61) 8 9758 7074; jobs@dtearth.com.au).

GRAPE HARVESTS IN AUSTRALIA

SOUTH AUSTRALIA

Clare-Watervale	February–April
Barossa Valley	February–April
Adelaide and Southern Vales	February–March
Coonawarra	February–April
Langhorne Creek	February–April
Riverland (Waikerie, Berri, Loxton, Renmark)	February–April

NEW SOUTH WALES

Orchard Hills	late January–mid March
Camden	early February–mid March
Wedderburn	mid February–mid March
Nolong	late February–April
Orange	March–April
Mudgee	late February–April
Hunter Valley (Pokolbin, Bulga, Denman, Broke, Muswellbrook)	early February–March
Murrumbidgee Irrigation area (Griffith, Leeton)	mid February–March
Dareton	January–April
Curlwaa	March–April
Buronga	February–June
Mid-Murray (Koraleigh, Goodnight)	late February–April
Corowa	February–March

VICTORIA

Goulburn Valley	February–March
Swan Hill	February–March
Lilydale	February–March
Mildura/Robinvale	February–March
Great Western-Avoca	February–March
Drumborg	February–March
Glenrowan-Milawa	February–March
Rutherglen	February–March

WESTERN AUSTRALIA

Swan Valley (near Perth)	February–April
Margaret River	February–April
Mount Barker	February–April

The Apple Harvest

Although apple picking is notoriously slow going for the beginner, you can usually pick up enough speed within a few days to make it rewarding. Seasonal pickers are needed in Western Australia throughout the year but especially between November and May, with the peak of the apple harvest falling in the summer. In harvests where the conditions seem at the outset to be unattractive it is not hard to get work especially when it is the time of year (normally February to May) when students return to college and the weather is getting colder.

Many travellers flock to the Western Australian harvest that takes place around Donnybrook, Manjimup and Pemberton. Brook Lodge Backpacker Accommodation at 3 Bridge St, Donnybrook, Western Australia (☎ (+61) 8 9731 1520; www.brooklodge.com.au) maintains a register of job vacancies in the area, though it doesn't get favourable reviews online. It can take between a couple of hours and seven to 10 days to find work locally, depending on the time of year. The season starts in November with thinning out the immature apples and plums and progresses to stone fruit picking December to March, though apple picking carries on until July. Other crops are grown in the vicinity such as tomatoes (picked January to March) and pears (February to April). During the picking season, a contract rate is the norm, ranging from $650 to $850 for a six-day week. Otherwise a straight hourly wage is paid of about $20. Transport to work is arranged by Brook Lodge for a charge.

Climatic conditions will determine what else you take in addition to a long novel to keep you amused until work materialises. High summer temperatures mean that you will need to take water, sunblock and a brimmed hat into the orchards. Later on warm clothes will come in handy as Armin Birrer discovered one chilly autumn: *'The only problem with the south of WA is that the wet season starts in May which lasts till August. And as the season progresses it gets colder and colder and more and more miserable.'*

Mary Anne Mackle spent six weeks picking in Manjimup and found that being paid by the bin was a great motivator to work long, hard hours. She and her companion started on a meagre three bins a day but by the end they were filling 16 a day, which shows what a difference some practice can make. By the time she finished, her clothes were in shreds and her body not far behind, but she had saved several thousand dollars.

Tasmania is not known as the 'Apple Island' for its shape alone. The apple harvest takes place between March and early May, though other fruit harvests start at the beginning of November with strawberries and apple thinning, followed by cherries and blueberries in late December. Grape picking is available in March/April. The work is available in the Huon region around Cygnet and Geeveston not far south of Hobart. Like many before him, Robert Abblett stayed at Huon Valley Backpackers, on Sandhill Road in Cradoc (☎ (+61) 3 6295 1551; www.huonvalleybackpackers.com) which doesn't get the most favourable reviews online though it does assist with fruit-picking work: *'As the main accommodation in the area, the hostel finds work for guests and provides transport too. I spent two months working hard for several different orchards, as the crop was intermittent. With previous experience, I saved £1,000. I was put with 20 other strange people for the whole season.'*

Other Harvests

From asparagus to zucchini there is an abundance of crops to be picked from one end of Australia to the other, and the energetic itinerant picker can do very nicely. Australia has such an enormous agricultural economy that there will always be jobs. Gordon Mitchell from Aberdeen is just one Briton who has worked out a profitable route:

> *I've been picking fruit in Australia for a few years. I make the best money between November and April/ May, starting at Young NSW picking cherries. When they finish I do the smaller cherry harvest in Orange NSW, then on to Shepparton Victoria in early January for the pear picking. When the sultanas start in Mildura in early February I do them, though most people stay in Shepparton to finish the pears and apples. This takes me to early or mid-March when the apples start in Orange and finish in late April or early May. Sometimes it's very hectic but that's when the picking is good.*

For application information on berry-picking opportunities in New South Wales as well as North Queensland, WA and Tasmania, send an enquiry to employment.blueberry@costagroup.com.au. Costa is Australia's largest producer and packer of fresh fruit and vegetables.

Queensland

As you travel north the produce, like the weather, gets more tropical so that citrus, pineapples, bananas and mangoes grow in profusion in the north, while stone fruits, apples and potatoes grow in the Darling Downs, 220km inland from Brisbane. In the tropics there are not always definite harvest seasons since crops grow year round.

Work in the Queensland harvests is strongly monopolised by the hostels. Farmers for the most part rely on hostel managers to supply them with a workforce, making it hard to fix up a job directly with a farmer and accommodation on farms is rare. Shuttle transport between hostel and farms is often laid on. Jobseekers are not always in a strong position to ensure they get paid a decent wage and pay a fair price for transport and accommodation.

About 400km north of Brisbane, the agricultural and rum-producing centre of Bundaberg absorbs a great many travelling workers. All the hostels in town advertise help with employment especially Federal Backpackers (☎ (+61) 7 4153 3711; federalbackpackers@hotmail.com) which has six buses to transport workers to the fields. The hostel at 64 Barolin St (☎ (+61) 7 4151 6097) calls itself the Bundy Workers and Divers Hostel, though it attracts more workers than divers. Bundaberg is such a magnet for working travellers that it is often bursting at the seams. Bridgid Seymour-East was not impressed with the scene: *'There are too many hostels and too few jobs to go around. Hostels take about 100 people each so lots of desperate people all together. Most people get only one or two days of work a week, just enough to pay for their hostel bed and food. You cannot choose your jobs and if you quit or get fired they might not give you a job for another week.'*

The town of Bowen, centre of a fruit and vegetable-growing region (especially tomatoes) 600km south of Cairns, is another well-known destination for aspiring pickers. All the hostels in Bowen cater for working travellers. As always, count on paying $140–$160 a week for a dorm bed.

The farmers usually provide a minibus once the picking really gets going, which costs a couple of dollars from Bowen or might even be thrown in with the cost of a long-stay bed. Otherwise a bicycle would be handy. If you're job-hunting farm to farm, go out on the Bootooloo or Collinsville Roads or to the Delta or Euri Creek areas. Apparently the tail end of the harvest in November can be a good time to show up, when lots of seasonal workers are beginning to drift south. If the farmers are desperate enough, they pay premium rates, sometimes even double.

Further north, Cardwell, Innisfail and Tully offer work in banana and sometimes sugar plantations. Farmers around Tully (the wettest place in Australia) organise transport between town and the properties. If you pay for one week's accommodation upfront plus a $300 deposit at the purpose-built working hostel Banana Barracks at 50 Butler St (☎ (+61) 7 4068 0455; www.bananabarracks.com/work.html), they will do their best to find you work. Since no hostel can absolutely guarantee work, some have complained that the deposit, often charged upfront by hostels for workers, is a potential rip-off. Henry Pearce describes his gruelling job as a banana cutter in October:

> *The bananas all grew together on a single stem which could weigh up to 60kg. The farmer cut into the trunk to weaken it and, once I had pulled the fruit down onto my shoulder, he cut the stem and I staggered off to place them on a 'nearby' trailer. The work was physically shattering and the presence of large frogs and rats inside the bunch (thankfully no snakes) jumping out at the last minute didn't do anything to increase my enjoyment. We were paid by the hour and worked an eight-hour day, five days a week which was standard for the area.*

Working with Queensland fruits seems to be an activity fraught with danger. If you decide to pick pineapples, you have to wear long-sleeved shirts and jeans (despite the sizzling heat between January and April) as protection from the prickles and spines. Caroline Perry advises anyone who packs rock melons to wear gloves; otherwise the abrasive skin rips your hands to shreds.

Southern Queensland has always been a reliable fruit-picking destination for backpackers; in November apples, peaches and pears are picked, and in January/February the tomato harvest takes place. A little north, inland from the Sunshine Coast, head for the strawberry harvest around Beerwah from May/June; try for example Gowinta Farms (www.gowinta.com.au) which has a caravan site for pickers and packers.

New South Wales

The southern part of the state around Wagga Wagga is known as the Riverina. Seasonal work opportunities can be found in Batlow, Jugiong, Leeton and Young as well as Darlington Point, Gundagai, Hay and so on.

The asparagus harvest at Jugiong on the Hume Highway north-west of Canberra attracts many seasonal pickers, as does the cherry harvest around Young half an hour north of Jugiong, which starts as the asparagus finishes. The packing season is a long one from about late September to at least mid-November. The work is notoriously backbreaking but can be lucrative. Whereas some have been disappointed with working conditions and earnings in the cherry harvest near Young between mid-November and Christmas, others recommend it. The unpredictable weather and piecework pay rates can make things difficult.

Of all the many picking jobs that Henry Pearce found, the best money was earned working on onions around Griffith, where he and his girlfriend saved an impressive $5,000 in 10 weeks between early January and March. You have to be lucky to find work in this harvest particularly if you don't have your own transport. Ask at all the onion-packing sheds in Griffith.

Victoria

The summer fruit harvests in northern Victoria annually attract many participants on working holidays. The best time to arrive is mid to late January and work should continue until the end of March. The National Harvest Labour Information Service mentioned above carries out much of the recruitment in Northern Victoria. Harvest Labour Offices can be found in Mildura, Robinvale, Swan Hill and Shepparton, and there is a harvest hotline ☎ (+61) 1 300 724788.

Mooroopna is just outside Shepparton and is a good place to look for work. Ask in the pub about tomato-picking possibilities in February and March. You might want to buy a second-hand bicycle from the shop on the main street of Shepparton to get around the area. Major employer R J Cornish & Co in Cobram report that changes in the market mean they are hiring fewer people. Plunkett Orchards in Ardmona in the Goulburn Valley contract out their seasonal hiring to Everlasting Agriculture Management in Shepparton who post harvesting and other vacancies on their site (www.eamanagement.com.au/jobs_listing.htm), and McNab & Son also in Ardmona (☎ (+61) 3 5829 0016; www.mcnab.com.au) are also worth a try as the season gets underway in January. Pickers coming to the area can stay at the Cobram Willows Caravan Park on the Murray Valley Highway where they will meet people earning more than $100 a day between December and March.

In the north-western corner of the state, Mildura (mentioned above as a centre for grape-growing) is a major agricultural district and Cardross across the river is also a promising destination. Work is available virtually year round (May is the slowest month) due to the sunny climate and epic irrigation schemes. A high proportion of the travellers staying in Mildura's hostels take advantage of the job-finding and transport-providing services of places such as Mildura International Backpackers (5 Cedar Avenue; ☎ (+61) 408 210132; www.workinghostels.com.au) where the majority of guests are working or looking for work. Although harvesting work is often not hard to get, some find it hard to make any money. The pear crates may look quite small at the outset but will soon seem unfillable with mysterious false bottoms. Many eager first-timers do not realise how hard the work will be physically, and give up before their bodies acclimatise. But you should have faith that your speed will increase fairly rapidly.

South Australia

The Riverland region of South Australia (not to be confused with the Riverina in NSW) consists of Renmark, Loxton and Waikerie but is centred on Berri where most of the backpacker accommodation and job agencies are located. MADEC, the government employment initiative, has an office in Renmark (harvest@madec.edu.au).

In recent years work has been available all year round due to the expansion of the wine and citrus industries, and the easing of the drought conditions with which the Murray Basin area has to battle. Berri Backpackers (☎ (+61) 8 8582 3144; www.berribackpackers.com.au) gets positive reviews from long-stay residents. Daniele Arena called this hostel 'the most wonderful probably in the whole world' since he greatly enjoyed their regular cheap barbecues.

According to an earlier report from Bridgid Seymour-East who also loved this hostel, landing some work is a bit of a free-for-all:

Whoever answers the phone first gets a job first, which can seem a bit daunting at first (survival of the fittest). We started on citrus picking for a big company Yandilla Park. Whilst the contract rate is high, you don't get that many hours in the long run because you can't pick citrus until the fruit is dry on the tree. Often you can't start picking until 11am or 12 noon, which can be very frustrating. But it gives you enough money to survive until the vine work begins. At the end of June I got a job cutting canes which involves taking a cutting from the grape vines, trimming it to size and bundling it in bunches of 100. Whilst extremely boring, I never made less than $120 a day after tax and on good days $200, so I was getting pay cheques of $800–$900 a week.

Hundreds of farms, big and small, need helpers. Other accommodation for pickers is available on campsites.

Nearer Adelaide, a major employer of travellers and casual cherry pickers is Torrens Valley Orchards in Gumeracha; (☎ (+61) 8 8389 1405; www.tvocherries.com), located just south of the Barossa Valley wine region and only a cheap bus ride from the state capital less than an hour away. Cherry picking and packing takes place in December/January for up to 25 backpackers at a time, while others are needed year round to plant trees, do pruning, maintenance and office work. Accommodation is available on-site for about eight workers.

Western Australia

There are over 100 vegetable and banana plantations around the cities of Geraldton and Carnarvon north of Perth, many of which are very short of pickers in the winter when they are busy supplying the markets of Perth. The tomato harvest lasts from early August until mid-November, with the month of September being the easiest time to find work. The banana harvest starts in October, but there is casual work available anytime between April and November. One way of meeting farmers is to go to the warehouses or packing depots where growers come to drop off their produce.

Agricultural development around Kununurra in the extreme north of the state is extensive, and every traveller passing through seems to stop to consider the possibility of working in the banana, melon, citrus or vegetable harvests. There are also jobs in sandalwood tree planting and pruning. Travellers are regularly hired during the first part of 'The Dry' (the dry season lasts from April to November) and beyond. If you can't fix up work through the Youth Hostel (half of whose beds are occupied by seasonal workers paying from $139 a week) or the Backpackers, contact Ord River Bananas and Oasis Bananas. For the melon harvest between the end of June and October contact Bluey's Outback Farm (☎ (+61) 8 9168 2177; blueysoutbackfarm@bigpond.com); the hourly pay for pickers starts at $20.

Not much harvesting takes place in the Northern Territory because of its climate. However plenty of people are needed to work on farms. In fact 85 per cent of all farm labourers working in the Territory are foreign backpackers.

NEW SOUTH WALES HARVESTS		
CROP	AREA	DATES OF HARVEST
Strawberries	Glenorie and Campbelltown	September–December
Cherries	Orange	November–January
	Young	October–December
Peaches and Nectarines	Glenorie	October–January
	Campbelltown	November–January
	Orange	February–March
	Bathurst	January–March
	Leeton and Griffith, Forbes	February–April
	Young	February–March

Plums	Glenorie	November–January
	Orange	January–March
	Young	January–March
Apricots	Leeton and Griffith	December–January
	Kurrajong	November
Apples and Pears	Oakland, Glenorie and Bilpin	January–April
	Armidale	February–May
	Orange	February–May
	Bathurst	March–May
	Forbes	February–April
	Batlow	February–May
	Griffith and Leeton	January–April
	Young	March–April
Oranges (Valencia)	Outer Sydney	September–February
	Riverina, Mid-Murray	September–March
	Narromine	September–February
	Leeton	December–January
Lemons	Outer Sydney, Riverina, Mid-Murray, Coomealla	July–October
Grapefruits	Mid-Murray	November–April
	Curlwaa	June–February
Asparagus	Dubbo, Bathurst, Cowra, Jugiong	September–December
Wheat	Narrabri, Walgett	November–December
Cotton	Warren and Nevertire, Wee Waa	November–March
Onions	Griffith	November–March
Corn de-tasselling	Narromine	January

SOUTH AUSTRALIA HARVESTS

CROP	AREA	DATES OF HARVEST
Apricots	Riverland (Waikerie, Barmera, Berri, Loxton, Renmark)	December–January
Peaches	Riverland	January–February
Pumpkins	Riverland	May–July
Oranges	Riverland	June–April

VICTORIA HARVESTS

CROP	AREA	DATES OF HARVEST
Pears and Peaches	Shepparton, Ardmona, Mooroopna Kyabram	January–March
	Invergordon, Cobram	January–March
Tomatoes	Shepparton/Mooroopna, Tatura	January–April
	Kyabram	January–April
	Echuca, Tongala	January–April
	Rochester	January–April
	Swan Hill	January–April
	Elmore	January–April
Tobacco	Ovens and Kiewa Valley	February–April
Potatoes	Warragul, Neerim	February–May
Cherries	Silvan, Lilydale, Warburton, Lilydale	November–December
Berries	Silvan, Wandin, Monbulk, Macclesfield, Hoddles Creek, Daylesford	November–February

Apples and Pears	Myrtleford	March–May
	Goulburn Valley	January–April
	Mornington Peninsula	March–May
Flowers and Bulbs	Emerald	January–December

WESTERN AUSTRALIA HARVESTS

CROP	AREA	DATES OF HARVEST
Apples and Pears	Donnybrook, Manjimup, Balingup, Pemberton	March–June
Oranges	Bindoon, Lower Chittering	August–September
Oranges	Harvey	June–July
Lemons	Bindoon, Lower Chittering	November–February
Grapefruit	Harvey	November–February
Apricots, Peaches and Plums	Kalamunda, Walliston, Pickering, Brook	December–March
Tomatoes, vegetables	Carnarvon, Geraldton	August–November
Bananas	Carnarvon	October
Melons, Bananas, etc	Kununurra/Lake Argyle	May–October

QUEENSLAND HARVESTS

CROP	AREA	DATES OF HARVEST
Bananas	Tully	October
Tomatoes	Bowen	August–November
Peaches and Plums	Stanthorpe	December–March
Watermelons	Bundaberg	November–December
Potatoes	Lockyer Valley	October–December
Onions	Lockyer Valley	September–October
Pineapples	Nambour, Maryborough, Bundaberg, Yeppoon	January–April
Apples	Stanthorpe	February–March
Citrus	Gayndah, Mundubbera	May–September
Strawberries	Redlands	July–November
Mangoes	Bowen	November–December
	Mareeba	December–January
Cucumbers, etc	Ayr	May–November
Courgettes	Mackay	August–September

INDUSTRY

Construction and Labouring

Darwin has always been a mecca for drifters, deportees and drop-outs looking for labouring work, though there are fewer job adverts in the Territory's papers than there once were. As the rains recede in May, the human deluge begins and competition for jobs is intense. It is better to be around at the end of the Wet (April) to fix something up beforehand.

Tradesmen of all descriptions usually find it easy to get work in Australia, especially if they bring their papers and tools. Plumbers, electricians and carpenters have been having a field day, especially in Sydney. A pair of steel-capped boots would also be a useful accessory.

TOURISM AND CATERING

This category of employment might include anything from cooking on tourist boats in the Whitsunday Islands in Queensland, to acting as a temporary warden in a Tasmanian youth hostel. You might find yourself serving beer at a roadhouse along the nearly uninhabited road through the Australian north-west or serving at a Sizzler diner (which claims to have invented 'casual dining in Australia'). Whatever the job, expect to present yourself as a serious candidate. According to Ken Smith who noticed plenty of 'Help Wanted' signs posted in restaurant and shop windows in Melbourne, *'even a job washing dishes usually requires several months' relevant experience'*.

Casual catering wages both in the cities and in remote areas are higher than the equivalent British wage. A new national minimum wage came into effect in July 2016 which can be checked after some searching on the website of Fair Work Australia (www.fairwork.gov.au). The award rate for casual waiting staff is 25% higher than the full-time minimum of $17.70 with weekend loadings that mean you should be paid $22.12 during the week, $26.55 on Saturdays, $31 on Sundays and $48.68 an hour on public holidays. Of course there will always be employers who try to flout the law and an article in the *Sydney Morning Herald* reported that 'a leading sushi restaurant chain has admitted it paid some foreign staff as little as $9 an hour, in what workplace experts warn is the tip of a "massive black economy" in Australia's hospitality industry'. If you are well informed about workplace law, you are less likely to be cheated by rogue businesses (but you might also find it harder to get a job).

Although tipping is not traditionally practised in Australia, it is gradually becoming more common and waiting staff in trendy city establishments can expect to augment their wages to some extent.

Standards tend to be fairly high especially in popular tourist haunts. A common practice among restaurant bosses in popular places from Bondi Beach to the Sunshine Coast is to give a jobseeker an hour's trial or a trial shift and decide at the end whether or not to employ them. Stephen Psallidas was taken aback when he approached a hospitality employment agency in Cairns: *'I was in Cairns in April and thought I'd have little trouble getting work. But though I had a visa and experience, I had no references, having worked as a waiter in Greece, where they wouldn't know a reference if one walked up and said "Hi, I'm a reference", so I was doomed from the start. The agency told me that if I'd had references they could have given me work immediately. Curses.'*

Queensland

Because of Queensland's attractions for all visitors to Australia, the competition for jobs comes mostly from travellers, who are more interested in having a good time than in earning a high wage. When employers need to fill a vacancy, they tend to hire whomever is handy that day, rather than sift through applications. For example if you phone from Sydney to enquire about possibilities, the advice will normally be to come and see.

If you want a live-in position, you should try the coastal resorts such as Surfers Paradise and Noosa Heads and islands all along the Queensland coast where the season lasts from March, after the cyclones, until Christmas. If Cairns is choc-a-bloc with jobseekers try the resort of Palm Cove just north of the city. Many of the small islands along the Barrier Reef are completely given over to tourist complexes. You might make initial enquiries at employment offices on the mainland for example in Proserpine, Cannonvale, Mackay or Townsville, though normally you will have to visit an island in person (and therefore pay for the ferry).

Among the many possibilities are the Kingfisher Bay Resort and Eurong Beach Resort on Fraser Island (☎ (+61) 7 4194 9386; www.kingfisherbay.com/jobs) where there is a high demand for food and beverage staff, as well as some jobs as tour guides and on the barges. Delaware North Australia Parks and Resorts run a few of Queensland's upscale resorts, ie on Heron Island, Lizard Island and tiny Wilson Island on the Great Barrier Reef as well as Kings Canyon Resort in the Northern Territory. The company also manages catering services at airports, cricket grounds, etc. They have a job board (google 'Delaware North Australia Career Opportunities') but each resort also recruits independently.

Vacancies crop up from time to time in resorts such as the Capricorn Resort (though it downsized not long ago) on the Sunshine Coast.

Tourist development along the Queensland coast has been rampant, especially with an eye to the Japanese market. Anyone who has travelled in Japan or who has a smattering of Japanese might have the edge over the competition (unless the competition happens to be a Japanese working holiday-maker of whom there are many in Cairns and elsewhere). James Blackman, who hadn't studied any Oriental languages, describes how he got his job at a resort in the Whitsunday Islands:

> *Giving up on Airlie Beach I went to Hamilton Island to search for work. I went to practically every establishment and was turned away. However, I persevered and the second last place gave me a job as a kitchen-hand in a restaurant which was on the beach front. Lots of different people staffed the resort and most were quite friendly, always asking, 'How're ya going?'*

Roger Blake was lucky in Airlie Beach when the initial fortnight of work as a handyman, gardener, labourer and jack-of-all-trades at some swanky apartments was extended to six:

> *I saved a tidy sum and figured I had enough to do the East Coast. I loved Airlie Beach and not without good reasons. Besides the obvious – the climate, crystal clear and turquoise Whitsunday waters and stunning ocean views – being a familiar face in this one-street town also had perks. I made good friends with many locals and was treated as one. For example, I qualified for cheap beers at a popular bar which otherwise charges absurd resort prices.*

The Gold Coast has a number of theme parks with opportunities for casual work during holiday periods, mainly in food and beverage and retail service. The industry was dealt a blow in October 2016 when a ride malfunctioned at Dreamworld on the Gold Coast resulting in the death of four people. The largest theme park in Australia re-opened six weeks later.

Wages are not high and you will have to pay for transport between a hostel and town. Check for adverts in the *Gold Coast Bulletin* or in the Brisbane *Courier Mail* on Saturdays. Alternatively, contact Warner Bros Theme Parks which recruits centrally for Movie World, Sea World, Wet 'n' Wild Water World and Australian Outback Spectacular. Many short-term vacancies occur in the holiday periods and are ideal for backpackers, ie Easter, a four-week period in September during school holidays and four to six weeks during the Christmas holidays.

Diving and Watersports

The dive industry is a substantial employer. Although not many visitors would have the qualifications – qualified mechanical engineer, diver and student of Japanese – which got Ian Mudge a job as Dive Master on the live-aboard cruiser *Nimrod* then operating out of Cooktown, his assessment of opportunities for mere mortals is heartening:

> *Anyone wishing to try their luck as a hostess could do no worse than to approach all the dive operators with live-aboard boats such as Mike Ball Dive Expeditions, Down Under Cruise & Dive, etc. 'Hosties' make beds, clean cabins and generally tidy up. Culinary skills and an ability to speak Japanese would be definite pluses. A non-diver would almost certainly be able to fix up some free dive lessons and thus obtain their basic Open Water Diver qualification while being paid to do so. Normally only females are considered for hostie jobs.*

The sailing season in Sydney lasts from October to April with the peak in December. There is no point in looking for work in the Antipodean winter. Some sailing schools may offer casual instructing work during school holidays to travellers who have experience in teaching dinghy sailing especially to kids.

Flying Fish (www.flyingfishonline.com) run a sail academy in Sydney and offer follow-up job assistance in the industry.

Ski Resorts

Another holiday area to consider is the Australian Alps where a ski industry flourishes although, with the changing climate, resorts have to rely more and more on snow-making machines. Perisher in the Snowy Mountains is the biggest ski resort in the southern hemisphere with a dedicated employment site www.perisherjobs.com.au. Jindabyne (NSW) on the edge of Kosciuszko National Park and Thredbo are the ski job capitals (about half an hour's drive apart), though Mount Buller, Falls Creek, Baw Baw and Hotham in the state of Victoria are relatively developed ski centres too. The big companies do their hiring between January and Easter, though you might be lucky if you show up in the resorts a couple of weeks before the season opens in June. Check out sites such as www.merlincareers.com.au for Falls Creek and Mount Hotham and http://totallyintoit.com.au or http://fsr.cvmail.com.au/thredbo for Thredbo.

Denise Crofts went straight from a waitressing job in Sydney to the large Arlberg Hotel in Mount Buller, where she had a terrific season, with excellent snow conditions. The hotel changed hands in 2016 but it is likely the new owners will continue to provide staff accommodation and full board at a reasonable cost. Henry Pearce's experiences looking for work were not very positive, despite heavy radio advertising:

> When we hitched to Cooma on June 2nd, we enquired about the progress of the applications we had sent in April. We were told that there had been 4,000 applications and two vacancies for bar staff to date. We carried on up to Thredbo and half-heartedly asked around a few chalets and hotels and it seemed most of them had already fixed up their basic requirements. We were told of several definite posts available once the snow fell. In Jindabyne we were hired to work at the 'highest restaurant in Australia' (at the top of the ski lift). But accommodation was uniformly expensive in Jindabyne as was the cost of lift passes and ski hire.

Fewer ski instructors are hired at the hiring clinics held in the big resorts before the season gets underway when there is an instructor training course on-site, as there is in Thredbo. Graduates of the Elite Instructor Training APSI Level 1 course (www.eliteskiinstructortraining.com) tend to get first dibs on the entry-level jobs. The company also offers internships combining full- or part-time work with training. Kosciuszko Thredbo Pty Ltd at the Alpine Ski Village in Thredbo hire the full range of ski resort staff in three categories: on-the-mountain, hotel and instruction. Applications must be made via various recruitment sites such as www.taw.com.au and www.totallyintoit.com.au by the beginning of April, and interviews take place in Sydney, Brisbane and Thredbo in early May. Lots of good information on working in Australian ski resorts can be found at www.snowseasoncentral.com.

The Interior

Uluru or Ayers Rock is a place of pilgrimage for more than a third of a million visitors a year. The nearest facilities are in the Ayers Rock Resort village about 20km north of the Rock. Ayers Rock Resort (formerly known as Yulara) is the fourth largest settlement in the Northern Territory and, since it employs 750 people, is a good place to look for a job. The resort is operated by Voyages Indigenous Tourism Australia whose employment website (www.voyages.com.au/careers) includes a detailed factsheet about living and working in Ayers Rock Resort. Staff accommodation is provided starting at $95 a week.

As the gateway to Uluru, Alice Springs is a popular tourist destination. One traveller who stayed at one of the many backpackers' lodges reported that eight out of the 12 women staying there were working as waitresses or bar staff. Occasional vacancies occur for hostesses to work on upmarket special interest tours. Personality and presentation are more important than qualifications and experience for jobs as hostesses and cooks.

If exploring Australia is your target rather than earning high wages, it is worth trying to exchange your labour for the chance to join an otherwise unaffordable tour. For example camping tour operators in Kakadu and Litchfield Park have been known to do this.

Coober Pedy (opal capital of Australia in the South Australian outback), Alice Springs, Kununurra and Broome are other places worth trying for tourist work in the Dry (May to October).

Cities

Melbourne is arguably better for work than Sydney, partly because it is less packed with working travellers who prefer Sydney's weather. Temp agencies are the first port of call for most jobseekers. Apart from restaurants and cafés, pubs and clubs, temporary catering jobs crop up in cricket grounds, theatres and yacht clubs. Function work is usually easy to come by via specialist agencies provided you can claim to have silver service experience.

Looking for work in a Sydney suburb apart from the ones inundated by backpackers might prove more successful. For example Danny Jacobson, a pizza chef from Chicago, had better luck in Newtown than he did in Bondi. He also was hired as a walking advertisement for a designer clothing sale.

The best opportunities for bar and waiting staff in Perth are in the city centre, Fremantle and Northbridge, the area around William and James Streets. Rhona Stannage and her husband Stuart Blackwell arrived in Perth in November, and having had chalet experience in the French Alps and restaurant experience in Cyprus en route, were in a strong position to find hospitality work:

> *Since there were lots of adverts around for bar/restaurant staff we didn't go door-knocking, but we did meet a Canadian guy who had been in Perth one week and who had immediately found work in North-bridge just by asking around in the restaurants, bars and nightclubs. We both got jobs fairly quickly – me within a week and Stuart a couple of weeks later. (I put my relative success down to the usual sexism in the hospitality trade since we have virtually the same experience.) I'm working in an Irish pub called Rosie O'Grady's (they prefer Irish accents but stretched a point when it came to my Scottish one). I would also recommend the 'traditional British pub' the Moon and Sixpence on Murray St in the City, since they seem to have only Poms and no Aussies working there.*

Rhona was also offered a job at the Burswood Entertainment Complex, now the Crown Perth, which is one of Western Australia's largest employers. Employees enjoy a range of benefits including free meals.

Catering agencies such as Pinnacle mentioned earlier (www.pinnaclepeople.com.au) and I Need Event Staff (www.ineedeventstaff.com.au) in Melbourne and other cities supply short-term staff to casinos, sporting and corporate events, as well as to other employers. The preference for females is strong in places such as Kalgoorlie where waitresses are sometimes known by the offensive name 'skimpies' (scantily clad bar maids). Partly because Darwin has such a small population (140,000), tourist bars and restaurants rely heavily on transients for their staff. As well as being easier to find work than in Sydney or Melbourne, the cost of accommodation is substantially less.

Bridgid Seymour-East thinks that new arrivals should be warned of the dangers that Sydney poses to the traveller: *'You may plan to stay a week or two and set off to travel or find work. However, one or two months later, after a lot of fun, you find yourself still there and your funds severely depleted. Sydney traps you because you do have so much fun. Jimmy and I met in a youth hostel in Glebe and love blossomed.'*

Holiday Language Courses

Travellers with a TEFL certificate can take advantage of the seasonal demand for English tuition created by 'study tours', popular among Japanese, Indonesian and other Asian students during their autumn and winter holidays. Demand for these holiday English courses has been increasing as middle-class prosperity has escalated in Pacific Rim countries and the Australian immigration authorities have relaxed the restrictions on visas.

When Barry O'Leary arrived in Sydney with a working holiday visa, he had very little money left so needed a job fast. He had emailed a number of language institutes in Sydney in advance and fixed up an interview the day after he arrived. Soon he found a job with an English language institute in an outer suburb of Sydney:

> *This was my first full-time job and I was thrown in at the deep end. Initially I was doing maternity cover and working 15 hours a week, but this later increased to 45 including preparation time. The wages were fantastic, I wasn't paying any tax because I set myself up as a contractor and I was paid $30 an hour (the*

going rate then) and $300 every two weeks for the evening business course I taught. I managed to save about $8,000 in three months which paid for a brilliant trip up the east coast of Australia. There was always a laugh in the staff room and a lot of banter between England and Australia. I really enjoyed the mixed classes because there was such a range of opinions and at times more challenging because each nationality would have different weaknesses.

Special Events

Special events such as Test matches and race meetings can be seen as possible sources of employment. If you happen to be in Melbourne for the Melbourne Cup (held on the first Tuesday of November which is a public holiday in Victoria) or for the Grand Prix in March, your chances of finding casual work escalate remarkably. An army of sweepers and cleaners is recruited to go through the whole course clearing the huge piles of debris left by 100,000 race-goers. Hotels, restaurants and bars become frantically busy in the period leading up to the Cup, and private catering firms are also often desperate for staff.

At a swanky backpackers in the hip suburb of St Kilda, an opportunity came up for Roger Blake to do some work. A company setting up exhibition stands at the Melbourne Exhibition Centre was short-staffed so came looking for casual workers. He worked for them on and off throughout his stay in Melbourne, which meant that he could move on to New Zealand with a few hundred dollars saved up. A couple of years ago Daniele Arena had the chance to work at the Phillip Island Grand Prix Circuit just south of Melbourne. They are especially keen to employ casuals before the Australian Motorcycle Grand Prix in October and the Superbikes in February. Odd jobs such as scrubbing floors, hosing the pit lanes and even painting tyre walls paid well and you get lots of hours.

All the major cities have important horse races. Rowena Caverly was hired for the Darwin Cup Races 'mainly to check that none of the Lady Members had passed out in the loos'.

Travelling fairs are popular and may have the odd vacancy. Geertje Korf was at first thrilled to land a job with a travelling fair but it wasn't all as exciting as she had hoped:

The work itself was good enough, helping to build up the stalls and working on the Laughing Clowns game. But the family I got to work for were not very sociable company. As a result, when we left a place and headed for the next I would spend time (about a week) until the next show day wandering lonely around incredibly hot and dusty little country towns where there was absolutely nothing to do while the showmen sat in a little circle drinking beer and not even talking to me. Also, the public toilets on the showgrounds were not usually open until showday, never cleaned since the last showday and usually provided some company (at last!) such as frogs, flies and redback spiders. I got paid $200 a week plus the use of a little caravan and evening meals, which was not bad. Apparently a Dutch guy had spent six months with them the year before and had a great time, so I suppose it all depends on your personality.

The Australian Pub

The tradition in male-dominated pubs of heavy drinking and barmaid taunting continues, so you should be prepared for this sometimes irritating (though almost always good-natured) treatment. You may get especially tired of hearing sporting comparisons between Australia and Britain.

Standards of service in pubs and restaurants are high and many hotel managers will be looking for some experience or training. Only those desperate for staff will be willing to train. Even if you have had experience of working in a British pub, it may take you some time to master the technique of pouring Australian lager properly. There is a bewildering array of beer glasses ranging from the 115ml small beer of Tasmania to the 575ml pint of New South Wales with middies, schooners, pots and butchers falling in between. Names and measures vary from state to state.

Working at a road station can be a lonely business. A typical station consists of a shop, a petrol pump and a bar, and they occur every couple of hundred miles along the seemingly endless straight highways through the Australian desert. The more remote the place (and these are often the ones that are unbearably hot) the more likely there will be a vacancy. If you see a job going in Marble Bar, for example, remind yourself that it is arguably the world's hottest inhabited town with summer temperatures occasionally nudging 50°C (122°F).

CHILDCARE

The demand for live-in and live-out childcare is enormous in Australia and a few agencies abroad cater to the demand, such as Childcare International in London (www.childint.co.uk). AIFS, the educational and travel company that operates the Au Pair in America programme has expanded to Australia. GET Australia's Au Pair in Australia scheme (www.nannyaustralia.com) places European and American candidates who have at least 200 hours of childcare experience in their destination of choice. Nannies and au pairs with more extensive experience qualify for elite programmes that pay higher wages. Programme fees vary but are currently reduced from US$900 to US$600 for Americans.

It is also easy to conduct the job-hunt on arrival. Applicants are often interviewed a day or two after registering with an agency and start work immediately. The trade association of au pair agencies is CAPAA (Cultural Au Pair Association of Australia) – see its website for links to its member agencies (www.capaa.com.au). Families post requests for live-in help on various classified ad websites; one to check is www.facebook.com/australianaupairfamilies.

Nanny and au pair agencies are very interested in hearing from young women and men with working holiday visas, though they do not like the rule that prohibits visa holders from working for more than six months for the same employer. Geertje Korf's experience in Tasmania illustrates the ease with which childcare work can be found: '*I decided to go to Tasmania for a cycling holiday. At the second place I stopped I got offered a job as a nanny to four children, just by mentioning I had been nannying in Sydney. The place had beautiful surroundings, restaurants, etc so I decided to accept. It was a good job and I left quite a bit richer.*'

A typical weekly wage in addition to room and board would be $175–$300 with some families paying up to $450 to live-in child carers who promise to stay for 12 months. A few au pair agencies place European and Asian women with working holiday visas in live-in positions, normally for a minimum of three months. Not all placements require childcare experience. Try any of the following:

Australian Nanny & Au Pair Network: ☎ (+61) 8 9206 4679; www.aupairnetwork.com.au. Places au pairs and demi pairs in the Perth area, who want to work fewer hours so they can spend more time learning English; placement fee $400.

Dial-an-Angel: ☎ (+61) 1300 859199; www.dial-an-angel.com.au. Long-established agency with franchised branches throughout Australia. Now focuses more on live-in elder care.

Family Match Au Pairs & Nannies: ☎ (+61) 2 4363 2500; www.familymatch.com.au. Agency places many working holidaymakers; 25–35 hours per week for pocket money of $180–$250 plus all live-in expenses.

People for People: ☎ (+61) 2 9971 1393; www.peopleforpeople.com.au. Welcomes working holidaymakers for positions in Sydney only. Starting wage of $240 per week (live-in) for 30 hours per week.

Smart Au Pairs: ☎ (+61) 2 9451 3888; www.smartaupairs.com.au. Places au pairs throughout Australia. Member of IAPA.

Most agencies will expect to interview applicants and check their references before placement. As in America, a driving licence is a valuable asset. As well as long-term posts, holiday positions for the summer (December–February) and for the ski season (July–September) are available. Matt Tomlinson worked as a nanny in a ski resort on the strength of the year he'd spent as an au pair in Paris: '*Being a male nanny in Australia was an interesting experience. I got used to being asked if I was a child molester. On the upside, I was also offered a number of live-in jobs in Melbourne. And in case you're wondering, yes, I did get a lot of ribbing from the guys when I told them what job I was doing.*'

Anyone considering a childcare position may be interested in Rowena Caverly's experiences: *'I looked after a 15-month-old boy at a permaculture farm set in a rainforest. The job taught me new skills daily, such as how to persuade a baby that the Huntsman Spider on the wall really does not want to play. My task in summer was to teach him to toddle heavily to scare off snakes. Otherwise a nasty situation might have developed (and my money would not necessarily be on the baby as the victim).'*

FISHING

It is sometimes possible to get work on prawn fishing vessels out of Broome, Darwin, Cairns, Townsville, Bowen or even Karumba on the Gulf of Carpentaria. You can either try to get work on smaller privately owned boats or with one of the big companies such as Raptis (crew@raptis.com.au; www.raptis.com.au) which operates 11 trawlers out of Karumba in Far North Queensland and three in South Australia from Adelaide and Port Lincoln.

There has also been a recent geographical shift from Darwin to Cairns. The prawn fleets usually spend eight to ten weeks from March catching banana prawns, and then go out in August/September for tiger prawns, with the season finishing by Christmas. Trawlers depart from the Frances Bay mooring basin in Darwin, invariably referred to as the Duck Pond, in mid-April and return at the beginning of June. The skippers complain that they can't get enough labour. A manager at one of the biggest companies Austral Fisheries (www.australfisheries.com.au) wrote: *'Working on our boats can be, and usually is, hard physical work with long hours that can be financially and personally rewarding. We are more than happy to give someone a start if they are prepared to commit themselves to the task. Going to sea can be a trip to self enlightenment or a trip from hell, it's all up to the individual.'* The website gives the names and email addresses of the people to contact if you are interested in an opportunity to join either their Southern Ocean fishing fleet or their Northern Prawn Fleet.

Any traveller who goes down to the docks at the beginning of the season has a chance of being taken on for a short trip, even without experience, though wages will be a fraction of those earned by the old hands, as Sam Martell learned:

> *After chatting to some Aussies in Darwin, the allure of $15,000 over six weeks was too tempting. So I trooped down to the harbour with a few beers to bribe my way and chatted to some fishermen and got shown around a couple of boats. Unfortunately I found that because I was 'green' I would not be paid what everyone else was. Rather than $2,500 a week it would be $300 – definitely not worth it as it works out at about $4 an hour. Only those who are gluttons for punishment or with experience should try the prawn trawlers. There are other fishing boats around though.*

The main jobs assigned to male deckhands are net mending and prawn sorting. Work is especially demanding during the banana prawn season of April/May, since banana prawns travel in huge schools which are caught in one fell swoop, requiring immediate attention. Much of the fishing for tiger prawns takes place at night. Women are taken on as cooks. They should make it quite clear before leaving harbour whether or not they wish to be counted among the recreational facilities of the boat, since numerous stories are told of the unfair pressures placed on women crew members at sea. In addition, some women complain that they are expected not only to cook but to help sort out sea snakes and jellyfish from the catch. Men are not immune to problems, of course: if the skipper takes a dislike to any of his crew, he can simply leave them stranded on an island or beach.

Pearling is an industry that takes place in relatively remote places and makes extensive use of itinerant labour, provided they are willing and strong. The inclusion of fishing and pearling on the list of kinds of work specified to make you eligible for a second working holiday visa proves that this is an industry chronically short of labour. Pearling gets its own heading on the working traveller job site: www.jobaroo.com/job-pearling. The capital is Broome where you can simply ask at the companies farming oysters. The harvest season lasts from April/May to September, though there are jobs year round. Work on the boats can be live-aboard or not, but in either case means very early mornings and hard physical work, which will be rewarded with a good wage with all expenses paid. Pearling companies operate out of Exmouth and Broome on the coast of WA north to the Coburg Peninsula near Darwin.

CONCLUSION

Ian Fleming sums up what many working travellers have observed about Australians:

> *The opinion that we formed regarding Australian employers is that they are hard but fair. They demand a good day's work for a fair day's pay, and if you do not measure up to their expectations they will have no hesitation in telling you so. I also found the Aussies to be much more friendly and helpful than antici-pated and very easy to socialise with (in spite of the fact that I was nicknamed 'P.B.' for Pommy Bastard).*

There is a marvellous range of jobs even if you are unlikely to repeat Sandra Grey's coup of being paid for three hours' 'work' testing a sunscreen on her lily-white back, or Jane Thomas's bizarre jobs, one in a sex-change clinic, the other in a morgue typing up the labels for dismembered parts of bodies.

Even after several setbacks with bosses and jobs, Louise Fitzgerald concludes: *'To anybody not sure about going, I'd say, go, you'd be stupid not to. Australia is a wonderful country and the Australians are great people, even if the males do have a tendency to be chauvinists. If you prove to them you're as good as they are, they tend to like you for it!'*

New Zealand

New Zealand is a charmingly rural country where four and a half million human beings are outnumbered by sheep by six to one, although it should be noted that the sheep-to-citizen ratio has fallen to less than a third of its level 25 years ago. While the main cities become more sophisticated by the year, they remain friendly and manageable in scale. Travellers have found hitch-hiking easy, the backpacker hostels congenial, camping idyllic (when it's dry) and the natives very hospitable. The minimum wage is NZ$15.25 (as of 2017) plus 8% holiday pay, equivalent at the time of writing to over £8.50. Unfortunately wages won't go as far as they used to since the cost of living has been steadily rising in recent years and the country is now ranked ninth in the world for cost of living, three places above Australia.

The country has still not recovered from the grievous blow it was dealt in February 2011 when the historic centre of Christchurch was devastated by an earthquake, killing several backpackers among the 172 confirmed dead. Recurring aftershocks have damaged attempts at repairing buildings and sewerage systems, and it will be a long time before Christchurch will regain its former status as a safe and welcoming haven for backpackers. The national unemployment rate dipped below 5% at the end of 2016, which is the lowest it has been since the 2008 financial crisis. Unemployment is lowest in the South Island, partly because so many people are employed in the Canterbury rebuild programme. Supplementing your travel funds with temporary jobs, cash-in-hand work, odd jobs or work-for-keep arrangements is usually not only quite easy in New Zealand but good fun as well. Camping on beaches, fields and in woodlands is generally permitted. Even more than elsewhere in the world, backpackers' accommodation in New Zealand is a good place to hear about local opportunities for casual work, particularly the ubiquitous fruit picking.

REGULATIONS

New Zealand deserves its national reputation for friendliness to visitors. Tourists from the UK need no visa to stay for up to six months, while Americans, Canadians and Europeans can stay for three visa-free months. Young travellers entering the country might be asked to show an onward ticket and about NZ$1,000 per month of their proposed stay. In practice, respectable-looking travellers are most unlikely to be quizzed at entry.

The UK Working Holiday Scheme has been deemed so successful in addressing severe labour shortages in seasonal work that the maximum duration is now 23 months (also for Canadians), and the quota has been removed. The scheme allows any eligible Briton aged 18–30 to obtain a working holiday visa, allowing her or him to do temporary or full-time jobs in New Zealand. Applicants must declare that they have at least NZ$4,200 with which to support themselves for a year, plus a flight out of New Zealand (or enough extra to cover it). Those who apply for the 23-month visa or who extend their 12-month visa while in New Zealand must obtain a medical certificate including chest X-ray from a doctor and radiology clinic on the government's approved list. On the two-year visa validity, participants are permitted to work for up to 12 months, either consecutively or cumulatively and are expected to travel the rest of the time. Admirably clear, comprehensive and up-to-date information can be obtained about working holiday and all visas from Immigration New Zealand's site www.immigration.govt.nz.

Applications for all working holiday schemes can be done online so that you can apply from anywhere in the world, and these will be finalised within 48 hours. The fee (currently NZ$208/£125) will be payable by credit card or bank draft at the time of application. Other working holiday schemes (maximum duration one year) are open to 42 other nationalities including Irish, American, German, Dutch and Japanese, mostly on a reciprocal basis. On most of these, there is a quota of participants starting from May or October, for example 100 Austrians and up to 1,150 Malaysians can join the scheme in any one year. Anyone who has worked for at least three months in horticulture or viticulture can apply to extend their working holiday visa by three months (for a fee of NZ$208).

An alternative to the working holiday visa for those who may not be eligible for a working holiday visa and who are prepared to 'plant, maintain, harvest or pack crops' in the horticulture and viticulture industries is the RSE visa scheme, which means you are given a permit to work for a Recognised Seasonal Employer for the length of time specified on the visa. A list of the 125 recognised employers can be consulted on Immigration New Zealand's website. The RSE category offers 9,500 places to overseas workers of all nationalities.

If you have contacts in New Zealand or special skills in short supply or a firm offer of employment before leaving the UK, you are entitled to apply for an Essential Skills Work Visa (for a non-refundable fee of £175). Your sponsoring employer in New Zealand may have to prove to Immigration New Zealand that it is necessary to hire a foreigner rather than an unemployed New Zealander. The work visa does not in itself entitle you to work, but does make it easier to obtain a work permit after arrival. If you are granted a work visa before departure it will allow you to stay for up to five years depending on your skills. (In general the term 'visa' is used for permission applied for from outside New Zealand, while 'permit' is for applications lodged within New Zealand.) If you think that permanent migration is a possibility, you must first submit an Expression of Interest (EOI) to Immigration New Zealand.

Special Schemes

BUNAC in London and in the USA (www.bunac.org) has a Work New Zealand programme that provides an 'IEP Work Exchange Visa' (unique to BUNAC) or ordinary working holiday visa, job assistance from BUNAC's partner organisation IEP in Auckland and other benefits for a programme fee of £600/US$645. Note that the upper age limit for the Work Exchange programme is 35 rather than 30 and it is open to people who have already had a working holiday visa. These visas, limited in number, are released in mid-December.

Specialist gap year agency Letz Live based on the Gold Coast of Queensland has recently teamed up with UK-based Tutors Worldwide to arrange for school leavers to spend an academic year at prep schools and high schools around New Zealand (www.letzlive.org/new-zealand). Posts involve a lot of coaching and supervision of sporting activities. The programme fee is A$2,450 in addition to the A$125 application fee; the closing date for British applicants falls in early January for a start date in July.

North Americans who want to join a programme to work in New Zealand can look into CCUSA's Work Adventures Down Under programme (www.ccusa.com) which charges a fee of US$750, while Canadians up to the age of 35 can be assisted by SWAP (www.swap.ca). A small company in

Wellington, Internship New Zealand (www.internship-nz.com), helps foreign graduates to fix up paid and unpaid positions in a variety of sectors including of course tourism and hospitality; the fee is in excess of US$1,000. The company's UK partner is IST Plus (www.istplus.com).

New Zealand Job Search (info@jobsearchnewzealand.com; www.workingholiday.co) is a specialist Job Search service for backpackers looking for employment in New Zealand. Located at Base Backpackers Auckland in the city centre (Level 3, 229 Queen Street; ☎ (+64) 800 462 396; auckland@stayatbase.com), Job Search packages includes a 12-month membership and other perks, eg a couple of nights' accommodation, airport transfer and mail service.

Anyone who has at least a year's experience on a dairy farm and is familiar with milking machines might make contact with NZ Dairy Careers in Canterbury (www.nzdairycareers.co.nz). They run an internship programme for international candidates who pay a fee from NZ$4,000 to cover work visa, training, career support and pastoral care throughout the year.

Tax

Employers will always expect to see a tax number from the Inland Revenue Department (IRD). Without a tax number you will be taxed at an emergency rate. Information about how to apply, including a downloadable application form (IR742) is available from the IRD site www.ird.govt.nz; the form together with your passport (with working holiday visa), proof of bank account and either a driving licence or an offer of employment in New Zealand must be taken for verification to a main post office or to an office of the Automobile Association. You must put down a physical address on the form, not a PO Box number; many hostels will be happy to allow you to use their address. Processing will take up to three weeks, though in other places it is just 48 hours. The IRD freephone (in NZ) number is ☎ (+64) 800 227774.

People who have worked for part of the year may be eligible for a tax rebate. Information about filing a tax return IR1005 on leaving New Zealand is available online. Make sure you keep all your Summary of Earnings slips, plus you will have to show proof of full payment for permanent departure out of the country. Any money due to you – as much as 20% of earnings – will be paid into a nominated bank account, ideally a New Zealand account. In Roger Blake's case the processing took three months but eventually a rebate of NZ$130 was posted to his home address in the UK which he thought worth the bother.

CASUAL WORK

Because New Zealand has a limited industrial base, most temporary work is in agriculture and tourism. As in Australia, backpackers' hostels and campsites are the best sources of information on harvesting jobs and other casual work. Farmers often make contact with hostels and backpackers' lodges looking for seasonal workers as Ian Fleming observed: *'During our travels around the North and South Islands, the opportunity to work presented itself on several occasions. While staying in the Kerikeri Youth Hostel, we discovered that the local farmers would regularly come into the hostel to seek employees for the day or longer. My advice to any person looking for farm work would be to get up early as the farmers are often in the hostel by 8.30am.'*

Alternatively local farmers cooperate with hostel wardens who collate information about job vacancies or they may circulate notices around youth hostels, for example, 'Kiwifruit Picking Work Bay of Plenty Available March–May; apply Bell Lodge Working Backpacker Hostel, Tauranga' so always check the hostel board. At the same time, be on your guard as Roger Blake warns:

> *After a couple of weeks in Auckland with a little work here and there I was barely breaking even as the cost of living is quite high. Acting on an ad I had seen on the YHA noticeboard, I phoned a hostel in Hastings that had placed an ad for 30 apple pickers 'needed immediately' which they confirmed. So the next day I jumped on a bus to Hastings. Although a few of the travellers there were working, the others were hanging on for another day as work was assured, 'maybe tomorrow'. After a week I had learned for myself that the season was late. A warning that hostels can and do use these tactics to fill their beds.*

The website www.backpackerboard.co.nz has lots of current job listings and tips on budget travel for backpackers in New Zealand. Two adverts spotted in 2017 were offering free accommodation in exchange for three hours of maintenance work a day at Geeky Gecko Backpackers in Dunedin and another urgently needed onion seed pickers near Wellington who were to be paid NZ$16.85 an hour. Similarly, the Noticeboard part of the Budget Backpackers Hostels group website (www.bbh.co.nz) includes job information, mainly in BBH hostels around the country. Decent discounts on hostel stays are available to BBH members; membership costs NZ$45.

A good resource is *Seasonal Work NZ* (www.seasonalwork.co.nz), which provides updated details on job vacancies. Try also www.seasonaljobs.co.nz where job listings are taken down after four weeks. The general site www.seek.co.nz can also be helpful.

After the engine of Roger Blake's camper van blew up, he scoured the hostel noticeboards of Wellington and fixed himself up with a cleaning job on a work-for-accommodation basis. Many travellers are dotted around New Zealand cleaning in hostels for three hours each morning six days a week in return for a free dorm bed.

Louise Hawkes spent more than a year doing a variety of transient jobs that kept her afloat:

> *The majority of work I did was in the hospitality industry, as a waitress, barmaid or barista. I even managed a backpackers' for six months in beautiful Kaikoura, which was a lovely change from waiting on tables. Other little jobs picked up along the way included working on a vineyard planting and guarding vines, driving a tractor on a farm, thinning kiwis on a kiwifruit farm and working in a barley field pulling out wild oats.*

Rural employers almost always give preference to hiring people with their own vehicle. Matt Tomlinson recommends buying a vehicle to travel and job-hunt in New Zealand. He bought one at a used car place in Manukau City. Also try the Ellerslie Car Fair in South Auckland every Sunday morning (www.carfair.co.nz) or online backpacker noticeboards as well as www.autotrader.co.nz where you might be lucky enough to find a decent vehicle for under NZ$2,000. The backpackers' car market that takes place at 20 East Street in Auckland city centre (www.backpackerscarmarket.co.nz) is praised by backpackers as a quick and efficient place to shop (or sell). Staff will help organise mechanical checks and advise on insurance and legalities. A similar market takes place in Christchurch, near the corner of Colombo and Battersea Streets. Look for a vehicle with a couple of months of WOF remaining (Warrant of Fitness, equivalent to MOT).

Greenpeace frequently recruits fundraisers (www.greenpeace.org/new-zealand). The job involves standing around in a busy shopping area and trying to persuade people to sign up for a monthly direct debit donation to Greenpeace. Telefundraisers are also in high demand; the starting wage in 2017 for all positions is just under $20 an hour.

If planning to be in or near Dunedin for a period of time, you could see if Zenith Technology is conducting any clinical trials in which you might be able to pick up a few hundred dollars for a weekend's volunteering (☎ (+64) 3 477 9669; www.zenithtechnology.co.nz).

RURAL AND CONSERVATION VOLUNTEERING

World Wide Opportunities on Organic Farms (WWOOF) NZ is active and popular, with more than 1,500 hosts mainly on farms and smallholdings, which welcome volunteers to work in exchange for food and accommodation. Membership in WWOOF NZ costs NZ$40 and gives online access to profiles of these hosts with whom you can arrange to stay (www.wwoof.co.nz). WWOOF hosts occasionally have leads for paid work in market gardens, nurseries and on conventional farms.

Another organisation matches working visitors with about 350 farmers throughout New Zealand. Farmstays can last from three days to several months. Farm Helpers in New Zealand in Palmerston North (www.fhinz.co.nz) charges NZ$25 for their membership booklet containing all the addresses. No experience is necessary and between four and six hours of work a day are requested. The coordinator advises that hosts in the Auckland area tend to be oversubscribed, so that it is best to head into the countryside. Another possibility is the free internet-based exchange of work-for-keep volunteers that can be found at www.helpx.net, where an impressive 4,792 hosts in New Zealand are listed. Originally set up by a British backpacker in New Zealand, the scheme is flourishing and expanding. Free membership allows you to list yourself as a willing volunteer, but in order to contact hosts directly, you must upgrade to premier membership for €20 for two years.

Adrienne Robinson and her partner and young son joined FHiNZ and arranged two enjoyable farmstays. Because they were looking for farms at the height of the summer and at Christmas, they found that many of the listed farms were already booked up for that period. Although finding hosts willing to accept children is more difficult, they found that the general picking, weeding and mulching work they were asked to do was fairly easy to manage alongside three-year-old Jordan.

Among travel bloggers who have described their WWOOFing experiences, Mark Coole is among the more enthusiastic as he moved from host to host. Typically he would be picked up at the nearest hostel to be driven deep into the bush, in one instance by German hosts who had spent a year sailing a yacht downunder and then settled. Another blogger from Finland expected a WWOOF place called Treehugger Organics to be alternative and hippy-ish but was surprised to find their motto was something like 'cheap food, meat, alcohol, and more meat and alcohol'. They were mildly disappointed, especially when they were set the less-than-glamorous task of picking and packing strawberries for six hours a day. But the other WWOOFers were 'super nice' and she decided she had found the best WWOOF job ever: bottle-feeding a piglet called Weeman.

The New Zealand Department of Conservation (DOC) carries out habitat and wildlife management projects throughout New Zealand involving volunteers and working with local communities. Their website www.doc.govt.nz/volunteer lists all sorts of interesting sounding volunteer projects from counting bats to cleaning up remote beaches and maintaining historic buildings. Most (but not all) require a good level of fitness. DOC also needs volunteer hut wardens at a variety of locations.

Conservation Volunteers New Zealand with offices in Auckland and Christchurch (www.conservationvolunteers.co.nz) is a not-for profit organisation which accepts overseas volunteers to monitor wildlife, plant trees, maintain tracks and so on. Overseas volunteers can book a package lasting from one week up costing approximately A$365 a week.

The easily confused New Zealand Trust for Conservation Volunteers (NZTCV) lists ongoing conservation projects of all kinds to counteract the loss of native bush and wildlife. Details are available at www.conservationvolunteers.org.nz. NZTCV has created a central database on which individuals can register in order to be put in touch with organisations running conservation projects.

PAUL BAGSHAW, FROM KENT, AND HIS GIRLFRIEND SPENT A THOROUGHLY ENJOYABLE WEEK ON AN UNINHABITED ISLAND IN MARLBOROUGH SOUND MONITORING KIWIS, THE FLIGHTLESS BIRD WHOSE NUMBERS HAVE BEEN SERIOUSLY DEPLETED. AN ONGOING PROGRAMME REMOVES THEM FROM THE MAINLAND TO SMALL ISLANDS WHERE THERE ARE NO PREDATORS:

The object of the exercise was to estimate the number of kiwis on Long Island north of Picton. As the kiwi is nocturnal, we had to work in the small hours. As it's dark, it's impossible to count them so we had to spread out and walk up a long slope listening for their high-pitched whistling call. During the day they hide in burrows and foliage so it is very rare to see one. One night, when we heard one rustling around our camp, my girlfriend went outside with a torch and actually managed to see it. She was so excited that she couldn't speak and resorted to wild gesticulations to describe its big feet and long beak. The island has no water source except rainwater that collects in tanks; all very basic. We lived in tents and prepared our own meals from supplies brought over from the mainland. Our one luxury was a portaloo.

FRUIT PICKING

The climate of New Zealand lends itself to fruit and vegetable growing of many kinds including not only the apples and kiwifruit well known from every British supermarket but carrots, citrus fruit and other produce. Just turning up in towns and asking around is usually a safe bet for work while the harvest is on. To give some idea of the scale, an estimated 25,000 seasonal workers are needed to harvest and pack the bumper crop of kiwifruit each year. Hourly rates start at the minimum wage of NZ$15.25, though most fruit and vegetable farmers or harvesting contractors pay contract rates (piecework) which will be less lucrative until you are experienced enough to work up some speed. Technically all workers should earn at least the minimum plus holiday pay of 8% of gross earnings, but it doesn't always work out this way. As always harvesters of premium grades of fruit such as the successful Gold variety will be paid hourly to discourage haste in picking that damages the fruit, while green kiwifruit pickers are paid piecework.

Below are some general guidelines as to what areas to head for. Motueka/Nelson, the Bay of Plenty (Tauranga/Katikati), Hawke's Bay and Northland (Kerikeri) are the favourites among travellers. Most farmers are able to provide some kind of shack or cottage accommodation (known as a 'bach' in the North Island, a 'crib' in the South), though the spring and summer weather is suitable for camping provided you have a good waterproof tent. Farmers often provide fresh fruit and vegetables, milk and sometimes lamb, or organise end-of-harvest barbecues with free drinks. As Roger Blake concluded after picking pears in Motueka, 'very nice people Kiwis!' If the farmer doesn't have accommodation, you can stay in backpackers' hostels or holiday parks/campsites. Long stays in the off-season can be as cheap as NZ$110 a week (as in the case of the Rotten Apple Backpackers in Hastings).

The abundance of work is astonishing. The following ad (from Trevelyan's Pack & Cool Ltd near the North Island town of Te Puke) is typical: 'There are all sorts of jobs available from mid-March to late October. All you need is a good attitude and a smile on your face and we will teach you the rest' (www.trevelyan.co.nz/#/employment). In fact most of the 1,200 seasonal staff of stackers, packers, tray liners, trolley operators and so on are taken on between April and June. Useful sites such as www.seasonaljobs.co.nz, www.seasonal-work.co.nz and www.backpackerboard.co.nz have already been mentioned. PickNZ has a number of regional seasonal labour coordinators in the relevant regions, namely Northland, Hawke's Bay, Waikato, Bay of Plenty, Marlborough, Wairarapa, Nelson and Central Otago with a centralised info line (☎ (+64) 800 PICKNZ/742569) and links to the regional email and office addresses from www.picknz.co.nz. Another good idea is to follow up some of the 125 Recognised Seasonal Employers listed on the Immigration New Zealand website such as Aongatete in Katikati (www.coolstore.co.nz/employment.html).

FRUIT AND VEGETABLE HARVESTS

AREA	CROP	SEASON
Nelson/Blenheim/Motueka	Apples (also pears, peaches)	February/March/April
Motueka	Apple thinning	mid-November/December
Blenheim	Cherries	late December/January
Wairau Valley (Marlborough area)	Cherries, grapes	December
Nelson/Tapawera	Raspberries	December
Kerikeri (Bay of Islands)	Peaches, apricots	December/January
	Citrus packing	October/November late
	Kiwifruit	April
Northland (peninsula north of Auckland)	Kiwifruit	May
	Strawberries	mid-October

Pukekohe (just south of Auckland)	Kiwifruit	May
Poverty Bay (Gisborne)	Kiwifruit	May
Poverty Bay Flats	Grapes	from February
Tauranga/Te Puke (Bay of Plenty)	Citrus	October/November
	Kiwifruit	May/July
	Avocadoes	October-March
Clive/Napier (Hawke's Bay)	Apples, pears and grapes	late February/April
	Pruning work	June
Hastings	Tomatoes, apples	late February/April
Ohakune	Carrots	June
Martinborough (north of Wellington in the Wairarapa area)	Grapes	March
Central Otago (Alexandra and Roxburgh)	Plums, apricots	January/February
	Apples, pears	March/April
Christchurch area	Peaches	March
	Apples, berries and mixed fruit	January–May
	Potatoes	January–March
Invercargill	Tulips	early December

Bay of Plenty

The Bay of Plenty is where the majority of New Zealand's kiwifruit is grown. The tiny community of Te Puke swells in number from 6,000 to 10,000 for the harvest that traditionally starts in late March (though it is best to arrive a week or two early to line up a job). One of the main sources of work info, Bell Lodge in Tauranga (www.bell-lodge.co.nz/kiwifruit_jobs.html), has links with contractors that form a triangle around Tauranga (Pyes Pa, Katikati, Paeangaroa). Picking in this area lasts six to eight weeks and the packing season extends to September. Farmers do not want to hire anyone who isn't planning to stay for at least a month. Workaholics can work evening shifts packing after a day in the orchards. An hourly wage is paid for this boring work (5pm–11pm). One employer to try is Aerocool south of Te Puke (jobs@aerocool.co.nz) which packs avocadoes over the Antipodean summer as well as kiwifruit in autumn and winter.

Hawke's Bay

The shortage of people to bring in the autumn harvests of apples and pears in the Hawke's Bay area can be acute. The area can absorb 15,000 workers, a seven-fold increase on the numbers needed outside the harvest times. Any working holidaymaker who shows up in early to mid-February at the apple orchards around Napier will almost certainly be taken on. Pruning work is also available in June.

Apollo Pac Ltd in Hastings and Whakatu (www.apolloapples.co.nz) operates a large apple pack-house and storehouse in Hawke's Bay employing several hundred graders and packers in the season between mid-February and July. The site for Mr Apple NZ Ltd in Hawke's Bay (www.mrapple.com/employment-opportunities) links to 15 orchards which welcome pickers and to a downloadable application form.

Travelling east, the largest carrot-producing region in the southern hemisphere is around Ohakune. Work is available for up to nine months of the year here. While waiting for the ski season to begin, Matt Tomlinson rang some farmers out of the *Yellow Pages* and was soon hired to pack carrots. High staff turnover means that hiring goes on continuously. The work is boring and hard and pays not much more than minimum wage.

Northland

The tropical far north of the country, which specialises in citrus growing, is another favourite destination. In addition to growers in the region, several major packing sheds employ a large number of casual workers in November/December. Contract pruning can be more lucrative than picking. Kiwifruit pickers normally work in gangs of 10 and are paid piecework, while kiwifruit packers and citrus pickers are paid by the hour. The six weeks between early April and mid-May is a busy kiwifruit season. For example Orangewood Ltd in Kerikeri (www.orangewood.co.nz/jobs) takes on seasonal staff to pack 1.5 million trays of kiwifruit between March and June. Any of the hostels in Kaitaia and Kerikeri will be able to advise such as Aranga Backpackers in Kerikeri (www.aranga.co.nz) which provides transport to the kiwifruit and mandarin orchards for a small fee and has tent sites which are available at discounted weekly rates in the off season; the weekly charge for a dorm bed is NZ$130. The hostel estimates that kiwifruit pickers will earn $12–$16 an hour in a good orchard, working five to eight hours a day. In Kaitaia, enquire about joining the mandarin gangs that work in the orchards managed by T&G (formerly Turner and Growers). T&G Global (https://careers.tandg.global) manages growing and packing around the country including citrus in Northland, glasshouse tomatoes south of Rotorua, and so on for which the company hires an army of seasonal workers each year. Mandarin thinning starts in early January and lasts four to six weeks.

Nelson/Motueka/Blenheim

The Nelson/Motueka area of the South Island is a great area for travellers for its jobs as well as its beaches. Many foreign travellers are hired for the apple harvest, and also at the apple packing and processing works in Stoke, just outside Nelson. One of the main employers of seasonal workers, whose numbers peak at 6,500 doing three shifts in the New Zealand autumn, is Enza Foods on Nayland Road in Stoke which hires its staff through T&G Global mentioned above. The season lasts from early March till September. Bonuses are paid for cleaning, night shifts and for completing the season. Note that workers must undergo a pre-employment urine test for drugs.

In Blenheim, make enquiries at the Grapevine hostel (29 Park Terrace; www.thegrapevine.co.nz) about local picking, packing and pruning work in local vineyards. Duncannon Backpackers (www.duncannon.co.nz) is allied with Hortus Ltd, a vineyard management and labour supply company which books out the whole hostel in the winter. However casual workers can find jobs in the summer in the Marlborough wine industry. Rob Abblett spent several months earning money in the South Island. Apple thinning between mid-November and Christmas was fairly lucrative though he fared less well with contract cherry picking around Blenheim for six weeks from late November or early December:

> *The season starts with select picking (on 20 November) on which nobody made any wages worth bothering about. Things picked up after the first two or three weeks but unfortunately many back-packers were paid by the kilo throughout the season, even on select picking. I was aghast to earn a pittance in the first week and not much more the second. Way too fickle a fruit. Yeah, in an excellent year with good pollination, ideal weather and a good orchard, it might be possible to earn NZ$800 a week (the figure used by the orchard owners to motivate the thoroughly disillusioned backpackers). But in a bad or average year, I would stick with apple thinning.*

Many employers can be found by trawling the internet as well as asking locally. For example the wine giant Pernod Ricard describes its staffing needs as 'endless' to prune and wrap vines in their Marlborough and North Canterbury vineyards from June to September and to carry out hand harvesting in March/April (www.pernod-ricard-nz.com/people/seasonal-work).

Roger Blake stayed on in 'Mot' (Motueka) until the season ended in June:

> *It has been three months since I arrived in this small town which is a haven for working travellers (plenty of hippies in these parts). Surrounded by the marvellous Mount Arthur, Motueka is the gateway to the*

world famous Abel Tasman National Park that has fantastic walking trails. I came to Mot to work with a friend and have been flat out ever since. The first job was a three-week stint picking pears that was good as it goes (fruit picking is really fun, not!) then I went to an orchard to pick apples. But I hated every minute of it and quit on my first day and was ready to up and leave the town, thoroughly disillusioned with this fruit-picking lark. As if by fate I got a job in a packing shed (apples and pears). The job is work as work is meant to be – monotonous and semi-hard labour. But for some reason I have enjoyed spending eight–14 hours a day for six days per week running back and forth between conveyor belts, sorting, standing tirelessly at a grader throwing out bad apples and (my preference) stacking the boxes after they are packed. And that for a pittance of a wage. Worked with a great crowd of people though which made work more of a social thing.

Although Roger calls his wage a pittance, he managed to save NZ$2,000 in three months, while living in a tent pitched at the holiday park on Fearon Street (☎ (+64) 3 528 7189; www.motuekatop10. co.nz) which gives seasonal workers a special affordable weekly rate.

Southland

Seasonal Solutions Co-op in Alexandra (17A Brandon St; www.ssco.co.nz) is the jobcentre for seasonal work in the region, and represents a large number of fruit and wine growing businesses in Central Otago. Current vacancies are listed on their Facebook page, though they are able to place only people who can register in person and are ready to start immediately. Cherries are picked in Otago over the winter with the peak period from just before Christmas to 20 January. Leaning Rock Cherries in Alexandra (www.leaningrockcherries.webs.com) accepts up to 200 pickers who camp on the farm, some of whom stay on for the apple harvest from mid-March to late April.

Massive investment in cherry production around Cromwell (not far from Alexandra) has created additional seasonal jobs for the area. For instance Orchard Fresh in Cromwell in Otago (www. 45s.co.nz/jobs.html) employ up to 350 picking and packing staff from mid-December to the end of January.

TOURISM

New Zealand is frequently voted the best country in the world in which to live or have a holiday. Enquiries in the US about migration to New Zealand surged by a factor of 24 right after Donald Trump won the US election. The tourist industry employs an enormous 7.5% of the country's workforce. Tourism creates many job opportunities, though most earn the minimum wage. Many tourist operations become very busy in February at the height of the cruise ship season. The tourist industry in New Zealand also adopts many adventurous and sporting guises. You might get taken on by a camping tour operator as a cook; or perhaps you could find a job on a yacht or in a ski resort (see below). One young British barista found lots of opportunities in his travels, from Wanaka in the South Island to a café at National Park railway station near Tongariro (www.thestationcafe.co.nz). He also enjoyed packing parachutes at a skydiving centre near Auckland.

New Zealand hoteliers and restaurateurs tend to be more relaxed than they are in Europe. Based on his experience of looking for catering work on the Auckland waterfront, Colm Murphy from Ireland recommends cold calling at all the bars and restaurants in the smart Viaduct Harbour, Princes Wharf, Parnell, Ponsonby and Jervois Road areas. Remember that the custom of tipping is relatively new to New Zealanders, though it is possible to make a little extra. Colm Murphy made up to NZ$100 a week in tips, especially when foreign tourists came to dine: *'Admittedly waiting on Kiwis is soul destroying. On numerous occasions I had big tables of 10–12 Kiwis and they never tipped me. They will thank you profusely for the service but they will not tip. To a certain type of Kiwi (especially those from south of the Bombay Hills, ie south of Auckland) tipping is an alien concept.'*

Well south of the Bombay Hills, the capital Wellington is not the first city you think of in the context of New Zealand tourism. But the base used by Peter Jackson in the making of the *Lord of the Rings* trilogy has brought fame and fortune to the city. It has a remarkably high ratio of cafés to citizens and a booming job market. Catharine Carfoot showed up there one November with a working holiday visa and easily found work first and accommodation second:

> I worked weekends driving for Wellington Cable Cars which has its ups and downs (cable car joke). And I was doing various things during the week, mostly temping through Select Appointments, and life modelling at the Inverlochy Art School and Vincents Art workshop. Bizarrely, I ended up practising my French conversation skills more than I had done for years, both at the Cable Car and with people met on the street asking for directions. It seems very odd that even the bigger hotels here don't always have a Francophone on duty.

Queenstown and the South Island

The lakeside resort of Queenstown is particularly brimming with opportunities. It is a town whose economy is booming due to both backpacker and general tourism and whose population is largely young and transient. Restaurants and bars (especially those that have been caught out in the past) invariably ask to see your working holiday visa.

Writing from Queenstown a few years ago, Roger Blake describes how he had set about the job-hunt:

> I arrived in Queenstown late one night with only NZ$90 in my pocket (and to my name). I immediately set about studying the internet café/backpackers noticeboards and phoned for every job going, no matter what. Early the following morning I got a call asking me if I could start work right away. (A mobile phone really is the most valuable asset to gaining work.) Since then I have been a builder's mate, a landscape gardener, deliveries off-sider, done house and furniture removals, dug holes for scientists, dug trenches, planted trees, been a refuse collector and much more besides. Generally only working Monday to Friday, my average week was around 45 hours (optional weekend work is available but I chose to enjoy them otherwise). Quite an achievement to save money in Queenstown with so much temptation and so many establishments willing to take your money. After four months here (and having had a damn good time in the process) I have saved a little over NZ$3,000.

Roger claims not to have met anyone who had a problem obtaining work in Queenstown whatever their nationality or visa status, though since then it has become tighter with no guarantees. As always in travellers' meccas, finding affordable accommodation is the main challenge. Roger shared a house with seven like-minded working travellers.

One of the perks of being a worker in Queenstown and therefore an honorary resident, is that workers can often get discounts on local activities such as rafting or bungee jumping. If you want to leave the scene behind, try ringing resort hotels in Milford Sound, Fox Glacier, Franz Josef and Mount Cook to ask about job vacancies.

Ski Resorts

The ski season lasts roughly from July to October. Of the dozen commercial ski fields in the country, the main ones on the South Island are Coronet Peak and the Remarkables (serviced by Queenstown), Mount Hutt and Treble Cone (with access from Wanaka). On the North Island, Mount Ruapehu is the main ski area, at least when its volcanic activity is dormant. The ski field at Turoa is serviced by the resort of Ohakune and the ski area of Whakapapa by the settlement called National Park; the former opens in the last week of June and the latter a week later.

Catering and related jobs are widely available in these resort towns. In addition to a wage, you may be given a lift pass and subsidised food and drink. Matt Tomlinson enjoyed his two jobs in Ohakune as a barman in the ski resort bar and a waiter in a restaurant, though he came to the conclusion that New Zealand bosses like to get their money's worth. When there weren't many customers, he was put to work building shelves, chopping wood and cleaning drains. He found the jobs by checking local noticeboards and asking around. Altogether the Ruapehu/Ohakune area absorbs hundreds of seasonal workers so there is plenty of scope. One of the main employers in the area is Ruapehu Alpine Lifts Ltd (Private Bag, Mount Ruapehu; www.mtruapehu.com; click on Jobs), which accepts applications until mid-April and interviews candidates in the weeks following. You will also have to keep your ears open if you are to find affordable accommodation.

The biggest company on the South Island is NZSki Ltd whose employment pages can be found at www.nzski.com/employment/NZSkiJobs.jsp covering opportunities at Coronet Peak, the Remarkables and Mount Hutt-Methven ski areas. Recruitment opens 1 March each year, though you can send in an expression of interest in the preceding summer. If you have a specific skill, eg ski or snowboard instructor, ski patroller, ski hire technician, snowcat/plough driver, then it is worth applying to the resort in advance. Opportunities also exist for carpenters and painters in the months before the season begins; ask around in the pubs. Most resorts are linked from http://skicentral.com/newzealand.html.

A level III BASI certificate (or the Irish equivalent IASI) is essential to get full-time instructing work. Part-timers or rookie instructors usually get a lift pass plus instructor training sessions and loggable hours of practice. Snowboard instructors are in demand. A number of New Zealand ski schools are beginning to offer instructor training to people from the northern hemisphere including Snow Trainers in Queenstown (www.snowtrainers.com) and the Rookie Academy in Wanaka (www.rookieacademy.com). These will cost a cool NZ$15,500–NZ$16,900 for 11 weeks.

Fishing

Fishing is a profitable business for New Zealand and fishermen (seldom fisherwomen) can be found in most coastal towns. Nelson is one of the important centres for fishing and fish processing, though in the past few years companies like Sealord have been scaling back operations and reducing staff. The giant seafood business Talley's (www.talleys.co.nz/careers/land-based-vacancies) might be a better bet. They hire workers to unload their boats at nine different depots around the South Island, which is a very tough job. The company also opens and packs mussels mainly between November and June, although a lot of mussel processing has moved to Tauranga in the North Island; try North Island Mussel Processors Ltd (www.nimpl.co.nz) who pay piecework rates, so it will take a while before you are adept at opening enough shells to make a reasonable wage; the season here lasts from January to June.

Of course recreational fishing creates work, as the American Chris Miksovsky describes:

> *Queenstown was such a nice place that I decided to stay for a while. I happened upon a job with a chartered fishing boat business. We'd take small groups of angler-wannabes out in a motorboat and try to help them catch some rainbow trout or lake salmon. I got to go on several outings but mostly I sat at a small desk by our dock in the town harbour giving information to people about the trips and getting a commission on the trips I booked. The money was excellent some days (NZ$150 was my record) and nil others, all paid cash in hand. It was probably the most relaxing and scenic job I've ever had, right on the water, surrounded by mountains, watching the tourists of the world go by. The only downside was that I often had to listen to die-hard fishermen go on and on about all the fish they'd caught around the world. The Americans were the worst: 'Now y'all see that there Barracuuuuda?' (pointing to photo), 'I caught that big ol' boy in Faayjaay. Tuk me fowr hours to brang that there sucker in.'*

Busking

Auckland and Wellington both purport to be busker-friendly cities and do not charge a fee for the necessary licence. Queenstown is said to be a goldmine for street performers. It is the kind of town where evening strollers, almost all tourists, will welcome and reward a short entertainment.

World traveller Anna Ling tried out her growing musical skills in the capital. She and some other musician-travellers with whom she had formed a band on the South Island decided to take Wellington by storm, but soon learned that it was not as easy to get gigs as they had hoped. Anna decided to supplement her income by busking with her guitar in a spot recommended by some people she had met at the Rainbow Gathering in New Zealand. Contrary to expectations, it wasn't a high-profile spot downtown, where you would be expected to have a busking licence from the Council, but a less prepossessing place outside a suburban shopping centre. It had the advantage of being not far from where she was staying, as a couchsurfer at a Maori marae. The advice she had been given proved sound, and she was happy with her earnings which often amounted to NZ$20 an hour. This allowed her to drop a few pennies into the *koha* jar at the marae. Koha is the Maori word for a gift, often given by guests to hosts, and the jar by the door was one to which a stream of couchsurfers contributed.

BUSINESS AND INDUSTRY

Experienced office support admin and clerical staff may be in demand in Auckland and Wellington by the big agencies such as Adecco (www.adecco.co.nz) that has 15 branches. Office temps in the main cities generally earn NZ$20–$25 an hour, though telemarketers and clerks start on the minimum wage. Holiday pay of 8% is accrued.

EMILIANO GIOVANNONI SPENT SEVERAL SUCCESSFUL MONTHS IN TELESALES IN WELLINGTON:

There are lots of opportunities for travellers in Wellington to get a little job. The big thing seems to be telesales and telemarketing. There are loads of agencies recruiting people for that sort of job and no particular skills are required but to be able to 'blag' it. The money is reasonably good for New Zealand and it is easy clean work.

Randstad and Kelly Services in Wellington, Auckland and Christchurch have ongoing vacancies for call centre staff among others, or search for 'Sales – Inbound' and 'Sales – Outbound' on www.seek.co.nz. You can register only if you will be staying for a minimum of three months. Without office experience, try market research and labouring agencies, which sometimes require only an IRD number. Labouring agencies can be a good bet such as Allied Workforce with 34 branches which is the largest casual labour supplier in New Zealand (www.awf.co.nz).

During his two-year working holiday in New Zealand, round-the-world traveller and unicyclist James from Wakefield did many jobs. One of the most enjoyable was a stint at the Cookie Time factory in Christchurch. This iconic New Zealand company was started nearly 35 years ago by a young New Zealander back from his own working holiday in the USA. He decided that the large American cookie would be popular in New Zealand and, with his brother, built up an enormously successful business that employs backpackers in its labour-intensive cookie-making process (see www.cookietime.co.nz/recruitment.html).

TEACHING AND AU PAIRING

Shortages of early childhood, primary and secondary teachers of maths, sciences, technology and special education are so much less common these days that all branches of teaching have been removed from Immigration New Zealand's skills shortage lists and the old international relocation grants and automatic two-year visas are no longer offered.

Au Pair Link in Auckland invites applications from young people from abroad who want to spend up to a year working for a family (☎ (+64) 800 287247; www.aupairlink.co.nz). Au pairs are paid NZ$180–NZ$230 per 40-hour week and a completion bonus of NZ$20 a week for the agreed minimum period of six, nine or 12 months. The agency charges a non-refundable fee of NZ$899 which covers screening and matching, and support throughout. The Auckland-based company International Working Holidays (www.iwh.co.nz) liaises with agencies abroad to place foreign au pairs with New Zealand families.

ANTARCTICA

Britain's research stations including the main ones at Rothera and Halley, and two research vessels in Antarctica are overseen by the British Antarctic Survey in Cambridge (www.bas.ac.uk/jobs). Vacancies are for scientists, PhD researchers, tradespeople such as plumbers and electricians, IT engineers and many others. All support staff hired by BAS must be suitably qualified or experienced and willing to sign a fixed-term or open-ended contract normally for six or 18 months.

As well as the highly trained scientists and others needed to run an Antarctic research station such as McMurdo Station, a certain number of dogsbodies are needed. The United States Antarctic Program, managed by the National Science Foundation, sends about 3,000 people to Antarctica, a good number of whom are women (www.usap.gov/jobsAndOpportunities/index.cfm). Even though the work schedule is nine hours a day, six days a week, the unskilled jobs are massively oversubscribed, so perseverance will be needed, plus excellent health (physical, mental and dental) and a willingness to travel at short notice. According to a contributor to the forum about jobs on www.coolantarctica. com, people hired for the menial jobs are usually over-qualified, and it is not unknown for judges and pharmacists to work as shuttle drivers and galley slaves. All of this is discouraging for those who want to land one of the four-, six- or 12-month contracts as a support worker.

In 2012 Raytheon Polar Services lost the recruitment contract in the USA, so recruitment is now done through specific companies and agencies working for the US government (see www.usap.gov/ jobsandopportunities). The primary contractor is Leidos, a defence company in Virginia (www.leidos. com/civil/antarctic-support-contract-asc?host=h). Most hiring takes place between March and August for the austral summer work period of October to mid-February.

United States of America

The great American Dream has beckoned countless people who have left their homelands in eager pursuit of the economic miracle. America's image that was enhanced in so many circles by the presidency of Barack Obama is now struggling in those same quarters with the election of Donald Trump who has adopted a tough stance on immigration to the US. It is too early to tell whether the rules and barriers around exchange programmes that Obama was beginning to dismantle will be extended. Trump inherits a strong economy with a low unemployment rate of 4.7%, but with dangers ahead from uncertainty in housing and currency markets.

Despite the wide open spaces and warm hospitality so often associated with America, their official policies can be discouraging for the traveller who plans to pick up some casual work along the way. The choice of the word 'alien' in official use to describe foreigners may not be intentionally symbolic; however, it does convey the suspicion with which non-Americans are treated by the authorities. It is difficult to get permission to work. But as we have found in so many other countries, there are some special provisions and exceptions to the rule.

The most important exception is the special work visa, the J-1, available through work and travel programmes such as the ones run by BUNAC in London (☎ (+44) 33 3999 7516; www.bunac.org). Various programmes, including the summer camp agencies, are described in detail since they arrange for large numbers of people to work legitimately in the USA.

Other possibilities include joining the one-year Au Pair in America Programme (see section on Childcare below) or joining one of the work exchange or internship programmes, which require you to find your own position in your field of study. According to the US State Department Office of Exchanges there are many designated sponsors of the J-1 visa programme, searchable at http://j1visa.state.gov/programs.

The other side of the coin is working without permission; this carries a number of risks and penalties to be carefully considered beforehand. As described below, the laws are always changing in order to tighten up on security in general and black work in particular. The missing link between you and a whole world of employment prospects is a social security number to which you will not be legally entitled unless you have a recognised work visa.

VISAS

Under the Visa-Waiver Program, citizens of the UK and 37 other countries who have a machine-readable passport do not need to apply for a tourist visa in advance for stays of less than 90 days. However, they have to obtain prior authorisation via ESTA, the Electronic System for Travel Authorization, including people who are only in transit at an airport. ESTA permission can easily be obtained online (the only way) but there is a fee of US$14 (all dollar prices in this chapter are in US dollars). Be sure to go to the official government site (website ending 'gov') and not a commercial site attempting to imitate the official site but charging a premium. Individuals entering on the visa waiver programme are prohibited from changing their visa status after arrival. And of course engaging in paid or unpaid employment in the USA is prohibited, as it is if you arrive with a visitor visa for business or tourism.

Applicants for any category of non-immigrant visa for work or study, including of course the J-1, or anyone planning a trip that will last more than 90 days must obtain a visa from the US Embassy, which involves completing a long and detailed form, scheduling a face-to-face interview and paying a non-refundable fee of $160/£130. Check the Embassy website (www.uk.usembassy.gov/) for visa information and application forms.

The J-1 visa, available to participants of government-authorised programmes, known as Exchange Visitor Programmes (EVP), is a valuable and coveted addition to any passport since it entitles the holder to take legal paid employment. You cannot apply for the J-1 without the right form and you cannot get form DS2019 without going through a recognised Exchange Visitor Programme (such as BUNAC and Camp America) which have approved sponsors in the USA. Many programmes are available only to registered students.

Other Visas (Non J-1)

Apart from the J-1 visa available to people on approved EVPs, several possible visa categories can be considered, all of which must be applied for by the employer on the applicant's behalf and will take at least three months. The H category covers non-immigrant work visas in special circumstances. The H2-B is for temporary or seasonal vacancies (excluding agricultural work) that employers have trouble filling with US citizens. For example, the chronic shortage of workers on the ski fields of Colorado means that some employers can obtain the necessary Labor Certification confirming that there are no qualified American workers available to do the jobs. Other industries that use a large number of H2-B visa holders include landscape gardening firms, shrimp processors in Louisiana, the crab-picking industry on the eastern shores of Maryland, and beach resorts in the Carolinas.

Petitions for H2-B visas must be submitted by the employer to the United States Citizenship and Immigration Services (USCIS), which is a bureau of the Department of Homeland Security. The duration of the H2-B visa is one year, though it can be extended for a maximum of three years. The quota is currently 66,000 a year. Half are issued in the first half of the fiscal year (October–March) and the other 33,000 are released after that. The USCIS allows you to see how many petitions have been granted and are pending. For example in January 2017, about 23,000 had already been issued with 7,600 pending, leaving only about 2,000 until the release of the next tranche on 1 April. Holders of the H2-B must work only for the employer that has petitioned for their visa. The seasonal work visa specifically for agriculture is the H-2A (see www.foreignlaborcert.doleta.gov/h-2a.cfm).

President Obama's administration sought higher wages for holders of the guest worker visa in order to cut down on exploitation. Some large employers which traditionally hired many H2-B holders, such as the Steamboat Ski Resort and the Aspen Ski Company in Colorado, were not happy with the increased wages and no longer use the programme (www.steamboat.com/employment), preferring to hire foreign workers with J-1 visas (though they cannot sponsor them themselves). Note that various specialist employment agencies help and advise employers to apply for the H2-B visa and may keep a roster of international candidates looking for work. For example Peak Season Workforce on Cape Cod (www.PeakSeasonWorkforce.com) runs its Mama Visa network on Facebook for international workers looking for H2-B placement in the US for seasonal work. Similarly ExpressH2B Seasonal Labor Solutions in DC (www.expressh2b.com) invites applicants to fill seasonal summer or winter jobs in national parks, hotels, ranches, restaurants, sports leagues, construction sites, ski resorts, theme parks, etc.

The non-immigrant Q-1 visa is the 'Cultural Exchange Visa', affectionately dubbed the 'Disney' visa, since it was introduced partly in response to their lobbying for representatives to work at the national pavilions at the Epcot Theme Park in Florida. If you find a job in which it can be argued that you will be providing practical training or sharing the history, culture and traditions of your country with interested members of the American public (as at Epcot), you might be eligible to work legally for up to 15 months. This is potentially possible in amusement parks, restaurants, museums, summer schools, etc. As usual this visa must be applied for by the prospective employer in the USA and approved in advance by USCIS.

A few years ago a new visa was introduced for Australian passport holders with university degrees. The E3 is for Australians going to work in a speciality occupation. In some cases extensive experience in the field will suffice. The quota is a generous 10,500. It is exceedingly difficult (not to mention expensive) to get permanent residency or a 'green card' that allows foreigners to live and work in the USA as 'resident aliens'. Nearly all the permanent resident visas that are issued each year are given to close relations of American citizens or world experts in their field. Money and love are not the only reasons to marry, though this course of action is too drastic for most.

Arrival

If you have a visa/visa waiver, a return ticket and look tidy and confident, chances are you will whizz through immigration and be granted the specified 90-day stay. Note that you can cross land borders with a Visa Waiver as long as the crossing takes place within 90 days of your return ticket from North America to Europe.

Whatever you do at immigration, don't mention the word 'work' in any context. (Scholars who have let slip that they have come to 'work' in a library have been hauled off for a thorough investigation.) Dress neatly but remember to look like a tourist, not an aspiring professional. If you are taken away to be interviewed, expect to have your luggage minutely examined. Be prepared to explain anything in your luggage that an average sightseeing tourist would be unlikely to have, such as smart clothes (for possible interviews). Better still, don't pack anything which could be incriminating such as letters of reference or letters from an American referring to jobs or interviews. Having written proof that you have a full-time job to return to, property ties or a guaranteed place in higher education in the UK are also an asset. It can be helpful to provide the border official with a travel itinerary, a list of places and people you want to see in your capacity of tourist.

If you don't have much money or an onward ticket, it is a good idea to have the names of Americans willing to put you up or a letter from a friend, undertaking to support you for a month or so. Laurence Koe had asked his grandmother to type up a list of all their family connections on the continent, which he showed to the suspicious immigration officer at Hawaii Airport, accompanying it with a touching story of how it had been his boyhood dream to circle the globe.

WORK AND TRAVEL PROGRAMMES

A welter of exchange organisations help candidates from round the world to obtain a J-1 visa. Participants on a Summer Work & Travel Exchange Visitor Programme can work on a J-1 visa in any job for up to four months between 1 June and 30 September or for the winter season between 21 November and 30 April (see section on Ski Resorts below). After the work period finishes, they are permitted a further 30 days for pure travel in the USA.

BUNAC (Priory House, 6 Wrights Lane, London, W8 6TA; ☎ (+44) 33 3999 7516; www.bunac.org) administers one of the longest established Summer Work Travel programmes. BUNAC's Work America programme offers several thousand places to full-time degree-level students who may take virtually any job anywhere in the USA over the summer, though they must receive a confirmed job offer before the visa will be granted. In addition to BUNAC's registration fee of £599 for first-time applicants, you must submit a letter from your principal, registrar or tutor on college headed paper showing that you are a full-time degree-level student. The programme opens in mid-September each year and closes on 1 June, though BUNAC's deadline falls on 1 April because of the eight-week processing time. You are also required to purchase comprehensive insurance (eg $258 for four months) and take at least $800 in support funds. To assist applicants in finding work, BUNAC publishes hundreds of job vacancies in its online Job Zone; employers from ice-cream sellers on Martha's Vineyard to ranchers in Wyoming register their wish to hire BUNAC participants from year to year. The employer may provide accommodation, particularly if a British student takes a job in the hospitality industry. BUNAC are very experienced at guiding applicants as gently as possible through the processes.

In addition to BUNAC, the principal work and travel programmes (as distinct from career-oriented internship programmes described in the next section) are broadly comparable. A premium is charged when the agency fixes up a job for you, for example IST Plus charges £529 if you arrange your own job or £629 if you have one arranged for you. UK programmes that provide full-time university students with the opportunity to live and work in the USA for a maximum of four months include CCUSA's Work Experience USA (www.ccusa.co.uk), IST Plus (www.istplus.com/watusa) and Global Choices (www.globalchoices.co.uk). Note that a number of other student travel organisations place students from around the world in similar work and travel programmes. For example Student Placement Australia New Zealand assists Antipodeans and also offers a 12-month working programme for the USA (www.workandtravelusa.com.au).

Internships

Internships provide a chance to get some work experience in your career interest as part of your academic course or at a later stage to develop your career. Several of the UK organisations mentioned above like BUNAC and IST Plus (among others) are authorised to help candidates find work placements in the USA and obtain a J-1 visa valid for three to 18 months.

Separate J-1 programmes cater to students/recent graduates and to established professionals. The J-1 Intern programme is open to students currently enrolled in a post secondary academic institution outside the US or who have recently graduated no more than 12 months prior to the desired internship start date. The J-1 Trainee programme is for those who have already graduated and completed at least one year of work experience in their occupational field, or those who have already worked for at least five years in their field.

An Intern placement can take place at any time during your studies, during the summer, as a sandwich year or up to 12 months after graduating. Although you are responsible for finding your own course-related position, the programme organisers supply practical advice on applying for work and often a searchable database of internships/work placements. Programme fees differ but may start at £600 for students who can fix up their own position but can top £4,000 for non-students who want a placement arranged for them. IST Plus's fees rise the longer the internship, so £1,060 for six months and £1,405 for 12. Fees charged by MyEducation UK (www.myeducationuk.co.uk) span £1,095 for a six-month DIY placement to £4,495 for an 18-month business placement.

It is also possible to apply directly to a sponsoring agency in the US; nearly 100 are listed at https://j1visa.state.gov/participants including the well regarded CCI Greenheart exchange organisation in Chicago (www.cci-exchange.com). Other established agencies include Cultural Vistas (www.culturalvistas.org), InterExchange (www.interexchange.org) and the Alliance Abroad Group (www.

allianceabroad.com), all accredited to grant J-1 visas to European candidates and H2-B visas in the case of the latter.

SUMMER CAMPS

Summer camps are uniquely American in atmosphere, even if the idea has spread to Europe. An estimated eight million American children are sent to 10,000 summer camps each year for a week or more to participate in outdoor activities and sports, arts and crafts and generally have a wholesome experience. The type of camp varies from plush sports camps for the very rich to more or less charitable camps for disabled or underprivileged children. British young people are especially in demand as soccer coaches on summer camps.

It is estimated that summer camps employ nearly a third of a million people. Thousands of 'counsellors' are needed each summer to be in charge of a cabinful of youngsters and to instruct or supervise some activity, from the ordinary (swimming and canoeing) to the esoteric (puppet-making and circus skills). Several summer camp organisations are authorised to issue J-1 visas, primarily Camp America and BUNAC, but some smaller ones are also mentioned below.

After camp finishes, counsellors have up to six weeks' free time and normally return on organised flights between late August and the end of September. Camp counselling regularly wins enthusiastic fans and is worth considering if you enjoy working with children and don't mind hard work. Some camps are staffed almost entirely by young people from overseas, which can be useful if you are looking for a post-camp travelling companion. If the idea of working at a remote lakeside or mountain location appeals to you but the responsibility of keeping children entertained and well-behaved 24 hours a day does not, you might be interested in a behind-the-scenes job in the kitchen or maintenance. Camp directors often find it difficult to attract Americans to do these jobs, partly because the wages are low, and Camp America and other approved exchange organisations can arrange this for British students and many other nationalities.

Bear in mind that your enjoyment of a summer camp job will be largely determined by the style of the camp, the standard of facilities and its proximity to interesting places to visit on your days off. One way of making an informed choice is to attend one of the recruitment fairs held in the New Year by Camp America where you can meet camp directors.

There is no guarantee of placement as one unlucky student discovered. Rachel Frayling-Cork applied to the Scottish company Wild Packs (though it might have been any of them) during her second year at Newcastle University, and jumped through all the hoops that camp counsellor applicants have to jump through, including travelling down to London for the J-1 visa interview and paying the fee. But she never boarded a plane to the USA:

> *Originally applying in about March I assumed that by May I would know where I was going. With no news of a camp placement the company encouraged me to sign an agreement called 'Up in the Air' which meant that they could leave it until very short notice to place me at a camp. I was unsure whether or not to sign the document but did so on the basis of their email that said 'Last year we placed 100% of people who went for the Up in the Air option'. In the end I wasn't placed although I waited until the last moment, which meant that I had no back up summer plans or jobs. I can't use the visa so that was money thrown down the drain, and I had to be quite forceful when insisting that the whole fee be refunded. Although it was my decision to sign the agreement I feel that they misled me to feel over-confident.*

To rub salt into her wound, the friend with whom she had applied and who was offered a place on a camp in Pennsylvania had a brilliant summer, proved by a stream of photos on Facebook.

Amy Jones, a student at Nottingham University, was not so satisfied with her camp where she was working an 85-hour week after the only American counsellor left, and the couple who ran the camp were intimidating, no doubt worried that there would be more desertions. One of the new rules they imposed was that the staff were not permitted to speak to each other unless about camp organisation.

Amy's conclusion was that, seen from one point of view, the recruitment agencies supply cheap labour that are not at liberty to leave because they then forfeit their free flight.

Camps have to impose rules and in many cases these are quite strict, such as no alcohol. (Apparently Irish and Australian counsellors, true to their reputations, are the most likely to be fined for drinking at camp.)

Camp America

Camp America (37 Queens Gate, London SW7 5HR; ☎ (+44) 20 7581 7373; www.campamerica. co.uk) is a major recruitment organisation in Britain and worldwide, which arranges for more than 7,000 people aged 18 or over from around the world to work on children's summer camps in the USA. The work is for nine weeks between June and August where you could be teaching activities such as tennis, swimming and arts and crafts. Camp America provides a free return flight from London to New York and guidance on applying for a J-1 visa. The camp provides free board and lodging plus pocket money that will range from US$650 to US$1,200 depending on experience and qualifications. Upfront charges include the registration fees of £599, which includes £212 to cover insurance but excludes the US visa fee of $160 and the compulsory police check (£53).

AFTER THE FIRST YEAR OF HER SOFTWARE ENGINEERING COURSE AT BIRMINGHAM UNIVERSITY, VICTORIA JOSSEL SPENT A WONDERFUL SUMMER IN THE USA WITH CAMP AMERICA WHICH SHE FELT REALLY ENHANCED HER CV:

On 9 June, I apprehensively boarded my flight to Blue Star camp in North Carolina. Not only did I have the privilege of bonding with the children in my cabin from whom you receive constant love, caring and attention, but I also met new people from all over the world and received amazing references for my future career. I learned how to organise, motivate and lead people as well as negotiate positive outcomes to conflicts. From a normal 19-year-old girl, I became a responsible, motivated, adaptable and independent person with 14 children who were my responsibility. I had never been camping and had never wanted to go camping. Yet it was the most amazing experience: I learned to start a fire on my own, cook food for all 14 girls and organise it so the kids all got exactly the same amount of Hershey's chocolate.

One way to secure a placement early and avoid last-minute uncertainty is to attend one of Camp America's recruitment fairs in London, Manchester and Edinburgh in January and February, which is what Colin Rothwell did: *'At the recruitment fair, you could actually meet the camp directors from all over the States and find out more about particular camps. If you are lucky, like me and a thousand others, you can sign a contract on the spot. Then you leave all the "dirty work" to Camp America and wait until they call you to the airport in June sometime.'*

Camp America's other summer programme is Campower, for degree-level students who would like to work in the kitchen/maintenance areas at camp and earn a little more ($1,200 for the summer, unchanged for some years).

Other Summer Camp Organisations

Some of the other companies give you a choice about whether you want to have a 'free' flight arranged or whether you want to earn more at camp and arrange your own flight. The well-respected Camp Counselors USA or CCUSA (www.ccusa.co.uk) works with hundreds of camps in most states of the union and since 1986 has placed more than 200,000 young people over 18 from over 60 countries. CCUSA's programme includes return flight to the USA, one night's accommodation in New York City, visas and insurance, full board and lodging during placement as well as slightly higher pocket money than on some of the other programmes. CCUSA tries to place counsellors at camps that suit their skills and personality. The CCUSA fee starts at £299 if you arrange your own flight or £525 if you go on a CCUSA flight. First year counsellors aged 18 earn $700 in pocket money for nine weeks while those over 21 receive $1,000 for the summer in addition to a free transatlantic flight. If you fix up your own flight, your pay will be higher: $1,285 for 18 year olds, $1,645 for older counsellors.

BUNAC places camp counsellors in cooperation with the J-1 visa sponsor CIEE. Other smaller programmes such as the following tend to charge lower fees:

Americamp: Salford and Glasgow: ☎ (+44) 161 312 3640/+44 141 258 3200; www.ameri camp.co.uk. Recommended by the student finance site www.savethestudent.org for having the lowest fees and highest pocket money.

Camp Leaders: Liverpool: ☎ (+44) 0151 708 6868; www.campleaders.com. Programme fees £299–£549 depending on flight arrangement; part of Smaller Earth global company.

Camp USA: Interexchange: New York; www.interexchange.org. Fee is $335. Stipends for 18 year olds whose airfare has been paid is $850, or $1,500 without airfare. Over-21s receive $1,100/$1,750.

USA Summer Camp: Offices in Solihull, Reading, Newcastle and Dublin; www.usasummer camp.co.uk. Fees of £300 (without flight) or £600; 10% discount for prompt payment.

Wild Packs: Rosyth, Fife; ☎ (+44) 1383 435991; www.wildpacks.com. £395 fee includes visa and medical insurance.

CASUAL WORK

A law stipulates that all employers must physically examine documents of prospective employees within three working days, proving that they are either a US citizen or an authorised alien (see Documents section below). All US employers are obliged to complete an I-9 form that verifies the employee's right to work. Employers who are discovered by the immigration authorities to be hiring illegal aliens are subject to huge fines. Yet it is estimated that there are thousands of British workers living and working illegally in California alone.

The law is considered to be unenforceable in seasonal industries such as fruit growing and resort tourism where it is still not uncommon for more than half of all employees to be illegal. Farmers and restaurateurs have claimed that they can barely stay in business without hiring casual workers without permits. Those who are caught working illegally run the risk of being deported, prohibited from travelling to the USA for five years and in some cases for good. If your place of work is raided and you are caught, you will be detained while your case is being 'processed', which can take up to three weeks. If you are 'in-status' (which means your tourist visa has not expired) you are given the option of departing voluntarily. If not, you will be automatically deported.

The law seems to be more strictly enforced in areas such as California, Texas and Florida that are traditional strongholds for illegal workers from Mexico and the rest of Latin America.

Documents

Every American can reel off his social security number by heart. J-1 visa holders are entitled to apply for one. Social security offices are required to check the J-1 visa with the USCIS database, which has caused delays, which in turn can mean delays in being paid by your employer. Other routes to obtaining a social security number apart from having an approved visa include getting one for the purposes of banking but this will be stamped 'Not Valid for Employment'.

False social security cards circulate, however the systems for uncovering these are becoming more sophisticated. Homeland Security's online E-Verify system allows employers to find out if their employees are eligible to work in the US. Alternatively SSNVS can find invalid social security numbers by matching records with tax and employment authorities.

Hostels

Round-the-world backpackers are sometimes shocked by the contrast between your average city hostel in the USA and in Australia/New Zealand.Therefore it might be wise to choose your accommodation with more care than elsewhere. There are of course travellers' hostels that will trade food and a bed for some work. Occasionally notices of casual jobs appear on the bulletin boards of youth hostels and backpackers' haunts. The Green Tortoise Hostel at 494 Broadway in San Francisco sometimes has strange odd jobs for pleasant and persistent travellers. One way to search for openings is to go to www.craigslist.org for the city where you want to work and search for 'hostel' in the Jobs pages. One ominous advert spotted in 2017 was for a 'Graveyard Hostel Clerk' to cover the night shift at the San Francisco International Hostel. The award-winning group of USA Hostels sometimes offers work exchanges for free accommodation (minimum one month) at its member hostels in San Francisco, Hollywood and two in San Diego (www.usahostels.com).

Carolyn Edwards had a discouraging time looking for work in Hawaii, but came across plenty of travellers spending four hours a day cleaning in hostels in exchange for bed and board. Richard Davies was given free accommodation and paid $10 an hour to clean toilets at his Los Angeles hostel which allowed him time to look for other work. Ask for work-for-keep openings at privately owned travellers' lodges in the Grand Canyon area. Mark Horobin patronised a different sort of hostel when he found himself skint in California:

Males who line up in the early afternoon outside the San Diego Rescue Mission have a good chance of being given a bed and meals for three days. If you need a longer stay you may consider signing up as a helper as I did, but to do this you'll have to explain your reason and attend a compulsory daily Bible study session. If you are accepted you work about four hours a day. Later I stayed at the Prince of Peace Monastery in Oceanside.

Drive-aways

The term 'drive-away' applies to the practice of delivering private cars within North America. Prosperous Americans and Canadians and also companies are prepared to pay large sums to delivery firms who agree to arrange delivery of private vehicles to a different city, usually because the car owner wants his or her car available at their holiday destination but doesn't want to drive it personally. The companies find drivers, arrange insurance and arbitrate in the event of mishaps. You get free use of a car (subject to mileage and time restrictions) and pay for all gas after the first tankful and tolls on the interstates. At peak times, depending on supply and demand, some drivers get their fuel paid for plus a cash bonus of several hundred dollars. Usually a deadline and mileage limit are fixed (eg 400 miles or 650km a day), though these are often flexible and checks lax.

A good time to be travelling north to south (eg Toronto to Florida, Chicago to Arizona) is October/November/early December when a massive number of retired folk head to a warmer climate. On the other hand, when there is a shortage of vehicles (eg leaving New York in the summer), you will be lucky to get a car on any terms.

The only requirements are that you be over 23, have a clean driving licence, plus preferably an International Driving Permit, and able to pay a deposit (generally $350–$400) which will be refunded by cheque on successful delivery. You may also have to produce references and/or an official motor vehicle driving record from your home country. (In the UK the DVLA allows you to share your driving record online via www.gov.uk/view-driving-licence for which you will need your National Insurance number as well as your licence.)

Check the *Yellow Pages* under 'Auto Transporters' for a local provider, though the company with national coverage is Auto Driveaway (☎ (+1) 800 346 2277; www.autodriveaway.com) which has dozens of franchised operators across the USA, from Salt Lake City to Philadelphia, Saint Louis to Seattle. Smaller companies like Custom Auto Delivery tend to use staff drivers with a US or Canadian licence rather than occasional ones. From Toronto, an established company is Toronto Drive-Away

Service (☎ (+1) 800 561 2658; www.torontodriveaway.com) whose website contains driver recruitment information; the minimum age is 30 and you must have references. The busiest season is mid-March to May when many Canadian cars need to be driven back from Florida, Arizona and to a lesser extent California. Occasionally the company promises that fuel will be covered plus an expense allowance of $300–$400 given. The agency says: *'Drive-away is not employment – just a Road Trip and an Adventure! So we welcome reliable, competent people but please – no fusspots!'*

An alternative is to ask at a travel information centre for car rental agencies which arrange delivery of rental cars to the places where there is a seasonal demand, for example to Florida or to ski resorts in the winter. The greater your flexibility of destination, the quicker you'll be out of town. Bridgid Seymour-East and Jimmy Henderson enjoyed a wonderful 'potluck' trip around the USA, picking up a car in Los Angeles and driving to a town in Minnesota. If you are travelling with one or more people, you can save money by splitting the cost of the gas. Some companies allow you to take co-drivers and/or passengers provided they register for insurance purposes. Others limit the number per vehicle to two since the owners are also transporting their belongings for the season, so trunk space is at a premium. The type of vehicle you are assigned and its gas consumption can make a significant difference to the overall cost. Few agencies store cars themselves so you will need to find your own way to the car's home. When you are introduced to the vehicle, check through a list of existing damage with the owner (or agent) and fill in a 'Condition Report'. Be very thorough, since otherwise you may be held liable for existing damage or faults. If you do have mechanical problems on the road, you pay for any repairs costing less than a specified sum, which you reclaim from the recipient of the vehicle. Many travellers have concluded that drive-aways are an excellent wheeze, among them Mig Urquhart:

> *One day somebody in Fort Lauderdale was talking about fishing in Alaska and about a week later three of us had a drive-away to Seattle. It was the most outstanding car to do the journey in – a Mitsubishi Montero, one of those big Jeep-type 4X4s. Only two of us could drive. We did 4,700 miles in nine days, which included a birthday party for me in Tampa, lunch in New Orleans, the Grand Canyon, Las Vegas, a weekend with a friend in San Francisco and finally the glorious drive from SF to Seattle. The trip cost each of us a couple of hundred dollars including food, gas, the motel in Vegas and a really nice meal in SF.*

THE JOB-HUNT

Working holidaymakers from Britain and countries worldwide can capitalise on current employee shortages during the summer season by participating in one of the approved Summer Work Travel programmes described earlier. Occasional newspaper headlines reveal the extent of the problem for employers: 'US ski resorts face severe staff shortages'; and the same is true of summer resorts too.

The majority of seasonal jobs will pay the national minimum wage of $7.25 (unchanged for the past four years), though some states have legislated a higher wage, eg California ($10), Massachusetts ($11) and Oregon ($9.75). Five southern states have no minimum wage. People in jobs that rely on tips earn a pittance since the minimum hourly wage for tipped employees in the USA starts at an appalling $2.13 in a number of states with an expectation that the rest will be made up from tips. These can be checked on the Department of Labor's website (www.dol.gov/whd/minwage/america.htm).

TOURISM AND CATERING

Labour demands in summer resorts and national parks sometimes reach crisis proportions especially along the eastern seaboard. Because tipping is so generous, employers in many states are allowed to pay next to nothing. This means that it is possible to earn from your employer the derisory wage of $15 for an evening shift but up to $300 in tips if you are waiting on tables. Bar staff also live on tips (but note that bar staff have to be the legal drinking age of 21). Apparently a British accent helps, except in the case of Briton Jane Thomas who was accused of putting it on to attract a higher tip! Even if you don't get a job serving drinks or as a 'waitperson', busboys (table clearers) are usually given a proportion of tips by the waiter whom they are helping, typically 10%.

Dozens of websites may prove useful in the job hunt: www.resortjobs.com, www.coolworks.com and www.jobmonkey.com are especially recommended for seasonal jobs in the tourist industry.

The recruitment needs of national and state parks can often be found on the internet, for example Glacier National Park in Montana near the Canadian border (www.glacierparkinc.com/careers), 15% of whose seasonal staff are overseas participants in Work and Travel programmes, and Denali Park in Alaska which hires 900 people each summer from early May to mid-September. See www.aramark. com/careers to search for vacancies in Denali as well as Glacier Bay National Park also in Alaska, and park resorts in Arizona, Colorado, etc. Aramark also recruits for up to 1,800 vacancies in California's Yosemite National Park (www.aramark.com/yosemitejobs). Facilities in some famous national parks such as Zion in Utah, Crater Lake in Oregon and Death Valley in California are run by Xanterra Parks & Resorts (www.xanterra.com). Xanterra also recruit for the even more famous Yellowstone National Park in Wyoming that offers 2,500 seasonal jobs (www.yellowstonejobs.com). Grand Canyon's facilities are managed by different companies; see the links at www.coolworks.com/grand-canyon-national-park-jobs.

Resorts in remote places always have trouble hiring enough staff. One that looks to countries around the world for its personnel is the Mount Rushmore Resort in the Black Hills of South Dakota (www.palmergulch.com) where they are in need of people to apply online for seasonal positions as waterslide attendants, cleaners, etc.

California is a magnet for Brits, though many find the cost of living higher than elsewhere in the States. Plenty of foreigners find work in Los Angeles, in the restaurants, bistros and cafés of Santa Monica, San Francisco and so on. Paying your way in Manhattan with a fast food or equivalent job will be a challenge. Jane Thomas solved this problem by getting on a housesitting circuit via contacts. Through a friend, she met various people who were only too glad to have a nice reliable English girl live in their houses while they were away on holiday, to discourage burglars, water the plants, etc. One of the places she stayed in was a luxury apartment overlooking Central Park. The incongruity of passing the commissionaire every morning arrayed in the orange polyester uniform of Burger Heaven struck her as highly amusing.

Seaside Resorts

Popular resorts are often a sure bet. Part way through her second year of a social anthropology degree at the University of Manchester, Julia Wilson realised that she did not want to fritter her summer away as she had the previous year, so a round-robin email from BUNAC caught her eye. She soon enrolled in the Work America programme and was emailing her CV to some employers listed by BUNAC. She received three job offers, and was shocked that two of them imposed a ceiling on tips earned. Instead she accepted a job at the West Chop Club in Martha's Vineyard; all Republican Senators, heiresses and spoilt kids. At first she was bowled over by the beauty of the place, so clean and well-groomed, near-pristine beaches. But the lack of spare time when working 40–50-hour weeks and the apartheid between guests and staff soon began to grate. When after a month her manager told her that she was sacking her because it was evident her heart was not in the job, Julia couldn't disagree and was given a scant 48 hours to vacate her room.

But she liked Martha's Vineyard enough to want to stay on the island, and scoured the local paper for accommodation and jobs. She soon found a room in the home of some colourful locals, bought a bicycle for $50 and juggled three part-time jobs that left her more free time and brought in more money than the pre-arranged job. She concluded that being fired was the best thing that happened to her. If she had stayed around for the $300 end-of-season bonus, she would have had to work up until 16 September and flown home on the 17th. Her jobs consisted of life-modelling for the local art society which paid $50 for two hours, working as a hostess in a restaurant (attached to a health spa which staff were allowed to use) and working in a boutique where she had plenty of time between customers to read books and use her laptop, while earning a generous $12 an hour.

According to Andrew Boyle, there seemed to be more BUNACers in the Maryland resort of Ocean City than natives, and he noticed considerable tension and a 'clash of ideologies' between the party-loving young workers and the older year-round residents. In fact a lot of young foreigners go to resorts like this simply to party and anyone who is willing to work really hard stands out and is usually treated better. Other popular resorts to try are Wildwood (New Jersey), Virginia Beach (Virginia), Myrtle Beach (South Carolina) and Atlantic Beach (North Carolina).

Boats

For a yachting job, Florida is the best place to look. Innumerable pleasure craft and also fishing boats depart from the Florida Keys (at the southern tip of the state) bound for the Caribbean, especially between Christmas and Easter. You might also try for work on a cruise ship (see the section in Working a Passage). There is usually plenty of bar and kitchen work in the Keys, the second largest gay centre in North America. Florida resorts are swamped by tens of thousands of students during their spring breaks, so accommodation is almost impossible to find in March and early April.

Fort Lauderdale creates plenty of casual work on yachts year round which regularly pays $11–$13 an hour. A good place to hear about day work on yachts, as well as opportunities in landscaping and restaurants, are the crew house hostels in town.

Ski Resorts

There truly is an abundance of winter work in ski resorts, especially in Colorado, between November and the 'Mud Season' in May. A standard seasonal commitment would be 21 November to 14 April. Aspen, Vail and Steamboat all have huge hiring needs.

The best time to look in person is October/November when the big resorts hold job fairs. Jobs are available as lift operators, restaurant workers, ticket clerks, basket check (such as left luggage for skiers), etc. As ever, the main problem is visas (see below) and after that a lack of affordable accommodation. Unless you arrange something in August/September, you will have to be very lucky to find a room of any kind. Check adverts in a local paper such as *Steamboat Pilot & Today* whose employment classifieds are posted online at www.yampavalleyjobs.com. Hundreds of 'help wanted' ads appear in the winter months and even more in the summer. Also check the resorts' websites some of which have links from the employment website www.coolworks.com/ski-resort-jobs.

You should also be aware that immigration raids are frequent, which make employers reluctant to hire people without papers even when desperate for staff. The website www.steamboat.com/employment posts some vacancies or email hr@steamboat.com. If in the resort visit the Human Resources office of the largest local employer, the Steamboat Ski and Resort Corporation (☎ (+1) 970 871 5132). Job Fairs are held around the first weekend of November where employers can meet jobseekers. Neil Hibberd worked a season as a ski lift operator for the Steamboat Corporation on a J-1 visa fixed up through an internship programme in London.

Condominiums or 'condos' are sometimes a good bet for casual employment. If you're just looking for occasional work, chopping wood in late autumn is a simple way of making a quick profit and contracts for clearing snow from roofs are sometimes available. Hotels aren't a big feature of American resorts (though two of the principal ones at Steamboat, the Sheraton and the Ptarmigan Inn, hire large numbers of non-local workers). Resort companies such as Mountain Resorts and the Steamboat Ski and Resort Corporation hire room cleaners, maintenance men, drivers, etc. It is common for one company to own all the facilities and control all employment in one resort, and in some cases provide accommodation to all staff.

In another of Colorado's famous resorts, try Vail Resorts which has a dedicated freephone jobs line (☎ (+1) 866 681 5455) and an employment website www.vailresortscareers.com. Aspen is another of the wealthiest resorts and supports a large transient working population. The Aspen Skiing Company is heavily involved with the hiring of foreign workers who can stay from mid-December till early April, through CCUSA, CIEE and similar; see www.aspensnowmass.com/we-are-different/employment. One of the major employers in Aspen for the summer as well as the winter season is the Gant Condominium Resort (www.gantaspen.com).

If you decide to show up in Aspen, visit the Cooper Street Pier bar and listen for foreign accents. Unfortunately, wages tend to be low in this setting and saving very difficult after you have paid for room and board, though ski pass and equipment rental are often a perk of the job. It is worth hanging on until the end of the season when many employers pay sizeable bonuses or distribute a share of the season's tips. Another major Colorado resort is Winter Park Resort (www.winterparkresort.com/employment), which despite its name also hires plenty of seasonal staff in the summer too.

Californian ski resorts that also hire in large numbers include Sugar Bowl in Norden (www.sugar bowl.com/employment) and Mammoth Mountain Resort (☎ (+1) 760 934 0654; www.mammothmountain.com/jobs) which recruits most international applicants for the following winter season as soon as the current one ends.

Theme Parks

Although British people are acquainted with fun fairs and theme parks, they will be amazed at the grand scale on which many American amusement parks and carnivals operate, sometimes employing up to 3,000 summer assistants to work on the rides and games, food service, parking lot and maintenance, warehouse, wardrobe and security. One chain of parks is Six Flags Theme Parks that have huge operations in nine states which together hire 2,500 international staff (www.sixflagsjobs.com). Representatives from Six Flags sometimes liaise with the major summer work agencies and recruit summer staff abroad. One of the biggest amusement parks is Cedar Point in Sandusky, Ohio (www.cedarpoint.com/jobs) that hires international students via BUNAC, CCUSA, etc. Make sure before applying that you are happy to conform to their 'Grooming Guidelines'. The opportunities afforded to young people looking for summer work by just one of these enormous commercial complexes are enormous and dwarf Butlins and Alton Towers entirely.

On a smaller scale, travelling carnivals and funfairs may need a few assistants to set up, operate and dismantle game stands and rides. Since the keynote of American business is to encourage competition and provide incentives, many of these carnival operators let you take home a cut of the profits on your particular stall, which can be stressful.

The Disney International Programs at the Walt Disney World Resort near Orlando in Florida (http://ip.disneycareers.com) are made up of several programmes including a summer Cultural Exchange programme for students and recent graduates who obtain a J-1 visa, and the one-year 'Cultural Representative Program' (Q visa). Participants in both programmes work in front line roles at Disney's theme parks and resorts. Specifically for the Cultural Representative Program, people from the UK and about a dozen other countries are hired to represent the culture, heritage and customs of their countries in themed pavilions and other areas of the resort. In the UK, the annual recruiting season starts in early October when initial screenings take place followed by a presentation and interview at the Yummy Jobs office in Essex and then interviews with Disney reps in London in November; for details contact Yummy Jobs (196a High St, Epping, Essex CM16 4AG; ☎ (+44) 3330 0629629; www.yummyjobs.com). The application and interview process takes place over months, and is very competitive: typically out of 3,500 applications, 220 will be accepted.

Yummy Jobs also recruit for the Universal Orlando Resort International Progam under the auspices of the J1 visa-approved agency Alliance Abroad Group.

Kevin Eastwood from Huddersfield participated as a Cultural Representative a few years ago and focused on the perks of the job:

> *The programme has been a fantastic opportunity for me and one I will remember forever. I worked in food and beverage at the UK Pavilion in Epcot ... Disney understands how sometimes it can be difficult being so far away from family and friends for so long, and has provided many resources, from computer labs to free internet access in our apartments, to housing events ... I now have friends from places such as Canada, Norway, China, Mexico, Italy, Japan, America and France. I also enjoyed all of the cast-*

exclusive opportunities available to us such as admission to Disney theme parks and discounts on resort accommodation and dining.

The gated staff apartments have lots of facilities and a buzzing social life. Rent for a shared room in an apartment costs $110–$130 a week and is deducted from wages. Other past Disney staff members have found it hard to cope with all the rules, and it is not unusual for anyone with a rebellious streak to be sent home. After checking out the feedback on the unofficial website for International Program alumni (www.wdwip.com), most of it very enthusiastic, Catherine Howard from Cork, Ireland decided to apply to work in Florida. Unfortunately, there is no separate Irish pavilion, but she sent an application off to Yummy Jobs anyway for their J-1 Cultural Program and, after she had paid the programme fee and various visa and criminal record check fees, they found her a front desk position at the Walt Disney World Swan and Dolphin Hotel next to Epcot but not owned by Disney. Interestingly, the literature from the sponsoring organisation in the USA made the training and visa scheme sound far more rigorous a process than it actually was and in the end her interview at the US embassy in Dublin lasted all of 60 seconds.

DESPITE SOMETIMES BAULKING AT AMERICAN BUSINESS CULTURE, CATHERINE HOWARD HAD A WONDERFUL 18 MONTHS:

I loved my job. Everyone was really nice and helpful, and I did actually enjoy chatting with guests. You are in Disney World after all, so for the most part, guests are usually happy to be there. Sometimes it was difficult to stomach the touchy-feely parts of corporate America. At pre-shift meetings, we would talk about 'core values' and making our guests feel special, and no pre-shift was complete without each of us reciting an example from our own lives where we were made to feel special as well. The Americans did this willingly without irony or self-consciousness, but it wrecked my head. The way I saw it, our time would be better spent fixing the actual problems the hotel had, instead of feeling special, but this attitude got me into trouble with the manager, so my advice would be to smile and suck it up instead! (This was the same manager, mind you, that introduced a directive whereby if a guest asked us how we were today, we had to reply with a word of three syllables or more, eg 'Good' was not allowed, but 'wonderful' or 'fantastic' was okay. My favourite was 'homicidal'.)

I loved my time in Florida and going there is one of the best decisions I ever made. But my first three months or so were one of the lowest points in my entire life, because I made one crucial mistake: I never learned to drive. I couldn't quite fathom what people meant when they said that in Orlando you couldn't walk anywhere. Not only was I a freak – the only person over the age of 16 in the entire state of Florida who couldn't drive a car – but when it came to finding an apartment, my options were severely limited. Four months in, I learned to drive, bought a car and moved into a much nicer apartment with one of my new best friends.

During my eighteen months in Orlando, I got to:

■ *See a Space Shuttle launch from Cape Canaveral – one of my top three dreams.*
■ *Spot celebrities: the best one was seeing Steven Tyler in the queue for Pirates of the Caribbean!*
■ *Attend a Hallowe'en screening of the Rocky Horror Show, in costume.*
■ *Watch fireworks every night on my way home from work (and the Seaworld fireworks from my patio every night in the summer).*
■ *Go to Mickey's Very Merry Christmas Party at the Magic Kingdom – twice.*
■ *Drink and eat my way around Epcot's Food and Wine Festival.*
■ *Go to Washington DC, Miami, Mardi Gras in New Orleans, New York at Christmastime, etc.*
■ *Wake up to sunshine almost every single morning.*

Subsequently she has written a hilarious book about her experiences called *Mousetrapped: A Year and a Bit in Orlando* which is highly recommended.

OTHER POPULAR JOBS

Selling

By reputation, anyway, American salesmen are a hardbitten lot. Some travellers have found that their foreign charm makes selling surprisingly effortless. (*'Are you really English? I just love that accent.'*) Americans are not as suspicious of salesmen as other nationalities and you may be pleasantly surprised by the tolerance with which you are received on the doorstep and, even more, by the high earnings which are possible. The J-1 programme prohibits jobs that do not pay at least minimum wage, so you cannot accept commission-only selling jobs.

Advertisements for sales positions proliferate. You may find telesales less off-putting than door-to-door salesmanship, but it will also be less lucrative. On the other hand, some working holidaymakers and gap year students do not shy away from the hard edge of selling and tackle commission-only jobs. Southwestern Advantage, with its headquarters in Nashville (www.southwesternadvantage.com), grew out of the oldest door-to-door sales company in the US and continues to sell educational books and software on doorsteps throughout the USA. They recruit thousands of students, including some from Europe, to become self-employed salespeople for the summer. The company has been embroiled in controversy for its grandiose claims of possible earnings for its sales force and has been banned from recruiting on several campuses in the US and UK.

Soccer Coaching

Soccer continues to gain popularity in North America, including among girls, and demand is strong for young British coaches (referred to as 'professional trainers') to work on summer coaching schemes. A number of companies recruit qualified coaches to work all over the States including Hawaii. Many recruit players to work regionally or throughout the country via British agencies.

Most companies prefer to hire candidates with a National Coaching Licence, eg Football Association Level 1 coaching which can be acquired after doing a course lasting 33–43 hours (see www.1st4sportqualifications.com). You are likely also to need an enhanced DBS check and emergency first aid certificate. Even if you are not up to the football standard, there may be ancillary job openings for general camp counsellors with some companies.

Challenger Sports: Lenexa, Kansas; www.challengersportsrecruitment.com. Originally set up as British Soccer Camps, this is the largest soccer camp operator in the USA and Canada; UK contact for coach applicants is Ben Beer (☎ (+44) 793 047 3289; benbeerchallenger sports@hotmail.co.uk). Recruitment sessions held in various places in February and March. Can also be arranged through BUNAC for £700.

Midwest Soccer Academy (MSA): Fenton, Michigan (www.midwestsoccer.net). Coaches needed for three and nine-month contracts.

Soccer Academy Inc: Manassas, Virginia; www.soccer-academy.com. European-based coaches should apply to Mark Jennings of Peak Active Sport in Derbyshire (☎ (+44) 7814 390740; mark@pas.uk.com); interviews for the summer take place in November and chosen candidates attend a training weekend in Manchester in April.

STA Soccer: New Jersey (www.stasoccer.com/staff). Employ staff mainly on long-term contracts.

UK Elite Soccer: Cedar Knolls, New Jersey; ☎ (+1) 844 893 1200; www.ukelite.com/employment. Offers soccer camps, coaching and programmes in 20 states, mainly on the east coast; seasonal coaches needed March to November and 70 summer coaches July to August.

UK International Soccer Camps/UKISC: Redlands, California; www.uksoccer.com. Employ many British coaches.

It is more important to be good at working with kids than to be a great football player, though of course it is easier to command the respect of the kids if you can show them good skills and a few tricks.

Dom Samuels was in the last year of his undergraduate programme when he decided to apply for a summer/fall coaching role in the USA.

After an initial assessment of applicants in Leeds (among other locations), I attended an intensive four-day course at Lilleshall, the National Sports Centre north of Telford, which encompassed various teaching/coaching techniques and forms of assessment. I was told to expect an email and I remember well the subject line of that email which read 'Welcome to LA ...'. Unbelievable!

Coaching children from the ages of three to 19 meant work was varied every day and I got the opportunity to really get to know some of the children. During the fall, coaching wouldn't commence until after school on weekdays and last from 4pm till 9pm or 10pm. Summer Camp hours were different, in the morning or all day. One of the most notable days was when, along with a handful of other coaches, I was sent to coach Hispanic children in downtown LA. Unbeknown to us, it was a heat wave that weekend and we were scheduled to coach from 8am till 3pm. It was 'extra work' but saw us paid for the extra hours, which is always nice in the next pay cheque. However, with the heat wave, not only did the children feel it, but so did we. We were coaching the children on Astro-turf. The rubber base of the turf was melting, and our feet were literally burning as we coached. When we got back to our host's house, we were greeted with two words: 'beer, pool'. If you're not a people-person, this job isn't for you.

I think the job is glamorised by some ... coach in the sunshine, party every weekend, meet great and like-minded lads and ladies, get put up in plush mansions and tipped by parents at the end of the camp. I connected with many families I stayed with and struggled emotionally to say goodbye. But that's the job. You go into a place, provide a service, get out and do it all again somewhere else. I have met and made friends and family for life. Utah and California are homes-from-home for me.

The time off we got was rare so I indulged when possible, usually taking a road trip. En route from Vegas to Arizona we saw a sign which said, 'Grand Canyon, 49 miles west ridge' which we assumed would be no more than a couple of hours out of our way, including time out for a few Kodak moments. Not quite. We drove and drove until the road actually ended. We were at the Colorado River. Seven lads, one with a geography degree and a map of the entire USA, and we couldn't navigate our way to the biggest hole in the planet. Hilarious!

Manual Work

Cash-in-hand work is more difficult to pin down, but it is usually possible to find casual work as a loader with removal firms, as security guards and in construction (especially for those with skills). The best time (for men) to look for removal work is just before the end of the month when many leases expire and more people tend to move house. Dan Eldridge worked at a hostel in San Francisco for a year and so knows the working scene well: *'An interesting option is to open up the phone book to "Movers" and personally visit them, especially any with Irish names. They all employ foreigners paying a decent hourly wage cash in hand. I sent many people to the moving companies and most quit after a couple of weeks, but were happy to have the cash.'*

Since houses throughout the States are wood-framed, carpenters can do well, even those without much experience. It is common practice to pay employees as contract labour, which leaves them with the responsibility of paying taxes, social security, etc; this is a definite advantage if your papers are not in order. Even if you can't find work building new houses, you can offer your painting or maintenance skills to any householder, preferably one whose house is looking the worse for wear.

A more definite but offbeat suggestion has been proffered by Mark Kinder who wrote from rural Maryland:

After spending the summer on the Camp America programme, a friend and I decided to do a parachute jump. Once you have made about 10 jumps, the instructors expect you to learn how to pack parachutes, which takes about five hours to learn. Once you have learnt how to pack you get paid a few dollars per chute cash and with a bit of practice can pack three or four chutes an hour which is good money. I would say that 90% of parachute centres in the USA pay people cash for packing the chutes but you generally have to be a skydiver to do the job. It is definitely a fun way of earning money. Skydivers are very friendly people and are thrilled to meet foreigners, so they will often offer a place to stay. If not, you can always camp at the parachute centre.

A list of the 231 parachute centres in the USA can be found in the Drop Zone (DZ) Locator section of the United States Parachute Association's website www.uspa.org/dropzonelocator.

Medical

Nurse shortages are chronic in the USA and qualified nurses might like to investigate possibilities through a specialist agency; more than 30 are listed at www.nursetogether.com/list-nurse-recruitment-agencies-us-based-employment, although the backlog of green card processing, known as retrogression, discourages some hospitals from sponsoring nurses. For people with a more casual interest in medicine, there is the possibility of testing new drugs as well as donating blood. While filling in the time until her flight out of Seattle, Mig Urquhart sold plasma at the Plasma Center. She was turned down on her first visit since there was too much protein in her urine (she reckoned it was because she had been living on peanut butter sandwiches). The current rates paid are $40–$60 per donation. You can earn more donating peripheral blood stem cells needed for transplants and medical research; a recent donor earned $800 in return for spending four hours on two days with needles in both arms.

When Lindsay Watt arrived in the USA, he intended to sustain himself with conventional kinds of employment. But almost immediately he discovered that the longish-stay male travellers staying at his hostel in New York were all earning money solely through medical studies. Invariably, a social security number is needed though it can bear the stamp 'Not Valid for Work'. Most studies pay about $200 for an overnight stay in a clinic. One spotted recently being run by BioTrial in New Jersey was seeking volunteers who passed a screening to spend three nights and two days in their clinic, and come for two outpatient visits afterwards, in order to earn up to $950. For longer term trials, you can earn thousands. There are Drug Research Centers in many American cities in Texas (especially Austin), Massachusetts, New York, New Jersey, Pennsylvania, Maryland and Florida. Women are seldom accepted unless they are sterile.

Two excellent sources of information on drug testing centres are the websites www.centerwatch.com, a listing service for clinical trials, and http://www.jalr.org (Just Another Lab Rat) which lists clinics and research centres that recruit healthy volunteers for Phase 1 trials. Try also www.clinicaltrials.gov which lists thousands of clinical studies sponsored by the National Institutes of Health, other federal agencies and the pharmaceutical industry; they indicate which ones are recruiting but mainly they are looking for people who are actually suffering from the relevant disorder or disease.

Alaskan Fishing

Fishing off the coast of Alaska and fish-processing are classic money-spinning summer jobs in the USA, still advertised in west coast newspapers, though the possible earnings are often exaggerated since the Alaskan salmon industry has been in decline for some time. It has been known for deckhands to weather full three-month seasons on mediocre boats and go home with no more than $3,000 for their effort, though $10,000+ is more typical.

Therefore think carefully before buying a one-way ticket to Alaska where the cost of living is very high and the competition for work intense. Be sure your expectations are realistic. There is no guarantee of finding a job on a productive boat and, even if you do get work, it's unlikely that you'll make any more than minimum wage considering the long hours. What is certain is that you will work harder, longer and faster than you ever have or ever will; you will be cold, beyond exhausted, made to feel stupid, and at times, miserable. Yet the determined can still succeed.

Do not rely on the promises of websites that offer to arrange jobs in the fishing industry for a fee. With profits and the safety of all onboard at stake, boat captains cannot afford to rely on email or long distance phone calls to size up potential crew. The only reliable way to land a deckhand job in Alaska is to show up two to four weeks before the season begins and beat the docks. You will have to obtain a commercial fishing licence that costs $277 for a non-resident, plus rubber boots and raingear. Novices can be found frequenting the docks at Kodiak, Ketchikan, Homer and Petersburg in Alaska as well as Astoria and Newport in Oregon. Due to the proximity to the mainland USA, work is generally harder to find in the ports of the South-west. Venturing further north to Kodiak Island or the Bristol Bay fisheries, which boast large fleets and are less accessible, holds more promise. In Kodiak, check the ever-popular job board at Harborside Coffee, perpetually plastered with post-it notes which, with luck, will read: 'Deckhand needed immediately, no experience necessary'.

The first halibut are caught over a 24-hour period in early May and this opens the fishing season. It is easier to pin down job openings between then and early June when salmon crews are doing pre-season gear work. Often a skipper will take inexperienced newcomers on a trial basis. If you are willing to do prep work without pay, eg mending nets, scrubbing hulls, chances are you will have the job when the season opens around 1 June. By putting in some hard time for free, a skipper can better discern if you have the necessary tenacity, as Jason Motlagh puts it, *'to grind through sleepless two-day benders, jellyfish facials, raw hands and screaming muscles'.*

This is a way of life for the boat owners, not a summer job. Try to convey that you will take your work seriously, but are easygoing enough to live with under cramped conditions for months at a time. Do not forget that taking orders and insults on the chin is a rite of passage; take it personally and you'll soon find yourself back on the dock.

Rejection is an inevitable part of the deckhand job search; never take no for an answer. Many skippers will turn you down several times before taking you on. If you can pass this initial test of your resolve, the prevailing logic is that it may reflect your work ethic, which will be tested like never before. If you start your job search late, be wary of boats with crew vacancies deep into the season. Some skippers are notorious for being abusive, reckless, withholding pay, or simply bad at catching fish. Ask around the docks to get the straight story on which boats are reputable and which ones to avoid. Deck-hands like to talk and you'll generally get a consensus. Boats talk too. If a vessel looks like it hasn't seen a fresh coat of paint since the Cold War, move on. Safety should be a top priority. Several hundred boats have sunk and more than 100 people died fishing Alaskan waters over the years. Each year a lot of fingers and a few lives are lost usually because of irresponsible captains cutting corners.

Most of the newcomers that flock to Alaskan ports each summer looking for deckhand jobs have no idea what they are letting themselves in for. Fishing is dangerous work in which adrenaline and fatigue are in constant conflict. Whereas seiners (the most lucrative) often have large crews, trollers and gillnetters tend to employ only one or two deckhands. On a salmon boat each member of the crew must pull his weight under monotonous, often brutal conditions that push the limits of physical and mental endurance. Amazingly, it is not impossible for women to find work as deckhands, though they will be spared none of the harshness of life at sea. Needless to say, privacy is in short supply, while crude language and pornography are not.

To remain in business fishermen must offset lower prices with higher volume, which translates to even longer hours. Unable to cope, many naïve hopefuls quit their jobs within the first few days, which is how Jason Motlagh managed to get a job on board a 'highliner'.

AFTER FINISHING A DEGREE IN FOREIGN AFFAIRS, AMERICAN JASON MOTLAGH CAUGHT THE FISHING BUG. ON RETURNING FROM KODIAK ONE AUTUMNS, HE WROTE ABOUT THE 'GRUEL-LING, TEDIOUS WORK ABOARD A COMMERCIAL FISHING VESSEL WITH REWARDS FEW OTHER JOBS COULD HOPE TO OFFER':

Like countless others before me, I decided to head north to be a 'greenhorn' for a crack at fortune and adventure as an Alaskan fisherman. Three months later, I returned to the lower 48 a lean-mean-fishing machine with a respectable pay cheque, a wealth of stories, and the self-knowledge that while I could brave 20+ hour work days on the water, 9 to 5 at a desk would never again be as easy.

Less than 10 hours after landing in Kodiak on a puddle jumper from Anchorage, with nothing more than a backpack and blind faith, I walked onto one of the top five boats in the entire fleet. A skipper who had come into port to refuel that morning got word on the dock that I was looking for deckhand work and told me he 'might be short a man, check back in two hours'. Apparently, after three rough weeks on the fish, one of his deckhands wanted off the boat. When I returned I was instructed to get some new rain gear and a fisherman's licence, as we'd be leaving in less than an hour. This was all the more remarkable as it was already weeks into the summer salmon season. The first guy I'd spoken with told me he had beaten the docks for eight days without success. But I didn't take his word for it, and neither should you. Make it happen.

If you can cook well, this is also the time to show your expertise in the galley. After a long day in foul weather, a tasty meal might be all a crew has to look forward to. Cooking duties invariably fall on greenhorns. Bad cooks are hated, skilled ones will be cut some slack. During my first weeks, when I could do no right on deck, some extra effort preparing meals kept me in my skipper's good graces.

If you are fortunate enough to find a job on the right boat, fishing can still be safe and lucrative. Thanks to a little bit of initiative and a lot of dumb luck, I walked away with just under $10,000 for 10 weeks' work on a boat that netted well over one million pounds of salmon for the season. But you must not forget that the good jobs are likely to be filled by return crew, who know just how rare they are.

But if you go in search of an experience that will sharpen life's edge, you will not be disappointed. Think of your pay cheque in terms of learning a real trade, earning the respect of hardened men, of gazing out over calm seas as humpback whales breach under a midnight sun. A moment's rest, a fresh cut of fish, the feel of solid land under your feet after two weeks on the water, will never be as sweet. And when the season comes to a close, you'll walk away with the unmistakable swagger of an Alaskan fisherman.

A detailed calendar of the varying seasons according to fish variety and location is published by the Alaska Department of Fish and Game (www.adfg.alaska.gov/static/fishing/PDFs/commercial/commercial_season_2.pdf).

Work in the fish factories is horrendous, with 5am starts, 18-hour shifts and appalling conditions. Most of the workers are from poor countries such as Somalia and El Salvador. Even if Lara Whitmore managed to earn (and save) $900 a week for three months, this snapshot of her experiences would not inspire many to follow in her footsteps:

The only good thing about this work station was the lack of a stench. It was too cold for the fish to smell. My hands were only covered by latex gloves as I reached for another fish fillet. It felt icy and mushy as I lay it on the bright table, checking it for worms and bones. I reached for the tweezers as I spotted a shadow in the fillet I was scanning. Gotcha, you little bastard. Piercing the raw flesh with the tweezers, I pulled out a worm about an inch long and added it to my growing pile. One worm down. A million to go. Once I pulled five or six worms out of a fillet the size of my palm before I tossed it down the drain. I swore I'd never eat cod again. After a time, I realised I couldn't feel my toes from the cold. There was also a throbbing knot in my left shoulder blade, but there was nothing to be done about that. I was cold, in pain, sleep-deprived, daydreaming, and in the sixteenth hour of my shift.

CHILDCARE AND DOMESTIC WORK

The US State Department administers the au pair placement programme that allows thousands of young people from around the world with childcare experience to work for American families for exactly one year on a J-1 visa. They apply through agencies in their country which are partnered with one of the 16 sponsoring organisations in the USA, which all follow the federal guidelines, so there is not much difference between them.

The basic requirements are that you be between 18 and 26, speak English, show at least 200 hours of recent childcare experience, have a full clean driving licence and provide a criminal record check.

The childcare experience can consist of regular babysitting, helping at a local crèche or school, etc. Anyone wanting to care for a child under two must have 200 hours of experience looking after children under two and must expect the programme interviewers to test their claims carefully. The majority of candidates are young women though men with relevant experience (eg sole care of children under five) may be placed. (It is still not unusual to have just a handful of blokes out of hundreds of au pairs.) The job entails working a maximum of 45 hours a week (including babysitting) with at least one and a half days off per week plus one complete weekend off a month. Successful applicants receive free return flights from one of many cities, a four-day orientation in New York and support from a community counsellor. The time lag between applying and flying is usually at least two months. The counsellor's role is to advise on any problems and organise meetings with other au pairs in your area. In some cases, applicants are required to pay a good faith deposit of $400 which is returned to them at the end of 12 months but which is forfeit if the terms of the programme are broken.

The fixed amount of pocket money for au pairs remains at $195.75 a week (now worth £160 with the fall in the value of sterling), which is a reasonable wage on top of room, board and perks plus a completion bonus of $200. On arrival participants must join a four-day orientation that covers child safety and development. Legislation has made first aid a compulsory component. A potential $500 is paid in addition by the host family to cover the cost of educational courses (three hours a week during term-time), which must be attended as a condition of the visa. Au pairs are at liberty to travel for a month after their contract is over and can renew the visa for a further year.

A separate programme exists for qualified child carers/nannies, called by Au Pair in America the 'Au Pair Extraordinaire' programme or 'Premiere Au Pairs', 'Au Pair Elite', etc by other companies. Candidates with the appropriate CACHE Diploma in Early Childhood Education, Edexcel-BTEC National Diploma or NVQ3 qualification, or who are over 20 with two years' verifiable childcare experience are eligible to earn $250 a week. Another 12-month programme is called Educare for students who want to have shorter working hours (up to 30 per week) and more time for formal studies. In this programme the pocket money is $146.81, the family's contribution to non-degree studies is up to $1,000 and the upfront fee plus airfare.

At any one time 12,000 American families are hosting a foreign au pair and the vast majority of placements are reasonably successful. This is not to say that problems do not occur, because it is not at all unusual for au pairs to chafe against rules, curfews and unreasonable expectations in house-work, etc. When speaking to your family on the telephone during the application period, ask as many day-to-day questions as possible, and try to establish exactly what will be expected of you, how many nights babysitting at weekends, restrictions on social life, use of the car, how private are the living arrangements, etc. The counsellors and advisers provided by the sending organisations should be able to sort out problems and in some cases can find alternative families.

Consider carefully the pros and cons of the city you will be going to. At first, Emma Purcell was unhapppy to learn she was to be sent to Memphis, Tennessee, which she had heard to be 'backward and redneck'; but she ended up thinking her family placement was a fortunate one:

> *I was a very naïve 18-year-old applying to be an au pair for a deferred year before university. I have been very lucky with my host family who have made me feel one of the family. I have travelled the USA and Mexico frequently staying in suites and being treated as royalty since my host dad is president of Holiday Inn. On the bad side, I have lost numerous friends who have not had such good luck. One was working 60 hours a week (for no extra pay) with the brattiest children, so she left. Another girl from Australia lasted six months with her neurotic family who yelled at her for not cleaning the toaster daily and for folding the socks wrong. Finally she plucked up the courage to talk to her host parents and their immediate response was to throw her out. A very strong personality is required to be an au pair for a year in the States.*

Au Pair in America (☎ (+44) 20 7581 7300; www.aupairamerica.co.uk) is the largest sending organisation, making in excess of 4,000 au pair and nanny placements throughout the country. The programme operates under the auspices of the American Institute for Foreign Study or AIFS

(37 Queens Gate, London SW7 5HR) though some of the selection has been devolved to independent au pair agencies such as Smaller Earth in Liverpool (☎ (+44) 151 702 6808; www.smallerearth.com/uk). Au Pair in America has appointed agent/interviewers throughout the UK and also has representatives in dozens of other countries.

Other active au pair Exchange Visitor Programmes in the USA are listed on the State Department website (http://j1visa.state.gov/participants). All are smaller than Au Pair in America but may be able to offer a more personal service. The norm is to send the US office a preliminary email to be put in touch with the partner agency in your country. A selection of US au pair agencies includes:

Agent Au Pair: San Francisco, California; ☎ (+1) 415 376 0202; www.agentaupair.com.

AuPairCare by Intrax: San Francisco, California; ☎ (+1) 800 428 7247; www.aupaircare.com; Europe offices in Berlin, etc: www.aupaircare.eu or phone ☎ (+44) 203 286 2042 for info in the UK.

Au Pair International: Boulder, Colorado; ☎ (+1) 720 221 3563; www.aupairint.com.

Cultural Care/EF: Cambridge, Massachusetts; www.culturalcare.com. UK agent: 22 Chelsea Manor St, London, SW3 5RL; ☎ (+44) 800 085 1950; www.culturalcare.co.uk.

EurAupair: Laguna Beach, California; ☎ (+1) 949 494 5500; www.euraupair.com; UK partners: Work in the USA, London; www.workintheusa.com or My Education UK, ☎ (+44) 238 0970 924; www.myeducationuk.co.uk.

goAUPAIR: Murray, Utah 84107; ☎ (+1) 201 859 0693; www.goaupair.com.

Interexchange Au Pair/Au Pair USA: New York; ☎ (+1) 212 924 0446; www.interexchange.org/au-pair-usa. Partner agency in Europe: Cool Agent with offices in Prague, London, etc; london@coolagent.net; www.coolagent.net/en/page-19-au-pair-in-the-usa.html.

US Au Pair, Inc: Oregon; ☎ (+1) 503 675 5333; www.usaupair.com.

It should be possible to fix up a job working with a family after arrival in the States, though the penalties for working illegally described earlier in this chapter apply equally. There are some job notices for au pairs and nannies on hostel noticeboards (especially in San Francisco) and in big city dailies, or you can look into online matching sites such as www.sittercity.com for which you need a US address.

Gerhard Flaig found a congenial employer by the simple expedient of pestering a contact he had (organist in the church next to his hostel in Los Angeles who had kindly let him play the organ) until he finally introduced him to the church secretary who did have an idea:

> *The secretary arranged a meeting with an old man who wanted someone to organise his files and house, to do some transcriptions and other odd jobs. He gave me my own room and free food plus paid me an hourly wage. I was overjoyed and left the hostel at once. After I'd done the transcribing, he wanted me to paint his rooms. His landlady was so satisfied with the job I did that she asked me to paint her house and then a friend of his asked me as well. I got one job after the other and was very busy working as a painter. I had a wonderful time in Hollywood and earned quite a lot of money to travel on. And I still keep in touch with the man.*

AGRICULTURE

Students of agriculture can find exchange schemes that allow them to receive further training in the USA (see information for instance on the International Agricultural Exchange Association in the introductory chapter on The Countryside). Also described in that chapter is the International Exchange Programme that allows equine and horticultural trainees to be placed in the USA by the international agency IEP-UK (www.iepuk.com).

Like everything else in America, many farms (often agribusinesses rather than farms) tend to be on a massive scale, especially in California and the Midwest. This means that the phenomenon of cycling along a country road, finding the farmer in his field and being asked to start work in an adjoining field is virtually unknown in the USA. Furthermore, it could be dangerous since anyone wandering up a farmer's driveway would be suspected of being a trespasser and liable to be threatened with a vicious dog or a gun.

In many important agricultural areas much of the fruit and vegetable harvesting has been traditionally done by gangs of illegal Mexicans or legal Chicanos (naturalised Americans of Spanish descent) for notoriously low wages. It is very common for an agent to contract a whole gang, so that there may be no room for individuals and pairs of travellers.

A gentler form of agriculture is practised on organic farms that flourish in many corners of the USA. WWOOF USA has established a national organisation (☎ (+1) 415 621 3276; www.wwoofusa.org); individual membership costs $30 for online access or $40 for a printed directory, which give access to the 1,683 member farms. Working for keep on a farm counts as employment for the purposes of immigration so it is important not to mention the word 'work' or 'employment' in any immigration context, but rather cultural exchange.

The National Centre for Appropriate Technology maintains a database of internships in sustainable agriculture at https://attra.ncat.org/attra-pub/internships which anyone can consult. They post a strict warning advising that interns research and visit the farm and check out living arrangements before engaging in any type of agreement, and obtain a written agreement of what is expected on both sides, should there be a dispute.

Work on dude ranches might be more congenial than heavy farm work and anyone with horse experience might find work as a wrangler. Michael Cooley moved from California to the Rockies with one thing in mind, apart from skiing and riding, and that was 'room and board' since both are so expensive in seasonal resort towns:

> I decided to look for work on a guest ranch (dude ranch) in April which is the right time. I picked up the Yellow Pages and started calling from A. Many wanted a season's commitment (mid-May to September), which was fine with me. One owner of a small ranch needed someone immediately, so I went for an interview the next day. Being from another country himself, he was nervous about hiring me, but he decided that I was OK for mucking out stalls, etc. I worked hard, he was pleased and I soon became the person who would answer the phone and talk to people looking for work themselves – how satisfying! I didn't make much money but I didn't spend anything either. The starting wage on most ranches is $400–$800 with the promise of a bonus for those who stay the whole season. It's hard work and long hours – you are there for the beauty of the area and fresh air, not for the $$ (I say this a lot to myself).

In the world of conventional agriculture, there is scope for finding work. In every state in the Union (except perhaps Nevada, Montana and Alaska) there is some fruit or vegetable being picked throughout the summer months. Both in large-scale harvests and on smaller farms there is a chance that no-one will be concerned about your legal status. This is what Jan Christensen from Denmark found when he looked for summer farm work in Minnesota some years ago:

> The farmers seemed to have a very relaxed attitude towards permits. The best places to look are along route 210 just off Interstate 94 at Fergus Falls, which is a rich farm area with good employment prospects from April/May till mid-October. But it's best to have some experience in tractor driving and combine harvester work. If you try to bluff, you will find yourself on the road PDQ. I found that my farmer expected me to know just about everything about farming and had no time to train me.

The correct visa for temporary agricultural workers is the H-2A work visa for temporary or seasonal agricultural work. But petitioning for these requires a long lead-in time and a lot of paperwork.

The apple harvest of eastern Washington State is massive, and there is a chronic shortage of pickers. An October headline in a Seattle paper read: 'Washington Apple Growers Scrambling to Find Workers'. The article quoted one farmer in despair about his unpicked apples who said that of the 149 people referred to him by the state's unemployment office, only half showed up on the first day, a quarter on the second day and just five lasted the distance. The work is tough and normally done by experienced gangs of Latinos but strengthened anti-illegal immigration laws are discouraging those on false documents. Last year growers were paying $25 a bin and a fast experienced picker can fill 10 a day (and a rookie a fraction of that). The towns to head for in the October picking season are along the Okanagon and Yakima Valleys including towns such as Quincy, Wenatchee, Wapato, Chelan and Okanogon. Look for the telltale signs *'Necesitos Piscadores'* (Pickers Wanted).

Another example of a large-scale harvest is the peach harvest in Western Colorado around Palisade. Several hundred pickers are suddenly needed between 20 July and 4 September and especially during the second fortnight in August. Cherries are also grown here and must be picked in June. Similarly the three-week cherry harvest around Traverse City, Michigan in late June/early July employs large numbers of non-locals.

California and Florida are the leading states for agricultural production, especially citrus, plums, avocados, apricots and grapes. Most of these are grown along the Central Valley particularly the San Joaquin Valley around Fresno. The work is notoriously poorly paid. Some have fared better in the Salinas Valley on the California coast, which is a huge vegetable growing area, again predominantly Spanish speaking.

VOLUNTEERING

The main workcamp organisations in the USA such as Volunteers for Peace (www.vfp.org) listed in the chapter Volunteering have incoming programmes. VFP have only a handful of projects in the USA, including rebuilding houses in the flood-damaged Lower Ninth Ward of New Orleans; the VFP joining fee is $500 and some projects incur extra costs. If there is sufficient interest BUNAC offers a Volunteer USA programme (www.bunac.org/uk/volunteer-abroad/usa) in association with American Conservation Experience (ACE) based in Flagstaff, Arizona in which volunteers are deployed in environmental projects, often in areas of outstanding beauty such as the Grand Canyon or Yosemite National Park. Certain eight-week projects are reserved for international volunteers; see www.usaconservation.org/programs/conservation-volunteers.

Voluntary opportunities in the USA range from the intensely urban to the decidedly rural. In the former category, you can build houses in deprived areas throughout the USA with Habitat for Humanity (www.habitat.org) or work with inner city youth, the homeless, etc in New York City with the Winant Clayton Volunteers. Every summer a number of British volunteers join the WCV exchange for eight weeks from mid or late June followed by two or three weeks of travel. For application info contact WCV based in East London (☎ (+44) 20 8983 3834; www.winantclayton.org.uk) in advance of the application deadline of 22 February. Participants must fundraise at least £1,750 and preferably more. If you want a less structured spell of volunteering in New York City, go along to the University Soup Kitchen in the Cardinal Spellman Center at 137 East 2nd Street, on Saturdays from 11.45am–3.30pm (www.streetproject.org). Volunteers receive a free lunch.

Working outside the big cities is an attractive prospect. For example the US Forest Service organises workcamps to maintain trails, campsites and wildlife throughout the country; volunteers should apply to the individual parks; state-by-state opportunities are posted on the internet at www.volunteer.gov. Interesting roles as historic homestead interpreters and astronomy volunteers are included. The American Hiking Society collates volunteer opportunities from around the United States to build, maintain and restore foot trails in America's backcountry. No prior trail work experience is necessary, but volunteers should be able to hike at least five miles a day, supply their own backpacking equipment (including tent), pay a $330 registration fee ($275 for AHS members) and arrange transport to and from the work site. Food is provided on some projects. For a schedule of Volunteer Vacations, go to www.AmericanHiking.org.

The ever-growing Student Conservation Association (www.thesca.org) places anyone 18 or older in conservation and environmental internships in national parks and forests nationwide. If accepted, interns are placed with a land-management agency (National Park Service, US Forest Service) anywhere in the US for three to six months. Positions range widely, from wildlife management to native plant restoration to wilderness rangering to trail work to fisheries. Travel expenses within the

USA, housing, training and a weekly stipend are provided. International applicants are accepted (www.thesca.org/serve/international-applicants) but SCA cannot sponsor a visa.

At a loose end after university, Emily Sloane decided to spend some time in the great outdoors:

> *I did a six-month internship in the glacier-covered North Cascades National Park in Washington state. I was a member of the native plant propagation team and spent my season taking care of nursery plants, gathering seeds and swinging pick-mattocks to loosen up restoration sites so that we could re-vegetate them. I had ample time to explore the mountains, picking up some mountaineering equipment and skills, and as an intern was given occasional special privileges, like a spot on an elite botanical expedi-tion for a nearby university and a ride over the mountains in my boss's friend's ultralight glider. My supervisors were lovably insane, leading us in pilates sessions at the beginning of every workday, screaming out classic rock songs as we planted in the November snow and (per my request) donning wigs for an entire workday as a birthday gift to me. One of my best summers EVER.*

Emily Sloane also worked for the Appalachian Mountain Club (www.outdoors.org) for two summers as a backcountry campsite caretaker, during which one of her more glamorous duties was mixing 60 gallons' worth of human faeces with a pitchfork (while wearing long rubber gloves, of course) to keep the composting outhouse operational. The AMC hires plenty of Europeans to work at its base lodge at Pinkham Notch at the foot of Mount Washington, New England's tallest peak (notorious for its horrendous weather). The work there might not itself be terribly exciting – kitchen or housekeeping duties, most likely – but it provides access to a very beautiful area and a community of rugged outdoorsy folks. It might be possible for a foreigner to score a backcountry job although, as these positions are much more competitive, it would be prudent to plan ahead (apply by December for the following summer). The busiest season at the AMC's facilities runs from late May to late August.

CONCLUSION

This chapter has only scratched the surface, but has been written in the hope that it will spark a few new ideas for your trans-American trip. As one of our less intrepid correspondents recalls: *'When we first arrived in the States we went immediately to visit the parents of a friend. I'd never met them before but they made us welcome. A good thing too, because America seemed so strange to me and expensive and complicated, that I just wanted to get on the first plane back.'*

There is no denying that it is preferable to qualify for an Exchange Visitor Programme such as BUNAC, Au Pair in America or Camp America. One of the advantages is that these approved agencies recommend a comprehensive insurance policy for you. If you go on your own, make sure you have purchased enough insurance cover since medical care is astronomically expensive in the USA.

You must balance caution with a spirit of adventure, accepting and even revelling in the bizarre. When Julia Wilson from Oxford found lodgings in ultra-posh Martha's Vineyard, she was alarmed at first that they had guns and would regularly go out hunting for skunk, not quite what she expected of a place so beloved of old Boston money. You may end up in some unlikely situations, but some of them may also lead to a few days of work helping a trucker with his deliveries, joining an impromptu pop group to perform at private parties, gardening on a Californian commune, building solar houses, and so on. If you aren't lucky enough to have the appropriate visa, you should grasp every opportunity to take advantage of offers of genuine hospitality.

You should be able to get some kind of job which will introduce you to the striking cultural differences between Europe and America and which will provide you with some capital with which to explore this amazing country.

Canada

Wide open spaces, a high standard of living and none of the excesses of south of the border, Canada is a very attractive prospect for the working traveller. Students and some other categories are eligible for visa schemes which make it possible to get round the 'Canada-only' immigration policies. Canadians are hospitable and eager for visitors to like their country. Despite a shocking fall in the Canadian dollar over 2015 and 2016, the economic prospects of the country have been described as 'sparkling' and the dollar seemed to be rallying as President Trump took up office. Even the province of Alberta is predicted to see some recovery after it took a hammering from a sharp contraction of the oil and gas industry due to the drop in world prices. The rate of unemployment there is well above the national average, 9% compared to 6.8%. But most working holidaymakers will have their sights set on Canada's major cities or its many holiday resorts which are flourishing.

RED TAPE

British citizens require only a valid passport to enter Canada. Normally on arrival they will be given permission to stay as tourists for six months; incoming tourists may be requested to show that they have sufficient funds, adequate medical insurance and a return ticket or, failing that, some Canadian contacts. Although Canadian Immigration is reputed to be less savage than its American counterpart, many young travellers without much money have been given a rough ride and are categorically prohibited from working, including working for keep.

The International Experience Canada (www.cic.gc.ca/english/work/iec/index.asp) working holiday programme is open to all Britons aged 18–30 (and to nationals from 33 other countries with varying rules). Participants do not need to be students nor must they fix up a job in advance. However, the application process is quite complicated and is over-subscribed. The first step is to submit your profile to the eligibility screening pool which opens in mid-October and which is free of charge. You then wait, hoping to receive an invitation to apply for a work permit. Invitations are sent in waves from late November to randomly selected candidates from the pool starting in December until the quota is used up, which is likely to be in February. The quota is 5,000 in the case of the UK. There is no guarantee that everyone in the pool will be invited to apply, though the website provides statistics of how many people are waiting and what their chances are in the next round.

Applicants must have Proof of Funds, currently C$2,500 (all dollar prices in this chapter are in Canadian dollars). Additional outlays will be a programme participation fee of $126, $250 for the work permit, plus police clearance from the previous six months and suitable insurance cover, which are both required. The IEC visa is valid for any job or internship within the 24-month life of the visa. The programme is of course open to Australians (for whom there is no quota) and New Zealanders (up to 2,500).

Americans are not allowed to enter Canada in order to look for work. Like all foreign nationals, they must fix up a job (before arrival) that has been approved by the employer's local ESDC (Employment and Social Development Canada).

A blogger at www.offtracktravel.ca has written a practical 100-page e-book called 'The Ultimate Guide to a Working Holiday (IEC) in Canada' (November 2016) which is worth the £2.99 investment, though much of the information can be found on the website.

Special Schemes

A good place to start to look for agencies is the Canadian government's list of Recognized Organizations for the IEC programme. Anyone looking for a place on the Young Professionals programme or an internship (also under the auspices of the IEC) will find plenty of opportunities, especially if they are training in the hospitality field.

BUNAC in London (www.bunac.org) offers a Work Canada package for those who want agency back-up. The basic package costs £359 and the one that comes with employer interviews before leaving the UK costs £599. BUNAC's partner in Canada is the long-established exchange organisation SWAP (www.swap.ca) whose walk-in resource offices in Toronto and Vancouver give support in the hunt for jobs, accommodation, bank accounts, etc as well as organising social events at which you can meet other workingholiday makers. Note that SWAP's job database is open to public consumption.

GO International in Vancouver (www.gointernational.ca) is a Canadian company that offers work abroad programmes to Canadians and also has incoming programmes. It works with employers across Canada to maintain an inhouse database of seasonal and part-time jobs that only participants can access. Positions are mainly in the Vancouver area, Whistler, the interior of British Columbia, the Rocky Mountain ski resorts of Banff, Jasper and so on, Calgary and Ontario. Another Vancouver-based internship and working holiday placement agency is Stepwest (www.stepwest.com) whose two programmes cover city jobs and resort jobs. A programme with guaranteed work placement in Vancouver starts at $990 at any time of the year, whereas a seasonal winter or summer placement in a resort in the Rockies will cost from $1,190. Yet another company is INTERNeX (www.internexworld.com) which specialises in organising work, internships and accommodation for international students interested in coming to Canada.

Specialist travel companies exist in Europe and the Antipodes that help people arrange working holidays such as WorknHoliday.com with offices in Vancouver and Toronto (as well as Melbourne, Sydney, Brisbane and Cairns) or Praktikawelten.de for Germans.

CASUAL WORK

Once you have obtained an IEC open work permit, you are entitled to apply for a Social Insurance Number. The SIN is comparable to the American social security number and is essential for finding any kind of job and for accessing bank accounts, employment offices, tax offices, etc. Many employers will be unwilling to consider you or, more importantly, pay you unless you have one.

If you decide to work without proper authorisation, you should be aware that you are breaking a law that is taken seriously in Canada with a very real danger of deportation. If you are working in a job known to hire large numbers of foreigners (eg ski resorts and fruit picking in British Columbia), there is a chance that the area will be raided by immigration control. Raymond Oliver could hardly believe their efficiency: at 10am he gave his British Columbia employer a made-up SIN, at noon a phone call came to say it was fake and at 11am the next day an immigration officer arrived to tell him he had to leave the country within a fortnight. More recently, some graduates from an expensive ski instructing course in the Rockies were discovered to be working on the slopes without the appropriate documents and were summarily sent home. It is rumoured that it is not difficult for people without permits to find winter work in ski resorts in the Rockies but not on the slopes. If you cannot fund your own departure, you will either be given a 'departure order' which gives you 30 days to leave the country, an exclusion order which means you are barred from returning to Canada for a specified period or, worst of all, a deportation order which permanently bars a return. Brigitte Albrech worked as a tree planter in Prince George, British Columbia using a SIN number given to her by her employer. But because she was German, it was hard to blend in and the authorities somehow heard of her (after she had been working for three months) and sent her a request in writing to leave within six weeks or face a court hearing.

Statutory minimum wages vary slightly by province but are mostly around $11 with the highest in Alberta (going up to $15 in 2018). People in tipped positions, eg liquor servers, often earn $1–$2 less per hour. Most working holidaymakers (like most Canadian students) earn the minimum wage, with an average weekly wage of $415 and average accommodation costs of $400–$600 a month in a shared house (more in Toronto and Vancouver). The government's searchable database of jobs, including a separate section for Youth & Student jobs, is at www.jobbank.gc.ca.

THE JOB-HUNT

It takes newly arrived jobseekers an average of between one and two weeks of concerted searching to find a job in Canada, which can be a dispiriting time. Even Canadian students find it hard to get summer jobs and there will be competition for most kinds of seasonal work. It will be necessary to look presentable, eager to please, positive and cheerful, even if the responses are negative or the employers rude. Ideally you will have some work references; even job ads for dishwashers often ask for a year's experience. On the other hand, some find the job-hunt relatively easy, as Australian Rebecca Wootten did, after spending seven months in Canada on a working holiday visa:

> *I worked in Vancouver and had a great time working for a float plane company called Westcoast Air. It isn't too hard to get a job. I joined an employment service straight after we were issued with our social insurance numbers, and handed out resumés. Lots of cafés are willing to hire Aussies and other foreigners. Also a great spot would have been the resort of Whistler, where you can work summer or winter.*

Toronto and other major cities have fleets of hand-pulled rickshaws or pedicab tricycles that employ runners/cyclists. The high season extends from the beginning of July to the end of the Labour Day weekend at the beginning of September. If interested, ask the vendors for the name and number of their boss. Matthew Shiel from the University of Swansea did it for the summer and at one point was saving an impressive $1,000 a week. Companies to try for a summer season job include Rickshaw Services of Toronto (www.rickshawservices.com), which markets rickshaw travel as the most eco-friendly mode of transport, and The Victoria Pedicab Company in Victoria (www.victoriatours.net) which invites applicants with a valid driver's licence to express interest via an online application form. Runners rent the rickshaw from the company and work as independent contractors. Tourism is booming in Victoria so the council is considering increasing the number of pedicab licences for 2017. The arrival of a cruise ship usually means a bonanza for runners.

As ever, youth hostel noticeboards are recommended for information on jobs. According to one informant, staff at the Edmonton Youth Hostel can advise on local work opportunities. Only students with working holiday permits will be allowed to work in hostels.

The Jericho Beach Youth Hostel in Vancouver sometimes recruits volunteers for particular roles such as leading ghost tours of Vancouver or bike tours of Stanley Park, but they cannot accept foreign nationals. Check out their employment board where notices from local companies and individuals offering employment may be posted. In addition, the front desk staff are a valuable resource for finding employment in the city.

In addition to Vancouver, the best cities to look for work are Toronto, Calgary and Edmonton. The majority of jobs in at least one jobs database (www.worknholiday.com) are hospitality jobs in the big cities with a few in Montreal for sandwich shop staff, etc. One possibility is to apply to branches of European retail companies such as the Body Shop and Gap. Tanufa Kotecha quickly learned that Canadian selling techniques are just as aggressive as American ones: *'I landed a job within a week in Toronto working in a French Canadian clothing store. In my store as soon as a customer walked in, they had to be greeted by a "sales associate" within 15 seconds! The North American way of selling is pushy and upfront, but it does get results. One must have confidence to sell.'* Almost all shop jobs of this kind pay the minimum wage.

TOURISM

For summer season jobs, British university students have an edge over their North American counterparts since they don't have to return to their studies until mid to late September rather than the beginning of September.

The Rocky Mountain resorts of Banff, Jasper, Lake Louise, Sunshine Mountain and Whistler are among the best places to try, both summer and winter. Whistler and in second place Banff seem to absorb the largest number of foreign workers as catering and chamber staff, ski staff, etc. Both are expensive towns in which to job-hunt, though in summer some people have been known to camp free well out of town.

Although most famous for its skiing and snowboarding, Whistler should not be overlooked in summer. Short-term housing rents drop dramatically, jobs are just as easy to find if you get there before the season starts and temperatures regularly exceed 30 degrees. Pete Thompson was so smitten by Whistler after spending a winter season there as a ski instructor that he couldn't resist staying on:

> *Whistler is one of a few resorts worldwide that is big enough and exciting enough to entertain visitors all year round. The atmosphere changes with the disappearance of the snow. Very early ski mornings are replaced by late-night partying in the forests, at full moon parties, or at casual evening barbecues, watching the sun set at around 10 or 11pm. Wildlife is everywhere, black bears being particularly easy to spot on walks or camping trips. So after you've enjoyed a Whistler winter, trade in your skis for a mountain bike, your board for board shorts and stay for the summer.*

The huge Fairmont Banff Springs Hotel alone employs 900 people, as do its sister hotels in the Fairmont group of luxury hotels such as Chateau Lake Louise, Jasper Park Lodge and Chateau Whistler. The Fairmont Group describes its recruitment needs and links to current vacancies at www.fairmontcareers.com. Also try Lake Louise Inn, Banff Lodging Company (www.bestofbanff.com/careers), Brewster Travel (www.brewster.ca/corporate/careers) and Athabasca Hotel in Jasper. One of the main employers in Jasper is Mountain Park Lodges; go to www.mpljasper.com/about/job_postings.html to find vacancies as line cooks, kitchen helpers and room cleaners. The standard wage at these hotels is the provincial minimum ($13.60 in Alberta, $11.25 in British Columbia). During the height of the season there may be very little time off. Employers will make a deduction for staff accommodation and/or meals, usually about $10 a day.

One traveller to Western Canada reported:

> *While on holiday in Banff, I met a lot of Australians and Britons staying at the youth hostel. All of them were just on holiday visas, and all of them had found work in the height of the tourist season. I was offered hotel work. There is a lot of work to be had in Canada and men in particular would have no trouble supporting themselves. Canadians are very warm towards foreigners and employers are generally prepared to risk hiring casuals 'black' if they can't get through the red tape. Wages are very good for this type of work.*

The CN Tower near the Toronto waterfront frequently advertises for staff to work as guides and crew on the Edgewalk where thrill-seekers walk outside on the roof of the main pod (www.cntower.ca/en-ca/about-us/careers/opportunities.html).

As always, special events such as the Calgary Stampede every June, result in a stampede of temporary workers. Anyone working front-of-house in the hospitality industry should be liable to earn a lot of tips in a short time. Check www.kijiji.ca for the town in which you want to work (Kijiji is the equivalent of Gumtree) and of course Craigslist. Tourist industry jobs in the cities will be hard to find out of season, since most openings are part-time and filled by local students. Any job that involves selling alcohol in Ontario requires Smart Serve certification and employers will ask about this at interview. You can do the course online or at one of many training centres for $40–$50 for three hours.

SKI RESORTS

Ski resorts throughout Canada create a great number of seasonal employment vacancies that can't be filled by Canadian students since they're all studying. As is the case throughout the world, affordable accommodation is in very short supply in the main ski resorts. Most of the accommodation in ski towns is full by October, well in advance of the start of the season.

Banff is always in desperate need of cheap labour; there are literally thousands of young travellers, mainly Canadian students, Australians, Kiwis and Brits in town. No-one seems to struggle to find employment, and as a result many employers are very flexible with hours. Many offer staff accommodation at subsidised rates, which is incredibly useful since rents in Banff are a killer. It's not unheard of for five people to share a two-bedroom flat to save money.

A few major employers cooperate with BUNAC to interview and hire in the UK in advance of the winter season, including the Four Seasons Resort in Whistler, Panorama Mountain Village Resort in British Columbia and Blue Mountain Resort in Ontario (mentioned below). Check details of the BUNAC 'Ultimate Work & Travel Package' on which three interviews are guaranteed.

For Banff, consider Sunshine Village Resort which employs about 400 seasonal staff, with limited basic accommodation provided depending on the position. Their website www.skibanff.com/jobs has lots of useful information for prospective staff including dates of their annual hiring fairs held in October.

Moving west to the Pacific, the Whistler Chamber of Commerce posts employment information at www.whistlerchamber.com/membership/employment-resources/working-in-whistler. The employment pages of the site www.whistlerblackcomb.com give details of the annual recruiting fair (usually first few days of November) although the bulk of available seasonal positions have already been allocated by this time, at recruitment sessions in Whistler and Ontario, both in September. It is also possible to apply online for jobs in retail, guest services, food and beverage, etc, although being available for a face-to-face interview is a huge advantage. A certain number of workers leave after the Christmas rush so it is possible to get a job once the season begins even if you haven't lined anything up at the main autumn hiring season.

James Gillespie spent the winter and summer of his gap year working in Whistler. After taking the beautiful train ride from Vancouver, it soon became clear that getting a place to stay would be a major problem. But soon he had a job as a ticket validator which came with a free ski pass and subsidised accommodation: *'It was an excellent job and, although sometimes mundane, it was often livened up by violent and abusive skiers trying to get on the lift for free. Going there was the best thing I've ever done and I hope to be living there permanently eventually. I came home with a diary full of experiences, a face full of smiles, a bag full of dirty washing and pockets full of ... well nothing actually. I was in debt, but it was worth it.'*

Applications for work in Ontario resorts such as Blue Mountain near Collingwood (www.bluemountain.ca/employment.htm) are normally considered in November, whereas the deadline is somewhat earlier for work in western resorts since the season starts earlier. Blue Mountain is operated by the international resort company Intrawest and the slogan on their centralised recruitment site (www.intrawest.com/careers/short-term-op) sums up the aims of the working traveller: WeWork2play. Blue Mountain employs up to 700 staff for the season, which is running on full steam from Christmas to the March break. If considering ski resorts in Québec such as Mount Tremblant knowledge of French is necessary.

Other popular holiday areas in summer are the Muskoka District of Ontario centred on the town of Huntsville, and the shores of the Great Lakes, particularly Lake Huron. Most of the holiday job recruitment in Ontario is done through Canadian universities, though someone willing to stay until mid or late September will be preferred. Among the biggest Muskoka resorts are Deerhurst (☎ (+1) 705 789 7113 ext 4236; www.deerhurstresort.com/careers), the Rosseau Marriott (rosseaujobs@marriott.com) and just nearby in Minett Ontario, Clevelands House (jobs@clevelandshouse.com). Most of the summer season hiring takes place between December and February.

TREE PLANTING

The archetype of the working Canadian is the lumberjack. Nowadays there are fewer jobs for tree-choppers than tree-planters. In areas that have been burnt or logged (increasingly to clear pine forests decimated by the mountain pine beetle), companies are required by law to re-plant. However, the industry has been in a decline since the 2008 recession when 17 sawmills closed in British Columbia alone. The northern BC town of Prince George used to be a mecca for mobs of young seasonal workers, but several of the silviculture companies have closed and the rest are struggling. Because there are fewer vacancies than in the industry's heyday, many companies will consider hiring only experienced planters.

On the other hand, there are still thousands of job vacancies with the companies that carry on, and every winter planting contractors recruit crews for the season, which begins in April. Most camps are set up in rugged backcountry locations so experience of wilderness camping is an asset, including how to protect yourself from bears. The internet is a goldmine of insiders' information with extensive listings of companies; see especially www.tree-planter.com and www.replant.ca.

The payment is piecework – so much per seedling planted. In good seasons in British Columbia, average rates of 17 cents have been on offer, but last summer in Ontario some companies were paying a basic eight cents per tree, with a premium of only one cent when planting on poor ground, even though it is miles slower when working on rough bushy terrain.

On decent terrain an experienced planter can plant on average 2,500 trees a day. At the extremes a hotshot can plant 4,000 and a rookie 1,500. Novices can usually earn $50–$150 a day after a few weeks' practice. A deduction is made for camp expenses including transport to the planting sites, usually the maximum allowed of $25 a day plus 5% GST, which can be a real killer to saving. Not all companies charge high camp expenses, but the more experienced planters tend to fill up the vacancies with the more generous companies. You will need a waterproof tent and work clothes including boots and waterproofs. Many firms do not lend out the equipment, so the cost of shovels and bags (which will run to between $200 and $600) are deducted from your wages. Transport is provided from camp to planting site, but the journey can take two to four hours out of the day, for which you are not paid.

Dates are uncertain due to weather. There is a spring and a much smaller summer season with two to four weeks in between. Some BC contractors start as early as late March and finish in July/August, though others don't begin until early May. Around Fort Frances and Thunder Bay in Ontario, the season is shorter, roughly 1 May to 1 July. An average season consists of 50 days of work.

A couple of summers ago, Canadian student Gabriel Keenleyside did a season of planting in northern Ontario. He came home with $1,200 for eight weeks of working 48 hours a week, but also had to spend $500 on equipment and $200 on transport to the camp. Hardly the pot of gold some have dreamed of.

FRUIT PICKING

British Columbia

The fruit-growing industry of Western Canada takes place in decidedly more congenial surroundings. The beautiful Okanagan Valley is tucked away between two mountain ranges in the interior of British Columbia and supports 26,000 acres of orchards. The Valley stretches north from the American border at Osoyoos for over 200km to Armstrong. Cherries, peaches, plums, pears, apricots, grapes and apples are all grown in the Valley, with a concentration of soft fruits in the south and hard fruits (apples, pears) in the north. All of these must be picked by hand.

The government's Service Canada centres in Penticton and Kelowna, which are one-stop shops for all government services including employment, might be able to advise. However most people learn about vacancies online, such as from www.okanagan.com/fruit-jobs.html, the BC Fruitgrowers' Association site, which will send vacancy alerts by email (www.bcfga.com) and general employment search engines like www.ca.indeed.com. Unfortunately not many farmers provide accommodation for their pickers, apart from holders of the Temporary Foreign Worker visa whom they are obliged to house. Lots of fruit pickers have no choice but to stay at the Loose Bay campground on the outskirts of Oliver, which is cheap but with inadequate facilities for the influx of migrant workers.

The harvests in Kelowna, a town approximately in the centre of the Valley, take place at the times given in the chart below.

FRUIT HARVESTS IN BRITISH COLUMBIA

CROP	APPROXIMATE STARTING DATE	APPROXIMATE DURATION
Cherries	25 June	through July
Apricots	mid-July	approx. 3 weeks
Vee peaches	5 August	2 or 3 weeks
Elberta peaches	28 August	2 or 3 weeks
Red Haven peaches	20 July	6 weeks
Prune plums	mid-August	until mid-September
Bartlett pears	12 August	until Sept/early Oct
Anjou pears	late September	October
Macintosh apples	early September	3–4 weeks
Spartan apples	late September	3–4 weeks
Newton apples	late October/November	3–4 weeks
Winesap apples	late October	3–4 weeks
Golden Delicious apples	September	3–4 weeks
Red Delicious apples	September	3–4 weeks
Rome Beauty apples	September	3–4 weeks
Fuji apples	September	3 weeks
Grapes	8 September	6 weeks

Once you arrive in a key fruit-growing area, you will soon hear about who is hiring. Some attempt is made to screen applicants through their social insurance number, etc to avoid hiring a picker who has caused trouble elsewhere. The BC Cherry Association (www.bccherry.com) has a centralised application system on its website and posts the contact details of its 35 member orchards together with usual picking dates and accommodation facilities. A late frost or poor pollination can drastically reduce the cherry harvest.

Professional migrant pickers (many of whom are from Québec) begin with the cherries in the south of the valley and move up the valley to pick only the peak cherries. The cherry harvest in Osoyoos begins in late June, but in Winfield 150km to the north, from late July. Then they come south again to work the apricots in the same way and so on. Hostility between migrant workers and locals is commonplace. Note that even when fruit pickers are paid piecework, they must earn at least the BC minimum wage of $11.25 an hour. Of course once your speed improves, it is to your advantage to be paid piecework. Most people's wages are paid directly into a bank account, which is a further difficulty for casual workers without proper papers.

Apples are the Okanagan's most famous export product. There is continuous picking of one variety or another from mid-August to the end of October. Apple picking can be slow and poorly paid. A basket is worn at the front of the body and this becomes very heavy as it fills up. Experience is not so important for the apple harvest. Especially towards the end of the harvest when all the students have returned to university (approximately mid-September) and the weather is getting colder, the farmers begin to take almost anyone.

Raspberry, blueberry and cranberry picking and pruning take place nearer Vancouver in Richmond, Chilliwack, Abbotsford, Aldergrove and Langley between June and August, though this work is notoriously badly paid. Warehouse bulb packing work is offered February–April by Van Noort Bulbs in Langley (www.vannoortbulb.com). Tales of mass exploitation of migrant farm labourers emerge from this area at intervals. Most growers do not provide accommodation and campsite charges are considerable relative to wages. There are pickers' huts but Asian immigrants mainly occupy these. A further problem is the controversy over pesticides that may harm skin. A trawl of the internet will result in directories of fruit farms such as the one at http://bcstrawberries.com. To take just one example, Driediger Farms in Langley (☎ (+1) 604 888 1665) employ an average of 150 pickers in the season to harvest blueberries, strawberries and raspberries.

Ontario, Québec and Eastern Canada

The microclimate in the fertile Niagara region bordering Lake Ontario is excellent for growing peaches, pears, plums, grapes (mostly for wine) and cherries. But local unemployment is high and it will be difficult to get a decent job, even though there is no shortage of fruit needing to be picked. To meet farmers, it is a good idea to go to the Saturday farmers' market at Sylvia Place in Niagara Falls, around the corner from the Service Canada office at the corner of Main and Peer Streets. Check what is in season at www.harvestontario.com with many links to farms and wineries.

The Maritimes

High unemployment in some Maritime areas has driven many locals west in search of employment. However, if you are travelling in the eastern provinces in early to mid-August, you might try to find paid work picking or 'raking' blueberries in the Nova Scotia towns of Parrsboro, Minudie, Amherst or Pugwash and elsewhere. Earlier in the summer (ie mid-June to mid-July), strawberry picking is available. In the autumn you can also look for work picking apples. Head for the Bay of Fundy coast of Nova Scotia around Annapolis Royal, Bridgetown and Middleton. The Nova Scotia Fruit Growers Association (www.nsapples.com/harvest.htm) in Kentville, NS may be able to refer enquirers to its members who need harvesting help. If you're lucky, fruit picking wages will be paid cash in hand.

Casual fruit pickers are sent to various farms on the outskirts of Montreal by registering with the Agri-job Agency (☎ (+1)514 273 1503; www.agrijob.info) which organises buses from several suburban metro stations to the farms. One picker found it all fairly joyless. A high proportion of pickers are from Francophone Africa.

OTHER FARM WORK

If you are interested in working your way from farm to farm and want to meet Canadians, you might consider volunteering for WWOOF-Canada (World Wide Opportunities on Organic Farms). You can access nearly 900 host farms at the WWOOF Canada website www.wwoof.ca after becoming a member. Membership costs $50 or $65 per couple for two years. All volunteers must have valid tourist visas. Canada permits volunteer work on farms in exchange for accommodation and meals, provided it is not the main object of the trip and that no stay on one farm exceeds four weeks. The WWOOF website provides masses of helpful information and examples of the documents that will help your case at the border.

CHILDCARE AND SUMMER CAMPS

Live-in nannies and mother's helps are in great demand in Canadian cities. However, domestic employment in Canada is governed by a number of carefully formulated regulations which are strictly enforced. Details of the 'Live-in Caregiver Program' may be obtained from the Canadian Immigration Department's website www.cic.gc.ca/english/work/caregiver/index.asp. Qualifying nannies must either have six months of full-time training in a related field (teaching, nursing, childcare) or 12 months' experience in full-time paid employment as a nanny, mother's help or caregiver within the previous three years, at least half of which must have been continuously for the same employer. The other main requirements are that the nanny must have a job contract from an employer in Canada, an LMIA (see below), have completed secondary school and speak English or French. Since 2014, employers must obtain a Labour Market Impact Assessment (LMIA) from Service Canada (at a cost of $1,000) to show that there is no Canadian worker available and that hiring a Temporary Foreign Worker will not have a detrimental effect on the Canadian labour market. The employer can obtain one of these before choosing the employee. With all these documents, the foreign nanny can apply for a work permit from IRCC (Immigration, Refugees & Citizenship Canada) before entering Canada.

The procedure for getting the permit usually takes between three and six months (longer for some countries) and will include a very strict medical examination by a private doctor on the Canadian list of panel physicians. There are only six locations in all of England, and expect to pay £300 for the check-up. The permit will be valid for one employer, though it can be changed within Canada as long as your subsequent job is as a live-in child carer. After two years as a caregiver (cumulatively within four years), it is possible to apply to become a permanent resident.

Working as a nanny or mother's help in Canada has more status attached to it than au pairing in Europe, and the conditions of work reflect this. Wages must be no less than the median wage paid in that category of employment in that location, which make fascinating browsing at www.jobbank.gc.ca. For example a low hourly wage for a live-in nanny in non-urban British Columbia is $10.85 an hour, a median wage $11 and a high wage $19. The federal and provincial governments set out guidelines for hours, time off and holidays. According to the terms of the programme, room and board must be free of charge to live-in nannies and earnings must be no less than the provincial minimum wage. See www.canada.ca/en/employment-social-development/services/foreign-workers/foreign-workers-hire-caregiver/working-conditions.html for province-by-province details.

A search of the internet will take you to many Canadian agencies offering the Caregiver programme, though some are more experienced at bringing in nannies from countries such as Peru, Mexico, the Philippines, Hong Kong, Ukraine and Slovakia rather than the UK. In all cases, nannies must satisfy the government's Live-in Caregiver requirements. Au pairs are also in demand and are easier for families to arrange because they can come as part of the IEC visa programme described earlier.

Here is a small selection of agencies that maintain databases of families looking for care, and caregivers/au pairs looking for families:

ABC Nannies Agency: Vancouver; ☎ (+1) 604 726 6501; www.abcnannies.ca. Live-in placements across Canada; live-out positions in Vancouver.

Diamond Personnel Inc: Toronto, Calgary, Vancouver; ☎ (+1) 888 886 8209; www.diamond-personnel.com. High demand for live-out nannies as well as live-in, especially in Calgary.

International Nannies & Homecare Ltd: Vancouver; ☎ (+1) 800 820 8308; www.internationalnannies.com. Matches European au pairs with families as well as live-in caregivers.

Nannies on Call: www.nanniesoncall.com. Based in Calgary with vacancies throughout Canada. Hoping to open an office in Halifax soon.

Niagara Caregivers & Personnel Ltd: Hamilton, Ontario; www.niagaracaregivers.com. Nanny and au pair openings across Ontario.

OptiMum Children & Nannies Inc: www.opti-mum.com. Nannies looking for work in and around Vancouver can add their details to a searchable internet database free of charge.

Scotia Personnel Ltd: Halifax, NS; ☎ (+1) 902 422 1455; www.scotia-personnel-ltd.com. Member of IAPA.

Trafalgar Personnel: Oakville, Ontario; http://trafalgarpersonnel.com/overseas-lcp-applicants.

Canadian children flock to summer camps in the great outdoors in huge numbers. Young people are needed to work as camp counsellors, swimming instructors, canoeing and wilderness guides and so on. Potentially useful online resources include www.ontariocampsassociation.ca and www.summer-campstaff.com. CCUSA (www.ccusa.co.uk) places British and other foreign counsellors and support staff on hundreds of camps in Canada, and cooperates with Nyquest Camp Canada based in Toronto (☎ (+1) 416 932 1370 or ☎ (+44) 20 3290 2358; www.go-nyquest.com) who organise hiring fairs in British cities in mid-January. The CCUSA programme fee for Britons is a reasonable £299 which includes up to ten weeks' insurance. Summer camp staff are paid between $1,500 and $1,900 at the end of the season.

VOLUNTEERING

Some interesting practical community projects are organised by Frontiers Foundation (☎ (+1) 416 690 3930; www.frontiersfoundation.ca/volunteer) in low-income communities in Canada, including aboriginal communities in isolated northern areas. Volunteers of many nationalities, who must be at least 18 and energetic, may join the Operation Beaver programme as tutors (eg of maths, science, English, music, drama), teaching assistants or recreation workers, along with assisting in First Nations offices. Most projects take place on wilderness camps for Native children or in schools in the three northern territories (Yukon, Northwest Territories and Nunavut). Education placements last 10 months from September whereas summer placements for house construction last at least three months starting in June and are for volunteers, preferably with relevant experience. All expenses are paid within Canada including domestic travel and medical insurance, plus pocket money of $50 a week.

ACCORDING TO EMILY SLOANE, WATCHING THE RIVERS BREAK UP IN THE SPRING WAS ONE OF THE MOST SPECTACULAR THINGS SHE HAS EVER SEEN, AND HER TIME WITH FF TURNED OUT TO BE ONE OF THE BEST EXPERIENCES OF HER LIFE:

From February to June I worked as an education volunteer in a Gwich'in village in the Northwest Territories through Frontiers Foundation. The school I worked in desperately needed help and positive energy. I became the teaching assistant in the grade 4–6 classroom, and I think that my presence allowed the overly stressed teacher to relax a bit. I eventually got to help design and implement parts of the reading and social studies curricula, too. And of course, being in the Arctic had its perks. I was able to attend a caribou hunting field trip in the Yukon in March, during which I got up in the middle of the night to use the outhouse in 60 below temperatures. I'd go cross-country skiing after school every day, sometimes with several husky puppies at my heels, and as the days grew longer, my skis were sometimes postponed until 10 or 11 at night. All in all, a thoroughly satisfying experience.

Another contributor stumbled (or rather strode) across a different way to experience the Canadian bush. Obbe Verwer from Amsterdam spent part of the summer hiking in British Columbia:

After enjoying my visits to a couple of farms listed by WWOOF, I went on by myself to Vancouver Island. I set off to hike through the rainforest along the Clayoquot Valley Witness Trail. When I came to the trailhead, I met the trail boss who was working with a group of volunteers to build boardwalks at both ends of the trail. This was to enable more people to walk part of the trail, which is important because this valley has to be saved from clearcut logging. I decided to join them. Actually you are supposed to go through the organising committee to become a volunteer worker but I just pitched my tent and joined on the spot.

All the wood to build the boardwalk had to be carried into the trail, steps, stringers, nails and tools. We worked till 4pm, but it was not strict at all. Sometimes it was pretty hard, but it was fun. The forest impressed me more and more. The big trees, the berries, the mushrooms and the silence in the mist. It was just amazing. It was very satisfying to be helping to save this forest.

The Western Canada Wilderness Committee can be visited at 46 East 6th Avenue in Vancouver (☎ (+1) 604 683 8220; www.wildernesscommittee.org). Volunteers should bear in mind that while working in rainforests one is bound to get wet. It also has offices in Victoria, Winnipeg and Toronto.

Travellers may find chances to subsidise an otherwise unaffordable wilderness experience by volunteering. For example a lodge in beautiful Algonquin Park in northern Ontario operates an Eco-Volunteer Programme in the summer. People who spend about four hours a day grooming trails, stacking wood, cutting grass, etc can get a 40% discount on accommodation and free meals (www.algonquincolodge.com/eco-volunteer).

A searchable database of volunteering opportunities in British Columbia and Alberta can be found at www.govolunteer.ca though most positions are not residential. This can be helpful for special events and annual festivals that need very short-term volunteers. An organisation in Ontario called Redleaf operates a nationwide volunteer placement programme, which mostly appeals to international candidates who want a chance to improve their English, though British volunteers can also be placed (http://red-leaf.com) on anything from an eco-gardening project to animal shelters, as well as many in seniors' residences and childcare centres. Accommodation is provided in private homes.

Clinical research is often carried out in university towns by university medical departments and teaching hospitals. The websites www.centerwatch.com and www.clinicaltrials.gov give easy-to-use links to major research centres in Canada such as the Clinical Research Centre at the McGill University Health Centre. Free newspapers in wide circulation in Toronto often carry ads for healthy volunteers aged 18–60, for example from Pharma Medica (☎ (+1) 416 759 5554; www.pharmamedica.com/tor). The website provides instant access to current studies, with levels of compensation offered, for example for three discrete weeks, non-smoking men and women aged 18–55 might be compensated up to $4,000. Another pharmaceutical company advertising trials in Toronto is Apotex (☎ (+1) 416 741 4256; www.apotex.com/ca).

Latin America

As a travel destination, South and Central America has been gaining popularity among Britons and Europeans faster than almost any other regional destination. Many gap year students as well as older travellers are setting their sights on a trip to Argentina or the Amazon or the Andes possibly in between a stint of teaching or volunteering.

Most Latin American nations do not need unskilled workers from abroad to perform the menial tasks associated with agriculture and industry. For every such job, there are several dozen natives willing to work for a pittance, and gringos (white Westerners) will not be considered for such work. However, people who can speak competent Spanish may find opportunities in the cities. Because Britain has few colonial ties with Central and South America, there is a general cultural and economic orientation towards Uncle Sam which means that Americans tend to occupy many jobs rather than Britons. Apart from volunteering opportunities, the main sphere of employment in which foreign travellers have any prospect of gaining acceptance is the teaching of the English language.

TEACHING

Spanning 75 degrees of latitude, the mammoth continent of South America together with the Caribbean islands and the eight countries of Central America, offer a surprising range of teaching opportunities. All but Brazil have a majority of Spanish speakers and, as in Spain itself, there is a great demand for English teaching, from dusty towns on the Yucatan Peninsula of Mexico to Punta Arenas at the southern extremity of the continent, south of the Falkland Islands.

The countries of most interest to the travelling teacher are Argentina, Chile, Mexico, Bolivia, Colombia, Ecuador, Peru and Brazil. Despite some economic uncertainty, demand for English language tuition continues to increase in the various kinds of institution engaged in promoting English, from elite cultural centres supported by the British and American governments to technical centres, from prestigious bilingual secondary schools to agencies which supply private tutors to businessmen. Experience is not always essential to land a teaching job on the spot.

It is advisable to take a professional approach, by having at your disposal a smartly turned out CV, qualifications and references, though not all schools will ask to see them. Obviously, you'll need a local contact number, so get yourself a mobile phone and then distribute your CV as widely as possible. When you drop your CV in, the school may ask you to take a written English test on the spot, which is sometimes quite elaborate with a composition section. If you pass the test, you may get invited to a group interview in which you will be asked to perform various tasks in small teams or pairs. If you are successful at this stage, you may then be asked to do a one or two-week training course (usually unpaid). Only once this has been completed will you be offered work. Some of the smaller companies will offer some hours if you pass their test and give a satisfactory demonstration lesson so try to bring some teaching materials with you.

You can also arrange jobs before arrival. Sheona Mckay managed to set up her own project as a volunteer teacher in Peru between March and June through a personal contact:

Especially for people wanting to teach English, I think it is easy enough to find out the names of some schools in an area you are interested in working in. Then you can email the school directly and hopefully come to an agreement with them.

A surefire way to get a teaching job is to do a TEFL training course in your destination country, such as with the US-based BridgeTEFL (www.bridgetefl.com) which offers a 120-hour proprietary certificate qualification called IDELT in Buenos Aires and Santiago (cost $1,995). EBC TEFL Training in Buenos Aires (www.ebcteflcourse.com/tefl-courses-jobs-buenos-aires-argentina) offers a month-long TEFL training course for €1,060 followed by a job placement programme, as does Maximo Nivel (www.maximonivel.com) in Cusco (Peru), Antigua (Guatemala) and San José (Costa Rica). Most courses last four weeks and cost between $1,200 and $2,000. An online recruitment agency Teachers Latin America based in Mexico City (www.teachers-latin-america.com) connects teachers with schools. Candidate teachers can upload their application to the site, and scour the jobs posted. More detailed information about teaching and training in Latin America can be found in the 2017 edition of my book *Teaching English Abroad* (Trotman).

THE JOB HUNT

In a land where baseball is a passion and US television enormously popular, American (and also Canadian) jobseekers have a distinct advantage. The whole continent is culturally and economically oriented towards the States and there is often a preference for the American accent and for American teaching materials and course books. On the other hand, many Britons have found themselves highly valued from Colombian universities to language agencies in Santiago. Business English is booming throughout the region and anyone with a business background will have an edge over the competition.

If you are looking for casual teaching work after arrival, check adverts in the English language press such as the *Buenos Aires Herald* or online communities. English language bookshops are another possible source of teaching leads. Ask in expatriate bars and restaurants, check out any building claiming to be an English School, however dubious-looking, and in larger cities try deciphering the telephone directory for schools or agencies which might be able to use your services.

The crucial factor in becoming accepted as an English teacher at a locally run language school may not be your qualifications or your accent as much as your appearance. You must look as professionally turned out as teachers are expected to look.

Travellers working their way around the world are more likely to find a few hours of teaching here and there earning $3–$15 an hour, and have to patch together hours from various sources in order to make a living. If you have a good education, are carrying all your references and diplomas and are prepared to stay for an academic year, it may be possible to fix up a relatively lucrative contract.

EXPERIENCED TRAVELLER LIBBY GOLDSMITH HAS BEEN ENJOYING MORE THAN FOUR YEARS OF TEACHING IN SOUTH AMERICA, FIRST IN SANTIAGO (CHILE) AND THEN IN BOGOTÁ (COLOMBIA). HAVING DONE A DISTANCE LEARNING TEFL COURSE AND A SUMMER OF TEACHING BEFORE DEPARTURE FROM ENGLAND, SHE FELT THAT SHE KNEW WHAT SHE WAS GETTING INTO:

I researched teaching institutes on the internet and cross-referenced these against online reviews. I then approached each institute with my CV by email or in person. I have seen two application processes in play. The first is the traditional approach where you send in your CV then await an invitation for an interview, which is usually fairly structured and standard, with questions relating to past experience, reasons for applying, etc. Upon a successful interview you are then invited back to teach a mock class on a designated topic. References are also required. The second process is based principally on a fellow teacher's recommendation, followed up with an informal interview to discuss requirements and teaching philosophies. Student feedback becomes the final character reference.

The majority of my teaching has been to business professionals, consequently the focus is on business language and business skills (eg emails, presentations, etc). Grammar is taught through functional language rather than directly. Peak teaching hours typically extended in bands across the week – anything between 6am and 9am were the morning slots; lunchtime slots extended from 11.30am to 2.30pm; and the evening between 4pm and 9pm. Working unsociable hours is a fact of life. Most of my classes are at business premises, which means I do quite a bit of travelling between classes; though I do enjoy this as it offers variation. Few institutes arrange accommodation but Facebook groups provide a support network and there are always noticeboards.

Wages are adequate in South America but it can be difficult to save much. Some weeks you can find yourself with lots of spare time due to a rash of cancellations and therefore feeling like a pauper.

The best part of EFL teaching is seeing students achieve their dreams and knowing that in part, you helped. The business students are all well-educated, extremely motivated and enthusiastic. Teaching is fun and extremely rewarding: watching a beginner with hardly any English in the first class learn to construct sentences and give basic opinions after as little as two or three months ... it is incredible. The highlight of the whole experience for me has been meeting some incredibly motivated and committed students who have such interesting stories and views of the world. The fascinating conversations you have can challenge your view of the world.

For a conventional pre-arranged teaching post, consider the British Council's Language Assistants Programme (www.britishcouncil.org/language-assistants). Applicants with at least A level Spanish and a degree, or undergraduates currently studying Spanish are placed for an academic year in Chile, Colombia, Ecuador, Mexico and Argentina (six months only from March). Deadlines and interview timetables are posted online.

Some US-based organisations arrange for paying volunteers to teach in South and Central America including WorldTeach at Harvard (www.worldteach.org) which sends volunteer teachers of EFL to Ecuador for a year and Brazil for a summer.

The country that has dropped off the radar of travelling workers is Venezuela. Reports of the state of the Venezuelan economy make for sobering reading and will deter all but the foolhardy from choosing it as a destination. Government policies together with the loss of revenue due to the fall in the price of oil have shattered the country. Severe shortages of commonplace goods have led to huge price increases plunging a huge percentage of the population, estimated to be as high as 80%, into poverty. Inflation is completely out of control at 180% with IMF forecasts that in 2017/8 it will top 700%. Not surprisingly this situation has led to social unrest and mass demonstrations, none of which will make the life of a foreign teacher feel safe or enjoyable. In fact most have fled.

Red Tape

Of course requirements vary from country to country but it is standard for work visas to be available only to teachers on long-term contracts after a vast array of documents has been gathered including notarised copies of teaching qualifications, police clearance, etc. This means that a high percentage of teachers work on tourist visas throughout Latin America. These must be kept up to date by applying for an extension from the immigration department or by crossing into and back from a neighbouring country. Occasionally extensions are available from the appropriate office, for example the 90-day visa given on entering Chile can in some cases be extended for a fee, though most long-stay Britons simply cross the border to Mendoza in Argentina every three months.

Libby Goldsmith describes the usual hassles she encountered in several countries:

> *Of course all the red tape is an issue – the obligatory work visa application, immigration and/or police formalities, identity card and so on. Based on my experience you have to have a 12-month contract in order to secure a work visa. I have started to hear of teachers with six-month contracts being turned down. After the visa, there's tax registration, setting up a bank account, health insurance, pension; and if you were looking to stay longer, residency application. If you approach a reputable institute, they offer support (though variable) with this process which is a life-saver!*

MEXICO

Companies of all descriptions provide language classes for their employees during all the waking hours of the week but especially in the early morning and at weekends. Roberta Wedge even managed to persuade a *'sleek head honcho in the state ferry service'* that he needed private tuition during the siesta and that busy executives and other interested employees of a local company needed English lessons at the same time of day.

Demand is not confined to the big cities but exists in the remotest towns, at least one of which must remain nameless in order to preserve Roberta Wedge's dreams:

> *After doing a 'taster' ESL course in Vancouver, I set out for Nicaragua with a bus ticket to San Diego and $500 – no guidebook, no travelling companion, no Spanish. On the way I fell in love with a town in Mexico (not for worlds would I reveal its name – I want to keep it in a pristine time warp so I can hope to return) and decided to stay. I found a job by looking up all the language schools in the phonebook and walking around the city to find them and keeping my eye out for English school signs. I had semi-memorised a little speech in Spanish, 'I am a Canadian teacher of English. I love your town very much and want to work here. This is my CV.' Within two days I had a job at a one-man school.*

Mexico City is a thousand times more polluted, yet offers the best prospects for language teachers, who have every chance of being invited to attend a disconcertingly informal interview.

AMERICAN BRADWELL JACKSON DIDN'T HAVE TO LOOK FAR FOR HIS FIRST TEACHING JOB IN MEXICO:

After reading Work Your Way Around the World, I made the decision to ... wander the earth freely. I wondered if it was really possible to get a job teaching English so easily. Well I found out that it is. I was sitting at a metro stop in Mexico City, trying to figure out what school to choose for my first planned job enquiry. After I decided that the particular school I had in mind was too far away, I looked up and saw an English school right across the street. Providence, I thought. I was right. I sauntered on upstairs, cheerfully asked if they needed an English teacher, and about an hour and a half later, I was told when to start my training. It really was that easy.

The starting wage at the large chains will be 80+ pesos per hour though opportunities exist to make more than double that at respectable institutes.

The red tape situation in Mexico is bound to cause headaches. Visitors are not allowed to work or engage in any remunerative activity during a temporary visit. The Free Trade Agreement makes it somewhat easier for Americans and Canadians but still not straightforward. British citizens can stay in Mexico for up to 180 days on the tourist card purchased for 500 pesos on arrival (sometimes included in your flight cost). The most respectable schools may be willing to help full-time contracted teachers with the paperwork to obtain a work visa outside the country, but won't pay the high cost. Among the required documents are a CV in Spanish, plus transcripts, diploma or certificate from your university, apostilled by the Mexican Consul or, in the USA, by the Secretary of State, in the state where you studied.

Among the many volunteer placement organisations in the UK that are active in Mexico, Outreach International (www.outreachinternational.co.uk) offers a range of teaching jobs as well as environmental and social projects. The £2,750 cost of a three-month placement with Outreach International includes insurance, online TEFL training (if needed) and Spanish language course. Sarah Elengorn from Middlesex wanted to learn Spanish and so was attracted to a six-month project with Outreach International, working with street children in their base city of Puerto Vallarta, Mexico. She was the only female and the only non-Mexican on her placement at a shelter for street boys, so her Spanish (albeit street Spanish) improved very quickly. Sarah did some work on the streets but mainly worked at the shelter, organising, teaching (including safe sex) and playing with the children. She stayed on in Puerto Vallarta working for various NGOs and charities.

BOLIVIA

Even the poorest of Latin American nations offers possibilities to EFL teachers, provided you are prepared to accept a low wage. In contrast to the standard hourly wage of $12–$20 in Europeanised cities such as Rio de Janeiro and Santiago, the wages paid by language schools in La Paz will be a lot less with a maximum of $11, which allows for a comfortable lifestyle in a country where a room in a hostel costs $5 and a meal in the market less than $2.

If you have a good standard of education, are carrying all your references and diplomas plus a CV translated into Spanish and are prepared to stay for an academic year, it is possible to fix up a teaching contract after arrival. Terms begin in early February and late September, so try to arrive a few weeks in advance of these dates. Try to find a list of language schools and *colegios* (private schools) and deliver your application dossiers by hand to the directors.

Miranda Crowhurst is one teacher (with a CELTA qualification under her belt) who fell immediately under the spell of Bolivia after arriving in the southern city of Santa Cruz in January a few years ago:

> *I arrived in Santa Cruz three years ago, with no Spanish, and no real idea of what to expect. It's often swelteringly hot, and always chaotic, with few traffic rules and building regulations, and although it's definitely not a tourist destination, it's a great place to live. People are friendly and relaxed here, and proud of where they come from. Plus, there are some fantastic off-the-gringo-trail places to visit nearby, like national parks and local villages. There's a famously riotous carnival, and some serious worshipping of short skirts, gyms and enormous cars. Like all large South American cities, you do have to be aware of crime, and muggings are common. You have to watch yourself in public places, as girls can receive unwanted attention, too. Having said that, nothing serious has happened to me yet!*
>
> *As for the teaching, schools vary hugely in their quality. While some pay peanuts, if you're a qualified and/or experienced native teacher, you should get a very good wage here (in Bolivian, rather than international terms). There is a real need for English teachers, as the expat community is pretty small, so schools are always hiring. Teaching here is great, mainly because of the students. They may have a typically Latino attitude towards homework ('Tomorrow, teacher!'), and to time-keeping, but they are very chatty in lessons, keen to participate, and happy to have fun and laugh. If you'd rather strike out on your own, you can charge a decent amount for private lessons, once you get your name around. Since I arrived, I've really come to enjoy the chaos, and the easygoing, friendly atmosphere, where drinking, barbecues and dancing are compulsory.*

The biggest language school in the country is the bi-national Centro Boliviano Americano (www.cba.edu.bo) that has a couple of locations in La Paz and schools in other cities such as Cochabamba (www.cbacoch.org), Sucre and Santa Cruz (www.cba.com.bo).

BRAZIL

The appetite for English has always been massive in Brazil though in the rush to prepare for the Rio Olympics, the demand increased exponentially and has since slumped a bit. Rio is bankrupt and wages and pensions have had to be slashed in the public sector in the wake of the Olympics and World Cup.

Although Brazil has traditionally done well at producing its own qualified English language teachers, there is always room for native speakers, as reported by a well-travelled TEFLer, Barry O'Leary. Barry arrived in Salvador (northern Brazil) just before Carnaval, which marks the break between terms every February.

BARRY O'LEARY BOUGHT A MAP, BORROWED A TELEPHONE DIRECTORY FROM HIS HOSTEL AND WALKED ROUND ALL THE 25 LANGUAGE ACADEMIES WITH HIS CV. MOST ACADEMIES COULDN'T TELL HOW MANY STUDENTS THEY WOULD HAVE UNTIL AFTER *CARNAVAL*, BUT BARRY EVENTUALLY SUCCEEDED:

I taught in three institutes, PEC (www.pec.com.br), Okey Dokey and AEC Idiomas. The business academy sent me to various offices that were all fully equipped and well organised. Generally working conditions were excellent and so was the pay; I received about $8 an hour, which was a good rate for Brazil. The pupils were a mixed bag, yet they all had a great sense of humour and participated in the lessons, though some students were there only because their boss wanted them to be and had little interest.

I worked at another academy one afternoon a week. The approach here was to teach English through music, followed by group conversation lessons. Each week the director would translate two or three songs for the students to sing along to in English. The students enjoyed this immensely, and I thought it was a very original way to learn. Most students seemed to be more interested in asking me questions about England and my life rather than pay attention to the lessons, but it was a good way for them to improve their fluency. I found Brazilian students very happy-go-lucky people, they were always smiling and interested in learning English.

I was lucky enough to live in the old quarter of Salvador called Pelourinho that was the hub of the night-life, but also the hub of any trouble. I lived in a house with 15 people including Brazilians, Nigerians, French and Irish, for which I paid $20 a month and had a brilliant three months.

If you want to study Portuguese, you can apply for a student visa that would make it easier to stay on. For example, many foreigners register at the Pontificia Universidade Católica in Rio de Janeiro. This is an excellent place to link up with students and advertise classes if you want to offer private lessons (which pay much better than working for an institute).

People under 30 from New Zealand, France and Germany are eligible to apply for a one-year working holiday visa to Brazil. Richard Ferguson from New Zealand studied Portuguese with a tutor in Belo Horizonte, but decided not to try to teach English. However, he did meet an American who gave private English lessons in São Paulo for a few months charging 50 reais an hour. He bemoaned the fact that the sprawling city was hard to get around and he also insisted that students should be asked to pay in advance because Brazilians are notorious for no shows, being late or last-minute cancellations. Hourly rates of pay for qualified and experienced teachers in institutes hover around R$50+.

Useful information on teaching can be found on the site BrazilianGringo.com maintained by an American whose site tries to match job-seeking teachers with teacher-seeking schools (www.braziliangringo.com/jobs-english-teachers-brazil).

ARGENTINA

Against expectations the Argentinian economy moved into recession in 2016, with inflation climbing which means the cost of living is rising, and many European visitors wonder how the local people can manage on the wages they earn. Eating out, taxis, etc are expensive in Buenos Aires but not basic services such as public transport and haircuts. Teachers are far more likely to secure a job once they are in Argentina than by applying from their home country. Anyone with a recognised qualification such as the CELTA will probably get snapped up, at least for a few hours a week initially, as Alan Chadwick did. He headed for Argentina's second city Córdoba where he handed round his CV to a few language schools, and was almost immediately offered some hours of teaching. The wage was a decent £10 an hour.

Cultural exchange programmes will appeal to those willing to teach as volunteers in rural areas, normally in state rather than private schools. For example, Voluntario Global (www.voluntarioglobal.org) feeds Spanish-speaking volunteers to worthy projects in schools, among others, in greater Buenos Aires, while Connecting Schools to the World (www.connectingschools.com.ar) invites university graduates to live for one or two semesters in a *pueblo* or city in the province of Córdoba. The programme fee of $2,000 is somewhat offset by the provision of homestay accommodation with a local family and a modest monthly stipend.

A number of companies accept untrained foreigners from North America and Europe as interns who are given free board and lodging with a family, free Spanish tuition, a small stipend and plenty of opportunities to travel and see the country.

BA Placements: Recoleta, Buenos Aires; www.baplacement.com/tefl.php. TEFL Certification Program with job assistance and access to internships.

Colonias de Inmersión al Idioma (CII): Buenos Aires; www.ecolonias.com. Offers TEFL Internships to university students or recent graduates.

Connecting Worlds: Buenos Aires and Mar de Plata; www.cwargentina.com. ESL Argentina Program in Mar del Plata, Bariloche and many other places in Argentina; volunteers stay for one or two semesters; programme fee of $1,299.

Expanish: Buenos Aires; www.expanish.com/spanish-courses/volunteer. Spanish language school with Volunteer English teaching programme. Volunteer placement fee of $95 plus donation of $100 following minimum two-week language course.

Pasantias Argentinas: Córdoba; www.pasantias-argentinas.com. Arranges professional internships in Córdoba including English teaching placements, equine therapy on ranches, etc; open to all native English speakers who have achieved a speaking knowledge of Spanish via a Pasantias language course.

Road2Argentina: Buenos Aires; www.road2argentina.com. Places English teaching assistants/interns for 4–24 weeks between mid-March and early December, as part of a cultural exchange and language-immersion programme. Programme fees start at $675 for one month and include accommodation in a shared homestay.

Luke McElderry from Texas and his girlfriend Jenny Jacobi spent hours researching potential teaching employers in Buenos Aires on the internet. After completing a training course, he sent a mass email with his CV attached to at least 40 addresses and waited for responses to trickle in, and ended up hearing from about a quarter. He describes his job-hunt:

> *The first interviews were varied, some in English, one in Spanish, but all fairly casual. Most take 30 minutes and they seem to care more about your availability than your experience. I was asked a couple of times if I had any visa/permit and said no, and the employers didn't seem to care at all. I have heard the biggest institutes are the ones that care, and ironically pay the least!*

Before long, they were working for an institute that sent them out to teach 90-minute classes in businesses. The wages were enough to take advantage of Buenos Aires's sophisticated social life, though prices were steadily rising while they were there. All went smoothly apart from finding accommodation, which was a real hassle.

After spending a few weeks investigating teaching possibilities in the capital, Alan Chadwick decided he was finding the city too hectic and dangerous to stay. Four or five mugging incidents were reported by people in his hostel, but the final straw came when a young Finnish traveller who had set off one afternoon to catch a long-distance bus returned within an hour having had all her bags, money and passport taken at gunpoint – possibly a toy gun but she couldn't be sure.

CHILE

More than most other South American economies, Chile's has been flourishing, though at the time of writing the unemployment rate was rising and stood at a shade under 7% (2017). The market for English language teaching is very healthy, with at least 30 major language schools in the capital Santiago alone. Short-term casual teaching is not well paid: non-contractual work starts at 6,000 pesos per hour but rises to 8,000 with experience. If you arrive in February at the beginning of the school year with a recognised TEFL certificate and preferably some teaching experience, it should be easy to find teaching work. Whereas some schools expect their teachers to cross the border to renew a tourist visa every three months; others provide a contract that is a prerequisite for a work visa (except for Australians, New Zealanders and Canadians who are eligible for one-year working holiday visas).

A few years ago, Doug Burgess went job-hunting in Santiago, armed with a CELTA and a bit of teaching experience:

> When I finished university I realised I wanted to learn another language and decided that Spanish was the one, as I love Latin culture. I decided the best way to do this was to teach abroad so I decided to do the CELTA at home in Cambridge and work in some institutes over the summer in order to save money and get some experience so that I wouldn't arrive in Chile as a green teacher. I chose Chile as it's probably the most developed country in South America, with a healthy currency and favourable exchange rate with other countries in South America.
>
> When I arrived in Chile I worked an exchange system for the first three months where I taught two classes of English and in exchange received two classes of Spanish every day for three months, which was great because I didn't speak any Spanish when I arrived and this saved me a lot of money.

Doug went on to be offered teaching work by some of the well-known institutes such as the prestigious Instituto Chileno Britanico (www.britanico.cl) with a number of branches in the capital.

TeachingChile in Santiago is an agency supplying native speaker teachers to various schools for a minimum of five months; it has contact numbers in North America (☎ (+1) 720 221 3831) and the UK (☎ (+44) 20 8150 6981); see www.teachingchile.com which sets out the programme fees, eg the full service costs $1,400.

On arrival in Chile, you will automatically be given a tourist visa valid for 90 days which you can renew by crossing the border. Once you find a job, the most common visa to apply for is the *Visa Sujeta a Contrato* (subject to contract visa), for which you will need to take a notarised copy of a contract from an employer that shows a minimum salary of 100,000 pesos a month to the Departamento de Extrajería. There is a huge differential in the fee for a work visa between nationalities: British nationals must pay about £1,000 for a work visa.

To find private clients, it may help to advertise. The best results are obtained by putting a small ad in *El Mercurio*, the leading quality daily or checking ads (mostly for part-time hours) on Craigslist (http://santiago.en.craigslist.org) or in the free ads paper *El Rastro*.

COLOMBIA

With the welcome news in September 2016 that FARC, the dreaded guerrilla movement, had signed a peace agreement with the Colombian government, perhaps now the world will stop associating Colombia only with crime and violence. With increasing security and the expansion of trade, interest in English has increased, especially among the business community. The Ministry of Education runs an ambitious programme to encourage bilingualism in the state education system. The national training service known as SENA recruits a large number of English Teaching Fellows from abroad to work for at least four months alongside local teachers, mainly in secondary schools throughout the country. Although TEFL experience/qualifications and a basic level of Spanish are preferred, the only absolute requirements for acceptance are being a native speaker aged 21–50 and able to pay the refundable US$400 deposit. A monthly living allowance of 1,500,000 pesos ($500) is paid in arrears to participants. SENA works with an organisation called Volunteers Colombia (www.volunteerscolombia. wordpress.com) who in turn work in partnership with various international recruiters like Flying Cows in the UK (www.flying-cows.com), ESLStarter.com (www.eslstarter.com/teach-english-in-colombia-public-school.php) and Greenheart in Chicago (www.greenhearttravel.org/program/adult/work/teach-in-colombia).

CELTA-QUALIFIED CHARLES BEACH APPLIED TO BECOME ONE OF THE FIRST VOLUNTEER PARTICIPANTS VIA THE NOTTINGHAM-BASED AGENCY FLYING COWS. AFTER PRE-SCREENING CANDIDATES FOR SUITABILITY TO THE PROGRAMME, FLYING COWS HANDLED ALL THE LENGTHY PRE-DEPARTURE PAPERWORK. CHARLES IS FULL OF PRAISE FOR THE PROGRAMME AND WAS HAPPY TO HAVE BEEN SENT TO THE SMALL CITY OF BUCARAMANGA:

I have two classes that total 20 hours of teaching a week. We are expected to spend another 20 hours a week planning lessons plus 5 hours are dedicated to a special project. In practice the working week is less than 45 hours, as sometimes lessons are cancelled or lesson-planning takes less time. Accommodation was found for us and paid for during the fortnight-long orientation and the first month in our placement city.

My pupils are mostly aged 17–18 and studying a vocational course provided by the state for young adults who can't afford education otherwise. There are some expected behaviour issues and their level of English is very low, but I genuinely like spending time with them and they are a lot of fun. Having to speak in front of 30 people every day is a tremendous confidence builder.

Colombia has been far easier to settle into than I expected. My life here in Colombia is pretty busy. In my spare time I go dancing, go hiking, practise Spanish, see classical music at the local university, hang out in student bars, etc.

Colombia is strongly oriented towards the USA with an extensive network of Colombian-American Cultural Centers around the country. Some global EFL companies have a strong presence in Colombia like EF (www.ef.com.co) and Berlitz (www.berlitz.com.co). When in 2015/16 Libby Goldsmith worked for both Bogotá Business English (www.BogotaBusinessEnglish.com/jobs) and First Class English also in Bogotá (www.fce.edu.co), she found it difficult to get hours outside the peak times of before and after the working day.

The main newspaper *El Tiempo* carries adverts for language schools in the capital. There are plenty of local language schools where untrained native English speakers can find work but with low pay; many schools start teachers off at 10,000 pesos an hour (about $3.50). One tip for anyone flying into Colombia is to have an address (eg a hostel) where you will be staying since you can be asked for this at the airport immigration desk. The immigration restrictions have become more manageable and it is no longer necessary to apply for a work permit from outside the country. The application with various apostilled documents can be made in Bogotá. Good employers will assist with the process and may even underwrite the $400 fee for a one-year visa.

ECUADOR

Ecuador represents an oasis of political stability with its currency not only pegged to the dollar but it actually is the US dollar. The demand for English thrives more than ever, particularly American English in the capital Quito and in the picturesque city and cultural centre of Cuenca in the southern Sierra. The majority of teaching is of university students and the business community whose classes are normally scheduled early in the morning (starting at 7am) to avoid the equatorial heat of the day and again in the late afternoon and evening. Many schools are owned and run by expatriates since there are few legal restrictions on foreigners running businesses.

Teaching wages have climbed back so that a respectable hourly wage now tops $6. Quito is not as large and daunting a city as some other South American capitals, though certain areas are dangerous. It should be easy to meet longer-term expats who can help with advice on teaching.

DAVINNA ARTIBEY FROM OREGON WENT TO ECUADOR IN THE SUMMER OF 2015, GOT A CELTA IN MONTAÑITA AND THEN A NINE-MONTH CONTRACT POSITION WITH CEDEI IN CUENCA (WWW.CEDEI.ORG).

My employer was the largest employer of English teachers in Cuenca, a nonprofit called CEDEI. There are usually about 40 English teachers on staff at any given time doing nine-month contracts that start in September, January and April. The pay was really low because all teachers are considered volunteers who receive a stipend. I earned about $350 per month, which wasn't enough to live on. In my estimate, to get by in Cuenca, around $700 to $800 per month would have been necessary. One thing CEDEI was really good at was professional development of its trainers. I learned and grew professionally from the ongoing work-shops provided. I absolutely loved living in Cuenca. It's a gorgeous, walkable city with a lot to do and very comfortable weather.

If you want to get away from commercial language schools in the cities like EF (www.ef.com.ec) and inlingua (www.lnlingua.com.ec) in Quito, many agencies in Ecuador place volunteer teachers in deprived settings. For example you can spend at least three months between September and June in the poor Andean region of Chimborazo (see http://ecuador.teach-english-volunteer.com). Through the Arajuno Road Project (www.arajunoroadproject.org), volunteers are given the opportunity to work and teach in schools in the Amazon jungle of central Ecuador.

Technically you shouldn't work on a tourist visa but there is little control. Britons and Americans can stay 90 days as tourists, though this can be extended by leaving the country. A tourist visa cannot be changed into another kind of visa without leaving the country. Many teachers work on an Intercultural visa (Category 12 VIII), valid for a year.

PERU

Lima has a sprinkling of language institutes, especially in the port area of Miraflores, which hire and pay a salary to native speakers. The other main cities such as Arequipa, Trujillo, Nazca and Piura also offer some opportunities. The town of Cusco is a favourite among travellers, many of whom settle down for an extended stay, possibly by swapping English lessons for Spanish at a school such as Excel (www.excelspanishperu.info) or for a room with a local family. Check the display adverts in the *'Seccion Empleos'* of the Sunday edition of the main daily *El Comercio*. A useful online resource can be found at http://thelajoblist.blogspot.co.uk/2009/12/peru.html although it is no longer maintained. The American teacher who compiled the list stresses how much easier it is to find teaching hours once you are in Peru than when you're trying to fix up a job from home. Many temporary visitors to Peru who lack a TEFL background end up doing some English teaching once they have established a base in the capital, usually earning about $5 an hour, which is a lot more than the local minimum wage of 4 soles, which is just over $1.

James Gratton arrived in Lima looking forward to what had sounded like a dream job. He had contacted some institutes ahead and was contacted enthusiastically by one (on the strength of a certificate earned from a one-week intensive TEFL training course in London and nine months of living and teaching in Venezuela the year before). Despite the job not living up to expectations (many of his employer's promises were not honoured), he concluded that the experience could be used as a stepping-stone to better opportunities. When he put a cheap advertisement (written in English) in *El Comercio* he immediately signed up two private clients.

CENTRAL AMERICA

If you keep your ears open as you travel through Central America, you may come across opportunities to teach English, especially if you are prepared to do so as a volunteer. Salaries on offer may be pitiful but if you find a congenial spot on the 'gringo trail' – for example many travellers fall prey to the charms of Antigua and Lake Atitlán in Guatemala – you may decide to prolong your stay by helping the people you will inevitably meet who want to learn English. Dozens of Spanish language schools in backpacker honeypots have links with local communities that welcome volunteer teachers. To take just one example, check out www.launion.edu.gt/volunteer-work/work-as-a-teacher.

As the wealthiest country in Central America, Costa Rica is sometimes referred to as the Switzerland of the region and there are plenty of private language academies in the capital San José. The school year runs from 1 March to 1 December. The *Tico Times* publishes its job classified ads online at www.ticotimes.net/classifieds.

VOLUNTEERING

Short-term voluntary work projects are scattered over this vast continent, though the two easiest countries in which to find organised projects are Ecuador and Costa Rica. Many of the opportunities that become widely known are concerned with conservation (treated separately below) and charge a substantial fee. But an approach to almost any environmental, health or childcare non-governmental organisation might be greeted warmly, especially if the enquiry is made in Spanish. The better funded of these projects might even be able to offer accommodation and expenses.

Patient searching of the web will unearth opportunities for volunteering, perhaps through one of the mainstream databases such as www.idealist.org or www.omprakash.org. The splendidly transparent site www.volunteersouthamerica.net is always worth scouring for *'grass-roots, zero-cost volunteer work'* in South and Central America as is www.truetravellers.org. Another Latin American specialist website with a similar ambition is www.volunteerlatinamerica.com; to contact any of the organisations in their searchable directory of grassroots projects, it is necessary to join at a cost of £9 for two years' basic membership or £18 which includes personalised assistance. The excellent online guide to Ecuador www.ecuadorexplorer.com has listings and links to teaching and voluntary projects as well as what to see and do. In some cases a centralised placement service makes choosing a project easier, though you will have to pay for the service as in the case of VolunteeringEcuador.org or Volunteer Bolivia (www.volunteerbolivia.org) located in Cochabamba. They encourage their clients to sign up for a month of Spanish tuition while staying with a local family before becoming a volunteer; a combined language course, homestay and volunteer placement programme costs $1,670 for one month or $2,450 for 12 weeks.

Spanish language course providers and cultural exchange organisations can often arrange interesting volunteer or internship programmes, though the fees charged will be much higher than if you can fix up a similar placement face-to-face with the grassroots organisations. Among the largest are the following:

Adelante LLC: Seal Beach, California; www.adelanteabroad.com. Internships, volunteer placements, teaching abroad and semester/summer study opportunities from one to 12 months in Costa Rica (San José), Mexico (Oaxaca), Chile (Vina del Mar/Valparaiso), Uruguay (Montevideo) and from 2017 Ecuador (Quito and Ambato); prices range from $3,475 to

$4,415 for three-month internships in various fields, and include language classes, various housing options and work assignment placement.

Amigos de las Americas: Houston, Texas; www.amigosinternational.org. Summer, semester or year-long volunteering programmes for high school, college and gap year students mostly in community health projects throughout Central and South America; participation fee is $12,950 for a semester, and a colossal $24,900 for a full year (2017) including airfares from the US; all volunteers must have studied Spanish at school or university and undergone training.

Caledonia Languages Abroad: Edinburgh; ☎ (+44) 131 621 7721; www.caledonialanguages. co.uk. Language travel agency which arranges Spanish courses in a range of countries and offers a combination of language and volunteering in Bogota. The fee is £700 for four weeks.

ESL Language Travel: London; ☎ (+44) 20 7451 0943; www.esl.co.uk. Destination countries for language and volunteering programmes include Panama (seldom targeted) as well as Argentina, Peru, Ecuador, Costa Rica and Mexico.

Individual language schools often have links with local projects and can arrange for students of Spanish to attach themselves to projects that interest them. Typically, Carisa Fey started her big trip round South America with a short language course in Quito, which led to some voluntary work afterwards teaching knitting to street kids. For example Mundo Verde Spanish School in Cusco, Peru (www. mundoverdespanish.com) has links with development projects in deprived urban areas and in the rainforest to which students can be assigned for no fee.

Argentina is among the most Europeanised countries in Latin America. A cultural exchange organisation, Grupo de Intercambio Cultural Argentino (www.gicarg.org), invites paying volunteers and interns from abroad (normally with a working knowledge of Spanish) to work in various sectors in Buenos Aires.

As you travel throughout the region you are bound to come across various charitable and voluntary organisations running orphanages, environmental projects and so on, some of which may be able to make temporary use of a willing volunteer. The Quaker-run peace and service centre in Mexico City, Casa de los Amigos, has information on a variety of volunteering opportunities throughout Mexico City and Mexico. The Casa also has its own volunteer programme for those who speak Spanish and are able to commit for nine months to a year, working for peace and social justice or in the hospitality programme at the Casa. A stipend of $100 a week is paid to full-time volunteers (voluntarios@ casadelosamigos.org) and the Casa provides simple accommodation in its guesthouse for which a donation will be expected, starting from £20 per night for a double.

The children's charity TASK Brasil (Trust for Abandoned Street Kids) has an office in London (☎ (+44) 20 7735 5545; www.taskbrasil.org.uk). They are looking for volunteers over 21 to work with street children in Rio.

Guatemala

Many travellers find that Lake Atitlán is the perfect place to use as a long-term base for chilling and volunteering. The small villages around the lake are all interconnected by launch boats, and the variety in atmosphere among these villages means that you can choose one that suits. Well-known party town San Pedro attracts many foreigners who come to attend one of the many Spanish schools. Hostel beds average about 50 quetzales (£5), though cheaper places can be found, and food is also very cheap. Anna Ling from Cambridge headed to laid-back Santa Cruz on her world travels, as she pursued her main interests, writing and performing music. She decided to stay for a while:

I am based at the Iguana Perdida hostel (www.laiguanaperdida.com), the first building near the launch stop. With the daily dinner shared on a long table, guests and workers together, it feels very much like a family. The hostel runs on the basis of voluntary work. I exchange five hours of work a day, six days a week for my bed and three meals a day, on top of various perks like free internet and half-price drinks. Work generally consists of sitting behind the bar, taking orders and chatting to guests. One of my responsibilities is to organise the dressing up clothes for the Saturday night Cross Dressing parties. The hostel almost always has positions opening and the owners ask only that you stay at least two weeks. I personally recommend this relaxed work-for-keep system above getting a paid bar job as wages barely cover living costs. (The cost of staying here for non-working guests is between 25–35 quetzals plus food is about 75 quetzals a day for cheaper meals.) My shifts start at 7.30am or 1pm, leaving the afternoon or evening free for joyous activities.

The local village is a wonderful place and home to the Amigos (www.amigosdesantacruz.org), a charity that has brought medical care and an outreach programme to the more remote villages. They have also built a library and a school offering free education to all children under 12, and scholarship programmes for older children. They are in the process of building a large new centre for vocational education. I went up to the village to see Pam, the brains behind the operation, and within the hour I was teaching an English class. I was soon given a classroom and started an enrichment afternoon with the local kids, doing arts, craft and music projects. The organisation is so well run that anyone willing to give some time will be put to good use, whether in teaching, construction or any other interests.

Language is no problem. Personally I'm trying to live very much on a tight budget and paid language lessons (25–50 quetzals per hour) would push me way over my daily price watch. But volunteering at the school has been the best opportunity for learning Spanish I could imagine. I take up a dictionary and the kids speak really slowly and clearly and it has helped so very much.

Almost any Spanish language school in Guatemala can help arrange a volunteer position. To find links to many of these language schools, visit www.xelapages.com/schools.htm, which also has a link to volunteering opportunities. The cultural institute Casa Xelaju in Quetzaltenango (www.casaxelaju.com) runs Spanish courses and refers clients to internships and voluntary work in Guatemala. The registration fee for volunteers is $80 plus $60 a week for homestay accommodation and all meals. The city of Quetzaltenango (known as Xela) offers many opportunities to do volunteer work in the community.

Conservation

An increasing number of organisations, both indigenous and foreign-sponsored, are involved in environmental projects throughout the continent. The highest concentration of projects is probably in Costa Rica where the National Parks and Communities Authority runs a voluntary programme Asociación de Voluntarios para el Servicio en las Areas Protegidas (ASVO). To be eligible you must be willing to work for at least 30 days, be able to speak at least minimal Spanish and provide a copy of your passport and a photo. The work may consist of trail maintenance and construction, greeting and informing visitors, beach cleaning, research or generally assisting rangers. There is also a possibility of joining a sea turtle conservation project. Details are available from the San José office (www.asvocr.org). Short-term volunteers who stay a week or more pay $38 a day for food and accommodation in addition to a $60 registration fee. Long-term volunteers who commit for a year pay nothing.

Trawling the internet for other eco-projects in Central and South America will turn up lots of lively possibilities, for example at www.greenvolunteers.com (access to database after joining for £4), www.workaway.info ($29 membership) and www.givingway.com (one-time membership of $10). To take an example at random, the San Rafael Reserve in Paraguay (www.faunaparaguay.com/volunteer.html) wants environmental volunteers although this one is pricey at $1,500 a month ($1,100 for students). Thousands of kilometres away on the Caribbean beaches of Costa Rica, you can monitor nesting sea turtles, go on night patrols to safeguard hatchlings and clean up beaches with the turtle protection charity ASTOP (www.parisminaturtles.org). They accept volunteers from February to October who pay $27 a day for a homestay for the first three weeks, after which the charges go down.

Among many other projects that give an idea of the range of opportunities, a rainforest research centre in the Brazilian state of Minas Gerais, Iracambi (www.iracambi.com), charges volunteers $800 a month to donate their time to monitor forests and streams as part of the overall ecosystem; a minimum of Portuguese is required.

One way of spending time in the famous Galápagos Islands is to become an International Volunteer with the Charles Darwin Foundation (www.darwinfoundation.org). Volunteers must be at least third-year undergraduates, preferably in environmental science, and able to stay for a minimum of six months. Without relevant scientific skills, international volunteers have to cover all their expenses including airfares to and from the islands, food and accommodation. The Galápagos islands have people as well as animals, and and the Galapagos Language Academy (www.galapagosla.com) sometimes hires native English teachers willing to stay for at least four months.

For animal lovers the Inti Wara Yassi wildlife reserve in Bolivia accepts volunteers to help care for injured animals (www.intiwarayassi.org). On Rob Harris's gap year, he was placed here by the UK agency Quest Overseas and divided his time between working in monkey quarantine (feeding, cleaning, looking after newly arrived capuchin monkeys before they were deemed adjusted enough to join the main group in the monkey park) and building the infrastructure of the new park to receive more animals in very remote and basic jungle living conditions. Sample prices for spending 15 or 30 nights at the project are $300 and $630 respectively.

Staying in Amazonia can be arranged by conservation NGOs such as the Fundación Fauna de la Amazonia (www.amazoniarescue.org) in Ecuador. A newly set up animal rescue and rehabilitation centre in the forests of eastern Ecuador cares for rescued animals and works to release them back to their natural habitat (centroderescatevallealto@gmail.com). Participation in the project costs $125 per week.

Organic farming has a healthy sprinkling of proponents in Latin America. The website www.wwoo-flatinamerica.com links the national branches in Argentina, Belize, Brazil, Chile, Colombia, Costa Rica, Ecuador, Guatemala, Mexico and Peru, all of which must be joined individually for $10–$38 if you want to exchange half a day of work for your keep in any of those countries.

THE IDEA OF VISITING ORGANIC FARMS APPEALED TO ROB ABBLETT:

I stayed on a WWOOF farm in Paraguay for two weeks, living and working with a Swiss-German family on a large isolated plot of land, learning about their many trials and tribulations as they struggled (in vain) to adapt from Swiss efficiency to Third World conditions. Afterwards I became the first WWOOFer a German woman host in Uruguay had ever had. She worked as a teacher in Montevideo and had integrated well into the country. She provided great food and wine for working on her large garden, picking strawberries, weeding and painting. But I didn't stay long: I'd been robbed in Paraguay, got scared in Buenos Aires and decided that eight years of working around the world has been fantastic and worthwhile but now I need to do something different.

OTHER OPPORTUNITIES

Apart from teaching, the only paid work available in Latin America tends to be for bilingual professionals. Engineers, business managers, highly specialised technicians have all found work in the private sector especially in international companies that operate in the mining, oil, hotel, banking and telecommunications sectors. Interesting volunteer opportunities are also available, as Sara Ellis-Owen discovered when she decided she needed to get out of London, and the law firm that employed her was sympathetic to her desire to take a break. Not only did they give her three months of unpaid leave but they also contributed financially to her placement by the Edinburgh-based charity Challenges Worldwide (www.challengesworldwide.com) with a legal NGO that advocated for the rights of all children in Belize. She was delighted to have plenty of free time to explore Belize which is an 'unspoilt, happy, relaxed place' and she loved every minute of it.

The Iko Poran Association in Rio de Janeiro (www.ikoporan.org) assigns several hundred volunteers in their 20s to various local development projects for three to 24 weeks. The programme fee for four weeks is $909, for 24 weeks $3,300 which covers volunteer lodging, 20 hours of Portuguese lessons and a donation to the project.

Work experience and volunteer placements in a number of fields can be arranged by several agencies in Ecuador such as ELEP (Experiential Learning Ecuadorian Programs) in Quito (www.elep. org). An interesting sustainable tourism company in Chile, La Bicicleta Verde, offers internships in their Santiago office (www.labicicletaverde.com/tour/internships). A sample price for a three-week placement with accommodation would be $480 plus registration fee of $160 and an intensive Spanish course (20 lessons) for $140. A volunteer/intern programme lasting nine weeks with three weeks of Spanish lessons costs $1,960.

Bilingual office support staff who can produce letters in proper English are in demand from commerce and law firms. Americans should find out if there is a local American Chamber of Commerce (as there is in Caracas) and Britons may do likewise. For example the website of the British-Chilean Chamber of Commerce (www.britcham.cl) links to hundreds of international companies in Chile.

Like Gibraltar and Malta, Costa Rica has become a location of choice for many online sports bookies because of the lack of government regulation. These companies hire English-speaking staff (preferably American) to take bets on sporting events over the telephone and do basic clerical work. However, the industry has been embroiled in scandal with several of the major companies closing suddenly owing large sums to clients and there are far fewer than the 400 companies that were based there in the industry's heyday.

Translators, particularly of scientific, medical and technical papers, tend to be well paid by universities and large industrial concerns. Both types of vacancy are advertised in English language newspapers, which may themselves need proofreaders and editors or know of companies that do. In many large cities there is a sizeable English-speaking expatriate community, predominantly involved in international commerce. The bars and restaurants that they frequent are good job-hunting grounds: not only might you hear about opportunities for temporary work in business, but you could also obtain work serving in the establishment itself.

As a student of modern languages, Andrew Cummings was keen to spend his year out in South America. He chose two very different destinations: the first an English language magazine in La Paz, Bolivia where he got journalistic work experience. The second was as a waiter at an upmarket restaurant in Buenos Aires, which he found very tough. The three months he spent at *Bolivian Express* (www. boliviaunlimited.org) afforded a wonderful glimpse into a rich culture and he loved getting acquainted with the fascinating capital city which he describes vividly:

> *La Paz itself is unique. High-rise apartment blocks and offices stand next to tiny restaurants and quaint squares, and the snow-capped mountains tower in the distance, always there to remind you of the stunning location (and the altitude!). There are some elements that might feel really familiar to a European visitor, and some completely alien: businessmen and cholitas (women in traditional dress) walk side-by-side on the pavements, whilst teenagers in high-tops and Ray Bans twiddle with their iPods during a festival celebrating an Aymara god. For me, the city had a lot more character than Paris or even Buenos Aires; it's one of the most amazing, stimulating places I've ever seen.*
>
> *The internship at the cultural publication Bolivian Express provided a very hands-on approach to journalism. It's very easy to get in contact with talented, influential people in La Paz, both because of the links the Bolivian members of the team already have and because of the accommodating nature of the people there. You'll find that you're given the tools to put together a fairly well-informed, interesting article very quickly. The first day we arrived, we were asked if we had any article ideas for the first issue of the magazine. Still mildly jet-lagged and vaguely suffering from altitude sickness, it's hardly surprising that we weren't feeling too creative. But if you walk down the street in La Paz there's a whole wealth of things that stick out, things that you might be able to write about; needless to say, at the next meeting, we had plenty of ideas up our sleeves. The cost of living in Bolivia is incredibly low, so it probably works out that even with the flight to South America, you spend no more than you would if you had to pay for accommodation, food and luxuries in Europe.*

The *Bolivian Express* offers participants some journalistic training and the chance to contribute an article or two on topics such as music, folklore, nightlife, sport and literature. The fee, which includes apartment accommodation, is $1,200 for one month, $3,000 for three months.

Tourism

Only highly able candidates who have extensive Latin American travel experience and knowledge of Spanish are hired as tour leaders and drivers with UK operators such as Tucan Travel (www.tucantravel. com/contact-us/employment) and Journey Latin America also in London (www.journeylatinamerica. co.uk/information/work-for-us). The company pays for food and accommodation plus a fee per tour. If you get to know an area well, you may be able to act as a freelance guide though, not surprisingly, this will probably incur the locals' resentment, as Mónica Boza found when she lived in Cusco, Peru:

> *If you have a good knowledge of the trails and want to become an outdoor guide, contact the tour agencies on arrival. But Peruvian guides are very jealous of foreign ones. I have known cases where they called the Migration Service and deportation followed. The adventure tour agencies are mainly along Plateros St or on the Main Square.*

Local opportunities may crop up in one of the many places where tourism is booming. The diving community of Roatan in Honduras takes on many scuba instructors and ancillary staff. Many expat-style bars and clubs employ foreigners, not to mention backpacker ghettoes in Cusco for example. Few corners of the world have escaped the fashion for Irish pubs. Mexico is another country in which travellers have been approached to work not as waiters or bar staff, but as hosts, entertainers and touts.

Anyone who can fix engines, especially on camper vans, should find no trouble earning a living in any touristy area of Mexico. You might be able to find day work on boats in harbours before the yachts set sail or perhaps an opportunity to boat-sit as Anne Wakeford did in Puerto Vallarta. She recommends asking boat owners to radio your request for work to their fellow yachtsmen in the morning. She also noticed that there might be work further south helping boats to navigate the locks of the Panama Canal.

At the other end of the continent, reports from the Falkland Islands indicate that jobs occasionally surface. Many of the tiny population have been drawn away from the countryside and into Stanley where a range of bars, shops and restaurants flourishes. The island government is worried about rural depopulation and abandoned farms, so hard-working people with agricultural experience might well be able to find work on the land. The few hotels there very occasionally recruit staff from abroad; the Sea Lion Lodge tends to employ Chilean staff and a British chef.

The Caribbean

The Caribbean is far too expensive to explore unless you do more than sip rum punch by the beach. A host of Britons, Australians, South Africans, etc are exchanging their labour, mostly on yachts, in order to see this exotic part of the world.

JOBS AFLOAT

Perhaps the easiest jobs to find are those working on the countless sailboats, charter yachts and cruise ships that ply the Caribbean each winter and spring. From November until May the Caribbean becomes a hive of marine activity. Since it marks the start of the main tourist season, Christmas is a particularly good time to look for work. The main requirement for being hired is an outgoing personality and perseverance in the search more than qualifications or experience. Hours are long and wages are minimal on a charter boat, but most do it for the fun. Board and lodging are always free and in certain jobs tips can be high. It would not be unusual to work for a wage of not much more than $100 a month and then earn 10 times as much in tips.

Cruise Ships

For general information about cruise ship work see the section Working a Passage. Contracts are normally for six to nine months and the hours of work are long, often 14 hours a day, seven days a week living aboard the passenger ship with all onboard facilities provided by the ship owner. Most cruise ships active in the Caribbean contract their staff from Florida-based personnel agencies (known as concessionaires), some of which liaise with UK and European agencies. Workers aboard passenger ships require a C-1/D seafarer's visa issued by the United States Embassy, which is only granted after a face-to-face interview (information at www.ustraveldocs.com/in/in-niv-typecandd.asp).

Charter Yachts

The charter season in the Caribbean is November to May when an experienced deckhand can earn $400 a week cash in hand plus tips. But there will be many weeks when the boat will not be chartered and the wage will fall away while you may have to hang around a boring marina. It is important to stress that a deckhand job is not compatible with a great vacation. It's a tough job with long working hours during which you must never stop smiling. When the guests are snorkelling on the reef, the deckhand will be helping the skipper repair the toilet. While the guests are hiking up a volcano, the deckhand is polishing the winches. The lack of a work permit can be a definite hindrance in the search for work with a charter company.

Immigration authorities are consistently tough throughout the Caribbean. When you leave any boat as a crew you sign off the crew list in immigration where they want to see a ticket not only out of the country but one that connects with a flight to your home country. They also want to see an address where you intend to stay and may ask to see sufficient funds.

Yacht charter companies are unwilling to publicise vacancies, both because they have enough speculative enquiries on the spot and also are forbidden by their respective island governments from hiring anyone without proper working papers. However, once you are on the spot, it is easier to hear of possibilities, and there are brokers and agents who match up crew with boats. Particularly in late October, these crew placement agencies may be able to help people on the spot, who complete an application form and pay the registration fee.

Jane's Yacht Services: English Harbour, Antigua; ☎ (+1) 268 460 3741; jane@jysglobalcrew. com; www.janesyachtservices.com and www.jysglobalcrew.com. Offers a crew placement service.

Nicholson Yacht Charters & Services Antigua: English Harbour, Antigua; ☎ (+1) 268 460 1530; www.nicholsoncharters.com. Charter captains of their fleet of 70 yachts (and others) turn to Nicholson to find suitable crew.

If you don't get anywhere with the agencies or charter companies, it will be a case of implementing all the tactics outlined in the Working a Passage chapter to commend yourself to skippers, by asking at docks, putting up notices, following up leads, frequenting bars and so on. One way of breaking into the world of Caribbean yachties is to help with the drudgery of maintaining boats when at anchor. Try to find out when and where boat shows and races are being held as people are always in a rush to get their boats looking first class.

JOBS ON LAND

People occasionally find work in nightclubs and hotels on the islands. The Cayman Islands are meant to be one of the best places to look for this sort of work, with over 1,500 Americans working there; the website www.caymanresident.com carries lots of practical information. Construction work may also be available on Grand Cayman; ask around at bars. Without a 'Gainful Occupation Licence' or work permit (difficult to obtain with hundreds of locals after the same jobs) you should not take for granted that you will be treated fairly. Plenty of horror stories circulate concerning maltreatment by employers, such as failure to pay wages and to honour agreements to provide a homeward flight. Keep your beach-scepticism handy, and don't hesitate to cut your losses and run, if you sense you're on to a bad deal.

The Dominican Republic has built up a flourishing package tour industry and people with hospitality experience or knowledge of several languages may find jobs. There are many hotels in the resort of Playa Dorada and Costa Dorado where you can ask for work which is unlikely to pay very much. Beware of promises of earning a fortune since these jobs will involve selling on commission.

There are some opportunities for voluntary service including in the Dominican Republic. The Bermuda Institute of Ocean Sciences (St George's GE01, Bermuda; ☎ (+1) 441 297 1880 ext 115; www.bios.edu/education/reu) offers some internships in marine science lasting 8, 10 or 12 weeks in the summer or for the autumn semester. Applicants (who are normally upper-level undergraduates or recent graduates in relevant subjects) should make personal contact with the faculty member(s) for whom they wish to work (see website). Note that immigration restrictions mean that the station cannot hire foreigners to carry out work other than research. Interns cover their living costs, ie $190 a week.

Gapforce (London SW6; www.gapforce.org) recruits fee-paying volunteers to help with a biodiversity marine project in the Bahamas. Projects involve protecting coral reefs and surveying endangered species and habitats. No previous experience is necessary as dive training is provided. The cost for a four-week stay is £1,700, the 10-week placement is £3,100, plus £300 for dive training plus flights.

Volunteers collaborate with marine biologists at the Bimini Biological Field Station in the Bahamas studying the behaviour of lemon sharks and other marine animals for at least a month. They also take on routine maintenance and catering chores. Volunteers contribute $875 per month (2017) to cover meals and housing (www.biminisharklab.com).

Despite the death of Fidel Castro and the easing of restrictions on travel and trade with the US, the Cuba Solidarity Campaign (London N4; www.cuba-solidarity.org.uk) still runs its work/study 'brigades' twice a year so that participants can 'experience the Cuban Revolution'. Cultural and educational visits are arranged and there may even be a chance for volunteers to undertake agricultural and construction work alongside Cubans. Volunteer work in Havana is included in the 20-day brigade taking place over Christmas 2017, at a cost of £650 plus flights and insurance.

St Eustatius National Parks Foundation in the former Netherlands Antilles has a volunteer programme to maintain park trails and a botanical garden, plus participate in a marine turtle-monitoring programme organised by the STENAPA Foundation. Volunteers from overseas available for one to three months should apply through the British-based www.workingabroad.com/projects/caribbean-conservation-volunteer. The cost for one month is from £720.

Africa

Into the second decade of the new millennium, Africa struggles with continuing challenges involving brutal suppression of democratic movements, ethnic violence, disputed elections, famine, Ebola and HIV. Chaos in the Democratic Republic of Congo and Somalia, border conflicts in Sudan, fear of terrorism in the Maghreb, criminal gangs in Johannesburg and unrest in many places persuade many travellers that some destinations on the continent are too difficult and dangerous to consider. Tunisia was a good-news story until terrorists killed 38 tourists on a beach in the resort of Sousse decimating the country's tourist industry overnight. Scrolling through the Foreign & Commonwealth Office's travel warnings with repeated 'advice against all but essential travel' in many regions is enough to put off many.

On the plus side the number of civil wars and violent coups across Africa is far less than it was. The real income per African citizen has increased by nearly a third over the past ten years, and there is a fast growing middle class. Social media has played a key role in promoting democracy as was seen in the (failed) Arab Spring and more recently in the free and fair presidential elections that have taken place in Nigeria and Gambia. Even in countries that undergo major upheavals it is amazing how resilient tour operators and development agencies can be in resuming their activities. Vast swathes of the continent are of course safe and marvellous, with an astonishing diversity of scenery and culture. South Africa, Tanzania, Kenya and Ghana are perennial favourite destinations for gap year students; all are stable and friendly countries with scores of volunteering opportunities.

It is impossible to generalise about countries as different from each other as Morocco, Uganda and South Africa; however, the level of paid employment opportunities is negligible throughout the continent and certainly does not warrant a country-by-country treatment here. The principal way to experience Africa other than as a gawking tourist is as a volunteer.

All travellers will have to come to their own conclusions about personal safety. Every so often a tragedy occurs in which someone is mauled by lions or a safari Jeep overturns in a ravine. Statistically, the level of violent crime in the urban areas of South Africa poses a more realistic threat, though victims tend to be the well-heeled types who stay in smart hotels.

TEACHING

Because English is or has been the medium of instruction in state schools in many ex-colonies of Britain including Ghana, Nigeria, Kenya, Zambia, Zimbabwe and Malawi, the majority of English teachers in these countries is local and the need for native speakers is much less than in Asia or Latin America. Still there is some demand for volunteers in secondary schools, especially in Ghana, Kenya and Tanzania.

The majority of foreigners teaching in Africa are not 'teacher-travellers' but on one or two year volunteer contracts fixed up in their home country, while a number of others are placed by recognised gap year organisations in the UK. Missionary societies have played a dominant role in Africa's modern history, and some religious organisations continue to be active in the field of education and teacher recruitment, such as Christians Abroad and the evangelical Africa Inland Mission. An estimated 24 million people are living with HIV/AIDS, mostly in Sub-Saharan Africa, and more than two million have died. In much of Africa the teaching of safe sex has become far more important than the teaching of English. Many agencies are working tirelessly to spread the message and volunteers may well find themselves involved in raising awareness of the dangers of spreading the virus.

Anyone who has fixed up a teaching contract should try to gather as much up-to-date information as possible before departure, preferably by talking to people who have been there. Otherwise local customs can come as a shock. A certain amount of deprivation is almost inevitable; for example teachers, especially volunteers, can seldom afford to shop in the pricey expatriate stores and so will have to be content with the local diet, typically a staple cereal such as millet usually made into a kind of stodgy porridge, plus some cooked greens, tinned fish or meat and fruit.

One gap year agency sent Sarah Johnson from Cardiff to Tanzania to teach English and geography at a rural secondary school:

> *The expectations which Zanzibari children have from school are worlds away from those of British school children. They expect to spend most of their lessons copying from the blackboard, so will at first be completely nonplussed if asked to think things through by themselves or to use their imagination. I found that the ongoing dilemma for me of teaching in Zanzibar was whether to teach at a low level which the majority of the class would be able to understand, or teach the syllabus to the top one or two students so that they would be able to attempt exam questions, but leaving the rest of the class behind. Teaching was a very interesting and eye-opening experience. I believe that both the Zanzibari teachers and I benefited from a cultural exchange of ideas and ways of life.*

The British Council has few teaching vacancies in sub-Saharan Africa but plenty in Egypt and some in Tunisia, while the Peace Corps in the USA (www.peacecorps.gov) recruits hundreds of volunteer teachers every year. The major gap placement agencies such as Lattitude, Project Trust and Africa & Asia Venture are active on the African continent (see Volunteering chapter).

A selection of other charities that recruit volunteer teachers includes the London-based Sudan Volunteer Programme (www.svp-uk.com) that needs volunteers to teach conversational English to university students and adults in Sudan for eight months from October or January. They recruit undergraduates and graduates with experience of travelling abroad (preferably in the Middle East) but not necessarily a TEFL certificate. Volunteers pay for their airfare (about £400) plus insurance for the first three months (£80), while local host institutions, most of which are in the Khartoum area, cover living expenses.

Egypt

After the euphoric celebrations that accompanied the Arab Spring, Egypt had a few turbulent years though is now returning to economic growth and more political stability. Even the cautious Foreign Office travel advice admits that most visits to Egypt are trouble-free, despite its assessment that the threat of terrorism is high. Life in Cairo and Alexandria continues relatively normally apart from frequent demonstrations that can turn violent. Egyptians want to learn and improve their English, just as before, and language teaching centres, both respectable and dubious, flourish side by side in the streets of the capital. Teaching jobs are not too hard to come by, especially if you have a Cambridge or Trinity Certificate in English language teaching. Many parents enrol their children to do intensive language courses in the summer, so this is a good time to look for an opening (assuming you can tolerate the heat).

The British Council in Agouza, Cairo (www.britishcouncil.org/eg) is one place to check for work. Normally they hire people already in Egypt with qualifications and two years' teaching experience after an interview and trial lesson, but may be less fussy for summer courses. During exam time there is also a need for paid invigilators. The US-based Amideast English Teaching Program occasionally hires teachers and support staff in Cairo and Alexandria (www.amideast.org/egypt/careers). An American traveller about to start law school posted the following on the Thorn Tree forum a couple of years ago:

> *Back in December I posted a message asking people if they thought it was possible to get short-term jobs abroad or if it was a good idea to possibly make tutoring flyers to put up around town. Both were ideas to supplement the money I already had saved and to have some new adventures/meet locals while travelling. I got a ton of negative responses telling me those ideas wouldn't work, etc, etc. Just wanted to post back on here six months later that it IS possible and my friend and I just did it. We got teaching jobs in Egypt that paid fairly well, without having work permits, without having TEFL, and the classes were for business professionals and thus were short terms (five weeks). Also, we put up tutoring flyers all over Cairo and made a decent amount of money doing private tutoring.*

Zamalek, along with Heliopolis and Maadi, are the best areas to look for private clients. The American University, centrally located at the eastern end of Tahrir Square in Cairo, is a good place to find work contacts or to advertise your availability to teach.

If you are looking for good causes to which you can volunteer your time, ask at All Saints Anglican Cathedral (www.episcocare.org/support-us/volunteer) behind the Marriott Hotel in Zamalek.

Ghana

As one of the most stable countries in Africa, Ghana supports a large number of organised schemes for volunteer teachers, since it has a long tradition of welcoming foreign students to participate in its educational and commercial life. Quite a number of exchange organisations, gap year agencies and charities operate to Ghana, though it is cheaper to apply directly to the Student and Youth Travel Organization in Accra (www.sytoghana.org). The Accra-based organisation Volunteer in Africa (www.volunteeringinafrica.org) arranges positions (among many others) as English and maths teachers in primary and junior secondary schools in Ghana for fee-paying volunteers; after an initial four-week stay costing $495, the weekly charge drops to $50.

The Volta Aid Foundation (www.voltaaidfoundation.org) places teaching volunteers in the eastern province of Ghana; the necessary qualifications are 'a big smile, warm heart and a good grasp of English'. Volunteers stay with local Ghanaian families and cover their living expenses by paying $500 for the first month and $350 for subsequent months.

Kenya

Kenya has had a shortage of secondary school teachers for some time, mostly in Western Province. With economic instability, inflation and drought, neither the government nor the farming communities can afford to employ more teachers despite the huge demand for education. It may still be possible to fix up an unpaid teaching assistant's job in a *Harambee* school (non-government self-help school) by asking in the villages, preferably before terms begin in September, January and April. Be prepared to produce your CV, diplomas and official-looking references. Basic accommodation will be provided, but probably no salary, even at local rates. According to the Kenyan immigration authorities (www. immigration.go.ke), all non-Kenyan citizens who wish to work must be in possession of an Entry Work Permit obtained by the employer from the Director of Immigration Services in Nairobi before they can take up paid or unpaid work.

You can link up with academies and charities listed on sites like www.idealist.org. For instance the Joyland Grace Academy in Busia near the Ugandan border welcomes travellers, couples and families who would like to donate their time at this school that educates orphans and other underprivileged primary aged children.

French West Africa

Even in ex-colonies of France, English is a sought-after commodity. World-traveller Bradwell Jackson discovered paid on-the-spot teaching opportunities in Mauritania, Mali and Senegal. Mauritania was not too long ago considered to have the potential for becoming a popular overland route from Morocco to Senegal; however, the Foreign Office warns of the high risk of kidnapping or terrorist attacks in the eastern and northern provinces, among others. The capital Nouakchott seems to be reasonably secure. Bradwell found a teaching job there by a *'happy accident of fate'*. On striking up a conversation with a Westerner walking on the other side of the street, he asked her about English language schools, and was promptly taken to the front door of The English Language Centre.

> *I was lucky enough to speak with the owner right away. I was talking to her while she was busy doing some other things, so it was not a formal interview. I did not have to fill out an application, though she asked me to write a letter explaining why I wanted to work in Mauritania. She seemed very interested, and asked me to come back in a couple of days to do a mock class in front of her teachers. I was hired based on this.*

Getting a work permit was refreshingly simple. The school simply took his passport to the employment office and paid for a one-year work permit. The students were a joy to work with, because they were hungry to learn.

Networks such as Couchsurfing (www.couchsurfing.com) have hosts registered all over Africa, who might be interested in exchanging hospitality for English lessons. Bradwell Jackson stayed with a couchsurfing host in Bamako, Mali, for two months.

TOURISM

Once again travellers' hostels are one of the few providers of casual work in the developing nations of the African continent. It is something that independent trans-Africa travellers can do for the odd week, from Dahab on the Red Sea to the backpackers' haunts of Johannesburg, and is a very nice way to have a break without having to pay for it. While cycling through Africa, Mary Hall stopped at a backpackers' hostel in Malawi where she was even offered a long-term job, but the road called.

Tourism is well established both on the Mediterranean coast of Africa and in the countries of East and Southern Africa where game parks are the major attraction. (Opportunities in South Africa are discussed separately below.) It is possible to find work in hotels and bars in resort areas; try the so-called trendy establishments rather than humble locally staffed ones. When you're in places such as Dahab on the Sinai Peninsula, keep an eye out for notices in bars and travel agencies for staff. Wages will be low, as will living expenses.

Anyone with a diver's certificate might be able to find work at Red Sea resorts such as Sharm el Sheikh and Hurghada. If you aren't sufficiently qualified but want to gain the appropriate certificates, the Red Sea might be a good place to train. Emperor Scuba Schools (www.emperordivers.com) have five schools on the Red Sea and run several Instructor Development Courses each year and a live-aboard internship programme for divers with a PADI and/or SSI Divemasters/Instructors qualification who want to gain experience on a dive charter. Another company to try is Sinai Divers (www.sinai divers.com/english.htm) with dive centres in Dahab, Marsa Alam and Sharm el Sheikh.

At local dive centres, you can sometimes get free lessons in exchange for filling air tanks for a sub-aqua club. It is possible to be taken on by an Egyptian operator (especially in the high season November to January); however, the norm is to be paid no wage and just earn a percentage of the take. Long-term possibilities may be available with overland companies. For tour leader work, applicants are required to have first-hand knowledge of travel in Africa or must be willing to train for three months with no guarantee of work. Requirements vary but normally expedition leaders must be at least 23 or 25 and be diesel mechanics with a truck or bus licence. Some African specialists are listed here.

Absolute Africa: London W4; ☎ (+44) 20 8742 0226; www.absoluteafrica.com/Work-For-Us.

Acacia Adventure Holidays: London W2; ☎ (+44) 20 7706 4700; www.acacia-africa.com. Most of their staff are Africans.

African Trails: Morecambe, Lancashire; ☎ (+44) 1524 419909; www.africantrails.co.uk/information/jobs.

Oasis Overland: Henstridge, Somerset; ☎ (+44) 1963 530113; www.oasisoverland.co.uk/work-for-oasis. Tour leaders and driver/mechanics.

OPPORTUNITIES IN SOUTH AFRICA

Economic and political instability plus frightening levels of urban crime continue to contribute to an enormous brain drain from South Africa. Hundreds of thousands of South Africans have emigrated over the past decade and more than two-thirds of skilled and educated South Africans have said that they have considered or are considering emigration, mainly to escape an unemployment rate that stubbornly remains above 25% (including people no longer looking for work). This means that it is very difficult for foreigners to land an unskilled or semi-skilled job (legally) that is capable of being done by locals. However those with 'critical skills' can apply for a 'quota visa' in areas of skills shortage, anything from sheep shearing to nursing, forestry technicians to urban planners.

Classified adverts in a range of South African papers can be accessed online via www.wegotads. co.za. Temporary employment agencies such as Kelly with 15 branches (www.kelly.co.za) might be willing to register likely candidates whom they are persuaded plan to settle in South Africa. Prospects are generally rosier outside the popular destination of Cape Town. In some of the more affluent urban areas, private childcare is commonplace, and a British nanny or au pair might find an opening through an online agency such as www.greataupair.com. Non-South African applicants must provide their own medical insurance and initial funds.

South African Student Travel Services in Cape Town; (☎ (+21) 424 3866; www.sasts.org.za) offer a Work South Africa programme to English-speaking students and recent graduates aged 18–25, and a Volunteer South African programme lasting 8–24 weeks and costing approximately $1,600–$4,800. Both programmes run throughout the year with two start dates a month.

Red Tape

Tourists can enter South Africa on a tourist visa for three months, renewable for a further three (for a fee) at one of the 11 Visa Facilitation Services (VFS) offices, provided the application is lodged at least 45 days before the original visa expires. It is no longer possible to change your status from visitor to worker without leaving the country and applying at an overseas embassy or consulate.

The South African government is (understandably) not keen to hand out work permits to Europeans and other nationalities when so many South African nationals are unemployed. Tony Forrester found the situation very discouraging: *'With affirmative action, it's a nightmare being a white male and looking for a job.'* The Department of Home Affairs (www.home-affairs.gov.za) takes the usual line of immigration authorities that *'the main consideration in dealing with work permits is whether a South African citizen/permanent resident cannot perform the employment task to be undertaken'*.

Furthermore the authorities have tightened up on casual workers and the fines for employers caught employing them are fierce.

Work South Africa is a working holiday programme no longer available to Britons (since the UK cancelled the working holiday visa for South Africans) but is available to Canadians who are full-time tertiary students aged 18–30 or graduates within six months of graduating. The majority of participants find work in the backpacking and tourist industry, usually Cape Town. Participants are allowed to take any job they can find, so must be able to show enough funds to support themselves for up to two months. The job-hunt can be tough, though easier in the high season between October and March.

Volunteering

An overwhelming number of companies and eco-tourism operations are marketing the South African wilderness to travellers with a conscience, as a place to learn skills and see big game, for big prices. One recent volunteer has noticed an exact correlation between price and number of big cats: *'lions, leopards and cheetahs attract tourists like bees to honey'*, according to Kirsten Shaw who volunteered at Daktari Bush School and Wildlife Orphanage (www.daktaribushschool.org). WorkTravelSA (Somerset West, South Africa; www.worktravelsa.org) arranges diverse volunteer work in both humanitarian and conservation areas, and also internships. Opportunities for paying volunteers in townships, game reserves and coastal marine reserves are all directly managed by WTSA. Most volunteer placements and internships – both general (for which no experience is needed) and customised or specialised – last two weeks to six months. Most placements are in the Western Cape region, Kruger Park and Sodwana Marine National Park.

Willing Workers in South Africa (WWISA; www.wwisa.co.za) is a community service volunteer organisation based in The Crags, near Plettenberg Bay. Whatever their age and skills, volunteers work on projects alongside local villagers according to their interests, options and available dates, in the areas for example of schooling and education, youth development, business development, healthcare and environmental research. Programmes are geared to the social and economic enhancement of the local rural community of Kurland Village. The participation fee is 380 rand per day (£23/$28). Another volunteer placement company is AVIVA (Africa Volunteering & Ventures Abroad) in Cape Town (www.aviva-sa.com). Its range of placements includes working with AIDS orphans, helping out at an alternative tourist lodge and working in Kruger National Park. Edge of Africa (www.edgeofafrica.com) offers volunteer experiences in wildlife, environmental, sports, medical and community projects in Madagascar as well as South Africa, mostly around Knysna on the famous Garden Route.

Cath Cooper and husband Steve from Doncaster made use of both these organisations (WWISA and AVIVA) during their brilliant seven-month stay in South Africa, part travelling, and part volunteering:

> *We booked a three-month project with AVIVA, with the option of staying longer. When we arrived in South Africa we expected to train for a month as field guides followed by mentoring local guides and assisting with their English language skills. We did the training, but as with many best-laid plans, there*

were no local guides to mentor. After some negotiation with a local school and the business sponsor, we set up an after-school sports project. It wasn't as planned. I never dreamed of teaching kids to play cricket! But it was the best experience of our lives. We were just outside Kruger National Park and on our last day in the area we managed to take a group of 60 children on their first ever safari.

For travelling in South Africa, we used a free booklet from Coast to Coast (www.coasttocoast.co.za) as our bible for finding hostel accommodation. It also had useful information on transport, attractions and some little known volunteering opportunities. One of the highlights of our time was Bulungula Lodge (www.bulungula.com) in the Eastern Cape, which had been recommended by everyone we met. It's not easy to get to but well worth the effort. A beautiful, peaceful place with volunteer opportunities available for those who want them.

Tourism

Cape Town is the tourist capital of South Africa including for backpackers, though jobs are harder to find here than elsewhere. The Backpack & Africa Travel Centre (☎ (+27) 21 423 4530; www.backpackers.co.za) has been recommended for its contacts with local projects in schools, etc. as well as a goldmine of travel info. Roger Blake expected to stay in South Africa for three months but ended up spending seven:

There are more than 100 hostels in South Africa, many of which 'employ' backpackers on a casual basis. Within two weeks of arrival I was at a hostel in George on a work-for-keep basis. Through contacts made here I also sold T-shirts at the beach for a small profit and I did a few days at a pizza place for tips only. Then I was offered a job at a hostel in Oudtshoorn (Backpackers Oasis). They gave me free accommodation and paid me a bit to run the bar and help prepare the ostrich braai (BBQ) that they have every evening. Also I did breakfasts for fellow travellers that was like being self-employed as I bought all the ingredients and kept all the profit. It was a small but worthwhile fortune after six weeks here.

A good hostel to try for spending a couple of months on a work-for-keep exchange basis is Atlantic Point in Greenpoint (www.atlanticpoint.co.za).

Everyone who has looked for a tourist job in Cape Town recommends Seapoint, a beach suburb lined with cafés, ice cream kiosks, snack bars and other places that have high staff turnovers, though wages are low. Ice cream is also sold from cycle carts; find out whom to contact for work by asking the sellers. Check job adverts on www.indeed.co.za, Gumtree and on the Careers page of the casino, hotel and entertainment group Tsogo Sun where current vacancies are posted (www.tsogosun.com/careers/vacancies).

Also try using the door-to-door approach in the flashy Victoria and Alfred Waterfront development, Camps Bay and the beaches along the Garden Route. Note that openings along the Garden Route are seasonal, ie the peak periods fall at Christmas and Easter. The summer season starts around the 10 December and so the best time to look for restaurant/bar work is the last week of November.

Bear in mind that these high-profile tourist meccas have been the target of immigration raids. Smart places downtown sometimes hire temporary staff, eg on posh Loop Street. Casual workers might prefer more discreet places. Suburban restaurants such as the Spur Steak Ranches (a leading South African franchise), Mike's Kitchen Family Restaurants and St Elmo's Pizzerias are often hiring, though the first two are liable to pay only commission. Suburbs in Cape Town to concentrate on are Observatory, Rondebosch, Wynberg and Plumstead.

Although Johannesburg is often maligned as a big, bad city, it is the earning capital of South Africa with better job possibilities than many other places. Unfortunately, some of the inner city areas (Yeoville, Brixton) have succumbed to the crime and grime for which the city is known. Now the areas to head for restaurant and pub work are the northern suburbs of Sandton, Rosebank and Dunkeld West.

Sandton is an area where within a 5km radius there are more than 60 restaurants and bars, five huge clubs, the Montecasino complex and backpackers' lodges. Travellers can sometimes get jobs waiting tables, working on the bar, etc. Resorts along the east coast between Cape Town and Port Elizabeth and even as far as the Ciskei provide employment opportunities, as does the Natal coast especially Durban and Margate. Particularly recommended on the east coast are George, Knysna, Jeffreys Bay, Plettenberg Bay and Port Elizabeth. As in the cities, the summer high season falls in December/January.

Tekweni Backpackers and Travel Info Centre in the Morningside area of Durban (www.tekweni backpackers.co.za) sometimes employs foreigners for free rent and a small wage (which soon gets swallowed up at the numerous night spots on Florida Road on the hostel's doorstep).

Work may be available in the boatyards of Cape Town and other places, especially doing the dogs-body jobs of sanding and painting. Activity peaks before the early January departure of yachts on the annual Cape to Rio Yacht Race.

Farm Work

The towns of Stellenbosch and Paarl to the east and north of Cape Town respectively are the centres of South Africa's massive wine industry. Around Stellenbosch the harvest begins in late January/early February and lasts four or five weeks. Further inland (eg around Worcester) it starts a few weeks later, and continues well into March. If you find a farmer willing to put you up and give you work the problem of work permits is unlikely to arise. The farm volunteer exchange website www.helpx.net records 103 properties in South Africa while WWOOF South Africa (www.wwoofsa.co.za) has about 250 properties looking for work-for-keep helpers.

BUSINESS AND INDUSTRY

If you are interested in joining a business in Africa (especially if you have a technical or managerial skill) start by surfing the internet. You can contact the Commercial Section of the embassy of the country that interests you for general information about job prospects. If you are on the spot, the expatriate community may be willing to offer advice or practical assistance.

Other work opportunities in Africa include translating business documents from and into French, German or English, depending on the particular country's position and trade. You could put an ad in the paper or visit firms.

VOLUNTEERING

Africa is still partially reliant on aid agencies and voluntary assistance. The majority of volunteers in Africa are trained teachers, medical staff, agricultural and technical specialists who have committed themselves to work with the support of their churches back home or through mainstream aid organisations such as VSO (www.vsointernational.org) and Skillshare International (Leicester, www.skillshare. org). Voluntourism trips to Africa can easily be searched online for example at www.responsibletravel. com searchable by country. After registering for £9 you can access volunteer jobs and internships across Africa on www.volunteer4africa.org.

The UK government-funded ICS (International Citizen Service) volunteer programme works through VSO and seven partner agencies including Restless Development and Y Care International. Volunteers aged 18–25 are recruited and paid for (apart from a requirement to fundraise £800) to spend 10–12 weeks working alongside local volunteers in anything from mentoring small businesses to sexual health education. Destination countries in Africa include Burkino Faso, Liberia and Togo as well as the usual suspects. All details can be found at www.volunteerics.org. Older candidates (aged 23–35) can consider applying to be team leaders.

Thirty-year-old Australian Paul Jones gave up a full-time position in the IT industry in order to go freelance and work and travel in Europe and beyond. While working in England, he came across a volunteer project in Tanzania which appealed:

I wish I'd known about these kinds of volunteer groups years ago because I would have done it then. The idea evolved from a pure holiday in Africa to some volunteer work mixed in with travel. I found out that the organisation supported a local NGO in the Singida region of Tanzania. At first I was surprised that I had to pay so much to participate in a four-week programme but learnt very quickly that it was my donation of money that was most important and my presence on the ground in Tanzania was secondary. Once I understood how it worked and that even charity organisations are businesses, even if not to make a profit, I set my sights on going and knew that while the outlay of money might seem a lot for me, it would mean a lot more to those I would be helping. You don't have to have any particular skills, but be willing to try something new, be flexible and get along with other people. I had every vaccination possible, got a medical test and police check which all added to the costs, but again you get over it. All transport was taken care of and language lessons were organised while in Tanzania. I'm still amazed at my experience in Tanzania. I can sit for hours at my computer and stare at my photos, remembering the village I worked in, my trek up Mount Kilimanjaro and the safari. There are such stark contrasts between different parts of Tanzania that I would recommend a similar experience to anybody.

With conservation and environmental issues such a priority, many organisations, large and small, are involved in protecting the magnificent wildlife and landscapes of Africa. A good starting point for locating interesting organisations is the website www.africanconservation.org which has a searchable database of elite organisations.

It may be possible to offer your services on a voluntary basis to any hospital, school or mission you come across in your travels, though acceptance is not guaranteed. Travellers who have found themselves in the vicinity of a famine crisis have often expressed shock when their offer of help has been turned down. Passers-by cannot easily be incorporated into ongoing aid projects.

If you have a useful skill and the addresses of some suitable projects, you are well on the way to fixing something up. Mary Hall had both, so wrote to a mission clinic in Uganda offering her services as a nurse:

There wasn't a doctor so the work was very stressful for me. After a couple of weeks I was helping to run the clinic, see and examine patients, prescribe drugs and set up a teaching programme for the unqualified Ugandan nurses.

We had no running water, intermittent electricity and a lack of such niceties as cheese and chocolate. Obviously adaptability has to be one of the main qualities. Initially I worked on my visitor's visa which wasn't a problem, but when it became apparent that I would be staying for longer, the clinic applied for a work permit for me. Quite an expensive venture (£100) and I think very difficult without a local sponsor. The local bishop wrote a beautiful letter on my behalf, so I got one. A white person is considered to be the be-all and end-all of everyone's problems, and I found it difficult to live with this image. I'd like to say that the novelty of having a white foreigner around wore off but it never did. Stare, stare and stare again, never a moment to yourself. Still it was a fantastic experience. I've learnt an awful lot, and don't think I could ever do nursing in Britain again. My whole idea of Africa and aid in particular has been turned on its head. Idealism at an end.

This professed disillusionment with aid work did not prevent Mary from pursuing a career in development in Africa and the Middle East.

A myriad of specialist programmes exists to encourage volunteer exchanges. For example volunteer sports coaches, phys ed teachers, recreation leaders and sports organisers are placed by a number of agencies. Paul Edmunds signed up with Sussex-based Travellers Worldwide (www.travellersworldwide.com) to join a cricket-coaching project on the outskirts of Accra in Ghana. He enjoyed the experience enormously and felt that it was extremely beneficial to the children to experience the structured framework of a sport. As well as bringing them pleasure, it also taught them discipline.

Sending Organisations

African Adventures: Eastleigh, UK; ☎ (+44) 23 8178 0957; www.volunteerinafrica.co.uk. Teaching, sports and building projects in Ghana, Kenya and Zanzibar.

Big Beyond: HQ in Cape Town; UK telephone: ☎ (+44) 1395 20656. Volunteer programme in Bwindi Impenetrable National Park of Uganda and in the Omo Valley of Ethiopia. Price from £995 for 2 weeks, £3,590 for 16 weeks.

Blue Ventures: London N7; ☎ (+44) 20 7697 8598; www.blueventures.org. Volunteers are needed from two weeks to six months to carry out marine research and community conservation at an expedition camp in South Western Madagascar; fee for six weeks about £2,500 for non-divers, slightly less for PADI divers.

BUNAC: London W8; ☎ (+44) 33 3999 7516; www.bunac.org. Volunteer South Africa programme offers choice of sports coaching, wildlife conservation or volunteering on a game reserve. £820–£995 for varying durations.

Challenge Africa: Bath; www.challengeafrica.org.uk. Projects in Kenya to tackle HIV and deficits in girls' education.

Community Centred Conservation: www.c-3.org.uk. Network of grassroots conservation projects in Madagascar that might accept paying interns.

Cross-Cultural Solutions: Brighton, East Sussex; ☎ (+44) 845 458 2781; www.crosscultural solutions.org. Volunteer vacations in Ghana, Tanzania and Morocco to teach English, provide skills training or enhance recreation programmes; sample fee is $6,000 for 6 weeks in Morocco.

Ecologia Youth Trust: ☎ (+44) 1309 690995; www.ecologia.org.uk. Personalised placements for volunteers at Kithoka Amani Community Home in Meru, Kenya run by small Scottish charity with local partner, International Peace Initiatives. IPI provides shelter to around 30 orphaned or vulnerable children, many living with or affected by HIV/AIDS and volunteers stay for 2–3 months.

Gapforce: London SW6; ☎ (+44) 20 7384 3028; www.gapforce.org. Recruits volunteers for Southern Africa and interns for Ghana in law, medicine, journalism, etc; sample price £1,500 for one month.

Global Vision International (GVI): Exeter, Devon; ☎ (+44) 1727 250250; www.gvi.co.uk. Projects in South Africa and marine conservation in the Seychelles.

Madventurer: Corbridge, Northumberland; ☎ (+44) 191 232 0625; www.madventurer.com. Charity that arranges development work in Ghana, Kenya, Togo, Tanzania, Uganda and South Africa.

Operation Wallacea: Spilsby, Lincolnshire; www.opwall.com. Academic marine and forest research projects in Madagascar and South Africa from £1,225 for a fortnight.

Reefdoctor.org: London SW15; www.ReefDoctor.org. Hands-on and scuba diving conservation programme in Madagascar, working with the local fishing communities of the Bay of Ranobe, part of the third largest coral reef system in the world; from three weeks to six months. Aquaculture internships cost £1,500 for two months; £2,500 for six months with three start dates per year.

Seed Madagascar: London W10; ☎ (+44) 20 8960 6629; info@azafady.org; www. madagascar.co.uk. 2–10 weeks working in community conservation and biodiversity research in Madagascar; fundraising target is £2,500 for 10 weeks excluding flights, visas, vaccinations, etc. Their Pioneer programme lasting 4–10 weeks involves construction and conservation and costs £2,000 for 10 weeks.

Street Child: London EC2; www.street-child.co.uk. International volunteering programme in Sierra Leone and possibly Liberia. Child protection work and teacher training. Volunteers contribute £5–£10 a day.

Volunteer Uganda: Hull, Yorkshire; www.volunteeruganda.org. Six- or 12-week placements in Kunungu district of south-west Uganda, mainly to teach and assist in local primary schools and do outreach work.

It is always sensible to do as much research as possible about a project and an organisation to which you intend to commit considerable time and money.

Short-term Projects

Thousands of small charities and NGOs accept volunteers to participate in rural and community development for varying periods. Invariably you have to finance your own travel and pay a registration fee to cover food and lodging, typically for three to six weeks. The work may consist of building, installing water supplies, conservation or assisting in homes for disabled or underprivileged children and adults.

In some cases, a national organisation fields applications from international volunteers who want to join a voluntary workcamp. For links to national workcamp agencies in Africa check the website of Service Civil International (www.sciint.ngo), though participation in these projects is normally arranged through the workcamp sending agency in your home country such as IVS in the UK.

Volunteers for Peace (see VFP in Volunteering chapter) for example lists information on workcamps in four African nations including Uganda and Togo. In recent years many African organisations have embraced the online world, which makes communication infinitely cheaper and easier.

If you decide to join a project once you are in an African capital such as Accra, Addis Ababa or Kampala, it should not be hard to track down the coordinating office. Foreign embassies might also be in a position to offer useful advice. They may have a Community Liaison Office that holds information about local charities and aid projects needing volunteers.

> **ROGER BLAKE SIMPLY MADE LOTS OF LOCAL ENQUIRIES WHEN HE TRAVELLED TO ETHIOPIA AND UGANDA:**
>
> *I had contemplated a 'voluntary' placement fixed up through an agency at home but I find the modern concept of paying to volunteer your services a crazy idea. So I decided that I would go it alone. I was in Ethiopia for almost two months and had a great time. On my return to Addis Ababa, I decided to ask around for any English teaching possibilities and was recommended to a charity that invited me to spend a short time supporting their qualified local teacher in the classroom with physically disabled children. I did not get paid but they did make it worth my while by giving me three excellent meals a day and I got to stay in a wonderful house in an idyllic countryside location with magnificent gardens. My 'employment' was unofficial, thus the short stay. I have ascertained that there are casual opportunities to teach here in Addis but you must search hard to find them.*

Continuing his trans-African journey, Roger next enquired about working possibilities in Kampala where he had already encountered the huge expatriate community and their attendant recreations – cinema, pubs, gyms and supermarkets:

> *On the noticeboard of the Red Chilli Hideaway, a backpackers' hostel and campsite, Kabira School had an advert for a youth worker at their youth centre. Nothing ventured, nothing gained, so I applied and got the job (for a trial period). I worked evenings and weekends with expat teenagers, in the same environment as a youth club at home. They would have been willing to arrange a work permit for me and pay me a very reasonable salary equivalent to $250 a month – enough to live on as I was staying in my tent at the hostel. I was tempted but I decided to move on with the African trip, mainly because I didn't want to lose my non-refundable onward air ticket to Australia.*

Uganda Lodge in Ruhanga in south-west Uganda (www.ugandalodge.com/uganda_volunteer.html) encourages travellers to get involved with a variety of local development projects while staying in the lodge's purpose-built volunteer accommodation for £105 a week.

Grassroots Organisations

Till Bruckner is another veteran world traveller who shares Roger Blake's fondness for fixing up teaching and voluntary placements independently rather than with the help of an intermediary:

> *My advice to anyone who wants to volunteer in Africa (or anywhere else) is to go first and volunteer second. That way you can travel until you've found a place you genuinely like and where you think you might be able to make a difference. You can also check out the work and accommodation for yourself before you settle down. If you're willing to work for free, you don't need a nanny to tell you where to go. Just go.*

However, for those who find this prospect daunting (and unless you are a mature and seasoned traveller you probably will), you might like to pursue the middle way which is to make contact with small local organisations in Africa which actively look for volunteers abroad, though make sure you do some research to avoid signing up with a bogus organisation. Always hunt for reviews and feedback online when considering a grassroots organisation.

Throughout Africa there are a great many volunteer workers with the mainstream aid agencies such as VSO and the Peace Corps in hospitals, schools and agricultural projects who are sometimes willing to assist travellers. Probably the more remote and cut-off the volunteers are, the more welcoming they will be, but be careful not to abuse or presume on their hospitality. Always offer to pay your way, or go armed with treats.

Conservation and Wildlife

A number of wildlife reserves in southern Africa have introduced programmes for paying volunteers, especially gap year students, to get close to the animals by monitoring them and protecting their environment. The costs which are usually substantial, sometimes at near tourist prices, are used to support projects on the conservation the reserves, many of which are privately owned.

Some overseas agencies involved with conservation in Africa have already been mentioned. African Conservation Experience with an office in Gloucestershire (☎ (+44) 1454 269182; www.conservationafrica.net) arranges conservation work placements lasting 4–12 weeks on game reserves in southern Africa including South Africa, Botswana, Namibia and Zimbabwe. Tasks may include darting rhino for relocation or elephant for fitting tracking collars, game capture, tagging, assisting with veterinary work, game counts, etc. Alien plant control and the re-introduction of indigenous plants is often involved. The cost for 12 weeks varies from £5,770 for monitoring wild dogs to £9,400 for a lion conservation project, including everything except flights.

One of the projects to which volunteer-sourcing agencies such as AVIVA (mentioned earlier in this chapter) send foreign volunteers is the seabird conservation organisation, the South African National Foundation for the Conservation of Coastal Birds. SANCCOB requires volunteers to help with the cleaning and rehabilitation of oil-soaked birds (mainly penguins) since oil pollution is a major problem in the coastal waters of South Africa. Volunteers stay at least six weeks which costs £478. Details are available from AVIVA or SANCCOB based in Cape Town (www.sanccob.co.za). If you book directly with SANCCOB, the fee is a modest 1,500 rand (£95) for six weeks but this doesn't include accommodation.

A well-publicised survey asked people to rank the 50 things they wanted to do before they died. Well over half of these dream trips involved contact with wildlife, particularly whales. An exotic location for conservation work is in the Comoros Islands off Madagascar. A marine mammal protection association that protects sea turtles and other species based on Moheli Island operates a volunteer programme. You can join expeditions at sea to research the humpback whale population through Moidjio CRCAD (http://sites.google.com/site/moidjio). This will cost £300 per week though other volunteer projects such as teaching cost a third as much. Living conditions are spartan.

African big game are a perennial attraction. Chris Giles and his wife Christine worked at Kwando Safari Camp in Botswana, where they did mainly menial work in the kitchen and the grounds but had plenty of thrilling brushes with the wildlife:

> *Our jobs were not strenuous or difficult but extremely important because it made us feel part of the team running the safari camp. Christine has been in the kitchen and I have been a waiter, scullery (washing up) and helped mend a walkway when an elephant wandered through during the middle of the night! As I have absolutely no practical skills, this was quite an achievement, although I'm not sure*

the maintenance manager, who showed great patience, was impressed with how long it took me. The scenery and wildlife in this remote part of northern Botswana are stunning so things that are normally mundane and routine suddenly become exciting. I was quite happy clearing plates, washing glasses, making fruit salad, serving drinks and chatting to guests from all around the world.

Other conservation volunteer opportunities are offered by the following:

African Impact: Cape Town, South Africa; www.africanimpact.com. Voluntourism opportunities on community projects (teaching, medical and sports) and on lion conservation projects in Zambia, Zimbabwe, South Africa, Zanzibar, Mozambique, Kenya, Malawi, Seychelles, etc.

APES (Animal Protection & Environmental Sanctuary): Kwazulu-Natal, South Africa; www. apes.org.za. Private centre for primate rehabilitation, rescue and animal care, especially vervet monkeys; volunteers pay £610 per month.

In Defense of Animals (IDA) Africa: Portland, Oregon; ☎ (+1) 503 730 8693; www.ida-africa. org. Sends volunteers over 21 who are fluent in either French or English and able to converse in the other language to a chimpanzee sanctuary in the Mbargue Forest of Cameroon, for a minimum of six months. Programme fee $300.

Limbe Wildlife Centre: Limbe, Cameroon; ☎ (+237) 9998 2503; www.limbewildlife.org and http://limbewildlifecentre.wildlifedirect.org. Runs a volunteer programme working with endangered Cameroonian wildlife including chimpanzees, gorillas, crocodiles, etc; volunteers stay one–three months and pay €750 a month.

Mnarani Marine Turtle Conservation Pond: Nungwi, Zanzibar; www.mnarani.com/volunteer. html. Volunteers help at a turtle aquarium where injured Green Turtles are cared for. Beach clean-ups are also involved. Volunteers pay $1,000 for the first month, $900 for the second and $800 thereafter.

Risette De Haas from the Netherlands ended up going as a volunteer coordinator at Daktari Wildlife Orphanage and Bush School near South Africa's Kruger National Park (www.daktaribushschool.org) whose mission is to educate underprivileged children to care for the environment through the medium of a wildlife orphanage. Her account sent from there gives a good flavour of the place:

I wanted to work with wildlife or children, and I wanted to do something 'good'. First I looked for jobs with big organisations, so maybe I could get a paid job. But those are very hard to find and they ask for experience or specific studies I didn't have. So I changed my online search to 'free' job, as a non-paying volunteer. After searching for about two months I found Daktari, so my two passions could be realised in one place, working with animals and with children. Daktari offers a few placements for volunteers over 18 who can speak English to stay for six months or longer. The placements are free and you get housing and food during the week. I made contact with the owner Michele and, after a few emails, and reading some blogs of previous volunteers, I decided that this was my opportunity. The only things Michele asked was whether my English was sufficient to do my job, and of course whether I was truly enthusiastic.

Because I am staying at Daktari for more than six months, I don't have to pay for my stay, as the short-term volunteers do. But you get more responsibilities, for me that was the job of volunteer coordinator/camp manager. I make sure that the volunteers and the children are happy and that the animals are taken care of. My weekends are officially off, but when we get a new volunteer I show them around and have an introduction meeting with them. It is hard work and quite long hours, but I love it and the thing I do here gives me so much energy that it is easy to keep up. The smiles of the kids, the attention with the animals and the 'family' of volunteers – perfect! Even when you work in the office at Daktari, you still have dogs, squirrels and warthogs running around.

We are in the bush here. There is no electricity and things are very basic, we have power and light via solar, but that sometimes runs out. For me coming to the bush was what I needed and put everything in perspective. I have another four months of my year here to go. Some kids just steal your heart and you want to know if they get all the best opportunities they deserve. I love the bush, I love Africa and I also love working for a charity. I know now that I made the best decision in my life by coming here. It changed everything.

Israel and the Palestinian Territories

Israel is not a happy country. After so much civilian bloodshed and so many failed peace initiatives, the conflict between the Israelis and Palestinians often seems beyond resolution. Israel has lost much of its appeal for travellers, and the number of young people choosing to head for what was a generation ago a favourite travellers' destination is drastically down. At present few opportunities exist in the Palestinian-governed Territories and many projects such as archaeological digs have been curtailed or cancelled. But behind all the shocking violence and retaliation in the headlines, thousands of individuals and groups are working towards a peaceful two-state solution. Spending time in this troubled region will enable people from outside to gain more insight into one of the world's most bedevilled trouble spots. Personal security is bound to be a consideration in a country where indiscriminate terrorist attacks are at times a real threat.

The prospects for finding paid work are much gloomier than they once were, partly because of a large resident population of cheap labour from Thailand, the Philippines, etc and because of a radical clampdown a few years ago on foreigners working without official work permits. The Israeli Law of Return which gives all people of Jewish heritage the automatic right to immigrate also means that job vacancies are few and far between. Employers caught employing illegal workers are heavily fined, so the managers of restaurants, hostels and other tourist establishments that at one time would have hired backpackers without a thought are now extremely reluctant to do so.

Fortunately, it is still possible to enter Israel as a volunteer. The number of volunteers heading for a kibbutz is way down from the heyday when half a million foreign volunteers were placed on Israeli kibbutzim between 1967 and 1985. However there has been a slight resurgence in the past few years and about 1,200 volunteers come every year from 50 countries.

REGULATIONS

For anyone without an Israeli passport who wishes to volunteer on a kibbutz or archaeological dig, it is obligatory for your sponsor to obtain a B4 Volunteer Visa from the Ministry of the Interior before you arrive in the country. This is an important change from the old days when travellers would simply show up as tourists and change their status to volunteer after arrival. The visa is valid for an initial three months (for a fee of NIS90/$23) and renewable for a further three months.

It is virtually impossible to obtain a work permit for the kind of casual work travellers tend to do in Israel and, as mentioned, it is increasingly risky working on a tourist visa. A working holiday programme (www.workingholiday.org.il) has been available to New Zealanders for a few years and in 2016 was extended to Australians, Germans, Austrians and South Koreans aged 18–30. There is no dedicated working holiday visa so participants receive a general B1 work visa valid for a maximum of one year.

KIBBUTZIM

From the 1960s to the 1990s, every self-respecting backpacker would at least have heard of the possibility of spending a few months on an Israeli kibbutz, exchanging his or her work for free living. But nowadays, the concept is not widely known among the travelling community, though the possibility still exists and thousands of volunteers continue to spend between 10 weeks and six expense-free months on one of the 27 kibbutzim in Israel that continue to accept foreign volunteers.

Originally a kibbutz was a communal society, usually based on agriculture, in which the means of production were owned and shared by the community as a whole. But this utopian concept has rather faded from view, and many kibbutzim have been partly or wholly privatised. A further change is that kibbutzim have increasingly become based on manufacturing rather than agriculture, and some kibbutzim are urban rather than rural.

Arranging a Job

The demand for volunteers fluctuates according to many factors including national politics, the time of year, competition from new Jewish settlers and so on though, in the present circumstances, demand for volunteers is likely to outstrip supply. Volunteers must be aged 18–35. For visa reasons, volunteers cannot be assigned to a kibbutz after arrival in Israel. They must register in advance through the Kibbutz Volunteer Program Center's website and pay $40 for application and visa processing. After arrival, volunteers proceed to the KPC office in Tel Aviv with their passport, photocopy of passport, medical certificate, airline ticket out of Israel and fees totalling NIS1,050 ($275) to cover registration and compulsory health insurance. The Volunteer Department of the KPC is at 13 Leonardo Da Vinci St, Tel Aviv 6473315; ☎ (+972) 3 524 6154/6; kpc@kibbutzvolunteers.org.il; www.kibbutz.org.il/volunteers. The office is open Sunday to Thursday 8.30am–2.30pm. The buses needed to reach the office are: numbers 5, 475 and 70 from the airport, 56 from the railway station and 70 from the Central Bus Station.

Only a tenth of the 270 kibbutzim operate volunteer programmes nowadays partly because so many have been privatised. This means you may not get much say in the kind of kibbutz you go to. A higher percentage of visitors on kibbutzim are Jewish than used to be the case. A number of kibbutzim are located in the fertile lands of northern and southern Israel. It is best to be prepared for the climate; for example the north can be cold and rainy in winter, whereas the Jordan Rift Valley can be one of the hottest and driest places in the world.

For contact details of representative offices in other countries, see www.kibbutz.org il/volunteers/repres.htm. North American applicants should contact the Kibbutz Program Center in New York (☎ (+1) 212 462 2764; www.kibbutzprogramcenter.org) which acts as a clearinghouse for American volunteers aged 19–35. The registration fee is $690.

South Africans can book kibbutz volunteer placements through one of the offices of OVC Work Study Travel throughout South Africa (www.ovc.co.za) or YDP (www.ydp.co.za).

Life on a Kibbutz

In return for their labour, volunteers receive free room and board and a small amount of pocket money, eg NIS400 (£85) a month. Most volunteers enjoy their stay, and find that some kibbutzim make considerable efforts to welcome volunteers. For example, the majority of kibbutzim try to provide occasional organised sightseeing tours for volunteers, sometimes every month. Yet kibbutzim expect volunteers to work hard for their keep. The average working day is up to nine hours on six days of the week, though hours may be reduced in the hot summer. Many kibbutzim give an extra two or three days off per month to allow their volunteers to travel (since travel is difficult on the sabbath when there is no public transport).

Jimmy Hill describes the variety of jobs he did in just two months at a small kibbutz south of Jericho: *'dining hall duties, chopping date trees, a lot of gardening, working in a vineyard, electrician, turkey chaser and guest house cleaner'*. New volunteers are often assigned the undesirable jobs though most volunteer organisers are willing to transfer a dissatisfied volunteer to a different job. Catherine Revell claims that if you are assertive and show willingness to work hard, you can find yourself doing more interesting work; among the jobs she did on three different kibbutzim were kitchen manager, shepherdess and a sculptor's assistant. Increasingly, work is in factories or of an industrial nature, though it is impossible to generalise and interesting options crop up. For example Allan Kirkpatrick from Glasgow spent an enjoyable six weeks at a kibbutz in northern Israel cleaning a theatre where a classical music festival was taking place. Agricultural jobs are still available at some kibbutzim. One unexpected hazard in the fields is the wildlife. The only job John Mallon was reluctant to do was to carry bunches of bananas since they housed rats and spiders. And although in most respects Deborah Hunter's kibbutz was no Garden of Eden, she recalls several shrieks and hasty descents of the ladder when volunteers encountered snakes in the fruit trees.

TOURISM

The current situation in Israel and the Middle East generally has put a big dent in the tourist industry, so work is not very plentiful. In general the best places for finding work in tourism have always been Eilat, Tel Aviv, Herzliya (a wealthy resort north of Tel Aviv) and, to a lesser extent, Haifa and Jerusalem. Many cheap hostels around Israel employ two or three travellers to spend a few hours a day cleaning or manning the desk in exchange for a free bed and some meals. In fact this is one of the few opportunities for spinning out an affordable stay in the country. Links to independent hostels around the country can be found at www.hostels-israel.com. If you prove yourself a hard worker, you may be moved to a better job or even paid some pocket money. Heather McCulloch worked for a hostel in Tiberias, the main resort on the Sea of Galilee (where at that time it was easy to find restaurant, beach or hotel work). The Abraham hostel in Jerusalem accepts volunteers for a minimum of six weeks to help promote its social programme, etc in exchange for free accommodation (www.abrahamhostels.com/jerusalem/volunteer). Note that there are Abraham hostels in Tel Aviv and Nazareth as well.

Casual jobs in cafés, restaurants, bars and hotels can be unearthed with difficulty. As in Greece, these jobs are much easier to get if you're female. The pay is usually low and sometimes non-existent, but you will get free food and drink, and tips. As throughout Israel, the price of a day's work has to be negotiated. Most working travellers recommend collecting your wages (and paying your own hostel bills) on a daily basis to prevent aggravation later. Also be aware that many travellers have had their money stolen from hostels including some who lost money entrusted to the hostel 'safe'.

The tourist season in Eilat lasts from late October to March, so it might be possible to fill a temporary vacancy in a hotel or cruise business. Because Eilat is an important yachting and diving centre, you can check for job notices posted on the gates to the Marina or on the Marina noticeboard, or talked about in the Yacht Pub. Work as crew or kitchen staff, cleaners or au pairs is usually found by asking boat to boat. Some years ago Sarah Jane Smith landed a job as a deckhand and hostess on a private charter yacht for scuba divers:

> *I was taken on cruises lasting between a week and a month to the Red Sea, Gulf of Suez, etc. to some of the best diving spots in the world. I was taught how to scuba dive and also did lots of snorkelling. I saw some of the most amazing sights of my life: the sun rising over Saudi Arabia as the moon sank into Egypt, coral reefs, sharks, dolphins, and so on. The social life on the marina was better than the kibbutz with hundreds of other travellers working on boats or in Eilat. Every night was a party and I hardly know how I survived it. The only bad thing is the low wages (if you get paid at all) and the hard work. But the harder you work and longer you stay, the better the wages and perks become.*

Over the years, thousands of travellers have spent some time working in the modern city of Tel Aviv doing everything from bouncing in clubs to au pairing. Work has been offered in bars, restaurants and beach cafés, especially to women. If you are considering doing a tips-only job, try to have a private conversation with the current staff before accepting. The cost of living is high, so Tel Aviv is not a good place to chill while waiting for something to crop up.

The hostels along Hayarkon Street were once valuable sources of job information or jobs themselves though it must be reiterated that the employment situation is much tighter now and in fact many of the hostels that used to maintain Work Lists have closed. One to try is Momo's Hostel at 28 Ben Yehuda St (☎ (+972) 3 528 7471; www.momoshostel.com) to which veteran traveller Jane Harris and her boyfriend Pete moved: *'Momo's had loads of work coming in, using a work list system. Pete got work loading and unloading containers, dishwashing and cleaning. I worked for Momo in the hostel. I'd recommend this hostel for work.'*

Things are not so easy now, but Momo's confirmed recently that *'there are still some business places which take a chance and employ tourists, including bars around the hostel and also some removals companies'*.

Buskers and sellers of handicrafts such as home-made jewellery have in the past reported good profits in Jerusalem. For example Leda Meredith sold woven string bracelets on Ben Yehuda Street.

OTHER PAID WORK

Professional and other vacancies are listed at www.janglo.net/index.php/taanglo which calls itself the largest online community for English speakers in Israel. Although the demand for live-in childcare is strong, the visa issue makes it next to impossible to work for longer than three months. Whereas there used to be several Israeli agencies actively placing foreign au pairs and nannies, now there are none. Your best chance is an online agency like GreatAuPair.com.

The startup and IT industry in Israel is flourishing; in fact the coastal areas around Tel Aviv (including Herzliya, Rehovot and Airport City) have been dubbed Silicon Wadi as having almost as high a concentration of high-tech industries as Silicon Valley in California. Those in a position to contract in the tech industry or who want to get involved in a startup should ask around.

Teaching

Because of the large number of English-speaking Jews who have settled in Israel from the USA, South Africa, etc, many native speakers of English are employed in the state education system and there is little active recruitment of foreign teachers. Wall Street English has 11 franchises in Israel including Tel Aviv, Ra'anona, Beer Sheba, Haifa and Nazareth which is the first to open in the Arab sector; the website www.wallstreet-english.co.il is in Hebrew only.

Shortly after reacquainting himself with a girl he knew in Tel Aviv, Tom Balfour started discovering possibilities:

I sent emails with my CV to various English schools, mostly branches of the two big companies Berlitz and Wall Street, explaining my situation – that I would be leaving Israel in a week to return to England for my summer job, but that I wanted to come back in September and teach English in Tel Aviv. Most of the schools simply sent me a reply saying 'get back to us when you return' but Wall Street in Tel Aviv invited me for an interview. In the interview I was asked various questions about teaching, and then the director pretended to be a low level student and asked me to explain various words to her. When she asked me what a model was, I said 'Naomi Campbell, Kate Moss' and then got up and did a pretend catwalk round the room. Although I'm sure that my qualifications helped, I think that might be what got me the job: knowing how to keep explanations simple, and being prepared to look silly if it helped. She told me that if I came back I would be offered a contract. I think that my Trinity TEFL qualification and my planned work at the summer school made me stand out from the native candidates, some of whom were hoping for a job simply on the strength of being English speakers.

Tom Balfour has no regrets about choosing Israel: *'Israel is an amazing country and Tel Aviv is a great, cosmopolitan city with a good beach and fantastic nightlife.'*

Even if you are an English speaker and experienced teacher, there is no guarantee that you will get a work visa, unless you improve your chances by being in a relationship with an Israeli (or Jewish).

VOLUNTARY OPPORTUNITIES

The volunteer agency GoEco (www.goeco.org) registers humanitarian and conservation volunteer openings in Israel as well as worldwide, for the benefit of international travellers willing to pay a participation fee. Examples include conservation of the coral reef reserve in Eilat and an eco-village building project in the Arava Desert; prices start at $480 for a fortnight. GoEco has contact phone numbers in the UK, Australia and USA.

The Jewish/Arab village of Neve Shalom/Wahat al-Salaam (meaning Oasis of Peace) between Tel Aviv and Jerusalem accepts a few volunteers over 20 to work in the guesthouse, kitchen, school or gardens attached to the community's School for Peace for a few months. See www.wasns.org/-volunteering for further details of volunteer and intern positions which provide a little pocket money.

To search for opportunities in a Jewish context that are open to visitors, go to Volunteering in Israel at www.ivolunteer.org.il/eng for a list of charities and organisations that accept volunteers.

Palestinian Projects

The political situation has made it impossible for projects to continue in Gaza (the FCO advises against all travel to Gaza) and difficult in the other Palestinian territories. The educational charity Unipal (Universities' Trust for Educational Exchange with Palestinians; www.unipal.org.uk) runs a summer programme of teaching English to teenagers in Jerusalem and the West Bank for three to five weeks. Volunteers pay for their flights plus £300 to cover food, accommodation and insurance. The deadline for applications is mid-February, interviews are in March and training is provided in April.

The Excellence Center in Hebron (www.excellencenter.org) hosts international volunteers, interns and students of Arabic for up to three months. Volunteers (over the age of 22) are expected to get to know the Palestinian community and write short articles about the culture in order to inform international readers. The registration fee for the scheme is $200 and homestay accommodation is provided. Travel to Hebron is straightforward: bus from Jerusalem's Damascus Gate to Bethlehem and shared taxi to Hebron.

The international network of work-for-keep opportunities maintained by Workaway.info lists 16 opportunities in Palestine, most of them helping in backpacker hostels and in other tourism-related capacities like helping to guide hiking trips near the Dead Sea.

Friends of Birzeit University, a UK-based charity that supports Palestinian education, has in the past been able to offer varied volunteer and interning positions in Ramallah, though none is available currently. Keep an eye on their website http://www.fobzu.org/get-involved/work-us if interested.

The British Council in the Palestinian Territories operates English language centres in Jerusalem and Ramallah, and occasionally runs adult and children's courses in other parts of the West Bank and Gaza (www.britishcouncil.ps).

Archaeology

Volunteers are needed to do the mundane work of digging and sifting. In the majority of cases, volunteers must pay a daily fee of $35–$70+ to cover food and accommodation (often on a nearby kibbutz) plus a registration fee (typically $70–$200). Most camps take place during university holidays between May and September when temperatures soar. Volunteers must be in good physical condition and able to work long hours in hot weather. Valid health insurance is required.

Information on volunteering at archaeological digs in Israel is available on the website of the Israel Ministry of Foreign Affairs (though it's a little difficult to locate; try googling 'MFA digs' and the year). After choosing an excavation of interest, you make contact directly with the person in charge of the research, some of them in the Department of Classical Studies at Tel Aviv University and others at universities elsewhere in Israel or abroad. A longstanding project is at the ancient port site of Yavneh Yam (tau.ac.il/~yavneyam) where the participation fee is $500 per week.

Long-term excavations are taking place at Ein Gedi Oasis, the only 6th century Jewish settlement to have been exposed on the shores of the Dead Sea. If interested in joining the excavations in January/February go to https://sites.google.com/site/eingediexcavations/home/call-for-volunteers where there is an application form. Participation costs are from $30 a night in a shared room at the field school or youth hostel plus $35 for meals.

Asia

For a continent as vast as Asia, this chapter may seem disproportionately short. That is simply because
there are not many kinds of work open to the traveller in developing countries, as has already been
noted in the chapters on Africa and Latin America. The kinds of job which travellers get in the developed world (seasonal farm work, tourist resorts, as nannies, etc) are not available in most of Asia.

The main exception is provided by those countries with a Western-style economy, principally China,
Taiwan, Korea (which in this chapter means of course South Korea), Japan and Singapore. One of
the most surprising economic miracles has been taking place in India, where Europeans are being
recruited to work alongside Indian professionals in business and other roles.

Having made your fortune in an industrialised country, you should be able to finance many months
of leisurely travel in the inexpensive countries of Asia such as Laos or Sri Lanka. In most of Asia it is
better to concentrate on travelling for its own sake rather than for the sake of working. The climate is
another factor. Although Robert Abblett had carefully planned his trip to India and had the addresses
of organic farms where he intended to work, he had not counted on the debilitating heat and decided
to enjoy a holiday instead.

However, described below are a number of ways to boost your budget between enjoying the temples
of Thailand and beaches of Turkey. Note that a one-year working holiday visa scheme operates for
young Britons going to Japan, Hong Kong, and Taiwan, a two-year permit is available for Korea and six
months in Singapore, plus young Australians and New Zealanders are eligible for a WH visa for Hong
Kong, Japan, Korea, Taiwan, Thailand, Vietnam and Singapore. Australians are also entitled to have
one-year working holidays in Turkey, Iran and Bangladesh, while New Zealand has reciprocal arrangements with Malaysia and China. Canadians can have legal working holidays in Hong Kong, Japan,
Korea and Taiwan, and Americans are entitled to work for six months in Singapore.

TEACHING

Although the English language is not a universal passport to employment, it can certainly be put to
good use in many Asian countries especially China, Japan, Taiwan, Korea, Thailand, Vietnam and
Turkey (dealt with in the next chapter). Thousands of people of all ages are eager for tuition in English
and native English speakers with a university degree or just a degree of enthusiasm have been cashing
in for a generation.

Working as a self-employed freelance tutor is more lucrative but hard to set up until you have been settled in one place for a while and have decent premises from which to work. By posting small adverts on online community sites or making contacts in universities, bookshops, etc, you should gradually build up a clientele of paying students.

Extensive detailed information on teaching English in the countries of Asia is contained in the 2017 edition of *Teaching English Abroad* by Susan Griffith. For a list of useful TEFL websites see the introductory chapter on Teaching in this book.

Japan

Despite repeated attempts to stimulate the Japanese economy, which has stagnated for decades, growth remains elusive. Wages never rise and deflation remains stubbornly in place. However in the run-up to the Tokyo Olympics in 2020, and ever increasing international tourists choosing Japan, a desire to master English is still in the ascendancy. The marketplace in which English-language academies are now competing may have shrunk since the glory days but it is still a flourishing industry. Groups of *eikaiwa* (conversation schools) remain in business, alongside thousands of English schools in Tokyo, Osaka and many other Japanese cities which hire *gaijins* (foreigners) to teach. A great many of these are willing to hire native speakers of English with no teaching qualification as long as they have a university degree and preferably some teaching experience.

Red Tape

As mentioned, Britons, Irish, Canadians, Australians and New Zealanders are eligible for a working holiday visa for Japan. The annual quota of working holiday visas for Britons aged 18–30 is 1,000. Visa holders may accept paid work in Japan for up to 12 months, provided it is incidental to their travels. Applicants must show that they have sufficient financial backing, ie savings of £2,500 or £1,500 plus a return ticket. Note that applications are accepted from April and once the allocation has been filled, no more visas will be granted until April of the following year. Further details are available by ringing ☎ (+44) 20 7465 6565 or on the embassy webpage (www.uk.emb-japan.go.jp/en/visa/working-holiday.html).

For those ineligible for a working holiday visa, the key to obtaining a work visa for Japan is to have a university degree and a Japanese sponsor. This can be a private citizen but most teachers are sponsored by their employers. Not many schools are willing to sponsor their teachers since they can safely rely on a stream of native speakers who already possess a visa that allows them to work. Documents that will help you to find a sponsor are the original or notarised copy of your BA or other degree and resumé.

The UK and US have a visa exemption arrangement with Japan whereby they can stay as visitors for up to 90 days with a possibility of extending for a further 90 days. It is possible to enter Japan, look for work and then apply for a work visa. Those found to be overstaying as tourists can be deported. Furthermore, employers caught employing illegal aliens as well as the foreign workers themselves are subject to huge fines, and both parties risk imprisonment.

Many participants make use of the services of the non-profit Japan Association for Working Holiday Makers (JAWHM; www.jawhm.or.jp/eng) whose head office is in Shinjuku-ku, Tokyo. Note that you must show your working holiday visa stamp to be eligible for their assistance; membership is free. In 2017, they launched what they call a 'job offer collection site' at www.job-board.info which lists mostly non-teaching jobs.

Finding a Teaching Job

Graduates should investigate the government's competitive JET (Japan Exchange & Teaching) Programme. Anyone with a bachelor's degree in any discipline who is under 39 and from the UK, USA, Ireland, Canada, Australia or New Zealand (plus a number of other countries) is eligible to apply. For

British applicants details may be obtained from the JET Desk at the Japanese Embassy (☎ (+44) 20 7465 6668; www.jet-uk.org). About 150 Britons join the programme each year. Applications in Britain are due by the last Friday in November for one-year contracts beginning in August. The annual salary is 3,360,000 yen (currently equivalent to about £24,000).

MARCUS STARLING SPENT TWO FANTASTIC YEARS WITH JET IN KAGOSHIMA, A CITY IN THE FAR SOUTH OF JAPAN, WHICH IS KNOWN AS THE 'NAPLES OF THE EAST' BECAUSE OF ITS SMOKING VOLCANO:

I had applied unsuccessfully for my ideal career job on the civil service fast stream, and wanted to gain some more post-university experience and independence before applying again. Having done a very varied gap year before university, I wanted to spend sufficient time in one place to learn a language and make it feel like a second home. I applied for two jobs abroad: one teaching English in a school in China, the other was the JET programme. JET paid far better, was well organised, internationally recognised, and looked to be a good opportunity to learn about the culture and language. I taught at four junior high schools (ages 12–15) on a rota basis, with occasional day visits to primary schools and leading kids' summer activity programmes. My travel experiences in Japan were unforgettable, particularly visiting some of the sub-tropical small islands off the coast.

JET pays for your flight to Japan (and the return flights at the end), so the initial cost is limited to your first month's rent and money you need to equip your new home and settle in. I found I spent £1,000 of my parents' money in the first month, but was able to pay them back within a couple of months by living a modest lifestyle on what seemed a very generous first salary. I should say that Japan isn't actually that expensive a place to live, providing you adapt your tastes (although it is an expensive place to travel). There's something special about Japan, hot spring baths, smoke from the volcano drifting over the bay, politeness and curiosity from people living down the street, small shrines hidden away in forests. Sometimes the curiosity and questions which were so welcome when I was a new visitor became a bit predictable when I had lived there for over a year and knew more of the language and culture – but this was far outweighed by the kindness behind these approaches.

A number of the largest language training organisations recruit graduates abroad as well as in Japan. Among the main employers are:

AEON Corp: www.aeonet.com. Actively recruits teachers abroad for its 320 branch schools; interviews are conducted at hiring days in American, Canadian and Australian cities and on a rolling basis through its recruitment offices in New York and Los Angeles.

Berlitz: http://teach.berlitz.co.jp. Must be already residing in Japan preferably with a work visa to be considered.

ECC Foreign Language Institute: with regional offices in Osaka, Tokyo and Nagoya; www. eccteachinjapan.com. Main hiring period is the autumn when recruitment events are held in London, Manchester, Toronto, etc.

Gaba Corporation: http://teaching-in-japan.gaba.co.jp. Operates 42 Learning Studios around Tokyo, Osaka and in Nagoya where clients are taught individually, and in off-site corporate settings.

Interac: www.interacnetwork.com/recruit. 2,000+ full-time ALTs (Assistant Language Teachers). Initial application must be done through global online system.

The most common means of recruitment is online, eg via websites such as www.alttokyo.com, www. recruiting.altmoot.com for ALTIA Central's recruiting page and www.jobsinjapan.com, by word of mouth among expat teachers and by advertising your services. GaijinPot (www.gaijinpot.com) is the largest job site for foreigners and has a near monopoly on the English teaching jobs in Japan among the English conversation schools, dispatch schools (for teaching in the public schools) and everything in between. The site stores more than 150,000 résumés, most of which are searchable by potential employers. GaijinPot is also a useful general portal for foreigners in Japan, with popular forums for sharing information, experiences and questions. Another potentially useful site is Tokyo Notice Board (www.tokyonoticeboard.co.jp). The twice-monthly free electronic newsletter *O-Hayo-Sensei* (which means 'Good Morning Teacher') has pages of teaching positions across Japan at www.ohayosensei. com. Many of these are open only to candidates who are already in Japan. To find private students try www.getstudents.net which, according to Joseph Tame, really works. Simply enter your details (what you teach, what area of Japan you teach in, how much you charge, etc), and the students will make contact. Other teacher–student matching services are at www.senseibank.com, www.findstudents.net and www.hello-sensei.com/en/sensei.

Note that a pub called Mickey House English Café near Takadanobaba Station (www.mickeyhouse. jp) holds regular social evenings and conversation exchanges when English speakers meet up with Japanese people, which could be a good way to meet potential students.

Travis Ball from Los Angeles travelled to Japan to make his fortune as an English teacher. He found a job with Geos, a huge chain of private English schools. There was no way that he could have foreseen that Geos would go bust a few months later:

I had no relevant experience aside from being a native speaker. One of the reasons I chose Japan was because it was supposed to be one of the easier countries to find work teaching English without any experience or certificates. I was basically sitting in my travellers' hotel room in Osaka sending out as many resumés as I could while attempting not to spend any money. I started by sending emails to every address listed in the chapter on Japan in your book about teaching English. I was asked if I could attend an interview in Tokyo, which took place over two days. The short-listing process included a couple tests, an actual interview, and a mock 20-minute lesson that we prepared the evening of the first day. Eventually I was told I was to teach in a small branch in the country.

I worked in a very small town, by Japanese standards. I hadn't expected to be stationed in the middle of nowhere, but tried to make the best of the situation. I would ride my bike around the nearby villages, try and organise day trips with my co-workers, and spent time teaching myself how to cook. I also took the time to develop a personal travel blog for flashpackers that I'm still working on to this day (www. flashpackerhq.com).

My pupils were awesome. They all gave me the benefit of the doubt when I started, and within a few months I was spending time outside work with many of my adult students. I still stay in touch with some. In the first two weeks, I made two separate children cry, which I felt awful about: one five-year-old because I tried to take his coloured pencil away, another who was struggling to make different sounds for 'B' and 'V'. This was a cultural thing that I had to get used to. All in all teaching English was an amazing experience and I highly recommend anyone considering it to go do it.

China

Recruitment of teachers for the People's Republic of China is absolutely booming in the private sector. (For information about teaching opportunities in the Hong Kong Special Administrative Region, see the section below.) However, the authorities have begun to tighten up the visa regulations, making it more difficult to pick up a teaching job on the spot and to sort out the paperwork later. This means that it is preferable to arrange a job in advance which allows you the chance to obtain the appropriate working visa before arrival. Fortunately the internet is plastered with any number of adverts from recruiters and language institutes.

Any web search or a trawl of the major ELT job websites is bound to turn up plenty of contacts. The majority of vacancies are for candidates who have a degree and a TEFL certificate; without the latter many agencies make it a requirement that you take at least an online TEFL course. Long-lived online agencies include http://jobs.echinacities.com, http://teachingchina.net, www.newworldesl.com and www.cathayteacher.com, which have long lists of jobs, all dated and described in detail. Most institutes will issue teachers with an invitation or letter of appointment. This together with other documents such as a medical report and criminal records check must be taken to the Chinese Consulate or Embassy to apply for a Z-visa (work visa) before arrival in China.

Round-the-world American traveller, Bradwell Jackson, landed a job with ease and was so satisfied with his conditions of work that he renewed his position, moving to a different province:

I was offered a job with Aston in China on the basis of a telephone interview and I am very happy with this. Aston is good to me, and my co-workers scramble to help me whenever I have even a mild matter that needs attention. I think it might be hard to convince Westerners to come and stay in an out-of-the-way city like Tangshan. Yet I feel as though I'm living the life of Reilly here. I've got nothing to complain about. The school has given me a free apartment complete with cable TV, washing machine, toaster oven, microwave, and refrigerator. Whenever I'm hungry, I just mosey on down to the street vendors and get some proper Chinese food for a friendly budget price. Who can ask for more?

By the end of his stay, he was conducting the training for newly recruited Western teachers. He passed on his tip about the three Ts that you can't talk about in China (Tiananmen, Taiwan and Tibet).

Some of the tried and tested old schemes are still in place and still work. The British Council places language assistants (who must be university graduates) to work with classes of up to 50 in secondary schools across China from September to July. Preliminary training is provided on a two-week expenses-paid induction course in Beijing. Participants receive free accommodation, a one-way flight back to the UK and an expert's salary from a lowly 4,000 yuan renminbi (net) per month. Details of the application procedure can be obtained from the Assistants Department at the British Council (www.britishcouncil.org/language-assistants/become/china).

Homestays combined with helping children to learn English and understand Western culture can be arranged by HHS Center Ltd in Beijing and other cities (www.hhscenter.com). Young foreigners live with a Chinese family for three, six or 12 months, and help out for 25 hours a week, looking after the children, teaching them some English and acting as an older sibling, usually with minimal household duties. In exchange they get free board and lodging, two Mandarin classes a week lasting three to four hours each, a monthly stipend of up to 4,000 yuan and a contribution to their airfare. Participants stay on an F-visa which does not permit paid work.

Taiwan

The hiring policy is virtually universal in Taiwan: almost anyone with a BA can land a job. The country remains a magnet for English teachers of all backgrounds. Hundreds of private language institutes or *buhsibans* continue to teach young children, cram high school students for university entrance examinations and generally service the seemingly insatiable demand for English conversation and English tuition.

Many well-established language schools are prepared to sponsor foreign teachers for a resident visa, provided the teacher is willing to work for at least a year. Only teachers with a university degree are eligible. Many people arrive on spec to look for work. It is usually easy to find a *buhsiban* willing to hire you but not so easy to find a good one. If possible, try to sit in on one or two classes before signing a contract. (If a school is unwilling to permit this, it doesn't bode well.) The majority of schools pay NT$550–$600 (roughly US$17–$19) per hour.

One of the best noticeboards is located in the student lounge on the sixth floor of the Mandarin Training Center of National Taiwan Normal University at 129 Hoping East Road. As always travellers' hostels will be helpful as reported by Bradwell Jackson after he investigated the teaching scene:

I couldn't believe all the English schools in Taipei. I presumed that the market must be saturated by now and that it would be too difficult to find a job, but after talking to the scuttlebutt-mongers at the Taipei Hostel (www.taipeihostel.com/teach.html), I found out that this was not the case. The hostel is English teaching central for foreigners and the common room is where all the newcomers meet to get the latest on the English teaching situation. Once you get the lowdown from the old hands there, just pick a direction and start walking. After passing about three corners, you'll definitely see an English school, probably two. Have your introduction ready, march on in there and sell yourself.

Many websites contain a wealth of detail about Taiwan and what it's like to teach there. Jobs and lots of information about teaching in Taiwan can be found at www.tealit.com (one of the best), www.orseek.com and www.englishintaiwan.com.

The following language schools all hire on a large scale:

Hess International Educational Group: Taipei City; www.hesseducation.com. Specialises in teaching children including kindergarten age; 600 Native Speaking Teachers (NSTs) in more than 180 branches; very structured teaching programme and curriculum; applicants must arrive with a police check from their home country.

Kidscamp/ALV: Tao-Yuan City; www.kidscamp.com.tw. Hires native speakers for summer and winter language camps; interviews via Skype are acceptable.

Kojen ELS: Taipei; www.kojenels.com. Employs around 300 teachers at schools, located mostly in Taipei but also Kaohsiung and Taichung; must have a degree but experience not needed.

Phoenix Group Asia: Taoyuan; www.phoenixgroup.asia. 50 teachers preferably North American. Gross salary is $1,700 per month.

Visas

Canadian, American, British, Australian and New Zealand passport holders do not need to apply for a visitor visa before coming to Taiwan. They are permitted to stay visa-free for 90 days (apart from Australians who can stay for only 30 days). If in that time you secure a job, your future employer will then apply for an Alien Resident Certificate (ARC), which should take three or four weeks to process if the application is in order. A compulsory health check at an approved hospital can be carried out after arrival and will cost NT$1,000–$1,700.

To qualify for an ARC, you must be assigned a minimum of 14 hours of work by one employer, and then can accept work from other sources up to a maximum of 32 hours.

Having discovered the joys of world travel at age 30, Stephanie Fuccio from the USA took the plunge and fixed up a teaching job with an English school in Tainan. She found that good money could be earned and the cost of living was really low, which had the disadvantage that many of the foreigners there were focussed on money to the exclusion of everything else. Her low overheads included $200 a month for a small apartment all to herself and a used scooter bought for $250. Meanwhile she was earning $17 an hour despite at that time having no teaching certificate or experience. She concluded that *'the whole country is simply gone mad with learning English'*.

Korea

Although South Korea does not immediately come to mind as a likely destination for British TEFLers, it has been long known in North America as a country which can absorb an enormous number of native speaker teachers, including fresh graduates with no TEFL training or experience.

Hundreds of language institutes (*hogwons*) can be found in Seoul the capital, Pusan (Korea's second city, five hours south of Seoul, sometimes transliterated Busan) and in smaller cities. The majority of these are run as businesses where profit takes precedence over education. Certificates and even degrees are in many cases superfluous, though a university degree will be needed in order to obtain the right visa. The English Program in Korea (EPIK) is a competitive scheme run by the Ministry of Education. Up to 3,000 foreign graduates are placed in state schools (mostly primary) and education offices throughout the country. Private recruiters are also involved and are chosen as official representatives by EPIK every spring. For 2017, the appointed agencies are Korvia Consulting in Seoul (www.korvia.com), Korean Horizons in Vancouver (www.koreanhorizons.com), Reach to Teach in the US (www.reachtoteachrecruiting.com), Gone2Korea.com and Canadian Connection (www.canconx.com). Many subscribe to the view that it is easier and faster to apply directly to EPIK (www.epik.go.kr) though its deadline for applications falls earlier than recruiters' deadline, for instance 1 February instead of 1 April for an autumn intake. The annual salary offered is 2 to 2.7 million won per month (depending on qualifications and experience) plus accommodation, flight reimbursement, visa sponsorship and medical insurance. Current information should be obtained from the EPIK website www.epik.go.kr. EPIK applicants need to have a 100-hour TEFL qualification, unless their degree is in Education.

A subsidiary government programme is called TALK or Teach and Learn in Korea (www.talk.go.kr), which is open to people with at least two years of university education. The teaching here takes place in after-school clubs in rural primary schools, the commitment is shorter (six months minimum instead of a year) and the pay is lower (1.5 million won a month).

In the UK, jobs in Korea can be fixed up in advance with an agency such as Flying Cows (www. flying-cows.com) which specialises in Korea and is willing to try to place anyone with a degree. Online agencies to try include www.teachkoreans.com, run by a young expat and his Korean wife, and www. peoplerecruit.com based in Pusan which calls itself a 'Competent Persons Database'. Signing up with an agency will assist with the visa process. Any person who arrives in Korea to teach English must get their final visa processing completed in their country of residence. This means that entering on a tourist visa for job-hunting is simply not possible, at least this is the official line. Note that an HIV test is compulsory (though controversial).

Dozens of agents in North America recruit EFL teachers, particularly in Canada. After doing a two-week evening course on TESL teaching in her final term of university, Jessie Cox from Ontario and her boyfriend scoured the job forums at www.eslcafe.com to find some decent recruiters for Korea who would not renege on their agreements. They sent their resumés (including the compulsory photo) to five different recruiters, and soon began receiving job offers, including some with split shifts, long working weeks, mean holiday entitlements and/or low wages. They simply chose the one offering the best working conditions.

YBM Education employ about 200 native English teachers for company-owned English Conversation Centers (ECC) branches and a further 450 at franchised schools which recruit independently throughout Korea. The headquarters are in Chongno-gu, Seoul (www.ybmecc.co.kr).

Despite signing contracts that promise good salaries, furnished apartments and other amenities, many teachers find they actually receive much less than they were promised; some do not even receive benefits required by Korean law, such as health insurance and severance pay. Teachers' complaints range from simple contract violations to non-payment of salary for months at a time. Teachers are advised to keep their passports in their possession after the visa processing has taken place.

Thailand

The word on the street is that it takes no more than a nanosecond to find a job in Thailand provided you arrive in the main hiring season (April is best) with the right passport and a degree. Bangkok and other Thai cities are a good bet for the casual teacher. Thailand is also the country where packaged teaching working holidays are most common, with youth tourism companies charging travellers vast sums to teach for a short time. Some of these are listed below for the benefit of gap year students who may be too nervous to go it alone.

One of the best all-round sources of information about English teaching in Thailand with an emphasis on Bangkok and on inside information about the main hiring companies is the website www.ajarn. com with stories and priceless tips on visas, accommodation, etc as well as many job vacancies. The site is run and constantly updated by a teacher who has been in Thailand for many years. The English language daily newspaper, the *Bangkok Post*, carries job advertisements (http://job.bangkokpost.com) though the jobs listings on Ajarn.com and Craigslist (http://bangkok.craigslist.co.th/odu) are more extensive. Many ads specify 'NES' status which simply means Native English Speaker.

The noisy Khao San Road is lined with expat pubs and budget accommodation, many with noticeboards offering teaching work and populated with other foreigners (known as *farangs*) well acquainted with the possibilities. Reports of foreigners working as touts for teacher agencies and language schools have been heard. They are paid a large commission when they deliver a newly arrived farang willing to teach full-time for less than the going rate, eg less than 35,000 baht (net) per month.

As usual, it may be necessary to start with part-time and occasional work with several employers, aiming to build up a decent number of hours in the same area to minimise travelling in the appalling traffic.

Teaching opportunities crop up in branches of the big companies such as ECC (www.tesol.ecc. ac.th/jobs) which is also a TEFL training centre, and AUA (www.auathailand.org) which employs 175 teachers for six branches in Bangkok and 10 upcountry, mainly at universities.

Outside Bangkok and tourist magnets such as Chiang Mai and Phuket, there is far less competition from *farangs* for work, particularly in lesser-known cities such as Nakhon Sawan, Khon Kaen, Udon Thani and Ubon Ratchathani. For a job in a university you will definitely have to show a strong teaching background. Among the best places are Hat Yai (the booming industrial city in the south) and Songkhla. Hotels are always worth asking, since many hotel workers are keen to improve their English. If you find a place which suits and you decide to stay for a while, ask the family which runs your guesthouse about local teaching opportunities.

The wages for newly arrived *farang* teachers are uniformly low. The basic hourly rate has risen only slightly over the past six years to 250–350 baht an hour though some professional schools and company work can pay considerably more. The norm is for schools to keep their staff on as part-time freelancers while giving them full-time hours; this is primarily to avoid taxes. Jobs that pay better often involve a lot of travelling, which in Bangkok is so time-consuming that it is necessary to work fewer hours. Most teachers conclude that it is just as lucrative and much less stressful to work at a single institute for the basic wage.

The Thai authorities keep changing the visa goalposts and enforcement is far stricter than it used to be. The paperwork forum of www.ajarn.com is a very good place to read about the evolving red tape situation and its practical (rather than theoretical) implications. The preferred alternative for people who have found a job from abroad is to apply for a non-immigrant B visa from any Thai Embassy. For this you will be asked to provide a copy of your degree certificate (now essential), police clearance and various documents from your prospective employer in Thailand such as a contract of employment. With this visa, the applicant can stay in Thailand for no longer than 90 days unless his or her employer obtains a teacher's licence for which you will need the original certificate of your Bachelor's degree and transcripts or a letter/email of confirmation of graduation from your university. If your degree is in education it will suffice but if in another subject, you will also need proof that you have a TESOL certificate. In addition you will need a criminal record check from your home country and from the Thai police and a medical certificate issued within the last month (obtainable from doctors in Thailand for a small fee).

One way round the visa problem is to join a volunteer teaching scheme. A number of specialist agencies and charities can help such as Volunthai (www.volunthai.com) and Volunteer Teacher Thailand (www.volunteerteacherthailand.org).

The following fee-charging placement agencies are primarily active in the field of voluntourism:

Camp Thailand: Manchester; www.summercampthailand.com. Also **Thai Jobs** (www.thaijobs. co.uk/tefl). Travel company with short summer teaching programme and longer-term one where participants receive a stipend. Sample fee £691 for three weeks.

International Volunteer HQ: New Zealand; www.volunteerhq.org/volunteer-in-thailand. 250 volunteers placed in Thailand every year including English teachers for young children, especially among hill tribes around Chiang Rai. Sample price $1,320 for 12 weeks (plus $279 registration fee).

IST Plus: London (www.istplus.com/teachinthailand). Teach in Thailand Programme fees from £995 for five months, £1,195 for 10 months.

Mundo Exchange Organization: Portland, Oregon, USA; www.mundoexchange.org. Volunteers teach English and computer skills to disadvantaged children and/or adults mainly in Isan province in North-Eastern Thailand. The placement costs are $400 for the first week (which includes two- to three-day orientation), $685 for two weeks, to $1,075 for eight weeks, then $105 per additional week. Fees include pre-arranged accommodation, travel within the project and support before and during the stay.

Openmind Projects: 43000 Nong Khai; www.openmindprojects.org. The fee for this volunteer teacher programme in different regions of Thailand starts at $295 for the first fortnight, and is $95 per week thereafter. Three-day orientation included. Teaching is taught by role play.

Starfish Volunteers: www.starfish-adventure.com. UK voluntourism company that places volunteer teachers in government schools in Surin. The 2017 fee is £800 for eight weeks.

Travel to Teach: T2T, 77/4 Chaitalay Road, Prachuap Khiri Khan 77000 (☎ (+66) 9 2818 5929; www.travel-to-teach.org). Thai-based organisation that provides volunteer teaching opportunities (among others) around Chiang Mai and mainly in the north. Sample fees £436 for a month, £1,213 for six months.

Indonesia

Most language schools in Indonesia (and Singapore) recruit only trained EFL teachers who are willing to stay for at least a year. Salaries paid by the schools that hire native speakers provide for a comfortable lifestyle including travel within Indonesia during the vacations and the possibility of saving. Most schools offer benefits packages and reasonable salaries of more than 16 million rupiah (nearly £1,000). If you plan to complete a one or two-year contract, enquire about reimbursement for airfares and a possible tax rebate. EF mounts a huge operation in the country across different groups, together hiring more than 700 teachers; information about the central recruitment system can be found at www.englishfirst.com/ESL-Jobs/teaching-english-in-Indonesia.

The most lucrative employment is in the oil company cities but opportunities exist in small towns too. At local schools unused to employing native speaker teachers, teaching materials may be in short supply. One of the problems faced by those who undertake casual work of this kind is that there is usually little chance of obtaining a work permit. Travellers have stumbled across friendly little schools up rickety staircases throughout the islands of Indonesia, as the German round-the-world traveller Gerhard Flaig describes:

> *In Yogyakarta you can find language schools listed in the telephone book or you just walk through streets to look for them. Most of them are interested in having new teachers. I got an offering to teach German and also English since my English was better than some of the language school managers. All of them didn't bother about work permits. The wages aren't very high, but it is fairly easy to cover the costs of board and lodging since the cost of living is very low.*

Vietnam, Cambodia and Laos

Vietnam is chronically short of language teachers due to its dizzying rate of economic growth (second only to China). One of the main reasons for this growth is the booming prosperity and an urgent ambition among parents for their children to master English. It is therefore relatively easy for native speakers to get a job in Hanoi or Ho Chi Minh City (HCMC) on the basis of a telephone interview. Schools will snap you up, especially if you have a bachelor's degree and a CELTA or Trinity certificate (or equivalent).

Furthermore, Vietnam has low living costs and high salaries, eg as much as $25 an hour at the quality schools such as ILA (www.teachenglishilavietnam.com), Apollo English (www.teachatapollo.com) and Language Link (www.llv.edu.vn/en/recruitment), while $16–$20 is the going rate at the more cheap and cheerful establishments. Stephanie Fuccio had no trouble getting work in Hanoi with Language Link after doing the CELTA course with them.

Often the best way to find work is simply to arrive in one of the major cities and look around. Check out Craigslist (http://vietnam.craigslist.org), which has scores of job ads and is useful for accommodation listings as well, and www.expat.com/en/jobs/asia/vietnam, which is also good for posting private tuition ads. The site vietnamteachingjobs.com enables you to target your search for Academic English, Business English, General English or young children. Other community sites for expats such as http://tnhvietnam.xemzi.com can be equally productive for jobs, accommodation, etc especially in Hanoi.

Other organised schemes include the estimable Teachers for Vietnam (www.teachersforvietnam. org) based in the US which covers travel expenses and accommodation for those accepted to teach at universities in Vietnam. Others charge substantial fees such as Teach and Travel in Vietnam (www. teachandtravelvietnam.com) and Smaller Earth (www.smallerearth.com/us/asia/tefl-in-vietnam) which costs $999 for a 5-month placement.

Cambodia is a relatively stable country, having emerged from the shadow of its past and of its neighbours and having rapidly developed its ELT market. Wages for casual teachers are at least $10 an hour in a country where you can live comfortably on $25 a day. Qualified EFL teachers can earn double or even treble that amount. Prospective teachers should arrive with extra passport photos and buy a Business E visa on arrival for $50 valid for one month. This can be extended at the Ministry of Foreign Affairs for up to a year at a time for $278. One of the longest established schools in Phnom Penh is the Australian Centre for Education or ACE (recruitment.cambodia@idp.com) which employs up to 200 teachers in Phnom Penh and Siem Reap. Teachers must have a degree and the CELTA or Trinity TESOL. With those same qualifications it is worth contacting the new teacher recruitment agency Teachers in Cambodia in Phnom Penh (www.teachersincambodia.com) which tries to place 100 native speaking teachers in schools for an academic year.

Another organisation to try is Volunteer in Cambodia (www.volunteerincambodia.org), which recruits volunteers to teach at Conversations With Foreigners (CWF), a local conversational English school in Phnom Penh (No 247C, Street 271, Toul Pumbung II). Money raised by the programme goes towards the Cambodian Rural Development Team, a local organisation working to improve livelihoods in rural communities. Volunteers do not pay to volunteer and stay for three months (there are specific group starting dates), but they do pay for their accommodation in the volunteers' house and meals, which currently costs $725 for three months. Teaching qualifications/experience are advantageous but not required.

HONG KONG

With the birth of the Hong Kong Special Administrative Region (HKSAR) of the People's Republic of China on 30 June 1997, Britons lost their preferential status. Britons must obtain a work visa or a working holiday visa prior to arrival if they wish to take up legal employment in Hong Kong.

Regulations

British citizens may visit the HKSAR without a visa for up to 180 days provided they can satisfy the immigration officer on arrival that they are entering as bona fide visitors with enough funds to cover the duration of their stay without working and, unless in transit to the Mainland of China or the region of Macau, hold onward or return tickets. USA citizens are given 90 days. The visa requirements are posted at www.immd.gov.hk/eng/services/index.html. Visitors are not normally allowed to change their status (eg from visitor to employment) after arrival except in special circumstances.

Applicants should complete application form ID-990A. The HKSAR Immigration Department is located on the 2nd Floor of Immigration Tower, 7 Gloucester Road, Wan Chai; enquiry@immd.gov.hk.

Teaching

The Hong Kong government has an official scheme by which hundreds of English speakers are employed to teach in the Chinese-medium state education system. The NET scheme is administered by the Hong Kong Education Bureau (netrecruit@edb.gov.hk; www.edb.gov.hk). Foreign teachers known as 'Netters' are assigned randomly and singly to government schools (primary and secondary) across Hong Kong and working conditions can be tough especially if you are assigned to a school with low-achieving pupils. On the other hand salaries and benefits are generous so acceptance is very competitive. The government rules stipulate that teachers recruited from overseas must be paid at least HK$20,000 a month. The monthly salary range for primary NETs is HK$26,700 (£2,500) to HK$45,230 (£5,250) and for secondary NETs even higher, HK$25,600 (£2,700) to HK$65,150

(£6,300). Superior qualifications are well rewarded in Hong Kong. Housing allowances and end-of-contract bonuses really bump up those earnings.

The Chatteris Educational Foundation in Kowloon (☎ (+852) 2520 5736; www.chatteris.org.hk) offers recent university graduates from English-speaking countries the opportunity to teach in Hong Kong. The wage of HK$14,000 per month for nine months has remained static for many years.

HK Education Provider Company Ltd (www.hkedu.com.hk) recruits ESL teachers from the seven English-speaking countries and places these university graduates in teaching positions in reputable public and private schools throughout Hong Kong. The agency provides training, shared accommodation with clubhouse facilities, teaching materials and online support. For a position as an Oral English Teacher, a Bachelor of Arts (BA) or Science (BS) degree is a prerequisite with a TEFL, TESOL or CELTA certificate.

Casual Opportunities

The entrance to the Star Ferry and the corridors of the Mass Transit Railway stations are favourite locations for buskers. Official hassle should be minimal as long as you don't block thoroughfares. Kim Falkingham recommends being able to sing some songs in Chinese. She looks back fondly on one listener who dropped the equivalent of £80 in her cap, but also remembers long days when nobody contributed anything.

Each spring the rugby sevens tournament draws huge crowds and many temporary bar staff are needed for a weekend before Easter. You get a commission for every jug of beer you sell and can drink as much as you like. Call the headquarters of the major breweries (Fosters, San Miguel, etc) before the event. People are also hired to sell commemorative shirts and souvenirs on the streets.

Disneyland Hong Kong employs several thousand staff but in almost all cases a good standard of Cantonese is required; http://hkdl.disneycareers.com/en/default carries recruitment information.

ENTERTAINMENT

Opportunities for film extras, buskers and models may crop up in Hong Kong if you are lucky (though adverts on Craigslist can sound decidedly dodgy). Here are some scattered suggestions in other countries of Asia.

Hollywood does not have the world monopoly on filmmaking. There is an enormous film industry in the Hindi, Chinese and Japanese speaking worlds and it is just possible your services will be required, especially if you're blonde. Foreign travellers hanging around certain backpackers' hostels in Mumbai, Chennai, Goa, Bangkok or Singapore might be invited by a film agent to become an extra. Danny Jacobson and his girlfriend Marion might have had a chance to be in a Thai movie a couple of years ago but never quite managed it:

> Early on in my time in Bangkok, I met an Australian guy who told me about possible work as an extra in Thai films. He gave me a cell number; I called, and a guy said come to such and such a café – 'plenty of work'. After a few calls on the cell phone he sat down at our table and explained there was a war film going to be shot up near Chiang Mai and they needed Westerners as extras. Food and accommodation plus 500 baht per day was the take. Not a lot of money, about US$11. But in Thailand that was enough to live very well on as a tourist for a day. We waited around while he made sporadic and seemingly pointless calls on his phone. He was the picture of what I assumed a casting agent would be like. Quick, up and down 'assessment' glances greeted all who approached him. Later the Dutch guy with us whispered to me that Mr Agent had been talking into a switched-off cell phone. So we hopped out of the taxi.

It is likely that agents like this do occasionally find work for extras but can't predict when or where until the very last minute. They keep their young hopefuls hanging around so that if the summons does come, they will be ready to supply the right kind of extras and collect their commission. Without the services of an agent, you will simply have to find yourself in the right place at the right time, which can happen to anyone. Even the author of this book, while travelling in the Swat Valley of Northern Pakistan, had to disappoint a Pakistani film director also staying at the Heaven Breeze Hotel who wanted her to mount a horse and impersonate a colonel's daughter.

Mumbai is probably the most promising destination for aspiring 'crowd artists' since every year hundreds of films are made in 'Bollywood'. Fast-talking agents with mobile phones sometimes lurk around the Salvation Army Red Shield Hostel on Mereweather Road or Leopold's Cafe on Colaba Causeway to sign up prospective extras. Do not be gulled into paying any money for a 'portfolio' since this will be no guarantee of a role and is probably just a con. If you are recruited by a genuine scout, you will probably be bussed to the shoot or take a rickshaw to Film City. First-time extras are typically paid about 1,000 rupees (£12) for the day plus meals. Expect to be kept hanging around much longer than originally told, often into the wee small hours.

Mimes, guitarists, dancers and musicians should go to Ginza in Tokyo or any Japanese city, especially in the evening. Once a few people gather, the Japanese herd instinct guarantees that the street will become all but impassable. Old Beatles and Simon and Garfunkel songs do well.

Hostessing

Some have found that a reasonably reliable way for a Western woman to make money in Japanese cities is to work as a hostess. Catherine Quinn, a freelance journalist, enjoyed her stint as a hostess in Tokyo several years ago and has kindly provided this description of how it works. According to Catherine, hostesses and hostess bars are widely misinterpreted in the West. Most accounts suffer in the translation, and are rendered at worst as a method to lure unsuspecting girls into prostitution, and at best as a dubious activity to be approached with great caution. This was highlighted in press coverage of Lucie Blackman, the English hostess who was murdered in Tokyo in 2000. Her tragic death was mistakenly reported in the Western media as a direct consequence of hostessing.

Hostess bars rely on a drinking culture completely alien to the West, where overworked salarymen pay for the company and attention of lively women. The preference is for European women, and prejudices can make it more difficult for 'non-Aryan' looking women. Generally, two types of hostess bar can be found. More traditional style bars open from about 8pm until midnight, pay around 2,500 yen an hour, and serve a small number of Japanese-speaking clientele. These bars are more often the choice of women with full-time English teaching jobs in the day, and often offer good chances to learn Japanese by talking with customers.

The second type of hostess bar is more in the style of a Western nightclub. These bars attract groups of Japanese businessmen on high incomes, in search of a night on the town; although they also attract a steady flow of single regulars. Many clubs run shorter hours (10pm–2am for example) if customers are scarce. Most clubs run a *dohan* (dinner date) reward system, which hostesses have to meet to earn serious money. Pressure to go on regular *dohan* has increased with economic necessity, with the strictest clubs operating fines for girls who don't make enough. Depending on the club, bonuses can be earned by drinking many drinks (these are charged to the customer) and persuading the customer to buy champagne. Many techniques abound for diluting the inordinate flow of alcohol, including the famous 'Lady's Special' (bar code for water), or the well-positioned pot plant in which to tip your drink.

Working hostesses are expected to wear nightclub style clothing which is glamorous rather than revealing, and to be well groomed. Appearance issues vary from club to club, with the top-end establishments often demanding a dizzying level of personal maintenance. Generally, work involves conversing with men who arrive at the bar, and acting as a drinking companion. Some clubs also like girls to sing karaoke with customers. For many hostesses, the major advantages of the job are the social company it provides and the unlimited drinks, a particular perk in a city where alcohol is so expensive. Although there is no guarantee that customers won't be tedious, to some extent your interest in the clientele will determine your enjoyment of the profession. Hours of speaking slowly can become tiring but, for some women, hostessing is an unrivalled method of earning money while experiencing another culture. Note that this kind of employment is forbidden under the terms of the working holiday visa scheme; as is bar work. The Japanese authorities have had bursts of clamping down on this work and as a result of this at one point many of the clubs were forced to close.

In Tokyo, hostess clubs are scattered throughout Roppongi and Ginza, and can be difficult to distinguish from normal bars, nightclubs and strip-joints, so tread carefully. The same applies in the new China where the new-found materialism has many businessmen trying to show off their wealth in karaoke bars. An instructive article called 'My Time as a Hostess in a Sleazy Chinese Karaoke Den' can be read on the Vice site (www.vice.com/en_us/article/i-sold-my-soul-to-ktv-300).

Modelling

Caucasian faces are sought after in the advertising industries of Singapore, Thailand, Japan, China, Korea, etc. Interested people should get some photos taken back home rather than risk being ripped off by agencies that charge you to put together a portfolio and then don't hire you. When you arrive, register with one of the numerous modelling agencies. Earnings are good if you average more than one or two assignments per week. Jaime Burnell couldn't believe how easy it was:

> *When I was in Thailand, I was approached by an American scouting for white/blonde girls to have their photos taken for adverts. White faces sell in Thailand so even me who is not model material usually got paid for one day's work at a rate of 5,000 baht. It was all done very professionally and the photos are kept in a photo library for future use. As long as you don't mind it being used two years later in a soap commercial then go for it. That money let me travel for over two months with some left over.*

Scouts have been known to hang around hostels on the Khao San Road in Bangkok. Try to track down modelling agencies such as CalCarrie Models and Elite Models to find work as a magazine model and a film extra.

Similar opportunities exist in Japan and Korea. Obvious tattoos will probably disqualify you since these have connotations of gangster status. There are big agencies in Tokyo, Osaka and Seoul; otherwise occasional jobs are passed on by word of mouth. The routine is you give them a call, go for an interview, they take your measurements, take a few photos and get you to sign a contract. Then they call you when they have work, most of which is very part-time. In Korea check for occasional adverts on www.craigslist.co.kr and www.worknplay.co.kr.

TOURISM AND BUSINESS

Some travellers find opportunities teaching scuba diving in Thailand or working as a croupier in Japan. Thailand affords the best chances as Vaughan Temby discovered:

> *We spent a great Christmas on the islands and although we weren't looking for work, we did come across some opportunities. On Koh Samui several bars along Chaweng beach needed staff during the peak season. The huge Reggae Bar Complex a little further inland hires some foreign staff. On Koh Pha'Ngan a friend of mine worked as a DJ and another as a waitress/kitchen helper in the excellent German-style bakery.*

Throughout Asia, there are many expat-run restaurants and hotels. Often these are the most popular places to stay since they are tuned into providing what Westerners want. Anyone who can obtain a long-term visa through local loopholes or by marrying a local, might try to capitalise on this situation.

The government of Singapore offers a Work Holiday Pass to well-qualified young foreign students and graduates who want to take up a job or internship in Singapore lasting up to six months. To be eligible you must be aged 18–25 years and studying in Australia, New Zealand, the UK, USA, France, Germany, Switzerland, Hong Kong or Japan, or have graduated from a university ranked in the top 200 in the world. The quota for the Work Holiday Programme is 2,000 and the visa fee is $150. See www.mom.gov.sg/passes-and-permits/work-holiday-programme for more details.

Japanese ski resorts provide openings for people with a 'basic understanding of the Japanese language'. Young foreigners are employed to operate the ski lifts, as waitresses, golf caddies and in fast food restaurants. Food and accommodation are normally provided in addition to a good salary.

SnowJapan (www.snowjapan.com/japan-ski-general-information/winter-season-jobs) has useful info about jobs in Japanese ski resorts, eg with companies such as Ski Japan Holidays (www.japanspecialists.com). San Consulting (www.sanconjp.com) provides hotel and resort positions throughout Japan for keen workers with a good knowledge of Japanese.

AUSTRALIAN REBECCA BARBER SUGGESTS VOLUNTEERING TO ASSIST WITH ONE OF THE MULTITUDE OF RAFTING TRIPS WHICH MANY COMPANIES RUN IN NEPAL:

When I went on a rafting trip (which are fantastic but expensive by Nepali standards: minimum $200 for 10 days), I met a guy who had just done two free trips as 'safety kayaker'. No qualifications were needed apart from being confident of your ability to paddle the river. When in Kathmandu, simply walk into every agency you see and offer to work. You would be unlikely to get full-time or long-term work but as a way of getting a few free trips, living at no expense and getting some great paddling experience, not to mention the chance of future employment, it's ideal.

The Cotswold-based specialist upmarket tour operator to Mongolia and Bhutan, Panoramic Journeys (www.panoramicjourneys.com) has been known to offer a classic working holiday: people who are willing to work behind the scenes to help run the tour can join it for free.

VOLUNTEERING

Many people who have travelled in Asia are dissatisfied with the role of tourist and would like to find a way of making a contribution. In very many cases this is laudable but naïve. It may be worth quoting Dominique Lapierre, author of *The City of Joy*, which movingly describes life in a Calcutta (now Kolkata) slum. Although he is talking specifically about India, a similar situation exists in all poor countries:

Many of you have offered to go to Calcutta to help. This is most generous but I am afraid not very realistic. Firstly because Indian authorities only give tourist visas of limited duration to foreign visitors. This is much too short a period for anyone to achieve anything really useful. Secondly because only very specialised help could really be useful. Unless you are a doctor or an experienced paramedic in the fields of leprosy, tropical diseases, malnutrition, bone tuberculosis, polio, rehabilitation of physically handicapped, I think your generous will to help could be more of a burden for the locals in charge than anything else. Moreover, you have to realise that living and working conditions on our various projects are extremely hard for unaccustomed foreigners.

It must be stressed that Westerners invariably have to make a financial contribution to cover food and accommodation as well as their travel and insurance. Some grassroots programmes will seem to Western eyes almost completely unstructured, so volunteers should be able to create tasks for themselves. If you have not travelled widely in the developing world you may not be prepared for the scruffiness and level of disorganisation to be found in some places. If this is potentially alarming, try to find an organisation with an office abroad which can provide briefing materials beforehand, though this means that you will end up paying a sizeable arrangement fee.

India

Mainstream commercial voluntourism companies are of course active in the region, placing unskilled paying volunteers in various settings in India and throughout the Subcontinent. Examples include International Volunteer HQ (www.volunteerhq.org) and Global Crossroad in the US (www.globalcrossroad.com). You can find hundreds of others online. For example, the review site GoOverseas.com lists more than 200 agencies working in India. At an opposite extreme from a cushy attachment to an English-medium private school is working for Mother Teresa's Missionaries of Charity in Kolkata. It is possible to become a part-time volunteer at Mother Teresa's children's home and other charitable houses, but no accommodation can be offered (www.motherteresa.org/07_family/volunteering/v_cal.html). The work may consist of caring for and feeding orphaned children, the sick and dying, mentally or physically disabled adults and children or the elderly. To register, take your passport to Shishu Bhavan, 78 A.J.C. Bose Road, at 3pm on Monday, Wednesday or Friday, or go directly to the Mother House at 54A A.J.C. Bose Road and get a day pass after morning mass.

The visa problem can prove a difficult one for people who want to commit themselves to stay longer term in India. If you do want to stay longer than the standard 180 days for tourists, you will have to leave the country and apply for a business or employment visa with an official letter of invitation from your Indian sponsor. In the UK, visas can be applied for through the specialist (fee-charging) VisaHQ agency (https://india.visahq.co.uk).

Development in Action based in central London (www.developmentinaction.org) arranges attachments to various Indian NGOs for interns to spend the summer or six months from September. Fees are £800 for two months July/August and £1,800 for the six-month placement.

Volunteers for Rural India with an office in London (www.vri-online.org.uk) may have volunteer openings in Amarpurkashi in Uttar Pradesh.

Dakshinayan (www.dakshinayan.blogspot.co.uk) works with tribal peoples in the hills of Rajmahal and nearby plains, though is less active than it once was. Volunteers join grassroots development projects and cover their living expenses plus a contribution.

GEOFFROY GROLEAU IS AN ECONOMIST AND CONSULTANT FROM MONTREAL WHO FOUND HIS WAY TO DAKSHINAYAN VIA THE INTERNET:

The application process is simple and can be conducted fully over the internet. The registration fee which must be provided before setting out for the project is the primary source of revenues for Dakshinayan. So there I was in early March stepping onto a train from New Delhi heading to Jharkhand. The project provides an opportunity to acquire a better understanding of the myths and realities surrounding poverty in the developing world, and specifically about the realities of rural India. The tribal people of these villages do not need or want fancy houses or televisions, but simply an education for their children and basic healthcare in order to improve the life they have been leading in relative isolation for centuries. It was interesting for me to see that they lead a quiet and simple life based on the rhythm of harvests and seasons, in marked contrast to most Westerners. The primary role for volunteers is to teach English for a few hours every day to the kids attending the three Dakshinayan-run schools. I should also mention the numerous unforgettable football games with enthusiastic kids at the end of another sunny afternoon. One should be aware that Dakshinayan is an Indian NGO fully run by local people, which in my view is another positive aspect. But it also means that volunteers will have to adapt to Indian ways.

The Kolkata-based SMILE Society (www.smilengo.org) arranges workcamps, internships and longer-term volunteering in teaching, health, street children projects, rural development, etc. Volunteers pay a registration fee and cover their basic living costs paid directly to the providers, often a homestay family.

Many travellers to India stay at monasteries, temples or ashrams, which are communities for meditation, yoga, etc. There may be no official charge or at least a very small one, but it may be assumed that you are a genuine seeker after enlightenment. The residential non-formal school Samanvay Ashram (Bodh-Gaya 824 231, Bihar; www.samanvayashram.org) has links with various educational and sanitation projects in the state to which it sends volunteers. WWOOF India (www.wwoofindia.org) lists 150 contacts in India and costs $40 to join.

Twenty-three-year-old Jenna Bonistalli wanted a complete change from her life as a student in New York so fixed up two voluntary placements in India, the first at a school in the Himalayas through Help-Education (listed below under 'Nepal') and later for an NGO that organised health and education outreach to a number of villages in rural Rajasthan:

After some travelling, a friend and I began our placement with the Veerni Project in Jodhpur, Rajasthan. Our role was as teachers in their Creative Literacy Programme, teaching remedial English through the Arts. This has been a very interesting placement, but also very difficult because the girls know very little English and most of them have been married off as children, so do not have much hope of continuing their studies past 15 or 16. The reason we chose this project was for its creative opportunities and its reasonable cost.

Another voluntary agency that works in rural Himalayan communities is iSPiiCE which stands for Integrated Social Program in Indian Child Education (www.volunteerindiaispiice.com) whose projects take place around Dharamsala, home in exile of the Dalai Lama. Participation prices start at £410 for a fortnight, rising to £1,075 for eight weeks in addition to a £150 application deposit.

The Sagreen International Educational Trust in Kerala (www.sagreenintl.com) claims to operate an ambitious volunteer teacher programme whereby more than 500 native speaker graduates can be placed throughout India for one or two terms of an academic year (June to March). Participants are promised training and a beach holiday on arrival in Kerala, help with obtaining an Employment Visa and even a monthly stipend for qualified teachers of 8,000–20,000 rupees (£95–£240). The programme fee is €650 for up to four months, €750 for up to eight months, and €850 for up to 12 months, which covers placement arrangements, accommodation and food.

Sri Lanka

A charitable foundation runs the SVS School for English in Colombo (www.svsenglish.org) which gives teachers who stay for the preferred six months free accommodation. Bond International Schools in Colombo, Trincomalee and Jaffna take on experienced teachers to prepare candidates for Cambridge ESOL exams (www.bond.lk/career.php). Kath McGuire decided to go travelling when she was 33 and found a volunteer teaching position in Sri Lanka:

The initial plan was to spend three months on a voluntary teaching placement followed by six weeks of travelling. But I loved it so much that I did a further two three-month projects with more travelling in between. There are too many highlights to mention. But the teaching has been so rewarding and so much fun, the people have been so loving and interesting and wonderful and I have seen some wonderful places: Mount Everest base camp, sunrise over the Annapurna mountain range in Nepal, climbing Sri Pada in Sri Lanka. The list does go on.

A tour agency (www.oceanislandholidays.com/volunteer-in-sri-lanka.html) offers volunteer placements in English teaching, turtle conservation and elephant welfare.

Maldives

In the recent past a privately run scheme affiliated to a travel agency in the Maldivian capital Male was promoting a volunteer programme with placements in teaching and sports coaching. However the company seems to have linked up with Ocean Island Holidays in Sri Lanka, just mentioned, which is offering a Cultural Immersion programme but with no sign of volunteering opportunities.

Nepal

Just as Nepal was becoming more stable after emerging from civil war between pro- and anti-Maoists and then abolishing its backward-looking monarchical system, the country was plunged into chaos by the destructive earthquake and its aftershocks of 2015. A number of agencies have stepped in to assist and some accept unskilled volunteers such as All Hands Volunteers with offices in Massachusetts and England (www.hands.org/projects/nepal-earthquake-recovery).

Once again most areas of Nepal are safe to visit and most schools are operating. In September 2015 a new constitution was agreed so Nepalis are hopeful that street protests and strikes will become less frequent. The price of basic food and travel has increased substantially over the past couple of years. Nepal Immigration operates an online visa application system, though tourist visas can still be purchased on arrival for $100 cash and are valid for 90 days (shorter stays for less money are also available) and can be extended for $2 a day thereafter, up to a maximum of 150 days. Return is prohibited until the next calendar year. Note that a hefty fine or even prison sentence can be imposed on foreigners found overstaying their visas.

A range of organisations makes it possible for self-funding volunteers to teach. Living expenses are very low by Western standards, though going through one of the mediating or gap-year organisations or booking through Nepali agencies listed here can increase the cost significantly. If you want to avoid an agency fee you can try to make direct contact with schools and NGOs on arrival.

Alliance Nepal: Kaski; www.volunteerworkinnepal.org. Opportunities to teach English, help in an orphanage, etc in the Pokhara Valley for two weeks to three months; prices from €200 for two weeks to €600 for 12 weeks.

Education & Health Nepal: www.ehn-nepal.org. NGO based in Kathmandu offering low-cost volunteering including teaching in rural schools and orphanage work. £80 admin fee plus £12 a day.

HELP (Himalayan Education Lifeline Programme): Whitstable, Kent; www.help-education. org. Volunteer teachers to teach in primary and secondary schools, work in poor communities in the Indian Himalayas (Sikkim, West Bengal, Ladakh and Uttarakhand) as well as Nepal, for between two and six months; volunteers pay an admin fee of £180, a donation of £300 (half for students) plus about £100 a month for board and lodging.

Hope And Home: Travel Program, Kathmandu; www.hopenhome.org. Community-oriented volunteer opportunities for international volunteers with homestay and cultural exchange; homestay accommodation and food from $400 for two weeks to $1,000 for 12 weeks plus registration fee of $200.

Insight Nepal: Pokhara; www.insightnepal.org.np. Development projects mainly in the Pokhara Valley; placements last seven weeks or three months starting year round for respective fees of $840 and $1,100.

KEEP (Kathmandu Environmental Education Project): Thamel, Kathmandu (www. keepnepal.org). KEEP is eager to recruit volunteers to help deliver English language training to guides and porters in July/August and December/January. KEEP also places volunteer teachers in government schools.

RCDP Nepal Volunteer: Kathmandu; www.rcdpnepal.org. Paying volunteers work on various programmes lasting one to 12 weeks, starting every other Monday, including teaching English; volunteers stay with families in villages; registration fee of $259 plus a weekly charge: $850 for 12 weeks in Kathmandu and Chitwan, $1,915 in Pokhara.

We Volunteer Nepal: Kathmandu; www.wevolunteernepal.org. Links international volunteers with range of teaching and other projects in Kathmandu Valley, Kavre, Langtang, Pokhara, Nawalparasi and Chitwan.

WWOOF Nepal is run by an energetic coordinator who has links with other NGOs and charities in Nepal (www.wwoofnepal.net). The WWOOF membership fee is $40 ($55 for a couple) which gives access to contact details for the organic farmers in Nepal. They have set up a sister organisation called Asian Cultural Exchange Programme (ACEP) with a broader range of hosts than merely farms.

South-east Asia

The mainstream London-based conservation expedition organisers all run projects in Asia. These expeditions are normally open to anyone reasonably fit who can raise the cost of joining (typically £2,500–£3,500 for three months excluding flights).

Barefoot Conservation: www.barefootconservation.org. Non-profit organisation working in marine conservation and engaging with local people in community projects; located on an Indonesian island in Raja Ampat; volunteers can join expeditions to carry out scientific survey dives and work in the community; cost of a sample four-week expedition is £1,895 or for 12 weeks £3,350 which includes dive training.

Coral Cay Conservation Ltd: www.coralcay.org. Recruits paying volunteers, expedition leaders, scuba instructors, etc for its marine and forest conservation projects in the Philippines (and Montserrat); 16 weeks costs £3,785.

Gapforce: www.gapforce.org. Sends paying volunteers to join many projects worldwide including adventures in Bali, Borneo, Thailand, India and Nepal. Also a marine conservation project in Fiji.

GoEco: www.goeco.org/area/volunteer-in-asia. Varied range of opportunities.

Orangutan Foundation: www.orangutan.org.uk. Arranges for volunteers to be based in Central Kalimantan, Indonesian Borneo for three weeks for £700 plus flight; tasks range from carrying out infrastructure repairs, trail cutting and constructing guardposts, but involves no direct work with orangutans.

Near Phuket at the southern end of Thailand, conservationists are working to protect marine turtles, mangrove forests and coral reefs on the island of Koh Phra Thong. Though projects in this area were badly hit by the 2004 tsunami, Naucrates has resumed its programme and recruits volunteers to help with rebuilding and education between December and April. Prices start at €795 for a fortnight. Prospective volunteers and student conservationists can obtain more details from the NGO Naucrates, based in Italy (www.naucrates.org).

Far East

Japan and Korea have WWOOF organisations, both of them web-based. It costs 5,500 yen to join WWOOF Japan (Sapporo; www.wwoofjapan.com) whose list of member farms comprises about 400 potential hosts; and $55 for the list of 75 Korean hosts from WWOOF Korea (www.wwoofkorea.org/en).

> **WHILE DOING HIS YEAR ABROAD OF A DEGREE IN JAPANESE AT SHEFFIELD UNIVERSITY AND ON PREVIOUS TRIPS, JOSEPH TAME HAS HAD A WONDERFUL TIME WWOOFING:**
>
> *I spent a few weeks in a beautiful little seaside village on the southern island of Shikoku, working as a volunteer for an organic tangerine cooperative. We would be picked up by local farmers at about 6am, work with them on the tangerine terraces until 11am when the heat got to be too much to bear. One particularly memorable day was when an Australian WWOOFer and I were given the job of picking caterpillars off the leaves of a huge field of organic Japanese potatoes. Over the course of three hours we collected two huge sacks of creepy crawlies, but at the end of the day forgot to tie the sacks up – when we returned to the field the following day we found the caterpillars had all escaped and returned to their former homes!*

WWOOF Japan is a good way to meet Japanese people, as it is popular among city dwellers eager to experience a quiet rural lifestyle. The WWOOF list also includes some paid employment since a few of their hosts run hostels, campsites or little schools (for which a working visa would be necessary).

Joining a short-term volunteer project can be a good way to visit an exotic place such as Mongolia. For example an NGO in Ulaanbaatar that places international volunteers is the New Choice Mongolian Volunteer Organization (www.volunteer.org.mn) which arranges short and long-term placements for volunteers to teach English, renovate buildings, etc for a fee of $250 per week, $1,445 for eight weeks.

The Middle East

With the tragic destruction of Syria and civil war raging in Yemen, some countries have been rendered virtually off-limits. Suicide bombings orchestrated by so-called Islamic State, seemingly intractable tensions between Israelis and Palestinians, and an escalation of anti-Western sentiment in some quarters have all dampened enthusiasm for travel and employment in the region. Unrest in Iraq and Afghanistan continue to render those countries off-limits, however Iran is a possibility and in fact there is a working holiday visa agreement between Australia and Iran. There are oases of calm such as the Gulf states and Jordan, so prospective travellers should not write off the whole of the Middle East due to anxieties about personal security.

The areas of employment to consider throughout the Middle East are English teaching, nannying/ nursing or a position in the petro-chemical or construction industries if you happen to have superior qualifications and relevant managerial experience. Simply Angelic (www.simplyangelic.co.uk) special- ises in placing qualified and experienced nannies, tutors and governesses with families worldwide and has regular vacancies in Dubai (where it has an office) and the rest of the United Arab Emirates, Bah- rain, Saudi Arabia, Kuwait, Lebanon and Turkey. Salaries for well qualified candidates can be stagger- ingly high eg £1,200 per week. Another agency for qualified nannies with an office in Dubai as well as London is Nannies Incorporated (www.nanniesinc.com/positions/Middle-east); vacancies are posted not just with VIP households but with VVIP families. Carfax Education headquartered in London has a steady demand for live-in tutors for families in the Middle East. Applicants with at least a bachelor's degree and some experience as a teacher or tutor should send enquiries to dubai@carfax-tutors.com (www.carfax-education.ae).

Countries in the Middle East vary greatly in degree of Islamic restrictiveness. Oman, Jordan, Leba- non and the United Arab Emirates, for example, have a relatively relaxed atmosphere. The wealthy countries of Saudi Arabia and the Gulf states generally employ teachers with top qualifications such as an MA in TESOL or Applied Linguistics with at least three years of experience, preferably at university level. Few casual opportunities can be found. Accepting a TEFL contract in an oil state usually means first-class accommodation in a luxury apartment complex, cheap shopping, etc.

Possible leads may be available from Amideast headquartered in Washington DC (www.amideast. org) which teaches American English at its field offices and centres in Oman, UAE, Iraq, Saudi, etc. Interestingly in 2017 it is running English courses in Yemen's port city of Aden.

Anyone interested in teaching English to the Palestinians scattered throughout the Arab World is likely to be very restricted in where they will be able to go. But Palestinian schools struggle on and anyone who supports their cause might pursue this idea through solidarity organisations (see section in chapter on Israel).

As usual it is always worth checking the opportunities on www.workaway.info and, if any of the 236 work-for-keep positions listed in the Middle East interest you, you can gain access to the contact details by buying a one year Workaway membership for $29. At the time of writing hosts offering places to stay were as varied as a hobby olive farm in northern Iran to a B&B at Petra, Jordan. There was even a young Bedouin tour guide looking for help with developing his website.

TURKEY

Turkey is a wonderful country to travel in, with a wealth of historic sites such as Troy and Ephesus, marvellous food and warm friendly people. But its tourist industry has been decimated by recent terrorist attacks, such as the mass shooting at an Istanbul night club on New Year's Day 2017. Deepening political unrest in the aftermath of the unsuccessful military coup and warnings of a 'high' terror threat have discouraged prospective tourists and teachers from choosing Turkey as a destination. The authoritarian and pro-Islamic tendencies of President Erdogan's government have killed Turkey's campaign to join the European Union by 2023, the centennial anniversary of the

Turkish Republic. Despite this, Turkey is a promising choice of destination for fledgling English teachers (with a university degree).

Teaching English

For several decades now, Turkey's prosperous classes have been eager to learn English. Expat teachers routinely earn good money for private English lessons. The boom in English is not confined to private language schools (*dershane*) that cram students for university entrance, but there are dozens of private secondary schools (*lises*) and a few universities where English is the medium of instruction.

Most of the mainstream schools will expect to see a TEFL Certificate of some kind, preferably the Cambridge (CELTA) or Trinity (TESOL) Certificate, in addition to a BA. This may apply to the established chains, but there are still dodgy operators and swashbuckling employers willing to hire (and exploit) others. One British teacher sets out what you should look for when choosing an employer: *'I worked at four different schools in Istanbul. You'll want a school that's professional (with good resources, support and teacher development), offers a good package (salary, accommodation, holiday entitlement) and has a timetable to suit you.'*

Although Istanbul is not the capital, it is the commercial, financial and cultural centre of Turkey, so this is where most of the EFL teaching goes on. On the negative side, there may be more competition from other travelling teachers here and also in Izmir than in Ankara or less obvious cities such as Mersin and Bursa. Among the main language teaching organisations in Istanbul are Kent School of English (www.kentenglish.com), English Time with 40 branches (www.englishtime.com) and English West (www.englishwest.com). Without a degree and a TEFL certificate it will not be possible for English teachers to get a residence/work permit which employers apply for on their employees' behalf.

A near-native-speaking English specialist who had been working for eight years in marketing communications decided it was time to change direction. Having learned that a TEFL qualification was a requirement for teaching in Turkey, she enrolled in a CELTA course and then moved to Istanbul:

> *Having travelled to Turkey as a tourist on a number of occasions, I decided to move there in the summer of 2015. Something drew me, even if I haven't found what it is. I had talked to an expat who was on leave in the Netherlands, and she advised me to become a teacher. She shared some of her experiences, not all of them rosy. I managed to arrange my first teaching hours within the first month of my stay and had already signed up with one of the top language schools a few months later. There is a real need for language teachers in Turkey and natives and near-natives (as in my case) are embraced. A lot of teaching in Turkey goes without contract, work permit and a set amount of teaching hours, so that one may get by in one month to fall short in the next. Many schools offer minimum wages. Classes may be at nights or weekends and split between teachers. Students may be very passive in their learning, unwilling to participate in activities and are sometimes in the wrong level, frustrating their learning process. In the end, however, that doesn't take away from the genuine interest – and need – that Turkish pupils have to learn English. They bond to their teacher like little puppies and, once they have gotten past the threshold of their limitations, love to discuss and are quite happy to go along with all you are offering. This, the fruits of teaching itself, makes teaching in Turkey rewarding, if you do not mind a few bumps along an uncertain road.*

Many casual teachers used to work on a tourist visa and cross out of Turkey to renew it on re-entry every three months. However, the regulations have been tightened up and are now in line with the Schengen system, which means that foreigners are allowed to stay 90 days within a period of 180 days.

It is no longer possible to process the residence/work permit after arrival in Turkey. As of 2016, all visa applications must go through an online Pre-Application System (www.turkishconsulate.org.uk/en/visa.asp) and at a later stage you submit originals of your job offer from a Turkish employer, university degree diploma, teaching/TEFL certificate plus a police check and proof of health insurance.

For short-term opportunities, the Education Department of the youth travel and exchange organisation, Genctur, in Galatasaray, Istanbul (☎ (+90) 212 244 62 30; www.genctur.com.tr) organises summer camps for children where English, German and French are taught by native speakers who work for two weeks in exchange for free board and lodging. Pocket money may also be given according to experience and skills. Applicants must have some experience of working with children.

The following are teacher placement agencies: the main indigenous language teaching organisations in Turkey plus one agent in the UK:

Boz Academy Consulting Services: Istanbul; hr@bozacademy.com; www.bozacademy.com. TEFL jobs in Turkey.

Marmaris Recruitment: (www.marmarisrecruitment.com). Admin fee of £40 to register. Deals with other kinds of vacancy including resort bar jobs, childcare and entertainment personnel.

Oxford as Academy: Bursa; www.teachingenglishinturkey.com.

Teach to Travel Ltd: London E1; www.teachtotravel.com. Up to 150 teachers with degree and TEFL certificate recruited for private and public schools and summer camps. Partner company in Istanbul is Teachers in Turkey (www.teachersinturkey.com); promised starting salary is 2,500 Turkish lira per month.

Childcare

Demand is steady for English-speaking au pairs and also among wealthy Turkish families for professional nannies who have studied childcare and child development. Most agencies in Turkey will expect candidates to be already resident in the country with a full valid residence permit, as specified by the Nanny Agency Istanbul (www.nannyagencyistanbul.com).

The high salaries sometimes quoted for nannies sound very attractive, though the life of a nanny can be frustrating because of cultural differences. Some nannies have had to get used to having their freedom and independence curtailed, and also the extent to which Turkish children tend to be spoilt and babied. But despite this, many have thoroughly enjoyed their stint in Turkey.

Tourism

There is a large population of seasonal travellers looking for casual employment, and many succeed. The main Aegean resorts of Marmaris, Kusadasi and Bodrum absorb a number of foreign travellers as workers. Other places firmly on the travellers' trail such as Antalya on the south coast and Goreme in Cappadocia are also promising. Antalya hostels regularly pay travellers $200 a month on top of a bed and one or two meals to man the desk or do other hostel chores. The best time to look is March or early April. Danny Jacobson met lots of foreign workers when he travelled in Turkey:

> *I would say Turkey is a hot spot. I met loads of travellers working in the south and even in Selcuk. In Fethiye, Oludenez, definitely in Olympos, it was like an Aussie/Kiwi resort complex. There are so many of them working and travelling down there, the Turkish people have started talking English with an Australian accent.*

Proprietors of bars, shops, travel agencies, etc aim to use native English speakers to attract more customers to buy their souvenirs or stay at their hotels. In the majority of cases, this sort of work finds you once you make known your willingness to undertake such jobs. However, if you want to try to fix up something sight unseen, consult the Scotland-based recruitment agency Marmaris mentioned above (www.marmarisrecruitment.com).

Major Turkish yachting resorts are excellent places to look for work, not just related to boats but in hotels, bars, shops and excursions. A good time to check harbourside noticeboards and to ask captains if they need anyone to clean or repair their boats is in the lead up to the summer season and the Yacht Charter Show in Marmaris in early May. Laura O'Connor describes what she found in Marmaris:

There's a large British community living there, retired and fed-up Brits who have sold their houses, bought a boat and are whooping it up. There's plenty of work opportunities in the Marina, especially for painting and varnishing in April. Also, girls can do hostessing on the boats. I was cleaning boats with a friend for enough money to cover my accommodation and evenings in the pub. Just walk around the Marina and ask.

If you can handle long hours, rich demanding guests and the politics of living and working with the same people for the four-month season, doing a season on a charter yacht is a good way to save money and see the Turkish coast.

Some UK tour operators hire childcare staff, watersports instructors, yacht crew, etc for Turkey. For example Sunsail, part of giant TUI Travel plc (www.tuijobsuk.co.uk), has a few openings for skippers, hostesses, mechanics/bosuns, dinghy sailors, etc for its sailing holidays based in Fethiye.

Voluntary Opportunities

The youth travel bureau Genctur mentioned above (www.genctur.com.tr) runs international workcamps for manual and social projects as well as acting as a youth and student travel bureau and coordinating summer camps where children learn English. GSM Youth Services Centre in Ankara (☎ (+90) 312 417 1124; www.gsm.org.tr/en) is another youth camp organiser with links to projects in Anatolia and throughout Turkey. Recruitment of volunteers for the fortnight-long camps takes place through the major workcamp organisations in the UK and worldwide.

Ecological farm stays are organised by the Bugday Association (the word means wheat in Turkish) through the TaTuTa Project (www.Tatuta.org) which is part of the international WWOOF association. At present there are nearly 100 member farms. Foreign volunteers can join for a fee of €30.

Pamukkale University sponsors a Sea Turtle Research, Rescue and Rehabilitation Centre in Dalyan called Dekamer (www.dekamer.org.tr/volunteering.html) which accepts long-term volunteers who need to pay €200 a month to cover food and accommodation (half price for bona fide students).

In Extremis

The best protection against getting into serious difficulties is to have a good travel insurance policy (see the Introduction). This is an expense that should not be shrugged off given the possible repercussions of not having cover. One of the benefits of the International Student Identity Card and International Youth Travel Card (for people under 30) is access to a toll-free emergency helpline on which medical, legal or financial advice can be sought in a crisis. However, they do not in any way replace the need for insurance. ISIC and IYTC cards can be bought online or from any branch of STA Travel for £12 or in the US for $25.

If you do end up in dire financial straits and for some reason do not have or cannot use a credit card, you should contact someone at home, if possible, who is in a position to send money.

TRANSFERRING MONEY

Ideally your account at home will remain in credit and you can access it via any ATM. If your card is lost, stolen or damaged, you should ring your bank's emergency number to request a replacement which will be sent to your home address, so you will have to ask someone to forward it to you securely. This of course will take some days, so you will need money in the interim. Your bank can wire money to a nominated bank in your destination. This will be easier if you have set up a telephone or internet bank account before leaving home since they will then have the correct security checks in place to authorise a transfer without having to receive something from you in writing with your signature.

Various products are on the market that aim to get round the problem, in the form of prepaid, reloadable cards that can be used at ATMs and in outlets worldwide. See the section on Money in the Introduction for a description of travel money cards.

Western Union offers an international money transfer service whereby cash deposited at one branch can be withdrawn almost immediately by you from any other branch or agency, which your benefactor need not specify. Western Union agents – there are 90,000 of them in 200 countries – come in all shapes and sizes, eg travel agencies, stationers, chemists. Unfortunately it is not well represented outside the developed world. The person sending money to you can do it online (www.westernunion. com), by phone (☎ (+44) 800 833833 in the UK) or in person at a Western Union counter. The service charge for an online transfer is £4.90 to send up to £500. Then they will let you know the tracking number (MTCN) which you will need along with your ID to collect the money.

Thomas Cook and the UK Post Office offer a similar service called Moneygram (www.moneygram. com) which is available from your mobile phone. Cash deposited at one of their foreign exchange counters is available within 10 minutes at the named destination or can be collected up to 45 days later at one of 350,000 cooperating agents in 200 countries. The fee starts at a modest £3.90 though these companies make money on the exchange rate as well. US citizens can ring Overseas Citizens Services (☎ (+1) 888 407 4747), part of the State Department, which can arrange for money wired in an emergency to a US Embassy abroad to be given to a named citizen for a fee of $30, but only if commercial options like Western Union are not appropriate.

Despite the popularity of online banking, you may still find it necessary to open a local account, for example if your employer pays by cheque. For this you will need proof of a local address and solid ID.

EMBASSIES AND CONSULATES

With luck you will never have to visit your consulate while travelling. But it is still a good idea to be aware of its location and services if you are travelling in an unstable country. The majority of people who do end up in consular waiting rooms are there because they have had their passports stolen or lost. In some cases it is easier to arrange replacement documents if you have a record of the passport number and date and place of issue; however you will have to start from scratch completing the application form and supplying original documents like a birth certificate (which won't be possible if you are abroad) and contact details for guarantors. You can be issued with a limited-validity emergency passport with a white cover. In an emergency, your consulate can help you get in touch with friends and relations if necessary, normally by arranging a reverse charge call. Consulates have the authority to make a cash advance after you have signed an Undertaking to Repay form. Do not pin too much faith in your consulate. When Jane Roberts turned to the British Consulate in Toronto after having all her money stolen, they just preached at her about how she should have thought about all this before she left home.

If you are really desperate and can find no-one at home or among your fellow travellers willing to lend you some money, do not expect your consulate to repatriate you. The updated version of the online guide 'Support for British Nationals Abroad' on the government's website uses the word 'repatriation' only in the context of bringing back dead bodies, and claims that even in a pandemic, consular repatriation is not an option.

The Foreign and Commonwealth Office of the UK government provides updated travel information and cautions for every country in the world and additional risk assessment of current trouble spots and advice on how to find consular help and legal advice. For detailed country-by-country risk assessments for travellers, go to www.gov.uk/foreign-travel-advice.

In the USA, the Department of State publishes travel alerts and travel warnings on its website www.travel.state.gov, highlighting any potential dangers to American travellers such as coups, terrorist activity, natural disasters, epidemics, etc.

LEGAL PROBLEMS

Everyone has heard hair-raising stories about conditions in foreign prisons, so think very carefully before engaging in illegal activities. Several thousand Britons are held in foreign prisons, at least half on drugs charges. If you do have trouble with the law in foreign countries, remain calm and polite, and insist on an immediate visit from a consular official. He or she can at least recommend a local lawyer and interpreter if necessary. If you are incarcerated, ask a parent or friend to inform the charity Prisoners Abroad (London N4; ☎ (+44) 20 7561 6820; www.prisonersabroad.org.uk), which liaises with consulates abroad and can make practical suggestions.

DIRE STRAITS

Try not to be too downcast if destitution strikes. Elma Grey had been looking forward to leaving Greece and rejoining her old kibbutz, but she was unexpectedly turned away from the ferry because of her dire shortage of funds. She describes the 'worst down' of her travels:

> *Back to the Athens hotel where I'd spent the previous evening, feeling utter despair. But I found that other people's problems have an incredible way of bringing out the best in total strangers. Everyone I came into contact with was full of sympathy, advice and practical suggestions regarding possible sources of work. And quite apart from this, the feeling of much needed moral support was probably what got me through the whole thing without my degenerating into a miserable heap. Although I'd never want to feel so stranded and desperate again, in a way it was all worth it just to experience the unique feeling of just how good fellow travellers can be in a crisis.*

Several travellers have insisted that when you get down to your last few dollars/pesos/euros, it is much wiser to spend them in a pub buying drinks for the locals who might then offer useful assistance than it is to spend the money on accommodation or food. David Irvine found himself in Tasmania with just $10 in his pocket. He walked into a pub and bet two men $20 each that he could drink a yard of ale, a feat he was fairly confident that he could accomplish.

Less than 24 hours after Ilka Cave from South Africa arrived in Tel Aviv, all her luggage, money and documents were stolen. One of the girls in the hostel suggested that she contact an au pair agency and soon she was living with a nice family and earning a salary. Michel Falardeau wanted to live rent-free in Sydney, so he offered his assistance to a number of charities, one of which gave him a place to live. Mark Horobin was down to his bottom dollar in San Diego and queued up outside the Rescue Mission. Several days later he had signed on as a kitchen helper and stayed for some time free of charge.

It is to be hoped that you will avoid the kind of disaster that will require the services of a lawyer, doctor or consul abroad. If you find yourself merely running short of funds, you might be interested in some of the following tidbits of information, intended for entertainment more than for practical advice.

HELP. Look out for churches that conduct services in English: the priest or vicar should be able to give you useful advice and often practical help. But be cautious about accepting help from fringe religious groups.

NIGHT SHELTERS. Most large towns and some railway stations in Western Europe and North America have a night shelter run by the Catholic organisation Caritas, the Salvation Army or similar which provides basic but free food and accommodation. They want to help genuine vagrants, not freeloading tourists, so you should be genuinely impoverished or a potential convert. You can find out where to find these hostels by asking around – any policeman on the night beat should know. Be warned that many of these organisations are run by religious movements, and you may be expected to show your gratitude by joining in worship.

Long-term traveller Bradwell Jackson had an overly romantic image of being a vagabond travelling without money, which the discomforts and horrors of living on the streets in Puerto Rico soon dispatched: *'There is nothing romantic about being homeless. I was never technically homeless myself (living on the street), but just seeing what those people go through made me so horrified that I'm still feeling shell shocked.'*

MONASTERIES and NUNNERIES. Monastic communities often extend hospitality to indigent wayfarers. Sometimes it is freely given but try to be sensitive as to whether or not a small donation is expected. Greek Orthodox monasteries are normally open to males only, for example Mount Athos accepts 10 non-Orthodox men a day, most of whom have requested a permit in advance.

JAIL. Travellers have on occasion found a free bed for the night by asking at police stations if there are any spare cells, though with the British prisons scandalously full to bursting at present, this is not a very promising possibility in the UK. According to US law, all people (including non-citizens) have the right to demand protective custody. You are most likely to be successful (and escape unharmed) in peaceful country towns.

SLEEPING OUT. It is illegal to sleep out on private property without the landowner's permission, except in Nordic countries which observe *Allemansratt*, which preserves the foot traveller's right to roam and to camp for one or two nights if not in view of a habitation. Most farmers will grant their permission if you ask politely and look trustworthy. In cities try public parks and also railway or coach stations, though some are cleared by security after the last train or bus or you may be asked for an onward ticket. Anna Ling felt safe sleeping in fenced parks in Seville (going to bed after dark) and also on a theatre porch with an overhanging roof, where there was a community of street people and young punks mainly from France. Some kind locals offered food and coffee. Many people try to camp discreetly near a proper campsite so that they can make use of the toilet and shower block. Ian Moody tried to avoid sleeping out on private property in Spain and one night chose a seemingly ideal shelter, a concrete covered ditch. At about 5am he was rudely awakened by a torrent of water which swept away his gear and nearly drowned him. Many people sleep on beaches; beware of early morning visits from the local constabulary and also large vacuum machines. Aaron Woods was nearly killed by a massive tractor raking the sand overnight on a beautiful beach in Sardinia where he was kipping. Jonathan Galpin recommends taking a mosquito net, not only as protection against biting insects but (when doubled over) from falling dew.

SQUATTING. Every city has a selection of abandoned buildings, many of which have been colonised by squatters. Finding a welcoming squat is a hit-and-miss business; some are more exclusive than others. Squatters are tough people who will not tolerate freeloaders, so you have to show that you can contribute something (cleaning, decorating, maintenance, etc). And be prepared for confrontation with the authorities. It is not unknown for long-stay squatters to make contact with the owner of the empty building and negotiate to stay there legitimately. Have a look at www.en.squat.net.

ANTI-SQUATTING. Large cities sometimes have an agency that finds tenants to live in vacant properties at minimal rent, in order to protect them from squatters. This is especially common in Utrecht and other Dutch cities because in the Netherlands buildings that have been empty for a year can be legally squatted, and owners then find it hard to repossess them for renovation or demolition. It's a great way of having a huge place to live very cheaply.

FREE KIPPING. Half-finished buildings usually provide enough shelter for a comfortable, uninterrupted kip. Robin Gray recommends garden huts in large garden centres which are often left open and provide a good night's shelter. Your luggage can be safely stowed in a locker at the station during the day.

FREE MEALS. Sometimes charities such as the Red Cross and Caritas give out free food, as David Bamford discovered when he was stranded in Villefranche unable to find a grape-picking job, along with scores of North Africans.

Restaurants may be willing to give you a free meal if you promise to recommend them to a guide-book or to correct the spelling on their menu (depriving future travellers of the delights of 'miscellaneous pork bowel', 'grilled chicken with swing' and 'vegetable craps'). It may also be possible to do an hour's work in exchange for a meal by going to the back door, possibly at fast food outlets. Some will even give a hand-out if you are brazen enough to request one.

DUMPSTER DIVING. Also known as skip-diving, urban foraging or freeganism, this refers to retrieving from skips decent food that has been discarded by supermarkets and shops. The 'free-cycle' culture is well established in most European cities and, once you become plugged into the network, you will discover the best places and times (eg Tuesdays after 10pm in Rotterdam). Beware of police looking for trespassers. See www.freegan.info for more information and Fallingfruit.org/dumpsters provides a world map on which you can zoom into markets and food-bearing dumpsters, with recommended times for raiding.

SCAVENGING FOOD. If you are not too fussy about what you eat (as above), you can look for stale or sub-standard food that has been discarded by shops, bakeries at the end of the day, market stalls or even restaurants. Fancy resort hotels are also prone to throw out good food on a regular basis.

BUFFET RESTAURANTS. In some countries such as Sweden, the USA and Australia, reasonable restaurants offer all-you-can-eat buffets. Diners have been known to share their second and third helpings with friends who have merely bought a soft drink.

FREE WINE. You may come across free tastings in wine producing areas from California to France (where these tastings are called *dégustations*). There will sometimes be something to eat – perhaps bread and cheese, or a local speciality.

FACTORY TOURS. Ask tourist offices if there are any food or drink factories nearby that offer free guided tours; these tours normally end with the gift of free samples of whatever is being produced. For example, distilleries in Scotland may hand out miniature bottles of whisky, and chocolate factories may dispense free treats. Note that some of the big mainstream factories now charge admission for their tours.

AGMs. We have heard of a Londoner who cannily bought a single share in hundreds of companies and feasted for a year on buffet lunches at AGMs.

HAPPY HOURS. To attract customers at off-peak times, bars and pubs sometimes offer free snacks as well as cut-price drinks.

FAIRS AND FESTIVALS. Watch for giveaways at local fairs and festivals. To take just one example in Italy, there are often free snacks at *sagre* (fairs).

RAIDING FRIDGES. When Roger Blake was broke in Brisbane, he became semi-reliant on the communal fridge at the backpackers hostel. Most hostels have a communal shelf for well meaning travellers to leave behind unwanted and perishable items. Apparently it is possible to live off unwanted food, especially in city hostels where there is a major departure airport.

WASHING UP. In hostels, everyone is expected to wash and dry his or her own dishes. If you make it known that you are willing to take over this chore in exchange for a small contribution, you may find lots of willing takers. Never underestimate the laziness of travellers. One night Roger Blake made $8 in 'tips' by doing this. He then asked the hostel owners whether he could set up as a 'dishy' for tips only. But they didn't welcome the idea as it went against their philosophy of getting everyone to muck in together.

SELF-SERVICE RESTAURANTS. The original publisher of this book had an odd experience in a huge New York self-service restaurant. Having eaten his Waldorf salad he went to the water fountain for a drink. On returning to his table to conclude his repast he found a tramp-like character, who had obviously assumed the customer had left for good, busily wolfing down the much anticipated apple pie; the unwanted guest promptly fled. On leaving the self-service emporium the victim spotted the culprit peering through the plate glass window with several pals, in search of customers who left their tables leaving uneaten remains still on the table.

FREELOADING. Couchsurfing (see Introduction) legitimises freeloading because there is an expectation that at some future time you will lend a sofa. The generosity of strangers should not be underestimated. Years ago, Dutchman Ramon Stoppelenburg set up a website www.letmestayforaday.com, from which he received 2,784 offers of free hospitality on his two-year tour. Journalist Paul Smith from Newcastle, aka the Twitch-hiker, set off to test whether social networking could possibly get a person round the world on the good will of people contacted solely through Twitter. Amazingly he got close to his destination, remote and uninhabited Campbell Island near Antarctica. He went on to write a book about it *Twitch-hiker: How One Man Travelled the World by Twitter* (still in print). More recently an impoverished Portuguese student called Diogo Bhovan left home to travel Europe with just €1 a day. He depended on the kindness of friends of friends of acquaintances to whom he explained his 'Vou ali e já venho' project, assisted by interest from the media.

PUBLICITY TRADING. Just as the Twitch-hiker exploited international publicity of his quest, so an enterprising Canadian called Kyle MacDonald accomplished an incredible feat. Starting with a red paper clip, he used the internet to offer to trade up, and in 14 trades he had a house in a nondescript town in Saskatchewan. You can read how he did it at http://oneredpaperclip.blogspot.co.uk.

CLAIMING BOTTLE DEPOSITS. In Denmark, Sweden, Norway, Mexico, France, Spain, Italy, Australia, Canada, the USA and many other countries you can earn some small change by taking wine, beer and coke bottles or aluminium cans for recycling back to shops for a refund of the deposit. It is best to look for bottles or cans after a beach party, a special event such as a festival, in the dustbins outside holiday villas early in the mornings or on city streets the night before rubbish collection day. In cities in Canada and elsewhere, people do this on a full-time basis.

AIRPORT TROLLEYS. In some airports, you have to insert a coin in order to have the use of a trolley. Many luggage-laden travellers do not bother returning their trolley to the trolley park for the return of their coin, and dump them by the taxi or bus stands.

TRICKS AND SKILLS. If you know that you can drink a yard of ale, juggle four plates or smoke 27 cigars simultaneously, you might find people willing to have a sporting bet with you. We have heard of a traveller who erected a sign on the pavements 'Jokes – 25 Cents Each' and another who actually set up a kissing booth in London while waiting to find a proper job.

WRITE A POEM. Charge a fee to write a poem, as seen in the charming scene from the film *Before Sunrise* in which a down-and-out fellow offers to write a poem for Julie Delpy and Ethan Hawke using a word of their choice (they choose 'milkshake') on a pay-what-you-like basis. In a similar vein, an itinerant poet called Ryan Ashley (www.untouchedpoetry.com) travels the USA setting up his folding table and typewriter (remember those?) at popular farmers' markets and festivals. Donations are welcome for his output.

ONLINE SERVICES. A global marketplace for the gig economy, Fiverr (www.fiverr.com) offers 'freelance services for the lean entrepreneur'. Anyone can offer to do any task you can think of starting at $5. Examples include: telling someone's girlfriend the relationship is over, filling someone in on missed episodes of *The Archers*, offering travel advice based on your experience, listening to someone's problems, doing a voice-over, designing a logo. The site keeps 20% of your takings.

MEDICAL RESEARCH. Private companies providing clinical trials to the pharmaceutical industry often pay healthy volunteers handsomely to test new drugs and techniques. Check www.centerwatch.com or www.clinicaltrials.gov for US studies. You might also enquire at university psychology departments, where there may be a need for participants for perception tests, etc. More information about research clinics can be found in the chapters on the US and UK.

SELLING PLASMA. Many countries pay blood and plasma donors handsomely, especially the USA and Middle East. Even if you donate your blood free of charge, you are always given a free drink and a snack. In the USA expect to be paid $40–$60 per donation and you can donate twice a week (see http://donatingplasma.org/donation/find-a-donor-center for links to 530 centres in the USA and Europe). Specialist clinics pay much higher compensation for donating stem cells.

SPERM DONATION. In many countries, fertility clinics pay (typically $50–$100) for sperm samples. Men should be aware that they will be invited to donate only after screening and analysis of potential fertility (which might be traumatic). In the UK, donors can no longer maintain anonymity (so that any children born subsequently can trace their genetic fathers) which has resulted in a sharp drop in the number of donors and sperm shortages for couples seeking assisted fertilisation. Men should take seriously the decision to take part and not focus merely on the immediate financial gain. One major player is Cryos International (see chapter on Denmark).

EGG DONATION. Egg donation is a much more serious business. Private fertility clinics in the USA have been offering $6,500–$15,000 for donated eggs which involves hormone treatment and surgery, whereas UK donors are paid 'compensation' of up to £750 per cycle (www.hfea.gov.uk/egg-donation-and-egg-sharing.html). According to another press report, high demand categories like Jewish donors or Oxbridge students can command very high fees. A simple web search reveals sites with names such as www.eggdonor.com.

SELLING BELONGINGS. Before setting off on your travels, sell your junk on eBay: everything from unwanted DVDs to your old table tennis table can make a tidy profit. By the end of your trip many of your belongings may have become expendable. You can try selling them to fellow travellers in hostels, to second-hand shops or in markets. Be ruthless about what you do and do not need: you have taken your photos, so you don't need your camera, and you can transfer your belongings from your expensive backpack to a cheaper bag. Be prepared to spend some time haggling.

THE LAST RESORT. Sell this book – but memorise the contents first! Peter McGuire sold this book's sister publication *Teaching English Abroad* for 5,000 won in Korea to someone who was immediately offered double that amount by someone else.

APPENDIX 1

SOME USEFUL PHRASES

English: Do you need a helper/temporary assistant?
French (F): Avez-vous besoin d'un aide/assistant intérimaire?
German (D): Brauchen Sie einen Helfer/einen Assistenten für eine begenzte Zeit?
Dutch (NL): Kunt U een helper/tijdelijke assistent gebruiken?
Spanish (S): ¿Necesita ayudante?
Italian (I): Ha bisogno d'un aiutante/d'un assistente provvisorio?
Greek (GR): Khryázeste kanénan ypálliyo/prosorynó voythó?

GB: Do you know if there is any work in the neighbourhood?
F: Savez-vous s'il y a du travail dans le quartier?
D: Wissen Sie, ob es in der Nachbarschaft irgendwelche Arbeit gibt?
NL: Weet u of werk is in de buurt?
S: ¿Sabe si hay trabajo por aquí?
I: Lo sa si c'è lavoro nella zona?
GR: Xérete an yaprkhy dhoulyá styn peryokhý?

GB: Where is the job centre/employment office?
F: Où se trouve l'agence pour l'emploi?
D: Wo ist das Arbeitsamt?
NL: Waar is het kantoor voor arbeidsvoorziening?
S: ¿Donde está la oficina de empleo?
I: Dove sta il centro per l'impiego?
GR: Poú ýno to grafýo (evréseos) ergasýas?

GB: What is the wage? Will it be taxed?
F: Quel est le salaire? Sera-t-il imposable?
D: Wie hoch ist der Lohn? Ist er steuerpflichtig?
NL: Hoe hoog is het loon? Is het belastbaar?
S: ¿Cuanto es el salario? ¿Será sujeto al pago de impuestos?
I: Qual'è la paga? Sarà tassata?
GR: Poso ýne to ymerornýsthyo? Tha forologhiyhý?

GB: Where can I stay? Will there be a charge for accommodation/food?
F: Où pourrais-je me loger? L'hébergement/les repas seront-ils payants?
D: Wo kann ich wohnen? Muss für Unterkunft und Verpflegung selbst gezahlt werden?
NL: Waar kan ik onderdak vinden? Moet ik betalen voor huisvesting en maaltijden?
S: ¿Donde me puedo alojar? ¿Hay que pagar por la habitación/la comida?
I: Dove posso passare la notte? Ci sarà una tariffa per l'alloggio/il cibo?
GR: Pou boró na mýno? Tha khreothó ya ty dhyamoný/to fagytó?

GB: Are there any cooking/washing facilities?
F: Est-ce qu'il y a des aménagements pour faire la cuisine/la lessive?
D: Gibt es Koch/Waschgelegenheiten?
NL: Is er kook/wasgelegenheid?
S: ¿Se puede cocinar/lavar la ropa?

I: Ci sono dei servizi per cucinare/lavorare?
GR: Ypárkhoun efkolýes ya magýrema/plýsymo?

GB: When will the harvest/job begin? How long will it last?
F: Quand commencera-t-elle la moisson/commencera-t-il le travail? Combien de temps durera-t-elle/il?
D: Wann beginnt die Ernte/Arbeit? Wie lange wird sie dauern?
NL: Wanneer begint de oogst/job? Hoe lang zal het werk duren?
S: ¿Cuando comenzará la cosecha/el trabajo? ¿Cuanto durará?
I: Quando comincerà il raccolto/il lavoro? Per quanto tempo durerà?
GR: Poté tharkhýsy o theryzmos/y dhoulyá? Póso tha dhyarkésy?

GB: What will be the hours of work?
F: Que sera l'horaire de travail?
D: Wie lange dauert die Arbeitszeit?
NL: Wat zijn de werkuren?
S: ¿Cual será el horario de trabajo?
I: Che sarà l'orario di lavoro?
GR: Pyéz tha ý ne y órez ergasýas?

GB: Thank you for your help.
F: Merci de votre aide.
D: Vielen Dank für Ihre Hilfe.
NL: Dank U voor Uw hulp.
S: Gracias por su ayuda.
I: Grazie del suo aiuto.
GR: Sas efkharystó ya tyn vóythýa sas.

APPENDIX 2

TRAVEL ITINERARIES

Anna Ling's Shoestring Travels

Cambridge
Departs home after A levels

↓

Granada, Spain
Squatted and busked, and then worked and lived free in a community in the hills

↓

West Country, England
12-hour shifts in an egg-packing factory

↓

Bought a van with boyfriend

↓

Epernay, France
Champagne harvest

↓

Paris
Fire poi busker

↓

Guatemala
Worked in hostel on Lake Atitlan

↓

New Zealand
Picked fruit in South Island and busked in Wellington while couchsurfing on a Maori marae

↓

Northern California
Worked on an organic farm

↓

Bolivia
Bar work in La Paz

Bradwell Jackson's Teaching Travels

Tampa, Florida
Left job as a drug abuse counsellor to work his way around the world

↓

Registered with Servas and Hospitality Club for free accommodation

↓

Mexico City
Found a teaching job at the second institute he approached and stayed for six+ months

↓

Registered with Couchsurfing for free accommodation

↓

Mauritania
Teacher at the English Language Center in the capital, Nouakchott

↓

Bamako, Mali
Stayed for two months with a couchsurfing host who paid him for English lessons

↓

Hebei Province, China
Teaching contract with Aston English Schools

↓

Oman
Investigated English language teaching scene in Oman

↓

France
Arrived in Marseille and as a personal challenge, staying free using night shelters

↓

Russia
After a further teaching contract in China and passing the CELTA course in London, he took up teaching in the small city of Shahkty in southern Russia

Richard Ferguson's Adventures

New Zealand
Started from home in Auckland

↓

Lisbon, Portugal
Worked in two pizzerias while living in the Bairro Alto (old district)

↓

Buenos Aires, Argentina
Freelance English tutor for 30 pesos per hour

↓

Barcelona, Spain
Unsuccessful job-hunt due to visa problems

↓

Palma de Mallorca
Pub job

↓

Faliraki, Rhodes
Barman in nightclub, with accommodation provided

↓

Obtained one-year Working Holiday Visa for Sweden

↓

Brussels, Belgium
Hostel cleaner and barman in exchange for bed, food and €100 a week

↓

Stockholm, Sweden
Worked in Galway Irish pub

↓

Moved to Berlin after travelling in India

APPENDIX 3

CURRENCY CONVERSION CHART

COUNTRY	£1	US$1
Argentina	20 peso	15.4 peso
Australia	A$1.70	A$1.33
Brazil	4 real	3.2 real
Bulgaria	2.3 lev	1.8 lev
Canada	C$1.73	C$1.35
Chile	830 peso	648 peso
China	8.8 yuan renminbi	6.9 yuan renminbi
Colombia	3,670 peso	2,865 peso
Czech Republic	32 koruna	25 koruna
Denmark	9 kroner	6.9 kroner
Ecuador	[uses US$]	
Egypt	23 Egyptian pound	18 Egyptian pound
Eurozone	1.19 euro	0.93 euro
Hong Kong	10 HK dollar	7.8 HK dollar
Hungary	374 forint	292 forint
India	83 rupee	65 rupee
Indonesia	17,000 rupiah	13,335 rupiah
Israel	4.69 new shekel	3.66 new shekel
Japan	140 yen	109 yen
Kenya	130 Kenya shilling	101 Kenya shilling
Korea	1,778 won	1,138 won
Malaysia	5.6 ringgit	4.4 ringgit
Mexico	24 peso	18.8 peso
Morocco	12.7 dirham	9.9 dirham
Nepal	130 rupee	102 rupee
New Zealand	NZ$1.82	NZ$1.42
Norway	11 krone	8.6 krone
Peru	4.11 new sol	3.2 new sol
Poland	5 zloty	4 zloty
Russia	72 rouble	56 rouble
Saudi Arabia	4.8 riyal	3.75 riyal
Singapore	1.8 Singapore dollar	1.40 Singapore dollar
South Africa	16.9 rand	13.2 rand
Sweden	11.5 krona	9.0 krona
Switzerland	1.28 Swiss franc	1.0 Swiss franc
Taiwan	39 Taiwan new dollar	30.7 Taiwan new dollar
Thailand	44 baht	34.3 baht
Turkey	4.6 lira	3.65 lira
USA	1.28 dollar	-

Current exchange rates can be checked at sites such as Oanda.com and the Universal Currency Converter at www.xe.com/ucc.

The following Eurozone countries use the euro: Austria, Belgium, Cyprus, Estonia, Finland, France, Germany, Greece, Ireland, Italy, Latvia, Lithuania, Luxembourg, Malta, Netherlands, Portugal, Slovakia, Slovenia and Spain. In addition, Kosovo and Montenegro also use the euro.

APPENDIX 4

INTERNATIONAL DIALLING CODES

INTERNATIONAL DIALLING CODES	
COUNTRY	**CODE**
Afghanistan	+93
Albania	+355
Andorra	+376
Antigua	+268
Argentina	+54
Australia	+61
Austria	+43
Bahrain	+973
Bangladesh	+880
Belgium	+32
Bermuda	+441
Bolivia	+591
Bosnia and Herzegovina	+387
Brazil	+55
Brunei	+673
Bulgaria	+359
Cambodia	+855
Cameroon	+237
Canada	+1
Chile	+56
China	+86
Colombia	+57
Costa Rica	+506
Croatia	+385
Cyprus	+357
Czech Republic	+420
Denmark	+45
Dominican Republic	+809
Ecuador	+593
Egypt	+20
Estonia	+372
Finland	+358
France	+33
Germany	+49
Ghana	+233
Greece	+30
Guatemala	+502
Hong Kong	+852
Hungary	+36
India	+91
Indonesia	+62
Ireland	+353
Israel	+972
Italy	+39

Japan	+81
Kenya	+254
Korea	+82
Kuwait	+965
Laos	+856
Latvia	+371
Lebanon	+961
Libya	+218
Lithuania	+370
Malaysia	+60
Maldives	+960
Malta	+356
Mauritania	+222
Mexico	+52
Morocco	+212
Mozambique	+258
Nepal	+977
Netherlands	+31
New Zealand	+64
Norway	+47
Oman	+968
Peru	+51
Poland	+48
Portugal	+351
Qatar	+974
Romania	+40
Russia	+7
Saudi Arabia	+966
Senegal	+221
Serbia	+381
Singapore	+65
Slovak Republic	+421
Slovenia	+386
South Africa	+27
Spain	+34
Sri Lanka	+94
Sweden	+46
Switzerland	+41
Syria	+963
Taiwan	+886
Tanzania	+255
Thailand	+66
Tunisia	+216
Turkey	+90
UAE	+971
Uganda	+256
Ukraine	+380
USA	+1
Venezuela	+58
Vietnam	+84
Yemen	+967

READERS' COMMENTS ON PREVIOUS EDITIONS

Emma Hames, UK (planning to go to America as a soccer coach): *Many thanks for this book, it is and will continue to be a source of inspiration and hope to lean upon during the 9–5 routine (for now …).*

Mommyof3, USA (Amazon review): *A long time ago this book caught my eye. I had always wanted to go to Europe. Empowered by this book, I bought a one-way ticket to Spain with no job prospects, nothing. Kinda crazy. I spent a year in Europe on my own, working as an au pair and teaching English. It really was a great experience, and this book was invaluable. I have not seen this edition, but yes, to me it was the Bible!! So inspirational and informative.*

James Curran, Graduate Job Podcast Presenter: *On a personal note, your book Work your Way Around the World inspired me to volunteer with a conservation charity in Australia before university and then to spend a year teaching English in China after university, and I would be honoured to have you on the show.*

D Thorpe (Amazon review): *This book is sure to make you want to just grab your stuff right now and leave, even if you have little money.*

Bohid_harma (Amazon review): *I almost want to give this book a negative review so no-one else will know about it! If you are tired of life, tired of the same monotonous routine, bored of your friends and of the same places and faces then buy this book. It will inspire you to throw off the shackles, to see uncertainty as an opportunity and not a reason to fear, to grasp your life which is slipping by and take that brave leap into the unknown. One of the best books I've ever purchased, it's inspired me to change my life and to take a chance and leave behind the home comforts. Once you set out on that path, you never know where it might lead!*

Nicole Gluckstern (American free spirit writing from Africa): *Hi there, how nice to find mail from a cult hero while in Burkina Faso, it's almost surreal! Love the book.*

Hillary Chura (New York Times journalist): Work your Way Around the World *was a great book and actually encouraged several of my friends and me to take off after college. I was abroad for two and a half years in London, Spain and Cairo … We all talk about what a great experience it was.*

Charlie Wetherall (runs the website The Runaway Trader): *I first met with Susan Griffith's work in the early 1980s when I … was attracted to the title because it offered a glimmer of hope that – someday – I could scrape up enough courage to escape the drudgery of my own existence and see some of the world, earning my way as I moved along … If you've got any kind of yen to get away from it all, check out Griffith's book. She may just plant a seed in your mind to make the Great Getaway, like she did in mine those many years ago.*

Amazon reviewer: *I picked up this book in a bookshop (in the 'olden days' before the internet!!) and was inspired by people's stories. I had always wanted to live in Switzerland, since seeing the children's drama 'Heidi' on TV. I thought 'why don't I just go for it?!' Things can't get worse, I've got nothing to lose!' … I quit my work and booked a flight to Zurich. The book actually was slightly negative about the possibility of finding official work in Switzerland … But after a great week of staying in hostels, meeting new people and walking miles through the snow in gorgeous Switzerland, knocking on hotel doors (that week alone was amazing), I eventually was offered a job as a chambermaid in Grindelwald and had a brilliant 3 months, earnt very good money, lived in a chalet with the other staff (mostly from Spain) … one of the best times of my life!*

Catherine Howard, Irish woman who worked at Disneyworld, Florida: *I'd like to commend you on your excellent publication,* Work Your Way Around the World. *I received a copy of it for Christmas and my only complaint is that after reading it you can't decide what you want to do because there's so much choice. Thanks again for your wonderfully informative book!*

Richard Ferguson (New Zealander working his way around the world): *I just want to say your book is great. Before leaving NZ I was full of apprehension. But after reading about so many people landing jobs all over, I was put at ease.*

Carisa Fey (from Stuttgart): *Thanks for your books, they helped me so much, especially the psychological effect. Everyone first told me that I was crazy and cannot do it, but so I knew, many others have done it before and so can I.*

Michael Jaczynski, London: *Learned Oracle: I have been in possession of* WYW *for less than 24 hrs but am already a fan. I just couldn't put it down last night and today feel much more confident about my impending adventure.*

Karen Martin from Grimsby who worked in the Netherlands, on a French farm and a winter season in the Alps: *I do feel that my time travelling – even if I didn't get to half as many places as I would like (still time though!!) – touched me in many ways and changed my life, confidence and outlook for the best ... and I will not forget the influence your book had on me!!*

Indu Shakya, Know Nepal: *We appreciate your hard work to bring people around the world together.*

Cath Cooper (administrator in Doncaster who decided to retrain as an occupational therapist after her travels in Africa and New Zealand): *After almost 20 years of dreaming, I eventually took the plunge, packed in a job I loved, persuaded Steve (my husband) to pack in a job he didn't love and set off for a grown-up gap year. I first came across* Work Your Way Around the World *in 1991 when I was 17. The following year I met Steve and my travelling dreams were put on the back burner whilst money was spent on our wedding and a house deposit. Much later, I bought an updated edition (though I still had my well-thumbed original). It took a couple more years researching and persuading before we made the decision to go. We were away for 10 months and did lots of different things we never dreamed of, such as teaching kids in South Africa to play cricket! But it was the best experience of our lives.*

Amazon.com reviewer: *Well done Susan Griffith ... awesome indeed to be able to help people achieve their ideas, dreams and goals for the future.*

Amazon.com reviewer: *Loved it! Very informative! I thought I was an experienced traveller but there were so many things in here that made me rethink the way that I travel. So much advice, great testimonies. Really is the Globetrotter's Bible.*